To David
with love
Ken ∙
Jeremy
and Sue

x

20.3.86

DOMESDAY BOOK

Suffolk

History from the Sources

DOMESDAY BOOK

A Survey of the Counties of England

LIBER DE WINTONIA

Compiled by direction of

KING WILLIAM I

Winchester
1086

DOMESDAY BOOK

general editor

JOHN MORRIS

34

Suffolk

edited by
Alex Rumble

from a draft translation prepared by
Marian Hepplestone, Barbara Hodge, Margaret Jones,
Judy Plaister, Catherine Coutts, Faith Bowers and Elizabeth Teague

(Part Two)

PHILLIMORE
Chichester
1986

1986
Published by
PHILLIMORE & CO. LTD.
London and Chichester
Head Office: Shopwyke Hall,
Chichester, Sussex, England

© Mrs. Susan Morris, 1986

ISBN 0 85033 480 2 (case)
ISBN 0 85033 481 0 (limp)

All rights reserved. No part of this publication may be reproduced, stored in a retrieval system, or transmitted in any form or by any means electronic, mechanical, photocopying, recording, or otherwise, without the prior permission of the publisher and the Copyright owner(s).

Printed in Great Britain by
Titus Wilson & Son Ltd.,
Kendal

SUFFOLK

(Part One)
Introduction

The Domesday Survey of Suffolk
(to Landholder XV, Archbishop Lanfranc)

(Part Two)

The Domesday Survey of Suffolk
(Landholder XVI, the Bishop of Bayeux to Holdings Elsewhere)
Bibliography and Abbreviations
Notes
Appendices
Index of Persons
Index of Places
Maps and Map Keys
Systems of Reference
Technical Terms

ȚRÆ baiocenſis epi̅. Riſebruge. H̃ In hauer hella. I. lib hō. xx. IIII.   . XVI.
ac̄. 7 dim̃. car̃. & ual&. III. ſot. h̃ ten̄. Tihell' de ep̄o. ſuus antec̄. t. r. e.
c̄m̃d. sc̄s. eadm̃. vi. forisfac̄turas.

. H̃. DE CARLEFORDA. In ſekeforda ten̄ Aluric̄' fili' Wluiet
com̄d heroldi. t. r. e. II. car̃ træ. p. man̄. Sēp. IIII. uiłłi. Tc̄. XIII. borđ.
m̊. xv. Sēp in dn̄io. II. car̃ tc̄ia poteſt fieri. &. hom̄. III. car̃. x. ac̄ p̄ti.
. I. molin̄. Tc̄. I. runc̄. m̊ n̄. 7. IIII. an̄. Tc̄. xxx. porc̄. m̊. n̄. Tc̄. c. ous̄.
m̊. xxx. vi. Tc̄ uał. IIII. lib̄. m̊. xl. ſoł. 7 ht in long̃. vi. qr̃. & vi. in lat̃.
7 de gelt̃. vii. đ. & obł. In eađ. IIII. libi hōes com̄d eidē. Alurici. de.
VIII. ac̄. I. ac̄ p̄ti. 7 dim̃. car̃. 7 uał. xvi. đ. h̃ ten̄. R. bigot. de ep̄o
In paruo belinges. ten̄. idē Aluric̄. t. r. e. L. ac̄. p. man̄. 7. II. borđ.
Tc̄. I. car̃. m̊ dim̃. III. ac̄ p̄ti. Tc̄. I. moł. m̊. n̄. Tc̄ uał. xx. ſoł. m̊. x.

LANDS OF THE BISHOP OF BAYEUX

RISBRIDGE Hundred

1 In HAVERHILL 1 free man; 24 acres. ½ plough.
Value 3s.
Tihel holds this from the Bishop. His predecessor before 1066 (had) the patronage, St. Edmund's (had) the 6 forfeitures.

Hundred of CARLFORD

2 In SECKFORD Aelfric son of Wulfgeat, under the patronage of Harold before 1066, held 2 carucates of land as a manor.
Always 4 villagers. Then 13 smallholders, now 15.
Always 2 ploughs in lordship; a third possible. 3 men's ploughs.
Meadow, 10 acres; 1 mill. Then 1 cob, now none; 4 cattle; then 30 pigs, now none; then 100 sheep, now 36.
Value then £4; now 40s.
It has 6 furlongs in length and 6 in width; 7½d in tax.
In the same (Seckford) 4 free men under the patronage of the same Aelfric, with 8 acres.
Meadow, 1 acre.
½ plough.
Value 16d.
R(oger) Bigot holds this from the Bishop.

3 In LITTLE BEALINGS Aelfric also held 50 acres as a manor before 1066.
2 smallholders.
Then 1 plough, now ½.
Meadow, 3 acres; then 1 mill, now none.
Value then 20s; now 10[s].

In ead̄ ten̄ Beor lib̄ hō . t . r . e . l . ac̄ . p . man̄ . 7 . iii . ac̄ p̄ti . 7 tc̄ ual & sep
viii . fol . hāc emit ipfe beorn lib̄ hō ab abbate . eo c̄untione qd̄ p̄ mor-
tē fuā rediret ad æcclīā . sc̄æ Æ ldred teftante hund . h̄ ten̄ . Ro . bigot.
de ep̄o . 7 W . de more de eo . h̄ tria maneria ten̄ . R . com̄s . die q̄ fe forifecit.
| 7 Ilari⁹ de eo.

373 b

H̃. DE WILEFORD . In Wikhā . R . bigot . i . lib̄u hōem cō
mdat . S . e . xxv . ac̄ . 7 fub eo . iiii . lib̄ hōes . vii . ac̄ . Tc̄ . i . car̄ . m̄ dimid̄.
ii . ac̄ p̄ti . 7 ual . v . fol . h̄ ten̄ . Radulfus . de fauenie . de . Ro bigot . de
feudo ep̄i . In debeis . xv . ac̄ . & p̄tinent ad cerfella . In ead̄ . lib̄u hōem
de dim̄ . ac̄.

H̃ . DE LOSA . In cerresfella . xiiii . lib̄i hōes . i . car̄ trǣ . Ro.
bigot . 7 Radulfus de faugno ten̄ de eo . 7 xiii . ac̄ . Tc̄ . v car̄ . m̄ . iii.
. i . ac̄ p̄ti . tres ex iftis . 7 . i . dim̄ fuer̄ . comd̄ . sc̄e eldrede . 7 edrici . de leffefella . W . mal& . fuit faifit die fui obitus . 7 alii . comd̄ ab̄bis tantū . tc̄
ual . lx . fol . m̄ fimilit̄ . In ead̄ . ii . foc̄ mans . sc̄e eldrede . vii . ac̄ in eod̄ p̄tio ſt.
In ead̄ . i . lib̄u hōem . marculf . comd̄ . Edrici . de leffefella . Wiłłm mal&
fuit faifitus die q̄ obiit . i . bord̄ . Tc̄ . i . car̄ . i . ac̄ p̄ti . 7 fub eo . iiii . lib̄i hōes
iiii . ac̄ . Tc̄ ual . x . fol . m̄ . v . 7 łt . viii . qr̄ . in long . 7 . vi . in lat̄ . xi . d̄ . de g̃.
alii ibi ten̄et.

In the same (Little Bealings) Beorn, a free man, held 50 acres before 1066 as a manor.

Meadow, 3 acres.

Value then and always 8s.

Beorn, the free man, himself bought this from the Abbot with the agreement that after his death it should revert to the Church of St. Etheldreda's as the Hundred testifies. Ro(ger) Bigot holds this from the Bishop, and W. *de More* from him.

Earl R(alph) held these three manors on the day he forfeited, and Hilary from him.

Hundred of WILFORD

4 In WICKHAM (Market) R(oger) Bigot [holds] 1 free man under the patronage of St. E(theldreda's); 25 acres. Under him, 4 free men; 7 acres. Then 1 plough, now ½.

Meadow, 2 acres.

Value 5s.

Ralph of Savenay holds this from Ro(ger) Bigot from the Bishop's Holding.

5 In DEBACH 15 acres; they belong to Charsfield.

In the same (Debach) 1 free man with ½ acre.

Hundred of LOES

6 In CHARSFIELD 14 free men; 1 carucate of land. Ro(ger) Bigot holds (it), and Ralph of Savenay holds (it) from him. And 13 acres. Then 5 ploughs, now 3.

Meadow, 1 acre.

Three of these (free men) and 1 half (free man), were under the patronage of St. Etheldreda's and of Edric of Laxfield; William Malet was in possession on the day of his death. The others were under the patronage only of the Abbot.

Value then 60s; now the same.

In the same (Charsfield) 2 Freemen of St. Etheldreda's; 7 acres. They are in the same assessment.

In the same (Charsfield) 1 free man, Marculf, under the patronage of Edric of Laxfield. William Malet was in possession on the day he died.

1 smallholder.

Then 1 plough. Meadow, 1 acre.

Under him, 4 free men; 4 acres.

Value then 10s; now 5[s].

It has 8 furlongs in length and 6 in width; 11d in tax. Others hold there.

⁷In gretingehā . I . libū hoem . balchi teñ . idē . Radulfus .
cōm . ad eftan . xxIIII . ac trae . I . ac p̃ti . tc . dim car . m̃ fimilit . IIII . fot
uat . In ead . I . lib hō . c̄omd . eidē . xxxvIII . ac . & dim . I . bord . II . ac
p̃ti . I . car . tc uat . xII . fot . m̃ fimit.

⁷In Kenetona . v . libi hoes . IIII . fuer c̄omd . S̃ . æ . 7 facxe antec . R . fa
uigno . de uno xxx . ac tre . Sep . I . car . Tc uat . x . fot . m̃ . vI . fot.
M̊ tenet . R . de fauigno . de . Ro . bigot;

⁷BANBERCA DVO . H̃ . In ilelega . III . libi hoes de foca Algari
Comit 7 c̄omdati m̃ teñ tehellus de herion de ep̄o . 7 hnt xxx . ac.
Tc . I . car . m̃ . dim . 7 dim ac p̃ti . 7 uat . v . fot.

⁷Branteftona teñ Alueua mat morchari . comit . T . R . E p̨ man

III . car terre . 7 . v . uilti . & . vI . bord . & . v . feru . Sep . II . car in dñio.
Tc & p . II . car houm . m̃ . I . 7 . IIII . ac p̃ti . Silu de . x . porc . Sep . II . eq.
in halla . Tc . v . añ . m̃ . III . tc . xx . porc . m̃ xxIII . Tc . c . ous . m̃ . cxx.
In ead . III . libi hoes . Alueue c̄omd 7 foc & faca f; pot uend fine licenc
xxIIII . ac trae . Sep uat . v . lib . ht . I . lḡ in loḡ . 7 . III . qr in lato . & de
gelto . vI . d . li man teñ Radulfus de curbefpina de ep̄o.

⁷StoV . H̃ . In Cratinga teñ Aluric fili brune . I . lib hō fub Vifgaro
c̄om tant . t . r . e . I . car trae in foca reḡ . m̃ teñ . Witts debee uilla de ep̄o.

7 In CRETINGHAM Ralph also holds 1 free man, Balki, under the patronage of Aethelstan; 24 acres of land.
    Meadow, 1 acre.
    Then ½ plough, now the same.
In the same (Cretingham) 1 free man under the patronage of the same man; 38½ acres.
    1 smallholder.
    Meadow, 2 acres.
    1 plough.
Value then 12s; now the same.

8 In KENTON 5 free men; 4 were under the patronage of St. E(theldreda's), and Saxi, R(alph) of Savenay's predecessor, (had patronage) over one; 30 acres of land. Always 1 plough.
Value then 10s; now 6s.
    Now R(alph) of Savenay holds (this) from Ro(ger) Bigot.

BABERGH Two Hundreds

9 In ELEIGH 3 free men under the jurisdiction and patronage of Earl Algar. Now Tihel of Helléan holds (them) from the Bishop. They have 30 acres. Then 1 plough, now ½.
    Meadow, ½ acre.
    Value 5s.

10 Aelfeva mother of Earl Morcar held BRANDESTON as a manor before 1066; 3 carucates of land.
    5 villagers; 6 smallholders; 5 slaves.
    Always 2 ploughs in lordship. Then and later 2 men's ploughs, now 1.
    Meadow, 4 acres; woodland at 10 pigs. Always 2 horses at the hall. Then 5 cattle, now 3; then 20 pigs, now 23; then 100 sheep, now 120.
In the same (Brandeston) 3 free men under the patronage and full jurisdiction of Aelfeva, but they could sell without permission; 24 acres of land.
Value always £5.
    It has 1 league in length and 3 furlongs in width; 6d in tax. Ralph of Courbépine holds this manor from the Bishop.

STOW Hundred

11 In CREETING (St. Peter) Aelfric son of Brown, 1 free man under the patronage only of Withgar before 1066; held 1 carucate of land in the King's jurisdiction. Now William of Bouville holds (it) from the Bishop.

Sep̃.v.borď.7.i.feru̓.Sep̃.i.cař in dñio.& ď.cař hoĩum.7 ĩtia pars
molin̄.&.IIII.ac̄ p̃ti.&.IIII.an̓.7 VIII.porc̓.Tc̄.VIII.oũs.m̃.XX.Sep̃
ual XX.fol̃.ḧt.I.lg̓.in long̃ & dim in lat̓.& de gelto.XXX.dẽn.Sʒ plur̓ ibi teñ.
& ibi.v.libi hões eidẽ alurici.cõm̃ tant de XVIII.ac̄.& dim̃.cař
& fuer̓ libati cũ mañ.& ual.II.fol̃. Rex & cõm̃ foca̅ 7 faca̅.

In newetona teñ.II.libi hões Alfi cõm̃datione tantũ LXXX.ac̄.ťræ.
in foc̓ regis & cõm̃.m̃ teñ Ro.bigot̓ de ep̄o fub Rog̃ Wareng̃.Tc̄.II.
borď.P̓ 7 m̃.I.Tc̄.I cař 7 dim in dñio.p̓ nult̃.m̃.I.7.III.ac̄ p̃ti.&
m̃.II.añ.&.VI.porc̓.&.XL.oũs.Sexta pars æcclíæ.X.ac̄.libæ ťræ
Tc̄ ual.XXX.fol̃.p̃.XX.fol̃.m̃.XL.fol̃.

In Rodehã.I.lib̃ hõ.faxonis.fub sc̃a aldreda.cõmd.T̃.R.e.X.ac̄
in foc̓ ĥ Sep̃ dim̃ cař.Roger̓ bigot̓ teñ de ep̄o.7 fub eo.Rađ de
fauiniaco.7 ual.II.fol̃.

Bofemera.H̃.In Crofelda teñ Wdebrun.lib̃ hõ cm̃dat̓ Edrico
anteceffori Rob̃ti mal&.XX.ac̄.p̓ mañ.Tc̄ 7 p̃.I.cař.m̃.nichil.
&.I.ac̄ p̃ti.Tc̄ 7 p̃ ual.V.fol̃.m̃.III.Rog̃ bigot̓ de ep̄o teñ.

In eađ.V.libi hões.XL.ac̄.Tc̄ 7 p̃.II.cař.modo nult̃.I.ac̄ p̃ti.ĥ ten& Ro.
bigot̓.Tc̄ ual.XVI.fol̃.m̃ XX.fol̃.

Always 5 smallholders; 1 slave.
Always 1 plough in lordship; ½ men's plough.
The third part of a mill; meadow, 4 acres. 4 cattle, 8 pigs; then 8 sheep, now 20.
Value always 20s.
It has 1 league in length and ½ in width; 30d in tax. But several hold there.
There also 5 free men of the same Aelfric under patronage only, with 18 acres. ½ plough. They were delivered with the manor. Value 2s.
The King and the Earl (have) full jurisdiction.

12 In (Old) NEWTON 2 free men of Alsi's, under patronage only, held 80 acres of land; in the jurisdiction of the King and the Earl. Now Roger Bigot holds (it) from the Bishop; Warengar [holds it] under Roger.
Then 2 smallholders, later and now 1.
Then 1½ ploughs in lordship, later none, now 1.
Meadow, 3 acres. Now 2 cattle, 6 pigs, 40 sheep.
The sixth part of a church, 10 acres of free land.
Value then 30s; later 20s; now 40s.

13 In RODEHAM 1 free man of Saxi's, under the patronage of St. Etheldreda's before 1066; 10 acres; in the jurisdiction of the Hundred. Always ½ plough.
Roger Bigot holds (it) from the Bishop; under him, Ralph of Savenay.
Value 2s.

BOSMERE Hundred

14 In CROWFIELD Woodbrown, a free man under the patronage of Edric, Robert Malet's predecessor, held 20 acres of land as a manor. Then and later 1 plough, now nothing.
Meadow, 1 acre.
Value then and later 5s; now 3[s].
Roger Bigot holds (this) from the Bishop.
In the same (Crowfield) 5 free men; 40 acres. Then and later 2 ploughs, now none.
Meadow, 1 acre.
Ro(ger) Bigot holds this.
Value then 16s; now 20s.

In ſtanhā . I . lib̄ hō . Lewin . c̄md̄at . Edrico de laxefella xx . ac̄ . p̄ man̄ t . r . e . & . II . bord . Sep̄ . I . car̄ . & . II . ac̄ p̄ti . & . II . Æcclie de . III . ac̄ . Tc̄ ual . v . ſol . & . IIII . d . m̄ . x . ſol 7 VIII . d . & . Ro . bigot ten̄ de ep̄o . Rex. 7 . c . ſocā : In Eadē . I . lib̄ hō . Aluric . xx . ac̄ . & . II . bord . 7 . I . ac̄ p̄ti .   : ex hoc fuit . Rob malet 7̄ par̄ e' die ſui obit .
Tc̄ . IIII . ſol . m̄ . ual . VIII . ſol . hic erat c̄omdat . ante ceſſori . Ricardi . filii Comitis . G . Rex . 7 ſocā . In ead . II . libi hōes . II . ac̄ . & . ual . VI . d .
In ead ten̄ Leuuric̄ . I . lib̄ hō . x . ac̄ . comdat Leuuino . Tc̄ dim car̄ ;
Tc̄ ual . III . ſol . m̄ . II . In ead . XI . libi hōes . LII . ac̄ 7 . x . ex h̄ fuer̄ c̄o m̄dati Leuino c̄omdato ante ceſſori . Rob̄ti malet . & XI .
noe Sperun fuit c̄omdat burcardo tēpore regis . e . 7 h̄t ex eadē tr̄a . Tc̄ . IIII . car̄ . poſt & m̄ . II . & . II . ac̄ p̄ti . Tc̄ ual . xx . ſol . m̄ . xxx .
h̄t . I . lḡ in long . 7 VI . qr̄ 7 dim . in lat . 7 xx . d . de gl̄ . Alii ibi tenent.
Rex . & . c . ſocā . In Vledana . I . lib̄ hō . Aluric c̄omd̄t Saxo . XVI . ac̄ . ſemp . I . car̄ . Tc̄ . I . bord . m̄ . null . Hc̄ Aluricū calūpniatur . Ro. de ramis tenuiſſe ſuo feudo p̄quā fuiſſent libati ep̄o Tc̄ . ſilua . de . xx .
IIII . porc . 7 VIII . por . 7 XXII . ōus . & . III . cap̄ . Tc̄ ual . x . ſol . m̄ . VIII . ſol.
In ead . VI . libi hōes . L . II . ac̄ . De uno & dimidio ex his ſcilic . Leuuino.
7 Thurmero . habuit Abb̄ ſc̄i eadmundi . c̄md̄t . t . r . e . 7 q̄da noe brictuolt . fuit c̄omdat Edrico antec̄ mal . Tc̄ int̄ tot . II . car̄ & dim . m̄ . II . Tc̄ ual . xx . ſol . 7 m̄ . Roḡ bigot ten̄ de ep̄o . & Gar̄ de illo .

374 b

15 In STONHAM 1 free man, Leofwin, under the patronage of Edric of Laxfield; 20 acres of land as a manor before 1066.
    2 smallholders.
    Always 1 plough. Meadow, 2 acres.
    2 churches with 3 acres.
    Value then 5s 4d; now 10s 8d.
    Ro(ger) Bigot holds (this) from the Bishop. The King and the Earl (have) the jurisdiction. Robert Malet was [in possession of] this, and his father on the day of his death.
In the same (Stonham) 1 free man, Aelfric; 20 acres.
    2 smallholders.
    Meadow, 1 acre.
    Value then 4s; now 8s.
    This (free man) was under the patronage of the predecessor of Richard son of Count Gilbert. The King and [the Earl] (have) the jurisdiction.
In the same (Stonham) 2 free men; 2 acres.
Value 6d.
In the same (Stonham) Leofric, 1 free man under the patronage of Leofwin, held 10 acres. Then ½ plough.
Value then 3s; now 2[s].
In the same (Stonham) 11 free men; 52 acres. 10 of these (free men) were under the patronage of Leofwin (who was) under the patronage of Robert Malet's predecessor. The eleventh, Sperun by name, was under the patronage of Burghard before 1066; he had 8 acres of this land. Then 4 ploughs, later and now 2.
    Meadow, 2 acres.
    Value then 20s; now 30[s].
    It has 1 league in length and 6½ furlongs in width; 20d in tax.
    Others hold there. The King and the Earl (have) the jurisdiction.

16 In 'OLDEN' 1 free man, Aelfric, under the patronage of Saxi; 16 acres.
    Always 1 plough.
    Then 1 smallholder, now none.
    Ro(ger) of Rames claims that he held this Aelfric in his Holding after (the men) were delivered to the Bishop.
    Woodland then at 20 pigs. 8 pigs, 22 sheep, 3 goats.
    Value then 10s; now 8s.
In the same ('Olden') 6 free men; 52 acres. Over one and a half of these, that is Leofwin and Thormar, the Abbot of St. Edmund's had patronage before 1066; one, Brictwold by name, was under the patronage of Edric, Malet's predecessor. Then between them all 2½ ploughs, now 2.
Value then and now 20s.
    Roger Bigot holds (this) from the Bishop; War(engar) [holds it] from him.

⁌In Cratingis. teñ Ofgot lib hō treginta ac̄. t. r. e. ꝑ mañ. sēp. I. bord. 7. I. car̄. vIII. porc̄. 7 Ix. oūs. 7. I. ac̄ p̃ti. sēp ual. xII. fol.

375 a

7 Rog̃ bigot teñ de epo. 7 Gar̃. de illo. Rex 7 C. de toto focā.
⁌In Burgeftala. I. lib hō. t. r. e. Aiōnus teñ. xIIII. ac̄. Ecclia. xxvI. ac̃
Sēp dim̃ car̄. &. I. ac̄ p̃ti. Tc̄ ual. x. fol. m̃ vIII. &. IIII. d.
⁌In ead lib hō. reg̃. e. Ailric̃. xIIII. ac̄. 7 dim̃ car̄. 7. I. ac̄ p̃ti. Tc̄ ual
v. fol. &. IIII. d. m̃. IIII. fol. In ead Vlui lib hō reg̃. II. ac̄. & tc̄
ual. v. d. m̃. vI. ht. vIII. qr̃ in lō. &. I. qr̃ 7 d in lat. & vI. d. 7 obol
de gelto. Rex 7. c. focā.
⁌In PAchetuna. III libi. hoes. reg̃. e. xxIIII. ac̄. femp. I. car̄. &. I. ac̄ p̃ti.
Tc̄ ual&. vIII. fol. & m̃ fimilit. In ead. I. lib hō. reg̃. e. 7 dim̃. v. ac̄ & dim̃.
& ual& xII. d. ⁌In Codeham. I. lib hō. nōe Almar com̃d Abbi de heli
lx. ac̄ tr̃æ ꝑ mañ. Tc̄. II. car̄. m̃. I. 7 dim̃. 7. I. bord. Tc̄ filua de. x. porc̄. m̃.
II. Semp ual. xxx. fol. Ecclia de. III. ac̄ & ual. vI. d.
⁌In ead. II. libi hoes Aluric̃ 7 Vluric̃. lx. ac̄. ꝑ. II. mañ. 7. I. uilt. 7. II.
bord. 7. II. car̄. 7 xl. oūs. 7. II. añ. &. IIII. ac̄ p̃ti. Tc̄ filua xxx. porc̄.

17 In CREETING Osgot, a free man, held 30 acres before 1066 as a manor.
    Always 1 smallholder;
    1 plough;
    8 pigs, 9 sheep. Meadow, 1 acre.
Value always 12s.
    Roger Bigot holds (this) from the Bishop; War(engar) [holds it]   375 a
from him.
The King and the Earl (have) jurisdiction over the whole.

18 In BURSTALL 1 free man, Ailbern, held 14 acres before 1066.
    A church, 26 acres.
    Always ½ plough. Meadow, 1 acre.
Value then 10s; now 8[s] 4d.
In the same (Burstall) a free man of King Edward's, Aethelric; 14 acres. ½ plough.
    Meadow, 1 acre.
Value then 5s 4d; now 4s.
In the same (Burstall) Wulfwy, a free man of the King's; 2 acres.
Value then 5d; now 6[d].
    It has 8 furlongs in length and 1½ in width; 6½d in tax. The King and the Earl (have) the jurisdiction.

19 In *PACHETUNA* 3 free men of King Edward's; 24 acres. Always 1 plough.
    Meadow, 1 acre.
Value then 8s; now the same.
In the same (*Pachetuna*) 1 free man and a half of King Edward's; 5½ acres.
Value 12d.

20 In CODDENHAM 1 free man, Aelmer by name, under the patronage of the Abbot of Ely; 60 acres of land as a manor. Then 2 ploughs, now 1½.
    1 smallholder.
    Then woodland at 10 pigs, now at 2.
Value always 30s.
    A church with 3 acres; value 6d.
In the same (Coddenham) 2 free men, Aelfric and Wulfric; 60 acres as 2 manors.
    1 villager; 2 smallholders.
    2 ploughs.
    40 sheep, 2 cattle. Meadow, 4 acres; woodland then at 30 pigs,

m̅ . xɪ . Tc̅ ual xxx . fol . m̅ . xʟ . Abbas de eli habuit co̅m̅d . In eade̅
ıı . libi . ho̅es Aluricus . & Wiſtricus . ıı . ac̅ . & . ual xıı . d̅ . Eccl̅ia . ɪ . ac̅ . 7
ual . ıı . d̅ Rex . 7 . c . de toto . foca̅ . / In ead heroldus lib̅ ho̅ in foca 7 in
comendatione ab̅b̅is de heli . xxx . ac̅ . p̸ man . t . r . e . femp . ıı . bord . &
. ɪ . car̅ . & . ıı . ac̅ p̅ti . filu̅ . x . porc . 7 ual . x . fol : In eade̅ . ııı . lib̅i ho̅es
: eccl̅ie . ıı . ac' . val . ııı ı . d̅ .
vıı . ac̅ & dim̅ . 7 dim̅ . car̅ . & . ual . ıı . fol . Rex . & . c . foc . In ead Leueua
liba femina . t . r . e . x . ac̅ . & . dim̅ . car̅ . & . ııı . bord̅ . 7 . ɪ . ac̅ p̅ti . & ual . ıııı . fol .
In ead xv . lib̅i ho̅es ʟxxx . ac̅ . ɪ . min . Ex hiſtis fuer̅ . vı . c̅m̅d faxo ante c̅
. Ra . piperelli . Tc̅ & p̸ . v . car̅ . m̅ . ɪ . filu̅ . x . porc . ıı . ac̅ p̅ti . Tc̅ & p̸ ual . xxx .
fol m̅ xx . Rex 7 . c . foca̅ .

375 b

/ In Vledana . vııı . lib̅i ho̅es . xʟ . ac̅ . Ex h̅ . fuere . ıııı . co̅m̅dti Saxo
ante ceſſori . Ra . pip̸ . hn̅ts . xx . v . ac̅ . Tc̅ int tot . ıı . car̅ . m̅ . ɪ . 7 . ɪ . ac̅
& dim̅ p̅ti . 7 . ɪ . runc . Tc̅ . vı . an̅ . m̅ . vıı . Tc̅ xx . vııı . ou̅s 7 m̅ xvıı . ou̅s .
: + Eccl̅ia de . vıı . ac̅ 7 dim' . 7 ual . xv . d̅ .
m̅ . xx . cap̅ . Tc̅ . v . porc . m̅ . xıx . | Tc̅ ual xx . fol . m̅ xxı . R . & . c . foc .
/ In Stanham tenuit Vluric lib̅ ho̅ . ʟx . ac̅ . p̸ man in co̅m̅d Ab̅b̅is
de eli Tc̅ . ıııı . bord . m̅ . ııı . Tc̅ . ıı . car in dn̅io . m̅ . ɪ . Tc̅ . ɪ . car hom̅ . m̅
d̅ . 7 . ııı . ac̅ p̅ti . Eccl̅ia . de . vıı . ac̅ & d̅ . 7 ual . xv . d̅ . Tc̅ ual . xʟ . fol . m̅ . xx .

now at 11.
Value then 30s; now 40[s].
The Abbot of Ely had the patronage.
In the same (Coddenham) 2 free men, Aelfric and Wihtric; 2 acres. Value 12d.
A church, 1 acre; value 2d.
The King and the Earl (have) jurisdiction over the whole.
In the same (Coddenham) Harold, a free man in the jurisdiction and patronage of the Abbot of Ely; 30 acres as a manor before 1066.
Always 2 smallholders;
1 plough.
Meadow, 2 acres; woodland, 10 pigs.
Value 10s.
2 acres belonging to the church; value 4d.
In the same (Coddenham) 3 free men; 7½ acres. ½ plough.
Value 2s.
The King and the Earl (have) the jurisdiction.
In the same (Coddenham) Leofeva, a free woman, before 1066; 10 acres. ½ plough.
3 smallholders.
Meadow, 1 acre.
Value 4s.
In the same (Coddenham) 15 free men; 80 acres less 1. Of these, 6 (free men) were under the patronage of Saxi, Ranulf Peverel's predecessor. Then and later 5 ploughs, now 1.
Woodland, 10 pigs; meadow, 2 acres.
Value then and later 30s; now 20[s].
The King and the Earl (have) the jurisdiction.

21 In 'OLDEN' 8 free men; 40 acres. Of these (free men), 4 who had 25 acres were under the patronage of Saxi, Ranulf Peverel's predecessor. Then in total 2 ploughs, now 1.
Meadow, 1½ acres. 1 cob; then 6 cattle, now 7; then 28 sheep, now 17 sheep; now 20 goats; then 5 pigs, now 19.
A church with 7½ acres; value 15d.
Value then 20s; now 21[s].
The King and the Earl (have) the jurisdiction.

375 b

22 In STONHAM Wulfric, a free man, under the patronage of the Abbot of Ely, held 60 acres as a manor.
Then 4 smallholders, now 3.
Then 2 ploughs in lordship, now 1; then 1 men's plough, now ½.
Meadow, 3 acres.
A church with 7½ acres; value 15d.
Value then 40s; now 20[s].

In eadē Aluoſ pbr . 7 Gōduí libī hóes cōmdati Saxo ante . c . Ra.
pip . XL . ac . p . II . man . t . r . e . sep . III . bord . Tc 7 p . II . car in dnio.
sep dim car hoiūm . 7 . I . ac & dim pti . Ecclia de . II . ac . & . ual
IIII . d . Tc ual . xxx ; ſol . m . XII . In eadē . xxvi . libī hoes . cōmdati
Saxo pt un . nōe Wiching CXL . II . ac . Tc . VII . car . m . V . 7 . I . ac
& dim pti . Tc ual . IIII . lib . m . XL . ſol . 7 IIII . d.
In ead . I . lib . ho . III . ac . 7 ual . X . d

/ In hamingeſtuna . II . libī hoes cōmdati . Saxo antec . pip . X . ac
& ual . XX . VIII . d . hoc tot ten& Radulfus de ſauigni de . R . bigot
& . Ro . de epo . Rex 7 . c . ſoca de toto.

/ In ead . II . libī hoes Brunnuin . & Godric . III . ac . & ual . VI . d . Id
Rog ten . R . 7 . c . ſoca

/ In Scaruestuna . III . libī . hoes . Leuuin . Leuuric Edric . IIII .
ac . 7 . II . bou . 7 ual . X . d . Rad . de ſauigni . ten de Roger

/ CLAINDVNE . H . In helminghehā tenuit . Durandus
                   . malet
lib ho cmdat . Edrico de laxefelda . antec . LXXX ac p man
T . r . e . sep . I . uilli . & . II . bord . Tc . II . car in dnio . P . I . m . nulla;

sep . I . car houm . & . II . ac pti . Tc ual . XXX . ſol . m . XX.
/ In Hmingeham ten . Balchi Cōmdat Aiſtan XL . ac . p man.
semp . IIII . bord . & . I . car in dnio . & . I . ac pti . & . I . runc . Tc . IIII.
an . m . II . Tc . XXX . porc . m . XX . VII . Tc . XL . ou . m . XXIIII . 7 ual . X . ſol.

In the same (Stonham) Alwold the priest and Godwy, free men under the patronage of Saxi, Ranulf Peverel's predecessor; 40 acres as 2 manors before 1066.
> Always 3 smallholders.
> Then and later 2 ploughs in lordship; always ½ men's plough.
>> Meadow, 1½ acres.
> A church with 2 acres; value 4d.

Value then 30s; now 12[s].

In the same (Stonham) 26 free men under the patronage of Saxi, except for one, Viking by name; 142 acres. Then 7 ploughs, now 5.
> Meadow, 1½ acres.

Value then £4; now 40s 4d.

In the same (Stonham) 1 free man; 3 acres.

Value 10d.

23 In HEMINGSTONE 2 free men under the patronage of Saxi, Ranulf Peverel's predecessor; 10 acres.

Value 28d.
> Ralph of Savenay holds the whole of this from R(oger) Bigot; Ro(ger) [holds it] from the Bishop.
> The King and the Earl (have) jurisdiction over the whole.

In the same (Hemingstone) 2 free men, Brunwin and Godric; 3 acres. Value 6d.
> Roger also holds (this).
> The King and the Earl (have) the jurisdiction.

24 In SHARPSTONE 3 free men, Leofwin, Leofric, and Edric; 4 acres.
> 2 oxen.

Value 10d.
> Ralph of Savenay holds (this) from Roger.

CLAYDON Hundred

25 In HELMINGHAM Durand, a free man under the patronage of Edric of Laxfield, Malet's predecessor, held 80 acres as manor before 1066.
> Always 1 villager; 2 smallholders.
> Then 2 ploughs in lordship, later 1, now none; always 1 men's plough. Meadow, 2 acres.

Value then 30s; now 20[s].

376 a

26 In HELMINGHAM Balki, under the patronage of Aethelstan, held 40 acres as a manor.
> Always 4 smallholders;
> 1 plough in lordship;
> Meadow, 1 acre. 1 cob; then 4 cattle, now 2; then 30 pigs, now 27; then 40 sheep, now 24.

Value 10s.

In ead lib hō Wichinc cōmdat. Burcardo. xxx. ac̄ ꝑ. mañ. t. r. e.
sep̄. I. car̄. &. I. ac̄ p̃ti. silu de. IIII. porc̄. & tc̄ ual. VI. sol. m̄. XIII. sol 7. IIII. d.
In ead lib hō. reg̃. e. Ailricus xxv. ac̄. & . I. bord. Tc̄ & p̄. I. car̄. modo
dim̄. Tc̄ ual. L. d. & fuit ad firmā ꝑ. x. sol. m̄ ual. IIII. sol. In ead
lib hō. Blacheman. dimidĩ cōmdat cuidā cōmdato. Edrici antec
mal&. & dimidi cōmdat. saxo XXIIII. ac̄ ꝑ mañ. sep̄. I. car̄. Tc̄
ual. v. sol. 7 fuit ad firm̄. ꝑ. xv. sol. m̄ ual. VIII. sol.
In ead Godric lib hō. dimid cōm̄d cuidā cōmdato Edrici. ante
cessori mal&. 7 dim̄. saxo. xx. ac̄. ꝑ mañ. &. I. bord. &. I. car̄ &
q̃rta pars æcclæ. I. ac̄ & dim̄ libæ t̃ræ. Tc̄ ual. VI. sol. &. IIII. d. 7
fuit ad firm̄ ꝑ XIIII. sol. m̄ ual x. sol. In ead lib hō Leue_
stan. cōmdat cuidā cōmdato. edrici. xx. ac̄. ꝑ. mañ. sep̄. I. car̄
& q̃rta pars æcclæ libæ t̃ræ. Tc̄ ual. VI. sol. & fuit ad firmā ꝑ.
XIIII. sol. m̄ ual. x. sol. In ead xI. libi hoēs. LXXI. ac̄ De duobᷣ
7 dimidio ex his. habuit sup̃dict saxo antecessor. Ra piperelli.
cōmdatiō. 7. I. Dimid fuit cōmdat cuidā cōmdato Ædrici
ante cessori. R. malet. Int eos habeb. tc̄. II. car̄. m̄. III. &. II. ac̄
p̃ti. 7 dim̄ æcclia. III. ac̄. Tc̄ ual. xx. sol. m̄ xx. Rex 7 com̄s de_
In Escaruestuna. xxvII. libi hoēs in soca 7 cōmdtoē toto soca.
Abbis de eli. I. car̄ t̃ræ. Tc̄ 7 p̄. IIII. car̄. &. m̄ III. &. II. ac̄ p̃ti,
. . . . sep ual xL. sol;

In the same (Helmingham) Viking, a free man under the patronage of Burghard; 30 acres as a manor before 1066. Always 1 plough.
   Meadow, 1 acre; woodland at 4 pigs.
Value then 6s; now 13s 4d.
In the same (Helmingham) a free man of King Edward's, Aethelric; 25 acres.
   1 smallholder.
   Then and later 1 plough, now ½.
Value then 50d; it was at a revenue for 10s; value now 4s.
In the same (Helmingham) a free man, Blackman, half under the patronage of someone under the patronage of Edric, Malet's predecessor, and a half under the patronage of Saxi; 24 acres as a manor. Always 1 plough.
Value then 5s; it was at a revenue for 15s; value now 8s.
In the same (Helmingham) Godric, a free man half under the patronage of someone under the patronage of Edric, Malet's predecessor, and half (under the patronage) of Saxi; 20 acres as a manor.
   1 smallholder.
   1 plough.
   The fourth part of a church, 1½ acres of free land.
Value then 6s 4d; it was at a revenue for 14s; value now 10s.
In the same (Helmingham) a free man, Leofstan, under the patronage of someone under the patronage of Edric; 20 acres as a manor. Always 1 plough.
   The fourth part of a church, ... of free land.
Value then 6s; it was at a revenue for 14s; value now 10s.
In the same (Helmingham) 11 free men; 71 acres. Over two and a half of these (free men) the above-mentioned Saxi, Ranulf Peverel's predecessor, had patronage; and 1 half (free man) was under the patronage of someone under the patronage of Edric, R(obert) Malet's predecessor. Between them, they had then 2 ploughs, now 3.
   Meadow, 2 acres.
   ½ church, 3 acres.
Value then 20s; now 20[s].
   The King and the Earl (have) jurisdiction over the whole.

27 In SHARPSTONE 27 free men in the jurisdiction and patronage of the Abbot of Ely; 1 carucate of land. Then and later 4 ploughs, now 3.
   Meadow, 2 acres; ...
Value always 40s.

In depbeham Goduï. 1. lib hō comdat saxo. XL. ac̃ ꝑ mañ. sep̃. II.
borđ 7. I. car̃. &. I. ac̃ p̃ti. & q̃rta pars eccłiæ. sc̃e mariæ. de. x. ac̃. & uał
xx. fol. Sc̃a Adeldreda. focā. 7. III. part eccłiæ sc̃i andreæ. I. ac̃. 7. đ. 7. IIII pars

In Vlueftuna. xv. ac̃. t. r. e. Idē Godui⁹ 7 jn Asfelda. VIII. ac̃. sep̃. III.
borđ. 7. I. car̃. In eadē. I. lib hō. Goda. Comdat. cuidā cōmdato. Edrici ante cefforis Robti malet xv. ac̃. tc̃. I. car̃. m̃ dim̃ 7. I. ac̃ p̃ti. H̃ tria
ſt ꝑ. uno manerio. m̃. IIII. añ. in dñio. 7. x. porc̃. 7 xxx. oūs. 7. XII. cap̃.
sep̃ uał xx. II. fol. Soca Abbis.

In Vlueftuna. Aluin⁹ pb̃r lib hō. 7 fexta pars cōmdationis fuæ
erat cuidā cōmdato. antecefforis mal& & quinq; partes faxo. ante
ceffori pip̃. xxxx ac̃. ꝑ mañ. sep̃. I. uił. &. I. pb̃r. &. II. borđ. &. II. ac̃
p̃ti. &. I. car̃ in dñio Tc̃ 7 p⁹ uał. xx. fol. m̃. x. Soc̃ abbis De quarta
parte ifti tr̃æ erat faifitus. Viłłm malet.. & de pb̃ro q̃ in ea manebat
die fui obitus. In ead Aluricus pb̃r lib hō ꝑ mañ. xxx. ac̃. in foca &
cōmdatiōe abbis. Tc̃. I. car̃. Tc̃ uał. x. fol. m̃. v.

In ead. II. libi. hōes. Cōmdati Saxo. Edric 7 Alnod. XL. ac̃. &. I. borđ
sep̃. I. car̃. m̃. II. uac̃. 7 XII. porc̃. 7 xx. oūs. 7 uał xx. fol.

28 In DEBENHAM Godwy, 1 free man under the patronage of Saxi; 40 acres as a manor.
    Always 2 smallholders;
    1 plough. Meadow, 1 acre.
    The fourth part of a church of St. Mary, with 10 acres.
    Value 20s.
    St. Etheldreda's (has) the jurisdiction.
    3 parts of a church of St. Andrew, 1½ acres. The fourth part of a church of St. Mary, 10 acres.

29 In ULVERSTON the same Godwy; 15 acres before 1066; and in ASHFIELD 8 acres.
    Always 3 smallholders;
    1 plough.
In the same (Ulverston) 1 free man, Goda, under the patronage of someone under the patronage of Edric, Robert Malet's predecessor; 15 acres. Then 1 plough, now ½.
    Meadow, 1 acre.
    These three are [held] as one manor.
    Now 4 cattle in lordship, 10 pigs, 30 sheep, 12 goats.
    Value always 22s.
    The jurisdiction (is) the Abbot's.

30 In ULVERSTON Alwin the priest, a free man the sixth part of whom was under the patronage of someone under the patronage of Malet's predecessor and five parts (were under the patronage) of Saxi, Ranulf Peverel's predecessor; 40 acres as a manor.
    Always 1 villager; 1 priest; 2 smallholders.
    Meadow, 2 acres.
    1 plough in lordship.
Value then and later 20s; now 10[s].
    The jurisdiction (is) the Abbot's.
    William Malet was in possession of a fourth part of this land, and of the priest who dwelt on it, on the day of his death.
In the same (Ulverston) Aelfric the priest, a free man in the jurisdiction and patronage of the Abbot; 30 acres as a manor. Then 1 plough.
Value then 10s; now 5[s].
In the same (Ulverston) 2 free men under Saxi's patronage, Edric and Alnoth; 40 acres.
    1 smallholder.
    Always 1 plough. Now 2 cows, 12 pigs, 20 sheep.
    Value 20s.

In ead Thure lib hō.xl.ac̄.p mañ.&.ii.bord.&.i.car.Tc̄ filua.viii.
porc.m̄.iiii. 7 ual.xx.fol. Soca 7 com̄datio abbis.
In ead Leuuin cilt lib hō.t.r.e.in foca 7 cōmendatione abbis.xl.
ac̄.p mañ.&.ii.uill.in alio hundret.Tc̄.i.car̄.7.i.ac̄ p̄ti.filu.xii.
porc.Tc̄ ual.xx.fol m̄.xv. h tot ten Rog bigot de ep̄o. 7 Rad
de fauigni.de illo. / x & ual&.iiii.d.
/ In depham.i.lib hō.Ailric com̄dat faxo in foca abbis dim ac̄ x

/ In mane wic. W de brun lib hō.in foca & com̄datione abbis.xxvii.
ac̄.sep̄.i.car̄.7.iii.bord. 7 dim ac̄ p̄ti.Tc̄ ual.x.fol.m̄.vi.
/ In Wineftuna.xx.i.libi.hōes.i.car̄ trǣ.7.ii.ac̄ ifti trǣ fuer̄ de dn̄io
faxi.t.r.e.anteceſſoris.Ran.pip̄.in depbenhā.un ex his.fuit cō
m̄dat sc̄o eadmund.cū.xii.ac̄. 7 fuit inde faifitus donec Rad forisfec̄.
sep̄.v.car̄.&.iiii.ac̄ & d p̄ti.Tc̄ ual xl.fol.m̄ xl.v.Ex.viii.habuit
Saxo com̄d & abbas de cli de aliis. 7 foca 7 com̄datione p̄t de duob;
fcili.Alwino 7 Leuino.com̄datis cuidā com̄dato.Edrici ant malet.

In the same (Ulverston) Thuri, a free man; 40 acres as a manor.
   2 smallholders.
   1 plough. Woodland then 8 pigs, now 4.
Value 20s.
   The jurisdiction and patronage (are) the Abbot's.
In the same (Ulverston) Young Leofwin, a free man before 1066 in the jurisdiction and patronage of the Abbot; 40 acres as a manor.
   2 villagers in another Hundred.
   Then 1 plough.
   Meadow, 1 acre; woodland, 12 pigs.
Value then 20s; now 15[s].
   Roger Bigot holds the whole of this from the Bishop; Ralph of Savenay [holds it] from him.

31 In DEBENHAM 1 free man, Aethelric, under the patronage of Saxi, in the jurisdiction of the Abbot; ½ acre.
Value 4d.

32 In *MANEWIC* Woodbrown, a free man in the jurisdiction and patronage of the Abbot; 27 acres. Always 1 plough.
   3 smallholders.
   Meadow, ½ acre.
Value then 10s; now 6[s].

33 In WINSTON 21 free men; 1 carucate of land. Before 1066, 2 acres of that land were in the lordship of Saxi, Ranulf Peverel's predecessor, in Debenham. One of these (free) men, with 12 acres, was under the patronage of St. Edmund's and was in possession of it until (Earl) Ralph forfeited. Always 5 ploughs.
   Meadow, 4½ acres.
Value then 40s; now 45[s].
   Saxi had patronage over 8 (free men) and the Abbot of Ely had jurisdiction and patronage over the others, except for 2, that is Alwin and Leofwin, (who were) under the patronage of someone under the patronage of Edric, Malet's predecessor.

⸿ In Asfelda Suarin̅ pbr lib hō in foca & cōmd abbis.xxx ac̄.femp.ıı.
bord.&.ı.car̄.7 ual.x.fol. Ex hoc pbro erat faifitus Galt̄ dedol
qdo forisfecit fuā trā. 7 cōms hugo poftea fic̄ hundret teftatur.
Et normannus dicit qd rex mifit ei. unū breuē ut faifiret Radulfū de fauigni ex oib; libis hominib; ex qb; Hubtus de portu faifierat
epm̄.& idō Normannus faifiuit Radulfū ex h̄ pbro f7 tm̄ nefcit
fi ubtus pus faifierat epm̄ de illo.& hc̄ inueneī barones regis in
pace int Rogum bigot 7 hugonē comitē. qdo uener in comitatū
& ita erit in pace donec fit derationatus.

⸿ SANFORT. H̄ & dim̄. In Burgheftala.ııı.libi hōes.xxx.
vıı.ac̄.Godinc.Vlmar.Aluiet.Vn Cōmdatus.Guert.7 alt̄.Alurico,
7 tci Salpo.Tc̄.ı.car̄.m̄.dim̄.7.ıııı.ac̄ pti.7 ual vııı.fol.Soca
in bcolt.In Ead Goduuin lib hō.Stigandi.xxx.ac̄.p man̄.
Tc̄ 7 p.ı.car̄.7.ı.molin m̄ d.& ual.vıı.fol.Saca in bcolt. pt
de domo fua.&.de.ııı.ac̄.In ead.ııı.libi hōes.xvııı.ac̄.Vluiet.
Brungar.Blacfune.fep dim̄.car̄.7 ual.ıııı.fol; h̄ tenet de epō.Ro.
⸿ bigot. 7 Ra de fauigni de illo.

⸿ SANFORT. H̄.7 dim̄.In Wenham.Algar lib hō.xx.ıııı
ac̄.p man̄.t.r.e.& ual.ıııı.fol. Soca in bcolt.In ead.ıııı.libi hōes
Brictuolt.Ofgot Ledmer.Godricus hn̄ts.L.ac̄.&.vı.bord.&
ual x.fol Soc̄ in bercolt;

34 In ASHFIELD Snaring the priest, a free man in the jurisdiction and patronage of the Abbot; 30 acres.
    Always 2 smallholders.
    1 plough.
    Value 10s.
    Walter of Dol was in possession of this priest when he forfeited his land, and afterwards Earl Hugh (was in possession), as the Hundred testifies. And Norman says that the King sent him a writ (stating) that he should put Ralph of Savenay in possession of all the free men of whom Hubert of Port had put the Bishop in possession. And so Norman put Ralph in possession of that priest; but however he does not know whether Hubert had first put the Bishop in possession of him. And the King's Barons kept the peace on this between Roger Bigot and Earl Hugh when they came into the County; and so it shall be at peace until there is a judgement.

SAMFORD Hundred and a Half

35 In BURSTALL 3 free men; Goding, Wulfmer (and) Alfgeat, one under the patronage of Gyrth, another (under that) of Aelfric, and the third (under that) of Scalpi; 37 acres. Then 1 plough, now ½.
    Meadow, 4 acres.
    Value 8s.
    The jurisdiction (is) in (East) Bergholt.
In the same (Burstall) Godwin, a free man of Stigand's; 30 acres as a manor. Then and later 1 plough and 1 mill, now ½.
Value 7s.
    The jurisdiction (is) in (East) Bergholt, except over his house and 3 acres.
In the same (Burstall) 3 free men, Wulfgeat, Brungar, and Blackson; 18 acres. Always ½ plough;
Value 4s.
    Ro(ger) Bigot holds this from the Bishop; Ra(lph) of Savenay [holds it] from him.

SAMFORD Hundred and a Half

36 In WENHAM Algar, a free man; 24 acres as a manor before 1066.
    Value 4s.
    The jurisdiction (is) in (East) Bergholt.
In the same (Wenham) 4 free men, Brictwold, Osgot, Ledmer (and) Godric, who have 50 acres.
    6 smallholders.
    Value 10s.
    The jurisdiction (is) in (East) Bergholt.

ꝟ In Reinduna tēn. Ednod liƀ hō. I. car̂ trē. &. c. aͨ. ꝑ man̂.
femp. III. uiƚƚ. 7 VI. borđ. &. I. car̂. & dim̂. in dn̄io. fep̄. I. car̂ hoīum,
& . IIII. aͨ p̃ti. filua x. porͨ. Quinta pars æcclīæ. de. v. aͨ. Tͨ
uaƚ. III. liƀ. m̂. IIII. liƀ. fed fuit ad firmā. ꝑ. VI. liƀ. Soca. in ƀ
colt hoc tēn. Ro. bigot de ep̄o.

ꝟ CLAINDVNE. H̃. In Vlueftuna. II. liƀi hoēs. Aluricus 7
Leuuinus. ifte fuit cōmdątus cuidā cōmdato edrici anteceffores
malet. 7 Aluricus cōm̂dąt Wifgaro. xxx. aͨ. 7. II. borđ. Tͨ
II. car̂. P̃. nichil. m̂ dim̂. &. II. aͨ p̃ti. Tͨ uaƚ. x. foƚ. ⋒. VIII. Roḡ
ten& de ep̄o. 7 garenḡ de illo. Soͨ aƀƀis. In eađ dimiđ liƀ homo
II. aͨ. 7 ſt in eođ p̃tio.
In petehaga. Siwardus liƀ hō. t. r. e. v. aͨ. 7 uaƚ. II. foƚ. foca aƀƀis
Idē Gar̂. ꝟ SANFORT. H̃. Et DIM.
Wenham tenuit. Tuneman. cōm heroldi. T. r. e. : reḡ. e. I.
car̂ træ. ꝑ man̂. Tͨ 7 VII. uiƚƚ. m̂. II. Tͨ. III. borđ. m̂. XVII. Tͨ. II
feruˀ. modo. I. fep̄. II. car in dn̄io. Tͨ. v. car̂. hoūm. P̃ 7 m̂. II. VI aͨ
p̃ti. Silua. VIII. porͨ. Ecclīæ. VI. aͨ. Tͨ. I. runͨ. m̂. II. Tͨ. IIII. an̂.
Tͨ xx. IIII. porͨ. m̂. XL. Tͨ. LX. oūs. m̂. LXX. Tͨ uaƚ. LX. foƚ. 7 m̂
fimiliͭ. Roḡ. bigot de ep̄o. Ht VI. qr̂ in lonḡ. 7. II. qr̂ & dim̂
in lat̂. 7. IIII. đ. In eađ. tēn Vluric liƀ hō. XL. aͨ. ꝑ man̂. t. r. e.

378 a

Tͨ. I. car̂. tͨ uaƚ. v. foƚ. m̂. VI. Haroldus focā Idē. Roḡ. de ep̄o.

37 In RAYDON Ednoth, a free man, held 1 carucate of land and 100 acres as a manor.
>Always 3 villagers; 6 smallholders;
>1½ ploughs in lordship. Always 1 men's plough.
>Meadow, 4 acres; woodland, 10 pigs.
>The fifth part of a church with 5 acres.
>Value then £3; now [£] 4; but it was at a revenue for £6.
>The jurisdiction (is) in (East) Bergholt.
>Ro(ger) Bigot holds this from the Bishop.

CLAYDON Hundred

38 In ULVERSTON 2 free men, Aelfric and Leofwin, the latter was under the patronage of someone under the patronage of Edric, Malet's predecessor, and Aelfric (was) under the patronage of Withgar; 30 acres.
>2 smallholders.
>Then 2 ploughs, later nothing, now ½. Meadow, 2 acres.
>Value then 10s; now 8[s].
>Roger holds (this) from the Bishop; Warengar [holds it] from him.
>The jurisdiction (is) the Abbot's.

In the same (Ulverston) a half free man; 2 acres.
They are in the same assessment.

39 In PETTAUGH Siward a free man before 1066; 5 acres.
>Value 2s.
>The jurisdiction (is) the Abbot's.
>Warengar also [holds this].

SAMFORD Hundred and a Half

40 Tuneman, a thane of King Edward's and under the patronage of Harold, held WENHAM before 1066; 1 carucate of land as a manor.
>Then 7 villagers, now 2; then 3 smallholders, now 17; then 2 slaves, now 1.
>The fourth part of a church.
>Always 2 ploughs in lordship. Then 5 men's ploughs, later and now 2.
>Meadow, 6 acres; woodland, 8 pigs.
>6 acres belonging to the church.
>Then 1 cob, now 2; then 4 cattle; then 24 pigs, now 40; then 60 sheep, now 70.
>Value then 60s; now the same.
>Roger Bigot [holds this] from the Bishop.
>It has 6 furlongs in length and 2½ furlongs in width; 4d [in tax].

In the same (Wenham) Wulfric, a free man, held 40 acres as a manor before 1066. Then 1 plough.
>Value then 5s; now 6[s].
>Harold (had) the jurisdiction.
>Roger also holds (this) from the Bishop.

Reindune tenuit. Edui lib hō . t . r . e . i . car tr̄æ . p man̄ . semp iiii . bord . & . i . car . v . ac̄ p̄ti . & . i . moliñ . Qnta pars æccłiæ . v . ac̄ . Tc̄ ual xxx . foł . 7 m̄ similit . sed fuit ad firmā . p lx . foł . łit . i . lḡ in lonḡ in lonḡ . & . viii . qr in lat̄ . 7 xxx d . de gt . alii ibi ten̄ .
In ead . ten̄ . lib hō Aluuiñ . lx . ac̄ . p . man̄ . Tc̄ . i . bord . sep . i . car & iiii . ac̄ p̄ti . Quinta pars æccłiæ . v . ac̄ . m̄ . iiii . an̄ . 7 xiii . porc . & xxx . vi . oūs . Tc̄ ual xx . foł . modo . xv . In ead lib hō Smeri xxx . ac̄ . p man̄ . t . r . e . c̄omdat Alurico capin antec̄ . Eudonis dapiferi . sēp . i . bord . Tc̄ dim̄ car . ii . ac̄ p̄ti . 7 ual . v . foł . In ea
★ d . lib hō Vluuiñ xxx . ac̄ . sēp . i . bord . 7 tc̄ dim̄ . car . m̄ . ii . bou . 7 ii . ac̄ p̄ti . 7 ual . v . foł . In ead lib hō Aluric xxx . ac̄ . p man̄ . sēp dim̄ car . & . ii . ac̄ p̄ti . 7 tc̄ ual . v . foł . m̄ . x . Soca in Bercolt.
In Reindune . i . lib hō . Aluricus . v . ac̄ . & ē in p̄tio de reinduna
In belefteda . tenuit Aluricus lib hō . xxx . ac̄ . p man̄ . 7 . ii . bord . Tc̄ . i . car . & ual . v . foł .
In Branthā . iii . libi hōes . Brun . Siricus . Godeftan 7 in Belenei . i . lib hō Burcheric . 7 in hechā . i . lib hō . Edricus łints lx . ac̄ . & . i . bord . & tc̄ . ii . car . m̄ . i . Tc̄ ual . x . foł . m̄ . xiiii .

41 Edwy, a free man, held RAYDON before 1066; 1 carucate of land as a manor.
>   Always 4 smallholders;
>   1 plough.
>   Meadow, 5 acres; 1 mill.
>   The fifth part of a church, 5 acres.
> Value then 30s; now the same; but it was at a revenue for 60s.
> It has 1 league in length and 8 furlongs in width; 30d in tax.
> Others hold there.
> In the same (Raydon) a free man, Alwin, held 60 acres as a manor.
>   Then 1 smallholder.
>   Always 1 plough. Meadow, 4 acres.
>   The fifth part of a church, 5 acres.
>   Now 4 cattle, 13 pigs, 36 sheep.
> Value then 20s; now 15[s].
> In the same (Raydon) a free man, Smeri, under the patronage of Aelfric Kemp, Eudo the Steward's predecessor; 30 acres as a manor before 1066.
>   Always 1 smallholder.
>   Then ½ plough. Meadow, 2 acres.
> Value 5s.
> In the same (Raydon) [1] free man, Wulfwin; 30 acres.
>   Always 1 smallholder.
>   Then ½ plough, now 2 oxen. Meadow, 2 acres.
> Value 5s.
> In the same (Raydon) a free man, Aelfric; 30 acres as a manor.
> Always ½ plough.
>   Meadow, 2 acres.
> Value then 5s; now 10[s].
>   The jurisdiction (is) in (East) Bergholt.
> In RAYDON 1 free man, Aelfric; 5 acres.
> It is in the assessment of Raydon.

42 In BELSTEAD Aelfric, a free man, held 30 acres as a manor.
>   2 smallholders.
>   Then 1 plough.
> Value 5s.

43 In BRANTHAM 3 free men, Brown, Siric, and Godstan; in BELENEI 1 free man, Burgric; in HIGHAM 1 free man, Edric; these have 60 acres.
>   1 smallholder.
>   Then 2 ploughs, now 1.
> Value then 10s; now 14[s].

⁊ In Boituna teñ Goduin̅ lib̅ hō . t . r . e . lx . ac̅ ꝑ mañ . iii . uill̄
& i . car̕ in dn̅io . 7 . i . car̕ hoiu̅m . filua . x . porc̕ . Q̊rta pars
æccliæ . vi . ac̅ . 7 ual̄ xx . fol̄ .

⁊ Alfildeſtunā . teñ . Alnold . lib̅ hō̕ . t̕ . r̕ . e̕ . ii . car̕ t̕ræ . ꝑ mañ .
Tc̅ . i . bord̄ . m̅ . v . Tc̅ . ii . car̕ in dn̅io . m̅ . i . 7 . i . ac̅ 7 dim̅ p̊ti . sc̄p . i . molin̄ .

378 b

7 ual̄ xx . v . fol̄ . ħt . vi . q̕r in long̕ . 7 . iii . in lat̕ . 7 . ii . d̄ 7 obl̄ de gelt̕ .
⁊ In tatituna teñ . Turgot lib̅ hō lx . ac̅ . ꝑ mañ . tc̅ . i . car̕ . 7 . i . ac̅ 7 dim̅
p̊ti . Tc̅ ual̄ . x . fol̄ . m̅ . iiii . Totu̅ teñ Ro . bigot de ep̄o . 7 de tota ē foca
in bercolt.

⁊ In Gẏpefwiz . i . domu̅ de dim̕ ac̅ . 7 In toft . Edui̊ lib̅ hō . ii . ac̅ &
dim̕ 7 ual̄ vi . d̄ . Ro . bigot . Soca in ƀcolt .

⁊ Hertefmara . H̄ . In efpala . xx . ac̅ . teñ . Leueua com̅mdata abƀi
de ʰeli 7 in foca ei̊ 7 ual̄ . iiii . fol̄ . ħ ten̄& Ro . bigot 7 Rad de fauigni
de Rog̅rio . In ead̄ . xii . ac̅ de dn̅io . de dephenhā . & . v . bord̄ . 7 in eod̄
pretio .

. XVII . ⁊ Tra Sc̄i Benedicti de Ramefeia . Duo Hund̄ de babenƀga . ✶
Laweffelam tenuit Sc̄s benedict t̕ . r̕ . e̕ . ꝑ Mañ . viii . car̕ t̕ræ c̄ foca .

378 a, b

44 In BOYNTON Godwin, a free man, held 60 acres as a manor before 1066.
    3 villagers.
    1 plough in lordship; 1 men's plough. Woodland, 10 pigs.
    The fourth part of a church, 6 acres.
  Value 20s.

45 Alwold, a free man, held ALFILDESTUNA before 1066; 2 carucates of land as a manor.
    Then 1 smallholder, now 5.
    Then 2 ploughs in lordship, now 1.
    Meadow, 1½ acres; always 1 mill.
  Value 25s.
    It has 6 furlongs in length and 3 in width; 2½d in tax.

46 In TATTINGSTONE Thurgot, a free man, held 60 acres as a manor.
  Then 1 plough.
    Meadow, 1½ acres.
  Value then 10s; now 4[s].
    Ro(ger) Bigot holds the whole from the Bishop.
    Jurisdiction over the whole is in (East) Bergholt.

47 In IPSWICH 1 house with ½ acre. In TOFT Edwy, a free man; 2½ acres.
  Value 6d.
    Ro(ger) Bigot [holds this].
    The jurisdiction (is) in (East) Bergholt.

  HARTISMERE Hundred

48 In ASPALL Leofeva, under the patronage of the Abbot of Ely and in his jurisdiction, held 20 acres.
  Value 4s.
    Roger Bigot holds this; Ralph of Savenay [holds it] from Roger. In the same Aspall 12 acres of the lordship of Debenham.
    5 smallholders.
  (It is) in the same assessment.

17   LAND OF ST. BENEDICT'S OF RAMSEY

  The Two Hundreds of BABERGH

1 St. Benedict's held LAWSHALL before 1066 as a manor; 8 carucates of land with the jurisdiction.

Tc̄.xiiii.uill.m̄.xvi.Tc̄.xii.bord.m̄.x.Tc̄.iiii.ser̾.m̄.v.Tc̄.ii.car̄ in
dn̄io.m̄.iii.Sēp.x.car̾ hom̄.viii.ac̾ p̄ti.Sēp.i.runc̾.M.x.anim̄.7
.xxx.porc̾.c.ou̾.7.xii.cap̾.Ecclia.xxx.ac̾ libæ træ.Tc̄ ual.viii.lib̄
m̄.xii.ħt.i.leu̾g in long̾.7 dim̄ in lat̾.7 de gelto.xv.d̄.

379 a

⸿TRÆ Willmi. Ep̄i DE TETFORT. BISCOPĪS. II. .XVIII.

Hoxanā tenuit Ailmarus ep̄s.t.r.e.p̄.mañ.ix car̾.træ.Tc̄ xl.uill
m̄.xx.Tc̄ xv.bord.m̄.l.i.Tc̄.iiii.serui; sēp.iii.car̾ in dn̄io.Tc̄.xl.car̾ hoñ.
m̄.xx.ii.& dim̄.7 xl ac̄ p̄ti.Silua.de.ccl.porc̾.Semp.ii.molin̄.&
.ii.runc̾.& xii.añ.7 lxxx.porc̾.7 xvii.ous̄.& xl.cap̾.In h̄ manerio
erat unū mercatū.t.r.e.7 p̄q̇.Willmus rex aduen̄; & sedebat in
sabbato.& W.malet fecit suū castellū ad eiam 7 eadē die q̇ erat
mercatū in manerio ep̄i.W.malet fecit aliū mercatū in suo castello
& ex hoc ita peioratū ē mercatū ep̄i: ut parū ualeat.& m̄ sedet die
ueneris.Mercatū aut̄ de heia sedet die sabbati.m̄ ten̄.Rob.de dono.reg̾s
⸿In h̄ mañ.ē æcclia sedes episcopatus de sudfolc.t.r.e.Tc̄ ual h̄ mañ
xxviii.lib.m̄.xx.sed erfasto reddidit.xxx.lib.ħt.i.lḡ in lō.7 viii.
q̄r in lat 7 xxii.d̄.& obol.de gt.In Wcibrada.i.soc̄.ii.ac̄.7 ual.x.d̄.
⸿In Wilebi.i.soc̄.xl.ac̄.7.i.bord.7.i.car̾.7.ii.ac̄ p̄ti.silu xx.porc̄.Tc̄ ual
x.sot.modo.viii.sot.

Then 14 villagers, now 16; then 12 smallholders, now 10; then 4 slaves, now 5.
Then 2 ploughs in lordship, now 3; always 10 men's ploughs.
Meadow, 8 acres. Always 1 cob. Now 10 cattle, 30 pigs, 100 sheep, 12 goats.
A church, 30 acres of free land.
Value then £8; now [£] 12.
It has 1 league in length and ½ in width; 15d in tax.

18   LANDS OF WILLIAM, BISHOP OF THETFORD

BISHOP'S Hundred

1 Bishop Aelmer held HOXNE as a manor before 1066; 9 carucates of land.
Then 40 villagers, now 20; then 15 smallholders, now 51; then 4 slaves.
Always 3 ploughs in lordship. Then 40 men's ploughs, now 22½.
Meadow, 40 acres; woodland at 250 pigs. Always 2 mills; 2 cobs, 12 cattle, 80 pigs, 17 sheep, 40 goats.
In this manor there was a market before 1066 and after King William came, and it took place on Saturdays. W(illiam) Malet made his castle at Eye and, on the same day that there was a market on the Bishop's manor, W(illiam) Malet established another market in his castle. Because of this, the Bishop's market declined so that it is worth little; and now it takes place on Fridays. However, the market at Eye takes place on Saturdays; Robert (Malet) now holds (it) by the King's gift.
In this manor is a church, the episcopal see of Suffolk before 1066.
Value of this manor then £28; now [£] 20; but it paid £30 to Erfast.
It has 1 league in length and 8 furlongs in width; 22½d in tax.

2 In WEYBREAD 1 Freeman; 2 acres.
Value 10d.

3 In WILBY 1 Freeman; 40 acres.
1 smallholder.
1 plough.
Meadow, 2 acres; woodland, 20 pigs.
Value then 10s; now 8s.

WANEFORDA. H.

HVmbresfelda . teñ Ælmer' eps . t . r . e . 1 . m̃ . de . v . car tr̃e . m̃ teñ eps W . sẽp . xvi . uilt . 7 sẽp . xii . bord . femp . iiii . feru' . Tc̃ . ii . car in dñio . m̃ iii . tc̃ . x . car omniũ hoiũ m̃ . v . 7 v . poffent ibi reftaurari xii . ac̃ p'ti tc̃ . filu' . ɔc . por m̃ . cc . i . mol . i . æcclia . xii . ac̃ . 7 . iii . eq' . qñ . rec̃ . & m̃ femp . vi . añ . Sẽp xxvi . porc' . cc . oũs . Tc̃ ual cũ foc̃ . xii . lib . m̃ . xvi . reddid Sup ferting de almehã lit W . eps . focã 7 facã p̃t h'oes Stigandi epĩ . 7 B . Abb . p teftimoniũ hundreti . Habuit breuẽ de . e . r' . qd ipfe habere debuit foc̃ 7 facã fup tr̃a sc̃i edmundi . & fui h'oes.

In barfhã . xvi . ac̃ . & . ii . bord . & dim' . car' . & . ual . ii . fol.

379 b

HERTESMARA . H̃. In Iacheflea . 7 in thrandeftuna teñ Almarus EPC . t' . r' . e' . i . car tr̃æ . p mañ . Sẽp . v . bord . & . i . car' . ii . ac̃ p'ti . 7 ual xx. fol . & p'tiñ ad æcclĩa de hoxna.

.XVIIII.
FEVDV' EP̃I DE TEDFORT;

In Seilanda . i . lib hõ . Stigandi . ii . car terræ . & xii . bord . & . ii . car' in dñio Tc̃ . iiii . car' . hoium . m̃ . ii . & . v . ac̃ p'ti . filua . de . lx . porc̃ . & . i . mol .

sẽp ual . lx . fol.

h̃ teñ Ailmar . Erfaftus.

WANGFORD Hundred
4 Bishop Aelmer held HOMERSFIELD before 1066; 1 manor at 5 carucates of land. Now Bishop William holds (it).
    Always 16 villagers; always 12 smallholders; always 4 slaves.
    Then 2 ploughs in lordship, now 3; then 10 men's ploughs, now 5, and 5 could be restored there.
    Meadow, 12 acres; woodland, then 600 pigs, now 200; 1 mill.
    1 church, 12 acres.
    3 horses when he acquired (it) and now. Always 6 cattle. Always 26 pigs; 200 sheep.
   Value then, with the jurisdiction, £12; now it pays [£] 16.
   Bishop William has full jurisdiction over the Ferthing of (South) Elmham, except over Bishop Stigand's men; and Abbot B(aldwin), according to the testimony of the Hundred, had a writ from King Edward (stating) that he himself ought to have full jurisdiction over St. Edmund's land and his men.

5 In BARSHAM 16 acres.
    2 smallholders.
    ½ plough.
    Value 2s.

HARTISMERE Hundred
6 In YAXLEY and in THRANDESTON Bishop Aelmer held 1 carucate of land as a manor before 1066.
    Always 5 smallholders;
    1 plough. Meadow, 2 acres.
    Value 20s.
    It belongs to the church of Hoxne.

19   THE BISHOP OF THETFORD'S HOLDING

[BISHOP'S Hundred]
1 In SYLEHAM 1 free man of Stigand's; 2 carucates of land.
    12 smallholders.
    2 ploughs in lordship; then 4 men's ploughs, now 2.
    Meadow, 5 acres; woodland at 60 pigs; 1 mill.
    Value always 60s.
    Aelmer held this, (and) Erfast.

/Menneham . teñ Vlfus teinn̄⁹ . tēpore . reḡ . e . I . cař
tr̄æ . p̄⁹ Ailmar⁹ & Erfaſtus . ſemp . I . uiłł . & . x . borđ . & . I . cař in dn̄io . Tc̄
III . cař . m̄ . I . & dim̄⁷ . 7 . VI . ac̄ p̄ti . ſilua de . LX . porc̄⁷ . 7 . I . molin̄ . & . II . liƀ hoc̄es⁷
XI . ac̄ cōmd & dim̄ . cař . Octaua pars eccłiæ . de XL ac̄⁷ . 7 dim̄ cař⁷ . Plus
tr̄æ ptin̄ ſed in breuiata in norfolc . Tc̄ uał . xxx . ſoł . m̄ LX .
/In denham . v . liƀi hoe⁷s . Almari⁹ cm̄da⁷ . LX . ac̄⁷ . & . I . cař⁷ . 7 uał . x . ſoł .
/In horan . VII . liƀi hoe⁷s . comd⁷ XLII . ac̄⁷ . 7 sēp . I . cař 7 dim̄ . Silua de XVI . porc̄⁷ .
/In Wilebi . I . liƀ hō . x . ac̄ In Ciccheliga . I . liƀ hō . XVI . ac̄⁷ . 7 . II . borđ . ſemp⁷
dimiđ . cař . Eccłia . de VIII . ac̄⁷ . Tot⁷ uał . xx . ſoł .
/In horan . II . liƀi hoe⁷s cōmd 7 ſoca . XIX . ac̄ & dim̄ . cař⁷ . 7 uał . III . ſoł 7 . x . đ .
/In Wilebey⁷ . I . liƀ hō . XL . ac̄⁷ cōmd⁷ . 7 ſoc̄ . ſemp . I . borđ . Tc̄ . I . cař⁷ . & . II . ac̄ p̄ti .
ſilua xx . porc̄ . Tc̄ uał . x . ſoł . m̄ . VIII .
/In Wighefelda . I . liƀ hō c̄om⁷ 7 ſoca . x . ac̄⁷ . 7 uał . xx . đ .
/In Cicheling⁷ . I . liƀ hō c̄omd . xx . VIII . ac̄⁷ . 7 . III . borđ . ſemp dim̄⁷ . cař⁷ 7

2 Ulf, a thane, held MENDHAM before 1066; 1 carucate of land. Later Aelmer and Erfast [held it].
   Always 1 villager; 10 smallholders;
   1 plough in lordship. Then 3 [men's] ploughs, now 1½.
   Meadow, 6 acres; woodland at 60 pigs; 1 mill.
   2 free men under patronage; 11 acres. ½ plough.
   The eighth part of a church with 40 acres. ½ plough.
   More land belongs, but (it is) listed in Norfolk.
   Value then 30s; now 60[s].

3 In DENHAM 5 free men; Aelmer (had) the patronage; 60 acres. 1 plough.
   Value 10s.

4 In HORHAM 7 free men under patronage; 42 acres. Always 1½ ploughs.
   Woodland at 16 pigs.

5 In WILBY 1 free man; 10 acres.
   In CHICKERING 1 free man; 16 acres.
   2 smallholders.
   Always ½ plough.
   A church with 8 acres.
   Value of the whole 20s.

6 In HORHAM 2 free men under patronage and jurisdiction; 19 acres.
   ½ plough.
   Value 3s 10d.

7 In WILBY 1 free man under patronage and jurisdiction; 40 acres.
   Always 1 smallholder.
   Then 1 plough.
   Meadow, 2 acres; woodland, 20 pigs.
   Value then 10s; now 8[s].

8 In WINGFIELD 1 free man under patronage and jurisdiction; 10 acres.
   Value 20d.

9 In CHICKERING 1 free man under patronage; 28 acres.
   3 smallholders.
   Always ½ plough.

uaɫ.v.foɫ.In ead̃ lib̃ hõ xl.ac̃.⁊ dim̃ car̃.filua de xii ⁊ porc̃.dim̃ ac̃
p̃ti.⁊ uaɫ.vi.foɫ.⁊.viii.d̃.In ead̃.i.liba femina.viii.ac̃.ante c̃ Rodb̃.
malet c̃m̃dation.t.r.e.⁊ uaɫ xvi.d̃.Almarus foc̃ ⁊ fac̃.

╔In badingelelda.ii.lib̃i hões.xxx.ac̃ com̃d̃.⁊.i.car̃.Tc̃ uaɫ.vi.foɫ.
m̃.x.

380 a

╔H̃.DELOSA.In Framalingaham.i.lib̃ hõ.com̃d̃.Almari ep̃i.xx.ac̃
tr̃æ.& dim̃ car̃.& uaɫ.iiii.foɫ.

╔Hertesmara.H̃.In acle.i.lib̃ hõ.Algarus com̃d̃.fc̃o Edmundo.t.r.
e.xiiii.ac̃.& dim̃ car̃.& dim̃ ac̃ p̃ti.& uaɫ.ii.foɫ.Drogo teñ de ep̃o

╔Waneforda.H̃.Humbresfelda.teñ.i.lib̃ hõ com̃d̃ Ælmari.xl
ac̃ p̃ mañ.Semp̃.ii.bord̃.Tc̃.ii.car̃.modo.i.ii.ac̃ p̃ti.i.æccl̃ia.de xxx.
ac̃.Tc̃ uaɫ.vi.foɫ.⁊ viii.d̃.m̃.ix.⁊.iiii.d̃.Adhuc in ead̃ uilla.xxiii.
lib̃i hões.lxxx.ac̃.Tc̃.vi.car̃.m̃.v.Tc̃ uaɫ.xl foɫ. Ⓜ xxx.& h̃t in
longo.i.l̃g.⁊ dim̃ in laɫ.⁊ de gelt̃ xx.d̃.

Value 5s.
In the same (Chickering) a free man; 40 acres. ½ plough.
Woodland at 12 pigs; meadow, ½ acre.
Value 6s 8d.
In the same (Chickering) 1 free woman; 8 acres. Robert Malet's predecessor (had) the patronage before 1066.
Value 16d.
Aelmer (had) full jurisdiction.

10 In BEDINGFIELD 2 free men under patronage; 30 acres. 1 plough.
Value then 6s; now 10[s].

Hundred of LOES 380 a
11 In FRAMLINGHAM 1 free man under the patronage of Bishop Aelmer; 20 acres of land. ½ plough.
Value 4s.

HARTISMERE Hundred
12 In OAKLEY 1 free man, Algar, under the patronage of St. Edmund's before 1066; 14 acres. ½ plough.
Meadow, ½ acre.
Value 2s.
Drogo holds (this) from the Bishop.

WANGFORD Hundred
13 1 free man under the patronage of Aelmer held HOMERSFIELD; 40 acres as a manor.
Always 2 smallholders.
Then 2 ploughs, now 1. Meadow, 2 acres.
1 church with 30 acres.
Value then 6s 8d; now 9[s] 4d.
Also in the same village, 23 free men; 80 acres. Then 6 ploughs, now 5.
Value then 40s; now 30[s].
It has 1 league in length and ½ in width; 20d in tax.

⌐ In halmehā . I . lib hō cōmd . 7 foc Ælmari epī . p man . XL ac . 7 . IIII .
bord . Sep . I . car . & . II . ac pti . filua ad VIII . porc . I . æcclia . VI . ac . 7 fub
eo . III . libi comd eide . VI . ac & dim . car . Tc ual . x . fol . m reddid XII .
In ead uilla . I . lib hō . Aluuin . cmd 7 foc . Almari XL . ac . p man . & . II . bord .
Tc . I . car . m dim . II . ac pti . Tc ual . VI . fol . m . X . 7 . VIII . d . Adhuc in ead
X . libi hoes cmd & foc eide LX. ac . Sep . I . car . II . ac pti . Tc ual . X . fol . m
reddid . XIIII . fol . In ead . X . libi hoes comd | eide . XXX . IIII . ac . Tc . III . car
m . II . Tc ual . X . fol . m reddid . XX . 7 ht in longo . I . lg 7 dim . in lato . &
de gelt . XX . d . Alii ibi tenent.
⌐ In flixtuna . I . lib hō . Ofketellus cōmd & foca . Stigandi epī . p man
XXX . ac . & . I . bord . Sep . I . car . II . ac pti . qnta pars uni mol . Tc ual . VIII . fol .
m . X . reddd . 7 . VIII . d . In ead . VIII . libi hoes cmd 7 foca 7 faca Almari
epī . c . 7 . VII . ac . Tc . II . car . m . I . 7 dim . dim æcclia XII . ac . Tc ual . X .
fol . m reddidit . XXXI . & . IIII . d .
⌐ Almea ten Willm de epo . Qd tenuit Aluuin . t . r . e . lib hō . cmd

380 b

In Wari tein . II . car træ . 7 . XX . ac . Tc uill . m . IIII . Tc . XI . bord . m . XX . Tc . IIII .
feru . Tc in dnio . III . car . m dim . I . runc . 7 . VII . an . 7 . XXX . porc . 7 . XIII . ous .
7 . XXX . cap . Tc houm . VI . car . m . III . 7 dim . 7 . XI . ac pti . filua ad XXX . porc .

14 In (South) ELMHAM 1 free man under the patronage and jurisdiction of Bishop Aelmer; 40 acres as a manor.
4 smallholders.
Always 1 plough.
Meadow, 2 acres; woodland at 8 pigs.
1 church, 6 acres.
Under him, 3 free [men] under the patronage of the same man; 6 acres. ½ plough.
Value then 10s; now it pays 12[s].
In the same (South Elmham) 1 free man, Alwin, under the patronage and jurisdiction of Aelmer; 40 acres as a manor.
2 smallholders.
Then 1 plough, now ½. Meadow, 2 acres.
Value then 6s; now 10[s] 8d.
Also in the same (South Elmham) 10 free men under the patronage and jurisdiction of the same man; 66 acres. Always 1 plough.
Meadow, 2 acres.
Value then 10s; now it pays 14s.
In the same (South Elmham) 10 free men under the patronage and jurisdiction of the same man; 34 acres. Then 3 ploughs, now 2.
Value then 10s; now it pays 20[s].
It has 1 league in length and ½ in width; 20d in tax. Others hold there.

15 In FLIXTON 1 free man, Askell, under the patronage and jurisdiction of Bishop Stigand; 30 acres as a manor.
1 smallholder.
Always 1 plough.
Meadow, 2 acres; the fifth part of one mill.
Value then 8s; now it pays 10[s] 8d.
In the same (Flixton) 8 free men under the patronage and full jurisdiction of Bishop Aelmer; 107 acres. Then 2 ploughs, now 1½.
½ church, 12 acres.
Value then 10s; now it pays 31[s] 4d.

16 William holds from the Bishop (South) ELMHAM. Alwin, a free man under the patronage of Ingvar, a thane, held it before 1066; 2 carucates of land and 20 acres.

380 b

Then 10 villagers, now 4; then 11 smallholders, now 20; then 4 slaves.
Then 3 ploughs in lordship, now ½ plough.
1 cob, 7 cattle, 30 pigs, 13 sheep, 30 goats.
Then 6 men's ploughs, now 3½.
Meadow, 11 acres; woodland at 30 pigs.

. I . æcclia . XL . ac libæ tr̄æ . 7 dim̄ . car̄ . Tc̄ ual . fol . m̄ . IIII . lib . In ead . I . lib homo
Bondus com̄d Ailmari ep̄i . LX . ac̄ p̄ man̄ . 7 . II . uilli 7 . II . bord . 7 . I . car in dn̄io.
Tc̄ houm . I . car . m̄ dim̄ . II . ac̄ p̄ti . 7 fub fe . II . libi hoes . VII . ac̄ . Tc̄ . I . car̄ . m̄
dim̄ . Tc̄ ual . X . fol . m̄ . XIII . Adhuc in ead . I . lib ho com̄d 7 foc̄ 7 facā . Sti—
gandi . XXX . ac̄ . p̄ man̄ . Sep̄ . II . uilt . 7 . I . car . & houm . I . car̄ . II . ac̄ p̄ti . Silua
ad VIII . porc̄ . Tc̄ ual . VIII . fol . m̄ . X . & . VIII . d . In ead . I . lib ho . Aluui . com̄d . Edrici
de laxefella . t . r . e . XXX . ac̄ p̄ man̄ . Tc̄ . II . bord . m̄ . III . Semper dimid car̄
. I . ac̄ p̄ti . Silua ad VIII . porc̄ . 7 fub eo . II . libi hoes . IIII . ac̄ 7 d . car̄ . Tc̄ ual . X . fol.
modo fimilit . Will malet . erat faifitus die qua obiit . In ead . XX . V.
lib hoes . com̄d Almaro ep̄o . I . car̄ terræ 7 dimid . Tc̄ . VIII . car̄ . m̄ . VI . 7 VI.
ac̄ p̄ti . filua ad XVI . porc̄ . Tc̄ ual . XXX . fol . m̄ XL . fol . III . æcliæ . XXX . ac̄.
7 ual . V . fol.

Fnflixtuna . I . lib ho Briht nothus . com̄datus Almaro . XXX . ac̄ . p̄ man̄ . 7 . IIII.
bord . Sep̄ . I . car̄ . 7 hou dim̄ . II . ac̄ p̄ti . filua ad IIII . porc̄ . Tc̄ ual . V . fol.
7 . IIII . d . m̄ . XX . fol . Adhuc . III . libi hoes . cm̄ 7 foc̄ 7 fac̄ . Almaro . XXXVIII . ac̄.
Sep̄ . I . car̄ . 7 dim̄ . filua ad . IIII . porc̄ . III . ac̄ p̄ti . Tc̄ ual . VI . fol . m̄ . XI . 7 VIII . d.

1 church, 40 acres of free land. ½ plough.
Value then ... ; now £4.
In the same (South Elmham) 1 free man, Bondi, under the patronage of Bishop Aelmer; 60 acres as a manor.
 2 villagers; 2 smallholders.
 1 plough in lordship; then 1 man's plough, now ½. Meadow, 2 acres.
 Under him, 2 free men; 7 acres. Then 1 plough, now ½.
Value then 10s; now 13[s].
Also in the same (South Elmham) 1 free man under the patronage and full jurisdiction of Stigand; 30 acres as a manor.
 Always 2 villagers;
 1 plough; 1 men's plough.
 Meadow, 2 acres; woodland at 8 pigs.
Value then 8s; now 10[s] 8d.
In the same (South Elmham) 1 free man, Alwy, under the patronage of Edric of Laxfield before 1066; 30 acres as a manor.
 Then 2 smallholders, now 3.
 Always ½ plough.
 Meadow, 1 acre; woodland at 8 pigs.
 Under him, 2 free men; 4 acres. ½ plough.
Value then 10s; now the same.
 William Malet was in possession on the day he died.
In the same (South Elmham) 25 free men under the patronage of Bishop Aelmer; 1½ carucates of land. Then 8 ploughs, now 6.
 Meadow, 6 acres; woodland at 16 pigs.
Value then 30s; now 40s.
3 churches, 30 acres; value 5s.

17 In FLIXTON 1 free man, Brictnoth, under the patronage of Aelmer; 30 acres as a manor.
 4 smallholders.
 Always 1 plough; ½ [men's] plough.
 Meadow, 2 acres; woodland at 4 pigs.
Value then 5s 4d; now 20s.
Also 3 free men under the patronage and full jurisdiction of Aelmer; 38 acres. Always 1½ ploughs.
 Woodland at 4 pigs; meadow, 3 acres.
Value then 6s; now 11[s] 8d.

h̄ totū ten̄ Wilmus de noers. de epo. Adhuc in ead uitt. 1. lib hō comd
7 soc Stigandi xxx. ac ꝑ man̄. Tc. 11. bord. m̄. viii. Tc. 1. car. m̄. 11. 11. ac p̄ti.
siluæ ad. iiii. porc. 7 sub eo. 1. lib hō xvi. ac. 7 dim̄. car. tc ꝉ modo. 11. bou.
Tc uat. x. sot. 7 m̄ simit. ide W.

⁊In barsht̄. x. libi hōes. ex eis habuit Aluric. 7 Guert comd. de. viii. 7 dim̄.

381 a

& ex aliis. Almari epi. lx. ac. Tc. 11. car. modo. 1. & dim̄. 11. ac p̄ti. tc uat. viii.
sot. modo. x. ⁊HERTESMARA. H̄. In Jachestea 7 in Thrandestuna
xl. libi hōes. 1. car. terræ. 7. xix. ac. Tc. 111. car. m̄. 111. 7 dim̄. 11. ac p̄ti.
Sep uat. xl sot. Eps soc 7 sacā. hoc ten̄. Othem de epo.

⁊In brō. 1. lib hō. comdatus. cuidā comd. Almari epi. vi. ac. 7 uat. xii. d.

⁊DIM̄. H̄. In flixtuna. tenuit scs michahel in elemosinā. t. r. e. 1. car
terræ. Tc. xiii. bord. m̄. viii. Sep. i. dn̄io. 1. car. Tc hōiū. iiii. car. m̄. 1.
Silua. ad viii. porc. iiii. ac p̄ti. dim̄ molin̄. Sep uat. xx. sot. Soca. Stigndo.

* ⁊TERRE EP̄I ROVENSIS. LACFORDA. Hundrct.   .XX.
Frakenaham ten̄ Orthi teinus heroldi. t. r. e. 7 pea derotionatus ē. Lan-
francus iussu regis. i epatū rouensem. ꝑ man̄. x. car træ. Semp xvi. uitt.
& viii. bord. 7. vi. seru. 7 semp. v. car. in dn̄io. 7. vi. car hoiu. sed. viii. pos̄s

William of Noyers holds the whole of this from the Bishop.
Also in the same village 1 free man under the patronage and jurisdiction of Stigand; 30 acres as a manor.
   Then 2 smallholders, now 8.
   Then 1 plough, now 2.
   Meadow, 2 acres; woodland at 4 pigs.
   Under him, 1 free man; 16 acres. Then ½ plough, now the same.
Value then 10s; now the same.
   William also holds (this).

18 In BARSHAM 10 free men; of these, Aelfric and Gyrth had patronage over 8 and a half, and Bishop Aelmer (had it) over the others; 60 acres. Then 2 ploughs, now 1½.
   Meadow, 2 acres.
   Value then 8s; now 10[s].

HARTISMERE Hundred

19 In YAXLEY and in THRANDESTON 40 free men; 1 carucate of land and 19 acres. Then 3 ploughs, now 3½.
   Meadow, 2 acres.
   Value always 40s.
      The Bishop (had) full jurisdiction.
      Otheri holds this from the Bishop.

20 In BROME 1 free man under the patronage of someone under the patronage of Bishop Aelmer; 6 acres.
   Value 12d.

Half-Hundred [of LOTHINGLAND]

21 In FLIXTON St. Michael's held in alms 1 carucate of land before 1066.
      Then 13 smallholders, now 8.
      Always 1 plough in lordship. Then 4 men's ploughs, now 1.
      Woodland at 8 pigs; meadow, 4 acres; ½ mill.
   Value always 20s.
      The jurisdiction belonged to Stigand.

20   LANDS OF THE BISHOP OF ROCHESTER

LACKFORD Hundred

1 Orthi, a thane of Harold's, held FRECKENHAM before 1066; later on Lanfranc by the King's command adjudged (it to be) in the Bishopric of Rochester; 10 carucates of land as a manor.
      Always 16 villagers; 8 smallholders; 6 slaves.
      Always 5 ploughs in lordship; 6 men's ploughs, but 8 could be

reſtaurari . 7 . xx . ac̄ p̄ti . 7 . i . mol̄ . 7 . ii . piſcar̄ . Ecclia . xx . ac̄ . 7 . iii . cq̄ . 7 . xi .
an̄ . & xl . porc̄ . & . cc . xxx . oūs . 7 . vi . uaſa apū . Tc̄ ual xii . lib̄ . m̄ . xiiii . h̄t
i leug in lōg . 7 dimid̄ in lato . & de gelto . xx . d̄ . Huic man̄ addidit
com̄s Rad̄ . iiii . lib̄os hōes q̄s inuaſit de . viii . ac̄ tr̄æ . Sep̄ dim̄ car̄ . 7 ual&
viii . d̄ . Soc̄ hui man̄ habeb̄ id̄ ep̄s . 7 de libis hōib; h̄t Sc̄s Edmundus.

381 b

.XXI. SVTHFVLC TR̄Æ SC̄E ALDREDE ; The*WARDESTREV*.

HVNDRET . Rateſdane ten̄ sc̄a Aldreda . t . r . e . p̄ . vi . car̄ terræ Semp xviii .
uilt̄ . Tc̄ xx . bord̄ . m̄ . xx . vii . Tc̄ . vi . ſerui . m̄ . iiii . Sep̄ . iii . car̄ in dn̄i .
Tc̄ . xii . car̄ hōiū . m̄ . iii . Silua . xx . iiii . porc̄ . 7 xvi . ac̄ p̄ti . Sep̄ . v . run .
Tc̄ m̄ xii . an̄ . 7 lxxx . 7 . x . oūs . xl . porc̄ . m̄ . xi . cap̄ . Semp ual . x . lib̄ .
. i . æcclia . xxiiii ac̄ . 7 . xv . ac̄ . ten̄ hunfridus hō . W . de . War . & goſce -
linus homo comitis . de moritonio . ii . h̄t . xvi . q̄r in longo . 7 x . in lato .
7 de gelto uiginti denarios . Soca sc̄e . ealdrede.

ᛘ In eadem . i . liber homo sc̄æ aldrede cōm̄d 7 ſoca . t . r . e . iii . ac̄ . &
ual . vi . d̄ . ᛘ In Rateſdana . i . liber homo sc̄e aldrede ſoca & ſaca
viii . ac̄ tr̄æ . 7 ual . ii . ſol . falco homo ſc̄i edmundi habuit has . viii .
ac̄ . dū abbatia sc̄e aldrede . ēet in manu regis & uſq; huc tenuit .
ſ; negat ſe detinuiſſe ſeruitiū.

ᛘ Drinceſtona ten̄ sc̄a . A . t . r . e . ii . car̄ terræ . 7 . i . æcclia . xii . ac̄
Tc̄ . xv . bord̄ . m̄ . vii . Tc̄ . vi . ſeru . m̄ . iiii . ſemp . ii . car̄ in dominio . Tc̄
iii . car̄ hominū . m̄ . i . Silu de . c . porc̄ . 7 vi . ac̄ p̄ti . Sep̄ . ii . æqui . in halla
. x . an̄ . xxx . ii . porc̄ . xxx . oūs . viii . cap̄ . Tc̄ ual xl . ſol . m̄ lx . ſ; fuit
ad firmā . c . ſol . & n̄ potuit reddere . h̄t . viii . q̄r in longo . & vii . i lato .
Et de gelto . xi . d̄.

restored.
Meadow, 20 acres; 1 mill; 2 fisheries.
A church, 20 acres.
3 horses, 13 cattle, 40 pigs, 230 sheep, 6 beehives.
Value then £12; now [£] 14.
It has 1 league in length and ½ in width; 20d in tax.
To this manor Earl Ralph added 4 free men with 8 acres of land, whom he annexed. Always ½ plough.
Value 8d.
The Bishop also has the jurisdiction of this manor; St. Edmund's has (jurisdiction) over the free men.

21 SUFFOLK LANDS OF ST. ETHELDREDA'S

THEDWESTRY Hundred

1 St. Etheldreda's held RATTLESDEN before 1066 for 6 carucates of land.
Always 18 villagers. Then 20 smallholders, now 27; then 6 slaves, now 4.
Always 3 ploughs in lordship. Then 12 men's ploughs, now 3.
Woodland, 24 pigs; meadow, 16 acres. Always 5 cobs. Then [and] now 12 cattle; 80 and 10 sheep; 40 pigs. Now 11 goats.
Value always £10.
1 church, 24 acres.
Humphrey, W(illiam) of Warenne's man, holds 15 acres; Jocelyn, the Count of Mortain's man, (holds) 2 (acres).
It has 16 furlongs in length and 10 in width; 20d in tax. The jurisdiction (is) St. Etheldreda's.
In the same (Rattlesden) 1 free man of St. Etheldreda's, under patronage and jurisdiction before 1066; 3 acres.
Value 6d.

2 In RATTLESDEN 1 free man of St. Etheldreda's, under full jurisdiction; 8 acres of land.
Value 2s.
Falc, a man of St. Edmund's, had these 8 acres while the Abbey of St. Etheldreda's was in the King's hand, and he has held (them) until now; but he denies that he has withheld the service.

3 St. Etheldreda's held DRINKSTONE before 1066; 2 carucates of land.
1 church, 12 acres.
Then 15 smallholders, now 7; then 6 slaves, now 4.
Always 2 ploughs in lordship. Then 3 men's ploughs, now 1.
Woodland at 100 pigs; meadow, 6 acres. Always 2 horses at the hall, 10 cattle, 32 pigs, 30 sheep, 8 goats.
Value then 40s; now 60[s]; but it was at a revenue for 100s and could not pay.
It has 8 furlongs in length and 7 in width; 11d in tax.

⌈*THINGOHOU*. H̃. In reda . xx . ać in dñio . & . IIII . borđ . II . ać p̃ti.
& dim̃ . car̃ foca & faca sc̃e aldrede . & ual . IIII . fol.

⌈*LACFORDE*. H̃. Brandona . teñ sc̃a . Aldrede . t . r . e . 7 m̃ . p . mañ.
v . car terræ . Semp . VIII . uilt . & . IIII . borđ . VII . ferui . femp . III.
★ car̃r in dñio . Tc̃ . IIII . car̃ . houm . m̃ . III . ać p̃ti . 7 . I . pifcar̃.

382 a

& . II . afini . & xI . añ . 7 . cc . oũs . 7 xx . por̃c . Ecctia . xxx . ać . Tc̃ ual . vI . liƀ.
m̃ . VIII . ħt . I . lḡ in lōgo . 7 dimiđ lati . 7 de gelto . xx . đ.

⌈Laringahetha . teñ sc̃a aldređ . t . r . e . p mañ . III . car̃r træ̃ . Sẽp
vI . uilt . & . v . borđ . & . IIII . ferũ . Tc̃ . III . car̃r in dominio . m̃ . II.
Semper . II . car̃r hou . 7 . v . ać p̃ti . 7 dim̃ moliñ . 7 . II . pifcar̃.
7 . II . æqui in halla . & . v . añ . c . oũs . 7 xvII . por̃c . Ecctia . LX . ać.
Tc̃ ual . IIII . liƀ . modo . vI . ħt . I . lḡ in longo . 7 dim̃ in lato . Et de gelto
xx . deñ . ⌈Lundale . I . car̃r terre . teñ sc̃a ald . 7 . III . borđ . 7 IIII.
ferũ . Semp . II . car̃r in dñio . 7 XIII . ać p̃ti . & . II . pifcar̃ . & . I . æq̃ . & xx.
IIII . añ . 7 LX . II . oũs . Semp ual . xx . fol . Ecctia fine tr̃a . ħt . II . q̃r in lōgo
& . II . in lato . Gelt̃ in Laringeheta.

⌈In dũhã dim̃ liƀ hō sc̃e aldređ cũ foca dim̃ car̃r træ̃ . 7 . III . borđ . 7 . I . ać
p̃ti . Sẽp dim̃ car̃ . 7 ual . v . fol.

THINGOE Hundred

4 In REDE 20 acres in lordship.
    4 smallholders.
    Meadow, 2 acres.
    ½ plough.
    The full jurisdiction (is) St. Etheldreda's.
  Value 4s.

LACKFORD Hundred

5 St. Etheldreda's held BRANDON before 1066, and now, as a manor; 5 carucates of land.
    Always 8 villagers; 4 smallholders; 7 slaves.
    Always 3 ploughs in lordship. Then 4 men's ploughs, now 3.
    Meadow, [3] acres; 1 fishery. 2 asses, 11 cattle, 200 sheep, 20 pigs.
    A church, 30 acres.
  Value then £6; now [£] 8.
    It has 1 league in length and ½ in width; 20d in tax.

382 a

6 St. Etheldreda's held LAKENHEATH before 1066 as a manor; 3 carucates of land.
    Always 6 villagers; 5 smallholders; 4 slaves.
    Then 3 ploughs in lordship, now 2; always 2 men's ploughs.
    Meadow, 5 acres; ½ mill; 2 fisheries. 2 horses at the hall, 5 cattle, 100 sheep, 17 pigs.
    A church, 60 acres.
  Value then £4; now [£] 6.
    It has 1 league in length and ½ in width; 20d in tax.

7 St. Etheldreda's held UNDLEY; 1 carucate of land.
    3 smallholders; 4 slaves.
    Always 2 ploughs in lordship.
    Meadow, 13 acres; 2 fisheries. 1 horse, 24 cattle, 62 sheep.
  Value always 20s.
    A church without land.
    It has 2 furlongs in length and 2 in width. Tax in Lakenheath.

8 In (Santon) DOWNHAM a half free man of St. Etheldreda's, with the jurisdiction; ½ carucate of land.
    3 smallholders.
    Meadow, 1 acre.
    Always ½ plough.
  Value 5s.

⁑In Liuermera.III.libi hões sc̄e.Aldrede commd̄.tn̄t.t.r.e.in soca sc̄i.e.
xxix.ac̄ tr̄æ.Sēp dim̄ car̄.7 ual.v.sol

⁑Babga duo h̄.Clamesford ten̄ sc̄a ald.t.r.e.&.m̄ p̄ manerio
viii.car̄ tr̄e.Sēp.xvi.uilt.7 xviii.bord.&.v.seru̇.semp.iii.car̄
in dn̄io.7 vii.car̄ hoiu̇.7 xii.ac̄ p̄ti.Silua.v.porc̄.&.i.molin̄.
semp.iii.eq̇.in halla.&.viii.an̄.&.m̄.cc.ou̇s.7.xxx.ii.porc̄.Eclia
de.xxx ac̄ libe tr̄æ.7.i.soc̄.de.viii.ac̄.Tc̄ ual.x.lib.m̄.xvi.ht.i.lḡ
in longo.7.viii.qr̄.in lato.& de gelto xv.d̄.

⁑Hertest ten̄ sc̄a Aldrede.t.r.e.p̄ man̄.v. car'.tr̄æ
semp xii.uilt.&.xiiii.
bord.7 iiii.seru̇.semp.ii.car̄ in dn̄io.Tc̄.v car̄ hoiu̇m.m̄.vi.7.x.
ac̄ p̄ti.Silua de.vi.porc̄.Sēp.iiii.equi.in halla.7 xx.animalia.

382 b

7 xx.v.porc̄.7 lx.ou̇s.Ecclia de lxxx.ac̄ libe terre.Tc̄ ual.vi.lib.m̄.xi.
lib.ht.i.lḡ in longo 7 dim̄ in lato.& de gelto.x.d̄.
In ead.iiii.soc̄.de xxx.ac̄ tr̄æ.7 dim̄.car̄.7 ual.v.sol.Adhuc ē.i.soca de.i.
car̄ tr̄æ.semp.i.car̄.7 ual xx.sol.hc̄ ten̄ bn̄er balistari de sc̄a Aldred.

⁑Stohu.II.In Ciltuna ten̄ sc̄a Aldreda.ii.soc̄.de.xxx.vi.ac̄.
sed n̄ pot uende.sine licn̄ca abbis.7.i.bord.Tc̄.i.car̄.m̄.nulla.7 dim̄
ac̄ p̄ti.7 ual.v.sol.

⁑In bukessalla.i.soc̄.de.x.ac̄.foresacte tr̄e.7.i.bord.de.v.ac̄ 7 ual
.x.d̄.In sinebga ten̄ Roger de oburuilla de sc̄a aldreda.iii.soc̄
de.xxx.iiii.ac̄ tr̄æ.7 ual.iiii.sol.In ead uilla vii.ac̄ de dn̄io.in
bkinges.saca 7 soca sc̄e aldre.

9 In (Great) LIVERMERE 3 free men of St. Etheldreda's, under patronage only before 1066, in the jurisdiction of St. Edmund's; 29 acres of land. Always ½ plough.
Value 5s.

BABERGH Two Hundreds
10 St. Etheldreda's held GLEMSFORD before 1066, and now, as a manor; 8 carucates of land.
 Always 16 villagers; 18 smallholders; 5 slaves.
 Always 3 ploughs in lordship; 7 men's ploughs.
 Meadow, 12 acres; woodland, 5 pigs; 1 mill. Always 3 horses at the hall, 8 cattle. Now 200 sheep, 32 pigs.
 A church with 30 acres of free land.
 1 Freeman with 8 acres.
Value then £10; now [£] 16.
 It has 1 league in length and 8 furlongs in width; 15d in tax.

11 St. Etheldreda's held HARTEST before 1066 as a manor; 5 carucates of land.
 Always 12 villagers; 14 smallholders; 4 slaves.
 Always 2 ploughs in lordship. Then 5 men's ploughs, now 6.
 Meadow, 10 acres; woodland at 6 pigs. Always 4 horses at the hall, 20 cattle, 25 pigs, 60 sheep.
 A church with 80 acres of free land.
Value then £6; now £11.
 It has 1 league in length and ½ in width; 10d in tax.
In the same (Hartest) 4 Freemen with 30 acres of land. ½ plough.
Value 5s.
 Also there is 1 [Freeman] with 1 carucate of land. Always 1 plough;
Value 20s.
 Berner the crossbowman holds this from St. Etheldreda's.

STOW Hundred
12 In CHILTON St. Etheldreda's held 2 Freemen with 36 acres; but they could not sell without the Abbot's permission.
 1 smallholder.
 Then 1 plough, now none. Meadow, ½ acre.
Value 5s.

13 In BUXHALL 1 Freeman with 10 acres of forfeited land.
 1 smallholder with 5 acres.
Value 10d.

14 In FINBOROUGH Roger of Auberville holds from St. Etheldreda's 3 Freemen with 34 acres of land.
Value 4s.
 In the same village 7 acres of the lordship of Barking.
  The full jurisdiction (is) St. Etheldreda's.

⌐ Dim. H. De gepeſwiz. Stoches tenuit. S. A. iii. car trae. p man.
t. r. e. ſemp. ix. uill. 7 tc. v. bord. modo. xv. Tc. i. ſeru. ſemp. ii. car in
dnio. 7 vi. car hoium. &. i. aecclia. de. xl. ac libe trae. 7. i. molin.
7 xx. ac pti. 7 xii. an. 7 xx. porc. 7 xx. iiii. oūs. &. xiiii. cap. & adhuc
ht ſca. Al. medietat ſoche quae e ult ponte. Tc ual. iiii. lib. m. c. ſol.
ht. vi. qr in long. 7 vi. in lat. 7. iiii. d. in gelto. de xx ſol

⌐ Boſemera. H. Berchingas ten. Sca. A. c ſoca 7 ſaca. t. r. e. p man.
vii. car trae. Tc xxvii. uilli. m. xxv. Tc. xx. iiii. bord. m. xxx. Tc
. v. ſeru. m. iiii. ſep. iii. car in dnio. Tc xx. iiii. car hominu. m. xv.
Ecclia lxxx. iii. ac libae trae 7. ii. car. 7. l. ii. ac pti. Silua. de. l. porc.
ſemp. i. mol. 7 una excluſa Alti molini. 7 in excluſa alti mol.
ht Rob. malet parte. 7. ii. arpen .... uinee. In dnio. xi. runc.
7 xx. iii. an. 7 xxx. porc. 7. c. oūs. 7 xlviii. cap. 7 iiii. libi.

383 a

Hoīes. de. vi. ac. 7 hnt. i. car. Iſti additi ſt huic manerio. t. r. e. Will.
& ual. ii. ſol. Rex & coms ſoca. Vnum 7 dim. ex his habuit harduiu
qdo forisfecit. m ten abbas. Tc ual manriu. xvi. lib. & abbas dedit
ad firma p. xx. lib. ht. i. lg. &. iiii. qr in longo 7. viii. qr. in lat. 7
xx. d. de gt.

⌐ In dermodeſduna. tenuer. xxv. lib libi hoes. i. car trae. ex quibz
habuit ſca. Al. com 7 ſoca. t. r. e. Tc. vi. car. modo. ii. &. iii. ac pti
7 ual. xx. ſol. Roger bigot tenet de abbate quia abbas eam derationauit ſup eu. cora epo de ſco Laudo ſz p tam tenebat de rege

⌐ In bchingas tenet. Rog. c. xviii. ac. de abbe de ſuo dnio. 7. i. aecclia
de. vi. ac. & ual. x. ſol.

Half-Hundred of IPSWICH

15 St. Etheldreda's held STOKE; 3 carucates of land as a manor before 1066.
> Always 9 villagers. Then 5 smallholders, now 15; then 1 slave.
> Always 2 ploughs in lordship; 6 men's ploughs.
> A church with 40 acres of free land.
> 1 mill; meadow, 20 acres. 12 cattle, 20 pigs, 24 sheep, 14 goats.
> Also St. Etheldreda's has the half of the jurisdiction which is beyond the bridge.
> Value then £4; now 100s.
> It has 6 furlongs in length and 6 in width; 4d in a tax of 20s.

BOSMERE Hundred

16 St. Etheldreda's held BARKING with full jurisdiction before 1066 as a manor; 7 carucates of land.
> Then 27 villagers, now 25; then 24 smallholders, now 30; then 5 slaves, now 4.
> Always 3 ploughs in lordship. Then 24 men's ploughs, now 15.
> A church, 83 acres of free land. 2 ploughs.
> Meadow, 52 acres; woodland at 50 pigs; always 1 mill, and a dam of another mill, and in the dam of the other mill Robert Malet has a share; 2 *arpents* of vines. In lordship 11 cobs, 23 cattle, 30 pigs, 100 sheep, 48 goats.
> 4 free men with 6 acres. They have 1 plough. These (free men) were added to this manor after 1066.
> Value 2s.
> The King and the Earl (have) the jurisdiction.
> Of these (free men), Hardwin had one and a half when he forfeited; now the Abbot (holds them).
> Value of the manor then £16; the Abbot granted it at a revenue for £20.
> It has 1 league and 4 furlongs in length, and 8 furlongs in width; 20d in tax.

383 a

17 In DARMSDEN 25 free men held 1 carucate of land; over whom St. Etheldreda's had patronage and jurisdiction before 1066. Then 6 ploughs, now 2.
> Meadow, 3 acres.
> Value 20s.
> Roger Bigot holds (this) from the Abbot, because the Abbot established his claim to it against him before the Bishop of St. Lô; but later, however, he held (it) from the King.

18 In BARKING Roger holds 118 acres from the Abbot in his lordship.
> 1 church with 6 acres.
> Value 10s.

↟In horſwalda . ı . lıb̃ hō . com̕ 7 ſoca . t . r . e . de . xx . ıı . ac̃ 7 dim̃ . 7 dim̃
car̃ . & dimid̃ . 7 uat̃ . ııı . ſot . hc̃ tenuit . Rog̃ de otburuilla
de rc̃ . 7 abbas derationauit ſup eū m̊ ten̄ de abb̃e.

↟In badeleia tenuit . sc̃a . A . xxx . ac̃ in dn̄io . t . r . e . hoc̃ in p̃tio de b̃
chingis

↟In hamingeſtuna . ı . ſoc̕ sc̃e . A . de . xıı . ac̃ . Witt de ſcoies . ten̄ de
abb̃e . & c̃ in p̃tio de blachā.

↟In hamingeſtuna . ı . lib̃ hō . Iricus . c̃omdatus abb̃i 7 in ſoca eı
xv . ac̃ . 7 . ıı . bord̃ . 7 uat̃ . ıı . ſot . 7 vı . d̃.

↟In Vledana . ı . lib̃ hō . Aluricus . com̃ tn̄t . ı . ac̃ . 7 d̃ . 7 uat̃ . ııı . d̃ . rex
7 . c . ſoc̕ . hoc eſt in dominio.

↟In Codenhā . xvı . ac̃ . dn̄ice trāe . & fuit in p̃tio de b̃cham.

↟In haſſa . ı . lib̃a femina . Liſteua . comendata abb̃i . ı . ac̃ . 7

ual& . ıı . den̄ . R . 7 . c . ſoc̃.

↟In ead̃ . ı . lib̃ hō com̃dation̄ tn̄t dim̕ . ac̃ . 7 uat̃ . ı . d̃ . R . 7 . c . ſoc̃.

↟*CLAINDVNE* . H̃ . Bercham tenuit sc̃a . A . t . r . e . ııɪɪ . car̃ tr̄e
p̃ man̄ . ſemp̃ xxııɪɪ . uitt . m̊ . ıx . bord̃ . Tc̃ . vı . ſeru . modo . ıı . Tc̃ . ııı .
car̃ in dn̄io . modo . ı . Tc̃ . vııı . car̃ hoıum . m̊ . vı . Eccl̃ia . de xvı . ac̃ .
ſemp̃ . ı . molin̄ . & . xıı . ac̃ p̃ti . Tc̃ ſilua . c . porc̃ . m̊ . xvı . m̊ . ıx . porc̃ .
7 xvıı oūs . 7 . ı . ſoc̃ . xxx . ac̃ . sep̕ . ı . carr̃ . Tc̃ uat̃ . xıı . lib̃ . modo . c . ſot .
ht̃ . ı . lg̃ in longo 7 vıı . qr̃ 7 dim̕ in lat̃ . 7 . xx . d̃ de gt̃ .

19 In HORSWOLD 1 free man under patronage and jurisdiction before 1066, with 22½ acres. ½ plough.
Meadow, ½ acre.
Value 3s.
Roger of Auberville held this from the King. The Abbot established his claim against him. Now he holds (it) from the Abbot.

20 In BADLEY St. Etheldreda's held 30 acres in lordship before 1066. This is in the assessment of Barking.

21 In HEMINGSTONE 1 Freeman of St. Etheldreda's, with 12 acres. William of Écouis holds (this) from the Abbot.
It is in the assessment of Blakenham.

22 In HEMINGSTONE 1 free man, Eric, under the patronage of the Abbot and in his jurisdiction; 15 acres.
2 smallholders.
Value 2s 6d.

23 In 'OLDEN' 1 free man, Aelfric, under patronage only; 1½ acres.
Value 3d.
The King and the Earl (have) the jurisdiction.
This is in lordship.

24 In CODDENHAM 16 acres of lordship land.
It was in the assessment of Barham.

25 In ASH(BOCKING) 1 free woman, Licteva, under the patronage of the Abbot; 1 acre.
Value 2d.
383 b
The King and the Earl (have) the jurisdiction.
In the same (Ashbocking) 1 free man under patronage only; ½ acre.
Value 1d.
The King and the Earl (have) the jurisdiction.

CLAYDON Hundred

26 St. Etheldreda's held BARHAM before 1066; 4 carucates of land as a manor.
Always 24 villagers. Now 9 smallholders. Then 6 slaves, now 2.
Then 3 ploughs in lordship, now 1; then 8 men's ploughs, now 6.
A church with 16 acres.
Always 1 mill. Meadow, 12 acres; woodland, then 100 pigs, now 16. Now 9 pigs, 17 sheep.
1 Freeman, 30 acres. Always 1 plough.
Value then £12; now 100s.
It has 1 league in length and 7½ furlongs in width; 20d in tax.

383 a, b

In ead. I. lib hō. xxx. v. ac. in foca & comdatione abbis. Tc. I. carr. modo dim. Tc. I. bord. m̅. II. 7. III. ac p̄ti. 7. I. moliñ. Tc ual. x. fol. m̅. xx. Rog̅ de otburuilla tenebat de rege m̅ de abbe.

In Efcarletuna. III. libi. hoes in foca 7 cōmd abbis. VIII. ac. 7. II. boū. Tc ual. xx. d m̅. II. fol. hoc tenuit. W. de fcoies de rege. m̅ de abbe.

Wineftunā tenuit fca. A. t. r. e. I. car tr̄æ in dn̄io. 7 XL. ac p man̄. sēp. VI. uill. 7. IIII. bord. Tc. II. car. m̅. I. sēp. III. car houm. VI. ac p̄ti. Tc filua. c. porc; m̅. LX. Ecclia. VIII. ac. II. runc. 7. IIII. an. & xx. porc. & L. ous. Tc. ual. IIII. lib. m̅. IIII. 7 x. fol. Et. I. lib homo additus Alsi. huic manerio xxx. ac. p man. in foca & commdtione abbis. femp. II. bord. 7. I. car. 7 ual. x. fol. ht. I. lg in longo. 7. III. qr in lat. 7 XIII. d. & obol de gl.

In Weftrefelda tenuit Aferet. I. foc abbis. xx. v. ac. sēp. I. car & . I. ac p̄ti. 7 ual. v. fol. Herueus ten de abbate iuffu regis. In ead. Turchillus lib hō com. VIII. ac. 7 ual. XVI. d. hc tenuit herueus de rege. & m̅ de abbe iuffu reg̅ fic ipfe dicit

384 a
Soca reg̅

In the same (Barham) 1 free man in the jurisdiction and patronage of the Abbot; 35 acres. Then 1 plough, now ½.
Then 1 smallholder, now 2.
Meadow, 3 acres; 1 mill.
Value then 10s; now 20[s].
Roger of Auberville held (this) from the King; now [he holds it] from the Abbot.

27 In SHARPSTONE 3 free men in the jurisdiction and patronage of the Abbot; 8 acres. 2 oxen.
Value then 20d; now 2s.
W(illiam) of Écouis held this from the King; now [he holds it] from the Abbot.

28 St. Etheldreda's held WINSTON before 1066; 1 carucate of land in lordship and 40 acres as a manor.
Always 6 villagers; 4 smallholders.
Then 2 ploughs in lordship, now 1; always 3 men's ploughs.
Meadow, 6 acres; woodland, then 100 pigs, now 60.
A church, 8 acres.
2 cobs, 4 cattle, 20 pigs, 50 sheep.
Value then £4; now [£] 4 10s.
1 free man, Alsi, in the jurisdiction and patronage of the Abbot, was added to this manor; 30 acres as a manor.
Always 2 smallholders;
1 plough.
Value 10s.
It has 1 league in length and 3 furlongs in width; 13½d in tax.

29 In WESTERFIELD Aseret, 1 Freeman of the Abbot's, held 25 acres.
Always 1 plough.
Meadow, 1 acre.
Value 5s.
Hervey holds (this) from the Abbot by order of the King.
In the same (Westerfield) Thorkell, a free man under patronage; 8 acres.
Value 16d.
Hervey held this from the King; now [he holds it] from the Abbot by order of the King, as he says.
The jurisdiction (is) the King's.

384 a

383 b, 384 a

In Petehaga Idē turchillus . dimͥ comͫ Abͣbi . t . r . e . & dimͥ.
Guert . xx . ac̄ . & . ı . ac̄ p̊ti . & . ı . uiłł . & dimͥ . carͥ . & uał . v . soł . hc̄ &iā
tenuit herueus de rege . & m̄ de abͣbe iuſſu regis ſīc ipſe dicit
Dimͥ ſoca abͣbis . & ante ceſſoris hugonis.

In dẹplohā dim̄ lib̄ hō ſoca & c̄om̄datioē . ııııı . ac̄ . & . uał . vııı . đ.
hc̄ teñuit . Robte . malet . de rege . m̄ de abͣbe.

In Aſſefelda . ı . lib̄ hō ſoͨc & commendatione . ııı . ac̄ . & uał
vııı . deñ.

In Henlea . ı . lib̄ . hō comͥđ . & ſoͨc . dimiđ . ac̄ . & . uał . ı . đ.

In torp . Alſi⁹ lib̄ hō . ſoca & commendͨc . x . ac̄ . 7 uał . xx . đ.

In Scaruetuna . ı . lib̄ homo ſoca & commendatioͥn . ıı . ac̄
& . uał . ıııı . đ . Galt̄ teñ.

PEREHĀ . DIMͥ . H̃ . In Blacheſſala . v . libi hoͥes
in ſoca & comendatioͥn Abͣbis . xx . vı . ac̄ . ſemper dimidia carͥ
7 ualet . ıııı . ſoł.

In Wanteſdena . xıı . ac̄ de dn̄io de Sutburne 7 uał . xx
ıııı dẹñ . In eadē teñ . Moruuinus lib̄ homo . ıı . ac̄ . & uał
ıııı . deñ . Idē moruuinus teñ de abͣbe.

30 In PETTAUGH the same Thorkell, half under the patronage of the Abbot and half (under that) of Gyrth before 1066; 20 acres.
Meadow, 1 acre.
1 villager.
½ plough.
Value 5s.
Hervey also held this from the King and now [holds it] from the Abbot by the King's order, as he says.
The jurisdiction (was) half the Abbot's and (half that) of Hugh's predecessor.

31 In DEBENHAM a half free man under jurisdiction and patronage; 4 acres.
Value 8d.
Robert Malet held this from the King; now [he holds it] from the Abbot.

32 In ASHFIELD 1 free man under jurisdiction and patronage; 3 acres.
Value 8d.

33 In HENLEY 1 free man under patronage and jurisdiction; ½ acre.
Value 1d.

34 In THORPE (Hall) Alsi, a free man under jurisdiction and patronage; 10 acres.
Value 20d.

35 In SHARPSTONE 1 free man under jurisdiction and patronage; 2 acres.
Value 4d.
Walter holds (this).

PARHAM Half-Hundred
36 In BLAXHALL 5 free men in the jurisdiction and patronage of the Abbot; 26 acres. Always ½ plough.
Value 4s.

37 In WANTISDEN 12 acres of the lordship of Sudbourne.
Value 24d.
In the same (Wantisden) Morewin, a free man, held 2 acres.
Value 4d.
Morwin also holds (this) from the Abbot.

Ƿ Plvmesgata. H̄. Sudburnhā teñ Sca. A. t. r. e.
p mañ. vi. car tre. femp. xiiii. uill. Tc xv. bord. modo xxi.
Tc. ii. feru. Tc. iii. car in dñio. m̄. i. Tc. xii. car. houm. modo.
vi. &. vi. poffent reftaur. iiii. ac pti. Silua. de xii. porc.
m̄. ii.
Tc. i. run: femp. vii. añ. 7 xvii. porc. &. c. xx. oūs. 7 sep
Ecclia. viii. ac.
ual. vii. lib. ht. i. lg in longo. & dimid in lato. 7 xx. d
|de gelto.

384 b

Ƿ Hertesmara. H̄. Weringhefeta. teñ. Sca. A. t. r. e. iiii. car.
terre p mañ. m̄ ten&. Rad de fauigni qrtā; de. R. peurel. femp
ii.
x. uill. &. ix. bord. Tc. iiii. feru. modo. sep. ii. car in dñio. &. iii. car
houm. &. iiii. ac pti. Tc filua. b. porc. m̄. cccc. Ecclia. xvi. ac. &
dim. car. &. ii. runc. &. viii. añ. 7 xxx. porc. &. c. vii. oūs. 7. xviii. cap.
Tc ual. x. lib. 7 m̄ fimilit. In ead. iiii. libi hoes com. Gotwinus
Brictmar. Ofulfus. DeRolfus. xl. ac. femp. ii. car. 7 ual. x. fol. Sca.
Ald. foca. ht. i. lg 7 dim in longo 7. i. lg in lat. 7. ix. deñ de gelto.
Alii ibi tenent.

Ƿ Risebrvge. H̄. Cedeberia. ii. car terre. p. ii. b3 maneriis
. ii. libi hoes. t. r. e. Tc. ii. bord. m̄. v. femp. iiii. feru. Tc. ii. car in dñio.
modo. iiii. 7 dim car hoium. viii. ac pti. filua. de xii. porc. hoc
teñ frodo de abbe. Quando recepit. iiii. runc. modo nullus.
Tc viii. añ. m̄. xiiii. Tc xx. oūs. Tota hec tra iacebat in dñio abbatiæ. tpr regis eduardi c oi confuet. pt fex forifactas sci. e. Tc ual
xl. fol. m̄. lx. & ht dim lg in longo. 7. iii. qr in lato. 7. i. deñ. 7. i.
ferdig. de g. Alii ibi teñ.
Ƿ In Copletuna. iii. libi hoes. xx. ac. Sca. A. foc 7 faca 7 com 7 ual. ii.
fol. Scs. e. vi. forifacturas.

PLOMESGATE Hundred

38 St. Etheldreda's held SUDBOURNE before 1066 as a manor; 6 carucates of land.
> Always 14 villagers. Then 15 smallholders, now 21; then 2 slaves.
> Then 3 ploughs in lordship, now 1; then 12 men's ploughs, now 6, and 6 could be restored.
> Meadow, 4 acres; woodland at 12 pigs. Then 1 cob, now 2.
> Always 7 cattle, 17 pigs, 120 sheep

Value always £7.

A church, 8 acres.
It has 1 league in length and ½ in width; 20d in tax.

HARTISMERE Hundred 384 b

39 St. Etheldreda's held WETHERINGSETT before 1066; 4 carucates of land as a manor. Now Ralph of Savenay holds a fourth (part) from R(anulf) Peverel.
> Always 10 villagers; 9 smallholders. Then 4 slaves, now 2.
> Always 2 ploughs in lordship; 3 men's ploughs.
> Meadow, 4 acres; woodland, then 500 pigs, now 400.
> A church, 16 acres. ½ plough.
> 2 cobs, 8 cattle, 30 pigs, 107 sheep, 18 goats.

Value then £10; now the same.
In the same (Wetheringsett) 4 free men under patronage, Godwin, Brictmer, Oswulf, Derwulf; 40 acres. Always 2 ploughs;
Value 10s.
> St. Etheldreda's (has) the jurisdiction. It has 1½ leagues in length and 1 league in width; 9d in tax. Others hold there.

RISBRIDGE Hundred

40 2 free men held CHEDBURGH before 1066; 2 carucates of land as 2 manors.
> Then 2 smallholders, now 5; always 4 slaves.
> Then 2 ploughs in lordship, now 4; ½ men's plough.
> Meadow, 8 acres; woodland at 12 pigs.

Frodo holds this from the Abbot.
> When he acquired it, 4 cobs, now none; then 8 cattle, now 14; then 20 sheep.

The whole of this land lay in the Abbey's lordship before 1066, with every customary due, except for the 6 forfeitures of St. Edmund's.
Value then 40s; now 60[s].
> It has ½ league in length and 3 furlongs in width; 1¼d in tax. Others hold there.

41 In CLOPTON 3 free men; 20 acres.
> St. Etheldreda's has full jurisdiction and patronage.

Value 2s.
> St. Edmund's (has) the 6 forfeitures.

҂DIM. H̃. de Cosforda Hecham . ten̄ . Sc̄a . A . t . r . e . xi . car҂
træ . Tc̄ xxx . uiłł . modo . xxx.vi . Tc̄ xviii . borđ . m̊ . xx . vi .
semp҂ . viii . seru҂ . Tc̄ . iiii . carr in dn̄io . modo . iii . Tc̄ xx .
car҂ hoi҂um . modo xvi . 7 xvi . ac̄ p̊ti . silua . de xx . porc҂ .
semp . xi . runc҂ . & . xxx . an̄ , 7 . clxxv . oūs . 7 lx . porc̄ . 7 xl . ii . cap҂.

385 a

& . ii . uasa apũ . Tc̄ uał . xx . lib̊ . modo xl . h̊t . i . lḡ . 7 . iiii . qr҂ in long҂ . 7
. i . lḡ in lat҂ . 7 xv . den̄ . de gelt . Alii ibi tenent.
҂Niedinḡa ten̄ . S . A . t . r . e . iii . car҂ træ . Tc̄ . viii . uiłł . m̊ . vi . Tc̄ . vi . borđ .
m̊ . ix . Tc̄ . iii . serui . m̊ . i . semp҂ . iii . car̄ in dn̄io . Tc̄ . ii . car҂ hoi҂um . m̊
. i . viii . ac̄ p̊ti . Silua vi . porc҂ . 7 . i . mot . 7 . ii . runc̄ . 7 xiiii . animał .
. c . oūs . & xx . porc҂ . 7 æcclia . vii . ac̄ . 7 . ii . soc̄ . de . xiiii . ac̄ . Tc̄ . i . car҂ .
modo . ii . boū . Tc̄ uał . iiii . lib̊ . m̊ . viii . h̊t . i . lḡ in longo . 7 . iii . qr҂ in lat҂ .
7 . ii . den̄ . & obol de gł.
҂In hecham . v . soc̄ . lx . ac̄ . Tc̄ . ii . car҂ . & . dim҂ . m̊ . i . 7 . iii . ac̄ p̊ti . 7 uał
x . soł . Roḡ bigot tenet . ҂In ead . . . cxx ac̄ de dn̄io . 7 . iii . borđ .
7 . i . carr҂ . 7 . i . ac̄ & dim҂ . p̊ti . 7 uał . x . soł . In ead . i . soc̄ . xl . ac̄ . 7 uał
. v . soł . hoc tenet . Ricard fili҂ . G . comitis.
҂Bisscopes . H̃ . Wineḃḡa ten̄ . lib̊ ho҂ de q҂ . sc̄a . A . c̄omend . t . r . e .
ii . carr҂ træ . 7 . vii . borđ . Tc̄ . ii . car҂ in dominio . m̊ . i . sēp . ii . car҂ houm .
xi . ac̄ p̊ti . silua . c . xl . porc҂ . Tc̄ . ii . runc̄ . m̊ . i . 7 . i . an̄ . Tc̄ . lx . porc҂ .
m̊ . xx . 7 xx . oūs . 7 . ii . rusc̄ . Ecclia xx . iiii . ac̄ . 7 uał . iiii . soł.

Half-Hundred of COSFORD

42 St. Etheldreda's held HITCHAM before 1066; 11 carucates of land.
    Then 30 villagers, now 36; then 18 smallholders, now 26; always 8 slaves.
    Then 4 ploughs in lordship; now 3; then 20 men's ploughs, now 16.
    Meadow, 16 acres; woodland at 20 pigs. Always 11 cobs, 30 cattle, 175 sheep, 60 pigs, 42 goats, 2 beehives.
    A church, 2 acres.
  Value then £20; now [£] 40.
    It has 1 league and 4 furlongs in length and 1 league in width; 15d in tax. Others hold there.

385 a

43 St. Etheldreda's held NEDGING before 1066; 3 carucates of land.
    Then 8 villagers, now 6; then 6 smallholders, now 9; then 3 slaves, now 1.
    Always 3 ploughs in lordship. Then 2 men's ploughs, now 1.
    Meadow, 8 acres; woodland, 6 pigs; 1 mill. 2 cobs, 14 cattle, 100 sheep, 20 pigs.
    A church, 7 acres.
    2 Freemen with 14 acres. Then 1 plough, now 2 oxen.
  Value then £4; now [£] 8.
    It has 1 league in length and 3 furlongs in width; 2½d in tax.

44 In HITCHAM 5 Freemen; 60 acres. Then 2½ ploughs, now 1.
    Meadow, 3 acres.
  Value 10s.
    Roger Bigot holds (this).
    In the same (Hitcham) 123 acres of [land in] lordship.
    3 smallholders.
    1 plough. Meadow, 1½ acres.
  Value 10s.
    In the same (Hitcham) 1 Freeman; 40 acres.
  Value 5s.
    Richard son of Count Gilbert holds this.

BISHOP'S Hundred

45 A free man, over whom St. Etheldreda's had patronage before 1066, held WINGFIELD; 2 carucates of land.
    7 smallholders.
    Then 2 ploughs in lordship, now 1; always 2 men's ploughs.
    Meadow, 11 acres; woodland, 140 pigs. Then 2 cobs, now 1; 1 cattle; then 60 pigs, now 20; 20 sheep; 2 [bee]hives.
    A church, 24 acres; value 4s.

384 b, 385 a

& xiii . libi hoes . lxxx . ac . ex uno habuit antec . Rob . male& cō
m . Tc . iiii . car . m . iii . Tc ual& . iiii . lib . 7 xiii . fol . 7 . iiii . d . m
iiii . lib . H reclamat Ro . bigot . de dono regis . fed abbas de eli de
rationauit fup eu . m ten . Rog p refpectu . foca in hoxa.
In Lon . i . Leug 7 . ii . qr . & . in lat . iiii . qr . & . xi . d . & obol . de gt
Alii ibi tenent.

In Saha . i . lib ho comdation . i . car . træ . & . ii . uilt . 7 . iii . bord.
femp . ii . car . & . v . ac . pti . filua . x . porc . Tc ual xx . fol . m . xxv.

385 b

foca In oxa . hoc tenuit Robt mal& . de rege ; Abbas derationau
& ea Rob de eo ten.

In blidinga . H . ten sca adeldrida Alnetne . p man . t . r . e . ii . car
træ . Tc . ix . uilt . modo . vii . femp . xiii . bord . femp . i . fer . femper
ii . car in dominio . 7 . iii . car hoium . 7 dim . Æcclia . de . ii . ac .
filua ad vi . porc . ii . ac pti . 7 . i . runc . & . viii . an . 7 xxviii . ous .
& viii . porc . 7 xvi . cap . Huic manerio ptinet lxxx . burgenfes.
* in dunewic . 7 manent . iii . xiiii . ac . fep ual . c . fol.
In ead . iii . libi hoes ptinent manentes in befemera de xiiii . ac .
& . i . car . & ual . iii . fol . S . A . foca . 7 faca.

H . Decolenesse . In moreftuna . i . lib ho . Vluiet
de . v . ac . comd . Æ . sca . t . r . e . 7 ual xvi . d . h ten& de sca . R . mal.

In tre lega . i . lib ho . Leuuricus . de xl . ac . p man . comd abbis.
t . r . e . hunc ten& Rog bigot de rege . Abbas derationauit & eam
. R . de eo ten& . 7 . i . car . 7 . iii . bord . i . ac pti . 7 . i . lib ho fub fe.
de . iiii . ac . 7 ual xx . fol.

13 free men; 80 acres. Robert Malet's predecessor had patronage over one of them. Then 4 ploughs, now 3.
Value then £4 13s 4d; now £4.
Roger Bigot claims this by the King's gift, but the Abbot of Ely established his claim against him. Now Roger holds (it) through a postponement.
The jurisdiction (is) in Hoxne. It has 1 league and 2 furlongs in length, and 4 furlongs in width; 11½d in tax. Others hold there.

46 In (Monk) SOHAM 1 free man under patronage; 1 carucate of land.
2 villagers; 3 smallholders.
Always 2 ploughs.
Meadow, 5 acres; woodland, 10 pigs.
Value then 20s; now 25[s].
The jurisdiction (is) in Hoxne.   385 b
Robert Malet held this from the King. The Abbot established his claim to it. Robert holds (it) from him.

In BLYTHING Hundred
47 St. Etheldreda's held *ALNETERNE* as a manor before 1066; 2 carucates of land.
Then 9 villagers, now 7; always 13 smallholders; always 1 slave.
Always 2 ploughs in lordship; 3 men's ploughs.
½ church with 2 acres.
Woodland for 6 pigs; meadow, 2 acres. 1 cob, 8 cattle, 28 sheep, 8 pigs, 16 goats.
To this manor belong 80 burgesses living in Dunwich; they dwell [on] 14 acres.
Value always 100s.
In the same (*Alneterne*) belong 3 free men who dwell in Bosmere, with 14 acres. 1 plough.
Value 3s.
St. Etheldreda's (has) full jurisdiction.

Hundred of COLNEIS
48 In MORSTON 1 free man, Wulfgeat, under the patronage of St. Etheldreda's before 1066, with 5 acres.
Value 16d.
R(obert) Malet holds this from St. (Etheldreda's).

49 In TRIMLEY 1 free man, Leofric, under the patronage of the Abbot before 1066, with 40 acres as a manor. Roger Bigot holds this (free man) from the King. The Abbot established his claim and Roger holds it from him. 1 plough.
3 smallholders.
Meadow, 1 acre.
1 free man under him, with 4 acres.
Value 20s.

385 a, b

In Waletuna . I . liba femina . Alueua . xvi . ac̄ . com̄d . abbis . & . II .
bord . 7 dim̃ . car̃ . & ual . III . fol . h . berruari ten& de abbate
& tenuit de rege . sed abbas derationauit . 7 In plūgeard . I . lib
hō . Æ . Edwin . de . II . ac̄ . 7 ual . IIII . d . 7 m̃ ten& id . H . de abbe .
In Kenebroc . I . lib hō . Edeldridæ . Godricus . VII . ac̄ . 7 II boū
7 ual . xx . d . hc̄ tenuit . Rog . bgot de rege . sed abbas derationauit . & eū . Rog . bigot . de eo ten̄ . sc̄a Edeldridā . focā
ex . v . hund . 7 dim̃ . 7 reddet illi XI . lib;

386 a

. H̃ . DE CARLEFORDA . Kyngestunā . ten̄ sc̄a . Ē . t . r . e .
II . car̃ terre . p man̄ . Tc̄ . VIII . uill . m̃ . v . m̃ . VIII . bord . Tc̄ . II . serũ .
m̃ . I . Sēp in dominio . II . car̃r . 7 . III . car̃r hom̃ . & . VIII . ac̄
& dim̃ pti . silua ad . v . porc̃ . Semp . I . runc . 7 . IIII . anial
& xxx oūs . 7 XII . porc̃ . semper ualet XL . fol . & ht in longo .
IIII . qr̃ . 7 . III . in lat̃ . 7 . III . d in gelt . Alii ibi tenent .
Brihtewella ten̄ . Sc̄a . t . r . e . p man̄ . II . car̃ . terre .
Tc̄ . vi . uill . m̃ . v . Semp . III . bord . Tc̄ . v . serũ . m̃ . II . Semp in
dn̄io . II . car̃ . Tc̄ hom̃ . IIII . car̃ . m̃ . III . 7 . I . æcclia . sine tr̃a .
& vi . ac̄ pti . 7 . II . molin̄ . Semp . I . runc . 7 . XL . oūs . 7 VIII . porc̃
& . I . foc̃ . de XII . ac̄ . & manet & manet in neubrumna . 7 semp
ual . XL . fol . & ht in longo . x . qr̃ . 7 vi . in lato . & de gelt . IIII . den̄ .
& . I . ferding . Alii ibi tenet .
In grundesburc . ten̄ Algar lib hō . S . e . t . r . e . I . car̃ terræ . p m̃ .
& . xxx . ac̄ . semp . II . uill . & . v . bord : semp in dn̄io . II . car̃ . 7 . houm .
. I . car̃ . IIII . ac̄ pti . Sēp . III . runc . 7 . vi . an̄ . 7 xvi . porc̃ . 7 LXX oūs .

50 In **WALTON** 1 free woman, Aelfeva, under the patronage of the Abbot; 16 acres.
2 smallholders.
½ plough.
Value 3s.
H(ervey) of Berry holds this from the Abbot. He held (it) from the King but the Abbot established his claim.

51 In 'PLUMGEARD' 1 free man of (St.) Etheldreda's, Edwin, with 2 acres.
Value 4d.
Now H(ervey) also holds (this) from the Abbot.

52 In **KEMBROKE** 1 free man of (St.) Etheldreda's, Godric; 7 acres. 2 oxen.
Value 20d.
Roger Bigot held this from the King, but the Abbot established his claim and Roger Bigot holds him from him.
St. Etheldreda's (has) the jurisdiction of the 5½ Hundreds; it is worth £11 to it.

Hundred of COSFORD

53 St. Etheldreda's held **KINGSTON** before 1066; 2 carucates of land as a manor.
Then 8 villagers, now 5; now 8 smallholders; then 2 slaves, now 1.
Always 2 ploughs in lordship; 3 men's ploughs.
Meadow, 8½ acres; woodland for 5 pigs. Always 1 cob, 4 cattle, 30 sheep, 12 pigs.
Value always 40s.
It has 4 furlongs in length and 3 in width; 3d in tax. Others hold there.

54 St. (Etheldreda's) held **BRIGHTWELL** before 1066 as a manor; 2 carucates of land.
Then 6 villagers, now 5; always 3 smallholders. Then 5 slaves, now 2.
Always 2 ploughs in lordship. Then 4 men's ploughs, now 3.
1 church, without land.
Meadow, 6 acres; 2 mills. Always 1 cob, 40 sheep, 8 pigs.
1 Freeman with 12 acres; he dwells in Newbourn.
Value always 40s.
It has 10 furlongs in length and 6 in width; 4¼d in tax. Others hold there.

55 In **GRUNDISBURGH** Algar, a free man of St. Etheldreda's, held before 1066; 1 carucate of land as a manor and 30 acres.
Always 2 villagers; 5 smallholders.
Always 2 ploughs in lordship; 1 men's plough.
Meadow, 4 acres. Always 3 cobs, 6 cattle, 16 pigs, 70 sheep,

& . III . uafa apū . Tc ual& xx . fot . m̃ . xL . fot . h̃ ten& herueus . deberuari͛ deberuarii . de . Sc̃a . ẽ . 7 ht . x . q͛r in longum
& . vi . in latũ . & de gelt͛ xv . d̃.

In Grundefburgh . III . dimidii . hões . cõm . Algari . t . r . e.
VII . ac̃ . 7 ual͛ XII . den̄.

In hafcetuna . xx . II . ac̃ . & . ual . IIII . fol.

In Thifteldena . ten̄ . I . lib̃ hõ . Vlmarus . cõm . sc̃e . ẽ . Lx . ac̃.
p̃ man̄ . 7 . v . libi hões fub fe . Ex his fuer͛ . II . cõm͛d ante . c . G . de magna uift.

386 b

Tc͛ . I . car͛ & dim̃ . m̃ . I . & . III . ac̃ p̃ti . Tc ual . x . fot . modo xII . Qñdo
recep͛ . I . runc͛ . 7 m̃ . Tc . v . añ . 7 m̃ ; xv . porc͛ . 7 L . oũs . 7 XII . cap̃.
7 . v . uafa apum.

In parua belinges . II . libi hões . de xx . ac̃ . cõm dat͛ . Sc̃e . E . 7 dimid.
car . & ual . III . folidoS.

In foxehola . xv . ac̃ . 7 ual . II . fot . In̄ buclefha͛ . v . ac̃ . 7 ual͛ vIII . dener͛.
In Rifhemara . ten̄ Turchillus lib̃ hõ . t . r . e . cõm͛d dim̃ sc̃e . Æ . &
dim . Guerti Lxxx . ac̃ trǣ . p̃ man̄ . Tc . I . car͛ . m̃ dim̃ . v . ac̃ p̃ti.
Tc ual . xx . fot . modo x . In eadẽ . I . lib̃ hõ . Edric͛ cõm͛d.
fic͛ ali͛ de . xx . ac̃ . Tc . I . carr . modo . dim̃ . 7 dimidia ac̃ . p̃ti.
Tc ual . x . fot . modo . vI . Ad huc in ead . v . libi . hões com . Turchillus
xv . ac̃ . Tc . dim̃ . car͛ . m̃ . nulla . Tc ual͛ . xxx . d̃ . m̃ . III . fot.

In Todenha͛ . I . lib̃ hõ . Aluric͛ . IIII . ac̃ . cõm͛d . cuiufda͛ cõm͛d . sc̃e . Æ.
7 ual . vIII . d̃ . hoc totum tenet heruéu deberruariū . de . sc̃a Æ.

3 beehives.
Value then 20s; now 40s.
> Hervey of Berry holds this from St. Etheldreda's.
> It has 10 furlongs in length and 6 in width; 15d in tax.

56 In GRUNDISBURGH 3 half [free] men under the patronage of Algar before 1066; 7 acres.
Value 12d.

57 In HASKETON 22 acres.
Value 4s.

58 In THISTLETON 1 free man, Wulfmer, under the patronage of St. Etheldreda's, held 60 acres as a manor.
> 5 free men under him; of these, 2 were under the patronage of Geoffrey de Mandeville's predecessor. Then 1½ ploughs, now 1.
Meadow, 3 acres.
Value then 10s; now 12[s].
> When he acquired it and now, 1 cob; then and now 5 cattle.
15 pigs, 50 sheep, 12 goats, 5 beehives.

59 In LITTLE BEALINGS 2 free men under the patronage of St. Etheldreda's, with 20 acres. ½ plough.
Value 3s.

60 In FOXHALL 15 acres.
Value 2s.

61 In BUCKLESHAM 5 acres.
Value 8d.

62 In RUSHMERE (St. Andrew) Thorkell, a free man half under the patronage of St. Etheldreda's and half (under that) of Gyrth, held before 1066; 80 acres as a manor. Then 1 plough, now ½.
Meadow, 5 acres.
Value then 20s; now 10[s].
In the same (Rushmere St. Andrew) 1 free man, Edric, under the same patronage as the other, with 20 acres. Then 1 plough, now ½.
Meadow, ½ acre.
Value then 10s; now 6[s].
Also in the same (Rushmere St. Andrew) 5 free men under the patronage of Thorkell; 15 acres. Then ½ plough, now none.
Value then 30d; now 3s.

63 In TUDDENHAM 1 free man, Aelfric, under the patronage of someone under the patronage of St. Etheldreda's; 4 acres.
Value 8d.
> Hervey of Berry holds the whole of this from St. Etheldreda's.

↯In Kalletuna teñ iſaac.viii.libo hoes comdat'.Sce.Æ.i.car' terre
&.ii bord.Tc.iii.car.m.i.iiii.ac pti.7 ual.xvi.ſol.7 hab& in
long.vi.qr.&.ii.in lat'.& de gelt'.ii.den'.& obolu.homo tent& Iſaac
de abbe.
↯In ingolueſtuna.i.lib homo.de.xvi.ac.7 dim.ac pti.7 dim.car.
7 ual.iii.ſol.hoc tenet.R.malet.de abb.
↯In isLeueſtuna.i.liba femina.comd.Sce.E.xxx.ac.Tc.i.car.m
dim.ii.bord.iiii.ac pti.7.i.lib homo.de.x.ac.7 ual.iiii.ſol.
↯In burh.vi.ac.7 ual xii.deñ.↯In biſchelea.iiii.ac.7 ual.viii.
d.↯In riſemara.i.lib homo.Leuric Comd.S.Æ.xl.ac.7 vii.bord.

387 a

&.i.car'.7 dim'.i.ac pti.7 ual.x.ſol.
★ ↯In finesford.i.liba femina keueua.comdat.Sce.Æ.xl.ac.7.i.car.
7 iiii.bord.7 ual.vi.ſol.
↯H.DE WILEFORDA.In Suttuna.Ro.mal&.teñ.dim.
lib ho.Goduuinus.comd.S.e.de.xii.ac.p man.7 dim bord.Tc
dim car'.7 modo.i.ac pti.Tc ual.ii.ſol.modo.v.In ead.ix.lib
ho ſub eo.7.i.lib ho comd Sce.Æ.xl.ac.Tc.i.car.m.ſimil.dim.
ac pti.Tc ual.iiii.ſol.modo.vii.

64 In *KALLETUNA* Isaac held 8 free men under the patronage of St. Etheldreda's; 1 carucate of land.
    2 smallholders.
    Then 3 ploughs, now 1. Meadow, 4 acres.
    Value 16s.
    It has 6 furlongs in length and 2 in width; 2½d in tax.
    Isaac [holds this] from the Abbot.

65 In *INGOLUESTUNA* 1 free man with 16 acres.
    Meadow, ½ acre.
    ½ plough.
    Value 3s.
    R(obert) Malet holds this from the Abbot.

66 In ISLETON 1 free woman under the patronage of St. Etheldreda's; 30 acres. Then 1 plough, now ½.
    2 smallholders.
    Meadow, 4 acres.
    1 free man with 10 acres.
    Value 4s.

67 In BURGH 6 acres.
    Value 12d.

68 In BIXLEY 4 acres.
    Value 8d.

69 In RUSHMERE (St. Andrew) 1 free man, Leofric, under the patronage of St. Etheldreda's; 40 acres.
    7 smallholders.
    1½ ploughs. Meadow, 1 acre.
    Value 10s.

70 In 'FINESFORD' 1 free woman, Leofeva, under the patronage of St. Etheldreda's; 40 acres. 1 plough.
    4 smallholders.
    Value 6s.

  Hundred of WILFORD

71 In SUTTON Ro(bert) Malet holds a half free man, Godwin, under the patronage of St. Etheldreda's, with 12 acres as a manor.
    A half smallholder.
    Then and now ½ plough. Meadow, 1 acre.
    Value then 2s; now 5[s].
In the same (Sutton) 9 free men under him and 1 free man under the patronage of St. Etheldreda's; 40 acres. Then 1 plough, now the same.
    Meadow, ½ acre.
    Value then 4s; now 7[s].

⁊ In Capeles . III . libi . hōes ⁊ dim̄ cōm̄d . Sc̄æ . e . xv . ac̄ . tr̄e . Tc̄ . I . car̄ .
m̄ dim̄ . Tc̄ . ual& . II . fot . modo . IIII . ⁊ In Scotefhā . I . lib hō ⁊ dimid
cōm̄d cidē . VII . ac̄ . ⁊ ual . XII . d.
⁊ In bramefwella . I . lib hō ⁊ dim̄ . cōmend . S . æ . VIII . ac̄ . dim̄ . car̄ .
⁊ ual . XVI . deñ . h ten& . R . mal& . de sc̄a Æ.
⁊ In bredefelda . III . libos hōes . integros . ⁊ . III . dim̄ ⁊ quarta parte . I . libi
XX . IIII . ac̄ . Tc̄ . II . car̄ . m̄ dim̄ . ⁊ ual . VI . fot . ⁊ II . deñ . Rob . malet . de sc̄a æ.
⁊ . I . lib hō . farmann . XII . ac̄ . in foc̄ . ⁊ cōm̄datione abbis . ⁊ ual . II . fot .
⁊ In baldefeia . II . libi cōm̄d . S . e . VII . ac̄ . ⁊ ual . XII . d . ⁊ In alretuna
XII . ac̄ . ⁊ ual& . II . fot . ⁊ In carsfelda . II . libi hōes cōm̄dat . S . e . XXX .
III . ac̄ . ⁊ . I . car̄ . I . ac̄ p̄ti . ⁊ ual . V . fot . ⁊ In Capeles . I . lib hō ⁊ in brade-
felda ali . XXX . II . ac̄ tr̄æ . ⁊ abbas de heli cōm̄d . Tc̄ . I . car̄ . m̄ dimid car̄ .
femper ual& . V . fot . hoc ten& Ro . malet de abbate de heli.

72 In CAPEL (St. Andrew) 3 free men and a half [free man] under the patronage of St. Etheldreda's; 15 acres of land. Then 1 plough, now ½.
Value then 2s; now 4[s].

73 In SHOTTISHAM 1 free man and a half [free man] under the same patronage; 7 acres.
Value 12d.

74 In BROMESWELL 1 free man and a half [free man] under the patronage of St. Etheldreda's; 8 acres. ½ plough.
Value 16d.
R(obert) Malet holds this from St. Etheldreda's.

75 In BREDFIELD 3 whole free men and 3 half [free men] and the fourth part of 1 free man; 24 acres. Then 2 ploughs, now ½.
Value 6s 2d.
Robert Malet [holds this] from St. Etheldreda's.
1 free man, Farman, in the jurisdiction and patronage of the Abbot; 12 acres.
Value 2s.

76 In BAWDSEY 2 free men under the patronage of St. Etheldreda's; 7 acres.
Value 12d.

77 In ALDERTON 12 acres.
Value 2s.

78 In CHARSFIELD 2 free men under the patronage of St. Etheldreda's; 33 acres. 1 plough.
Meadow, 1 acre.
Value 5s.

79 In CAPEL (St. Andrew) 1 free man and in BREDFIELD another; 32 acres of land. The Abbot of Ely (has) the patronage. Then 1 plough, now ½ plough.
Value always 5s.
Ro(bert) Malet holds this from the Abbot of Ely.

Meltuna habbis de heli . II . car̃ tr̃æ . p mañ . Tc̃ . XVIII . uiłł . m̃ . IX .
Tc̃ . VI . borđ . modo . XIII . Tc̃ . II . feru . m̃ . null . femper . II . car in dñio .
Tc̃ . V . carr̃ hoĩum . m̃ . III . 7 dim̃ . XVII . ãc p̃ti . I . runc . 7 . I . moliñ .

387 b

XI . porc . XXX . VII . oũs ; & huic manerio ptinet Balderefeia . bereuuita .
& enumerata . & . IIII . fochemanos ; de XXX . II . ãc terræ . terrã dare non
potuer̃ nec uenđe . Tc̃ . II . car̃ . m̃ . I . & dim̃ . II . ãc p̃ti . Sep XL . fot . uał .
7 łit . I . łḡ . I . łḡ in longo . 7 . IX . qr̃ de dim̃ de łat . 7 XXVII . deñ . de gelt .
In eađ balderefeia . V . libi hões XIX . ãc tr̃æ abbas de eli cõmđ femp uał
In hoi . I . łib hõ de XIX ãc tr̃æ femp dim̃ car̃ . I . ãc p̃ti . sẽp vał . v / XL . deñ .
In hundeftuf . I . łib homo de . VI . ãc terre . Abbas de eli cõmđ . XII . deñ uał .
In brumefuelle . II . libi hões de . X . vi . ãc tr̃e . 7 abb̃ de eli cõmđ . XII . đ uał .
In eađ uilla . I . æcclia de . XVI . ãc terræ & uał . II . fot . E hoc eft
dominiũ abbatis . Et in eađ uilla teñ herueu . LXX . libo hões .
unđe abb̃s habuit foca & faca 7 õms confuetudines Ex his habuit
antec̃ . R . bigot . cõmđ . de . I . cũ . VI . ãc . 7 modo XL . V . II . car̃
terræ . 7 XVI . ãc . Tc̃ . XII . car̃ . modo . VI . 7 . III . ãc p̃ti . Tc̃ uał . XL . fot .
7 modo LX . In eadem . IIII . libi . homines cõmđ abb̃i . LX . & XVI .
ãc tr̃æ . Tc̃ . IIII . car̃ . modo . III . 7 . IIII . ãc p̃ti . 7 . II . runc . VI . porc .
L . VII . oũs . Tc̃ uał . XX . fot . 7 modo fimił .
In berdesfella . III . libi . hões . cõmđ abb̃ . LXX . VI . ãc tr̃æ . Tc̃ . III .
car̃ . modo . II . 7 fub eis . III . libi homines de . V . ãc . dim̃ ãc prati .
Tc̃ uał . XV . fot . modo . XX .

80 The Abbot of Ely's MELTON; 2 carucates of land as a manor.
>   Then 18 villagers, now 9; then 6 smallholders, now 13; then 2 slaves, now none.
>   Always 2 ploughs in lordship. Then 5 men's ploughs, now 3½.
>   Meadow, 17 acres. 1 cob. 1 mill. 11 pigs, 37 sheep.

387 b

To this manor belongs an outlier, BAWDSEY, and [it has] been counted.
>   4 Freemen with 32 acres of land. They could not grant or sell the land. Then 2 ploughs, now 1½.
>   Meadow, 2 acres.
>   Value always 40s.
>   It has 1 league in length and 9[½] furlongs in width; 27d in tax.

In the same BAWDSEY 5 free men; 19 acres of land. The Abbot of Ely (has) the patronage.
Value always 40d.

81 In HOO 1 free man with 19 acres of land. Always ½ plough.
>   Meadow, 1 acre.
>   Value always 5s.

82 In 'HUNDESTUF' 1 free man with 6 acres of land. The Abbot of Ely (has) the patronage.
Value 12d.

83 In BROMESWELL 2 free men with 10 acres of land. The Abbot of Ely (has) the patronage.
Value 12d.
In the same village, 1 church with 16 acres of land; value 2s.
>   This is (part of) the Abbot's lordship.
In the same village Hervey holds 70 free men over whom the Abbot had patronage, full jurisdiction and all customary dues. Of these (free men), R(oger) Bigot's predecessor had patronage over 1 with 6 acres. Now 45 [with] 2 carucates of land and 16 acres. Then 12 ploughs, now 6.
>   Meadow, 3 acres.
>   Value then 40s; now 60[s].
In the same (Bromeswell) 4 free men under the patronage of the Abbot; 60 and 16 acres of land. Then 4 ploughs, now 3.
>   Meadow, 4 acres. 2 cobs, 6 pigs, 57 sheep.
Value then 20s; now the same.

84 In BREDFIELD 3 free men under the patronage of the Abbot; 76 acres of land. Then 3 ploughs, now 2.
>   Under them, 3 free men with 5 acres.
>   Meadow, ½ acre.
>   Value then 15s; now 20[s].

⁋In berdefelda . vi . ac qte ante . Ro . mal& . modo ten&.
Herueu de berruarius de abb . hoc totum ten& herueus de abb.
Adhuc in ead . i . æcclia xxx . i . ac . libe terræ . & . ii . ac pti . & ual
⁋In bromefwella herueus . ii . libi hoes . comd . Sce . e . ⁋ . v . fot.
xxii . ac . Tc . ii . car . modo dim . i . ac dim ae pti . Tc ual . iiii . fot.
⁋ m . v .

388 a

⁋In bradefelda . herueus . ii . libi . comd . S . e . iiii . ac . & ual . xii d.
⁋In brumefwella . R . malet ten& . iii . libo . hoes . comend . S . e .
iiii . ac . & ual . ii . fot . In Scotefha . i . ac . & ual . ii . den.
⁋In usforda ten p man . Almar lib ho . t . r . e . comd . Edrici
dim . 7 dim sce . e . lx . ac . Tc . iiii . bord . modo . ii . Tc . i . car.
& dim . m dim . iiii . ac . pti . & . i . molin . Seper ual . x . fot.
⁋In ead . ix . libi hoes . comd eid . pt . ii . Ipfi fuer comd . S . e .
xxv . ac . & . ii . ac pti . Sep . i . car . Semp ual . iiii . fot.
⁋In Ludha . dim lib homo . Morewinus . comd sce . e . xx . ac 7
dim bord . & dim . car . 7 . vii . libi hoes . fub eo . de xx . ac . ii . ac . & dim
pti . Tc . i . car . modo dim . Semp ual . x . fot.
⁋In hora pola . dim . ii . libi hoes . de xiii . ac & dim . & ual xx . den.

85 In BREDFIELD 6 acres which Ro(bert) Malet's predecessor held. Now Hervey of Berry holds (it) from the Abbot.
    Hervey holds the whole of this from the Abbot.
    Also in the same (Bredfield) 1 church, 31 acres of free land.
        Meadow, 2 acres.
    Value 5s.

86 In BROMESWELL Hervey [holds]; 2 free men under the patronage of St. Etheldreda's; 22 acres. Then 2 ploughs, now ½.
        Meadow, 1½ acres.
    Value then 4s; now 5[s].

87 In BREDFIELD Hervey holds; 2 free men under the patronage of St. Etheldreda's; 4 acres.   388 a
    Value 12d.

88 In BROMESWELL R(obert) Malet holds 3 free men under the patronage of St. Etheldreda's; 4 acres.
    Value 2s.

89 In SHOTTISHAM 1 acre.
    Value 2d.

90 In UFFORD Aelmer, a free man half under the patronage of Edric and half under (that of) St. Etheldreda's, held 60 acres as a manor before 1066.
        Then 4 smallholders, now 2.
        Then 1½ ploughs, now ½.
        Meadow, 4 acres; 1 mill.
    Value always 10s.
    In the same (Ufford) 9 free men under the patronage of the same man, except for 2 who were under the patronage of St. Etheldreda's; 25 acres.
        Meadow, 2 acres.
        Always 1 plough.
    Value always 4s.

91 In LOUDHAM a half free man, Morewin, under the patronage of St. Etheldreda's; 20 acres.
        A half smallholder.
        ½ plough.
        7 free men under him, with 20 acres.
        Meadow, 2½ acres.
        Then 1 plough, now ½.
    Value always 10s.

92 In HARPOLE half 2 free men, with 13½ acres.
    Value 20d.

⁊In meltuna . I . lib hō . S . e . II . ac̄ . ⁊ ual . IIII . den̄.

⁊In horepolo . dim̄ . lib homo . S . e . xv . ac̄ . ⁊ tc̄ . dimidia carr . modo nulla . ⁊ ualet . III . fol.

⁊ . H̃ . DELOSA . HOV . tenuit s̄ca . e . t . r . e . ꝑ man̄ . III . car̄ terræ . Tc̄ xvIII . uitt . modo . x . Tc̄ . I . bord . modo . xvI . Tc̄ . vI . ſeru̅ . modo . II . Tc̄ . in dn̄io . III . car̄ . modo . II . Tc̄ . vI . car̄ hominū . m̄ . v . Silua ad . xx . porc̄ . vII . ac̄ ꝑti . I . molin̄ . & vII . an̄ . xxIIII . porc̄ . & xxx . ou̅s . ⁊ xL . capre . Tc̄ ual . c . fol . m̄ . IIII . lib . ⁊ . I . ex his carr̄ . cep̄ . W . debu uilla . . I . pq̊ derationata ē p p̄ceptū regis . ⁊ faifita æcctiæ . fed dominiū ſuum G . de magna uilla reuocat ad tutore . ⁊ dedit inde uade . modo eſt t̄ra in manu regis . Huic manerio iacent . IIII . libi hoes . comdat S . Æ . vI . ac̄ t̄re . & ual . xII . d . I . æcctia . vIII . ac̄ ⁊ dimid . & ual xvI . den̄.

388 b

⁊ lit in longo . vIII . qr̄ . ⁊ in lato . IIII . ⁊ de gelt̄ . III . den̄ & obot.

⁊In brandeftuna . I . lib hō . ten̄ herueus de bituricenfis . S . Æ . vIII . ac̄ . ⁊ ual . IIII . fot . ⁊In Letheringaham . III . ac̄ & dim̄ . de dn̄io & ual . vI . den̄.

⁊In gretingahā . I . uitta xvI . ac̄ ⁊ dim̄ . car̄ . ⁊ ual . III . fot . ⁊In dalingehou IIII . libi hoes . comd . S æ . dim̄ . car̄ terræ . Tc̄ . II . car̄ . modo . I . ac̄ ꝑti . Tc̄ ual . vIII . fot . modo fimilit̄.

⁊In vdebriga . vII . libi hoes . t . r . e . modo . II . commend . S . Æ . xL . ac̄ . Tc̄ . I . car̄ . Tc̄ ual . vI . fot . modo . v . In ead uilla . Ro mal& . I . lib hō xvI . ac̄ . ⁊ dim̄ . ⁊ dim̄ car̄ . ⁊ ual . v . fot.

⁊In dalingahou . dim̄ lib hō . xvI . ac̄ . ⁊ ual . II . fot . ⁊ . vIII . d.

93 In MELTON 1 free man of St. Etheldreda's; 2 acres.
Value 4d.

94 In HARPOLE a half free man of St. Etheldreda's; 15 acres. Then ½ plough, now none.
Value 3s.

Hundred of LOES

95 St. Etheldreda's held HOO before 1066 as a manor; 3 carucates of land.
Then 18 villagers, now 10; then 1 smallholder, now 16; then 6 slaves, now 2.
Then 3 ploughs in lordship, now 2; then 6 men's ploughs, now 5.
Woodland for 20 pigs; meadow, 7 acres; 1 mill. 7 cattle, 24 pigs, 30 sheep, 40 goats.
Value then 100s; now £4.
W(illiam) of Bouville took 1 of these carucates. It was afterwards adjudged by the King's command and put in the possession of the Church; but he recalls his lord, G(eoffrey) de Mandeville, as guarantor and he gave a pledge for it. Now the land is in the King's hand.
To this manor belong 4 free men under the patronage of St. Etheldreda's; 6 acres of land.
Value 12d.
1 church, 8½ acres; value 16d.
It has 8 furlongs in length and 4 in width; 3½d in tax.   388 b

96 In BRANDESTON Hervey of Bourges holds; 1 free man belonging to St. Etheldreda's; 8 acres.
Value 4s.

97 In LETHERINGHAM 3½ acres of lordship (land).
Value 6d.

98 In CRETINGHAM 1 villager; 16 acres. ½ plough.
Value 3s.

99 In DALLINGHOO 4 free men under the patronage of St. Etheldreda's; ½ carucate of land. Then 2 ploughs, now 1.
Meadow, [1] acre.
Value then 8s; now the same.

100 In WOODBRIDGE 7 free men before 1066, now 2, under the patronage of St. Etheldreda's; 40 acres. Then 1 plough.
Value then 5s; now 5[s].
In the same village, Ro(bert) Malet [holds]; 1 free man; 16½ acres. ½ plough.
Value 5s.

101 In DALLINGHOO a half free man; 16 acres.
Value 2s 8d.

dim̄ lib̄ hō . vi . āc . 7 ual . xii . d . ᚹ In vdebrige . ii . bord . x . āc . & ual . ii . fol.
ᚹ In mungedena . i . lib̄ hō . 7 in ceres felda . alt . xviii . āc . 7 ual . iii . fol.
ᚹ In reslefhā
ᚹ PLŪGATA . H̄ . In aldeburc . v . āc . 7 eſt in dn̄io . 7 ual . x . d . Normann.

.XXII. ᚹ TRA . Giflebti epī . ebroicenfis . Wilefort Hund . Vdehā
tenuit Turmod p uno man . de . ii . car . træ . Tc̄ . ii . uill . m̄ . vii . Sep
. ii . car . in dn̄io . 7 . i . car . hom . 7 . x . āc . p̄ti . i . mol . i . runc . vii . an.
lvi . porc . Tc̄ ual . xl . fol . m̄ . xii . lib.
ᚹ Capefciā tenuit brictmar . i . foc . sc̄e Adeld . l . āc . p . ꝏ . 7 n̄ potuit
uend l dare trā . fuā . sep . i . uill . 7 . iii . bor . tc̄ . i . car . ii . āc . p̄ti . Tc̄ . i . mol.
7 . reddit . xxxv . fol . in fupiori p̄tio . In Ludham xxx libi hōes
cōm̄d Turmodo . ex h fuere . xv . cōm̄dati Edrici . 7 un fuit cōm̄d . Sc̄æ
. A . c̄ . xx . āc . it totū . hn̄t . i . car tr̄e . 7 . d . tc̄ . vi . car . m̄ . iii . vi . āc . p̄ti . Val.
viii . lib . 7 . i . eccla . lx . āc . 7 . ual . v . fol . plures ibi parciunt.

389 a
⋆ ᚹ TRA ABBIS DE BERNAI ; STOV . H̄ . In cratinga . i . lib̄ hō . de xx . āc .XXIII.
dim̄ ecclia . x . āc . 7 . i . uill . 7 . ii . bord . Semp . i . car . inī oēs . & . ii . āc p̄ti.

102 In RENDLESHAM a half free man; 6 acres.
Value 12d.

103 In WOODBRIDGE 2 smallholders; 10 acres.
Value 2s.

104 In MONEWDEN 1 free man and in CHARSFIELD another; 18 acres.
Value 3s.

PLOMESGATE Hundred
105 In ALDEBURGH 5 acres. It is in lordship.
Value 10d.
Norman [holds this].

22   LAND OF GILBERT, BISHOP OF EVREUX

WILFORD Hundred
1 Thormod held 'UDEHAM' as one manor at 2 carucates of land.
Then 2 villagers, now 7.
Always 2 ploughs in lordship; 1 men's plough.
Meadow, 10 acres; 1 mill. 1 cob, 7 cattle, 56 pigs.
Value then 40s; now £12.

2 Brictmer, 1 Freeman of St. Etheldreda's, held CAMPSEY (Ash); 50 acres as a manor. He could not sell or grant his land.
Always 1 villager; 3 smallholders.
Then 1 plough.
Meadow, 2 acres; then 1 mill.
It pays 35s in the above assessment.

3 In LOUDHAM 34 free men under the patronage of Thormod. Of these, 15 were under the patronage of Edric and 1 was under the patronage of St. Etheldreda's with 20 acres. Between them all they have 1½ carucates of land. Then 6 ploughs, now 3.
Meadow, 6 acres.
Value £8.
1 church, 60 acres; value 5s.
Several have a share there.

23   LAND OF THE ABBOT OF BERNAY

STOW Hundred
1 In CREETING (St. Peter) 1 free man with 20 acres.
½ church, 10 acres.
1 villager, 2 smallholders.
Always 1 plough between them all. Meadow, 2 acres.

Apptiata eſt in cratinga in alio. h. In cad. I. lib hō. de. v. ac. aptiata ē
Rex dedit. de feudo harduini.

/ BOSEMERA. H. Cratingas tcn̄ Aluricus lib homo. I. carr̄ terræ
& dim. p man̄. ſemp. IIII. uilli. 7 XII. bord. &. II. ſeru. Tc. II. carr in dn̄io.
m̄. I. Tc. II. carr houm. m̄. I. &. IIII. ac pti. 7 VI. an̄. 7 XV. porc. Tc. c. ous.
m̄. XXX. VI. Tc ual. c. ſol. modo. VI. lib. Niuetuna. ten Aluuricus. I. carr
træ. p man̄. t. r. e. ſemp. III. uill. 7 XII. bord. 7. I. ſeru. 7. I. car in dominio.
Tc. II. car hoium modo. I. v. ac pti. ſilua de. VI. porc. 7. II. mol. 7 ual. LX. ſol.
/ In Cratingas. XX. IIII. libi hōes. I. carr̄ terræ. 7. I. uirg. Tc. III. car. modo
. I. & dimid. 7 ual XX. ſol. Æcclia. de. XII. ac Niuetuna ht. VI. qr in lōgo
7. III. in lat. &. V. den̄ de gelt. Rex & comes de toto ſoca In Vledana Aluuin
. II. lib hōes. XI. ac. Tc dim. car. in nichil. in eod ptio;

* / TRE ABBATIÆ. DE CETE.. HT. DIMID. H. de cosfort.   ; XXIIII;
Careſeia tenuit. Sca maria t. r. e. III. car træ. 7 dim. ſemp. VI.
uilli. 7 XVIII. bord. 7. I. ſeru. &. II. car in dominio. 7. IIII. car houm. &.
. IIII. ac pti. ſilua. LX. porc. 7. I. molin. 7. I. runc. &. X. an̄. &. XXX. VI.
porc. 7. c. XL. ous. 7. III. uaſa ap. Ecclia. III. ac. &. I. ſoc. II. ac. 7. I. lib hō
XX. ac. 7. I. ucar. 7. I. ac pti. Tc ual h man. IIII. lib. modo. c. ſol. 7
Lib hō. IIII. ſol. IIII. d. min. ht. VIII. qr in longo. 7. VI. in lato. 7 VII.
den̄ & obol de gelt;

It has been assessed in Creeting in another Hundred.
In the same (Creeting St. Peter) 1 free man with 5 acres.
It has been assessed.
The King gave (this) from Hardwin's Holding.

BOSMERE Hundred

2 Aelfric, a free man, held CREETING (St. Mary); 1½ carucates of land as a manor.
Always 4 villagers; 12 smallholders; 2 slaves.
Then 2 ploughs in lordship, now 1; then 2 men's ploughs, now 1.
Meadow, 4 acres. 6 cattle, 15 pigs; then 100 sheep, now 36.
Value then 100s; now £6.

3 Aelfric held (Old) NEWTON; 1 carucate of land as a manor before 1066.
Always 3 villagers; 12 smallholders; 1 slave;
1 plough in lordship. Then 2 men's ploughs, now 1.
Meadow, 5 acres; woodland at 6 pigs; 2 mills.
Value 60s.

4 In CREETING 24 free men; 1 carucate of land and 1 virgate. Then 3 ploughs, now 1½.
Value 20s.
A church with 10 acres.

5 (Old) Newton has 6 furlongs in length and 3 in width; 5d in tax.
The King and the Earl (have) jurisdiction over the whole (of it).

6 In 'OLDEN' Alwin; 2 free men; 11 acres. Then ½ plough, now nothing.
(It is) in the same assessment.

LANDS OF THE ABBEY OF CHATTERIS

Half-Hundred of COSFORD

1 St. Mary's held KERSEY before 1066; 3½ carucates of land.
Always 6 villagers; 18 smallholders; 1 slave;
2 ploughs in lordship; 4 men's ploughs.
Meadow, 4 acres; woodland, 60 pigs; 1 mill. 1 cob, 10 cattle, 36 pigs, 140 sheep, 3 beehives.
A church, 3 acres. 1 Freeman, 2 acres.
1 free man, 20 acres. 1 plough.
Meadow, 1 acre.
Value of this manor then £4; now 100s. (Value) of the free man 4s less 4d.
It has 8 furlongs in length and 6 in width; 7½d in tax.

.XXV. **TERRÆ RICARDI FILII COMITIS. GISLEBERTI.**

Rifebruge. h. Claram tenuit Aluricus. p man. xxiiii. car terræ
t. r. e. Tc. xl. uilli. Poſt xxx. v. modo xxx. Tc & p. x. bord. modo xxx. ſep
xx. feru. Tc xii. car in dnio. Poſt. vi. modo. vii. Tc xxx. vi. car hoim.
Poſt xxx. modo xxiiii. xxx. vii. ac pti. ſilua de. xii. porc. ſemper
. i. mol. M. v. arpenni uineæ. ſemp. vi. runc. Tc. x. an. modo. xiiii.
Tc. xii. porc. m lx. Tc. lx. ous. m. cccc. lxxx 7 xii. uaſa apum.
Semp unu mercatu. modo. xl. iii. burgenſes. H maneriu dedit
Aluricus fili Wiſgari Sco Johanni. t. r. e concedente filio ſuo. & quen-
dā ſacerdotē Ledmaru. & alios cū illo impoſuit. Facta etiā carta
æcclīam. & omnē locu Leueſtano abbi ad cuſtodiendū cmiſit. &
in cuſtodia Wiſgari filii ſui. Clerici u hanc. tra nec dare l foris facere
a ſco ihoe poterant. Poſtqua aut Rex W. adueuit. ſaiſiuit ea in manu
ſua. Huic man ſemp adiacent. v. ſoc. cū oi conſuetudine. i. car tre
& dim. ſemp. i. car. 7 dim. vi. ac pti. Tc ual xl. lib. & m ſimilit.
Et ht. ii. lg. in log. 7. i. in lat. 7. xv. den de gelt.

HVNENDANA. Wiſgar. t. r. e. p man. xx. v. car terre. & xx ac.
Tc. 7 poſt. l. iiii. uilli. M. xl. i. ſemp xxx. bord. 7. xiiii. ſeru. Tc.
ix. car in dnio. P. iiii. m. vii. Tc xxx. i. car homn. P & modo xx
iii. & . xlv. ac pti. Silua de. c. lx. porc. ſemp. i. molin. Ecclia
dimid car libæ træ 7 alia. æcclia. iiii. ac. & dim. ſemp. i. car. 7. iii.
ac prati. Tc. ii. runc. m. vi. Tc. xiiii. an. m. xxx. i. Tc. c. xxx. porc.
m. c. 7 lx. Tc. lxxx. ous. m. cccc. lxxx. M. xvii. uaſapu. Tc
ual xxx. lib. P 7 modo. xl. 7 iiii. ſol. &. ht. ii. lg. & . ii. qr in logo

& . i. lg in lat. & . xv. d. de gelt. Alibi tenent.

LANDS OF RICHARD SON OF COUNT GILBERT

RISBRIDGE Hundred

1 Aelfric held CLARE as a manor; 24 carucates of land before 1066.
   Then 40 villagers, later 35, now 30; then and later 10 smallholders, now 30; always 20 slaves.
   Then 12 ploughs in lordship, later 6, now 7; then 36 men's ploughs, later 30, now 24.
   Meadow, 37 acres; woodland at 12 pigs; always 1 mill. now 5 *arpents* of vines. Always 6 cobs. Then 10 cattle, now 14; then 12 pigs, now 60; then 60 sheep, now 480; 12 beehives.
   Always 1 market; now 43 burgesses.
   Aelfric son of Withgar gave this manor to St. John's before 1066 with the assent of his son and placed therein a certain Ledmer the priest and others with him. When a charter had been made, he committed the Church and the whole place to the custody of Abbot Leofstan and into the protection of his son Withgar. The clerics could not grant this land or alienate it from St. John's. But after King William came, he took possession of it into his own hand. To this manor have always belonged 5 Freemen with every customary due; 1½ carucates of land. Always 1½ ploughs.
   Meadow, 6 acres.
Value then £40; now the same. It has 2 leagues in length and 1 in width; 15d in tax.

2 HUNDON; Withgar [held it] before 1066 as a manor; 25 carucates of land and 20 acres.
   Then and later 54 villagers, now 41. Always 30 smallholders; 14 slaves.
   Then 9 ploughs in lordship, later 4, now 7; then 31 men's ploughs, later and now 23.
   Meadow, 45 acres; woodland at 160 pigs; always 1 mill.
   A church, ½ carucate of free land. Another church, 4½ acres. Always 1 plough.
   Meadow, 3 acres. Then 2 cobs, now 6; then 14 cattle, now 31; then 130 pigs, now 160; then 80 sheep, now 480; now 17 beehives.
   Value then £30; later and now [£] 40 4s.
   It has 2 leagues and 2 furlongs in length, and 1 league in width; 15d in tax. Others hold there.

Deſelingā tenuit. Wiſcar̄. ꝑ man̄. t. r. e. xx. car̄ terræ. ſemp̄
xxviii. uill̄. 7 lxxx. xi. bord̄. 7 xx. ſeru̅. &. x. car̄ in dn̄io. 7 xxx.
ii car̄. hominū. &. xv. ac̄ p̄ti. Silua lxxx. porc̄. Tc̄. v. molin̄. m̄.
iiii. Duæ æcclīæ. i. car̄ terræ 7 dimid. 7. i. car̄ & dim̄. Tc̄. viii. runc̄.
m̄. v. Tc̄. xviii. an̄. m̄. xl. tc̄. c. porc̄. modo lxxx. Tc̄ dccc. xl. oūs. m̄. dccccl͞x
&. ix. uaſa apū. Tc̄ ual̄. xxx. lib̄. P̄ 7 modo. xl. Sed tn̄ dedit cuidā
p̄poſito ad firmā ꝑ lx. v. lib̄. ſed maneriū non potuit pati. Et h̄t
. ii. lḡ 7 dim̄ in longo. 7. i. lḡ in lat̄. 7 xxx. vii. den̄ de gelto. in duobȝ h̄.

h̄ · ten̄ · Rob.
In danerdeſtuna. i. ſoc̄. ii. car̄ terræ. 7. x. ac̄. ꝑ man̄. 7. iii. bord̄.
7. ii. ſeru̅. Tc̄. iii. car̄. modo. ii. &. ii. ac̄ p̄ti. ſilua. de. x. porc̄. modo
ii. runc̄. 7 xiii. an̄. 7 xx. viii. porc̄. 7 xxx. ii. oūs. 7. iiii. cap̄. Tc̄ 7 p̄
ual̄ xl. ſol̄. modo. l.

In Cleptuna. ii. ſoc̄. i. car̄ terre. 7 lxxx. 7. i. ac̄. & dimid. &
. ix. bord̄. &. ii. ſeru̅. Tc̄. ii. car̄ in dn̄io. m̄. iii. & dimidia. car̄ hoūm.
&. iii. ac̄ p̄ti. ſilua de. iiii. porc̄. ſemp̄. ii. runc̄. Tc̄. vi. an̄. m̄. xii. m̄
xxx. porc̄. Tc̄ xl. oūs. modo. lxxx. &. iii. uaſa apū. Tc̄ ual̄ xx. ſol̄.
m̄. xl. Danardeſtuna h̄t. i. lḡ in lonḡ. &. iii. qr̄. in lat̄. 7. ii. &
obol. de gelt. Et Cloptuna h̄t. i. lḡ in longo. &. iii. qr̄. in lat̄.
&. vi. d. & obol de gelt.

In dalham. i. ſoc̄. ii. car̄ terre. &. i. uill̄. &. v. bord̄. &. ii. ſeru̅. &. ii.
car̄ in dn̄io. Tc̄. ii. car̄ hominū. modo. i. & dimidia. &. ii. ac̄ p̄ti.
ſilua lx. porc̄. ſemp̄. ii. runc̄. &. x. an̄. modo. xvi. Tc̄ xxiiii. porc̄.
m̄. xxx. Tc̄. c. oūs. modo. cl. 7. l. cap̄. Tc̄ ual̄ xl. ſol̄. m̄. lx. i. æcclīa

xl. ac̄ libæ t̄ræ & dimidia car̄. 7 ual̄. v. ſol̄. H ten̄ Willmus peccatū.
In denhā. ii. ſoc̄. iii. car̄ terre. ſemp̄. v. uill̄. &. xiii. bord̄. &. i. ſeru̅. Tc̄.
iiii. car̄ in dominio. modo. iii. ſemp̄. iiii. car̄ hom̄. vi. ac̄ p̄ti. ſilua xx.
porc̄. Ecclia abſqȝ t̄ra. h̄ ten̄ &. W. hurant. Tc̄. i. eq̄. m̄. ii. m̄. iiii.
an̄. Tc̄ xv. porc̄. modo. xxx. iii. 7 lxxii. oūs. 7 xxx. viii. cap̄. Tc̄ ual̄
iii. lib̄. modo. iiii. 7 x. ſol̄.

3 Withgar held DESNING as a manor before 1066; 20 carucates of land.
Always 28 villagers; 91 smallholders; 20 slaves;
10 ploughs in lordship; 32 men's ploughs.
Meadow, 15 acres; woodland, 80 pigs; then 5 mills, now 4.
2 churches, 1½ carucates of land. 1½ ploughs.
Then 8 cobs, now 5; then 18 cattle, now 40; then 100 pigs,
now 80; then 840 sheep, now 960; 9 beehives.
Value then £30; later and now [£] 40; nevertheless he gave it to a
reeve at a revenue for £65, but the manor could not bear it.
It has 2½ leagues in length and 1 league in width; 37d in tax in
two Hundreds.
Robert holds this.

4 In DENSTON 1 Freeman; 2 carucates of land and 10 acres as a manor.
3 smallholders, 2 slaves.
Then 3 ploughs, now 2. Meadow, 2 acres; woodland at 10 pigs.
Now 2 cobs, 13 cattle, 28 pigs, 32 sheep, 4 goats.
Value then and later 40s; now 50[s].

5 In CLOPTON 2 Freemen; 1 carucate of land and 81½ acres.
9 smallholders, 2 slaves.
Then 2 ploughs in lordship, now 3; ½ men's plough.
Meadow, 3 acres; woodland at 4 pigs. Always 2 cobs. Then 6
cattle, now 12; now 30 pigs; then 40 sheep, now 80; 3 beehives.
Value then 20s; now 40[s].

5a Denston has 1 league in length and 3 furlongs in width; 2½d in tax.
Clopton has 1 league in length and 3 furlongs in width; 6½d in tax.

6 In DALHAM 1 Freeman; 2 carucates of land.
1 villager; 5 smallholders, 2 slaves.
2 ploughs in lordship; then 2 men's ploughs, now 1½.
Meadow, 2 acres; woodland, 60 pigs. Always 2 cobs. [Then] 10
cattle, now 16; then 24 pigs, now 30; then 100 sheep, now
150; 50 goats.
Value then 40s; now 60[s].
1 church, 40 acres of free land. ½ plough. Value 5s.
William Peche holds this.

7 In DENHAM 2 Freemen; 3 carucates of land.
Always 5 villagers; 13 smallholders; 1 slave.
Then 4 ploughs in lordship, now 3; always 4 men's ploughs.
Meadow, 6 acres; woodland, 20 pigs.
A church, without land.
William Hurant holds this.
Then 1 horse, now 2; now 4 cattle; then 15 pigs, now 33; 72
sheep, 38 goats.
Value then £3; now [£] 4 10s.

⁊In auo Keduna.I.foc̄.I.car̛ terræ.femp.&.II.uill.⁊.I.ferư.&.I.car̛. in dn̄io.⁊ dim̛ car̛ houm̛.⁊ ual.xx.fol.hoc ten̄ Gifleb.

⁊In auo Keduna.I.foc̄.I.car̛ terræ.&.modo.III.bord.&.I.feru.femp .I.car̛ in dn̄io.&.IIII.ac̄ p̃ti.femp ual.xx.fol. Hoc ten& fulkeredus.

⁊In Wratinga.I.foc̄.I.car̛ terræ.femp.I.uill.&.III.bord &.I.car̛ [⁊.I.feř.] in dominio.Tc̄ dim̛.car̛ hom̛.modo.II.boư.⁊.IIII.ac̄ p̃ti.Eclia xxx.II.ac̄.libæ tr̄æ.femp.ual.xx.fol.Vlmarus femp tenet.

⁊In ftanesfelda.I.foc̄.I.carr̛ tr̄æ.⁊.II.bord.⁊ femp.I.car̛.⁊.III.ac̄. prati.Rog̃ ten̄.Quando recepit.III.runc̄.⁊ modo fimilit̄. Tc̄.IIII.an̛.modo.VI.Tc̄.VII.porc̄.modo.xxx.Tc̄ xL.ōus.m̂.Lxxx. Tc̄ ual.xx.fol.modo.xxx.

⁊In hvnedana.I.foc̄.I.car̛ terræ.femp.II.bord.&.I.car̛ Hamo ten̄ Tc̄ xxx.ōus.modo.L.⁊ ual& xx.folidos.In ead̄e.x.foc̄.I.car̛ terræ.femp.I.car̛.&.II.ac̄ p̃ti.⁊ ual.xx.fol. ⁊In faRleia.I.foc̄ VII.ac̄.& ual xIIII.d̛.In brochola.I.foc̄.dim̛.car̛ terræ.femp.I.car̛ &.II.ac̄ p̃ti.Tc̄ ual.VIII.fol.m̂.xvI.

⁊In Kidituna.I.foc̄.xxx.ac̄ & d̛.car̛.⁊ ual v.fol.

8 In HAWKEDON 1 Freeman; 1 carucate of land.
    Always 2 villagers; 1 slave;
    1 plough in lordship; ½ men's plough.
  Value 20s.
    Gilbert holds this.

9 In HAWKEDON 1 Freeman; 1 carucate of land.
    Now 3 smallholders; 1 slave.
    Always 1 plough in lordship. Meadow, 3 acres.
  Value always 20s.
    Fulcred holds this.

10 In WRATTING 1 Freeman; 1 carucate of land.
    Always 1 villager; 3 smallholders; 1 slave;
    1 plough in lordship. Then ½ men's plough, now 2 oxen.
      Meadow, 4 acres.
    A church, 32 acres of free land.
  Value always 20s.
    Wulfmer has always held it.

11 In STANSFIELD 1 Freeman; 1 carucate of land.
    2 smallholders.
    Always 1 plough. Meadow, 3 acres.
  Roger holds (this).
    When acquired, 3 cobs, now the same; then 4 cattle, now 6; then
      7 pigs, now 30; then 40 sheep, now 80.
  Value then 20s; now 30[s].

12 In HUNDON 1 Freeman; 1 carucate of land.
    Always 2 smallholders.
    1 plough.
  Hamo holds (this).
    Then 30 sheep, now 50.
  Value 20s.
  In the same (Hundon) 10 Freemen; 1 carucate of land. Always 1 plough.
    Meadow, 2 acres.
  Value 20s.

13 In FARLEY 1 Freeman; 7 acres.
  Value 14d.

14 In BROCKLEY 1 Freeman; ½ carucate of land. Always 1 plough.
    Meadow, 2 acres.
  Value then 8s; now 16[s].

15 In KEDINGTON 1 Freeman; 30 acres. ½ plough.
  Value 5s.

ac̄.&.iii.bord.sēp.i.car̆.&.ii.ac̄ p̃ti.7 ual̆.x.fol̆. ⁊In Stoches.i.foc̆.

/In boituna.i.foc̄.lx.

391 a

xxx.vii.ac̄.Tc̄ dimid.car̆.modo.ii.boū.7.iii.ac̄ p̃ti.7 ual̆.vi.fol̆. &.ii.d. Hos fochemanos tenuit Wifgar.t.r.e.cū ōi c̄fuetudne. ı̃t.vi.forisfacturas sc̄i eadmundi.

⁊Risebrvge.H̃.In Wimundeftuna.iii.foc̆.lxv.ac̆.& dim̃. car̆.7 ual̆.x.fol̆. Ex his hab.fuus ante c̄ omēm.c̄fuet̆.⁊Dim̆.H̃. De cofort. In Wecefhā teñ Vluricus lib̄ hō.t.r.e.lxxx.ac̄. hoc eft de feudo phinci.femp.iii.bor.&.i.ferū.&.i.car̆ in dñio.&.i.ac̄ & dim̄ p̃ti.Tc̄.iii.runc̆.m̃.v.Tc̄.viii.añ.m̃.xi.Tc̄.iii.porc̆.modo xx.v.m̊ lxxx.oūs.7 ual̆.xx.v.fol̆.Sc̄s.e.focā. In ead.i.lib homo.xv, ac̄.& ual.ii.fol.7 vi.d. Wifgarus focā.Sc̄s.e.vi.forisfacturas; ⁊In hetchā.ii.libi hōes.i.car̆ terræ.iiii.bord.&.ii.ferui.Tc̄.ii.car̆ m̃.i.&.iiii.ac̄ p̃ti.7 ual̆.xx.fol̆.hoc tenet Ailuardus filius belli.

⁊Blake.brune.H̃.In bdeuuella.i.lib hō c̄om̃d.xxx.ac̆.&.i.bord. Tc̄ dim̃.⁷ᶜᵃʳ & ual̆.v.fol̆. ⁊In Stou.i.foc̆.xxviii.ac̆.tc̄.dim̃ car̆ & ual iii.fol̆.H̃ ten& Rob.blund.sc̄s.edmund foc̄.⁊

16 In BOYTON 1 Freeman; 60 acres.
   3 smallholders.
   Always 1 plough. Meadow, 2 acres.
   Value 10s.

17 In STOKE (by Clare) 1 Freeman; 37 acres. Then ½ plough, now 2 oxen.   391 a
   Meadow, 3 acres.
   Value 6s 2d.
   Withgar held these Freemen before 1066 with every customary due, except for the 6 forfeitures of St. Edmund's.

RISBRIDGE Hundred

18 In WIMUNDESTUNA 3 Freemen; 65 acres. ½ plough.
   Value 10s.
   His predecessor had every customary due from these (Freemen).

Half-Hundred of COSFORD

19 In WATTISHAM Wulfric, a free man, held 80 acres before 1066. This is part of Finn's Holding.
   Always 3 smallholders; 1 slave.
   1 plough in lordship.
   Meadow, 1½ acres. Then 3 cobs, now 5; then 8 cattle, now 11; then 3 pigs, now 25; now 80 sheep.
   Value 25s.
   St. Edmund's (has) the jurisdiction.
   In the same (Wattisham) 1 free man; 15 acres.
   Value 2s 6d.
   Withgar (had) the jurisdiction. St. Edmund's (has) the 6 forfeitures.

20 In HITCHAM 2 free men; 1 carucate of land.
   3 smallholders; 2 slaves.
   Then 2 ploughs, now 1. Meadow, 4 acres.
   Value 20s.
   Aethelward son of Bell holds this.

BLACKBOURN Hundred

21 In BARDWELL 1 free man under patronage; 30 acres.
   1 smallholder.
   Then ½ plough.
   Value 5s.

22 In STOW (LANGTOFT) 1 Freeman; 28 acres. Then ½ plough.
   Value 3s.
   Robert Blunt holds this.
   St. Edmund's (has) the jurisdiction.

ᴟ *WILEFORD*. $\tilde{H}$. In Bredefella . xii . ac tr̃æ . 7 . i . uill . & ual
. ii . fol . h̃ tẽn . Normannus . de . R .

ᴟ *HER*tefmera . h̃ . In cotetuna . tẽn . fader . vii . ac̃ . 7 ual . xiiii . d̃ .
Galt̃ diaconus ten&.

ᴟ *THEWARDESTRE*. $\tilde{H}$. In timeworda . i . lib̃ hõ . Withgari . t.
r . e . antecefforis Ricardi cõmdatiõn tantũ . lx . ac̃ . Tc̃ . i . car̕ . 7 ual̃
. x . fol . Soc̃ fc̃i Edmundi . In raftedena . ii . foc̃ . vii . ac̃ 7 ual xii . dẽn .

ᴟ *THINGEHOV*. $\tilde{H}$. In Weftlea . iii . lib̃i h́oes . Withgari . cóm̃d̃ . lxxx .
ac̃ cũ foca p̃t . vi . forefacturas . fc̃i edmundi . 7 . i . bord̃ . Semp . ii . car̕ .

391 b
& . ii . ac̃ p̃ti . Ecclia viii . ac̕ . Silua de ix . porc̕ . 7 due partes . i . mol .
& ual . x . fol . In ead̃ uilla . i . lib̃ hõ . fc̃i . e . c̃omd̃ . cũ foca dim̃ car̕ terræ .
. iii . ac̃ p̃ti . Sẽp . i . car̕ . Semp ual . x . fol . ᴟ In Saxham . i . foc̃ . Wifgari .
de xv . ac̃ . Semp dim̃ car̕ . & ual . iii . fol . ᴟ In horningeferda . i . foc̃ . ei
d̃e de . xx . ac̃ . 7 . ii . bord̃ . femp . i . car̕ . & ual . iiii . fol . ᴟ In herfteda . ii .
lib̃i h́oes . Wifgari cũ faca fed poterant uend̃e fine licencia . xv ac̃ .
Semp dim̃ car̕ . & ual . iii . fol .

WILFORD Hundred
23 In BREDFIELD 12 acres of land.
   1 villager.
   Value 2s.
   Norman holds this from Richard.

HARTISMERE Hundred
24 In COTTON Fathir held 7 acres.
   Value 14d.
   Walter the deacon holds [this].

THEDWESTRY Hundred
25 In TIMWORTH 1 free man, under only the patronage of Withgar, Richard's predecessor, before 1066; 60 acres. Then 1 plough.
   Value 10s.
   The jurisdiction (is) St. Edmund's.

26 In RATTLESDEN 2 Freemen; 7 acres.
   Value 12d.

THINGOE Hundred
27 In WESTLEY 3 free men under the patronage of Withgar; 80 acres, with the jurisdiction except for the 6 forfeitures of St. Edmund's.
   1 smallholder.
   Always 2 ploughs. Meadow, 2 acres.
   A church, 8 acres.
   Woodland at 9 pigs; two parts of 1 mill.
   Value 10s.
   In the same village 1 free man of St. Edmund's, under patronage with the jurisdiction; ½ carucate of land.
   Meadow, 3 acres.
   Always 1 plough.
   Value always 10s.

391 b

28 In SAXHAM 1 Freeman of Withgar's, with 15 acres. Always ½ plough; Value 3s.

29 In HORRINGER 1 Freeman of the same man's, with 20 acres.
   2 smallholders.
   Always 1 plough.
   Value 4s.

30 In HAWSTEAD 2 free men of Withgar's, with the jurisdiction but they could sell without permission; 15 acres. Always ½ plough.
   Value 3s.

In maneſtuna . I . lib hō dim̄ car̄ terræ
ſub Witgaro . cū ſoca . t . r . e . Tc̄ . III . bord . modo . I . Tc̄ & p̄ . I . car̄ . m̄ dim̄.
& . II . ac̄ p̄ti . 7 ſemp ual . x . ſot . In Redā . VII . libi hōes . Wiſḡ . cū
ſoca & ſaca ſed poſſant uende . I . car . terræ . & . VI . bord . Tc̄ & poſt . III.
car̄ . modo . I . & dim̄ . & . IIII . ac̄ p̄ti . Silua . III . porc̄ . Tc̄ & p̄ ual xxx
ſot . modo . xL . Ecctia XII . ac̄ tērræ libere.

LAC . FORDA . H̄ In b̄tona ten̄ . godeua . I . liba femina
Wiſgari com̄ tantū in ſoca ſc̄i . edm̄ . t . r . e . Lx . ac̄ t̄ræ & . IIII . bord.
& . I . ſeru . ſemp dim̄ . car̄ in dn̄io . 7 . I . ac̄ p̄ti . 7 ual . v . ſot . In ead
. I . ſoc̄ Witḡ . LX ac̄ . & . IIII . bord . Sēp dim̄ . car̄ . & . I . ac̄ p̄ti . & ual
. v . ſot . Witḡ . ſoc̄ . Haluedona ten̄ Leuiet . lib hō ſub Wit-
garo . t . r . e . com̄d . tantū in ſoca ſc̄i . e . p man̄ . II . car̄ terræ
Tc̄ . IIII . uitt . m̄ . II . & ſemp . III . bord . 7 . I . ſeru . Tc̄ . II . car̄ in dn̄io.
p̄ 7 m̄ . I . 7 dimid . car̄ hom̄ . & qrta pars piſc̄r . ſemp . I . æq . &
XII . porc̄ . 7 . c . L . ous . Tc̄ ual . ſot . xxx . & p̄ 7 modo ſimilit . Æc
ctia . xv . ac̄ libe t̄ræ ; Canauathā ten̄ Wigar ante
ceſſor . Ricardi b̄wita in defelinga p . v . car . terræ . cū foca . ſēp
xx . v . uitt . 7 . v . car̄ . Æcctia . Lx . ac̄ lib terre . & . tē . v . mot . m̄ . IIII.

& . III . ac̄ p̄ti . lit . I . leūg in longo . & . IIII . qr̄ in lato . & de gelto . xx . d ;

31 In MANSTON 1 free man under Withgar, with the jurisdiction before 1066; ½ carucate of land.
    Then 3 smallholders, now 1.
    Then and later 1 plough, now ½. Meadow, 2 acres.
    Value always 10s.

32 In REDE 7 free men of Withgar's, with full jurisdiction but they could sell; 1 carucate of land.
    6 smallholders.
    Then and later 3 ploughs, now 1½.
    Meadow, 4 acres; woodland, 3 pigs.
    Value then and later 30s; now 40[s].
    A church, 12 acres of free land.

  LACKFORD Hundred

33 In BARTON (Mills) Godiva, 1 free woman under only the patronage of Withgar [but] in the jurisdiction of St. Edmund's before 1066, held 60 acres of land.
    4 smallholders, 1 slave.
    Always ½ plough in lordship. Meadow, 1 acre.
    Value 5s.
    In the same (Barton Mills) 1 Freeman of Withgar's; 60 acres.
    4 smallholders.
    Always ½ plough. Meadow, 1 acre.
    Value 5s.
    Withgar (had) the jurisdiction.

34 Leofgeat, a free man only under the patronage of Withgar before 1066 [but] in the jurisdiction of St. Edmund's, held ELVEDEN as a manor; 2 carucates of land.
    Then 4 villagers, now 2. Always 3 smallholders; 1 slave.
    Then 2 ploughs in lordship, later and now 1; ½ men's plough.
    The fourth part of a fishery. Always 1 horse; 12 pigs; 150 sheep.
    Value then 30s; later and now the same.
    A church, 15 acres of free land.

35 Withgar, Richard's predecessor, held CAVENHAM as an outlier in (the lands of) Desning for 5 carucates of land, with the jurisdiction.
    Always 25 villagers;
    5 ploughs.
    A church, 60 acres of free land.
    Then 5 mills, now 4; meadow, 3 acres.
    It has 1 league in length and 4 furlongs in width; 20d in tax.

392 a

In Lakingahethe . I . car̄ terræ . & . VIII . uill. Tc̄ . I . car̄ in dn̄io. modo . I . & dim̄ . & . IIII . pifcar̄ . in eli . 7 . I . nauis ad pifcandum . & . I . ac̄ p̄ti . hæ . II . terre sī in p̄tio de defilinges. Totenhā ten̄ id antec̄. comine Ricardi . I . car̄ terræ 7 dim̄ . 7 . IX . uilli . Sēp . II . car̄ . 7 . ac̄ & dim̄ p̄ti . & Reddit . L . fol. In b̄tona xxx . ac̄ tr̄e in dn̄io . Wit gari . & . II . bou . & ual . III . fol. In mudenehalla . II . foc̄ de . LX . ac̄. 7 . I . bord . & femp . II . car̄ . & ual . v . fol. & p̄tin̄ in defelinga . & non pot̄ uend̄. In hernigawella . III . foc̄ . Wit . de LX . ac̄ Semp dim̄ car̄ . ap̄p̄tiata ē . in defelinga . In ead . I . foc̄ . Wisḡ cū medietat̄ tr̄æ . foca . tefte . hund̄ . 7 medietat̄ s̄ci . edm̄ . cū foca . & h̄t . I . car̄ tr̄æ & . v . bord . Semp . I . car̄ . int̄ oēs . 7 ual . xv . fol.
In Wamforda . IIII . foc̄ eidē cū foca de . I . car̄ tr̄æ . & . I . bord . Sēp . II . car̄ . int̄ om̄s . & . III . ac̄ p̄ti . 7 ual . x . fol . & iacēt in defilinges.

36 In LAKENHEATH 1 carucate of land.
    8 villagers.
    Then 1 plough in lordship, now 1½.
    4 fisheries in Ely; 1 fishing-boat; meadow, 1 acre.
   These 2 lands are in the assessment of Desning.

37 Richard's same predecessor held TUDDENHAM; 1½ carucates of land.
    9 villagers.
    Always 2 ploughs. Meadow, 1½ acres.
   It pays 50s.

38 In BARTON (Mills) 30 acres of land in Withgar's lordship. 2 oxen.
Value 3s.

39 In MILDENHALL 2 Freemen with 60 acres.
    1 smallholder.
    Always 2 ploughs.
   Value 5s.
    It belongs in (the lands of) Desning. They could not sell.

40 In HERRINGSWELL 3 Freemen of Withgar's, with 60 acres. Always ½ plough.
   It has been assessed in Desning.
    In the same (Herringswell) 1 Freeman of Withgar's with a half of the land and the jurisdiction, as the Hundred testifies; and a half of the land (is) St. Edmund's with the jurisdiction. He has 1 carucate of land.
    5 smallholders.
    Always 1 plough between them all.
   Value 15s.

41 In WANGFORD 4 Freemen of the same man, with the jurisdiction, with 1 carucate of land.
    1 smallholder.
    Always 2 ploughs between them all. Meadow, 3 acres.
   Value 10s.
    It lies in (the lands of) Desning.

⁊BABERGA.DVO.H̃. In bure ten&. Witg̃.T.R.E.xviii.libi hões. de cõmd ⁊ foca ⁊ faca ⁊ poterant uend trã.T.R.E. fine licencia ei &.iiii.foc qui non poterant uende.&. xviii.hnt.i.car trae ⁊ dim.&.iii.foc.i.car.&. dim tre.⁊ hi tres hnt fubfe i uilt.⁊.vii. bord.⁊ iii.carr.⁊.iiii.ac p̃ti.⁊ ual.xxx.fol.⁊ hi xviii libi hnt. fub fe.x.bord. Semp.ii.car.⁊.iiii.ac p̃ti. Silua.vi.porc. ⁊ i.molin ⁊ ual.xxx.fol. Bura ht.i.lg̃ in longo ⁊ dimid in lato.⁊ de gelto xxiiii.d. S⁊ alii ten ibi. Ecclia de.xviii. ac libe trae. ⁊In cormerda.vii.libi hoes Wifgari cõmd &. focã &. faca.t.r.e.ii.car trae.⁊.i.bord.Tc.iii.car p̃.&. m̃.ii.

⁊.v.ac prati.⁊ ual&. xxvi.fol.⁊.viii.den. ⁊In Coresfella.vii.libi cõmd ⁊ fac ⁊ foc eidd.iii.car.⁊ dim terrae.xxv.ac.⁊ x.bord. Semp iii.car.inter oms.&. xiii.ac p̃ti.&. ual.iii.lib. ⁊In ilelega.vii.libi hões comd ⁊ fac ⁊ foc eid lx.ac trae. Semper.i.car inter omnes.&. .i.mol.⁊ ual.x.fol. ⁊In Waldinga fella.iii.libi hoes comd ⁊ focã ⁊ facã eid.i.car terrae.⁊ xlv.ac.⁊ ix.bord.Tc.iii.car.p.ii.m̃.i. ⁊.iii.ac p̃ti.⁊.i.runc.⁊.ii.an.⁊ lxxx.xiii.ous. Silu de.iii.porc. ⁊ ual.l.fol. M ten elinant.tcia pars.aecclie.x.ac libae trae.

BABERGH Two Hundreds

42 In BURES Withgar [held] 18 free men before 1066, with the patronage and full jurisdiction; they could sell the land before 1066 without his permission. Also 4 Freemen who could not sell. The 18 (free men) have 1½ carucates of land. 3 Freemen (have) 1½ carucates of land.
    The 3 (Freemen) have under them
        1 villager, 7 smallholders.
        3 ploughs. Meadow, 4 acres.
    Value 30s.
    The 18 free men have under them
        10 smallholders.
        Always 2 ploughs.
        Meadow, 4 acres; woodland, 6 pigs; 1 mill.
    Value 30s.
    Bures has 1 league in length and ½ in width; 24d in tax. But others hold there.
    A church with 18 acres of free land.

43 In CORNARD 7 free men under the patronage and full jurisdiction of Withgar before 1066; 2 carucates of land.
    1 smallholder.
    Then 3 ploughs, later and now 2. Meadow, 5 acres.
    Value 26s 8d.

392 b

44 In *CORESFELLA* 7 free men under the patronage and full jurisdiction of the same man; 3½ carucates of land [and] 25 acres.
    10 smallholders.
    Always 3 ploughs between them all. Meadow, 13 acres.
    Value £3.

45 In ELEIGH 7 free men under the patronage and full jurisdiction of the same man; 60 acres of land.
    Always 1 plough between them all. 1 mill.
    Value 10s.

46 In WALDINGFIELD 3 free men under the patronage and full jurisdiction of the same man; 1 carucate of land and 45 acres.
    9 smallholders.
    Then 3 ploughs, later 2, now 1.
    Meadow, 3 acres. 1 cob, 2 cattle, 93 sheep. Woodland at 3 pigs.
    Value 50s.
    Now Elinant holds (this).
    The third part of a church, 10 acres of free land.

In Ranauadiſc . ix . liƀi . hoes comd . 7 ſoca 7 ſaca eide . iii . carr træ & . v . borđ . 7 . i . ſeru . 7 . iii . car . 7 xiiii . ac p̃ti . 7 . iiii . an̄ . 7 . i . æquus m̃ . xv . porc . 7 xl . vi . ous . 7 ual . iii . liƀ . Rog de s̄co germ̄ . ten̄.

In herterſt . ii . liƀi hoes . com & ſoca 7 ſaca eide de . ii . car terræ 7 . iii . borđ . Semp . ii . car . & . viii . ac . p̃ti . 7 ual . ii . liƀ.

In Walingaſella . ii . liƀi hoes & . un̄ fuit rotƀti . filii Witmarce . comd . abo Wiſgari 7 ſoca 7 ſaca & . hnt . ii . car . terræ . & . ix ac p̃ti . 7 . ii . car . m̃ . ix . an̄ . 7 xxxvii . porc . 7 lxix . ous . & . xi . cap̃ . 7 ual . l . ſol . hr . iiii . qr . in longo . & . iiii . in lato . & de gelto . vi . đ . qui cūq; ibi tenent . In grotena . i . liƀ ho . comd 7 ſaca . & ſoca 7 lit . x . ac træ . 7 ual . xx . đ .   *STOHV . HVND.*

In Sellanda ten̄ find . . antec Ri . xx . iii . ac . 7 . iiii . borđ . ſemp dimidia car . & . ii . bou . 7 ual . v . ſol . *DIMIDIVM . H.*

Degepeſwiz . In burgo de gepeſwiz tenuit Wiſgarus . i . æccliā sc̄i petri . t . r . e . cui pertinebant . Tc 7 m̃ . vi . car træ ꝑ man̄.

47 In CAVENDISH 9 free men under the patronage and full jurisdiction of the same man; 3 carucates of land.
    5 smallholders, 1 slave.
    3 ploughs.
    Meadow, 14 acres. 4 cattle, 1 horse; now 15 pigs; 46 sheep.
    Value £3.
    Roger of St. Germain holds (this).

48 In HARTEST 2 free men under the patronage and full jurisdiction of the same man, with 2 carucates of land.
    3 smallholders.
    Always 2 ploughs. Meadow, 8 acres.
    Value £2.

49 In WALDINGFIELD 2 free men; one was under the patronage of Robert son of Wymarc, both (were) under the full jurisdiction of Withgar. They have 2 carucates of land.
    Meadow, 9 acres.
    2 ploughs.
    Now 9 cattle, 37 pigs, 69 sheep, 11 goats.
    Value 50s.
    It has 4 furlongs in length and 4 in width; 6d in tax, whoever holds there.

50 In GROTON 1 free man under patronage and full jurisdiction. He has 10 acres of land.
    Value 20d.

STOW Hundred

51 In SHELLAND Finn, Richard's predecessor, held 23 acres.
    4 smallholders.
    Always ½ plough and 2 oxen.
    Value 5s.

Half-Hundred of IPSWICH

52 In the Borough of IPSWICH Withgar held 1 church, St. Peter's, before 1066 to which belonged, then and now, 6 carucates of land as a manor.

Tc 7 p̄⁹ vɪ. uilt. modo. vɪɪɪ. Tc &. p̄⁹. v. borđ. m̃. xv. Tc. ɪɪɪɪ. feru᷄. fēper

393 a

ɪɪ. caŕ in dominio. Tc. ɪɪɪ. caŕ. modo. ɪɪɪɪ. Tc filu᷄. vɪɪɪ. porc̃. m̃
ɪɪɪɪ. femper. ɪ. molin̄. 7. ɪɪɪ. ac̃. p̃ti. m̃. ɪ. run̄. &. ɪ. an̄. 7. ɪx. porc̃.
7 ʟxxx. ou᷄s P̱tinent adhuc huic æccliæ. v. burgenfes. 7. in burgo.
xv. ac̃ libe tr̃æ. 7 vɪ. manfure uacue. Ex fup̃dictis. vɪ. caŕ tr̃e. ca-
lu᷄pniat́. Roger uicecomes. c. ac̃. 7. v. uilt. &. ɪ. mol. ad manc̃riu᷄
regis de branfort. &. v. uilt. de eodē manerio teftantur ei. &. offert
legē qualē quis iudicauerit. fed dimidiu᷄ hundret de gepefwiz teftantur qđ hoc iacebat ad eccliā. ẗ. e. & Wifgar tenebat. & offert
derationari. Tc ual. c. fol. modo. xv. lib. cu᷄ aliis terris que iacent
huic æccliæ. In eod̄ burgo h̄t Ricardus. xɪɪɪ. burgenfes. quos tenuit
Phin. t. r. e. fuper. ɪɪɪɪ. ex his habebat focā & facā. 7 comd̄. un eoꝫ
ē feruus. 7 fup xɪɪ. comd́ tn̄t fed manebant in fua ꝓpa tr̃a. & red-
debāt in burgo totā confuetudinē. 7 Hoc eft de honore fint.

Ⅴ Bosemara. H̃. Badeleiā ten̄ Afchil. t. r. e. modo. R. in dn̄io
ꝑ ɪɪ. carŕ terræ. 7 xx. ac̃. ꝑ man̄. femp. ɪɪɪɪ. uilt. 7. ɪɪɪɪ. borđ. 7. v. feru᷄.
7. ɪɪ. caŕ in dominio 7. ɪɪ. carŕ hominu᷄. vɪɪɪ. ac̃ p̃ti. 7 dim̄ molin̄. 7.
ɪɪ. run̄c. & xx. vɪ. anial. 7 xxx. ɪɪ. porc̃. Tc. ʟx. ou᷄s. modo. c. Ecclia. xɪɪɪɪ.
ac̃. Tc ual ʟx. fol. modo. ɪɪɪɪ. lib. Ex hac tr̃a calu᷄pniat́ Ab̄b dim̄. caŕ.
tefte. h̄. Rex & comes focā. Huic manerio additi ſt. t. r... xx. vɪ. uilli
libi hoe᷄s. ɪ. caŕ terræ 7 xʟ. v. ac̃. hos om̄s ten̄ Ricaŕ. ad hoc maneriu᷄
quod tenuit fint. 7 ipfe phin tenebat eos p acommodationē. | Tc 7 p⁹
v. caŕ. modo. ɪɪ. Tc ual xʟ. fol. modo. xʟ. vɪɪ. Rex 7 comes focā & facā.
h̄t. x. qŕ in longo. &. v. in lato. 7. x. den̄ de gelto.

Ⅴ In ftanham. v. ac̃ terræ. 7 filua. ɪɪɪɪ. porc̃. in p̃cio. de. xv. lib. eft.

Then and later 6 villagers, now 8; then and later 5 smallholders, now 15; then 4 slaves.

Always 2 ploughs in lordship. Then 3 [men's] ploughs, now 4. Woodland, then 8 pigs, now 4; always 1 mill. Meadow, 3 acres. Now 1 cob, 1 cattle, 9 pigs, 80 sheep.

393 a

Also to this manor belong 5 burgesses, 15 acres of free land in the Borough and 6 empty dwellings.

Of the above-mentioned 6 carucates of land, Roger the Sheriff claims 100 acres, 5 villagers and 1 mill for the King's manor of Bramford, and 5 villagers of the same manor testify for him and they offer (to prove it by) any law, whoever should give judgment. But the Half-Hundred of Ipswich testify that this belonged to the church before 1066 and Withgar held it, and they offer (to let it) be proven.

Value then 100s; now £15, with other lands which belong to this church.

In the same Borough, Richard has 13 burgesses whom Finn held before 1066. Over 4 of these, (Finn) had full jurisdiction and patronage. One of them is a slave. Over 12 (he had) only the patronage, but they dwelt on their own land and they paid the whole of the customary due in the Borough. This is (part) of Finn's Honour.

BOSMERE Hundred

53 Askell held BADLEY before 1066, now Richard [holds it] in lordship, for 2 carucates of land and 20 acres as a manor.

Always 4 villagers; 4 smallholders; 5 slaves.

2 ploughs in lordship; 2 men's ploughs.

Meadow, 8 acres; ½ mill. 2 cobs, 26 cattle, 32 pigs; then 60 sheep, now 100.

A church, 14 acres.

Value then 60s; now £4.

Of this land, the Abbot claims ½ carucate as the Hundred testifies. The King and the Earl (have) the jurisdiction.

To this manor 26 free men were added after 1066; 1 carucate of land and 45 acres. Richard holds all these men for this manor which Finn held. Finn himself held them on lease from the Sheriff, as the Sheriff himself says. Then and later 5 ploughs, now 2.

Value then 40s; now 47[s].

The King and the Earl (have) full jurisdiction. It has 10 furlongs in length and 5 in width; 10d in tax.

54 In STONHAM 5 acres of land.

Woodland, 4 pigs.

It is in the assessment of £15.

Flochetunā tenuit Godmanus.t.r.e. Wifgarus habuit comd
7 rex & comes focā. hoc ten& Germundus. de. R. p man. & . II. car
terræ. femp. IIII. bord. & . I. feru. & . II. carr in dominio. 7 . IX. ac pti.
Tc. I. runc. Tc. IIII. an. m. VIII. Tc. IIII. porc. Tc. XV. ous. modo LX.
Tc ual. IIII. lib. modo. LX. fol. ht dim lg in longo. 7 . IIII. qr in lato.
& . II. den de gelto. Huic manerio addidit Germundus. XV. ac. t.r.
Willi. qs libe tenebat quidā pbr.t.r.e. in foca regis 7 comit. & ual
II. fol. & . VI. den. Briefeta ten. Bondo lib hō. t.r.e. 7 regina
edeua habuit comd tant. fed. R. clamat ad feudū Wifgari 7 Rex
& coms focā. modo. Rog. p. I. car træ. 7 p man. femp. i. uilt. & . I. bord.
& . I. car in dominio. & . tc. I. car houm. Tc ual. XX. fol. modo XXX.
Hanc terrā reclamat. Rog deramis de dono regis & inde faifitus
fuit. In eade ide ten. Rog de orhec. II. liberos. hoes. de XV. ac. & ual
XXX. d. hoc etiā calupniatur Rg de ramis. fic fuperius. f7 Ric Re-
clamat ad feudū Wifgari. In ead ten& . Ran piperellus. IIII. ac. quæ
iacebant fupdicto manerio. t.r.e. Hoc reclamat ad feudū phin.
In Rignefeta tenuit Hardechinus lib hō. c. ac. p m. t.r.e. modo
ten& Goisfridus. femp. II. uilt. & . IIII. bord. & . I. car in dominio
Tc dimidia car hominū. VII. ac pti. Silua. tc XXX. porc. modo XVI.
Et ual. tc. XX. fol. modo XXX. v. In ead tenet Godricus lib hō. t.r.e.
LX. ac. p man. femp. I. car. Tc ual. X. fol. modo . XX. In ead Codui
lib hō tenuit LX. ac. p man. Tc. I. car. Tc ual. X. fol. modo. XV.

55 Godman held FLOWTON before 1066, Withgar had the patronage and the King and the Earl (had) the jurisdiction. Germund holds this from Richard as a manor and 2 carucates of land.

 Always 4 smallholders; 1 slave;
 2 ploughs in lordship.
 Meadow, 9 acres. Then 1 cob; then 4 cattle, now 8; then 4 pigs, then 15 sheep, now 60.

Value then £4; now 60s.

 It has ½ league in length and 4 furlongs in width; 2d in tax.

To this manor after 1066, Germund added 15 acres which a priest held freely before 1066 in the jurisdiction of the King and the Earl. Value 2s 6d.

56 Bondi, a free man, held BRICETT before 1066; Queen Edith had only the patronage; but Richard claims (it) for Withgar's Holding. The King and the Earl (have) the jurisdiction. Now Roger [holds this] for 1 carucate of land, as a manor.

 Always 1 villager; 1 smallholder;
 1 plough in lordship. Then 1 men's plough.

Value then 20s; now 30[s].

 Roger of Rames claims back this land by the King's gift and he was in possession of it.

In the same (Bricett) Roger of Orbec also holds 2 free men, with 15 acres.

Value 30d.

 Roger of Rames claims this too, as above, but Richard claims (it) back for Withgar's Holding.

In the same (Bricett) Ranulf Peverel holds 4 acres which belonged to the above-mentioned manor before 1066. This he claims back for Finn's Holding.

57 In RIGNESETA Hardekin, a free man, held 100 acres as a manor before 1066. Now Geoffrey holds (it).

 Always 2 villagers; 4 smallholders;
 1 plough in lordship. Then ½ men's plough.
 Meadow, 7 acres; woodland, then 30 pigs, now 16.

Value then 20s; now 35[s].

 In the same (*Rigneseta*) Godric, a free man, [held] 60 acres before 1066 as a manor. Always 1 plough.

Value then 10s; now 20[s].

 In the same (*Rigneseta*) Godwy, a free man, held 60 acres as a manor. Then 1 plough.

Value then 10s; now 15[s].

Totū tenɫ Goisfridus 7 dedit ad firmā ꝑ LXX. fol. fed n̄ pot habe
nifi LX. fol. Huic manerio addidit phin. t. r. Witt. III. libos.

394 a

hões de xx. ac̄. Tc̄. I. car. hoc ē in eod ptio. ht. VIII. qr̄ in longo. &. III.
in lat̄. &. v. den̄ de gelto. Rex & comes focā. In facheduna. I. lib
hō Comitis Algari. tenɫ xxx. ac̄. t. r. e. m̄ Vlmar de Ricardo. femp
. I. car & ual. v. fol. rex & comes focā. Affiam tenuit Vluricus
lib hō. LX. ac̄ ꝑ man̄ femp. II. uitt 7. II. foc̄. de. VII. ac̄. &. II. bord.
&. I. car in dominio. & dimidia car hoūm. &. II. ac̄ pti. Tc̄ ual
xx. fol. modo xxx. 7 Rex & comes focā. In ead ten̄ Iric lib homo
LX. ac̄ ꝑ man̄. &. II. bord. & femp. I. car. &. I. ac̄ pti. 7 ual. xxx.
fol. R. 7. c. focā In ead tenɫ Edricus. lib hō. t. r. e. XL ac̄ ꝑ man̄.
Tc̄. I. car. &. I. ac̄ pti. Rex 7 comes ht focā. 7 ual xx. fol. huic manerio addidit phin. t. r. Witti. VIII. libos hões. de xxx. v. ac̄. & foc̄.
de. XII. ac̄. qui n̄ potuit recedere de sc̄a aeldreda. 7 int eos
habebant. Tc̄. III. car. modo. II. Tc̄ ual. xv. fol. modo xx. Totū
ten̄ Osbnus de wanceio. & Ricardus reclamat ad feudū phin.
Rex & coms focā. Duos ex his libis hōibȝ calūpniatur Rog
de ramis ad fuū feudū. & inde faifitus fuit. Tot ht̄. VI. qr̄ in longo
7. II. in lato. 7 VI. den̄. de gelt. Ex hoc toto nichil habuit
Phin. tr̄e. regis. e.

Geoffrey holds the whole of this and gave it at a revenue for 70s; but he could only have 60s.

To this manor after 1066, Finn added 3 free men with 20 acres. Then 1 plough.

This is in the same assessment.

It has 8 furlongs in length and 3 in width; 5d in tax. The King and the Earl (have) the jurisdiction.

394 a

58 In *FACHEDUNA* 1 free man of Earl Algar's [held] 30 acres before 1066. Now Wulfmer [holds it] from Richard. Always 1 plough. Value 5s.

The King and the Earl (have) the jurisdiction.

59 Wulfric, a free man, held ASH(BOCKING); 60 acres as a manor.

Always 2 villagers; 2 Freemen with 7 acres; 2 smallholders; 1 plough in lordship; ½ men's plough. Meadow, 2 acres.

Value then 20s; now 30[s].

The King and the Earl (have) the jurisdiction.

In the same (Ashbocking) Yric, a free man, held 60 acres as a manor.

2 smallholders.

Always 1 plough. Meadow, 1 acre.

Value 30s.

The King and the Earl (have) the jurisdiction.

In the same (Ashbocking) Edric, a free man, [held] 40 acres as a manor before 1066. Then 1 plough.

Meadow, 1 acre.

The King and the Earl have the jurisdiction.

Value 20s.

To this manor after 1066, Finn added 8 free men with 35 acres, and a Freeman with 12 acres who could not withdraw from St. Etheldreda's. Between them they had then 3 ploughs, now 2. Value then 15s; now 20[s].

Osbern of Wanchy holds the whole of this and Richard claims it back for Finn's Holding.

The King and the Earl (have) the jurisdiction.

Roger of Rames claims two of these free men for his own Holding and was in possession of them.

The whole has 6 furlongs in length and 2 in width; 6d in tax.

Finn had nothing of the whole of this before 1066.

CLAINDINE.H. In Toroluestuna in dñio. xviii. libi hões. Ex
his fuer̄. xii. 7 dim̄ com̄dati Alurico pro com̄dato Wisgari
int̄ tot̄ h̄nt. lxiiii. ac̄. Et ex aliis scil̄. v. & dim̄. n̄ hab ante
cessor Ricardi. com̄m̄d. de alurico. Walduino. Haroldo. Go-
duino. Vlmaro. Alurico. Isti habebant. xxiiii. ac̄. t. r. e. hos
hões ideo tenet Ricardus quia eos tenebat Arfastus ep̄c.

394 b
qdo Ricardus derationauit æcclīa sc̄i petri de gipeswiz sup eū.
sed modo nesciebat eos n̄ ptinere ad suū feudū. Int̄ totū h̄nt. semp. iii.
car. & . i. ac̄ p̄ti. Supiores. xii. ual&. Tc̄ vi. sol̄. &. viii. denarios. & Alii.
iiii. sol̄. &. i. den̄. Rex 7 com̄s h̄t soc̄a de toto.
In helminghea de tr̄a sin tenuit Turi teinn̄. reḡ. E. i. car tr̄æ
p man̄. semp. i. car. & . ii. car houm. 7 . iii. uill. & v. bord. & . iii. ac̄ p̄ti.
Tc̄ silua. de. xx. porc̄. m̊. x. &. ii. runc̄. &. iiii. an̄. &. xx. iiii. porc̄. 7 xl
ous. 7. ii. uasa apū. Tc̄ ual xvi. sol̄. m̊ xx. h̄t. i. lḡ in longo. &. vii. in-
lato. 7 xx. den̄ de gelt. Alii ibi ten̄. Rex. 7 com̄s h̄t soc̄a. Galt de cadomo.
In Tvrol uestuna. lxxxxi ac̄. ptinentes æccliæ sc̄i petri de
Gipewiz. 7 ual. xv. sol̄. 7 h̄ ē in p̄tio de sup̄dic̄tis. xv. lib. h̄t. x. qr̄ in
longo. &. vi. in lato. 7 xx. den̄. de gel. alii jbi tenet.
Sanfort.H. 7 dim̄. Alwartunā ten̄ de tr̄a phin Turi
teinnus reḡ. p man̄. i. car tr̄æ. 7 dim̄. Tc̄. viii. uilli. m̊. iii. Tc̄. iiii. bord.
modo. vii. semp. i. car. 7 dim̄ in dn̄io. Tc̄. iiii. car in dn̄io. modo. i.
& . iii. ac̄ p̄ti. tcia pars piscinæ. Tc̄. i. runc̄. m̊. ii. Tc̄. an̄. modo
viii. Tc̄. xx. porc̄. modo. xxvi. semp. lxxx. ous. modo. iiii.
cap. Tc̄ ual. xl. sol̄. modo. xxx. Roḡ ten&. de Ricardo. Idē Tu
Ri soc̄a.

CLAYDON Hundred

60 In THURLESTON 18 free men in lordship. Of these, 12 and a half were under the patronage of Aelfric father of Withgar; in total, they have 64 acres. Of the others, that is 5 and a half, Richard's predecessor did not have patronage over Aelfric, Waldwin, Harold, Godwin, Wulfmer (and) Aelfric; these had 24 acres before 1066. Richard holds these men because Bishop Erfast held them when Richard established his claim to the church of St. Peter's, Ipswich, against him, but now (he says that) he did not know that they did not belong to his Holding. In total, they have always had 3 ploughs.

394 b

    Meadow, 1 acre.
Value of the above 12 (free men) then 6s 8d; (value of) the others 4s 1d.
    The King and the Earl (have) jurisdiction over the whole.

61 Of Finn's land, Thuri, a thane of King Edward's, held 1 carucate of land in HELMINGHAM as a manor.
    Always 1 plough; 2 men's ploughs;
    3 villagers; 5 smallholders.
    Meadow, 3 acres; woodland, then at 20 pigs, now 10. 2 cobs,
        4 cattle, 24 pigs, 40 sheep, 2 beehives.
Value then 16s; now 20[s].
    It has 1 league in length and 7 furlongs in width; 20d in tax.
Others hold there. The King and the Earl (have) the jurisdiction.
    Walter of Caen [holds this].

62 In THURLESTON 91 acres which belong to the church of St. Peter's, Ipswich.
    Value 15s. This is in the assessment of the above-mentioned £15.
    It has 10 furlongs in length and 6 in width; 20d in tax. Others hold there.

SAMFORD Hundred and a Half

63 Of Finn's land, Thuri, a thane of the King's, held ERWARTON as a manor; 1½ carucates of land.
    Then 8 villagers, now 3; then 4 smallholders, now 7.
    Always 1½ ploughs in lordship. Then 4 ploughs in lordship, now 1.
    Meadow, 3 acres; the third part of a fish-pond. Then 1 cob, now 2; then 6 cattle, now 8; then 20 pigs, now 26; always 80 sheep. Now 4 goats.
Value then 40s; now 30[s].
    Roger holds (this) from Richard.
    Thuri also (had) the jurisdiction.

In Scoteleia tenuit Celeolt.t.r.e. com̄dat̄ Alurico
LX.ac̄ ꝑ man̄.semp.I.uill.&.I.bord.& dim.car̄.& ual.x.sol.Idē
Roḡ; Soca in bcolt.In torp.tenuit Osbnus lib̄ hō Alurici.c.ac̄.ꝑ man̄
t.r.e.semp.III.bord.&.I.car̄.7.III.ac̄ p̄ti.7 ual.xx.sol.Soca in bcolt.
Idē Osbnus de ricardo.Purte p̄yt ten̄ jd̄ Osbnus.t.r.e.LX.ac̄
ꝑ man̄.semper.III.uill.&.II.bord.&.II.seru̅.& dim car̄ in dn̄io.

395 a

&.II.car̄ hom̄.7 ual.x.sol.Idē Osbnus Soca in bcolt;
In Cherchetuna tenuit.Edmundus lib̄ hō LX.ac̄.ꝑ man̄.t.r.e.
semp dimid.car̄.&.I.ac̄ p̄ti.7 tc̄ ual xx.sol.modo xx.III.sol.&
II.den̄.In ead Strangulfus lib̄ hō.tenuit.LX.ac̄ ꝑ man̄.t.r.e.
semp dimidia.car.& ual.IIII.sol.In Eadē Turi lib̄ hō.Guert
LX.ac̄.ꝑ man̄.t.r.e.semp.IIII.bord.& dimidia.carr̄.Tc̄
ual.x.sol.modo.xI.sol.7.v.den̄.In ead.II.libi.hoes.Hun̄.
7 Godric.xv.ac.t.r.e.7.II.bou.Tc̄.ual.v.sol.modo.vIII.
Soca in bcolt.ħt.vI.q̄r in longo.7.v.in lato.7.IIII.d.de gelto.
In Eure Wardestuna tenuit Ailbnus lib̄ hō.LX.ac̄.ꝑ maner.
semp dim.car̄.7 ual.vIII.sol.In eduinestuna.tenuit Godric
lib̄ homo.xxx.ac̄.ꝑ m̄.semp dimidia.car̄.Tc̄ ual.v.sol.modo
III.Soca in bcolt.

64 In SHOTLEY Ceolwold, under the patronage of Aelfric, held 60 acres as a manor before 1066.
> Always 1 villager; 1 smallholder;
> ½ plough.
> Value 10s.
>> Roger also [holds this].
>> The jurisdiction (is) in (East) Bergholt.

65 In TORP Osbern, a free man of Aelfric's, held 100 acres as a manor before 1066.
> Always 3 smallholders.
> 1 plough. Meadow, 3 acres.
> Value 20s.
>> The jurisdiction (is) in (East) Bergholt.
>> The same Osbern [holds this] from Richard.

66 Osbern also held PURTEPYT before 1066; 60 acres as a manor.
> Always 3 villagers; 2 smallholders; 2 slaves;
> ½ plough in lordship; 2 men's ploughs.
> Value 10s.

395 a

>> The same Osbern [holds this].
>> The jurisdiction (is) in (East) Bergholt.

67 In KIRKTON Edmund, a free man, held 60 acres as a manor before 1066. Always ½ plough.
> Meadow, 1 acre.
> Value then 20s; now 23s 2d.
> In the same (Kirkton) Strangwulf, a free man, held 60 acres as a manor before 1066. Always ½ plough.
> Value 4s.
> In the same (Kirkton) Thuri, a free man of Gyrth's; 60 acres as a manor before 1066.
>> Always 4 smallholders.
>> ½ plough.
> Value then 10s; now 11s 5d.
> In the same (Kirkton) 2 free men, Hun and Godric; 15 acres before 1066. 2 oxen.
> Value then 5s; now 8[s].
>> The jurisdiction (is) in (East) Bergholt. It has 6 furlongs in length and 5 in width; 4d in tax.

68 In ERWARTON Ailbern, a free man, held 60 acres as a manor. Always ½ plough.
> Value 8s.

69 In EDUINESTUNA Godric, a free man, held 30 acres as a manor.
> Always ½ plough.
> Value then 5s; now 3[s].
>> The jurisdiction (is) in (East) Bergholt.

394 b, 395 a

Et in hundret ħt Ric̃ . iii . libo hões . Godric.
Edwinũ . Leuric . xxx . iii . ac̃ . femp . dim̃ . car̃ . Tc̃ ual . v . fol.
modo . vi . fol . 7 . vi . deñ . Soca in bcolt . ⁄ In burgheftala teñ
Aluric̉ ftari . com̃d . Guert . xl . ac̃ . p . mañ . t . r . e . femp
ii . bord . Tc̃ . i . car̃r . modo . dim̃ . ii . ac̃ p̃ti . 7 ual . viii . fol . ⁄ In boituna . Lueuftan̉ teñ lib hõ . commendat̃ fin . t . r . e . l . ac̃ . femp
iii . bord . Tc̃ . i . car̃ . modo dim̃ . & . iii . ac̃ p̃ti . Tc̃ ual . x . fol . modo
xi . fol . 7 v . deñ . Soca in bcolt . ⁄ In Toft . Aluin̉ lib hõ commendatus efgaro . ftalre . xx . ac̃ . In ead Aluiet . lib hõ . viii . ac̃ . femp dim̃
car̃r . 7 ual . tc̃ . v . fol . m̃ . xx . 7 . iiii . d . Soca in bcolt.
⁄ In Reindune teñ Leuricus lib hõ . xxx . ac̃ . p mañ . femp dim̃
car̃ . 7 . ii . ac̃ p̃ti . Tc̃ . v . fol . ual . modo . xi . fol . 7 . v . d hoc totum ten&

Ricardus in dominio . ⁄ 7 In̉echam tenuit Godricus lib homo
. i . car̃ terræ . p mañ . t . r . e . femp . i . uilt . & . ii . bord . & . i . car̃ in dñio.
& . vi . ac̃ p̃ti . Ecclie . iiii . ac̃ . Tc̃ ual . xx . fol . modo . xx . v . Osbnus
teñ . Ex his oĩbʒ libis hominibʒ nichil habuit . t . r . e . Phin . Ante-
ceffor Ricardi p̃t de uno folo . com̃d tantũ . Soca de toto
in bercolt . Et eos ten& . Ricardus ad honorẽ phin.
⁄ FRESETVNAM . tenuit Rob filỉ Wimarc . t . r . e . Rog̃ de.
aRbernum ten& . vi . car̃ træ . p . mañ . femp xx . iiii . uilt . & . iiii bord.

70 Also in the Hundred, Richard has 3 free men, Godric, Edwin, Leofric; 33 acres. Always ½ plough.
Value then 5s; now 6s 6d.
The jurisdiction (is) in (East) Bergholt.

71 In BURSTALL Aelfric Starling, under the patronage of Gyrth, held 40 acres as a manor before 1066.
Always 2 smallholders.
Then 1 plough, now ½. Meadow, 2 acres.
Value 8s.

72 In BOYNTON Leofstan, a free man under the patronage of Finn, held 50 acres before 1066.
Always 3 smallholders.
Then 1 plough, now ½. Meadow, 3 acres.
Value then 10s; now 11s 5d.
The jurisdiction (is) in (East) Bergholt.

73 In *TOFT* Alwin, a free man under the patronage of Asgar the Constable; 20 acres.
In the same (*Toft*) Alfgeat, a free man; 8 acres. Always ½ plough.
Value then 5s; now 20[s] 4d.
The jurisdiction (is) in (East) Bergholt.

74 In RAYDON Leofric, a free man, held 30 acres as a manor. Always ½ plough.
Meadow, 2 acres.
Value then 5s; now 11s 5d.
Richard holds the whole of this in lordship.

395 b

75 In HIGHAM Godric, a free man, held 1 carucate of land as a manor before 1066.
Always 1 villager; 2 smallholders;
1 plough in lordship. Meadow, 6 acres.
A church, 4 acres.
Value then 20s; now 25[s].
Osbern holds (this).
From all these free men, Finn, Richard's predecessor, had nothing before 1066 except for patronage only over one alone. The jurisdiction of the whole (is) in (East) Bergholt. Richard holds them as of Finn's Honour.

76 Robert son of Wymarc held FRESTON before 1066. Roger of Abenon holds 6 carucates of land as manor.
Always 24 villagers; 4 smallholders;

395 a, b

&.ıı.caŕ in dominio. Tc̄.vııı.caŕ hom̄.modo.vı.vııı.ac̄.p̊ti.&.
.ı.mol.Quedā æcclia.Tc̄.xı.an̄.m̊.ııı.Tc̄.xʟ.porc̄.modo.ııı.
Tc̄.c.xʟ.oūs.m̊.cı.Tc̄ ual vııı.lib̄.modo.xı.&.x.fol.h̄t.ı.lḡ
in long.7 dim̊ in lato.&.x.den̄.de gelto.Idē Rob̄.focā.

⁊In Burgheſtala.Leuricus.commendatus Algaro Comiti.t.r.
e.xvıı.ac̄.7 ual.ııı.fol.ħ Reuocat Ricardus ad īrā fin.Vlmar̊
ten̄ de ricardo.foca in b̄colt.

⁊Risebrvge.H̃.Iſti ś libi hoēs qui.t.r.e.poterant terras fuas
uendere & donare.Wifgar̊ ante ceſſor Ricardi habuit comm̄d
& focā & facā p̄t vı.foris facturas.sc̄i eadmundi. ⁊In Stanesfelda
ten̄ Edric̊ fpuda.ı.lib̄ hō.ıı.caŕ.terræ.&.ıı.bord.7.ııı.ferui.
femp.ıı.caŕ.&.ıı.ac̄ p̊ti.m̊.xıııı.an̄.Tc̄.ıııı.oūs.modo.ʟxxx.
& xxv.porc.Tc̄ ual.xʟ.fol.modo.ʟx.ħ tenet Giflebertus.

⁊In ead.ten̄ Vlflet.ı.lib̄ hō.ı.caŕ terræ.femp.ı.caŕ.&.ıııı.ac̄
p̊ti.Tc̄ ual.xx.fol.modo.xxx.Rob̄.ten&.In ead Crawa
.ı.lib̄ hō.ʟx.ac̄ trǣ.&.ı.ferů.femp.ı.car.&.ıııı.ac̄.& dim̄ p̊ti.

femper.ı.molin̄.& tc̄ ual.x.fol.modo.xv.ħ tenet.Roḡ.
Ecclia de xv.ac̄ libæ trǣ.Tota ſtenesfelda.h̄t xıı.qr̄ in longo.&.vı.
in lato.&.xııı.d & obolū de gl.

2 ploughs in lordship. Then 8 men's ploughs, now 6.
Meadow, 8 acres; 1 mill.
A church.
Then 11 cattle, now 3; then 40 pigs, now 3; then 140 sheep, now 101.
Value then £8; now [£] 11 10s.
It has 1 league in length and ½ in width; 10d in tax.
Robert also (had) the jurisdiction.

77 In BURSTALL Leofric, under the patronage of Earl Algar before 1066; 17 acres.
Value 3s.
Richard avouches this as Finn's land. Wulfmer holds (it) from Richard.
The jurisdiction (is) in (East) Bergholt.

RISBRIDGE Hundred
THESE ARE THE FREE MEN WHO COULD SELL AND GRANT THEIR LANDS BEFORE 1066; WITHGAR, RICHARD'S PREDECESSOR, HAD PATRONAGE AND FULL JURISDICTION (OVER THEM), EXCEPT FOR THE 6 FORFEITURES OF ST. EDMUND'S.

78 In STANSFIELD Edric Spud, 1 free man, held 2 carucates of land.
2 smallholders, 3 slaves.
Always 2 ploughs.
Meadow, 2 acres. Now 14 cattle; then 4 sheep, now 80; 25 pigs.
Value then 40s; now 50[s].
Gilbert holds this.
In the same (Stansfield) Wulfled, 1 free man, held 1 carucate of land. Always 1 plough.
Meadow, 4 acres.
Value then 20s; now 30[s].
Robert holds (this).
In the same (Stansfield) Crawa, 1 free man; 60 acres of land.
1 slave.
Always 1 plough.
Meadow, 4½ acres; always 1 mill.
Value then 10s; now 15[s].
Roger holds this.
A church with 15 acres of free land.
The whole of Stansfield has 12 furlongs in length and 6 in width; 13½d in tax.

396 a

In depdana ten&. Brictric
blacus. I. lib hō. II. car terræ. semp. VII. bord. &. I. seruus. &. II. car in dnio.
Tc dimidia car hominū. 7. III. ac pti. modo. I. runc. Tc. VII.
an. modo XIIII. Tc. XV. porc. modo XXX. tc XXX. VII. oūs. modo
LXXX. modo. X. cap. &. III. uasa apū. Semp. ual. LX. sol. Frodo
fr Abbis ten&. In eadē. II. libi hoes. Blacuinus 7 Godwinus
II. libi hoes. II. car terræ. &. III. bord. Tc. I. car. &. dim. modo. II.
&. III. ac pti. Tc. I. runc. Semp. VI. an. Tc XVI. porc. m. XX. VI. tc
XL. oūs. Tc ual XXX. sol. modo. L. Osbnus ten.
In Cloptuna ten Leuiet. I. lib hō. I. car & dim træ. &. I. uilt. &.
. I. bord. 7. III. seru. Tc. I. car. modo. II. 7. IIII. ac pti. semper. I. runc.
7. X. an. m. XXX. IIII. porc. 7 LXXX. III. oūs. Tc ual. XX. sol. modo
XXX. Rog ten&. In Vratinga. Goda. I. liba femina. II. car
træ. 7 XXX. ac. semp. IX. bord. 7. II. car in dominio. & dimidia car.
hom. VII. ac pti. 7. I. molin. Tc. I. runc. modo. II. Tc. IIII. an. m
X. Tc. I. porc. m. L. II. Tc LXXX. oūs. m. C. Tc. IIII. cap. modo. XL.
Tc ual. XXX. sol. m. XL. Paganus ten&. Tota ht. I. lg in longo
& dim in lato. &. XII. den de gelto. In hauer hella ten& frede-
bnus. I. lib hō. V. bord. & hnt LXXX. ac. 7. I. car in dnio. 7. II. boū
hoium. 7. II. ac pti. Tc ual. XIII. sol. &. IIII. d. modo. XV. sol. Idē
paganus ten&. In haningehæc. ten Alvvinus. I. lib hō. C. ac.
&. I. bord. &. I. car. &. II. ac pti. Tc ual. X. sol. modo. XV;

79 In DEPDEN Brictric Black, 1 free man, [held] 2 carucates of land.
Always 7 smallholders; 1 slave;
2 ploughs in lordship. Then ½ men's plough.
Meadow, 3 acres. Now 1 cob; then 7 cattle, now 14; then 15 pigs, now 30; then 37 sheep, now 80; now 10 goats; 3 beehives.
Value always 60s.
Frodo, the Abbot's brother, holds (this).
In the same (Depden) 2 free men, Blackwin and Godwin; 2 carucates of land.
3 smallholders.
Then 1½ ploughs, now 2.
Meadow, 3 acres. Then 1 cob; always 6 cattle. Then 16 pigs, now 26; then 40 sheep.
Value then 30s; now 50[s].
Osbern holds (this).

80 In CLOPTON Leofgeat, 1 free man, held 1½ carucates of land.
1 villager; 1 smallholder; 3 slaves.
Then 1 plough, now 2.
Meadow, 4 acres. Always 1 cob; 10 cattle. Now 34 pigs; 83 sheep.
Value then 20s; now 30[s].
Roger holds (this).

81 In WRATTING Goda, 1 free woman; 2 carucates of land and 30 acres.
Always 9 smallholders.
2 ploughs in lordship; ½ men's plough.
Meadow, 7 acres; 1 mill. Then 1 cob, now 2; then 4 cattle, now 10; then 1 pig, now 52; then 80 sheep, now 100; then 4 goats, now 40.
Value then 30s; now 40[s].
Payne holds (this).
The whole has 1 league in length and ½ in width; 12d in tax.

82 In HAVERHILL Fridebern, 1 free man, [held] 5 smallholders; they have 80 acres.
1 plough in lordship; 2 men's oxen. Meadow, 2 acres.
Value then 13s 4d; now 15s.
Payne also holds (this).

83 In HANCHET Alwin, 1 free man, held 100 acres.
1 smallholder.
1 plough. Meadow, 2 acres.
Value then 10s; now 15[s].

In Vrdresfelda. Vlmarus tenͨ . ɪ . liƀ hō . ʟ . ɪ . acͨ . & . ɪ . borđ . & dimͨ
carͨ . & . ɪ . acͨ prati . 7 ual . ᴠɪɪɪ . fol . Idē Paganus ten& . In eađ . ɪ . liƀ
hō Leuiara . c . acͨ . 7 . ɪ . borđ . 7 . ɪ . carͨ . 7 ual . xx . fol . Godart tenet.
In eađ . ɪ . liƀ hō Aluuinus . ɪɪɪ . carͨ trӕ . & . ɪɪ . uilł . & . xɪ . borđ . & . ɪɪɪ . ferū.
& . ɪɪɪ . carͨ in dn̄io . Tcͨ . ɪ . carͨ homͨ . m̂ . dimͨ . & . ɪɪ . acͨ . p̃ti . filua . xx . porcͨ.
Tcͨ . ɪɪ . runcͨ . modo . ɪɪɪ . Tcͨ xx . ɪɪ . an̄ . m̂ . xx . Tcͨ ʟx . porcͨ . modo xʟ . v.
Tcͨ ʟx . ous̄ . modo . cxxɪɪɪ . Tcͨ . ʟx . cap̄ . m̂ . ʟᴠɪɪ . Sēp ual . ʟx . fol . Wilarđ
ten& . Tota ħt . ɪ . lḡ in longo 7 dimͨ in lato . 7 ᴠɪ . đ . de gelto.

In Wratinga . ɪ . liƀ hō alƀnus . ɪɪɪ . carͨ trӕ . & . ᴠ . uilłi . & . x . borđ . Tcͨ
ɪɪɪ . carͨ in dn̄io . modo . ɪɪ . femper . ɪ . carͨ homͨ . & . xɪɪ . acͨ p̃ti . Silua
ᴠɪɪɪ . porcͨ . 7 . ɪ . molīn . Tcͨ . ɪɪ . runcͨ . modo . ɪɪɪ . Tcͨ . ɪx . an̄ . m̂ . xɪɪɪ.
Tcͨ xx . ɪɪɪɪ . porcͨ . modo . xʟ . ᴠɪɪɪ . Tcͨ . ʟx . ous̄ . m̂ . ᴠɪɪ . c . 7 . ᴠɪ . uafa apū.
7 fub eo . ɪx liƀi hoēs dimͨ carͨ trӕ . Tcͨ dimͨ . carͨ . & . ɪ . acͨ p̃ti . Ӕcclia . xɪɪɪ.
acͨ . Tcͨ ual . ʟ . fol . m̂ . ʟx . In cileburna . tenͨ . Godwin9 . ɪ . liƀ hō
ɪɪ . carͨ terrӕ . ɪ . uilł . & . ɪɪɪɪ . borđ . Tcͨ . ɪɪ . carͨ . m̂ . ɪ . 7 . ᴠɪ . acͨ . p̃ti . & . ɪ . mol.
femp . ɪ . runcͨ . Tcͨ ual . xʟ fol . modo . ʟ . Goisfridus fili9 hamonis ten&.

In Poflingeorda . ɪ . liƀ hō . edricus . xxx . ᴠ . acͨ . & dimͨ carͨ . & . ɪɪ . acͨ
p̃ti . & ual ᴠɪɪɪ . fol Loher9 ten& . In boituna . ɪ . liƀ hō Vlgar . ᴠɪɪɪ.
acͨ . 7 ual xᴠɪ . đ . Radulfus ten&.

84 In WITHERSFIELD Wulfmer, 1 free man, held 51 acres.
   1 smallholder.
   ½ plough. Meadow, 1 acre.
   Value 8s.
      Payne also holds (this).
   In the same (Withersfield) 1 free man, Leofwaru; 100 acres.
   1 smallholder.
   1 plough.
   Value 20s.
      Godard holds (this).
   In the same (Withersfield) 1 free man, Alwin; 3 carucates of land.
   2 villagers, 11 smallholders, 3 slaves.
   3 ploughs in lordship; then 1 men's plough, now ½.
   Meadow, 2 acres; woodland, 20 pigs. Then 2 cobs, now 3; then 22 cattle, now 20; then 60 pigs, now 45; then 60 sheep, now 123; then 60 goats, now 57.
   Value always 60s.
      Wilard holds (this).
   The whole has 1 league in length and ½ in width; 6d in tax.

85 In WRATTING 1 free man, Ailbern, 3 carucates of land.
   5 villagers, 10 smallholders.
   Then 3 ploughs in lordship, now 2; always 1 men's plough.
   Meadow, 12 acres; woodland, 8 pigs; 1 mill. Then 2 cobs, now 3; then 9 cattle, now 13; then 24 pigs, now 48; then 60 sheep, now 700; 6 beehives.
   Under him, 9 free men; ½ carucate of land. Then ½ plough.
   Meadow, 1 acre.
   A church, 13 acres.
   Value then 50s; now 60[s].

86 In CHILBOURNE Godwin, 1 free man, held 2 carucates of land.
   1 villager, 4 smallholders.
   Then 2 ploughs, now 1.
   Meadow, 6 acres; 1 mill. Always 1 cob.
   Value then 40s; now 50[s].
      Geoffrey son of Hamo holds (this).

87 In POSLINGFORD 1 free man, Edric; 35 acres. ½ plough.
   Meadow, 2 acres.
   Value 8s.
      Lother holds (this).

88 In BOYTON 1 free man, Wulfgar; 8 acres.
   Value 16d.
      Ralph holds (this).

⁊In alia boituna teñ Ajuuar̛ . I . lib̃
Hõ . XXIIII . āc . ⁊ ual . IIII . fol . W . peret̛ . teñ . ⁊In hauo keduna . Teñ
Aluuin̛ . I . lib̃ hõ . XL . āc . ⁊ dim̛ . car̛ . ⁊ . II . āc . p̛ti . & . ual . VI . fol . & . VIII . d.
Folkered̛ teñ . ⁊In CloPtuna . I . lib̃ . hõ . Roc . de . XIII . āc . & ual.
II . fol . Willm̛ peccatũ teñ . ⁊In Bradeleia . femp . II . libi hoes̛ . LX.
VIIII . āc . ⁊ . I . āc ̛p̛ti . Semp . I . car̛ . & ual . XVII . fol . & . VI ̛. d.

397 a

⁊In Tridiauua femp . X . libi hoes̛ . I . car̛ trǣ . & . I . car̛ . ⁊ . I . āc p̛ti . Æc-
clia XXVIIII . āc . ⁊ ual . X . fol . Tota ħt . I . lg̃ in longo . & . I . qr̛ in lato . &
XII . đ de gelto . ⁊In Kidituna . femp . X . libi . hoes̛ . I . car̛ terræ . & . II.
car̛ . & . ual . XX . fol . ⁊In hauerhella . femp . XIII . libi hoes̛ . I . car̛ terræ
⁊ LX . āc . ⁊ . I . car̛ ⁊ dim̛ filua . VII . porc̃ . ⁊ ual& . XXX . fol .
⁊In Wedresfelda . IX . libi hoes̛ . I . car̛ terræ . ⁊ dim̛ . femp . II . car̛
& dim̛ . Tc̃ ual XX . fol . modo . XXX . ⁊In ftoches femp . XX . I . libi hoes̛
. I . car̛ terræ . LX . VIII . āc . Tc̃ . I . car̛ . & . dim̛ . modo . II . & . X . āc . p̛ti.
Tc̃ ual . XX . fol . modo . XXX . I . ⁊ . IIII . deñ . Ecclia LX . āc . & ual . X.
fol . ⁊In poflingewrda femp . VI . libi hoes̛ . LXXX . V . āc . & . III . bord.
& . I . carr̛ . & ual& . XIIII . fol . & . II . đ .

89 In the other BOYTON Ainuar, 1 free man; 24 acres.
Value 4s.
William Peret holds (this).

90 In HAWKEDON Alwin, 1 free man, held 40 acres. ½ plough.
Meadow, 2 acres.
Value 6s 8d.
Fulcred holds (this).

91 In CLOPTON 1 free man, Roc, with 13 acres.
Value 2s.
William Peche holds (this).

92 In BRADLEY always 2 free men; 69 acres.
Meadow, 1 acre.
Always 1 plough.
Value 17s 6d.

93 In THURLOW always 10 free men; 1 carucate of land. 1 plough. 397 a
Meadow, 1 acre.
A church, 29 acres.
Value 10s.
The whole has 1 league in length and 1 furlong in width; 12d in tax.

94 In KEDINGTON always 10 free men; 1 carucate of land. 2 ploughs.
Value 20s.

95 In HAVERHILL always 13 free men; 1 carucate of land and 60 acres.
1½ ploughs.
Woodland, 7 pigs.
Value 30s.

96 In WITHERSFIELD 9 free men; 1½ carucates of land. Always 2½ ploughs.
Value then 20s; now 30[s].

97 In STOKE (by Clare) always 21 free men; 1 carucate of land [and] 68 acres. Then 1½ ploughs, now 2.
Meadow, 10 acres.
Value then 20s; now 31[s] 4d.
A church, 60 acres; value 10s.

98 In POSLINGFORD always 6 free men; 85 acres.
3 smallholders.
1 plough.
Value 14s 2d.

⁊ In Wichā . ſemp . I . lib homo
LX . aē . 7 . II . bord́ . 7 . I . car̕ . 7 . IIII . aē p̄ti . 7 ual̕ & . x . ſol̕ . ⁊ In Stra
teſella ſemp . XVI . libi . ho̕es . I . car̕ terræ . ſemp . III . car̕ . & . II . aē p̄ti.
& ual̕ & . xx . ſol̕ . Æcclia . xxx . aē . & ual̕ . v . ſol̕ . ⁊ In hauokeduna
ſemp . VIII . libi ho̕es xxx . aē . & . II . bord́ . 7 . I . car̕ . 7 ual̕ . xIII . ſol̕ . ⁊ . IIII d́ .
⁊ In hauerha . II . libi ho̕es xxvI . aē . 7 ual̕ . IIII . ſol̕ . & dim̕ . Iſti
om̕s pot̕ uende ⁊ dare t̕ras ſuas . ſed Wiſgarus h̄t . t . r̕ . e . ⁊ ſocā ⁊
ſacā p̄t . vI . forisfaēturas ſc̄i eadmundi . ut ſupius diximus.
⁊ In bradeleia . IIII . libi . ho̕es . Vluuinus . Leuricus . ⁊ Leuuinus . & h̄nt
xv . aē . Quartus bundo . & . h̄t . I . car̕ . terræ . ſemp . II . car̕r . 7 . II . aē
prati . 7 ual̕ . xx . II . ſol̕ . 7 vI . den̄ . Ex his n̄ habuit ante c̄ Ricardi .
c̄om̄d́ . t . r . e . Sc̕s . edm̕ . totā ſocā . ⁊ In Tridlauua . II . ſoē . edeuæ
cū om̄i c̄ſuetudine . q̕s tenebat . Rad́ qdo forisfecit . & h̄nt xxv .
aē . & ſemp dim car̕ . & . ual̕ IIII . ſol̕ . & . IIII . den̄ . h̄ ten̄ Widardus.

⁊ In Wimundeſtuna . vI . libi ho̕es . de ſexto qui uocatur briētricus .
neſcit hund́ ſi potuit t̕rā ſuā uende t̕ . non . t . r . e . ſed teſtatur
qd́ uider̄ eū iurare qd́ non poterañt dare uende t̕rā ſuā ab ante
ceſſore Ricardi . & h̄nt . II . car̕ . terræ . 7 xI . aē . ſemp . II . car̕ . vII . aē
p̄ti . m̂ . II . runc̄ . Tc̄ . II . uaē . modo . III . Tc̄ . vI . por̕c . modo xxx . Tc̄ .
xvI . oūs . modo . LxII . Tot̕ ual̕ xL . ſol̕ . hoc ten̄ . Giroldus.

⁊ DIMIDI . H̃ . *DE COSFORT* . In hechā . xIIII . libi ho̕es . Lx . aē
Tc̄ . II . car̕ . modo . I . & . II . aē p̄ti . 7 ual̕ . x . ſol̕.

99 In WICKHAM(BROOK) always 1 free man; 60 acres.
    2 smallholders.
    1 plough. Meadow, 4 acres.
    Value 10s.

100 In STRADISHALL always 16 free men; 1 carucate of land. Always 3 ploughs.
    Meadow, 2 acres.
    Value 20s.
    A church, 30 acres; value 5s.

101 In HAWKEDON always 8 free men; 30 acres.
    2 smallholders.
    1 plough.
    Value 13s 4d.

102 In HAVERHILL 2 free men; 26 acres.
    Value 4½s.

All these (free men) could sell and grant their lands but Withgar had full jurisdiction before 1066, except for the 6 forfeitures of St. Edmund's, as we said above.

103 In BRADLEY 4 free men. Wulfwin, Leofric and Leofwin; they have 15 acres. The fourth, Bondi, has 1 carucate of land. Always 2 ploughs.
    Meadow, 2 acres.
    Value 22s 6d.
    Over these (free men), Richard's predecessor did not have patronage before 1066; St. Edmund's (had) full jurisdiction.

104 In THURLOW 2 Freemen of Edeva's with every customary due. (Earl) Ralph held them when he forfeited. They have 25 acres. Always ½ plough.
    Value 4s 4d.
    Widard holds this.

105 In WIMUNDESTUNA 6 free men. Concerning the sixth, called Brictric, the Hundred does not know if he could sell his land or not before 1066 but it testifies that they saw him swear that he could not grant or sell his land away from Richard's predecessor. They have 2 carucates of land and 11 acres. Always 2 ploughs.   397 b
    Meadow, 7 acres. Now 2 cobs; then 2 cows, now 3; then 6 pigs, now 30; then 16 sheep, now 62.
    Value of the whole 40s.
    Gerald holds this.

  Half-Hundred of COSFORD

106 In HITCHAM 14 free men; 60 acres. Then 2 ploughs, now 1.
    Meadow, 2 acres.
    Value 10s.

* ⁊In halefheia. vi. libi hões. i. car̃ terræ. &. vi. borđ. &. ii. car̃. &. ii. ac̄
prati. &. ual. xx. fol. ⁊In carefeia. i. liƀ. v. ac̄. 7 ual. x. đ. fuus antec̄
foca & cõm̃. ⁊In brettham. viii. libi hões. xxx. ac̄. &. i. car̃. & ual
v. fol. ⁊In Rifebroc. ii. libi hões. x. ac̄. & ual. xx. đ.
⁊In Watefelda. iii. libi hões lx. ac̄. &. iii. borđ. Tc̄. i. car̃. & dim̃. modo
. ii. 7 ual. x. fol. Ex ħ. haƀ fuus ante c̄ cm̃đ. t. r. e. 7 foca & faca. Ŝ. e.
vi. forisfacturas. ⁊In Stanefïrada. i. liƀ homo. xxiiii. ac̄. & ual
iiii. fol. Ante c̄. dimiđ. com̃đ. & Aƀƀ. de eli aliã. Dim̃ hanc
terrã calũpniat̃. R. peurel 7 fuit ei libata in Lofa. Ŝ. E. focã;

398 a

⁊TERRE WILL̃MI DE WARENA :~ Thewardefïreu. H̃.   .XXVI.
In ratefdana tenuer̃. ii. libi hões. fc̄e aldrede ; c̄ foca 7 faca.
un eoʒ poterant uendere terrã. 7 alt̃ n̄ poterat. Qui po
terat uendẽ. habebat. xl. ac̄. 7. v. borđ. & alt̃ qui non poterat
lx. Semper. ii. borđ. Semp int̃ eos. ii. carr̃. &. ii. ac̄ p̃ti. 7 ual. xx.
           ten& humfrid' fil' Roderici.
fol. & ē de efcangio Lewes. Hoc ⁊In gedinga. ii. libi hões fc̄i. e. cõm̃
7 foca lx. ac̄. tr̃æ. &. iii. borđ. Tc̄. i. car̃. modo nulla. &. v. ac̄ p̃ti.
& ual. v. fol. DE efcangio Lewes.

107 In LINDSEY 6 free men; 1 carucate of land.
6 smallholders.
2 ploughs. Meadow, 2 acres.
Value 20s.

108 In KERSEY 1 free man; 5 acres.
Value 10d.
His predecessor (had) the jurisdiction and patronage.

109 In BRETTENHAM 8 free men; 30 acres. 1 plough.
Value 5s.

110 In RUSHBROOKE 2 free men; 10 acres.
Value 20d.

111 In WHATFIELD 3 free men; 60 acres.
3 smallholders.
Then 1½ ploughs, now 2.
Value 10s.
Over these (free men) his predecessor had patronage before 1066, and full jurisdiction. St. Edmund's (had) the 6 forfeitures.

112 In STONE STREET 1 free man; 24 acres.
Value 4s.
His predecessor (had) half the patronage and the Abbot of Ely (had) the other half.
R(anulf) Peverel claims half this land and it was delivered to him in Loose.
St. Edmund's (has) the jurisdiction.

26   LANDS OF WILLIAM OF WARENNE   398 a

THEDWESTRY Hundred

1 In RATTLESDEN 2 free men of St. Etheldreda's held with full jurisdiction. One of them could sell the land, the other could not. The one who could sell had 40 acres; 5 smallholders. The other who could not (sell had) 60 (acres); always 2 smallholders. Always 2 ploughs between them.
Meadow, 2 acres.
Value 20s.
It is in exchange (for) Lewes.
Humphrey son of Rodric holds this.

2 In GEDDING 2 free men of St. Edmund's under patronage and jurisdiction; 60 acres of land.
3 smallholders.
Then 1 plough, now none. Meadow, 5 acres.
Value 5s.
(It is) in exchange (for) Lewes.

*LACFORDA. H̃. *In heluedana tēn . I . lib̃ homo s̃ce Aldrede comd tantū . in foca s̃ci . e . II . car̃ terræ p efcangio de Lewes . qd̃ tēn Nicolaus . de . W . Tc̃ & p̃ . IIII . uiłł . modo . III . Semp . II . bord̃ . & . I . feru. Tc̃ & p̃ . II . car̃ in dominio . modo . I . Semp . I . car̃ hom̃ . & quarta pars pifcariæ . & . I . æccłiæ . xv . ac̃ . terræ . Tc̃ . IIII . porc̃ . modo . II . Tc̃ cc . ous̃ . modo . ccc . Tc̃ . L . cap̃ . m̊ . c . vI . minus . tc̃ & p̃ uał . xxx . fol. modo . L . fol. *In herninga wella tēn& (Rogrus tēn&) p̃pofitus 7 fuit tohe lib̃ ho f7 non poterat . uend̃ . I . car̃ terræ . & . II . bord̃ . Semp . I . car̃r & LX . ous̃ . & uał xvI . fol . De feudo frederici in foca s̃ci . ed. In ead tēn lib̃ homo antc̃ frederici in foca s̃ci . e . xL . ac̃ . qd̃ tēn& nicolaus de . W . Tc̃ dim̃ car̃ . modo nulla . & uał . xL . den̄.

*STOV. H̃. In bureffalla tēn& (hunfrid̃) monulfus p̃fbit̃ (hō) s̃ce aldrede com̃ - d in foca regis dimidia car̃ terræ . & xx . ac̃ . m̊ tēn Wiłłmus p efcangio Lewes . tc̃ & p̃ . II . bord̃ . modo . vII . Tc̃ 7 femp . I . car̃ in do- minio . Semp . II . boũ houm̃ . & . II . ac̃ p̃ti In ead . IIII . lib̃i hões eid monulfi com̃d . II . ac̃ . & . uał . xII . fol.

398 b

*BOSEMARA. H̃. Toneftała (nicolauˢ tēn) tenuit . Lefwinus lib̃ homo . I . car̃ terræ . 7 xx . ac̃ p man̄ . t . r . e . femp . I . uiłł . Tc̃ . II . car̃ in dominio . P̃ 7 modo . I . & . II . ac̃ p̃ti . modo . I . runc̃ . 7 . I . uac̃ . Tc̃ . xxx . ous̃ . modo . Lx . Tc̃ uał xxIIII . fol . modo . xxv . Rex & comes focā

LACKFORD Hundred

3 1 free man of St. Etheldreda's, under patronage only (but) in jurisdiction of St. Edmund's, held in ELVEDEN; 2 carucates of land in exchange for Lewes. Nicholas holds (it) from William.
  Then and later 4 villagers, now 3. Always 2 smallholders; 1 slave.
  Then and later 2 ploughs in lordship, now 1; always 1 men's plough.
  The fourth part of a fishery.
  1 church, 15 acres of land.
  Then 4 pigs, now 2; then 200 sheep, now 300; then 50 goats, now 100 less 6.
  Value then and later 30s; now 50s.

4 Roger holds in HERRINGSWELL; a reeve [held], he was a free man of Toki's but could not sell; 1 carucate of land.
  2 smallholders.
  Always 1 plough; 60 sheep.
  Value 16s.
  It is (part) of Frederick's Holding, in the jurisdiction of St. Edmund's.
  In the same (Herringswell) a free man of Frederick's predecessor, in the jurisdiction of St. Edmund's, held 40 acres. Nicholas holds it from William. Then ½ plough, now none.
  Value 40d.

STOW Hundred

5 Humphrey holds in BUXHALL; Munulf the priest, a man of St. Etheldreda's under patronage (but) in the jurisdiction of the King, [held] ½ carucate of land and 20 acres. Now William holds (it) in exchange (for) Lewes.
  Then and later 2 smallholders, now 7.
  Then and always 1 plough in lordship; always 2 men's oxen.
  Meadow, 2 acres.
  In the same (Buxhall) 4 free men of the same Munulf's under patronage; 2 acres.
  Value 12s.

BOSMERE Hundred

6 Nicholas holds in TUNSTALL; Leofwin, a free man, held (it); 1 carucate of land and 20 acres as a manor before 1066.
  Always 1 villager.
  Then 2 ploughs in lordship, later and now 1. Meadow, 2 acres.
  Now 1 cob; 1 cow. Then 30 sheep, now 60.
  Value then 24s; now 25[s].
  The King and the Earl (have) the jurisdiction.

⁊ In Gratingis . Hunfridus
teñ de Wiltmo . I . lib hm . xxxviii . ac̄ . femp . I . car̄ . Tc̄ ual . viii . fol . modo . x.

⁊ BRADEMARA . H̄ . BERHAM . teñ Hugo fili goldæ quod tenuit
Bofteinn . t . r . e . Dim̄ car̄ . træ . p mañ . femp . iii . bord . & . ii . ſerui .
& . i . car̄ in dn̄io . Tc̄ dim̄ . car̄ hom̄ . modo . ii . bous . Tc̄ . ii . runc̄ .
modo . i . Tc̄ . xiii . porc̄ . Tc̄ lxxx . v . ous . Modo . x . c . ⁊ iii . libi hoes .
iiii . ac̄ . & . dim̄ . car̄ . ex his habuit fuus anteceſſor com̄d . Tc̄ ual
xvi . fol . Modo . xx.

⁊ RISEBRVGE . H̄ . DE FEVDO FEDRICI . --
Depdanā teñ hugo de Wanceio qd̄ tenuit Toka teinnus . t . r . e . p m̄ .
iii carr̄ terræ . femp xvi . uilt . ⁊ vii . bord . Tc̄ . iiii . feru . Tc̄ & p
ii . carr̄ in dominio . modo . iiii . femper . iiii . car̄ hom̄ . xii . ac̄ p̄ti .
Silu . de . c . porc̄ . femper . ii . runc̄ . Tc̄ xx . ii . añ . modo . xvii .
Tc̄ . xl porc̄ . m̄ . lxx . ii . Tc̄ . xxiiii . ous . modo . c . xii . modo
xiii . uafa apū . Eccl̄ia . xx . iiii . ac̄ . libæ træ . Tc̄ ual . iiii . lib .
Modo . vi . ht . i . leg . in longo . & . viii . qr̄ . in lat . ⁊ . v . d . ⁊ oblu de gelto.

⁊ Wedresfeldā . teñ . Wimer quā tenuit idē . t . r . e . p manerio
ii . car̄ terræ . femp . v . uilt . & . v . bord . Tc̄ . iii . feru . Tc̄ . ii . car̄
in dominio . modo . iii . femper . i . car̄ . hominū . ii . ac̄ prati .
Silua . xx . porc̄ . Tc̄ . ii . runc̄ . modo . iii . Tc̄ . iiii . añ . modo .
xii . Tc̄ xx . porc̄ . modo . xxx . Tc̄ lxxx . ous . Modo . c . femp

xvi . cap̄ . ⁊ vi . uafa apū . Tc̄ ual lxx . fol . modo . iiii . lib . In cadē
. i . lib hō . xx . iiii . ac̄ . femp dim̄ carr̄ . ⁊ ual . iiii . fol .

⁊ In Cloptuna teñ . hugo . quam tenuit idē tocha . i . carr̄ . træ
femper . i . carr̄ . & . ii . ac̄ . prati . Semper ual & . xx . fol .

7 In CREETING Humphrey holds from William 1 free man; 38 acres. Always 1 plough.
Value 8s; now 10[s].

BRADMERE Hundred
8 Hugh son of Gold holds BARNHAM; Bosten held it before 1066; ½ carucate of land as a manor.
    Always 3 smallholders; 2 slaves;
    1 plough in lordship. Then ½ men's plough, now 2 oxen.
    Then 2 cobs, now 1; then 13 pigs; then 85 sheep, now 90.
3 free men, 4 acres. ½ plough. Over these (free men) his predecessor had patronage.
Value then 16s; now 20[s].

RISBRIDGE Hundred
(PART) OF FREDERICK'S HOLDING
9 Hugh of Wanchy holds DEPDEN; Toki, a thane, held it before 1066; 3 carucates of land as a manor.
    Always 16 villagers; 7 smallholders. Then 4 slaves.
    Then and later 2 ploughs in lordship, now 4; always 4 men's ploughs.
    Meadow, 12 acres; woodland at 100 pigs. Always 2 cobs. Then 22 cattle, now 17; then 40 pigs, now 72; then 24 sheep, now 112; now 13 beehives.
    A church, 24 acres of free land.
Value then £4; now [£] 6.
It has 1 league in length and 8 furlongs in width; 5½d in tax.

10 Wigmer holds WITHERSFIELD; he also held it before 1066; 2 carucates of land as a manor.
    Always 5 villagers; 5 smallholders. Then 3 slaves.
    Then 2 ploughs in lordship, now 3; always 1 men's plough.
    Meadow, 2 acres; woodland, 20 pigs. Then 2 cobs, now 3; then 4 cattle, now 12; then 20 pigs, now 30; then 80 sheep, now 100. Always 16 beehives.

399 a

Value 70s; now £4.
In the same (Withersfield) 1 free man; 24 acres. Always ½ plough.
Value 4s.

11 Hugh holds in CLOPTON; Toki also held it; 1 carucate of land. Always 1 plough.
    Meadow, 2 acres.
Value always 20s.

HVND DE BLEDINGA. Wretham tenuit. Edricus
lib hō. t. r. e. ii. carr. terræ. p mañ. femp. v. uilt. femp xi. bord.
Tc. vi. ferui. modo. iii. Tc car & dim in dnio. modo. ii. Tc. iii.
car houm. modo. ii. femp filua ad xx. porc. femper. ii. ac prati.
mo. ii. runc. modo xiii. an. modo. xii. porc. modo; c. xiii. ous.
modo xx. cap. 7 v. uafa apū. 7. i. æcclia. de. xl. ac. femp ual. xl. fol.
7 iftu maneriū ten Rodbtus de petro ponte de eo. In eadē uilla
tenuit Turchillus. lib hō. t. r. e. femper. ii. carr. terræ. p. i. ma
nerio 7 femper. v. uilt. 7 femp xi. bord. ii car. poffunt fieri in
dominio. 7. i. quando recepit. ii. ac. pti. filua ad xx. porc.
femp ual. xl. fol. Et hanc terrā ipfe met. R. ten&.
*In ead villa. ten Wluric lib homo. ii. car terræ p manerio.
femp. v. uilt. 7 xi. bord. i. car in dominio. & altera poteft fieri.
&. ii. carr. hominū. ii. ac prati. filua ad xx. porc. femp ual. xl.
fol. 7. i. æcclia. de. viii. ac. 7 hoc ten ide. R.
In eadē Villa. xx. libi homin manfer. de. ccc. lx. ac. &. ii. bord.
7 femp. vi. car in dominio. femp ual. lx. fol. In. i. de iftis hominibȝ
ht Cōms Alanus dim emendatione. 7 dim tra 7 foca & faca.
7 totū h ht Rodbtus de Willmo. de Warena. de tota hac tra iac
foca & faca in blideburg. *H̃.*

*Adhuc ht Willm in eadē uilla. i. maneriū. iii. car tre quod tenuit halden
. i. lib homo. Tc. vi. uilt. 7 mo. iiii. Tc xi. bord. modo. xiii. Tc. iii. feru.
modo. i. femp. iii. car in dominio. Tc & modo. ii. car houm. ii.
ac pti. filua ad xl. porc. modo. vii. an. modo. xxiiii. porc.
qual xxti. ous. modo. xxx. cap. T. R. E. ual. iiii. lib. & modo
iii. 7 hoc ten Willmus fili Rainaldi. de. W. de Warene.

Hundred of BLYTHING

12a Edric, a free man, held WRENTHAM before 1066; 2 carucates of land as a manor.
>Always 5 villagers; always 11 smallholders. Then 6 slaves, now 3. Then 1½ ploughs in lordship, now 2; then 3 men's ploughs, now 2.
>Woodland, always for 20 pigs; meadow, always 2 acres. Now 2 cobs, now 13 cattle, now 12 pigs, now 113 sheep; now 20 goats, 5 beehives.
>1 church with 40 acres.

Value always 40s.
>Robert of Pierrepont holds this manor from him.

In the same village Thorkell, a free man, held before 1066; always 2 carucates of land as 1 manor.
>Always 5 villagers; always 11 smallholders.
>2 ploughs possible in lordship; when acquired, 1.
>Meadow, 2 acres; woodland for 20 pigs.

Value always 40s.
>The same Robert holds this land.

In the same village Wulfric, a free man; 2 carucates of land as a manor.
>Always 5 villagers; 11 smallholders;
>1 plough in lordship, another possible; 2 men's ploughs.
>Meadow, 2 acres; woodland for 20 pigs.

Value always 40s.
>1 church with 8 acres.
>Robert also holds this.

In the same village dwell 20 free men, with 300 acres.
>2 smallholders.
>Always 6 ploughs in lordship.

Value always 60s.
>Over 1 of these men, Count Alan has half the patronage, half the land and full jurisdiction.
>Robert has the whole of this from William of Warenne.
>The full jurisdiction over the whole of this land lies in Blythburgh.

12b Also in the same village William has 1 manor; 3 carucates of land. 399 b
Haldane, 1 free man, held it.
>Then 6 villagers, now 4; then 11 smallholders, now 13; then 3 slaves, now 1.
>Always 3 ploughs in lordship. Then and now 2 men's ploughs.
>Meadow, 2 acres; woodland for 40 pigs. Now 7 cattle; now 24 pigs; fourscore sheep; now 30 goats.

Value before 1066 £4; now [£] 3.
>William son of Reginald holds this from William of Warenne.

In eadē villa manſit . I . lib̄ hō . 7 dimidia . car̄ terre ten̄ ꝑ manerio . 7 ſubſe habuit . II . libo homines . de . X . ac̄ . & . I . bord̄ . ſemp . I . car̄
in dominio . 7 dimid̄ car̄ hoūm . ſilua . ad . IIII . porc̄ . 7 dīm ac̄
prati . II . runc̄ . VI . an̄ . X . porc̄ . XXX . oūs . XX . cap̄ . Tc̄ ual . X . ſol.
7 modo ſimiliī . ⁊In eadē uilla ten̄ Aluricus de ſanford
. L . ac̄ ꝑ manerio . ſemp . II . bordarii . ſemp . I . car̄ . in dominio
. I . ac̄ prati . 7 . I . runc̄ . IIII . an̄ . VIII . porc̄ . LX . oūs . VII . cap̄.
ſemp ualuit . X . ſol . ⁊In eadē uilla manent . VIII . libi hōes
7 tenēt . car̄ 7 dim̄ . 7 . X . ac̄ terræ . 7 . tenē . I . bord̄ . ſemp . II.
car̄ in dominio . ſemper ual . XII . ſol . 7 hoc totū ten&
uuilłmus fili rainaldi . ſub . W . de uuarena.
⁊Henestedē . I . bereuuite de uueretehā . I . car̄ terræ . ſemp.
IIII . uilłi . 7 ſemper . IX . bord̄ . 7 ſemp . I . car̄ in dominio . 7 ſemp
II . car̄ hominū . 7 . VI . an̄ . 7 . XL . oūs . XII . porc̄ . XX . cap̄ . ſemp
ual . XX . ſol . 7 modo ſunt additi . II . libi . hōes . de . XXX . ac̄ trǣ.
7 hn̄t . I . car̄ . in dominio . 7 ual . III . ſol . 7 has . II . terras ten&
Godefridus de ponte . ſub . Willmo de Warenna . Et om̄s hæ
terræ . hn̄t . III . lḡ in longo . & . II . de lato . 7 reddit . II . ſol . de geldo

regis ꝑ totā hanc terrā ht Rex ſocā 7 ſacā p̄t dominium
Aldani . 7 de terra hac s̄t ablate . VI . ac̄ . terræ . comiti . Alano
q̄s homines Willmi ſibi abſtuler̄ teſte hundreto . 7 Turkil de uue-
reteham fuit hō edrici antececſoris Rodb̄ti malet.

In the same village 1 free man dwelt and held ½ carucate of land as a manor. He also holds it.
>Under him he had 2 free men, with 10 acres. 1 smallholder.
>Always 1 plough in lordship; ½ men's plough.
>Woodland for 4 pigs; meadow, ½ acre. 2 cobs, 6 cattle, 10 pigs, 30 sheep, 20 goats.

Value then 10s; now the same.
In the same village Aelfric of *Sanford* held 50 acres as a manor.
>Always 2 smallholders.
>Always 1 plough in lordship.
>Meadow, 1 acre. 1 cob, 4 cattle, 8 pigs, 60 sheep, 7 goats.

Value always 10s.
In the same village 8 free men dwell and hold [1]½ carucates and 10 acres of land. They hold
>1 smallholder.
>Always 2 ploughs in lordship.

Value always 12s.
William son of Reginald holds the whole of this under William of Warenne.

12c HENSTEAD, 1 outlier of Wrentham; 1 carucate of land.
>Always 4 villagers; always 9 smallholders.
>Always 1 plough in lordship; always 2 men's ploughs.
>6 cattle, 40 sheep, 12 pigs, 20 goats.

Value always 20s.
Now 2 free men have been added, with 30 acres of land. They have 1 plough in lordship.
Value 3s.
Godfrey of Pierrepont holds these two lands under William of Warenne.

12d All these lands have 3 leagues in length and 2 in width; 2s in the King's tax.
>Through the whole of this land the King has full jurisdiction, except (in) Haldane's lordship.
>From this land 6 acres of land were taken away from Count Alan which William's men took away for themselves, as the Hundred testifies.
>Thorkell of Wrentham was a man belonging to Edric, the predecessor of Robert Malet.

⁊MIdeltuna . tenˊ Rannulfus nepos |qd tenuit. Aluricus . I . libˊ homo ,p . I.
manerio . modo W . de Warena . in dnio tenˊ . II . carˊ terræ . sem-
per . II . uilli . semp . VIII . bordˊ . Tcˊ . IIII . serui . ⁊ . modo . I . Tcˊ . II . carˊ
in dnio . ⁊ in dimˊ . carˊ homˊ . VI . acˊ pˊti . Tcˊ . I . runcˊ . ⁊ modo . II . ⁊
modo . II . uaccas . ⁊ XX . porcˊ . ⁊ L . ousˊ . ⁊ tcˊ ual . XL . sol . ⁊ modo . &.
. I . æcclia de XV . acˊ . ⁊ ual . II . sol . ⁊ huic manerio stˊ additi . V . libi hoesˊ
⁊ dimˊ pbˊr . ⁊ tenˊ . L . V . acˊ . ⁊ dimˊ . & . I . carˊ ⁊ dimid in dnio . ⁊ . II . acˊ
pˊti . ⁊ . X . sol ual . ⁊ htˊ . VIII . qrˊ in longu ⁊ . VII . in latˊ quicuq, ibi
terrā hab& . ⁊ Reddit . VII . dˊ . & obolū . ⁊ sup hos . VI . hoesˊ hab& Rex
& Comes socā ⁊ sacā . ⁊ Aluricus qui hunc maneriū tenˊ
fuit homo Edrici ante cessoris Rodbˊti . & Willˊ mal& . ⁊ Rodbˊti . ⁊
fuerunt saisiti . de trˊa hac.

⁊Torintuna . tenˊ Aluricus libˊ homo . ,p manˊ . t . r . e . mˊ
ten& Godefridus de petroponte de Willˊ . de uarena semper
II . carˊ terræ . semp . V . uillˊ . XI bordˊ . Tcˊ III . seruˊ . modo . II . Tcˊ . II . carˊ &
modo III . in dominio . & semper . IIII . carˊ homˊ . silua ad VI . porcˊ . II.
acˊ prati . ⁊ VI . anˊ . otiosa . ⁊ XL . porcˊ . ⁊ . c . ⁊ XX . ousˊ . & . IIII . uasa apum.
⁊ ual LX . sol . Et hanc terrā reclamat Rodbˊtus malet sicut
alterā . hoc testatur hundret . ⁊ Rex ⁊ Comes socā ⁊ sacā

⁊Norhals tenˊ . t . r . e . Edricus libˊ hō ,p . I . manerio . II . carˊ trˊæ.

400 b

Tcˊ . V . bordˊ . modo . VI . Tcˊ . I . seruˊ . Tcˊ . II . carˊ in dominio . modo carˊ & dimˊ
⁊ dimid carˊ homˊ . I . acˊ pˊti . Tcˊ . I . runcˊ . ⁊ modo . I . ⁊ VIII . porˊc.
⁊ . c . V . ousˊ . ⁊ tcˊ ual XL . sol . & . modo . XX . huic manerio sunt ad
dite . c . acˊ terræ qˊs tenueˊr XIIII . libˊ omines . Tcˊ . II . carˊ . modo . modo
. I . ⁊ . I . acˊ pˊti . ⁊ ual . X . solidos . Et totā hanc terrā tenˊ Willˊmus fili9
Rainaldi . de . W . de Warena . ⁊ II . dimidios de istis . XIIII . hominibȝ
sint sasitos hoesˊ Willˊelmi sup comitē Alanū.

13 Ranulf, his nephew, held MIDDLETON. Aelfric, 1 free man, held it as 1 manor. Now William of Warenne holds (it); 2 carucates of land.
>Always 2 villagers; always 8 smallholders. Then 4 slaves, now 1.
>Then 2 ploughs in lordship; now ½ men's plough.
>Meadow, 6 acres. Then 1 cob, now 2; now 2 cows, 20 pigs, 50 sheep.
>Value then and now 40s.
>1 church with 15 acres.
>Value 2s.
>To this manor were added 5 free men and half a priest. They held 55½ acres. 1½ ploughs in lordship.
>Meadow, 2 acres.
>Value 10s.
>It has 8 furlongs in length and 7 in width, whoever has land there; it pays 7½d. The King and the Earl (have) full jurisdiction over these 6 men.
>Aelfric who held this manor was a man belonging to Edric, the predecessor of Robert and of William Malet, and of Robert; they were in possession of this land.

14 Aelfric, a free man, held THORINGTON as a manor before 1066. Now Godfrey of Pierrepont holds (it) from William of Warenne. Always 2 carucates of land.
>Always 5 villagers; 11 smallholders. Then 3 slaves, now 2.
>Then 2 ploughs in lordship, now 3; always 4 men's ploughs.
>Woodland for 6 pigs; meadow, 2 acres. 6 idle cattle, 40 pigs, 120 sheep, 4 beehives.
>Value 60s.
>Robert Malet claims this land back like the other; the Hundred bears witness to this.
>The King and the Earl (have) full jurisdiction.

15 Edric, a free man, held COVEHITHE before 1066 as 1 manor; 2 carucates of land.
>Then 5 smallholders, now 6; then 1 slave.
>Then 2 ploughs in lordship, now [1]½ ploughs; ½ men's plough.
>Meadow, 1 acre. Then 1 cob, now 1; 8 pigs, 105 sheep.

400 b

>Value then 40s; now 20[s].
>To this manor were added 100 acres of land which 14 free men held. Then 2 ploughs, now 1.
>Meadow, 1 acre.
>Value 10s.
>William son of Reginald holds the whole of this land from William of Warenne. Of the 14 free men, William's men have 2 half (free men of whom) they have taken possession from Count Alan.

⊩ H̃. DE EARLAFORDA. In burhe . tenuit Alricus lib homo
t . r . e . 1 . car̕ . terræ . 7 xx . ac̄ . ꝑ mañ . Tc̄ . 11 . borđ . modo . vii . Tc̄
. 1 . car̕ . modo . ii . Tc̄ . hoḿ diḿ . car̕ . modo . 1 . iiii . ac̄ prati . 7 . 1 . runc̕ .
& . vii . aniał . Tc̄ . xvi . porc̄ . modo . xii . 7 xvii . oūs . Tc̄ uał . xx . soł
modo . xxx . In eadē . xi . libi hoes̕ . integros . & . iii . diḿ . Cōmđ eid̋
Alrici . de . l . ac̄ . 7 . ii . borđ . Tc̄ . ii . car̄ . modo . 1 . dimiđ . ac̄ . p̕ti .
Tc̄ uał . x . soł . modo . viii . soł . h̃ totū recep̄ . W . ꝑ . 1 . car̕ . terræ
& . R . de glā uilł de eo . 7 . 1 . æcclia . de . viii . ac̄ . 7 plures h̃nt

⊩ H̃. DE WILEFORDA.   ⊩ partem.
   Robt̕ ten&
In bulges . 1 . lib homo . cōmđ . Ailrici . t . r . e . 7 . xiii . ac̄ . 7 diḿ
car̕ . 7 uał . ii . soł . ⊩ In depebecs . 1 . lib hō . cōm̄ eidē̇ . iiii . ac̄ .
7 uał . viii . đ . ⊩ In torſtaneſtuna . vi . ac̄ . 7 uał xii . deñ . hoc
ten& . R . de glam uilla . de . W . de uarena
⊩ In bdefelda teñ Ailric̊ lib hō . iii . ac̄ . & . uał . vi . đ . Idē Rob .

⊩ TR̃A SVANI DESCESSE JN SVDFVLCH.   . XXVII .
TINGOOV . H̃ . In Riete . 1 . foc̄ . de xx . ac̄ . & . 1 . borđ . & . diḿ . car̕ .
& . 1 . ac̄ p̕ti . & uał . v . soł . Socā sc̄s . e .
⊩ In maneſtuna . 1 . foc̄ . de . xx . ac̄ . & . 1 . borđ . & . dimiđ . car̕ . & . 1 . ac̄
prati . 7 . uał . v . soł .

Hundred of CARLFORD
16 Aethelric, a free man, held in BURGH before 1066; 1 carucate of land and 20 acres as a manor.
Then 2 smallholders, now 7.
Then 1 plough, now 2; then ½ men's plough, now 1.
Meadow, 4 acres. 1 cob; 7 cattle; then 16 pigs, now 12; 17 sheep.
Value then 20s; now 30[s].
In the same (Burgh) 11 whole free men and 3 half (free men) under the patronage of the same Aethelric, with 50 acres.
2 smallholders.
Then 2 ploughs, now 1. Meadow, ½ acre.
Value then 10s; now 8s.
William acquired the whole of this as 1 carucate of land, and R(obert) of Glanville [holds it] from him.
1 church with 8 acres. Several have a share.

Hundred of WILFORD
17 Robert holds in BOULGE; 1 free man under the patronage of Aethelric before 1066; 13 acres. ½ plough.
Value 2s.

18 In DEBACH 1 free man under the patronage of the same man; 4 acres.
Value 8d.

19 In 'TORSTANESTUNA' 6 acres.
Value 12d.
R(obert) of Glanville holds this from William of Warenne.

20 In BREDFIELD Aethelric, a free man, held 3 acres.
Value 6d.
Robert also [holds this].

27   SWEIN OF ESSEX'S LANDS   401 a

THINGOE Hundred
1 In REDE 1 Freeman, with 20 acres.
1 smallholder.
½ plough. Meadow, 1 acre.
Value 5s.
St. Edmund's (has) the jurisdiction.

2 In MANSTON 1 Freeman, with 20 acres.
1 smallholder.
½ plough. Meadow, 1 acre.
Value 5s.

BAbegA: DIO. H. Stokes tenet Rotbt. t . r . e . p man
IIII . car træ cu foca. Tc. xx. v . uilt. modo . xv. Tc. xxx. II . bord.
modo xxIII . Tc. vIII . feru . modo . vI . Tc. II . carr in dnio. modo. IIII.
Tc. xII . car hominu . modo . vII . modo . II . molin . 7 . xx . v . ac . pti.
Silua . Lx . porc . modo . III . equi . modo . vIII . an . modo xx . porc . modo
Lxx . ous . modo . IIII . cap. Tc uat . x . lib . modo . xII . Ecclia de . Lx . ac
libere . terræ . In ead uilla . xI libi . homines Rotbti comd . 7
foca jnt oes . I . car . terræ . fed pot uende . 7 . I . lib . homo . de . xII .
ac comend. Rot . f7 faca 7 foca . sci . e . jnt oes . I . car . 7 dim tc .
modo . I . 7 uat& . xxx . fot . ht . vIII . qr . in longo . 7 . IIII . in lato .
& . de gelto . xx . den.

Withermers ten Rotb pat fueni . t . r . e . p . man . IIII . car
terræ . cu foca. Tc. xx. vII . uilt. modo . xx . IIII . Tc. xxx . II.
bord . modo . xxvII . Tc. II . feru . modo . I . Tc. III . car in dominio.
modo . II . Tc. xIII . car. hominu . modo . vIII . Semp . I . molin . 7
xxx . ac . pti . m . II . equi . 7 xx . an . modo . xx . IIII . porc . 7 xv . æq
filuatice . modo . Lxxx . ous . Tc uat . x . lib . modo . xII . ht vIII . qr in
longo . 7 IIII . in lato . 7 de gelto xx . d.

Polefteda ten id Rotbtus pat fueni . t . r . e . p man . IIII . car

401 b

car terræ cu foca. Tc. xx. vI . uilt. modo . xx . I . Tc. xxx . vI . bord.
modo xxx . femp . I . feru Tc . 7 femp . II . car in dnio . Tc . xv . carr
hominu . modo . Ix . Semper . I . mol . Silua . Lxxx . porc.
. xxx
7 . I . ac prati . modo . vIII . equi . in halla . modo xxvIII . an . modo
xL . porc . modo c . L . ous . Tc uat . x . lib . modo . xII . lib . ht vIII .
qr in longo . 7 IIII . jn lato . 7 de gelto . xx . d . quicuq ibi ten.

BABERGH Two Hundreds

3 In STOKE (by Nayland) Robert [held] before 1066; 4 carucates of land as a manor, with the jurisdiction.
   Then 25 villagers, now 15; then 32 smallholders, now 23; then 8 slaves, now 6.
   Then 2 ploughs in lordship, now 3; then 12 men's plough, now 7.
   Now 2 mills; meadow, 25 acres; woodland, 60 pigs. Now 3 horses; now 8 cattle; now 20 pigs; now 70 sheep, now 4 goats.
   Value then £10; now [£] 12.
   A church with 60 acres of free land.
   In the same village 11 free men under the patronage and jurisdiction of Robert; 1 carucate of land between them all, but they could sell. 1 free man with 12 acres, under the patronage of Robert but the full jurisdiction (was) St. Edmund's.
   Between them all, then 1½ ploughs, now 1.
   Value 30s.
   It has 8 furlongs in length and 4 in width; 20d in tax.

4 Robert, Swein's father, held WITHERMARSH before 1066 as a manor; 4 carucates of land, with the jurisdiction.
   Then 27 villagers, now 24; then 32 smallholders, now 27; then 2 slaves, now 1.
   Then 3 ploughs in lordship, now 2; then 13 men's ploughs, now 8.
   Always 1 mill. Meadow, 30 acres. Now 2 horses; 20 cattle; now 24 pigs; 15 wild mares; now 80 sheep.
   Value then £10; now [£] 12.
   It has 8 furlongs in length and 4 in width; 20d in tax.

5 Robert, Swein's father, also held POLSTEAD before 1066 as a manor; 4 carucates of land, with the jurisdiction. 401 b
   Then 26 villagers, now 21; then 36 smallholders, now 30; always 1 slave.
   Then and always 2 ploughs in lordship; then 15 men's ploughs, now 9.
   Always 1 mill. Woodland, 80 pigs; meadow, 31 acres. Now 8 horses at the hall; now 28 cattle; now 40 pigs; now 150 sheep.
   Value then £10, now £12.
   It has 8 furlongs in length and 4 in width; 20d in tax, whoever holds there.

/ Eilanda teñ idē Rodbť pat̄. fueñ. t. r. e. p̄. mañ. ii. car̄ terræ
cum foca. Semp. vi. uitł. Tc̄. xx. borđ. modo. xvii. Tc̄. vi. ferū.
modo. ii. Semp. i. car̄ in dominio. Tc̄. iiii. car̄ hominū. m̄.
iii. Semp. i. moliń. 7. x. ac̄ prati. modo. iii. equi in halla.
modo. xxx. i. animał. modo. xl. v. porc̄. modo. lxxx. ous. modo
xxxv. cap̄. Tc̄ uał. vi. liƀ. modo. viii. liƀ. ht̄ dim̄ lḡ in lango.
7. ii. qr̄. in lato. 7 de gelto. xii. deñ.

/ Aluenelega teñ brungar liƀ hō Rotƀti com̄d tantum.
t. r. e. p̄ mañ. i. car̄ tr̄æ. cū foca Semp. i. uitł. 7. x. borđ.
femp. ii. car̄ in dn̄io. 7 dim̄ car̄ hominum. Silua. vi. porc̄.
7 iiii. ac̄ prati. 7. i. moliñ. 7. i. æquus in halla. 7 modo. xiiii.
amał. modo xl. ix. porc̄. 7 lxxx. vii. ous. Tc̄. uał. xx
fot. p̄ 7 modo. xxx. fot. ht̄. vi. qr̄ in longo. 7 iii. in lato
7 de gelto. iii. deñ. Sup̄ hanc habuit. ses̄. e. foc̄ & facā. t. r. e.
7 Rodƀtus fili Wimarce 7 pat̄ fueni. com̄d tantū. Eodē
tp̄r fuer̄ furati equi inuenti. in domo ifti brungari. ita
qđ abbas cuius fuit foca 7 faca & Rodƀt qui habuit com
datione sup ifti. uener̄ de hoc furto ad placitū 7 fic̄ H. teftat̄.

402 a
Difceffer̄ amicabilit̄ fine iuditio qđ uidiffed hundr̄t.

/ DIMID. H. DEGEPES Wiz. In burgo habuit. Roƀ.
t. r. e. xli. burgenfes cū foca 7 faca. 7 com̄d. 7 rex habebat̄
alias confuetudines. Ex itł mortui funt. xv. amifit commendatione fed foca 7 faca hab &. & de aliis fimilit̄. & rex alias con
fuetudines. hab.

/ SANFORT. H. Stratfort tenuit Roƀ. t. r. e. p̄ mañ
iii. car̄ terræ. femp xx. uitł. Tc̄. viii. borđ. modo. x. Tc̄. iiii. ferū.
Tc̄. ii car̄ in dominio. modo. i. Tc̄. x. car̄. hominū. modo. v. 7. v. poffent
reftaurari. 7. xvi. ac̄ pti. filua xvi. porc̄. femp. i. moliñ. Ecc̄lia. xx
ac̄. libæ terræ. 7 dim̄. car̄. &. i. runc̄. &. vi. aniał. 7 xxx. vi. porc̄. 7
l. ous. femp uał. vi. liƀ. Roƀ de eo. Sueñ. focā. ht̄ vii. qr̄ in longo
&. v. in lato. 7. ix. deñ de gelto.

6 Robert, Swein's father, also held NAYLAND before 1066 as a manor; 2 carucates of land, with the jurisdiction.
    Always 6 villagers. Then 20 smallholders, now 17; then 6 slaves, now 2.
    Always 1 plough in lordship. Then 4 men's ploughs, now 3.
    Always 1 mill. Meadow, 10 acres. Now 3 horses at the hall; now 31 cattle; now 45 pigs; now 80 sheep; now 35 goats.
  Value then £6; now £8.
  It has ½ league in length and 2 furlongs in width; 12d in tax.

7 Brungar, a free man under the patronage only of Robert, held AVELEY before 1066 as a manor; 1 carucate of land, with the jurisdiction.
    Always 1 villager, 10 smallholders.
    Always 2 ploughs in lordship; ½ men's plough.
    Woodland, 6 pigs; meadow, 4 acres; 1 mill. 1 horse at the hall; now 14 cattle; now 49 pigs; 87 sheep.
  Value then 20s; later and now 30s. It has 6 furlongs in length and 3 in width; 3d in tax.
  Over this (land), St. Edmund's had full jurisdiction before 1066 and Robert son of Wymarc, Swein's father, (had) patronage only. At that time stolen horses were found in the home of Brungar, and so the Abbot, who had full jurisdiction, and Robert, who had patronage over him, came about this theft to the assembly, as the Hundred testifies. They left in a friendly manner without a trial that the Hundred had seen.

402 a

Half-Hundred of IPSWICH

8 In the Borough (of IPSWICH) Robert had 41 burgesses before 1066 with the full jurisdiction and the patronage, and the King had the other customary dues.
    Of these (burgesses), he has lost the patronage over 15 (who) are dead but he has full jurisdiction, and the same with the others; the King has the other customary dues.

SAMFORD Hundred

9 Robert held STRATFORD (St. Mary) before 1066 as a manor; 3 carucates of land.
    Always 20 villagers. Then 8 smallholders, now 10; then 4 slaves.
    Then 2 ploughs in lordship, now 1; then 10 men's ploughs, now 5, and 5 could be restored.
    Meadow, 16 acres; woodland, 16 pigs; always 1 mill.
    A church, 20 acres of free land. ½ plough.
    1 cob, 6 cattle, 36 pigs, 50 sheep.
  Value always £6.
    Robert holds [this] from him.
  Swein (has) the jurisdiction. It has 7 furlongs in length and 5 in width; 9d in tax.

⁊Painetunā ten&. Roḃ. T.R.E.
II.car̛ terræ. ꝑ man̄. Tc̄. III. uiłł. femp. III. borđ. Tc̄. II. car̛ in dominio.
modo. I. Tc̄. III. car̛. hominū. &. X. ac̄ p̄ti. Ecctie. III. ac̄. liḃe. t̄re.
modo. I. falina. &. VIII. aniał. &. XX. porc̄. ⁊ LXXX oūs. ⁊ XX. VIII.
cap̄. Tc̄ uał. XL. fot. modo. XXX. Ht̄. V. qr̄ in long̛. &. IIII. in lat̛.
&. IIII. đ. &. I. ferding̛ de gł. Roḃt̛ foc̄ Algarus de fueno.
⁊Weruefta tenuit Toli liḃ ho̅. commendatus. Roḃto. I. car̛ terræ
&. I. borđ. &. I. car̛. &. III. ac̄ p̄ti. &. V. porc̄. ⁊ XXX. oūs. &. XIIII.
cap̄. Tc̄ uał. X. fot. ⁊ modo fimiłr̄. Suen̛ in dn̄io.
⁊In frifetuna. ter̄. Roḃ. t. r. e. XXX. ac̄. de dn̄io. femp. I. car̛. &. I.
ac̄ p̄ti. ⁊ uał. X. fot. Ernulfus de fueno. Idē Roḃ focā;

402 b

⁊H̄. DE WILEFORDA Peituna tenuit Godricus
com̄đ heroldi. t. r. e. ꝑ man̄. III. car̛. terræ. Tc̄. X. uiłł. modo VIII.
Tc̄. IIII. borđ. ⁊ modo; Tc̄. I. feru̅. Semp in dn̄io. II. car̛. & hom̛.
. III. car̛. III. ac̄ prati. ⁊. I. molin̄. Tc̄. II. runc̛. Tc̄. IIII. an̄. modo. II.
Tc̄. I. porc̄. modo. VI. ⁊ XXVII. oūs. Tc̄ uał. LX. fot. modo XL. ⁊ ht̄
in longo. I. leugā. ⁊. in lat̛. IIII. qr̄. ⁊ de gelto. XIII. den̄. ⁊ oḃlū.
In eadē ꝑtinent. XX. liḃi. hoes. com̄đ eidē. LXXX. ac̄. t̄ræ. ⁊
II. ac̄ p̄ti. Semp. II. car̛. Tc̄ uał XIII. fot. modo. XV.

10 Robert [held] PANNINGTON before 1066; 2 carucates of land as a manor.
  Then 3 villagers; always 3 smallholders.
  Then 2 ploughs in lordship, now 1; then 3 men's ploughs.
  Meadow, 10 acres.
  A church, 3 acres of free land.
  Now 1 salt-house; 8 cattle, 20 pigs, 80 sheep, 28 goats.
  Value then 40s; now 30[s].
  It has 5 furlongs in length and 4 in width; 4¼d in tax.
  Robert (had) the jurisdiction.
  Algar [holds this] from Swein.

11 Toli, a free man under the patronage of Robert, held WHERSTEAD; 1 carucate of land.
  1 smallholder.
  1 plough.
  Meadow, 3 acres. 5 pigs, 30 sheep, 14 goats.
  Value then 10s; now the same.
  Swein [holds this] in lordship.

12 In FRESTON Robert held before 1066; 30 acres in lordship. Always 1 plough.
  Meadow, 1 acre.
  Value 10s.
  Arnulf [holds this] from Swein.
  Robert also (had) the jurisdiction.

Hundred of WILFORD

13 Godric, under the patronage of Harold, held PEYTON before 1066 as a manor; 3 carucates of land.
  Then 10 villagers, now 8; then and now 4 smallholders; then 1 slave.
  Always 2 ploughs in lordship; 3 men's ploughs.
  Meadow, 3 acres; 1 mill. Then 2 cobs; then 4 cattle, now 2; then 1 pig, now 6; 27 sheep.
  Value then 60s; now 40[s].
  It has 1 league in length and 4 furlongs in width; 13½d in tax.
  In the same (Peyton) 20 free men, under the patronage of the same man; 80 acres of land.
  Meadow, 2 acres.
  Always 2 ploughs.
  Value then 13s; now 15[s].

.XXVIII. **TERRÆ EEVDONIS DAPIFERI IN SVTFVLC.**
Lacforda . h . Herefwella ten godwinus teinus . reg . E . p̄
man̄ . vi . car̄ træ . Tc xi . uitti . p̄ . x . modo . xi . 7 femp . iiii . bord.
Semp . xi . feru . Tc 7 p̄ . v . car̄ in dn̄io . modo . iii . Semp . v . hom̄.
7 xiiii . ac̄ p̄ti . & . ii . mot . 7 dim̄ . Ecctia . lx . ac̄ træ . ii . pifcar̄.
Semp . ii . equi in halla . Tc . xx . an̄ . modo . xiii . Tc xl . porc̄ . m̄ . xx.
Tc . o . cccc . ou . m̄ . o . ccc . Tc & p̄ uat . x . lib . m̄ . xvi . ht . i . lg in log.
7 . vi . qr̄ in lato . 7 de gelto . x . d . Huic iac& . i . beuita cocles-
worda . viii . car̄ . terre . Ecctia lx . ac̄ . Tc 7 poft . xv . uitt . modo
xi . uitt . Semp . iiii . bord . Tc 7 p̄ . xi . feru . modo . viii . 7 xx . ii.

403 a

ac̄ prati . ~~Tc 7 p̄ v̄ cai~~ . Tc & p̄ . v . car̄ . in dominio . modo . iiii.
Tc 7 poft . vi . car̄ . homin̄ . modo . v . 7 . ii . equi . in halla . Tc . cc . ou̇s.
modo . o . cccc . xx . minus . Tc & p̄ uat xii . lib . modo . xxiiii.
ht . i . lg in longo . 7 . viii . qr̄ in lato . 7 de gelto . vii . d.
Soca & faca . sc̄s edm̄.

In Lakingaheda 7 in brantona . vi . foc̄ . Aldrede cū foca qd n̄
pot uende . Libati fuer lifie ante ceffori eudonis . p . ii . car̄ terræ
fed tam̄ poftea recognou de sc̄a aldreda 7 Eudo tenuit eos cū
foca & faca . 7 . iiii . bord . femp . iii . car̄ . 7 . iii . ac̄ . p̄ti . 7 . ii . pifcr̄.
Tc 7 poft uat . xxx . folidos modo reddit lxx . fot.

Todenhā ten Canut lib ho comit algari p man̄ . iii . car̄ træ
Tc . vi . uitt . p̄ iiii . m̄ . vi . 7 Tc . iiii . feru . modo . i . Tc . iii . car̄ in dominio . p̄ dim̄ . modo . ii . 7 . i . car̄ . 7 dim̄ homin̄u . 7 . iii . ac̄ . p̄ti.
7 . i . molin̄ . i . pifcina fuit f7 modo n̄ ē . Ecctia . xxx . ac̄ . modo . x.
equi . in halla . 7 modo . xl . porc̄ . 7 . xi . an̄ . Tc . cc . ou̇s . modo . lx.

EUDO THE STEWARD'S LANDS IN SUFFOLK

LACKFORD Hundred

1a Godwin, a thane of King Edward's, held ERISWELL as a manor; 6 carucates of land.
>Then 11 villagers, later 10, now 11; always 4 smallholders; always 11 slaves.
>Then and later 5 ploughs in lordship, now 3; always 5 men's ploughs.
>Meadow, 14 acres; 2½ mills.
>A church, 60 acres of land.
>2 fisheries. Always 2 horses at the hall. Then 20 cattle, now 13; then 40 pigs, now 20; then 900 sheep, now 800.
>Value then and later £10; now [£] 16.
>It has 1 league in length and 6 furlongs in width; 10d in tax.

1b To this (manor) belongs 1 outlier, CHAMBERLAIN'S HALL; 8 carucates of land.
>A church, 60 acres.
>Then and later 15 villagers, now 11 villagers; always 4 smallholders. Then and later 11 slaves, now 8.
>Meadow, 22 acres.
>Then and later 5 ploughs in lordship, now 4; then and later 6 men's ploughs, now 5.
>2 horses at the hall; then 1200 sheep, now 900 less 20.
>Value then and later £12; now [£] 24.
>It has 1 league in length and 8 furlongs in width; 7d in tax. St. Edmund's (has) full jurisdiction.

2 In LAKENHEATH and in BRANDON 6 Freemen of (St.) Etheldreda's with the jurisdiction [who] could not sell. They were delivered to Lisois, Eudo's predecessor, for 2 carucates of land; but nevertheless, later on they were acknowledged (to be) St. Etheldreda's. Eudo held them with full jurisdiction.
>4 smallholders.
>Always 3 ploughs.
>Meadow, 3 acres; 2 fisheries.
>Value then and later 30s; now it pays 70s.

3 Canute, a free man under the patronage of Algar, held TUDDENHAM as a manor; 3 carucates of land.
>Then 6 villagers, later 4, now 6; then 4 slaves, now 1.
>Then 3 ploughs in lordship, later ½, now 2; 1½ men's ploughs.
>Meadow, 3 acres; 1 mill; there was 1 fish-pond but now there is not.
>A church, 30 acres.
>Now 10 horses at the hall; now 40 pigs; 11 cattle; then 200 sheep, now 60.

Tč. 7 p̄ ual̃. iiii. lib̃. m̃. c. fol̃. Et h̃t. i. lḡ in longo 7 vi. q̄r̃ in lato.
7 de gelto xx. d̃. ⁄ In Ranauahā. i. lib̃ homo Canuti com̃d̃
tant in foca sc̄i. edm̃. lx. ac̃. i. bord̃. femp. i. car̃. Semp ual̃. v. fol̃.

⁄ SANFORT. H̃. & dim̃. In Rienduna. ten̄ Suertingus lib̃
homo. xvii. ac̃. 7 ual̃. iii. fol̃. Osb̄n ten̄. de eudone Soca in Ecolt.

⁄ PLVMESTGATA. HVNDRET. Glemhā ten̄
Vluricus dim̃ Com̃d. Ab̃bi de eli 7 dimidi ante c̃ mal&. ii. car̃
terræ p man̄. t. r. e. 7 Willt. mal&. inde faifitus fuit femp
vii. bord̃. 7. ii. car̃ in dominio. 7 dim̃ car̃ hominū. 7 viii. ac̃ p̃ti,

403 b
&. i. molin̄. 7 dim̃ æcclia. x. ac̃. Tc̃. ix. porc̃. modo. xvi. Tc̃
v. oūs. modo. xl. Tc̃ ual̃. xl. fol̃. modo. l. In Ead̃e additi sī
x. libi. hoes. com̃d̃ ulurico. l. iii. ac̃. &. 7. i. car̃. 7 ual̃. x. fol̃. 7. x. d̃.

⁄ Pirot ten̄ de eudone. Soca ab̃bis de eli. de toto fuit faifitus
Willmus malet. h̃t xii. q̄r̃ in longo 7 vi. 7 dim̃ in lato. & xx. d̃.
Reddit de gelto.

⁄ DIMIDI H̃. DE COSFORT. LEIham tenuit
Aluricus campa. t. r. e. iiii. car̃. terræ p man̄. femp. xv.
uilli. 7. iii. bord̃. 7. i. fer. femp. ii. car̃ in dominio. Tc̃. vi. car̃
homin̄. P 7 modo. iii. xii. ac̃. prati. filua. x. porc̃. 7. i. molin̄.
Ecclia xl. ac̃. 7. i. ac̃. p̃ti. 7. i. car̃. femp. i. runc̃. 7 xx. an̄. 7 xxxvi.
porc̃. 7 c. lxxx. oūs. 7 xxiii. cap̃. femp ual̃. vi. lib̃. &. viii. q̄r̃
in longo. & vi. in lato. & vii. d̃. & obol̃. de gelto;

Value then and later £4; now 100s.
It has 1 league in length and 6 furlongs in width; 20d in tax.

4 In CAVENHAM 1 free man under the patronage only of Canute (and) in the jurisdiction of St. Edmund's; 60 acres.
1 smallholder.
Always 1 plough.
Value always 5s.

SAMFORD Hundred and a Half
5 In RAYDON Swarting, a free man, held 17 acres.
Value 3s.
Osbern holds [this] from Eudo.
The jurisdiction (is) in (East) Bergholt.

PLOMESGATE Hundred
6 Wulfric, half under the patronage of the Abbot of Ely and half (under that) of Malet's predecessor, held (Great) GLEMHAM; 2 carucates of land as a manor before 1066. William Malet was in possession of it.
Always 7 smallholders;
2 ploughs in lordship; ½ men's plough.
Meadow, 8 acres; 1 mill.
½ church, 10 acres.
Then 9 pigs, now 16; then 5 sheep, now 40.
Value then 40s; now 50[s].
In the same (Great Glemham) were added 10 free men under the patronage of Wulfric; 53 acres. 1 plough.
Value 10s 10d.
Pirot holds [this] from Eudo.
The jurisdiction (is) the Abbot of Ely's.
William Malet was in possession of the whole of it.
It has 12 furlongs in length and 6½ in width; it pays 20d in tax.

403 b

Half-Hundred of COSFORD
7 Aelfric Kemp held LAYHAM before 1066; 4 carucates of land as a manor.
Always 15 villagers; 3 smallholders; 1 slave.
Always 2 ploughs in lordship. Then 6 men's ploughs, later and now 3.
Meadow, 12 acres; woodland, 10 pigs; 1 mill.
A church, 40 acres. Meadow, 1 acre. 1 plough.
Always 1 cob, 20 cattle, 36 pigs, 180 sheep, 23 goats.
Value always £6.
(It has) 8 furlongs in length and 6 in width; 7½d in tax.

403 a, b

.XXIX. **TERRA ROGERI DE OBVRVILLA.** *STO HVND.*

In finebga teñ Leuefuna lib hō gut mundi ante c̄ hugoñ
de monte forti commd̄ tant̄. ii. car̄ t̄re. 7 Tc̄. iiii. bord̄. p̃ 7 m̄
iii. Semp. ii. car̄ in dn̄io. Silu de. xii. porc̄. 7 xvi. ac̄ p̃ti.
7. i. molin̄. Ecclia de. xxx. ac̄ libe. terræ. 7. i. ac̄ p̃ti. Tc̄. i. runc̄;

404 a

M nuli. Semp viii. an̄. Tc̄. xx. porc̄. modo. vi. Tc̄ xxx. oūs. mc̄do.
. c. Tc̄ ual. iiii. lib. p̃. ii. m̄. lx. fol. ht̄. i. lḡ in longo. & viii. qr̄
in lato. 7 de gelto xx. ii. deñ. & obolū. In eod̄ manerio. xviii. libi
homines eid̄e Leuefune commendant̄. tant̄. i. car̄ terræ. i. foc̄. reḡ
7 comit̄. Tc̄ 7 p̃ ∴ iii. car̄. modo. i. 7. iii. ac̄ p̃ti. 7 dim̄. Hos ten& Roḡ
p̄ efcangio. In ead. vi. foc̄ ptinentes in tornei manerio regis. Ed.
cū com̄d 7 faca 7 foca 7 fumagio. 7 hnt̄ lx. v. ac̄ 7 dim̄. terræ. &
. i. bord̄. Tc̄ & p̃. iii. car̄. int̄ oēs modo. i. 7. iii. ac̄ p̃ti. & hos ten& p̄
efcangio. In ead. ii. libi hōes gut mundi ante hugonis com̄dat̄
tant̄ lxxx. ac̄ in foca reḡ 7 comit̄. Tc̄. i. car̄ & dim̄. p̃ 7 modo. nuli.
& hos ten& fimilit̄. Adhuc in ead. i. lib hō com̄d ante c̄ euftachii
iiii. ac̄. In ead. i. lib homo Leuftani de Iofa com̄d. iiii. ac̄. In ead
. i. lib hō Adhuc reḡ com̄d 7 foca 7 faca in hund̄. xx. ac̄. Tc̄ dim̄ car̄.
7. i. ac̄ p̃ti. In ead. i. lib homo Wifgari Ante Ricardi com̄d. fed | in
hund̄. xxx. ac̄. 7. i. uilt Tc̄. i. car̄. p̃ 7 modo nichil. &. ii. ac̄ p̃ti.
In ead. iiii. libi hōes. foca in hund̄ xvi. ac̄. Tc̄. i. car̄. 7 dim̄. p̃ 7
modo. nichil. hos ten& p̄ efcangio. Tc̄ 7 p̃ ual oms ifti libi. iiii.
lib. modo. xl. fol.

LAND OF ROGER OF AUBERVILLE

STOW Hundred

1 In FINBOROUGH Leofson, a free man under the patronage only of Guthmund, Hugh de Montfort's predecessor, held 2 carucates of land. Then 4 smallholders, later and now 3.
Always 2 ploughs in lordship.
Woodland at 12 pigs; meadow, 16 acres; 1 mill.
A church with 30 acres of free land. Meadow, 1 acre.
Then 1 cob, now nothing; always 8 cattle. Then 20 pigs, now 6; then 30 sheep, now 100.
Value then £4; later [£] 2; now 60s.
It has 1 league in length and 8 furlongs in width; 22½d in tax.
In the same manor 18 free men under the patronage only of the same Leofson (and) in the jurisdiction of the King and the Earl; 1 carucate of land.
Then and later 3 ploughs, now 1. Meadow, 3½ acres.
Roger holds these (free men) by exchange.
In the same (Finborough) 6 Freemen who belong to King Edward's manor of Thorney, with the patronage, full jurisdiction and carrying-service, have 65½ acres of land and 1 smallholder.
Then and later 3 ploughs between them all, now 1.
Meadow, 3 acres.
He holds these (Freemen) by exchange.
In the same (Finborough) 2 free men, under the patronage only of Guthmund, Hugh's predecessor (and) in the jurisdiction of the King and the Earl; 80 acres. Then 1½ ploughs, later and now none.
He holds these (free men) in the same way.
Also in the same (Finborough) 1 free man under the patronage of Eustace's predecessor, 4 acres.
In the same (Finborough) 1 free man belonging to Leofstan of Loes, under patronage; 4 acres.
In the same (Finborough) 1 free man still under the patronage of the King; the full jurisdiction (is) in the Hundred; 20 acres. Then ½ plough.
Meadow, 1 acre.
In the same (Finborough) 1 free man belonging to Withgar, Richard's predecessor; under patronage, but the jurisdiction (is) in the Hundred; 30 acres.
1 villager.
Then 1 plough, later and now nothing.
Meadow, 2 acres.
In the same (Finborough) 4 free men; the jurisdiction (is) in the Hundred; 16 acres. Then 1½ ploughs, later and now nothing.
He holds these (free men) by exchange.
Value then and later of all the free men £4; now 40s.

Bosemara. H. Sumersham in dnio. ten. Leffcilt
. 1. car terre . p manen . tpr. e. femp . 1. car . & . 1. ac prati . & ual&
. xxx. fot. *P*lLebga ten& dot lib ho. lx. ac. p man. t. r. e.
modo. R. in dominio. 1. bord. femp. 1. car. & . 1. ac pti. 7 ual xx. fot.
Rex & comes foca. In ead. v. libi. xxx. ac. In eod ptio. R. 7. c. foca.
In Flochetuna in dominio. 1. lib homo. Godmannus. xx. ac. tenuit

t. r. e. & adhuc ten& de Rogo. & ual. xl. d. In ead in dnio. 11. libi
hoes Wilgripus. & Edricus. unus. xl. ac. & alt de . x . ac. femp . 1. car.
& . 1. ac pti . 7 ual xvi. fot. Rex & comes foc.
In Blacham. in dnio ten Vlwart. xxx. ac. 1. lib homo femper di-
m car. & . 1. ac prati. 7 ual. xiiii. fot. In Ella in dominio. 1. lib ho
Aluiet. xii. ac. 7. ii. bou. 7 ual. vii. fot. In ead. 1. lib homo. iii. ac. 7
est in ptio de fumersha. In Offetuna. 1. lib ho Walduinus. comdat
Leurico hobbefuna. & ht xx. ac. & . 1. bord. Tc dim car. Tc ual. xl.
den. M. iiii. fot. Will ten de Rogo.
In Briefeta. 1. lib ho Leuricus. commendt. Godrico de Ringeshala
ante ceffori Willo de oburuilla. & ht. x. ac. Tc. ii. bou. 7 ual. xx. d. Gis
lebtus. ten de Rogo. Rex. 7. Coms foca.

BOSMERE Hundred

2 Leofcild held SOMERSHAM in lordship; 1 carucate of land as a manor before 1066. Always 1 plough.
   Meadow, 1 acre.
   Value 30s.

3 Dot, a free man, [held] *PILEBERGA*; 60 acres as a manor before 1066. Now Roger [holds it] in lordship.
   1 smallholder.
   Always 1 plough. Meadow, 1 acre.
   Value 20s.
   The King and the Earl (have) the jurisdiction.
   In the same (*Pileberga*) 5 free men; 30 acres.
   (It is) in the same assessment.
   The King and the Earl (have) the jurisdiction.

4 In FLOWTON Godman, 1 free man, held 20 acres in lordship before 1066 and still holds (them) from Roger.
   Value 40d.
   In the same (Flowton) 2 free men, Wilgrip and Edric, one (with) 40 acres, the other with 10 acres. Always 1 plough.
   Meadow, 1 acre.
   Value 16s.
   The King and the Earl (have) the jurisdiction.

404 b

5 In BLAKENHAM Wulfward, 1 free man, held 30 acres in lordship. Always ½ plough.
   Meadow, 1 acre.
   Value 14s.

6 In ELLA 1 free man, Alfgeat; 12 acres in lordship. 2 oxen.
   Value 7s.
   In the same (*Ella*) 1 free man; 3 acres.
   It is in the assessment of Somersham.

7 In OFFTON Waldwin, 1 free man, under the patronage of Leofric Hobbeson. He [had] 20 acres.
   1 smallholder.
   Then ½ plough.
   Value then 40d; now 4s.
   William holds (this) from Roger.

8 In BRICETT Leofric, 1 free man, under the patronage of Godric of Ringshall, William of Auberville's predecessor. He [had] 10 acres.
   Then 2 oxen.
   Value 20d.
      Gilbert holds (this) from Roger.
      The King and the Earl (have) the jurisdiction.

⁊In horſwalda.ıı.libi hões hardinc̄.⁊ toui com̄dati regis.ten̄.xx.ıı.ac̄.⁊ dim̄.modo Witt.ten̄ de Rog̃o.ſemp dim̄ car̃.& dim̄.ac̄ p̃ti.⁊ ual.v.ſol.⁊.x.den̄.Rex & Com̄s.ſocā.hanc trā ten̄ Roger de abbe de eli p̃cepto ep̄i de s̄co Laudo.ut ipſe Rog̃ dicit.   ⁊In Langhedana.ı.lib homo Wlbolt xxııı.ac̄.p mañ.&.ı.ac̄ &.dim̄ p̃ti.⁊ in t̄cio anno qrta pars mol.⁊ ual.⁊ ualuit.v.ſol.⁊.vııı.den̄.

⁊CLAINDVNE.H̃.Henleiā tenūit Tepechinus lib homo t.r.e.com̄d heroldo.ıı.car̃ terræ.p man̄.⁊ xvı.bord.Tc̄.ıııı.ſerui. Tc̄.ııı.car̃ in dominio.modo.ıı.Tc̄.ıııı.car̃ hom̄.modo.ııı.vııı. ac̄.p̃ti.ſilua.vı.porc̄.⁊.vıı.an̄.⁊.xıııı.porc̄.⁊ xxx.oūs.Eccliæ .ıı.ac̄.Tc̄.ual.ıııı.lib.modo.ııı.Eudo dapifer ten& in ſuo dn̄io. In ead.ıııı.libi homines additi.vııı.ac̄.&.ıı.boū.⁊ ual.ıı.ſol.Rex ⁊ com̄s
                                                              ⁊ſocam;

405 a
⁊DĪMID.H̃.DE COSFORT.Elmeſtā ten̄ Thou. teinnus p man̄.t.r.e.vı.car̃.trǣ.⁊ xl.ac̄.Tc̄ & p̃.xı.uilt.m̄ .ıı.ſemp.xıı.bord.Tc̄.ıııı.ſeru.ſemp.ıı.car̃.in dn̄io.Tc̄ & p̃. xıı.car̃ hominū.modo.ıııı.Ecclia.de.xv.ac̄.⁊ dim̄.car̃.Tc̄.ıı.run̄. Tc̄.xvı.an̄.m̄.ıııı.Tc̄.xxx.porc̄.modo.xx.Tc̄.cc.xl.oūs.modo. .cc.Tc̄ ual.x.lib.m̄.vıı.ht̄.x.qr in longo.⁊ vıı.in lat̄.⁊.xv.den̄ den̄ de gelto.Sc̄s.e.dim̄ ſocam.
⁊In Wateſelda.ı.lib hō.lx.ac̄.⁊.ıı.bord.Tc̄ ⁊ poſt.ı.car̃.modo dim̄.⁊.ı.ac̄.p̃ti.⁊ ual.x.ſol.ſc̄s.e.com̄d ⁊ ſoca.

9 In HORSWOLD 2 free men, Harding and Tovi, under the patronage of the King, held 22½ acres. Now William holds (it) from Roger. Always ½ plough.
Meadow, ½ acre.
Value 5s 10d.
The King and the Earl (have) the jurisdiction.
Roger holds this land from the Abbot of Ely by command of the Bishop of St. Lô, as Roger himself says.

10 In *LANGHEDANA* Wulfbold, a free man; 24 acres as a manor.
Meadow, 1½ acres; in (every) third year, the fourth part of a mill.
The value is and was 5s 8d.

CLAYDON Hundred
11 Tepekin, a free man, under the patronage of Harold, held HENLEY before 1066; 2 carucates of land as a manor.
16 smallholders; then 4 slaves.
Then 3 ploughs in lordship, now 2; then 4 men's ploughs, now 3.
Meadow, 8 acres; woodland, 6 pigs. 7 cattle, 14 pigs, 30 sheep.
A church, 2 acres.
Value then £4; now [£] 3.
Eudo the Steward holds (this) in his lordship.
In the same (Henley) 4 free men (were) added; 8 acres. 2 oxen.
Value 2s.
The King and the Earl (have) the jurisdiction.

Half-Hundred of COSFORD
12 Tovi, a thane, held ELMSETT as a manor before 1066; 6 carucates of land and 40 acres.
Then and later 11 villagers, now 2; always 12 smallholders. Then 4 slaves.
Always 2 ploughs in lordship. Then and later 12 men's ploughs, now 4.
A church with 15 acres. ½ plough.
Then 2 cobs; then 16 cattle, now 4; then 30 pigs, now 20; then 240 sheep, now 200.
Value then £10; now [£] 8.
It has 10 furlongs in length and 7 in width; 15d in tax.
St. Edmund's (has) half the jurisdiction.

13 In WHATFIELD a free man; 60 acres.
2 smallholders.
Then and later 1 plough, now ½. Meadow, 1 acre.
Value 10s.
St. Edmund's (has) the patronage and the jurisdiction.

H̃. DE CARLEFORD. In Finesford. teñ. Tepekin. xxiiii. ac̃.
&. i. ac̃ prati. Tc̃ dim̃. cař. 7. i. liƀa femina de dim̃. ac̃. Semp ual. iiii. fol.

★ *TRA WILL̃I FR̃IS. ROGERI DE OTBURVILLA.* .XXX.
Bofemara. *H̃*. Ringefhalam tenuit Godui liƀ homo. i. cař terræ
7 XL. ac̃. ꝑ mañ. Tc̃. i. uill. Tc̃. ii. cař modo dim̃. & iiii. borđ. 7. vi.
ac̃ prati. filua. viii. porc̃. dim̃ Ecclia. xii. ac̃. Tc̃. iiii. runc̃. modo.
. i. 7 xiii. porc̃. & LX. oũs. 7 xxxii. cap̃r. 7 ual XL. vii. fol. Ex hac terra teñ quidā commd̃tus abbatis sc̃i. eadm̃. xi. ac̃. t. r. e; De hoc
manerio teñ hugo. XL. ac̃. 7 in eod̃ p̃tio ual. v. fol. In ead. i. liƀ homo
Vluricus teñ. LXXX. ac̃. ꝑ mañ. Tc̃. i. cař. 7. iiii. ac̃ prati. Tc̃ ual&
. XX. fol. modo. viii. Fulcho ten& de Willmo. Rex 7 Coms̃ focā.

405 b
In ead̃ Trumuinus liƀ hõ regis. tenuit xviii. ac̃. t. r. e. modo
Will. in dñio. Tc̃ dim̃ cař. & ual. iii. fol. *In* Ringhes hala. Edric̃
liƀ homo. comd̃ ante ceffori. Willi. ten&. v. ac̃. m̃ Will. in dominio
7 ual& xii. deñ; *In* Briefeta Fulcho tenet de Willo. Anfchillus
liƀ homo comd̃ Leurico obbefune ten& LX ac̃. t. r. e. ꝑ mañ. Ex his
ħt Willmus XL. ac̃ fed totũ fimul fibi liƀatũ fuit in hac terra. eft.
. i. borđ. & femp. i. cař. 7 ual. x. fol. Rex & coms̃ focā. Ex fupiorib;
LX. ac̃. tulit hugo de hofdenc XX. ac̃ ut Willmus dicit. 7 hund̃
fed ipfe hugo ẽ in captione regis & id̃o non potuit dare refponfũ.

Hundred of CARLFORD

14 In FINESFORD' Tepekin held 24 acres.
> Meadow, 1 acre.
> Then ½ plough.
> 1 free woman with ½ acre.

Value always 4s.

30   LAND OF WILLIAM BROTHER OF ROGER OF AUBERVILLE

BOSMERE Hundred

1 Godwy, a free man, held RINGSHALL; 1 carucate of land and 40 acres as a manor.
> Then 1 villager. Then 2 ploughs, now ½. 4 smallholders.
> Meadow, 6 acres; woodland, 8 pigs.
> ½ church, 12 acres.
> Then 4 cobs, now 1; 13 pigs, 60 sheep, 32 goats.

Value 47s.
Of this land, a man under the patronage of the Abbot of St. Edmund's held 11 acres before 1066.
Of this manor, Hugh held 40 acres.
(It is) in the same assessment; value 5s.
In the same (Ringshall) Wulfric, 1 free man, held 80 acres as a manor. Then 1 plough.
> Meadow, 4 acres.

Value then 20s; now 8[s].
> Fulk holds (this) from William.
> The King and the Earl (have) the jurisdiction.

In the same (Ringshall) Trumwin, a free man of the King's, held 18 acres before 1066. Now William [holds it] in lordship. Then ½ plough.

Value 3s.

2 In RINGSHALL Edric, a free man under the patronage of William's predecessor, [held] 5 acres. Now William [holds it] in lordship. Value 12d.

3 In BRICETT Fulk holds from William. Askell, a free man under the patronage of Leofric Hobbeson, [held] 60 acres before 1066 as a manor. Of these, William has 40 acres, but the whole (of it) was delivered to him altogether. On this land is
> 1 smallholder.
> Always 1 plough.

Value 10s.
> The King and the Earl (have) the jurisdiction.

Of the above 60 acres, Hugh of Houdain took 20 acres so William and the Hundred say; but Hugh himself is under the King's arrest and has therefore not been able to give a reply.

.XXXI. ꝼTERRÆ.HVGONIS DE MONTE FORTI. ꝼBRADEmara. H̃.
In berham in dominio . ix . libi homines . xvi . ac̄ . & dim̃ . car̃.
ꝼIn Watefelda in dñio . ix . libi homines . xvi . ac̄ . & dim̃ car̃ . & ualēt
xv . fot . Sc̄s eadmundus foc̄ . Duo ex his fuer̃ sc̄i eadm̃ . ad com̃d . t . r . e.
& . vii . ante cefforis hugonis comitis.

ꝼBISSCOPES. H̃ . SAHAM . ten̄ . Oflac teinnus . t . r . e . ꝑ man̄
. i . car̃ terre Roḡ de Candos ten̄ . femp . i . uitt . & . iii . bord . & . i . feru̇.
& . i . car̃ in dominio . & dim̃ . car̃ hom̃ . & . iiii . ac̄ p̃ti . filua x . porc̄.

406 a

Tc̄ . x . porc̄ . modo . xii . 7 . v . an̄ . Tc̄ . iiii . oūs . modo . xii . femp ual xx . fot.
★ Soca epi. ꝼIn borant . ide ten̄ . i . lib homo com̃d . xiiii . ac̄ & dim̃
car̃ . & ual . iii . fot.   ꝼIn badinga felda . v . libi homines . com̃d
lx . ac̄ . 7 . ii . bord . & . i . car̃ . 7 dim̃ . 7 . ii . ac̄ p̃ti . 7 ual . x . fot . Ep̃s foca.
ꝼIn Badingafelda . id . vii . uitt . lx . ac̄ . & . i . car̃ 7 dim̃ . filua . xl . porc̄.
h̃ iac& inacolt . 7 in p̃tio foca epi.
ꝼIn Blidinga . H̃ . In Stouone ten& Hugo de montfort in dñio . l.
ac̄ . trę . q̃s tenuer̃ . iiii . libi hōes . t . r . e . 7 modo . iii . dim̃ . ac̄ p̃ti.
& . i . car̃ in dñio . 7 vii . fot . & dim̃ . ual . femp . 7 . c . allec̃tia . 7 rex
7 comes habuer̃ focā 7 facā fup hos . iiii . hōes.

LANDS OF HUGH DE MONTFORT

BRADMERE Hundred

1 In BARNHAM in lordship, 9 free men; 16 acres. ½ plough.

2 In WATTISFIELD in lordship, 9 free men; 16 acres. ½ plough.
Value 15s.
St. Edmund's (has) the jurisdiction.
Two of these (free men) were St. Edmund's as regards the patronage before 1066, and 7 (were) Earl Hugh's.

BISHOPS Hundred

3 Oslac, a thane, held (Monk) SOHAM before 1066 as a manor; 1 carucate of land. Roger of Candos holds (it).
Always 1 villager; 3 smallholders; 1 slave;
1 plough in lordship; ½ men's plough.
Meadow, 4 acres; woodland, 10 pigs. Then 10 pigs, now 12; 5 cattle; then 4 sheep, now 12.
Value always 20s.
The jurisdiction (is) the Bishop's.

4 He also holds in HORHAM; 1 free man under patronage; 14 acres. ½ plough.
Value 3s.

5 (He) also (holds) in BEDINGFIELD; 5 free men under patronage; 60 acres.
2 smallholders.
1½ ploughs. Meadow, 2 acres.
Value 10s.
The Bishop (has) the jurisdiction.

6 (He) also (holds) in BEDINGFIELD; 7 villagers; 60 acres. 1½ ploughs.
Woodland, 40 pigs.
This belongs to Occold and (is) in the assessment.
The jurisdiction (is) the Bishop's.

In BLYTHING Hundred

7 In STOVEN Hugh de Montfort holds 60 acres of land in lordship.
4 free men held it before 1066 and now 3 [free men hold it].
Meadow, ½ acre.
1 plough in lordship.
Value always 7½s, and 100 herrings.
The King and the Earl had full jurisdiction over these 4 men.

405 b, 406 a

҃H. *DE COLONESSE.* In nachetuna tenuit in dñio. Gut mund᷉
t.r.e.ıı.car̍ terræ ꝑ mañ. Semp. vı. uiłł. Semp in dominio. ıı. car̄.
Tc̄. ııı car̍ hoɱ. modo. ıı. filu᷉ ad. vııı. porc̄. ıı. ac̄ p̍ti. Tc̄. ı. moł.
m̃. nułł. Tc̄. ıııı. runc̍. m̃. ı. &. ı. añ. Tc̄. vııı. porc̄. modo nułł. Tc̄
xxııı. oūs. modo. c. 7 xx. ııı. Tc̄. xxx. cap̄. m̃ nułł. femp ual & ua
luit. lxx. foł. & łıt. ı. lḡ & dim᷉ in longo. 7. ı. in lato. 7 de gelto. ıı. d.

★ ⁄ In brihtolueftana xvııı. libi hōes c̄omendati. Guthmund. de. ı. car̍
terræ. 7 xx. ac̄. ıııı. bord. Tc̄. x. car̍ m̃. ᵛ. ıı. ac̄ p̍ti. filua de. ıı. porc̄.
æcclia. de. vı. ac̄ hī dim᷉ lḡ in lōg. 7. ıı. qr̄. in lato. 7. x. d de gelto.
In Leuentona. ııı. libi hōes. xx. ac̄. c̄omd̍ati eid̄. tc̄. ıı. car̍. modo. ı.
⁄ın culuerdeftuna. v. libi homines c̄omd̍ eid̄. xx. ı. ac̄. 7 dim᷉. tc̄
.ıı. car̍. medo. ı. łıt. ııı. qr̄ in longo. 7. ıı. in lato. ıı. d de gelto.
⁄ In ifte uertona. ıııı. libi hōes. c̄omd̍ eid̄. xvııı. ac̄. Tc̄. ıı. car̍. modo.
. ı. &. ı. ac̄ p̍ti. & ual. ıııı. lib. &. x. foł. fup totā hanc terrā sc̄a eldreda
⸝ focā.⸜

⁄ In Waletuna. ı. lib hō. Lurc nōe c̄omd̍ eid̄. N. xxıııı. ac̄. 7 ual
ııı. foł. Normannus teñ de hugone. sc̄a. e. focā. 7 iftud fup̍dictū
maneriū nachetuna teñ Gut mundus. dei q̍ rex edwardus obiit.
de sc̄a edeldryda. ita qd n̄ potuit uende nec dare. de ecclia. ꝑ iftᷓ
conuentionē. qd p̍ morte fuā debebat redire in ecclia in dñio.
& hoc teftatur hundret.

⁄ ҃H. *DE CARLEFORDA.* In bifchelea. in dñio. ııı. libi hōes
c̄omdati. Gud mundi. t.r.e. xxıx. ac̄. 7. ı. car̍. ı. ac̄. p̍ti. 7 ft in p̄tio
de brithtolueftuna.

Hundred of COLNEIS

8 In NACTON Guthmund held in lordship before 1066; 2 carucates of land as a manor.
Always 6 villagers.
Always 2 ploughs in lordship. Then 3 men's ploughs, now 2.
Woodland for 8 pigs; meadow, 2 acres; then 1 mill, now none.
Then 4 cobs, now 1; 1 cattle; then 8 pigs, now none; then 23 sheep, now 123; then 30 goats, now none.
Value always is and was 70s. It has 1½ leagues in length and 1 in width; 2d in tax.

9 In [*BRIHTOLUESTUNA*] 18 free men under the patronage of Guthmund, with 1 carucate of land and 20 acres.
4 smallholders.
Then 10 ploughs, now 5.
Meadow, 2 acres; woodland at 2 pigs.
A church with 6 acres.
It has ½ league in length and 2 furlongs in width; 10d in tax.

10 In LEVINGTON 3 free men under the patronage of the same man; 20 acres. Then 2 ploughs, now 1.

11 In *CULUERDESTUNA* 5 free men under the patronage of the same man; 21½ acres. Then 2 ploughs, now 1.
It has 3 furlongs in length and 2 in width; 2d in tax.

12 In *ISTEUERTONA* 4 free men under the patronage of the same man; 18 acres. Then 2 ploughs, now 1.
Meadow, 1 acre.
Value £4 10s.
St. Etheldreda's (has) jurisdiction over the whole of this land.

13 In WALTON 1 free man, Lurk by name, under the patronage of N.; 24 acres.
Value 3s.
Norman holds (this) from Hugh.
St. Etheldreda's (has) the jurisdiction.

406 b

13a Guthmund held the above-mentioned manor of NACTON from St. Etheldreda's in 1066 in such a way that he could not sell or grant it away from the Church, (and) on the agreement that after his death it ought to return to the Church in lordship; the Hundred testifies to this.

Hundred of CARLFORD

14 In BIXLEY in lordship; 3 free men under the patronage of Guthmund before 1066; 29 acres. 1 plough.
Meadow, 1 acre.
They are in the assessment of *Brithtoluestuna*.

⁊ In burg.I.lib hō.comd dim.sc̄e.e.t.r.e.
⁊ dim antecessoris.Rob.malet.modo.III.hoes.xx ac̄.terræ.Tc̄.I.car̄.
modo.dim.II.ac̄ p̄ti.Tc̄ ual.x.sol.modo.v.In eadē.I.lib homo
comd.dimid.sc̄e.æ.⁊ dim.Edrici grimma de.x.ix.ac̄ terræ.⁊.I.
bord.Tc̄.I.car̄.modo dim.I.ac̄ p̄ti.⁊ ual.IIII.sol.⁊.IX.den.
⁊ In Parua belinges.I.lib hō.comdat dim.Sc̄e.æ.⁊ dim.Edrici.IIII.
ac̄.⁊ dim.⁊ ual.VIII.den.⁊ In clopetuna.II.lib hō.⁊ dim comd
Sicuti alii ut.sup.xIIII.ac̄.Tc̄ dim.car̄.m̄.null.& ual.II.sol.⁊ VII.d.

⁊.H.de Wileford.In Keresfelda in dn̄io.x.libi homines comd Edrici.
& dim.Sc̄e.Æ.LX.ac̄.&.I.ac̄ p̄ti.Tc̄.II.car̄.modo.I.Tc̄ ual xxIIII.sol.
modo xx.II.sol.& VIII.den.

⁊.H. DE LOSA.In ceres felda.II.libi hoes.com.S.e ⁊ de.I.comd
habuit dim ante c̄.hugonis de monte forti.VII.ac̄.⁊ ual XVI.d.
⁊ In gretingahā tenuit Aluric lib hō heroldi.t.r.e.II.car terræ ⁊ dim.
⁊ xv.ac̄.Semp.VI.uill.⁊ xxI.bord.Tc̄.II.ser.⁊.in dn̄io.II.car̄.⁊.VI.
car hom.⁊ VIII.ac̄ p̄ti.Silua ad VIII.porc̄.I.molin.Tc̄.I.runc̄.⁊.II.an̄.

407 a
⁊ xx.ous.⁊ xx.porc̄.Tc̄ ual.c.sol.modo.VIII.lib.⁊.I.uncea auri.&
ht in longo.I.lḡ.⁊.III.q̄r in lato.&.de gelto.xI.d.Alii ibi tenent.
In cad.x.libi homines.comd eid xLVI.ac̄.IX.ac̄ & dim.calūpniatur.
Willmus de arcis.&.II.dim hoes.Semp.I.car.& ual.xx.sol.I.ex istis.fuit
comd.Edrici de laxa fella.⁊ Will.malet inde fuit saiat die qua
obiit.h ten&.R.de hugone.

15 In BURGH 1 free man before 1066, half under the patronage of St. Etheldreda's and half (under that) of Robert Malet's predecessor's; now 3 men; 20 acres of land. Then 1 plough, now ½.
    Meadow, 2 acres.
    Value then 10s; now 5[s].
In the same (Burgh) 1 free man, half under the patronage of St. Etheldreda's and half (under that) of Edric Grim, with 19 acres of land.
    1 smallholder.
    Then 1 plough, now ½. Meadow, 1 acre.
Value 4s 9d.

16 In LITTLE BEALINGS 1 free man, half under the patronage of St. Etheldreda's and half (under that) of Edric; 4½ acres.
Value 8d.

17 In CLOPTON 2 free men, half under patronage like the others above; 14 acres. Then ½ plough, now none.
Value 2s 7d.

    Hundred of WILFORD

18 In CHARSFIELD in lordship; 10 free men, half under the patronage of Edric and half (under that) of St. Etheldreda's; 60 acres.
    Meadow, 1 acre.
    Then 2 ploughs, now 1.
Value then 24s; now 22s 8d.

    Hundred of LOES

19 In CHARSFIELD 2 free men under the patronage of St. Etheldreda's and Hugh de Montfort's predecessor had half the patronage over 1; 7 acres.
Value 16d.

20 Roger of Candos holds in CRETINGHAM; Aelfric, a free man of Harold's, held (it) before 1066; 2½ carucates of land and 15 acres.
    Always 6 villagers; 21 smallholders. Then 2 slaves.
    2 ploughs in lordship; 6 men's ploughs.
    Meadow, 8 acres; woodland for 8 pigs; 1 mill. Then 1 cob, 2 cattle, 20 sheep, 20 pigs.
Value then 100s; now £8 and 1 ounce of gold.   407 a
    It has 1 league in length and 3 furlongs in width; 11d in tax.
Others hold there.
In the same (Cretingham) 10 free men under the patronage of the same man; 46 acres. William of Arques claims 9½ acres and 2 half (free) men. Always 1 plough.
Value 20s.
    One of these (free men) was under the patronage of Edric of Laxfield; William Malet was in possession on the day he died.
    Roger holds this from Hugh.

WANNEFORDA. H̄. In Willinga hā tēn in dn̄iū . xv . libi hões
com̄ Burcardi . t . r . e . I . car terræ 7 dim̄ . 7 xviii . ac̄ . Semp . II . uill.
Tc̄ . vii . car . modo . vi . filua ad x . porc . I . ac̄ . pti . I . æcclia . xl . ac̄ . 7 ual . vii.
fol. plures ibi participantur. Tc̄ ual . lx . fol . modo xxx . fol . 7 xxx . d.
7 . III . mill allectiū . Rex 7 Com̄s foca.

In Weftuna . I . lib hō . xvi . ac̄ . com̄d eid . & dim car . 7 ual . v . fol.
& . cccc . allectium . *In* Wellingaham . I . lib hō com̄d . Burckardi
7 non potuit uendere terrā nec dare . III . ac̄ libe terræ . 7 . ual xviii .
d . 7 . c . allecti . In atheburgfelda . vi . libi hões . comm̄dti Burcardo
lx . ac̄ . Tc̄ . II . car . modo . I . & dim . Tc̄ ual . x . fol . modo . xi . 7 viii . den̄.
7 . d . cccc . allecti . *In* Warlingahā . v . libi hões . 7 dim . com̄d.
Guerti . lx . ac̄ . Semp . II . car . & . I . bord . II . ac̄ prati . Semp ual . x . fol.
7 . vi . d . 7 . I . mill . allecti

LVDINGA. H̄. In beketuna in dn̄io . vi . libi hões . com̄d . Burchardi.
. l . ac̄ tre . Tc̄ . I . car . modo dim . Tc̄ ual . IIII . fol . modo xxi . 7 IIII . d . 7 I.
mill 7 dim . allecti.

In Keffingelanda . I . lib hō . com̄d . Edrici de Laxefella . xxx . ac̄ . p m.
Semp . I . car . & . I . ac̄ pti . Tc̄ ual . v . fol . modo . viii . fol . In ead . IIII . libi hões.

407 b

. I . com̄datus Edrici . & . III . com̄dati . Burckardi . t . r . e . lxxx . 7 x.
ac̄ . & . II . bord . Semp . II . car . 7 . I . ac̄ pti . Tc̄ ual . x . fol . modo . xxii.
mill allecti .

WANGFORD Hundred
21 In WILLINGHAM in lordship; 15 free men under the patronage of Burghard before 1066; 1½ carucates of land and 18 acres.
Always 2 villagers.
Then 7 ploughs, now 6.
Woodland for 10 pigs; meadow, 1 acre.
1 church, 40 acres; value 7s. Several have a share there.
Value then 60s; now 30s 30d and 3000 herrings.
The King and the Earl (have) the jurisdiction.

22 In WESTON 1 free man under the patronage of the same man; 16 acres. ½ plough.
Value 5s and 400 herrings.

23 In WILLINGHAM 1 free man under the patronage of Burghard; he could not sell the land nor grant; 3 acres of free land.
Value 18d and 100 herrings.

24 In *HATHEBURGFELDA* 6 free men under the patronage of Burghard; 60 acres. Then 2 ploughs, now 1½.
Value then 10s; now 11[s] 8d and 900 herrings.

25 In WORLINGHAM 5 free men and a half under the patronage of Gyrth; 60 acres. Always 2 ploughs;
1 smallholder.
Meadow, 2 acres.
Value always 10s 6d and 1000 herrings.

LOTHING Hundred
26 In *BEKETUNA* in lordship; 6 free men under the patronage of Burghard; 60 acres of land. Then 1 plough, now ½.
Value then 4s; now 21[s] 4d and 1500 herrings.

27 In KESSINGLAND 1 free man under the patronage of Edric of Laxfield; 30 acres as a manor. Always 1 plough.
Meadow, 1 acre.
Value then 5s; now 8d.
In the same (Kessingland) 4 free men, 1 under the patronage of Edric and 3 under the patronage of Burghard before 1066; 80 and 10 acres.
2 smallholders.
Always 2 ploughs. Meadow, 1 acre.
Value then 10s; now 22[s and] 1000 herrings.

407 b

⁊In Rodenhala.ı.lib hō Aſlacus.com̃d Burcardi xl.ac̃.p man̄.Semp.ıııı.bord.Semp in dominio.ı.car.⁊ hou dim̃ car.ſilua ad.ııı.porc̃.ı.ac̃ & dim̃ p̃ti.Tc̃ ual.v.ſol.modo.ıx.⁊ vı.centos allecti.Totum in dn̄io.

⁊In Wimundahala.ıı.libi hões com̃d Burckardi.xıı.ac̃.Semp dim̃ car.Tc̃ ual.ıı.ſol.modo.ııı.⁊ dim̃ mill allectii.

In Giſleha.ıı.lib hō com̃d eid.ı.ac̃.⁊ dim̃.⁊ ual.ıı.ſol.⁊ vı.den̄. ⁊.cc allecti.In ead.ı.lib hō com̃d eid.vı.ac̃.⁊ dim̃ car.⁊ ual.v.ſol. ⁊ ccc.allecii. ⁊In hornes.ı.lib hō.c̄omendation̄.Guerti.t.r. .v.ac̃.⁊ ual.ııı.ſol.⁊.c.⁊ lx.allectii.

⁊In carletuna.ıı.libi hões com̃d.Burchardi.xxx.ac̃.Semp.ı.carr. & ual.ııı.ſol.cccc.allec̃.In ead.ı.lib hō com̃d.eide.xxx.ac̃.Tc̃ .ı.car.modo null.dimid ac̃ p̃ti.Tc̃ ual & modo.v.ſol.⁊.ccc.allecti

⁊In kirkelea.ı.lib homo com̃d.dim.Burchardi ⁊ dimid.vlſi.xıı. ac̃.Tc̃ dim̃ car.modo null.Tc̃ ual.ıı.ſol.modo.ııı.⁊.cc.allecti.

⁊In riſcemara.ı.lib homo.c̄om.Guerti.xvı.ac̃.Tc̃.ı.car.modo dim̃. & ual.v.ſol.⁊.ccc.allecti.H totū ten̄.H in ſuo dominio.⁊ q̃rta pars.ı.æcclię.vııı.ac̃.⁊ ual.xvı.d.Rex ⁊ Comes ſocā.quattuor ex his ſupradictis hoib3 teſtatur hund qd Walter de doai.fuit ſaiatus die qua ſe foriſfecit.⁊ pt hug Com̄s.modo ten̄ hugo de monte forti.ſed n̄ ten& p libatione teſte hund.⁊ hões hug de mut. dicunt qd ipſe.W.tenuit de eo.

28 In *RODENHALA* 1 free man, Aslac, under the patronage of Burghard; 40 acres as a manor.
    Always 4 smallholders.
    Always 1 plough in lordship; ½ men's plough.
    Woodland for 3 pigs; meadow, 1½ acres.
Value then 5s; now 9[s] and 600 herrings.
    The whole (is) in lordship.

29 In *WIMUNDAHALA* 2 free men under the patronage of Burghard; 12 acres. Always ½ plough.
Value then 2s; now 3[s] and 500 herrings.

30 In GISLEHAM 2 free men under the patronage of the same man; 1½ acres.
Value 2s 6d and 200 herrings.
In the same (Gisleham) 1 free man under the patronage of the same man; 16 acres. ½ plough.
Value 5s and 300 herrings.

31 In *HORNES* 1 free man under the patronage of Gyrth [before 1066]; 5 acres.
Value 3s and 160 herrings.

32 In CARLTON (Colville) 2 free men under the patronage of Burghard; 30 acres. Always 1 plough.
Value 3s [and] 400 herrings.
In the same (Carlton Colville) 1 free man under the patronage of the same man; 30 acres. Then 1 plough, now none.
    Meadow, ½ acre.
Value then and now 5s and 300 herrings.

33 In KIRKLEY 1 free man half under the patronage of Burghard and half (under that) of Wulfsi; 12 acres. Then ½ plough, now none.
Value then 2s; now 3[s] and 200 herrings.

34 In RUSHMERE 1 free man under the patronage of Gyrth; 16 acres. Then 1 plough, now ½.
Value 5s and 300 herrings.
    Hugh holds the whole of this in his lordship.
    The fourth part of 1 church, 8 acres; value 16d.
    The King and the Earl (have) the jurisdiction.
The Hundred testifies that Walter of [Dol] was in possession of four of the above-mentioned men on the day he forfeited; later Earl Hugh (was in possession); now Hugh de Montfort holds [them]. But he does not hold them through a delivery, as the Hundred testifies; and Hugh de Montfort's men say that William himself held (them) from him.

HERTESMARA. H̃. In cotintuna. I. lib hō Saxwinus
cõmd. Buchardi. xx ac̄. t. r. e. Tc̄. I. car. modo dimid. dim
ac̄ prati. filua ad II. porc. 7 ē in p̄tio in dn̄io de neutūn.
⁊In Wluertheftuna. ten̄ herueus. II. libo hoes cõmd Burchardi
XVIII. ac̄. filua ad. II. porc. 7 ual. IIII. fol.
⁊In caldecoten ten̄. in dn̄io. I. lib hō. II. ac̄ & dim. 7 ual. VI. den̄.
⁊In Giſlingahā. ten̄ Giſleb. I. libā feminā c̄m. Gutmundi. xv.
ac̄. 7. I. ac̄ p̄ti. 7 ual. II. fol. In caldecotan. in dn̄io. III. ac̄ 7 dim
7 ual. VI. d.

⁊LACFORDA. H̃. LIuermera ten& hugo de beuerda ten& de
hugone quā tenuit Gutmundus. t. r. e. fub sc̄a aldreda q̄d non
poter̄ uende p manerio. II. car terræ. Semp IIII. uilli. &. III. bord.
Tc̄. III. ferui. modo. I. Semp II. car in dn̄io. Tc̄ & p:̄ II. car. hom.
modo. I. 7 IIII. ac̄ p̄ti. 7. I. pifcar. Semp. I. eq. 7. III. an̄. Tc̄. x. porc.
modo. III. CLX. ous. modo. C. Soc 7 fac sc̄a aldred. &. III. libi hoes
gutmundi cõmd 7 foc 7 fac sc̄i edm. LXXX. ac̄ terræ 7 medietatē
cõmdt uni cū tr̄a habuit scs. e. t. r. e. Int oes femp. II. car &. I. ac̄
p̄ti. Man ual. XL. fol. 7 libi homines XIII. fol. ht VI. qr̄ in longo
&. IIII. in lato. & de gelto. IIII. d.

HARTISMERE Hundred

35 In COTTON 1 free man, Saxwin, under the patronage of Burghard; 20 acres before 1066. Then 1 plough, now ½.
　　Meadow, ½ acre; woodland for 2 pigs.
　It is in the assessment of the lordship of (Old) Newton.

36 In WYVERSTONE Hervey holds 2 free men [who were] under the patronage of Burghard; 18 acres.
　　Woodland for 2 pigs.
　Value 4s.

37 In *CALDECOTEN* he holds in lordship; 1 free man; 2½ acres.
　Value 6d.

38 In GISLINGHAM Gilbert holds 1 free woman [who was] under the patronage of Guthmund; 15 acres.
　　Meadow, 1 acre.
　Value 2s.

39 In *CALDECOTAN* 3½ acres in lordship.
　Value 6d.

LACKFORD Hundred

40 Hugh de *Beuerda* holds (Great) LIVERMERE from Hugh; Guthmund held (it) before 1066 under St. Etheldreda's, so that he could not sell; 2 carucates of land as a manor.
　　Always 4 villagers; 3 smallholders. Then 3 slaves, now 1.
　　Always 2 ploughs in lordship. Then and later 2 men's ploughs, now 1.
　　Meadow, 4 acres; 1 fishery. Always 1 horse; 3 cattle. Then 10 pigs, now 3; [then] 160 sheep, now 100.
　　The full jurisdiction (is) St. Etheldreda's.
　He also holds 3 free men of Guthmund's under the patronage and full jurisdiction of St. Edmund's; 80 acres of land. Before 1066 St. Edmund's had the half of the patronage of one (free man) with the land. Always 2 ploughs between them all.
　　Meadow, 1 acre.
　Value of the manor 40s; (value of) the free men 13s.
　　It has 6 furlongs in length and 4 in width; 4d in tax.

⊽ B.ABERGA DVO. H̃. Stanefteda ten̄ i dn̄io gutmund̊ hugo
teinn̾.t.r.e.p man̄.v.car̾ terræ cū foca.Tc̄.IIII.uiłł.p̊ 7 m̄
.III.7.x.bord̄.Tc̄ 7 p̊r̾ x.ferū.modo.VI.Tc̄.IIII.car̾ in dn̄io.
p̊ 7 modo.III.Semp.II.car̾ hominū.&.XVI.ac̄ p̊ti.&.I.molin̄.
Silua de.xx.porc̾.Tc̄.III.equi.modo.IIII.Semp̾ XVI.an̾.

408 b
&.LX.porc̄.7.c.oūs Tc̄ ual &.p̊.VI.lib̄.m̄ reddit.XII.lib̄.hr̃.I.lḡ in
longo.7 IIII.qr̃ in lato.7 de gelto.VII d̄ & obolū.quicuq; ibi ten&.
Ecc̄lia de xx.v.ac̄ libæ terre.

⊽ STOV. H̃.Hagala ten̄ Gut mundus.fub.R.E.p manerio.VIII.
car̾ terræ cū foca & faca.fup dn̄ium hallæ tn̄tū.Tc̄ xxx.II.uiłł.
p̊ 7 modo xxx.7.VIII.bord̄.7 tc̄.x.ferū̾.p̊ VI.m̄.III.Semp.IIII.car̾.
in dn̄io.Tc̄ 7 poft XXIIII.car̾ hoīum.modo.VIII.Silua.cc.porc̄.7
XLII.ac̄ prati.Ecc̄lia de.xxxI.ac̄ libe terræ.7 dim̄ ac̄ prati.
Semp.VI.equi in halla.7 XVIII.an̾.7 LXXX.porc̄.L̶X̶X̶X̶X̶V̶I̶.oūs.
7 LXXX.cap̊.7 in dn̄o.VI.foc̄.eid̄e Gut mundi de quib; foca eft.in
hund̄ 7 n̄ pot uend̄e tr̄a.Tc̄ dim̄ car̾ terræ.7 xx.ac̄.7 femper.Tc̄ 7
p̊.II.car̾.modo nulla.Tc̄ totū ual.XVI.lib̄.p̊ XII.modo xx.lib̄.
De h̄ man̄.ten̄ herueus.I.car̾.&.xxx.ac̄.7 ual.LXIII.fol.7 Radul-
fus.I.car̾.de.xx.fol.Turoldus.I.car̾.de xxx.fol.Pefferera.dim̄.car̾
de.x.fol.Rotb̾t.xx.ac̄.de.v.fol.Ricard.xxx.ac̄.de.v.fol.Totū ē
in p̃tio manerii.łt.I.lḡ in longo 7 dim̄ in lato.& de gelto XVII.d̄.

⊽ In daga worda ten̄ hugo in dn̄io.VII.libos homines quā ten̄uit
Gutmundus Ante cū hugon̄ comd̄ tantū.II.car̾ terræ in foca reg̾
& comit̾ 7 fub eis XVII.bord̄.Tc̄.7 p̊.v.car̾.in̄t oēs.modo.IIII.Silua
XII.porc̄.&.VIII.ac̄ p̊ti.Tc̄ & p̊ ual.XL.v.fol.7 modo XL.v.

BABERGH Two Hundreds
41 Hugh holds STANSTEAD in lordship; Guthmund, a thane, [held it] before 1066 as a manor; 5 carucates of land, with the jurisdiction.
  Then 4 villagers, later and now 3; 10 smallholders; then and later 10 slaves, now 6.
  Then 4 ploughs in lordship, later and now 3. Always 2 men's ploughs.
  Meadow, 16 acres; 1 mill; woodland at 20 pigs. Then 3 horses, now 4; always 16 cattle, 60 pigs, 100 sheep.
  Value then and later £6; now it pays £12.
  It has 1 league in length and 4 furlongs in width; 7½d in tax, whoever holds there.
  A church with 25 acres of free land.

408 b

STOW Hundred
42 Guthmund held HAUGHLEY under King Edward as a manor; 8 carucates of land, with full jurisdiction only over the lordship of the hall.
  Then 32 villagers, later and now 30; 8 smallholders; then 10 slaves, later 6, now 3.
  Always 4 ploughs in lordship. Then and later 24 men's ploughs, now 8.
  Woodland, 200 pigs; meadow, 42 acres.
  A church with 31 acres of free land. Meadow, ½ acre.
  Always 6 horses at the hall; 18 cattle, 80 pigs, 146 sheep, 80 goats.
  Also in lordship, 6 Freemen of the same Guthmund's, jurisdiction over whom is in the Hundred; they could not sell the land. Then and always ½ carucate of land and 20 acres. Then and later 2 ploughs, now none.
  Value then of the whole, £16; later [£] 12; now £20.
  Of this manor, Hervey holds 1 carucate and 30 acres; value 63s. Ralph (holds) 1 carucate of land at 20s. Thorold (holds) 1 carucate [of land] at 30s. Pesserera (holds) ½ carucate [of land] at 10s. Robert (holds) 20 acres at 5s. Richard (holds) 30 acres at 5s.
  The whole is in the assessment of the manor.
  It has 1 league in length and ½ in width; 17d in tax.

43 In DAGWORTH Hugh holds in lordship 7 free men; Guthmund, Hugh's predecessor, held it with only the patronage, in the jurisdiction of the King and Earl; 2 carucates of land.
  Under them, 17 smallholders.
  Then and later 5 ploughs between them all, now 4.
  Woodland, 12 pigs; meadow, 8 acres.
  Value then and later 45s; now 45[s].

408 a, b

☞ In daga warda eadē tenͣ in dnͣio . vi . foc̄ ptinentes in tornei . man̄ reḡ.
de regiōe cū omͣi confuetudine . & hͣnt inͣt omͣs . i . car̓ terræ . & . iiii . bord̄.
Tc̄ 7 poſt . iii . car̓ . modo . ii . 7 . v . ac̄ p̓ti . Tc̄ & p̄͢ ual . xxx . fol . modo xx.
dim' æcclia . de xxv . ac̄ libæ terræ
7 hoes . vi . foc̄ reclamat hugo ex libͣatione ; Daga worda hͣt . i . lḡ 7 dim̓

409 a
in lato . & de gelto xxx . d̄ . Quicūq; ibi teneat.
   ī dnͣio
☞ In Watͣdena xvii . libͣi hoͣes gut mundi antc̄ hugonis com̓d tnͣt.
& hͣnt . ii . car̓ terræ in foca regis 7 comit̓ . Tc̄ . x . bord̄ . 7 femp . Tc̄ . v .
car̓ . poſt . iiii . modo . v . inͣt omͣs . Silua . iiii . porc̓ . 7 . vi . ac̄ p̓ti . Tc̄ & p̄͢
ual . l . fol . modo xl . hͣt . i . leug̓ . in longo 7 dim̓ in lato & de gelto xxv .
den̄ . quicūq; ibi tenͣ.
☞ In erueſtuna . x . libͣi homines gut mundi antec̄ . . . . hugon̓ . cō
mendat tnͣtū dim̓ car̓ terræ in foca reḡ 7 comit̓ . 7 ii bord̄.
Tc̄ & p̄͢ . iii . car̓ inͣt omͣs . modo uix hͣnt . i . car̓ . 7 iiii . ac̄ p̓ti . Tc̄
& p̄͢ ual . xx . fol . modo . x . Ecclia . x . ac̄ . libæ terræ . hͣt . x . qr̓ in
longo . & . vi . in lato . 7 de gelto . x . den̄ . q̓cūq; ibi tenͣ.
☞ In torpe . xvi libͣi hoͣes antec̄ com̓d tnͣtū . i . car̓ tr̓æ in fac̓ reḡ 7 comit̓.
7 . ii . bord̄ . fub eis . Tc̄ 7 p̄͢ . iii . car̓ . inͣt omͣs . modo . i . 7 . iii . ac̄ . prat̓.
Tc̄ 7 p̄͢ ual . xxx . fol . modo . uix ual . x . fol . hͣt . v . qr̓ . in longo . 7
. iii . in lato . & de gelto . viii . d̄ . quicūq; ibi tenͣ.
       ī dnͣio
☞ In Vltuna . iii . libͣi hoͣes eidͣ gudmund̄ comm̓ tnͣtū . dim̓ car̓ terræ
in foca reḡ 7 comͣs . 7 xiii . ac̄ Tc̄ 7 p̄͢ . iii . bord̄ . modo . i . Semp . i . car̓.

44 In the same DAGWORTH he holds in lordship 6 Freemen who belong to the King's manor of Thorney, belonging to the Realm, with every customary due. They have between them all 1 carucate of land.
    4 smallholders.
    Then and later 3 ploughs, now 2. Meadow, 5 acres.
    Value then and later 30s; now 20[s].
    ½ church with 25 acres of free land.
    Hugh claims [to hold] these 6 Freemen by a delivery.
    Dagworth has 1 league [in length] and ½ in width; 30d in tax, whoever holds there.

45 In WETHERDEN in lordship; 17 free men belonging to Guthmund, Hugh's predecessor, under patronage only, in the jurisdiction of the King and the Earl. They have 2 carucates of land.
    Then and always 10 smallholders.
    Then 5 ploughs, later 4, now 5 between them all.
    Woodland, 4 pigs; meadow, 6 acres.
    ½ church with 15 acres of free land. Meadow, 1 acre.
    Value then and later 50s; now 40[s].
    It has 1 league in length and ½ in width; 25d in tax, whoever holds there.

46 In ERUESTUNA 10 free men belonging to Guthmund, Hugh's predecessor, under patronage only, in the jurisdiction of the King and the Earl; ½ carucate of land.
    2 smallholders.
    Then and later 3 ploughs between them all, now they have scarcely 1 plough. Meadow, 4 acres.
    Value then and later 20s; now 10[s].
    A church, 10 acres of free land.
    It has 10 furlongs in length and 6 in width; 10d in tax, whoever holds there.

47 In TORPE 16 free men [of Hugh's] predecessor, under patronage only, in the jurisdiction of the King and the Earl; 1 carucate of land.
    Under them, 2 smallholders.
    Then and later 3 ploughs between them all, now 1. Meadow, 3 acres.
    Value then and later 30s; value now scarcely 10s.
    It has 5 furlongs in length and 3 in width; 8d in tax, whoever holds there.

48 In VLTUNA in lordship; 3 free men of the same Guthmund's, under patronage only, in the jurisdiction of the King and the Earl; ½ carucate of land and 13 acres.
    Then and later 3 smallholders, now 1.
    Always 1 plough.

7 . IIII . ac p̄ti . 7 . I . moliñ . ſed medietatē calūpniatur . Coms de mo
retoñ . 7 . H̄ . teſtatur . Tc & p̄ ual xII . ſol . & modo ſimilit̄ .

⸿ In Ciltuna 7 in torſtuna tenḋ hugo in dn̄io . ex libatione ut dic̄ .
xvi . ſoc̄ qui p̄tinebant in tornei maner̄ regis . e . cū ōi conſuetudiñ
teſte hund . & hn̄t . I . car̄ terræ 7 . VII . borḋ . Tc 7 p̄ . IIII . car̄ . int̄ om̄s .
modo . III . 7 . vi . ac p̄ti . Tc 7 p̄ ual . L . ſol . modo xxx . Tot̄ ht̄ . IIII .
q̄r in longo . & . III . in lato . & de gelto . VIII . d . Et oēs iſti . libi hoc̄s ē

409 b

7 ſoca fuer̄ libati ſic̄ om̄s hugonis dicunt ꝑ . II . man̄ . v . car̄t tr̄æ .
⸿ In dagaworda ten̄ breme lib ho . Reḡ . e . qui fuit occiſ in bello ha-
ſtingenſi & ht̄ . I . car̄ terræ 7 dim̄ ſed libata fuit hugoñ ꝑ dimid car̄
de eſcangio . 7 ſoca reḡ . 7 com̄s . Semp . xi . borḋ . 7 III . ſeru̇ . Tc 7 ſemp
II . car̄ . in dn̄io . Tc & p̄ . II . car̄ hominū . modo . I . Silua Lx . porc̄ . 7 IX .
ac prati . & . I . moliñ . I . Ecclia ſine terra 7 dim̄ ecclia . xxx . ac terræ .
★ Tc . I . ac & dim̄ prati . Tc xIII . añ . modo . x . 7 xII . porc̄ . 7 xvI . oūs .
7 xL . cap̄ . Semp ual . Lx . ſol . In eod manerio . I . lib ho bremere
com̄d tantū . 7 ht̄ . xI . ac & dim̄ . & . I . borḋ . Tc & p̄ dim̄ . car̄ . modo
nulla . 7 ual . III . ſol . hoc man̄ tenḋ . Wiłł fili groſſe de hugone
de monte forti .

⸿ In newetuna . tenḋ Alwinus de melleſſam . I . libū hōe dim̄
car̄ terræ modo tenḋ hugo ꝑ eſcangio . ſub eo . II . borḋ . Semp
. I . car̄ . 7 . I . ac 7 dimid p̄ti . & modo . xL . oūs . & . III . porc̄ . Semp
ual . xL . ſol . In ead ten̄ hugo in dn̄io . ex libat̄ ꝑ eſcangio . II .
libos hōes de quibȝ ſoc̄ erat in hundret & hn̄t xxvII . ac . Semp
dim̄ car̄ . & ual . v . ſol . ⸿ In dago Worda ten̄ hugo . dim̄ libū homi-
nē . xx . ac . & ual . III . ſol .

Meadow, 4 acres; 1 mill, but the Count of Mortain claims a half and the Hundred testifies [to this].
Value then and later 12s; now the same.

49 In CHILTON and in *TORSTUNA* Hugh holds in lordship, by a delivery so he says, 16 Freemen who belonged to King Edward's manor of Thorney with every customary due, as the Hundred testifies. They have 1 carucate of land.
    7 smallholders.
    Then and later 4 ploughs between them all, now 3. Meadow, 6 acres.
Value then and later 50s; now 30[s].
The whole has 4 furlongs in length and 3 in width; 8d in tax.
All these free men, ... and the jurisdiction were delivered, as all of Hugh's (men) say, for 2 manors, 5 carucates of land.

409 b

50 In DAGWORTH Breme, a free man of King Edward's, held, who was killed in the Battle of Hastings; he had 1½ carucates of land but it was delivered to Hugh for ½ carucate by an exchange. The jurisdiction (is) the King's and the Earl's.
    Always 11 smallholders; 3 slaves.
    Then and always 2 ploughs in lordship; then and later 2 men's ploughs, now 1.
    Woodland, 60 pigs; meadow, 9 acres; 1 mill.
    1 church without land. ½ church, 30 acres of land. Meadow, 1½ acres.
    Then 13 cattle, now 10; 12 pigs, 16 sheep, 40 goats.
Value always 60s.
In the same manor 1 free man; Breme had only the patronage. He has 11½ acres.
    1 smallholder.
    Then and later ½ plough, now none.
Value 3s.
William son of Gross holds this manor from Hugh de Montfort.

51 In (Old) NEWTON in lordship; Alwin of Mendlesham [held] 1 free man; ½ carucate of land. Hugh now holds (it) by exchange.
    Under him, 2 smallholders.
    Always 1 plough.
    Meadow, 1½ acres. Now 40 sheep, 3 pigs.
Value always 40s.
In the same (Old Newton) Hugh holds in lordship by delivery 2 free men by exchange, jurisdiction over whom was in the Hundred. They have 27 acres. Always ½ plough.
Value 5s.

52 In DAGWORTH Hugh holds a half free man; 20 acres.
Value 3s.

*In torneia tēn Rog̃. de candos. 1.
car' terræ de hugone. que fuit de dñio manerio foca regis. tē : pore
. r. e. fed fuit libata. p. 1. car' terræ. hanc habuit. Rad' ftalra in ua
dimonio de uice comite. Toli. ut hundreto audiũ dr̃e f7 non uidit
breues neq; libatorē. & tenebat die qua rex. e. fuit mortuus. & p
Radulfus filius ei. & ht. IIII. uill. 7. III. bord. &. II. fer. Tc. II. car'
in dominio. m̃. I. femp. II. car' hoim. &. IIII. ac prati. &. I. moliñ

410 a

Silua. IIII. porc'. modo. x. porc̃. & xxx. oũs. Semp ual LX fol.
Et in ead id. tēn. II. libi hoes. xx. ac. Tc & poft. I. car'. modo dim̃.
& ual. xL. deñ. Hæc eft de efcangio.

*THEWARDESTEU. H̃. In begatona. tēn. I. lib hō Ediue
diuitis. xL. ac tr̃æ. t. r. e. modo tēn hugo de monte forti p efcang'.
Semp dim'. car'. 7 ual. v. fol.

*DIMID'. H̃. DEGERES WIZ. In burgo ht. Hugo in dñio
. I. manfurā 7 iacet in nechetuna. Rex ht totā confuetudinē.

*BOSEMARA. H̃ BETESFORT. ten& Rog̃ de candos de. hug'.
quā tenuit Aluricus lib hō. t. r. e. p man̄. I. car'. terræ. femp. VIII.
bord. Tc. II. car' in dominio. modo. I. & dim'. car'. hom. VI. ac p̃ti.
filua de xx. porc̃. Dim' ecclia. xx. ac. modo. I. runc'. 7 IIII. animal.
& xII. porc̃. &. xxI. oũs. &. IIII. cap̃. 7 ual. xxx. fol. Huic man̄.
addidit hugo. v. libos hoes. I. car' terræ. &. x. ac. III. bord.
Tc. III. car'. modo. I. car' & dim'. vI. ac p̃ti. filua.
v. porc̃. 7 ual. xx. fol. h e p efcangio de tr̃a fc̃i au-
guftini. Rog̃ de candos tēn. Rex. 7 Com̃s focā.
ht. x. qr̃ iu longo. &. v. in lato. Alii ibi tenent.
7. x. deñ. de gl.

53 In THORNEY Roger of Candos holds 1 carucate of land from Hugh which was in the lordship of the manor in the jurisdiction of the King before 1066, but it was delivered for 1 carucate of land. Ralph the Constable had this in pledge from the Sheriff, Toli, as the Hundred has heard say, but it did not see the writs nor a deliverer; he held (it) in 1066. Later Ralph, his son [held it]. It has
    4 villagers, 3 smallholders, 2 slaves.
    Then 2 ploughs in lordship; now 1; always 2 men's ploughs.
    Meadow, 4 acres; 1 mill; woodland, 4 pigs. Now 10 pigs, 30 sheep.
Value always 60s.
In the same (Thorney) he also holds; 2 free men; 20 acres. Then and later 1 plough, now ½.
Value 40d.
    This is by exchange.

410 a

THEDWESTRY Hundred

54 In BEYTON 1 free man of Edeva the Rich's held 40 acres of land before 1066. Now Hugh de Montfort holds (it) by exchange. Always ½ plough.
Value 5s.

Half-Hundred of IPSWICH

55 In the Borough (of IPSWICH) Hugh has 1 dwelling in lordship and it belongs to Nacton.
    The King has the whole of the customary due.

BOSMERE Hundred

56 Roger of Candos holds BATTISFORD from Hugh; Aelfric, a free man, held it before 1066 as a manor; 1 carucate of land.
    Always 8 smallholders.
    Then 2 ploughs in lordship, now 1; ½ men's plough.
    Meadow, 6 acres; woodland at 20 pigs.
    ½ church, 20 acres.
    Now 1 cob, 4 cattle, 12 pigs, 21 sheep, 4 goats.
Value 30s.
To this manor Hugh added 5 free men; 1 carucate of land and 10 acres.
    3 smallholders.
    Then 3 ploughs, now 1½ ploughs.
    Meadow, 6 acres; woodland, 5 pigs.
Value 20s.
    This is by exchange for land of St. Augustine's.
    Roger of Candos holds (this).
    The King and the Earl (have) the jurisdiction.
    It has 10 furlongs in length and 5 in width. Others hold here; 10d in tax.

⁊ In dermo—desduna. Vluricus . I . lib
homo . com̃d . t . r . e . xviii . ac̃ . & dim̃ car̃ . & . ual . ii . fol.
⁊ . vii . d̃.

⁊ CLAINDVNE. H̃. In Weſtrefelda . ten̄ hugo . in dn̄io.
quem tenuit Ordricus lib̃ ho̅ . viii . ac̃ . & ual xvi . den̄ . In Saham
ii . ac̃ tr̃æ de dn̄io . ⁊ ual iiii . den̄.

410 b

⁊ HERTESMere H̃. Acolt. tenuit Gutmundus de ulurico fr̃e ſuo
abb̃e de eli . i . car̃ terræ ⁊ xl . ac̃ . pro man̄ m̃ ten& Rog̅ de candos
de hugone . ſemp . v . uill̃ . ⁊ viii . bord̃ . Tc̃ . ii . ſerui . Tc̃ ⁊ p̃ . ii . carr̃
in dominio . m̃ . i . Tc̃ . ii . car̃ hom̃ . P̃ ⁊ modo . i . ⁊ dim̃ . & . iii . ac̃ p̃ti.
ſilua . xl porc̃ . Ecclia de . viii . ac̃ . ⁊ dim̃ car̃ . ſemp . i . runc̃ . Tc̃ . viii.
an̄ . Tc̃ . lx . porc̃ . modo . xiii . Tc̃ . xl . ou̅s . modo . xxviii . & xxi.
cap̃ . Tc̃ ual . lx . fol . Poſt . iiii . lib̃ . modo . c . fol . Et huic manerio
additi ſunt . viii . lib̃i ho̅es xl . ac̃ . Tc̃ & poſt . ii . car̃ modo . i . & dim̃.
Ecclia xii . ac̃ . ⁊ ual . x . fol . Gudmundus de toto ſoca̅ . ht x . qr̃.
in longo . & . viii . in lato ⁊ . ix . den̄ de gelto ;

411 a

⁊ TRA GOSFRIDI DE MAGNA VILLA.
Stohu . H̃ . In cratinga ten̄ Witgarus lib̃ homo abbis de eli com̄
d̃ tn̄tu̅ . t . r . e . ii . car̃ terræ . in ſoca regis ⁊ comit̃ . Gosfridus ht
p̃ man̄ . ex dono reg̃ . & ſub eo Witt̃mus de boe uilla ſed non per-
tenuit ad feudu̅ anſgari ante c̃ goſfridi . Semp . vi . bord̃ . Semp
ii . car̃ in dn̄io . Tc̃ ⁊ p̃ dim̃ car̃ hominu̅ . m̃ nichil . ⁊ v . ac̃ p̃ti.
⁊ q̃rta pars . i . mol̃ . ⁊ medietas alt̃ri mol̃ . ſemp . ii . equi . in halla
⁊ v . an̄ . & . viii . por̃ . Tc̃ xx . ou̅s . modo xxx . Semp ual x̶x̶x̶ . v . fol.

57 In DARMSDEN Wulfric, 1 free man under patronage before 1066; 18 acres. ½ plough.
Value 2s 7d.

CLAYDON Hundred
58 In WESTERFIELD Hugh holds in lordship what Ordric, a free man, held; 8 acres.
Value 16d.

59 In (Earl) SOHAM 2 acres of land in lordship.
Value 4d.

HARTISMERE Hundred 410 b
60 Guthmund held OCCOLD from his brother Wulfric, the Abbot of Ely; 1 carucate of land and 40 acres as a manor. Now Roger of Candos holds (it) from Hugh.
   Always 5 villagers; 8 smallholders. Then 2 slaves.
   Then and later 2 ploughs in lordship, now 1; then 2 men's ploughs, later and now 1½.
   Meadow, 3 acres; woodland, 40 pigs.
   A church with 8 acres. ½ plough.
   Always 1 cob. Then 8 cattle; then 60 pigs, now 13; then 40 sheep, now 28; 21 goats.
Value then 60s; later £4; now 100s.
To this manor were added 8 free men; 40 acres. Then and later 2 ploughs, now 1½.
   A church, 12 acres.
Value 10s.
   Guthmund (had) jurisdiction over the whole. It has 10 furlongs in length and 8 in width; 9d in tax.

32 LAND OF GEOFFREY DE MANDEVILLE 411 a

STOW Hundred
1 In CREETING (St. Peter) Withgar, a free man of the Abbot of Ely's under patronage only, in the jurisdiction of the King and the Earl, held before 1066; 2 carucates of land. Geoffrey has it as a manor by the King's gift, and William of Bouville under him; but it did not belong to the Holding of Asgar, Geoffrey's predecessor.
   Always 6 smallholders.
   Always 2 ploughs in lordship. Then and later ½ men's plough, now nothing.
   Meadow, 5 acres; the fourth part of one mill, and a half of another mill. Always 2 horses at the hall; 5 cattle, 8 pigs.
   Then 20 sheep, now 30.
Value always 40s.

410 a, b, 411 a

7 in ead . v . libi homines eide Witg comd tntu . ix . ac terræ in foca
regis 7 comit . & dim car . & ual& . ii . fol . In eod man . i . lib ho
edrici . antec . Rotbti mal& comd tant . modo ten Willm de
boeuilla fub gosfrido . 7 ht . xvi . ac . & . i . bord . & dim car . & . i . ac
pti . 7 ual& . xxx . vi . den .

CLAINDVNE . H̃ . In Weftrefelda tenuit Langfere
lib ho comd haldein xiiii . ac . & ual . ii . fol . Id Will . Rex 7 coms
foca . *SANFORT . H̃ .* 7 dim . Holetuna ten Aufgar .
t . r . e . ii . car terræ . p man . femp . xiii . uill . & . ii . bord . Tc . iiii . feru .
modo . iii . femp . ii . car in dominio . Tc . v . car hom . modo . iii . &
xxiiii . ac prati . Eclia . Tc . ii . runc . modo . i . & . ii . an . Tc . xii .
porc . modo . vi . Tc lx . ous . m lxxiiii . Tc ual . lx . fol . m . xl .
ht . vi . qr in longo . & . iiii . in lato . 7 . vii . den de gelto . Id Aufgar foca .
Reinduna ten& . Angar . ii . car terræ . p man . t . r . e . femp
viii . uilli . & . iii . bord . & . iii . feru . & . ii . car in dominio . Tc . vii .
car hom . modo . iiii . vi . ac pti . filu . xvi . porc . Tc . ii . runc .

modo . i . Semp . v . an . & . xii . porc . Tc . xxx . ous . modo . l . Semp ual
viii . lib . In dnio . *De* eade terra ten& Aluredus . i . uill . de
xxx . ac . 7 ual& . v . fol . Angarus foca . Dead terra ten& Gislebt
pbr . i . uill . de . xxx . ac . 7 dimid car . & ual . v . fol .

In the same (Creeting St. Peter) 5 free men of the same Withgar's under patronage only, in the jurisdiction of the King and the Earl; 9 acres of land. ½ plough.
Value 2s.
In the same manor 1 free man belonging to Edric, Robert Malet's predecessor, under patronage only. Now William of Bouville holds (him) under Geoffrey. He has 16 acres.
   1 smallholder.
   ½ plough. Meadow, 1 acre.
Value 26d.

CLAYDON Hundred
2 In WESTERFIELD Langfer, a free man under the patronage of Haldane, held 14 acres.
Value 2s.
   William also [holds this].
   The King and the Earl (have) the jurisdiction.

SAMFORD Hundred and a Half
3 Asgar held HOLTON (St. Mary) before 1066; 2 carucates of land as a manor.
   Always 13 villagers; 2 smallholders. Then 4 slaves, now 3.
   Always 2 ploughs in lordship. Then 5 men's ploughs, now 3.
   Meadow, 24 acres.
   A church. Then 2 cobs, now 1; 2 cattle; then 12 pigs, now 6; then 60 sheep, now 74.
Value then 60s; now 40[s].
   It has 6 furlongs in length and 4 in width; 7d in tax. Asgar also (had) the jurisdiction.

4 Asgar [held] RAYDON; 2 carucates of land as a manor before 1066.
   Always 8 villagers; 3 smallholders; 3 slaves;
   2 ploughs in lordship. Then 7 men's ploughs, now 4.
   Meadow, 6 acres; woodland, 16 pigs. Then 2 cobs, now 1. Always 5 cattle; 12 pigs. Then 30 sheep, now 50.
Value always £8.
   (It is) in lordship.
Of the same land, Alfred holds 1 villager with 30 acres.
Value 5s.
   Asgar (had) the jurisdiction.
Of the same land, Gilbert the priest holds 1 villager with 30 acres.
½ plough.
Value 5s.

ꝑ In belesteda tenuit Olf. & adhuc ten& lib hō.t.r.e.cōm
dt̅ Ansgaro. LXXX,ac̄.semp.I.uill.&.II.bord.Tc̄.I.car.modo
dim.& II.ac̄ p̄ti.Tc̄.I.molin. Quarta pars æccliæ.Tc uat.x.sol
modo.VII. Soca in bcolt.

ꝑ Scottunā teñ Rainelmus ten& de Gosfr. quā tenuit frieber-
nus teinnus reḡ.t.r.e.II.terræ.ꝑ mañ.semper.II.uill.&.x.
bord.Tc̄.II.seru.modo.semp.I.car in dominio.&.I.car hom.
&.IIII.ac̄ p̄ti. Tercia paRs eccliæ.de xv.ac̄.m̊.VII.añ.Tc̄.II.por.
modo.XIII. 7 LX.ous. 7.I.sat. 7.II.uasa apū.& uat.sol.ht.VI.
qr̄ in longo.& IIII.qr̄ in lato.&.IIII.deñ.de gl.Id Frieb.soca

ꝑ In Gipe Wiz.I.mansurā.& ꝑtin& in mosa.

ꝑ In rienduna.Eduinus. 7 Brictmarus libi homines cōmdti
Ansgaro.t.r.e.&.dim.car. 7 uat.v.sot. Soca in bcolt.

ꝑ H̄.DE WILEFORD. In cerefelda.I.liba femina. Le
ueua cōmdatus. Haldeini.t.r.e.xxx.ac̄. 7 II.bord.Semp
.I.car.II.ac̄ p̄ti.Tc̄ & semp uat.x.sot. In ead.I.lib homo
cōmdatus eidē.XI.ac̄.& uat.II.sot.

ꝑ In depeBek.I.lib hō.cōmd.cuiusdā cōm.R.stalra.VI.ac̄.
& uat.XII.deñ. ꝑ In bulges.I.lib hō.cōm.haldeini XVI.ac̄.
Tc̄.I.car.modo.II.bou. 7 uat.II.sot. In ead.I.lib homo cōmd.

Haldeini. 7 Vlurici.VI.ac̄.& uat.XII.deñ.

5 In BELSTEAD Vlf, a free man under the patronage of Asgar before 1066, held and still holds 80 acres.
    Always 1 villager; 2 smallholders.
    Then 1 plough, now ½.
    Meadow, 2 acres. Then 1 mill.
    The fourth part of a church.
    Value then 10s; now 7[s].
    The jurisdiction (is) in (East) Bergholt.

6 Rainalm holds STUTTON; he holds (it) from Geoffrey. Fridebern, a thane of the King's, held it before 1066; 2 [carucates] of land as a manor.
    Always 2 villagers; 10 smallholders. Then 2 slaves, now .... .
    Always 1 plough in lordship; 1 men's plough. Meadow, 4 acres.
    The third part of a church with 15 acres.
    Now 7 cattle; then 2 pigs, now 13; 60 sheep; 1 salt-house; 2 beehives.
    Value 40s.
    It has 6 furlongs in length and 4 furlongs in width; 4d in tax.
    Fridebern also (had) the jurisdiction.

7 In IPSWICH 1 dwelling; it belongs to Moze.

8 In RAYDON Edwin and Brictmer, free men under the patronage of Asgar before 1066; 15 acres. ½ plough.
    Value 5s.
    The jurisdiction (is) in (East) Bergholt.

Hundred of WILFORD

9 In CHARSFIELD 1 free woman, Leofeva, under the patronage of Haldane before 1066; 30 acres.
    2 smallholders.
    Always 1 plough. Meadow, 2 acres.
    Value then and always 10s.
    In the same (Charsfield) 1 free man under the patronage of the same man; 11 acres.
    Value 2s.

10 In DEBACH 1 free man under the patronage of someone under the patronage of R(alph) the Constable; 6 acres.
    Value 12d.

11 In BOULGE 1 free man under the patronage of Haldane; 16 acres.
    Then 1 plough, now 2 oxen.
    Value 2s.
    In the same (Boulge) 1 free man under the patronage of Haldane and of Wulfric; 6 acres.
    Value 12d.

℣ In Wikam . I . lib̃ homo com̃end' heldeini . III . ac̃ . & ual& . VI . deñ ;
℣ In meltuna . II . libi hões . com̃d' . heldeini . IIII . ac̃ . & ual& . VIII . deñ.
h̃ ten& . W . fili' fahuala . de . G . de magna uilla.

℣ . H̃. DE LOSA. Ledringaham tenuit . haldeinus . t . r . e . heroldi.
LXXX . ac̃ ꝑ mañ . Tc̃ . V . bord' . modo . X . Tc̃ . I . feru . modo . II . Semp
in dominio . II . car' . 7 hoũ . II . car' . Silua ad . IIII . porc' . VI . ac̃ p̃ti . I . mot.
Semp . II . run' . 7 . VI . añ . 7 XXX . porc' . 7 LXXX . cap̃ . 7 . V . uafa apũ . I.
æcclia . de XX . ac̃ . 7 ual . XL . d' . Tc̃ ual& . XX . fol . modo fimil.
In ead' . XIII . libi hões 7 . II . dim' . com̃d' eid' . p̃t . VI . fueŕ com̃d' . S̃ . æ-
deldrýde . LX . ac̃ . Semp . IIII . car' . II . ac̃ p̃ti . Tc̃ ual XVII . fol . m̃ fimil.
Adhuc in ead' . I . lib̃ hõ . com' dim' S̃ æ . 7 dim' haldeini . LX . ac̃ . ꝑ mañ
7 II . bord' . 7 . I . car' . IIII . ac̃ p̃ti . Semp ual . XX . fol.
℣ In udebrige . II . libi hões com̃d' eid̃ haldeini . XXXIII . ac̃ . & dim'
car' . & . I . bord' . & ual . III . fol . h̃ ten& id̃ . Wiłłmus . de . G . de magna uilł.
℣ WAINEFORDA . H̃ . Scadena fella . ten& haldein . lib̃ homo . co
m̃d' heroldi . I . car' terræ ꝑ mañ . Semp . I . uiłł . 7 X . bord' . Tc̃ in dñio . II.
car' . modo . II . Semp hoũ . I . car' . IIII . ac̃ p̃ti . filua ad . XX . porc' . & . I . ru'.
& . XI . porc' . 7 LXXX . oũs . 7 . II . uafa apũ . Tc̃ ual& . X . fol . modo . XX.

12 In WICKHAM (Market) 1 free man under the patronage of Haldane; 3 acres.
Value 6d.

13 In MELTON 2 free men under the patronage of Haldane; 4 acres.
Value 8d.
W(illiam) son of Saxwalo holds this from Geoffrey de Mandeville.

Hundred of LOES

14 Haldane held LETHERINGHAM before 1066 under the patronage of Harold; 80 acres as a manor.
Then 5 smallholders, now 10. Then 1 slave, now 2.
Always 2 ploughs in lordship; 2 men's ploughs.
Woodland for 4 pigs; meadow, 6 acres. 1 mill. Always 2 cobs, 6 cattle, 30 pigs, 80 goats, 5 beehives.
1 church with 20 acres; value 40d.
Value then 20s; now the same.
In the same (Letheringham) 13 free men and two half (free men) under the patronage of the same man, except for 6 who were under the patronage of St. Etheldreda's; 60 acres. Always 4 ploughs.
Meadow, 2 acres.
Value then 17s; now the same.
Also in the same (Letheringham) 1 free man half under the patronage of St. Etheldreda's and half (under that) of Haldane; 60 acres as a manor.
2 smallholders;
1 plough. Meadow, 4 acres.
Value always 20s.

15 In WOODBRIDGE 2 free men under the patronage of the same Haldane; 33 acres. ½ plough.
1 smallholder.
Value 3s.
William also holds this from Geoffrey de Mandeville.

WANGFORD Hundred

16 Haldane, a free man under the patronage of Harold, [held] SHADINGFIELD; 1 carucate of land as a manor.
Always 1 villager; 10 smallholders.
Then 2 ploughs in lordship, now 2; always 1 men's plough.
Meadow, 4 acres; woodland for 20 pigs. 1 cob, 11 pigs, 80 sheep, 2 beehives.
Value then 10s; now 20[s].

In ead̃.ı.lib̃ hõ com̃d̃.Stigandi ẽpi.ı.car̃.terræ.ꝑ mañ.Tc̃.ı.uill
modo fimilit̃.Tc̃.v.bord̃.modo.ıııı.Tc̃ in dominio.ı.car̃.Tc̃ hoũ.ıı.
car̃.modo.ı.Tc̃ ual&.xx.fol̃.m̃ fimilit̃.Hic hõ fuit derationatus
⁊ faiatus ad opus regis. ⁊ poftea faifiuit.eũ Waleram̃. ⁊ inde dedit uadẽ.
Adhuc in ead̃.ıı.libi hões cm̃d̃ haldeini.xxxıı.ac̃ ⁊ dim̃ ꝑ mañ.Semp

412 b

dim̃ car̃.& ual̃.v.fol̃.⁊.vııı.d̃.
⸿In Weftuna.ı.lib̃ hõ.v.ac̃.⁊ ual& xvı.d̃.⸿In Wichedis.ı.lib̃ hõ.ı.ac̃.&
ual&.ıııı.d̃.⸿.H̃.DE BLIDIGGA.Turintuna ten& aldenus
t.r.e.ııı.car̃ terræ ꝑ mañ.Tc̃ vııı.bord̃.modo.xııı.femp.ıı.ferũ.
Tc̃.ıı.car̃ in dñio.modo.ııı.femp.ııı.car̃ hoũ.filua ad xx.porc̃.
vıı.ac̃ p̃ti.Tc̃.ı.runc̃.modo.ıı.⁊ modo.xıııı.porc̃.Tc̃ lx ⁊ xıı.oũs.
modo.q̃t xx ⁊ xıı.⁊ modo.ıııı.uafa ap̃u.⁊ xv.cap̃.⁊.ı.molin̄.⁊
.ı.æcclia de.vııı.ac̃.Tc̃ ual xl.fol̃.modo lx.Willmus de boe uilla
ten& de.G.de magna uilla.⁊ non ẽ de honore Anfgari.
⸿Huic manerio iac&.ıı.libi hões.de.c.ac̃.⁊ xx.terræ.ıı.bordarii
ıııı.ac̃ p̃ti.Tc̃.ıı.car̃ in dñio.m̃ null.Tc̃ ual.ı.marcã.m̃.vııı.fol̃.
Il terra ht̃.ı.lg̃.& dim̃ in long̃.⁊ in latũ leugã & dim̃.⁊ vıı.d̃
& obolũ reddit de geldo.
⸿In norhals.xx.ac̃ terræ.q̃s teñ.ı.lib̃ homo.t.r.e.de ftigando.
modo teñ.W.de boe uilla.de.G.de magna uilla.femp dim̃.car̃.
⁊ ual.ıııı.fol̃.
⸿.H̃.DE CARLEFORDA.In torp tenet halden lib̃ hõ.t.r.e.
.ııı.car̃ terræ.ꝑ mañ.Semp.ıııı.uill.⁊ xı.bord̃.Tc̃ ıı.ferũ.modo.
.ı.Semp in dñio ıı.car̃.Tc̃ hoũ.ıı.car̃.modo.ı.vıı.ac̃ p̃ti.&.ıı.
runc̃.⁊ vıı.añ.⁊ xıı.porc̃.⁊.c.oũs.Tc̃ ual xx.fol̃.modo.xl.&

In the same (Shadingfield) 1 free man under the patronage of Bishop Stigand; 1 carucate of land as a manor.
   Then 1 villager, now the same; then 5 smallholders, now 4.
   Then 1 plough in lordship; then 2 men's ploughs, now 1.
   Value then 20s; now the same.
   This (free) man was adjudged and taken for the King's use; later on Waleran was in possession of him and gave a pledge for him.
   Also in the same (Shadingfield) 2 free men under the patronage of Haldane; 32½ acres as a manor. Always ½ plough.
   Value 5s 8d.

412 b

17 In WESTON 1 free man; 5 acres.
   Value 16d.

18 In WICHEDIS 1 free man; 1 acre.
   Value 4d.

Hundred of BLYTHING

19 Haldane [held] THORINGTON before 1066; 3 carucates of land as a manor.
   Then 8 smallholders, now 13; always 2 slaves.
   Then 2 ploughs in lordship, now 3; always 3 men's ploughs.
   Woodland for 20 pigs; meadow, 7 acres. Then 1 cob, now 2; now 14 pigs; then 60 and 12 sheep, now fourscore and 12; now 4 beehives; 15 goats. 1 mill.
   1 church with 8 acres.
   Value then 40s; now 60[s].
   William of Bouville holds (this) from Geoffrey de Mandeville. It is not (part) of Asgar's Honour.
   To this manor belong 2 free men, with 120 acres and 20 of land.
   2 smallholders.
   Meadow, 4 acres.
   Then 2 ploughs in lordship, now none.
   Value then 1 mark of silver; now 8s.
   This land has 1½ leagues in length and 1½ leagues in width; it pays 7½d in tax.

20 In COVEHITHE 20 acres of land which 1 free man held from Stigand before 1066. Now W(illiam) of Bouville holds (it) from Geoffrey de Mandeville. Always ½ plough.
   Value 4s.

Hundred of CARLFORD

21 In THORPE Haldane, a free man, [held] before 1066; 3 carucates of land.
   Always 4 villagers; 11 smallholders. Then 2 slaves, now 1.
   Always 2 ploughs in lordship. Then 2 men's ploughs, now 1.
   Meadow, 7 acres. 2 cobs, 7 cattle, 12 pigs, 100 sheep.
   Value then 20s; now 40[s].

412 a, b

hr̄ in longo . VIII . qr̃ . 7 VI . in lat̃ . & . XV . đ . de gelt̃ . Alii ibi tenent.
/ In burcg . VIII . libi hões . cõmđ eid . halden . LIIII . āc . Semper
II . car̃ . II . āc prati . 7 ual̃ . X . fol̃ .
/ In grundes burg . IIII . libi hões cõmđ . halden . T . r . e . de XXVI . āc

413 a

trrę . 7 . I . car̃ . dim̃ āc p̃ti . 7 ual̃ . IIII . fol̃ . In eađ . I . lib̃ hō . Almarus
cõmđ Eilrici de burg . de . VIII . āc . dim̃ āc prati . 7 ual̃ XVI . đ .
/ In hafhetuna . III . dim̃ hões . 7 . I . integrũ . cõm halden . t . r . e . de XXII
āc . terrę . & . I . car̃ . & dim̃ āc p̃ti . & ual̃ . III . fol̃ .
★ / In netkemara . II . libi hões cõmđ . Alden . de XX . āc . 7 dim̃ car̃ . dim̃ āc
p̃ti . & ual̃ . II . fol̃ . / In ingolueftuna . I . lib̃ homo . Godric cõm dimiđ
halden . 7 dim̃ . Sc̃a . Æ . XX . āc terrę . II . āc p̃ti . & ual̃ . II . fol̃ .
/ In Ifleueftuna . I . fochemañ . halden . XV . āc . & . I . borđ . Tc̃ . I . car̃ . modo
. I . bou . I . āc p̃ti . 7 ual̃ . II . fol̃ . In burg . III . libi hões . t . r . e . cõmđ hal
den . L . āc terre . Tc̃ . II . car̃ . m̃ . I . I . āc 7 dim̃ p̃ti . 7 ual̃ . X . fol̃ . In eađ
. I . lib̃ hō . Brichtricus . cõmđ Alric deburch . X . āc . 7 ual̃ . XX . đ . Adhuc
in eađ . I . lib̃ hō . Brihtuoldus mufla . cõmđ dim̃ . ante c̃ . herueu
deberũ . 7 dim̃ ante c̃ . R . mal& . XXIIII . āc . Tc̃ . I . car̃ . modo ñ . I . āc p̃ti .

It has 8 furlongs in length and 6 in width; 15d in tax. Others hold there.

22 In BURGH 8 free men under the patronage of the same Haldane; 54 acres. Always 2 ploughs.
   Meadow, 2 acres.
   Value 10s.

23 In GRUNDISBURGH 4 free men under the patronage of Haldane before 1066, with 26 acres of land. 1 plough.
   Meadow, ½ acre.
   Value 4s.
   In the same (Grundisburgh) 1 free man, Aelmer, under the patronage of Aethelric of Burgh, with 8 acres.
   Meadow, ½ acre.
   Value 16d.

413 a

24 In HASKETON 3 half (free) men and 1 whole (free man) under the patronage of Haldane before 1066, with 22 acres of land. 1 plough.
   Meadow, ½ acre.
   Value 3s.

25 In [NECKEMARA] 2 free men under the patronage of Haldane, with 20 acres. ½ plough.
   Meadow, ½ acre.
   Value 2s.

26 In INGOLUESTUNA 1 free man, Godric, half under the patronage of Haldane and half (under that) of St. Etheldreda's; 20 acres of land.
   Meadow, 2 acres.
   Value 2s.

27 In ISLETON 1 Freeman of Haldane's; 15 acres.
   1 smallholder.
   Then 1 plough, now 1 ox. Meadow, 1 acre.
   Value 2s.

28 In BURGH 3 free men before 1066 under the patronage of Haldane; 50 acres of land. Then 2 ploughs, now 1.
   Meadow, 1½ acres.
   Value 10s.
   In the same (Burgh) 1 free man, Brictric, under the patronage of Aethelric of Burgh; 10 acres.
   Value 20d.
   Also in the same (Burgh) 1 free man, Brictwold Muffle, half under the patronage of Hervey of Berry's predecessor and half (under that of) R(obert) Malet's predecessor; 24 acres. Then 1 plough, now none.
   Meadow, 1 acre.

412 b, 413 a

7 uat. v. fot. & fit in longo. ix qr. & vii. in lato. 7 xv. d de gelt. Alii ibi tenent. ⁊In culfola. iii. libi hoes. ii. com halden. & 7 icius com. Scæ Edeld. xxx. ac træ &. i. bord. Tc. ii. car. modo nulla. ii. ac pti. & uat. v. fot.

⁊In hobbeſtuna. i. lib ho comd. e. 7 uxor ei. comd. halden. t. r. e. xxx. ac. Tc. i. car. modo. n. i. ac pti. Semp uat. v. fot. In ead. i. foc. Topi. com S. æ. xv. 7 uat. iii. fot.

⁊In finlesforda. ii. ac. halden. t. r. e. 7 uat. iiii. d. fi totu ten&. Willm fili fahala debou uilla. de. G. de magna uilla. sca. Æ. p tota focha huius hundreti;

413 b

.XXXIII.⁊ TRÆ RADVLFI. BAIGNARDI. RISEBRVGE. H.

Kiditunam tenuit Ailad. t. r. e. p man. v. car. terræ. Tc & p xiii. uill. modo. xi. Tc & p. i. bord. modo. ii. Tc & p. ix. fer. modo nullus. Tc & p. iii. car in dominio. modo. ii. Tc & p. viii. car hominum. modo. ii. & dim. xx. ac. pti. Tc. i. molin. Tc. iiii. runc. modo. iii. Tc. xv. an. modo. iiii. Tc xxvii. porc. modo. xviii. Tc. lii. ous. modo. c. l. modo. vi. uafa apu. Tc uat. vi. lib. modo vii. &. v. fot.

Value 5s.
It has 9 furlongs in length and 7 in width; 15d in tax. Others hold there.

29 In CULPHO 3 free men, 2 under the patronage of Haldane and the third under the patronage of St. Etheldreda's; 30 acres of land.
1 smallholder.
Then 2 ploughs, now none. Meadow, 2 acres.
Value 5s.

30 In *HOBBESTUNA* 1 free man under the patronage of (St.) E(theldreda's) and his wife under the patronage of Haldane before 1066; 30 acres.
Then 1 plough, now none.
Meadow, 1 acre.
Value always 5s.
In the same (*Hobbestuna*) 1 Freeman, Topi, under the patronage of St. Etheldreda's; 15 acres.
Value 3s.

31 In 'FINLESFORDA' 2 acres; Haldane [held it] before 1066.
Value 4d.
William son of Saxwalo of Bouville holds the whole of this from Geoffrey de Mandeville.
St. Etheldreda's (has) the whole of the jurisdiction of this Hundred.

33 THE LANDS OF RALPH BAYNARD 413 b

RISBRIDGE Hundred
1 Aethelgyth held KEDINGTON before 1066 as a manor; 5 carucates of land.
Then and later 13 villagers, now 11; then and later 1 smallholder, now 2; then and later 9 slaves, now none.
Then and later 3 ploughs in lordship, now 2; then and later 8 men's ploughs, now 2½.
Meadow, 20 acres; then 1 mill. Then 4 cobs, now 3; then 15 cattle, now 4; then 27 pigs, now 18; then 52 sheep, now 150; now 6 beehives.
Value then £6; now [£] 7 5s.

In Ead̄ xxv. libi hōes. ii. cař terræ. &. v. bord. &. ii. ferū. femp
xi. cař. 7 vi. ac̄ p̃ti. & ual xl fol. fuus ante c̄ com̄d 7 focā &
facā. p̄t vi. forisfacturas sc̄i eadmundi. & de uno habuit ante
c̄. Ricardi filii gisleḃti. comitis com̄d. S 7 baign totū reclamat
p efcangio. Ecc̄lia de. xl ac̄ libæ træ. 7. i. ac̄ & dim̄ p̃ti. 7 ual. vi.
fol. ħt in longo xii. qr̄. 7 vi. in lato. 7 xii. den̄. de gelto. Alii ibi tenēt.

In Poflingewrda. iii. libi. hōes. de iftis duob; habuit fuus antec̄
com̄. t. r. e. 7 focā & facā. p̄t vi. forisfact. sc̄i. e. 7 idē. sc̄s eadmund
com̄ de tc̄io. t. r. e. & rex conceflit ei. t̄ra. ex ħ uidimus breuē
& lint. i. cař terræ. &. xx. ac̄. &. vii. bord. &. i. cař & dim̄. filua de
. v. porc̄. femp ual xxx. i. fol. In eadē. i. lib̄ .hō. i. cař terræ & dimid. femp. vi. bord. 7. i. cař in dn̄io. ħ ten̄ Noriolt. Tc̄. ii. run̄.
7 modo fimilit̄. 7 vi. an̄. 7 xvi. porc̄. &. xx. ōus. Tc̄ ual xx. fol.
modo xxv. In ead. i. lib̄ hō. i. cař terre & dim̄. &. iii. bord.
7. i. cař & dim̄. &. iiii. ac̄ p̃ti. modo. ii. runc̄. 7. iiii. an̄. 7 xx.
porc̄. 7 xxviiii. ōus ħ ten̄. Walt. 7 ual. xxx. fol. In ead. ii.
libi hōes. c. lx. ac̄. 7 viii. bord 7. i. cař. 7 ual xxvi. fol. &. viii. d.

414 a

H ten & Ricer̃. Ecc̄lia. xl. ac̄ libæ terræ & ual. vi. fol. Sc̄s. e. vi.
forisfacturas. baign̄. focā. ħt xiii. qr̄ in longo. 7 xii. in lato.
& xv. d. de gelto. Alii. ibi tenent. ħ eft p efcangio.

In the same (Kedington) 25 free men; 2 carucates of land.
5 smallholders; 2 slaves.
Always 11 ploughs. Meadow, 6 acres.
Value 40s.

His predecessor (had) the patronage and the full jurisdiction, except for the 6 forfeitures of St. Edmund's; and of one, the predecessor of Richard son of Count Gilbert had the patronage. But Baynard claims the whole by exchange.

A church with 40 acres of free land. Meadow, 1½ acres. Value 6s.

It has 12 furlongs in length and 6 in width; 12d in tax. Others hold there.

2 In POSLINGFORD 3 free men. Of these, his predecessor had the patronage over two before 1066 and the full jurisdiction, except for the 6 forfeitures of St. Edmund's; St. Edmund's also had patronage over the third before 1066. The King granted the land to him; and we have seen the writ for this. They have 1 carucate of land and 20 acres.
7 smallholders.
1½ ploughs. Woodland at 5 pigs.
Value always 31s.
In the same (Poslingford) 1 free man; 1½ carucates of land.
Always 6 smallholders;
1 plough in lordship.
Norigold holds this.
Then 2 cobs, now the same; 6 cattle, 16 pigs, 20 sheep.
Value then 20s; now 25[s].
In the same (Poslingford) 1 free man; 1½ carucates of land.
3 smallholders.
1½ ploughs.
Meadow, 4 acres. Now 2 cobs, 4 cattle, 20 pigs, 29 sheep.
Walter holds this.
Value 30s.
In the same (Poslingford) 2 free men; 160 acres of land.
8 smallholders.
1 plough.
Value 26s 8d.
Richere holds this.
A church, 40 acres of free land; value 6s.
St. Edmund's (has) the 6 forfeitures; Baynard (has) the jurisdiction. It has 13 furlongs in length and 12 in width; 15d in tax. Others hold there.
This is by exchange.

ꝻWlteſkeou ten&. Godwinus. teinnus. t. r. e. ꝑ manꝫ. III. car̃ terre.
& xv. ac̄. ſemp. vi. uiłł. Tc̄. IIII. borđ. modo. v. Tc̄. vi. ſerū. modo.
. IIII. Tc̄ 7 p̊ III. car̃ in dominio. modo. II. ſemp. II. car̊. & diṁ
homꝫ. ſilua. x. porc̃. XII. ac̄ p̃ti. ſemp. I. molin̄. Tc̄. II. runc̃.
Tc̄. XXIIII. an̄. modo XII. Tc̄ XL porc̃. modo. XII. Tc̄ LX. ous̄. modo
XL. &. v. uaſa apū. Ectia. v. ac̄. &. II. libi hões XXV. ac̄. I. car̃.
&. I. ac̄ p̃ti. Suus ant̄ comđ. 7 ſoc̃. S̊. e. vi. forisfacturas. Tc̄ & p̃
uał LXXX. III. ſoł. & modo ſimiłit̃. ħt dim lḡ in longo. &. III.
qr̃ & dim̃ in lato. 7 III. den̄. de gelto. Alii ibi tenent.
ꝻBIDINGA. H̃. Riendunā ten& Toret. v. car̃ terræ. tc̄ 7 p̊
XIIII. uiłł. modo. v. Tc̄ & p̊ XVI. borđ. modo. XX. Tc̄. II. ſerui.
modo. I. Tc̄ 7 p̊ III. car̃ in dn̄io. modo. II. Tc̄ & p̊. XI. car̃ homꝫ. iñ
VII. ſilua de. LX. porc̃. Tc̄. II. runc̃. modo. I. Tc̄. XII. añ. modo. v.
Tc̄ XL. porc̃. modo. XXX. ſep̃. c. x. ous̄. modo. XV. cap̃. Tc̄ uał. c. ſoł
modo. VII. lib̃. 7 x. ſoł. In ead̃. XXX. libi hões. II. car̃ terre. &. v. ac̄.
&. II. borđ. Tc̄ 7 p̃. VIII. car̃. modo. VI. 7 uał. XII. lib̃. 7 x. ſoł. ex. ħ
ſuus ante c̄ comđ & ſoc̃ & ſacā. t. r. e. In ead̃. II. libi hões comđ
XVI. ac̄. & dim car̃. & uał. x. ſoł. Rex & coms̄ ſocā. hoc eſt ꝑ eſcangio
ħt. I. leug̃. 7. III. qr̃ in longo. 7. I. lḡ in lato. 7. III. pcas. 7. VI. đ
& oboł͞u de gelto. II. eccliæ. I. car̃. tr̃e. uał. x. ſoł.

3 Godwin, a thane, [held] WIXOE before 1066 as a manor; 3 carucates of land and 15 acres.
  Always 6 villagers. Then 4 smallholders, now 5; then 6 slaves, now 4.
  Then and later 3 ploughs in lordship, now 2; always 2½ men's ploughs.
  Woodland, 10 pigs; meadow, 12 acres; always 1 mill. Then 2 cobs; then 24 cattle, now 12; then 40 pigs, now 12; then 60 sheep, now 40; 5 beehives.
  A church, 5 acres.
Also 2 free men; 25 acres. 1 plough.
  Meadow, 1 acre.
  His predecessor (had) the patronage and jurisdiction; St. Edmund's (had) the 6 forfeitures.
Value then and later 83s; now the same.
  It has ½ league in length and 3½ furlongs in width; 3d in tax.
Others hold there.

BLYTHING Hundred
4 Thored [held] REYDON; 5 carucates of land.
  Then and later 14 villagers, now 5; then and later 16 smallholders, now 20; then 2 slaves, now 1.
  Then and later 3 ploughs in lordship, now 2; then and later 11 men's ploughs, now 7.
  Woodland at 60 pigs. Then [3] cobs, now 1; then 12 cattle, now 5; then 40 pigs, now 30; always 110 sheep; now 15 goats.
Value then 100s; now £7 10s.
In the same (Reydon) 30 free men; 2 carucates of land.
  2 smallholders.
  Then and later 8 ploughs, now 6.
Value £12 10s.
  Over these (free men) his predecessor had patronage and full jurisdiction before 1066.
In the same (Reydon) 2 free men under patronage; 16 acres. ½ plough.
Value 10s.
  The King and the Earl (have) the jurisdiction.
  This is by exchange.
  It has 1 league and 3 furlongs in length and 1 league and 3 perches in width; 6½d in tax.
  2 churches, 1 carucate of land; value 10s.

͡ In brantuna . xi . libi hōes comd̄ . t . r . e . m̄ . x . ii . car̄ tr̄æ.

& lx ac̄ . Tc̄ . ii . uilł . modo . i . Tc̄ viii . bord̄ . modo xvii . Tc̄ . ix . car̄ . m̄ vii . filua xx . porc̄ . & . ii . ac̄ p̄ti . Tc̄ ual̄ xxx . fol̄ . modo xl . Rex & coms̄ foc̄ . p escangio . In ead̄ . i . foc̄ . ii . car̄ terre . & . ii . uilł . & . viii . bord̄ . & . iii . car̄ . filua . iii . porc̄ . & . ii . ac̄ p̄ti . & ual̄ & xxx . fol̄ . Ecclia xvi . ac̄ . 7 ual̄ . xvi . d̄ . Rex & coms̄ focā.

͡ Froxedena ten& toret . p man̄ . iii . car̄ terræ . t . r . e . femp x . uilli . Tc̄ xiiii . bord̄ . modo . xx . Tc̄ . ii . feru̅ . femp . ii . car̄ in dominio . femp . i . port maris . Tc̄ & p̄ ix . car̄ hom̄ . modo . vii . filu̅ xl porc̄ . Tc̄ . i . nulla . & . iii . ac̄ p̄ti . Tc̄ . ii . runc̄ . modo . i . Tc̄ . x . an̄ . modo . vi . Tc̄ lx . porc̄ . m̄ xiii . 7 lx . ous̄ . 7 xx . iiii . cap̄ . 7 . ii . uafa apū . femp ual̄ . iiii . lib̄ . Rex 7 Coms̄ focā vi . forisfacturas . In ead̄ . viii . libi hōes . t . r . e . modo . iii . c . xiii . ac̄ . Tc̄ . iii . car̄ . modo . i . & dim̄ ac̄ p̄ti . Tc̄ ual̄ . x . fol̄ . m̄ . xiiii . p escagio . Rex & Coms̄ focā . In longo . i . lḡ . 7 xx . iiii . pcas . 7 in lat̄ . x . qr̄ & . vii . pcas . 7 . iiii . d̄ . de gelto . Ran̄ ten̄ . ii . eccliæ . xxviii . ac̄ . ual̄ . iii . fol̄

͡ Wankefordā ten̄ . Toret . p man̄ . t . r . e . ii . car̄ terræ femp . viii . uilł . Tc̄ & poft . xiii . bord̄ . modo . xxi . Tc̄ . ii . feru̅ . femp ii . car̄ in dn̄io . Tc̄ . viii . car̄ hom̄ . m̄ . vii . filua lx . porc̄ . & . ii . ac̄ prati . femp . i . mol̄ . Tc̄ . i . falina . Tc̄ . ii . runc̄ . Tc̄ xxiiii . an̄ . m̄ . xvii . Tc̄ . xxx . v . porc̄.

5 In BRAMPTON 11 free men under patronage before 1066, now 10; 2 carucates of land and 60 acres.

414 b

>Then 2 villagers, now 1; then 8 smallholders, now 17.
>Then 9 ploughs, now 7.
>Woodland, 20 pigs; meadow, 2 acres.
>Value then 30s; now 40[s].
>The King and the Earl (have) the jurisdiction.
>(This is) by exchange.

In the same (Brampton) 1 Freeman; 2 carucates of land.
>2 villagers; 8 smallholders.
>3 ploughs.
>Woodland, 3 pigs; meadow, 2 acres.

Value 30s.
>A church, 16 acres; value 16d.
>The King and the Earl (have) the jurisdiction.

6 Thored [held] FROSTENDEN as a manor; 3 carucates of land before 1066.
>Always 10 villagers. Then 14 smallholders, now 20; then 2 slaves.
>Always 2 ploughs in lordship. Always 1 seaport. Then and later 9 men's ploughs, now 7.
>Woodland, 40 pigs; then 1 salt-house, now none; meadow, 3 acres. Then 2 cobs, now 1; then 10 cattle, now 6; then 60 pigs, now 13; 60 sheep, 24 goats, 2 beehives.

Value always £4.
>The King and the Earl (have) the 6 forfeitures.

In the same (Frostenden) 8 free men before 1066, now 3; 113 acres. Then 3 ploughs, now 1.
>Meadow, ½ acre.

Value then 10s; now 14[s].
>(This is) by exchange.

The King and the Earl (have) the jurisdiction. It has 1 league and 24 perches in length, and 10 furlongs and 7 perches in width; 4d in tax.
>Ranulf holds (this).
>2 churches, 28 acres. 1 plough. Value 3s.

7 Thored held WANGFORD as a manor before 1066; 2 carucates of land.
>Always 8 villagers. Then and later 13 smallholders, now 21; then 2 slaves.
>Always 2 ploughs in lordship. Then 8 men's ploughs, now 7.
>Woodland, 60 pigs; meadow, 2 acres; always 1 mill. Then 1 salt-house. Then 2 cobs; then 24 cattle, now 17; then 35 pigs,

modo . xvii . Tc̄ . c . oūs . m̄ lxxx . 7 viii . cap̄ . & . v . uafa apū . ābold .
ten& . femper ual . iiii . lib̄ . jn lōg . i . lḡ . 7 . i . qr̄ . in lat̄ . ix . qr̄ . 7 . vii .
d̄ . de gelto . alii ibi tenent . Rex 7 Coms̄ . vi . forisfacturas.

¶ In henhā . i . lib̄ . homo Aluin c̄md̄ . i . car̄ tr̄æ ,p man̄ . femp̄ . iiii .
uilt . Tc̄ . xi . bord . modo . xiiii . Tc̄ . ii . car̄ in dn̄io . p̄ . i . m̄ . ii . Tc̄ 7
poft . v . car̄ hominū . modo . iii . filu . xl . porc̄ & dim a ͞c prati.

415 a

femp̄ . i . molin̄ . modo . i . runc̄ . 7 . viii . an̄ . Tc̄ . iiii . porc̄ . m̄ . xiiii.
Tc̄ xx . oūs . modo . xl . femp̄ . xvi . cap̄ . modo . iiii . uafa apū . femp̄
ual . xl . fol . Rex 7 coms̄ foca . h̄ ten̄ . Rob̄ de blideburc . h̄ ē ,p efcago.

¶ Blidinga: H̄ . Vpbeftunā . ten̄ . toret . t . r . e . ,p man̄ . iii . car̄ .
: tc̄ . iiii . bor . Poft . v . m̄ . xx . tc̄ . ii . fer' . m̄ . i . tc̄ 7 p' . ii . car' in dn̄io . m̄ . iii.
tr̄æ . Tc̄ xv . uilt . p̄ vii . modo . iii . Tc̄ 7 p̄ ix . car̄ hom . m̄ . x . filua
de . clx . porc̄ . 7 vii . a ͞c p̄ti . Tc̄ . i . runc̄ . modo . ii . Tc̄ xvi . an̄ . modo
xviiii . femp̄ xxx . porc̄ . Tc̄ . xii . oūs . m̄ . lxxxii . femp̄ ual . c . fol.
In huic man̄ iacent . iii . libi hōes de . xlii . a ͞c . 7 . i . bord . 7 . i . car̄ 7 filu
ad xvi . porc̄ . & . i . a ͞c . p̄ti . Tēpore . r . e . ual . vi . fol . 7 viii . d̄ . modo .
viii . fol 7 . i . æcc̄lia . de . iii . a ͞c . 7 ual . iii . d̄ . 7 tota hæc terra hab&
vii . qr̄ in longo . & iiii . in lato . & reddit de geldo regis . iii . den̄.

now 17; then 100 sheep, now 80; 8 goats; 3 beehives.
Anbold holds (this).
Value always £4.
(It has) 1 league and 1 furlong in length, and 9 furlongs in width; 7d in tax. Others hold there. The King and the Earl (have) the 6 forfeitures.

8 In HENHAM 1 free man; Alwin, under patronage; 1 carucate of land as a manor.
Always 4 villagers. Then 11 smallholders, now 14.
Then 2 ploughs in lordship, later 1, now 2; then and later 5 men's ploughs, now 3.
Woodland, 40 pigs; meadow, ½ acre; always 1 mill. Now 1 cob, 8 cattle; then 4 pigs, now 14; then 20 sheep, now 40; always 16 goats. Now 4 beehives.
Value always 40s.
The King and the Earl (have) the jurisdiction.
Robert of Blythburgh holds this. This is by exchange.

BLYTHING Hundred

9 Thored held UBBESTON before 1066 as a manor; 3 carucates of land.
Then 15 villagers, later 7, now 3; then 4 smallholders, later 5, now 20; then 2 slaves, now 1.
Then and later 2 ploughs in lordship, now 3; then and later 9 men's ploughs, now 10.
Woodland at 160 pigs; meadow, 7 acres. Then 1 cob, now 2; then 16 cattle, now 19; always 30 pigs. Then 12 sheep, now 92.
Value always 100s.
In this manor belong 3 free men, with 42 acres.
1 smallholder.
1 plough.
Woodland for 16 pigs; meadow, 1 acre.
Value before 1066, 6s 8d; now 8s.
1 church with 3 acres; value 3d.
The whole of this land has 7 furlongs in length and 4 in width; it pays 3d in the King's tax.

415 a

414 b, 415 a

In Cratafelda tenuit tored̃. T.r.e. III. car̃ & dim̃. terræ. p man̄. semp. v. uill. Tc̃ & p. IX. bord. 7 m̃o. XXXI. senp. I. ser̃. sep. in dn̄io . II. car̃. Tc̃ hom̃. VII. car̃. modo. x. filua ad. cc. & dim̃ porc̃. III. ac̃ & dim̃ p̃ti. Tc̃ 7 modo. I. runc̃. Tc̃. VIII. an̄. modo. XIIII. Tc̃ XL. porc̃. modo XLVII. Tc̃ XX. VI. cap̃. modo. XXXII. 7. I. æcclia. de. VI. ac̃. 7 ual. VI. d. semp. IIII. lib. 7 huic manerio iacent. v. franci. hões. de XXVI. ac̃. 7 semp. II. car̃. & filua ad VI. porc̃. 7 ual. VI. sol. 7 VIII. den̄. Et isti redd soca huic man̄ p̃terea. II. hões. de. XL. ac̃. 7. I. car̃. 7 ual v. sol. 7 soca de istis duob; in bledeburc. Et has. II. mansiones ten& uuilielmus bainardus de radulfo auunculo ei. In ead uilla ten& quidã francus. I. Man̄. de. XL. ac̃. 7. III. bord. semp. I. car̃. filua ad VI. porc̃. . I. ac̃ & dim̃ p̃ti. T. R. e. ual. x. sol. modo. XX. Et istud man̄ est in dn̄iũ radulfi. Et tota h̃ terra h̃t. VIII. qr in longo. 7. v. in lato. 7 reddit

415 b
de gelto regis. III. den̄. 7 obolum.

V. H̃. de Wanneford. Inscadenafella. I. lib homo. Toredi. XX. ac̃ tre Tc̃. I. car̃. modo. nulla. & ual&. III. sol.

V THEWARDESTREV. H̃. In stanfella ten̄ elslet. I. liba femin̄. sub sc̃o. e. t. r. e. I. car̃ terræ. M̃ ten& bainardus. p escangio. Tc̃ . I. bord. modo. III. Tc̃. II. seru. modo. I. tc̃. II. car̃ in dominio. p dim̃. modo. I. 7. v. ac̃ p̃ti. modo. I. molin̄. Tc̃ ual XXX. sol. modo. XL. In ead. III. libi hões. eid̃e efflet c̃omd. XXX. ac̃. tre in soca sc̃i. E. semp. I. car̃. &. I. ac̃ p̃ti. semp ual&. v. sol.

10 In CRATFIELD Thored held before 1066; 3½ carucates of land as a manor.
>   Always 5 villagers. Then and later 9 smallholders, now 31.
>> Always 1 slave.
>   Always 2 ploughs in lordship. Then 7 men's ploughs, now 10.
>   Woodland for 250 pigs; meadow, 3½ acres. Then and now 1 cob; then 8 cattle, now 14; then 40 pigs, now 47; then 26 goats, now 32.
>   1 church with 6 acres; value 6d.

[Value] always £4.
To this manor belong 5 free men with 26 acres. Always 2 ploughs.
>   Woodland for 6 pigs.

Value 6s 8d.
>   And the (freemen) pay suit to this manor.

In addition, 2 men with 40 acres. 1 plough.
Value 5s.
>   Over these two (men), the jurisdiction (is) in Blythburgh.
>   William Baynard holds these two manors from Ralph, his uncle.

In the same village a free(man) [held] 1 manor, with 40 acres.
>   3 smallholders.
>   Always 1 plough.
>   Woodland for 6 pigs; meadow, 1½ acres.

Value before 1066, 10s; now 20[s].
>   That manor is in Ralph's lordship.
>   The whole of this land has 8 furlongs in length and 5 in width; it pays 3½d in the King's tax.

415 b

Hundred of WANGFORD

11 In SHADINGFIELD 1 free man of Thored's; 20 acres of land. Then 1 plough, now none.
Value 3s.

THEDWESTRY Hundred

12 In STANNINGFIELD Aelfled, a free woman, held under St. Edmund's before 1066; 1 carucate of land. Now Baynard holds (it) by exchange.
>   Then 1 smallholder, now 3; then 2 slaves, now 1.
>   Then 2 ploughs in lordship, later ½, now 1.
>   Meadow, 5 acres; now 1 mill.

Value then 30s; now 40[s].
In the same (Stanningfield) 3 free men under the patronage of the same Aelfled, in the jurisdiction of St. Edmund's; 30 acres of land. Always 1 plough.
>   Meadow, 1 acre.

Value always 5s.

415 a, b

BABENBERGA. duo hund̄. Simplinga ten̄ ailith liba
femina ſub gloſo. R. e. p̄ man̄. vi. car̄ terræ. 7 dim̄. Tc̄ ix. uitt
modo. xii. Tc̄ xii. bord̄. modo xvi. Tc̄ iii. ſerui. modo. null Tc̄
& p̄. iiii. car̄ in dominio. modo. iii. Tc̄. vii. car̄ hom̄. modo. vi.
Silua. c. porc̄. 7 xvii. ac̄ p̄ti. Tc̄. iiii. eq̄. modo. v. Tc̄. vii. an̄.
modo. v. Tc̄ lx. porc̄. m̄ xxx. iii. Tc̄ lxxx. ou͡s. modo. c. Tc̄ xvi.
cap̄. modo xxiiii. Eccl̄ia de. lx. ac̄ libæ tr̄e. &. i. bord̄. &.
. i. car̄. 7 dim̄ ac̄ p̄ti. Tc̄ uat. x. lib̄. p̄ 7 modo. xii. ħt. i. lḡ in lōg.
7 dim̄ in lato. & de gelto. xv. d̄. In ead̄ uitta. i. lib̄ hō Alith
com̄d in ſoca sc̄i. e. xxx. ac̄. &. i. bord̄. ſemp̄. i. car̄ 7. i. ac̄ 7 dim̄
★ prati. Semper uat x. ſot. 7 hc̄ bainardus p̄ eſcangio;

416 a
*T*ERRE RANVLFI PEVRELLI *LACFORDA*. H̃. . XXXIIII.
In etclingaham ten̄ Sewardus de melduna ſub rege. e. ſed ſoca
& ſaca. sc̄i. e. p̄ man̄. iii. car̄ terræ Semp̄. vi. uitt. Tc̄. ii. bord̄. modo.
. i. Tc̄ & poſt. iiii. ſerui. m̄. iii. Semp̄. iii. car̄ in dominio. 7. ii. car̄ hom̄.
&. i. molin̄. Tc̄. i. æqus. modo nullus. 7 tc̄. iii. an̄. modo. ii. Tc̄ xxx.
porc̄. modo. xxi. tc̄. cc. l. ou͡s. modo. ccc. l. Tc̄ & p̄ uat. iiii. lib̄.
modo. c. ſot. Soc̄a sc̄s. e.

BABERGH Two Hundreds
13 Aethelgyth, a free woman, held SHIMPLING under the illustrious King Edward as a manor; 6½ carucates of land.
>Then 9 villagers, now 12; then 12 smallholders, now 16; then 3 slaves, now none.
>Then and later 4 ploughs in lordship, now 3; then 7 men's ploughs, now 6.
>Woodland, 100 pigs; meadow, 17 acres. Then 4 horses, now 5; then 7 cattle, now 5; then 60 pigs, now 33; then 80 sheep, now 100; then 16 goats, now 24.
>A church with 60 acres of free land.
>1 smallholder.
>1 plough. Meadow, ½ acre.
>Value then £10; later and now [£] 12.
>It has 1 league in length and ½ in width; 15d in tax.
In the same village 1 free man of Aethelgyth's under patronage, in the jurisdiction of St. Edmund's; 30 acres.
>1 smallholder.
>Always 1 plough. Meadow, 1½ acres.
>Value always 10s.
>Baynard [has] this by exchange.

34 LANDS OF RANULF PEVEREL

LACKFORD Hundred
1 In ICKLINGHAM Siward of Maldon held under King Edward, but the full jurisdiction (was) St. Edmund's; 3 carucates of land as a manor.
>Always 6 villagers. Then 2 smallholders, now 1; then and later 4 slaves, now 3.
>Always 3 ploughs in lordship; 2 men's ploughs.
>1 mill. Then 1 horse, now none; then 3 cattle, now 2; then 30 pigs, now 21; then 250 sheep, now 350.
>Value then and later £4; now 100s.
>St. Edmund's (has) the jurisdiction.

Baberga.h̄. ARetona ten̄ fewardus de meldona teinnus
t.r.e.p̄ man̄.xii.car terræ cū foca & faca.Semp.xxiiii.uilł.sēp
xxx.viii.borđ.femp.xvii.ferū.Tc̄ viii.car.in dominio.p̄.& m̄.vi.
Tc̄ xx.car hominū.p̄.7 m̄ xiiii.&.l.ac̄ prati.Silua.xl.porc̄.
Tc̄ & p̄.ii.molin̄.modo.i.Tc̄.viii.eq̃ in halla.modo.xi.Tc̄ xxx
iiii.an̄.modo.xxxi.Tc̄.cc.porc̄.modo.clx.Tc̄.ccc.oūs.modo
cccc.xxiii.oūs.Tc̄.ix.uafa apū.modo.vii.Eccłia cui adiacent
xxx.ac̄.libæ terræ.Tc̄ & p̄ uał.xx.lib̄.modo.xxx.In Aratona.iiii.
lib̄i hōes quos ranulfus recep̄ p̄ terra.l.ac̄.In Walingafella.v.lib̄i
hom̄s.lxx.ii.ac̄.In altera Walingafella.iii.de l.ac̄.In honilega.i.
de l.ac̄.In manetuna.i.lib̄ hō.de.l.ac̄.Inī om̄s ħnt.vii.borđ.
Tc̄ & p̄.v.car.modo.iiii.Ifti lib̄i tc̄ & p̄ uał.iiii.lib̄.modo lx.foł.
De his ōib; poterant.xi.uenđe terras fuas.&.iiii.non poterant
fed de ōib; habuit antec̄ Rannulfi com̄đ 7 facā excepto uno qui ē
in foca fc̄i edm̄.Ranulfus recepit om̄s p̄ terra.Achetuna ħt.i.łḡ in lōḡ
&.i.in lato.& de gelto xiii.đ.

Afetona ten̄ iđ Sewardus antec̄.Ran̄ p̄ man̄.viii.car terræ cū

foca & faca.t.r.e.Tc̄ & p̄ xiiii.uilł.modo.v.Tc̄ & p̄ xx.i.borđ.
modo.lv.Tc̄ & p̄ xiiii.ferui.modo.xii.Tc̄ & p̄ vii.car in dn̄io.
modo vi.Tc̄ & p̄ xiii.car hom.modo.xii.Silua.xxx.porc̄.7 xv.ac̄
p̄ti.7.i.molin̄.Tc̄.vi.eq̃.in halla.m̄.v.Tc̄ xxiiii.an̄.modo.xxiii.
Tc̄.c.porc̄.modo lx.Tc̄.cc.x.oūs.modo lxxxx.Tc̄ xiiii.uafa apum.
modo.vi.modo.xii.cap̄.Ecclia de xxx.ac̄.libæ terræ.In eađe.v.
lib̄i hom̄s eiđ Sewardi com̄ 7 foc̄.fed non poterant uendere t̄ra
fuā in foca tam̄ remanentēs.& ħnt inī om̄s.xxx.ac̄ t̄ræ.&.i.ac̄.p̄ti.

BABERGH Hundred[s]

2 Siward of Maldon, a thane, held ACTON before 1066 as a manor; 12 carucates of land, with full jurisdiction.

 Always 23 villagers; always 38 smallholders; always 17 slaves.

 Then 8 ploughs in lordship, later and now 6; then 20 men's ploughs, later and now 14.

 Meadow, 50 acres; woodland, 40 pigs; then and later 2 mills, now 1. Then 8 horses at the hall, now 11; then 34 cattle, now 31; then 200 pigs, now 160; then 300 sheep, now 423 sheep; then 9 beehives, now 7.

 A church to which are attached 30 acres of free land.

Value then and later £20; now [£] 30.

In ACTON 4 free men whom Ranulf acquired for land; 50 acres. In WALDINGFIELD 5 free men; 72 acres. In the other WALDINGFIELD 3 (free men), with 50 acres. In *HONILEGA* 1 (free man), with 50 acres. In MANTON 1 free man, with 50 acres.

 Between them all they have 7 smallholders.

 Then and later 5 ploughs, now 4.

Value of the free men then and later £4; now 60s.

 Of all these (free) men, 11 could sell their lands and 4 could not; but Ranulf's predecessor had patronage over them all, and jurisdiction, except for one who is in the jurisdiction of St. Edmund's.

 Ranulf acquired them all for land.

 Acton has 1 league in length and 1 in width; 13d in tax.

3 Siward, Ranulf's predecessor, also held ASSINGTON as a manor; 8 carucates of land with full jurisdiction before 1066. 416 b

 Then and later 14 villagers, now 5; then and later 21 smallholders, now 55; then and later 14 slaves, now 12.

 Then and later 7 ploughs in lordship, now 6; then and later 13 men's ploughs, now 12.

 Woodland, 30 pigs; meadow, 15 acres; 1 mill. Then 6 horses at the hall, now 5; then 24 cattle, now 23; then 100 pigs, now 60; then 210 sheep, now 90; then 14 beehives, now 6; now 12 goats.

 A church with 30 acres of free land.

In the same (Assington) 5 free men under the same Siward's patronage and jurisdiction, but they could not sell their land while still remaining in the jurisdiction. Between them all they have 30 acres of land.

 Meadow, 1 acre.

Semp . I . car̷ . Adhuc in eadē . I . liƀ hō liƀatus ꝑ terra fed n̄ ptin&
man̄ de q̊ antec̄ Ran̄ habuit com̄d cū foca . & ħt . xxx . ac̄ . femp
. I . car̷ . Tc̄ ual̷ x . liƀ . 7 p̊ xii . modo xx . fed n̄ pot̷ redde . de . c . fol̷.
De iftis xx . liƀ . st̄ xx . fol̷ . fup iftos liƀos hoes . ħt . I . lḡ in longo . viii . qr̷
in lato . & de gelto . vii . đ.

⁋ In Clamesforda . ten̄ blacuin̊ . com̄datus . Siwardo . xxx . ac̄ . ꝑ m̊
t . r . e . & ual& . vi . fol̷ . Garinus tenet . Sc̄a . A . focā.

⁋ LOSAM ten& Leuftan̄ ten̄ fub rege gloriofo . e . ꝑ man̄ . I . car̷ . & dim̷
terræ dei car̷ fuit foca | sc̄æ trinitatis in cantuariā . Semp . vi . bord̷ . Tc̄ . ii.
feru̷ . Semp ii . car in dominio . & nulla hou̷ . 7 vi . ac̄ p̷ti . Tc̄ . ii . equi.
modo nullus . Tc̄ . x . an̄ . m̊ null̷ Tc̄ . xxx . porc̷ . m̊ . null̷ . Tc̄ lx . iiii . ou̷s
modo nullus . Tc̄ & poft ual̷ xl . fol̷ . 7 modo . ħt dim̷ lḡ in longo & . iiii.
qr̷ in lato . & de gelto . I . đ.

⁋ Stohu . ħ . Anuhus ten̄ ketel tegn̊ . Reg̷ . e . ꝑ . I . car̷ & dim̷ . & xx . ac̄.
cū foca . Semp . viii . bord̷ . & . iiii . feru̷ . Tc̄ & p̷ ⸝ iii . car̷ in dn̄io . modo . ii.
& femp . I . car̷ hom̷ . & . xii . ac̄ p̷ti . Silua de . vi . porc̷ . & . I . runc̷ . &

vi . an̄ . Tc̄ xvi . porc̷ . modo . xxx . Tc̄ xl . ou̷s . m̊ . lxxx . vii . 7 xxii . cap̷.
Ecc̄lia de . iii . ac̄ liƀæ terre . Tc̄ & p̊ ual xl fol̷ . modo . l . ħt . v . qr̷ in
longo . & . iii . in lato . & de geldo . vi . đ & obolū.

⁋ In Aneus ptinuer̄ . t . r . e . xxvi . ac̄ . & modo ten& osƀtus mafculus
in æcc̄lia ftou . & tenuit anteq̊ Ranulfus habuiff& man̄ anuhus.

* ⁋ BOSEMARA . H̄ . Burgheftalā . ten̄ Rad̷ de fauigncio . de . Radulfo.
quā tenuit Turchillus teinnus . t . r . e . ꝑ man̄ . xxviii . ac̄ . modo . ii . bord̷.
femp . I . car̷ in dominio . & . ii . ac̄ p̷ti . femp . I . runc̷ . & . I . an̄ . modo . ix.
porc̷ . Tc̄ . xiiii . ou̷s . modo . xxx . Tc̄ ual̷ . v . fol̷ . & . iiii . đ . m̊ . viii . fol̷.

Always 1 plough.
Also in the same (Assington), 1 free man delivered for land, but he does not belong to the manor over which Ranulf's predecessor had patronage with jurisdiction. He has 30 acres. Always 1 plough. Value then £10; later [£] 12; now [£] 20, but it could not pay (this amount) by 100s. Of the £20, 20s is on account of the free men.
It has 1 league in length, 8 furlongs in width; 7d in tax.

4 In GLEMSFORD Blackwin held under the patronage of Siward; 30 acres as a manor before 1066.
Value 6s.
Warin holds (this).
St. Etheldreda's (has) the jurisdiction.

5 Leofstan holds LOOSE; he held (it) under the illustrious King Edward; as a manor, 1½ carucates of land. The jurisdiction over 1 carucate belonged to (the Church of) the Holy Trinity in Canterbury.
Always 6 smallholders. Then 2 slaves.
Always 2 ploughs in lordship; no men's [plough].
Meadow, 6 acres. Then 2 horses, now none; then 10 cattle, now none; then 30 pigs, now none; then 64 sheep, now none.
Value then and later 40s; and now (the same).
It has ½ league in length and 4 furlongs in width; 1d in tax.

STOW Hundred

6 Ketel, a thane of King Edward's, held ONEHOUSE for 1½ carucates and 20 acres, with the jurisdiction.
Always 8 smallholders; 4 slaves.
Then and later 3 ploughs in lordship, now 2; always 1 men's plough.
Meadow, 12 acres; woodland at 6 pigs. 1 cob, 6 cattle; then 16 pigs, now 30; then 40 sheep, now 87; 22 goats.
A church with 3 acres of free land.
Value then and later 40s; now 50[s].
It has 5 furlongs in length and 3 in width; 6½d in tax.
26 acres in ONEHOUSE belonged there before 1066. Now Osbert Male holds (them) in the lands of the Church of Stow(market); he held (them) before Ranulf had the manor of Onehouse.

417 a

BOSMERE Hundred

7 Ralph of Savenay holds BURSTALL from [Ranulf]. Thorkell, a thane, held it before 1066 as a manor; 28 acres.
Now 2 smallholders. Always 1 plough in lordship.
Meadow, 2 acres. Always 1 cob; 1 cattle. Now 9 pigs; then 14 sheep, now 30.
Value then 5s 4d; now 8s.

⁋In briefeta teñ Rađ filiꝰ brien . ɪ.lib̄ hō q̇ud tenuit Lefſtanꝰ . t . r . e . ɪɪ . car̓
terræ . 7 ɪɪɪɪ . āc ꝑ mañ . ſemp . ɪ . uiƚƚ . & . x . borđ . & . ɪɪ . ſeru . & . ɪɪɪ . car̓
in dominio . 7 . vɪ . āc p̓ti . ſilu . x . porc̓ . Tc̄ . ɪɪ . car̓ hom̄ . modo . ɪ . De hac
tr̄a iacebant cuidā eccłiæ . ʟ . ɪɪɪɪ . āc qs modo teñ . Rađ filiꝰ brien
in ſuo dn̄io . Tc̄ . ɪɪ . runc̓ . modo . v . Tc̄ . x . añ . modo . xv . Tc̄ . xxx . porc̄ .
modo . ʟ . Tc̄ ʟxxx . oūs modo . c . xʟ . In eađ . ɪɪɪɪ . ſoc̄ . de xʟ . ɪ . āc . 1c̄ . ɪ . car̓
& dim̄ . modo . ɪɪ . car̓ hom̄ . Rex & coms̄ focā . Tc̄ uaƚ . ʟx . ſoƚ . modo . c .
⁋Codeham teñ hunfridus filiꝰ Alb̄ici teñ de ʀ . quā tenuit Le
uricus lib̄ hō . t . r . e . ʟx . āc . ꝑ mañ . ſemp . ɪɪɪ . borđ . 7 ɪɪ . car̓ . & . ɪɪɪɪ . āc
p̓ti . Silu de . ʟx . porc̓ . Quedā Quedā pars triū æccłiarū . & . ɪ .
runc̓ . tc̄ vɪɪɪ . añ . modo . vɪ . 7 xɪɪɪɪ . porc̓ . & . xɪɪ . oūs . Tc̄ uaƚ&
xx . ſoƚ . modo xʟ . Eccłia . ɪɪɪ . āc . 7 vɪ . deñ .
⁋In Mucelfelda teñ Rađ . de ſauigni xɪɪ . āc . & . ɪɪɪ . borđ . & dim̄ æc
cłia . & . ɪɪ . āc & dim̄ . & s̄t in p̄tio de olueſtuna . Rex & Coms̄ de toto
focā . In ſtanham q̄rta pars æccłiæ . vɪɪ . āc . & . dim̄ . & uaƚ xv . đ .

417 b

⁋Claindune . H̄ . Depheam tenuit Saxo . ɪ . car̓ terræ . ꝑ mañ . & xxɪɪ .
āc . De his xxɪɪ . āc habuit ante Rob̄ti mal& . t . r . e . vɪɪɪ . āc . in foca
& com̄ ab̄bis . Tc̄ . ɪɪɪɪ . uiƚƚ . modo . ɪɪ . ſemp xɪx borđ . Tc̄ . ɪ . ſeru̓ . ſemp
ɪɪ . car̓ in dn̄io . Tercia pars ſc̄æ mariæ æccłiæ de . x . āc . Tc̄ & poſt . ɪɪɪ . hom̄ .
car̓ . modo . ɪɪ . & . ɪɪɪɪ . āc p̄ti . Tc̄ filua . de . c . porc̓ . modo xʟ . Tc̄ . ɪ .
runc̓ . 7 ɪɪɪɪ . añ . xʟ . porc̓ modo . xxvɪɪɪ . 7 xxvɪɪ . cap̄ . Tc̄ xʟ . oūs . modo
xxx . 7 xxx . āc de dn̄io in Loſa hund . Tc̄ uaƚ& . ʟx . ſoƚ . modo . ʟ . Rađ
de ſauigni ten&

8 In BRICETT Ralph son of Brian holds what Leofstan held before 1066; 2 carucates of land and 4 acres as a manor.
Always 1 villager; 10 smallholders; 2 slaves;
3 ploughs in lordship.
Meadow, 6 acres; woodland, 10 pigs.
Then 2 men's ploughs, now 1.
Of this land, 54 acres belonged to a church. Ralph son of Brian now holds them in his lordship.
Then 2 cobs, now 5; then 10 cattle, now 15; then 30 pigs, now 50; then 80 sheep, now 140.
In the same (Bricett) 4 Freemen, with 41 acres. Then 1½ ploughs, now 2 oxen.
The King and the Earl (have) the jurisdiction.
Value then 60s; now 100[s].

9 Humphrey son of Aubrey holds CODDENHAM; he holds (it) from Ranulf. Leofric, a free man, held it before 1066; 60 acres as a manor.
Always 3 smallholders;
2 ploughs.
Meadow, 4 acres; woodland at 60 pigs.
A part of 3 churches.
1 cob; then 8 cattle, now 6; 14 pigs, 12 sheep.
Value then 20s; now 40[s].
A church, 3 acres; value 6d.

10 In MICKFIELD Ralph of Savenay holds 12 acres.
3 smallholders.
½ church, 2½ acres.
They are in the assessment of Ulverston.
The King and the Earl (have) jurisdiction over the whole.

11 In STONHAM the fourth part of a church, 7½ acres; value 15d.

CLAYDON Hundred

417 b

12 Saxi held DEBENHAM; 1 carucate of land as a manor, and 22 acres. Of these 22 acres, Robert Malet's predecessor had 8 acres before 1066 in the jurisdiction and under the patronage of the Abbot.
Then 4 villagers, now 2; always 19 smallholders. Then 1 slave.
Always 2 ploughs in lordship.
The third part of St. Mary's Church, with 10 acres.
Always 2 ploughs in lordship. Then and later 3 men's ploughs, now 2.
Meadow, 4 acres; woodland then at 100 pigs, now 40. Then 1 cob, 4 cattle. [Then] 40 pigs, now 28; 27 goats; then 40 sheep, now 30.
30 acres in lordship in Loes Hundred.
Value then 60s; now 50[s].
Ralph of Savenay holds (this).

⁊Vlueſtune tenuit Idē Saxo . 7 eod̄ modo ꝑ man̄.
. I . caŕ terræ . t . r . e . Tc̄ . & p̽ . III . uiłł . modo . I . Tc̄ & p̽ ꝉ IX bord̄ . modo
XIIII . Tc̄ & p̽ . II . caŕ in dn̄io . modo . I . Tc̄ & p̽ . III . caŕ hom̄ . modo
II . Tc̄ . I . runc̄ . Tc̄ XIIII . an̄ . Tc̄ LX . porc̄ . modo XXII . Tc̄ XXII . ōus .
modo . XXX . Tc̄ & p̽ uał . XL . fot . modo XXX . Huic man̄ ptinebant
VIII . ac̄ . de dominio . t . r . e . q̓s modo ten& mat̄ Roḃti malet.
ħt . I . lḡ in longo . & . VII . q̄r in lato . & . XXVI . d̄ & oḃ . de geldo Alii ibi ten̄.
⁊Dim̄ . ħ . DE COSFORT . In Watefelda . XX . ac̄ . tenuit . Leſtanus &
uał XX . d̄ . sc̄s . e . foca

⁊H̄ . DE CARLEFORD . In Clopetuna . ten̄ . Edric̄ grim . t . r . e.
. I . caŕ terræ . 7 XLII . ac̄ . com̄d dim̄ . S æ . 7 dim̄ ante c̄ . R . malet.
Semp . II . uiłł . & XIII . bord̄ . Tc̄ in dn̄io . III . caŕ . modo . II . fed poteſt fieri,
Tc̄ hom̄ . II . caŕ . m̊ . I . v . ac̄ ꝑti . filua ad . x . porc̄ . & . I . runc̄ . Tc̄ . VIII .
an̄ . modo . III . modo . XXX . porc̄ . T& LXXX . ōus . modo XX . Tc̄ uał
LX . fot . modo . L . hoc ten̄ . Toroldus . de . R . I . æccłia . XV . ac̄ . de quat
tuor dominationiḃ & . uał . II . fot.

⁊ H̄ . DE WILEFORDA . In depebes . XV . ac̄ . & ptinent ad clopetuna

& uał . III . fot.

⁊HERTESMARA . H̄ . In Tufemera . I . caŕ terræ . de dn̄io abb̃is de eli.
qd̄ tenuit faxo . t . r . e . ꝑ fuis folidatis . Tc̄ & p̽ . I . caŕ . modo nichil.
& tc̄ uał XX . fot . modo . X . Rad̄ de fauigni ten̄.
⁊In Afpella XVI . ac̄ . de dn̄io . Vlueſtune . 7 IIII . bord̄ . & dim̄ caŕ.
In ead̄ tc̄ia pars æccłiæ . & tc̄ia pars feriæ.

13 Saxi also held ULVERSTON in the same way as a manor; 1 carucate of land before 1066.
    Then and later 3 villagers, now 1; then and later 9 smallholders, now 14.
    Then and later 2 ploughs in lordship, now 1; then and later 3 men's ploughs, now 2.
    Then 1 cob; then 14 cattle; then 60 pigs, now 22; then 22 sheep, now 30.
    Value then and later 40s; now 30[s].
    To this manor before 1066 belonged 8 acres in lordship. Now Robert Malet's mother holds them.
    It has 1 league in length and 7 furlongs in width; 26½d in tax. Others hold there.

Half-Hundred of COSFORD

14 In WHATFIELD Leofstan held 20 acres.
    Value 20d.
    St. Edmund's (had) the jurisdiction.

Hundred of CARLFORD

15 In CLOPTON before 1066 Edric Grim, half under the patronage of St. Etheldreda's and half (under that) of R(obert) Malet's predecessor, held 1 carucate of land and 42 acres.
    Always 2 villagers; 13 smallholders.
    Then 3 ploughs in lordship, now 2, but [another] possible; then 2 men's ploughs, now 1.
    Meadow, 5 acres; woodland for 10 pigs. 1 cob; then 8 cattle, now 3; now 30 pigs; then 80 sheep, now 20.
    Value then 60s; now 50[s].
    Thorold holds this from Ranulf.
    1 church, 15 acres from four lordships; value 2s.

Hundred of WILFORD

16 In DEBACH 15 acres; they belong to Clopton.
    Value 3s.

HARTISMERE Hundred

17 In TUSEMERA 1 carucate of land of the Abbot of Ely's lordship. Saxi held it before 1066 as his wages. Then and later 1 plough, now nothing.
    Value then 20s; now 10[s].
    Ralph of Savenay holds (this).

18 In ASPALL 16 acres of the lordship of Ulverston, and in the assessment.
    4 smallholders.
    ½ plough.
    In the same (Aspall) the third part of a church. And the third part of a fair.

TRÆ ALBERICI DE VER. BABENĞA DVO. H̃. .XXXV.

Lauenham teñ Vlwinus teinñ . reğ . e . ₽ mañ . vi . car̛ . terræ .
cū faca & foca . Tc̃ & p̊ xi . uiłł . modo vii . Tc̃ & p̊ xxiiii . bord̛ . modo
xxx . viii . Semp̛ . vi . ferư . Semp̛ . iiii . car̛ in dominio . Tc̃ & poft
ix . car̛ hom̛ . modo vii . & . x . ac̃ p̃ti . Silư . de . c . porc̛ . Tc̃ . v . eq̛ . in halla
modo . i . Tc̃ xxiiii . añ . modo xxv . Tc̃ c . lx . porc̛ . modo lx . v . Tc̃ &
femper . cc . oũs . Tc̃ lx . cap̛ . modo . lxxx . Tc̃ . v . uafa apū . modo . vi .
i . arpentū uineæ . & . i . foc̃ q̛ non pot̛ dare nec uende . de . i . car̛ r̃æ
& . v . bord̛ . Semp̛ . ii . car̛ . modo . i . mol̛ . & . iii . ac̃ p̃ti . Tc̃ 7 p̊ totū
ual̛ x . lib̛ . m̃ . xv . ħt . i . leğ in longo . & dim̛ in lato . & de gelto . vii . d̛ & obol̛ .

418 b

Walingafella teñ idē ulwinus antec̛ albrici . fub rege . e . ₽ mañ .
ii . car̛ terræ cū foca & faca . Semp̛ . iiii . uiłł . & . x . bord̛ . & . iiii . ferư femp̛
. ii . car̛ in dñio . & . ii . car̛ hom̛ . & iiii . ac̃ p̃ti . Silua de . iiii . porc̛ . Semp̛
. i . eqư in halla . 7 iii . añ . 7 xvi . porc̛ . Semp̛ . c . oũs . Semp̛ ual̛ . v . lib̛ . ħt
xii . qr̛ in longo . & . iii . in lato . & de gelto . vi . d̛ .

SANFORT . H̃ . Belfted̃a tenuit Tocha lib̛ ho͂ com̛d̛ . tantū .
lxxx . ac̃ ₽ mañ . Tc̃ . ii . uiłłi . modo . ii . bord̛ . femp̛ . i . car̛ . & . ii . ac̃ p̃ti .
Tc̃ . i . moliñ . Tc̃ ual̛ xvi . fol̛ . p̊ 7 m̃ xv . fermeus ten& . Soca in ɓcolt .
In eade͂ teñ Turgifus lib̛ homo . com̛d̛ tantū . lxxx . ac̃ . ₽ mañ . se͂p̛
. ii . uiłłi . & . i . bord̛ . Tc̃ & p̊ . i . car̛ . m̃ . nichil . & . ii . ac̃ p̃ti . Tc̃ ual̛ . xvi .
fol̛ . P̊ & modo xv . Soca in ɓcolt . ħt . v . qr̛ in longo . & . iii . in lato . & vi . d̛
& obol̛ de gelto . hæc duo mañ derationata funt . Rad̛ taillebofc .
7 Phin in manu reğ . & poft accepit ea . Albicus fine libatione . fic
p̄pofit . & hund̛ . dic̃ .

LANDS OF AUBREY DE VERE

BABERGH Two Hundreds

1 Wulfwin, a thane of King Edward's, held LAVENHAM as a manor; 6 carucates of land, with full jurisdiction.

Then and later 11 villagers, now 7; then and later 24 smallholders, now 38; always 6 slaves.

Always 4 ploughs in lordship. Then and later 9 men's ploughs, now 7.

Meadow, 10 acres; woodland at 100 pigs. Then 5 horses at the hall, now 1; then 24 cattle, now 25; then 160 pigs, now 65; then and always 200 sheep; then 60 goats, now 80; then 5 beehives, now 6. 1 *arpent* of vines.

1 Freeman who could not grant or sell, with 1 carucate of land. 5 smallholders.

Always 2 ploughs.

Now 1 mill. Meadow, 3 acres.

Value of the whole then and later £10; now [£] 15.

It has 1 league in length and a ½ in width; 7½d in tax.

2 Wulfwin, Aubrey's predecessor, also held WALDINGFIELD under King Edward as a manor; 2 carucates of land, with full jurisdiction.

Always 4 villagers; 10 smallholders; 4 slaves.

Always 2 ploughs in lordship; 2 men's ploughs.

Meadow, 4 acres; woodland at 4 pigs. Always 1 horse at the hall; 3 cattle; 16 pigs; always 100 sheep.

Value always £5.

It has 12 furlongs in length and 3 in width; 6d in tax.

SAMFORD Hundred

3 Toki, a free man under patronage only, held BELSTEAD; 80 acres as a manor.

Then 2 villagers; now 2 smallholders.

Always 1 plough.

Meadow, 2 acres; then 1 mill.

Value then 16s; later and now 15[s].

Fermeus holds (this).

The jurisdiction (is) in (East) Bergholt.

In the same (Belstead), Thorgils, a free man under patronage only, held 80 acres as a manor.

Always 2 villagers; 1 smallholder.

Then and later 1 plough, now nothing. Meadow, 2 acres.

Value then 16s; later and now 15[s].

The jurisdiction (is) in (East) Bergholt.

It has 5 furlongs in length and 3 in width; 6½d in tax.

These 2 manors were adjudged from Ralph Tallboys and Finn into the King's hand; later Aubrey received them without a deliverer, so the reeve and the Hundred say.

In Canepetuna tẽn Brunnuiṅ ſochemaṅ de bcolt manerio regis. . iiii . ac̄ . & ual xii . d̄.

HERTESMERA. H̃. Burgatā tenuit Vluuinus lib̃ hō . t . r . e. ꝓ mañ . v . car̉ terre & ſemp xxii . uiłł . 7 xxxiii . bord̄ . Tc̄ . iiii . ſeru̇. ſemp . iii . car̉ in dominio . Tc̄ 7 ṗ xv . car̉ . modo . x . 7 iii . ac̄ & dimid. p̃ti . Tc̄ ſilua . c . porc̉ . modo xl . Æccliæ . de . xxix . ac̄ . & dim̉ car̉. Tc̄ vii . añ . modo . xii . Tc̄ xxiii . porc̄ . modo lxxx . Tc̄ lxiii . oūs. m̃ clxxvi . Tc̄ xl . cap̃ . m̃ . lvii . & . ix . ſoc̄ . cxlii . ac̄ . & . iiii . bord̄. ſemp . v . car̉ . & . iii . ac̄ & dim̉ p̃ti . ſilua de . vi . porc̉ . Qrta pars æccliæ . i . ac̄ . Tc̄ ual totũ . xvi . lib̃ . modo xix . 7 iiii . ſol . ħt . i . lg in lõgo

419 a

7 vii . qr̉ in lato . 7 . v . deñ . de gelto . Vluuiṅ habuit ſocā . Totũ ten&̃ Adel:ṁ de albico.

DIM̃. H̃. de cosfort . Ialelham tẽn . Vluuinus . t . r . e . ꝓ mañ. v . car̉ terræ & dim̉ . Tc̄ vii . uiłł . modo . iiii . Tc̄ vi . ſeru̇ . modo . ii . Tc̄. iiii . car̉ in dñio . modo . iii . Tc̄ vi . car̉ hom̃ . modo . iiii . vii . ac̄ p̃ti. Silua viii . porc̉ . ſemp . ii . moliñ . & iii . runc̉ . Tc̄ . x . añ . modo . xviii. Tc̄ lxxx . porc̉ . modo lx . Tc̄ . c . xl . oūs . M lx . Ecclia . de . vii . ac̄ . Tc̄ ual . viii . lib̃ . modo xv . In cadẽ . i . lib̃ hō . v . ac̄ . com̃ tantũ . ses ead ſocā 7 ual . x . deñ . ħt viii . qr̉ in longo . & vii . in lato ; & v . deñ de gelto ;

4 In *CANEPETUNA* Brunwin, a Freeman from the King's manor of (East) Bergholt, held 4 acres.
Value 12d.

HARTISMERE Hundred
5 Wulfwin, a free man, held BURGATE before 1066 as a manor; 5 carucates of land.
Always 22 villagers; 33 smallholders. Then 4 slaves.
Always 3 ploughs in lordship. Then and later 15 [men's] ploughs, now 10.
Meadow, 3½ acres; woodland, then 100 pigs, now 40.
... churches with 29 acres. ½ plough.
Then 7 cattle, now 12; then 23 pigs, now 80; then 63 sheep, now 176; then 40 goats, now 57.
9 Freemen; 142 acres.
4 smallholders.
Always 5 ploughs.
Meadow, 3½ acres; woodland at 6 pigs.
The fourth part of a church, 1 acre.
Value of the whole then £16; now [£] 19 4s.
It has 1 league in length and 7 furlongs in width; 5d in tax.
Wulfwin had the jurisdiction.
Adelelm holds the whole (of this) from Aubrey.

Half-Hundred of COSFORD
6 In ALDHAM Wulfwin held as a manor before 1066; 5½ carucates of land.
Then 7 villagers, now 4; then 6 slaves, now 2.
Then 4 ploughs in lordship, now 3; then 6 men's ploughs, now 4.
Meadow, 7 acres; woodland, 8 pigs; always 2 mills. 3 cobs; then 10 cattle, now 18; then 80 pigs, now 60; then 140 sheep, now 60.
A church with 7 acres.
Value then £8; now [£] 15.
In the same (Aldham) 1 free man, under patronage only, St. Edmund's (had) the jurisdiction; 5 acres.
Value 10d.
It has 8 furlongs in length and 7 in width; 5d in tax.

HERTESMERA. H̃. In burgata liba femina. milda 7 Iin
wordam. ix. libi hoes Befo. Aluuin. Godwinus Vluiet Botius.
Ordricus. Stanart. Godric. *In Strandeftuna. ii. libi hoes
Fulcardus. Aluin. *In metles. iiii. libi homines. & dim. Leuric.
Godric. Vluara. Leuuin. benne. Furcardus dim. *In torham
. i. lib hō. Vlmar. In Richinge hala. i. lib hō. Brictmar. In gis
lingehā lib hō Edricus. *In Wordhā. i. lib hō. Colemanus. In metles
. i. liba femina Menleua. & habebat. xiiii. ac. libæ terræ. 7. t. r. e.
concefferat. illā terrā sc̄o eadmundo. Int totū hnt alii lxxxx. ac
femp. vi. car. & dim. &. i. ac p̃ti. Semp ual lx. fol. Totū ten&
Adelalmus de albico. ex his libis hominibʒ habuit ante c̄ Albici
focā. & comd. t. r. e. *In Giflinghehā. iii. libi hoes. Vlmar. Leftan,
Lefquena xxiii. ac. &. i. car. 7 ual iiii. fol. 7 viii. den. Idē Adelalm
ten& de abico.

.XXXVI. *TERRA ROBERTI GRENONIS. S Anfort. h̃. & dim.
Cercesfort tenuit Scapi teinnus Haroldi. p man. i. car terræ.
t. r. e. modo ten& Willm de alno. de Robto. Tc̄ vi. uill. modo
iiii. Tc̄. iiii. bord. modo. iii. Tc̄. ii. feru. m̃. i. Tc̄. ii. car in dnios
modo. i. Tc̄. i. car & dim hom. modo. i. vii. ac p̃ti. modo. i. mol.
Tc̄. ii. runc. & vi. an. & c. xl. ous. modo nichil. Tc̄ & p ual lx.
fol. modo. xl. ht. vi. qr in longo. &. ii. in lato. &. iiii. den.
de gelto. Scapi habuit focā fub Haroldo.
*Stotunā tenuit Idē Scalpi t. r. e. ii. car terræ. p man.
Tc̄. viii. uill. modo. v. Tc̄. iiii. bord. modo. v. Tc̄. vi. feru. modo. iii.

HARTISMERE Hundred

7 In BURGATE a free woman, Mild; and in WORTHAM 9 free men, Besi, Alwin, Godwin, Wulfgeat, Boti, Ordric, Stanhard, Godric. In THRANDESTON 2 free men, Fulcard, Alwin. In MELLIS 4 free men and a half (free man); Leofric, Godric, Wulfwaru, Leofwin Benne, and Fulcard the half (free man). In THORNHAM (Magna) 1 free man, Wulfmer. In RICKINGHALL (Superior) 1 free man, Brictmer. In GISLINGHAM a free man, Edric. In WORTHAM 1 free man, Coleman. In MELLIS 1 free woman, Menleva; she had 14 acres of free land, and before 1066 she had given that land to St. Edmund's. Between them all the others have 90 acres. Always 6½ ploughs.

Meadow, 1 acre.
Value always 60s.
Adelelm holds the whole (of this) from Aubrey.
Over these free men Aubrey's predecessor had jurisdiction and patronage before 1066.

8 In GISLINGHAM 3 free men, Wulfmer, Leofstan, Leofcwen; 23 acres. 1 plough.
Value 4s 8d.
Adelelm also holds (this) from Aubrey.

36   LAND OF ROBERT GERNON

SAMFORD Hundred and a Half

1 Scalpi, a thane of Harold's, held CHURCHFORD as a manor; 1 carucate of land before 1066. Now William *de Alno* holds (it) from Robert.

Then 6 villagers, now 4; then 4 smallholders, now 3; then 2 slaves, now 1.
Then 2 ploughs in lordship, now 1; then 1½ men's ploughs, now 1.
Meadow, 7 acres; now 1 mill. Then 2 cobs, 6 cattle, 140 sheep; now nothing.
Value then and later 60s; now 40[s].
It has 6 furlongs in length and 2 in width; 4d in tax. Scalpi had the jurisdiction under Harold.

2 Scalpi also held STUTTON before 1066; 2 carucates of land as a manor.
Then 8 villagers, now 5; then 4 smallholders, now 5; then 6 slaves, now 3.

Tc & p̃.ii.car in dñio.modo.i.femp.ii.car hom.v.ac p̃ti.filua
xvi.porc.femp.i.mol.&.ii.falinæ.dim ecclia xv.ac.Tc.ii.
runc.Tc xvi.añ.modo.ii.Tc xl.porc.modo.xiiii.Tc.clxxxx.
oũs.modo xxxv.Tc & p ual vi.lib.modo.lx.fol.ht vi.qr
in longo.&.iiii.in lato.&.iiii.d de gelto.Ide Willm.Soca eod m̃.

⸿ In branthā.i.lib hō Mauua comd tantũ.v.ac & dim.7 ual
xii.d.Ide Will haroldus foca.

⸿ Manesfort tenuit Scs benedictus de ramefeia in dñio.t.r.e.
modo ide.W.p mañ.i.car terræ.7 dim femper.ii.uill.Tc.iiii.
bord.modo.v.Tc & p ii.car in dñio.modo.i.Semp.i.car hom.
iii.ac p̃ti.&.i.mol.Tc.ii.runc.Tc.v.añ.modo.iii.Tc xv.
porc.modo.v.femp.xxx.oũs.Tc & p ual xl.fol.modo.xx.
ht vi.qr in longo.&.iii.in lato.7 iii.den &.i.ferding de gelto.
Scs.benedictus.focam.

420 a

⸿ In alfildeftuna.tenuit.Aluuin lib comdatus Alurico ante ceffori
Robti.xxx.ac terræ p mañ.t.r.e.femp dim car.& ual&.iiii.fol.
Haroldus foca.Ide W.

⸿ TVRchetleftuna ten Grimmus lib hō coindatus Guert.i.car
terræ p mañ.t.r.e.femp.ii.uill.&.ii.bord.Tc & poft.i.car.modo
nichil.7.ii.part pifcariæ.femp.i.car hom.Tc ual xl.fol.modo
xxx.viii.Ide W.hoc Reuocat Rob p efcang.de terra hugonis
de monte forti.haroldus foca.

Then and later 2 ploughs in lordship, now 1; always 2 men's ploughs.
Meadow, 5 acres; woodland, 16 pigs. Always 1 mill; 2 salt-houses. ½ church, 15 acres.
Then 2 cobs; then 16 cattle, now 2; then 40 pigs, now 14; then 190 sheep, now 35.
Value then and later £6; now 60s.
It has 6 furlongs in length and 4 in width; 4d in tax.
William also [holds this].
The jurisdiction [was held] in the same way.

3 In BRANTHAM 1 free man, Mawa, under patronage only; 5½ acres. Value 12d.
William [holds this].
Harold (had) the jurisdiction.

4 St. Benedict's of Ramsey held MANESFORT in lordship before 1066. Now William also [holds it] as a manor; 1½ carucates of land.
Always 2 villagers. Then 4 smallholders, now 5.
Then and later 2 ploughs in lordship, now 1; always 1 men's plough.
Meadow, 3 acres; 1 mill. Then 2 cobs; then 5 cattle, now 3; then 15 pigs, now 5; always 30 sheep.
Value then and later 40s; now 20[s].
It has 6 furlongs in length and 3 in width; 3¼d in tax. St. Benedict's (had) the jurisdiction.

5 Alwin, a free man under the patronage of Aelfric, Robert's predecessor, held ALFILDESTUNA; 30 acres of land as a manor before 1066. Always ½ plough.
Value 4s.
Harold (had) the jurisdiction.
William also [holds this].

420 a

6 Grim, a free man under the patronage of Gyrth, held TURCHETLESTUNA; 1 carucate of land as a manor before 1066.
Always 2 villagers; 2 smallholders.
Then and later 1 plough, now nothing. 2 parts of a fishery. Always 1 men's plough.
Value then 40s; now 38[s].
William also [holds this]. Robert claims this by exchange with the land of Hugh de Montfort.
Harold (had) the jurisdiction.

Brantham tenuit Idē Grimus. LX. ac̄. ṗ man̄. t. r. e. femp
. I. bord̄. Tc̄ & poft dim̄ car̄. modo. II. bou̅. I. ac̄ p̄ti. Tc̄ & p̊ ual. x.
fol. & VIII d̄. m̄. v. fol. Idē W. hoc &iā reuocat Rob̄ eod m̄. harol-
In hulfereftuna ten& Aluret com̄datus Scalpio / dus focam.
LXXX. ac̄. ṗ man̄. t. r. e. m̄ Rob̄ in dominio. femp III. bord̄.
Tc̄ & poft. I. car̄. in dn̄o. modo dim̄. &. I. ac̄ p̄ti. Tc̄ ual XVI. fol.
modo. x.
In tatiftuna. Trumuin̊ 7 ulfius libi hos com̄d. c. xx. ac̄. ṗ
. II. man̄. t. r. e. femp. I. bord̄. Tc̄ & p̊. II. car̄. modo. I. &. II. ac̄ p̄ti.
Tc̄ ual. x. fol. modo. VIII.
In Stuttuna ten̄ Ætnod lib̄ hō c̄m̄d. LX. ac̄. ṗ man̄. t. r. e. Tc̄
& p̊. I. car̄. m̄ dim̄. &. I. ac̄ p̄ti. Tc̄ ual. x. fol. m̄. VIII.
In branthā. tela. liba femina. com̄d. xxx. ac̄ ṗ man̄. t. r. e.
femp. I. bord̄. & dim̄ car̄. &. I. ac̄ p̄ti. Tc̄ & p̊ ual. v. fol. m̄. III.
7 VI. den̄. &. obol. / In tatiftuna. ten̄ Aluricus lib̄ homo.
com̄d. xxx. ac̄ ṗ man̄. 7. II. bord̄. Tc̄ & p̊ dim̄. car̄. modo. II. bou̅.

420 b

&. I. ac̄ p̄ti. Tunc ual XL den̄. modo XL. II.
In herchefteda. Aluric̊ lib̄ hō com̄d. xxx. ac̄. pro man̄. t. r. e.
Tc̄ & p̊ dim̄ car̄. modo. II. bou̅. & dim̄ ac̄ p̄ti. Tc̄ ual. v. fol. m̄ XLII. d̄.
In eduineftuna Spieta lib̄ hō com̄d. xxx. ac̄. ṗ man. t. r. e. Tc̄
dim̄ car̄. Tc̄ ual. v. fol. m̄ XL. II. d̄. In h̄ hundreto. h̄t. VII. lib̄ hōes
com̄d Rob̄ in dn̄io. cxx. ac̄. femp. III. car̄. Tc̄ ual xx. fol. m̄ xxv.
Haroldus focam.

7 Grim also held BRANTHAM; 60 acres as a manor before 1066.
  Always 1 smallholder.
  Then and later ½ plough, now 2 oxen. Meadow, 1 acre.
  Value then and later 10s 8d; now 5s.
  William also [holds this]. Robert claims this in the same way.
  Harold (had) the jurisdiction.

8 In WOLVERSTONE Alfred, under the patronage of Scalpi, [held] 80 acres as a manor before 1066. Now Robert [holds it] in lordship.
  Always 3 smallholders.
  Then and later 1 plough in lordship, now ½. Meadow, 1 acre.
  Value then 16s; now 10[s].

9 In TATTINGSTONE Trumwin and Wulfsi, free men under patronage; 120 acres as 2 manors before 1066.
  Always 1 smallholder.
  Then and later 2 ploughs, now 1. Meadow, 2 acres.
  Value then 10s; now 8[s].

10 In STUTTON Ednoth, a free man under patronage, held 60 acres as a manor before 1066. Then and later 1 plough, now ½.
  Meadow, 1 acre.
  Value then 10s; now 8[s].

11 In BRANTHAM Tela, a free woman under patronage; 30 acres as a manor before 1066.
  Always 1 smallholder;
  ½ plough. Meadow, 1 acre.
  Value then and later 5s; now 3[s] 6½d.

12 In TATTINGSTONE Aelfric, a free man under patronage, held 30 acres as a manor.
  2 smallholders.
  Then and later ½ plough, now 2 oxen. Meadow, 1 acre.
  Value then 40d; now 42[d].

420 b

13 In HARKSTEAD Aelfric, a free man under patronage; 30 acres as a manor before 1066. Then and later ½ plough, now 2 oxen.
  Meadow, ½ acre.
  Value then 5s; now 42d.

14 In EDUINESTUNA Spieta, a free man under patronage; 30 acres as a manor before 1066. Then ½ plough.
  Value then 5s; now 42d.

15 In this Hundred Robert has in lordship 7 free men under patronage; 120 acres. Always 3 ploughs.
  Value then 20s; now 25[s].
  Harold (had) the jurisdiction.

Ϝ Cosfort . H̃. In Latham xx . ac . de dñio de ciresfort qď
tenuit Scapi⁹. & ual . iii . fol. Will de alno ∴ ten&.
Ϝ In Colenes . hund . i . liƀ hō . ii . ac . libæ terræ . & ual . iiii . d . Idē ten&.

.XXXVII. *Ϝ Tr.æ petri de valonis . brademera . H̃.*   ★

Fachenham tenuit Aleſtan⁹ teinnus p̱ man̄ . v . car̄ terræ . ſemp
xiiii . uill . & vii . bord . 7 . x . fer̄ . 7 ſemp . v . car̄ in dn̄o . 7 iiii . car̄ hom.
xvi . ac p̱ti . ſilua de . viii . porc̄ . ſemp . i . molin̄ . Tc̄ . iiii . runc̄ . m̄ . iii.
7 xvi . equæ ſiluatice . ſemp . xii . an̄ Tc̄ xl . porc̄ . m̄ . xx . ſep̄ . ccc . ous̄.
Duæ æcclie xl . ac . 7 . i . car̄ . & dim̄ ac p̱ti . huic man̄ iacent . vi . foc̄
7 dim̄ . xxx . ac . ſemp . i . car̄ . ſemp xiii . liƀ . ht . i . lḡ in longo . & . viii.

421 a

qr̄ in lato . 7 . ii . ſol de gelto . In ead . xx libi hōes de qbȝ habuit Aleſtan⁹
comd . lxxx . ac . ſemp . ii . car̄ . & . iii . ac prati . & ual xx . ſol . hoc reclamat de dono regis . *Ϝ* In torp . i . liƀ hō . Spauoc . xxx ac . hic fuit hō
regine edit . & dedit eū . petro . p̱ morte ei⁹ conceſſit ei . rex . ut dict̄ ſui hōes.
Ϝ In Sapeſtuna . iii . libi hōes . xiii . ac . 7 dim̄ terræ int̄ eos ſemp . i . car̄.
7 . i . ac p̱ti . hoc eſt de dono regis . & ual . v . ſol.

COSFORD Hundred

16 In LAYHAM 20 acres of the lordship of Churchford. Scalpi held it.
Value 3s.
William *de Alno* holds (this).

17 In COLNEIS Hundred 1 free man; 2 acres of free land.
Value 4d.
He also holds (this).

37 LANDS OF PETER OF VALOGNES

BRADMERE Hundred

1 Alstan, a thane, held (Great) FAKENHAM as a manor; 5 carucates of land.
Always 14 villagers; 7 smallholders; 10 slaves.
Always 5 ploughs in lordship; 4 men's ploughs.
Meadow, 16 acres; woodland at 8 pigs; always 1 mill. Then 4 cobs, now 3; 16 wild mares; always 12 cattle. Then 40 pigs, now 20; always 300 sheep.
2 churches, 40 acres. 1 plough. Meadow, ½ acre.
To this manor belong 6 Freemen and a half; 30 acres. Always 1 plough.
[Value] always £13.
It has 1 league in length and 8 furlongs in width; 2s in tax.
In the same (Great Fakenham) 20 free men over whom Alstan had patronage; 80 acres. Always 2 ploughs.
Meadow, 3 acres.
Value 20s.
He claims this by the King's gift.

2 In (Ixworth) THORPE 1 free man, Sparrowhawk; 30 acres. He was a man of Queen Edith's and she granted him to Peter. After her death the King assigned (him) to him, as his men say.

3 In SAPISTON 3 free men; 13½ acres of land between them. Always 1 plough.
Meadow, 1 acre.
This is by the King's gift.
Value 5s.

4 In BARNINGHAM Alstan held 1 carucate of land as a manor.
Then 5 villagers, now 2; 1 slave.
Always 1 plough in lordship. Then ½ men's plough, now 2 oxen.
Meadow, 2 acres. Always 1 cob. Then 30 sheep.
Value 20s.
6 free men, (subject to) fold-rights and patronage; 12 acres. ½ plough.
Value 5s.

In b̄nichā . I . car̊ terræ . ꝑ mañ . teñ Aleſtan⁹ . Tc̄ . v . uiƚƚ . modo . II . 7
. I . ſeru̇ . ſemp . I . car̊ in dn̄io . Tc̄ dim̊ car̊ . hom̊ . m̊ . II . boū . & . II . ac̄ p̊ti.
7 ſemp . I . runc̊ . Tc̄ . xxx . oūs . 7 uaƚ . xx . ſoƚ . 7 . VI . libi hōes . ſoca falde
& c̄omd̊ XII . ac̊ . 7 dim̊ car̊ . 7 uaƚ . v . ſoƚ.

In Wicā teñ Alan̊ . t . r . e . ꝑ mañ . I . car̊ . t̊ræ . ſemp . v . bord̊ . Tc̄ . II .
ſerui . modo . I . Tc̄ . I . car̊ in dn̄io . m̊ . II . 7 . III . ac̄ p̊ti . ſilua . de . VIII .
porc̊ . 7 . II . boū hom̊ . m̊ . I . runc̊ . Tc̄ . III . añ . modo . XI . Tc̄ . VII . porc̊ .
modo . XIII . Tc̄ XL . oūs . m̊ . C . 7 . II . ſoc̊ . x . ac̊ . ſemp . II . boū . Tc̄ uaƚ
xx . ſoƚ . modo . xxx . In ead̊ . VIII . libi . hōes . c̄md̊ . I . car̊ t̊re . 7 XI . bord̊ .
ſemp II . car̊ . & III . ac̄ p̊ti . ſilua . II . porc̊ . Tc̄ uaƚ . x . ſoƚ . modo . xx .
hos h̊t de libatione . 7 ꝑ terra.

Riſeurd̊a teñ Alti⁹ Ketel . libi hōes teigni . t . r . e . II . car̊ terræ
Tc̄ . II . car̊ in dominio 7 m̊ . IIII . ac̄ . p̊ti . modo . I . runc̊ . Tc̄ . I . añ . m̊.
. V . Tc̄ XI . oūs . modo . LXXX . 7 IIII . uaſa apū . hanc terrā tenuer̊ iſti
. t . r . e . ꝑ duob⁊ maneriis . Semp uaƚ . xxx . ſoƚ . In ead̊ VIII . libi hōes
. I . car̊ terræ . 7 IX . ac̊ . c̊omd̊ ſup VII . ſocā faldæ . 7 c̊omd̊ ſup unū
tm̄ . Tc̄ & p̊ . II . car̊ . m̊ . I . & . IIII . ac̄ p̊ti & uaƚ . x . ſoƚ . & h̊t VI . qr̄ in
longo . & . III . qr̄ in lato . 7 XI . d̊ . & . I . ferding de gelto . Sc̄s eadmundus
de toto hund ſocā.

421 b

Hertesmera . H̄ . In Weſt torp . I . lib̊ hō . c̊om Alti⁹ . IX . ac̄ . ſilua
ad II . porc̊ . 7 uaƚ XVIII . d̊.

XXXVIII. TERRA ROGERII DE RAMIS. BABENBGA DVO. H̄.

In bura teñ com̊s Algarus . I . car̊ terræ . m̊ . Roḡ . & . I . uiƚƚ . & . III .
bord̊ . & . I . ſeru̇ . & . I . car̊ in dn̄io . & . I . car̊ hom̊ . & . II . ac̄ p̊ti . Tc̄
dim̊ moƚ . m̊ nulƚ⁹ 7 . ſēp . I . equ⁹ . 7 xxx . porc̊ . & . c . oūs . 7 uaƚ . xx . ſoƚ

5 In WYKEN Alan held 1 carucate of land as a manor before 1066.
   Always 5 smallholders. Then 2 slaves, now 1.
   Then 1 plough in lordship, now 2. Meadow, 3 acres; woodland at
      8 pigs. 2 men's oxen.
   Now 1 cob; then 3 cattle, now 11; then 7 pigs, now 13; then 40
      sheep, now 100.
   2 Freemen; 10 acres. Always 2 oxen.
   Value then 20s; now 30[s].
   In the same (Wyken) 8 free men under patronage; 1 carucate of land.
   11 smallholders.
   Always 2 ploughs.
   Meadow, 3 acres; woodland, 2 pigs.
   Value then 10s; now 20[s].
   He has this by a delivery and for land.

6 Auti and Ketel, free men (and) thanes, held RUSHFORD before 1066;
   2 carucates of land. Then 2 ploughs in lordship; now (the same).
   Meadow, 4 acres. Now 1 cob; then 1 cattle, now 5; then 11 sheep,
      now 80; 4 beehives.
   Those men held this land before 1066 as two manors.
   Value always 30s.
   In the same (Rushford) 8 free men; 1 carucate of land and 9 acres.
   7 under patronage and subject to fold-rights, and 1 under patronage
   only. Then and later 2 ploughs, now 1.
   Meadow, 4 acres.
   Value 10s.
   It has 6 furlongs in length and 3 furlongs in width; 11¼d in tax.
   St. Edmund's has jurisdiction over the whole Hundred.

HARTISMERE Hundred
7 In WESTHORPE 1 free man under patronage, Auti: 9 acres.
   Woodland for 2 pigs.
   Value 18d.

38   LAND OF ROGER OF RAMES

BABERGH Two Hundreds
1 In BURES Earl Algar held 1 carucate of land. Now Roger [holds it].
   1 villager, 3 smallholders, 1 slave.
   1 plough in lordship; 1 men's plough.
   Meadow, 2 acres; then ½ mill, now none. Always 1 horse, 30 pigs,
      100 sheep.
   Value 20s.

⁋In linhou . ten& uluric̅⁹ . fub alurico cā́po . t . r . e . 7 poterant uendere . xxx . ac̅ . & . iiii . bord . & . iii . bou̅ . & ual . xviii . fol . Socā
7 facā . sc̅s . e.

⁋Dimid . H̃. De gepefwiz . In uilla de gepefuiz ht . Rog̃
. i . ecc̅l̅ia sc̅i georgii . 7 . iiii . burg̃nfes . 7 . vi . uaftatas manfuras
una ex his derationata . fuit ad op̅ ab̅bis⁹ de eli . & . inde faifit
fuit . tefte hund̃ . fed Rog̃ dicit q̃d ten& de rege . Sup̃ dic̅te ecc̅liæ
ptin& . i . ac̅ . tr̅e . Totū ual . x . fol . Rex ht confuetudine̅.

⁋Bosemera . H̃. In Crofelda . ten̅ Edricus lib̅ ho̅ . t . r . e.
xx . ac̅ . Tc̅ . i . car . 7 m̃; Tc̅ . iiii . tunc . modo nullus . Tc̅ . ii . an;
Tc̅ xii . porc . 7 . v . ou̅s . m̃ int̅ totū nichil femp ual xl . den̅.
In ead ten̅ Wicolfus . lib̅e . t . r . e . xxxv . ac̅ q̃s tenebat ille . Edric⁹
cū fua terra q̃do lib̅ata fuit Rog̃o . femp iiii . bord . filua . x.
porc . & . ii . ac̅ p̃ti . & . ual . viii . fol.

422 a

⁋In Codehā . iii . lib̅i . hoes . xxx . ac̅ . & . i . bord . Tc̅ & p̃⁹ . i . car . modo
dim̃ . & . i . ac̅ & dim̃ p̃ti . Tc̅ ual . vi . fol . modo . v . & q̃rta pars æcc̅lie
& q̃rta pars ex hoc q̃d ecc̅liæ ptin& . hanc tr̅a tenuit Warenger
de Rogero fed ipfe defaifiuit . Rex & com̅s foca de toto.

⁋Eftenā ten̅ . i . lib̅ ho̅ . Ailmarus fub Edrico ante ceffore Rob̅ . mal&
com̃d tn̅tū . t . r . e . p̃ man̅ . lx . ac̅ . femp . i . bord . Tc̅ & poft . i . car.
modo nulla . & . ii . ac̅ p̃ti . filua . de xxx . porc . Ecclia . de xiiii.
ac̅ . Tc̅ ual . xx . fol . m̃ . xv.

2 In *LINHOU* Wulfric [held] under Aelfric Kemp before 1066; they could sell; 30 acres before 1066.
4 smallholders.
3 oxen.
St. Edmund's (has) full jurisdiction.

Half-Hundred of IPSWICH
3 In the town of IPSWICH Roger has 1 church, St. George's; 4 burgesses; and 6 destroyed dwellings. One of these (dwellings) was adjudged to be for the use of the Abbot of Ely and he was put in possession of it, as the Hundred testifies, but Roger says that he holds (it) from the King. To the above-mentioned church belongs 1 acre of land.
Value of the whole, 10s.
The King has the customary due.

BOSMERE Hundred
4 In CROWFIELD Edric, a free man, held 20 acres before 1066. Then 1 plough; now (the same).
Then 4 cobs, now none. Then 2 cattle; then 12 pigs, 5 sheep; now nothing at all.
Value always 40d.
In the same (Crowfield) before 1066 Wigulf held freely 35 acres which the same Edric held with his land when it was delivered to Roger.
Always 4 smallholders.
Woodland, 10 pigs; meadow, 2 acres.
Value 8s.

5 In CODDENHAM 3 free men; 30 acres.
1 smallholder.
Then and later 1 plough, now ½. Meadow, 1½ acres.
Value then 6s; now 5[s].
The fourth part of a church and the fourth part of what belongs to the church.
Warengar held this land from Roger but he dispossessed (him).
The King and the Earl (have) jurisdiction over the whole.

6 Aethelmer, 1 free man under patronage only held STONHAM (Aspal) before 1066 under Edric, Robert Malet's predecessor, as a manor, 60 acres.
Always 1 smallholder.
Then and later 1 plough, now none.
Meadow, 2 acres; woodland at 30 pigs.
A church with 14 acres.
Value then 20s; now 15[s].

In ead . I . lib hō . Aluuin in foca regis . LXXXX . ac̄ . p mañ . femp . I .
uilt & . I . borđ . 7 tc̄ . II . car̄ . in dn̄io . modo . I . & . IIII . ac̄ p̃ti . filu
xx . porc̄ . Tc̄ ual xL . fol . modo . xxv . Rex & Cōms focā .
In ead . lib hō . de Lx . ac̄ . & . I . borđ . & . I . uilt . Tc̄ . & p . I . car̄ . modo
dim . Tc̄ . I . car̄ hom̄ . modo dim . & . I . ac̄ p̃ti . filua . xx . porc̄ . Tc̄
ual xx . fol . m̄ . xv . Rex & cōms focā . In ead lib hō de xxx . ac̄
& . I . borđ . Tc̄ & . p . I . car̄ . modo dim . Silua de . x . porc̄ . Tc̄ ual . x .
fol . modo . v . Rex & cōms focā . In ead . VIII . libi hoēs . xxx . ac̄ .
duo ex his fuer̄ cōmdati cuidā hōi cōmdato ante cefſori Rob.
mal& . & Willm pat̄ fuus inde faifitus fuit . Int̄ eos om̄s h̄nt
. I . car̄ . & ual . v . fol . h̄ totū ten̄ milo de Rog . & recepit . IIII . eq̃s
m̄ . I . Tc̄ . III . an̄ . m̄ . III . Tc̄ . XIIII . porc̄ . modo . xxxvI . Tc̄ xxxvI .
oūs . m̄ nult . h̄t dim l̄g in longo . & dim in lato . & . vI . đ . de gelto .
Alii ibi tenent . Rex | cōms . focā .

In ead . R . h̄t in dn̄io Eftuna . XII . libi hoēs . de . xL . ac̄ . in foca
reḡ . & comitis . Tc̄ & p . II . car̄ . m̄ . I . car̄ & dim . & . I . ac̄ p̃ti .

422 b
& ual& . xv . fol .
In briefeta . ten& Anfchetillus de Rogo . I . car̄ terræ p mañ in
foca regis & comitis q tenuit Goduuin lib hō . t . r . e . Tc̄ . II . borđ .
modo . v . Ecclia de xv . ac̄ . femp . I . car̄ . in dn̄io . modo . II . boū . hom .
& . II . ac̄ p̃ti . 7 xL . II . oūs . 7 xv . porc̄ . Tc̄ ual . xx . fol . modo xxv . Tota
h̄t . I . l̄g in longo . & dim in lato . & vI . đ & obolū de gelto . alii ibi tenēt .

In the same (Stonham Aspal) 1 free man, Alwin, in the King's jurisdiction; 90 acres as a manor.
>Always 1 villager; 1 smallholder.
>Then 2 ploughs in lordship, now 1.
>Meadow, 4 acres; woodland, 20 pigs.

Value then 40s; now 25[s].
>The King and the Earl (have) the jurisdiction.

In the same (Stonham Aspal) a free man, with 60 acres.
>1 smallholder, 1 villager.
>Then and later 1 plough, now ½; then 1 men's plough, now ½.
>Meadow, 1 acre; woodland, 20 pigs.

Value then 20s; now 15[s].
>The King and the Earl (have) the jurisdiction.

In the same (Stonham Aspal) 1 free man, with 30 acres.
>1 smallholder.
>Then and later 1 plough, now ½. Woodland at 10 pigs.

Value then 10s; now 5[s].
>The King and the Earl (have) the jurisdiction.

In the same (Stonham Aspal) 8 free men; 30 acres. Two of these were under the patronage of a man (who was) under the patronage of Robert Malet's predecessor, and William (Malet), his father, was in possession of that (patronage). Between them all they have 1 plough.

Value 5s.
>Miles holds the whole of this from Roger.
>He acquired 4 horses, now 1; 3 cattle, now 3; then 14 pigs,
>>now 36; then 36 sheep, now none.

>It has ½ league in length and ½ in width; 6d in tax. Others hold there. The King and the Earl (have) the jurisdiction.

7 In the same STONHAM (Aspal) Roger has in lordship; 12 free men, with 40 acres, in the jurisdiction of the King and the Earl. Then and later 2 ploughs, now 1½ ploughs.
>Meadow, 1 acre.

Value 15s.

422 b

8 In BRICETT Ansketel holds from Roger 1 carucate of land as a manor, in the jurisdiction of the King and the Earl. Godwin, a free man, held it before 1066.
>Then 2 smallholders, now 5.
>A church with 15 acres.
>Always 1 plough in lordship. Now 2 men's oxen.
>Meadow, 2 acres. 42 sheep, 15 pigs.

Value then 20s; now 25[s].
>The whole has 1 league in length and ½ in width; 6½d in tax. Others hold there.

In Langhedana ten̄ filia Rōg . I . lib̄ hm̄⁷ . IX . ac̄ . & ual xvIII . đ.
In Codenhā . I . lib̄ hō Aluuin⁹ . I . ac̄ . & ual . II . đ . & in ead . IIII . ac̄
de dn̄io &   appciate ſunt.

CLAINDVNE . H̃. Achrehā tenuit Goduinus pb̄r . lib̄ hō

t . r . e . I . car⁷ tr̄æ . 7 xx . ac̄ ꝑ man̄ . modo filia Rōg . Tc̄ in dn̄io . II . car⁷.
m̄ . III . & . IIII . ac̄ p̄ti . & . II . runc⁷ . & . VII . an̄ . & ⁷tres partes æccliæ xxI . ac̄./ VI . porc⁷ . Tc̄ ual . xx
IIII . ſol . & m̄ ſimilit̄ . In ead̄ . ͞Guert I . lib̄ hō . Gotwin⁹ . c . ac̄ . ꝑ man̄ . Tc̄.
III . borđ . 7 modo . I . Tc̄ . I . car⁷ . & modo . & . II . ac̄ & dim p̄ti . Tc̄ ual xvI.
ſol . modo . xIx . 7 IIII . đ . In ead . I . lib̄ hō Aluricus . c̄omdatus ſaxo ante
ceſſori piperel⁷ xL . ac̄ . ſemp . I . car⁷ . & . I . ac̄ p̄ti . Tc̄ ual . vI . ſol . 7 VIII . đ.
modo . x . In ead Sunwin⁹ lib̄ hō tenuit Guert . c̄omđ . xxx⁷ . ac̄vI.
ꝑ man̄ . t . r . e . Tc̄ . I . car⁷ . & . I . ac̄ & dim p̄ti . & . ual . VI . ſol.
In ead Turbnus pb̄r lib̄ hō tenuit . xxx . ac̄ . ꝑ man̄ . t . r . e . Tc̄ . I . car⁷.
Tc̄ . I . borđ . Tc̄ ual . v . ſol . m̄ . x . 7 . x . đ . Rex & com̄s ſocā . & c̄omđ.
In ead . xxxv . libi hōes . cc . & . III . ac̄ . & dim . & . II . ac̄ p̄ti . Tc̄ . vII . car⁷
m̄ dim Tc̄ ual xL . ſol . modo . v . lib̄ . & . Ix . ſol . Rex et C . ſocā . hɼ . I . lḡ
in longo . & . vII . qɼ in lato . 7 xx . đ de gelto.

In Weſtrefelda . III . libi hōes⁷ . xx . vIII . ac̄ . Tc̄ & ⁹p⁷ . I . car⁷ . modo

nichil . & . I . ac̄ p̄ti . & . ual . x . ſol . Rex & com̄s ſocā.

In toddenham . xx . ac̄ in dn̄io de totdenhā . & c̄ in p̄tio.

9 In *LANGHEDANA* Roger's daughter holds 1 free man; 9 acres.
Value 18d.

10 In CODDENHAM 1 free man, Alwin; 1 acre.
Value 2d.
In the same (Coddenham) 4 acres in lordship.
They have been assessed.

CLAYDON Hundred

11 Godwin the priest, a free man, held AKENHAM before 1066; 1 carucate of land and 20 acres as a manor. Now Roger's daughter holds (it).
Then 2 ploughs in lordship, now 3.
    Meadow, 4 acres. 2 cobs, 7 cattle, 6 pigs.
    Three parts of a church, 12 acres.
Value then 24s; now the same.
In the same (Akenham) Godwin, a free man [under the patronage of] Gyrth; 100 acres as a manor.
    Then 3 smallholders, now 1.
    Then 1 plough, now (the same). Meadow, 2½ acres.
Value then 16s; now 19[s] 4d.
In the same (Akenham) 1 free man, Aelfric, under the patronage of Saxi, (Ranulf) Peverel's predecessor; 40 acres. Always 1 plough.
    Meadow, 1 acre.
Value then 6s 8d; now 10[s].
In the same (Akenham) Sunwin, a free man under the patronage of Gyrth, held 36 acres as a manor before 1066. Then 1 plough.
    Meadow, 1½ acres.
Value 6s.
In the same (Akenham) Thorbern the priest, a free man, held 30 acres as a manor before 1066. Then 1 plough.
    Then 1 smallholder.
Value then 5s; now 10[s] 10d.
    The King and the Earl (have) the jurisdiction and the patronage.
In the same (Akenham) 35 free men; 203½ acres.
    Meadow, 2 acres.
    Then 7 ploughs, now ½.
Value then 40s; now £5 9s.
    The King and the Earl (have) the jurisdiction. It has 1 league in length and 7 furlongs in width; 20d in tax.

12 In WESTERFIELD 3 free men; 28 acres. Then and later 1 plough, now nothing.
    Meadow, 1 acre.
Value 10s.
    The King and the Earl (have) the jurisdiction.

13 In TUDDENHAM 20 acres of the lordship of Tuddenham.
It is in the assessment.

�ножIn Weſtrefelda . v . libi hões . xx . iii . aē . & . i . uirga . Tē & p̄ . i . car̃.
modo nult̃ . 7 ual . iiii . fol . Giroldus ten& . In ead . i . lib hō . xvi.
aē . Tē & p̄ dim̃ . car . modo . nul . & ual . xxx . ii . d . Rex & coms̃ focā.
Ernaldus ten̄ de eo.

In li hund̃ . xx . aē quē ptinent eccliæ de totdenham.

Niuuetunā ten̄ ernaldus de rog̃ . quē ten̄ Brictmarus lib hō
t . r . e . c . ii . aē . p man̄ . t . r . e . Tē & p̄ . ii . uilli . & . ii . bord̃ . modo . iiii.
bord̃ . femp . i . car in dn̄io . Tē & p̄ . ii . car̃ hom̃ . m̂ nichil . & . ii . aē
p̃ti . & . i . run̄ . Tē xx . porc̃ . modo xvi . Tē xx . oūs . modo xii.
7 ual . xx . fol . In ead ten̄ Leuefunus . lib hō com̄d . Stigando . xl.
aē . p man̄ . t . r . e . Tē & p̄ . i . car̃ . m̂ . ii . boū . & . i . aē . p̃ti . Tē ual . xx . fol.
modo . x . Rad̃ de Rog̃ Rex & coms̃ de toto focā.

In Codeham ten̄ . Rog̃ in dn̄io . vi . libos hoēs . xxvi . aē . in foc̃ reg̃
& comitis . Tē & p̄ . ii . car̃ . modo . i . & . i . aē . p̃ti . 7 ual . xii . fol . ii . d̃ . min̄.

In helminchā . i . lib hō Leuredus . xx . aē . Tē & p̄ . i . car̃ . modo nichil.
7 ual . iii . fol . 7 . i . d . Rex & coms̃ de toto focā.

In eſtuna . xv . aē dn̄icæ terræ . & . in p̃tio . milo ten& de rog̃o.

In Codehā ten̄ Aluric̃ . 7 boti . libi hoēs . boti ix . aē . & dim̃ . Tē . dim̃
car̃ . m̂ . ii . boū . 7 ual . iii . fol . Idē milo.

14 In WESTERFIELD 5 free men; 23 acres and 1 pole. Then and later 1 plough, now none.
Value 4s.
    Gerald holds (this).
In the same (Westerfield) 1 free man; 16 acres. Then and later ½ plough, now none.
Value 32d.
    The King and the Earl (have) the jurisdiction.
    Arnold holds (this) from him.

15 In this Hundred, 20 acres which belong to the church of Tuddenham.

16 Arnold holds NEWTON from Roger; Brictmer, a free man, held it before 1066; 102 acres as a manor before 1066.
    Then and later 2 villagers and 2 smallholders; now 4 smallholders.
    Always 1 plough in lordship. Then and later 2 men's ploughs, now nothing.
    Meadow, 2 acres. 1 cob; then 20 pigs, now 16; then 20 sheep, now 12.
Value 20s.
In the same (Newton) Leofson, a free man under the patronage of Stigand, held 40 acres as a manor before 1066. Then and later 1 plough, now 2 oxen.
    Meadow, 1 acre.
Value then 20s; now 10[s].
    Ralph [holds this] from Roger.
    The King and the Earl (have) jurisdiction over the whole.

17 In CODDENHAM Roger holds in lordship 6 free men, in the jurisdiction of the King and the Earl; 26 acres. Then and later 2 ploughs, now 1.
    Meadow, 1 acre.
Value 12s less 2d.

18 In HELMINGHAM 1 free man, Leofred; 20 acres. Then and later 1 plough, now nothing.
Value 3s 1d.
    The King and the Earl (have) jurisdiction over the whole.

19 In STONHAM (Aspal) 15 acres of lordship land.
(It is) in the assessment.
    Miles holds (this) from Roger.

20 In CODDENHAM Aelfric and Boti, free men, held 9½ acres. Then ½ plough, now 2 oxen.
Value 3s.
    Miles also [holds this].

/ S̄ANFORT . H̃ . & dim̃ . In heihā . ten̄ . firic̓ liƀ hō . xxx . ac̄ . p̄ man̄ .
t . r . e . femp dim̄ car̓ . & tc̄ ual& . v . fot . modo . viii . Garengerus ten̄,
haroldus focā in ƀcolt.

423 b

* / H̃ . De CARLEFORDA . In tudenhā Geroldus . i . liƀ h̃m Aluric
diaconū com̓d Saxæ . de aƀƀe . t r . e . xii . ac̄ . p̄ man̄ . iii . bord.
Semp . i . car̓ . ii . ac̄ p̃ti . Tc̄ . i . runc̓ . 7 femp . ii . an̄ . & . xi . porc̓ . & xl .
oūs . & uat . iii . fot . 7 jn ead . ii . liƀi hoes . com̓d . i . fce Æ . & alter
com̓d . heroldi . x . ac̄ . 7 dim̄ car̓ . & uat . ii . fot . h̃ ten& . Geroldus.
de . R.

/ In Grundefƀur Raulfus . xx . ac̄ & p̃tinent ad neutuna . & in
p̃tio jn finlesford . vi . ac̄ . i . ac̄ de p̃to & p̃tinent ad neutuna in
aliā hund . hoc ten& Radulfus.

/ In oteleia . iiii . ac̄ . & p̃tinent ad eftuna . & in p̃tio h̃ ten Milo de-
belefol.

/ COLENESSE . H̃ . In kirketuna . ii . ac̄ . & uat . iiii . d̄.

/ LOSA . H̃ . In udebrige . i . liƀ hō . com̓d Aluuini . xi . ac̄ . dim̄
ac̄ p̃ti . & uat xxvii . d̄.

SAMFORD Hundred and a Half

21 In HIGHAM Siric, a free man, held 30 acres as a manor before 1066. Always ½ plough.
Value then 5s; now 8[s].
Warengar holds (this).
Harold (had) the jurisdiction in (East) Bergholt.

Hundred of CARLFORD 423 b

22 In TUDDENHAM Gerald [holds] 1 free man, Aelfric the deacon, under the patronage of Saxi from the Abbot (of Ely) before 1066; 12 acres as a manor.
3 smallholders.
Always 1 plough.
Meadow, 2 acres. Then 1 cob. Always 2 cattle, 11 pigs, 40 sheep.
Value 3s.
In the same (Tuddenham) 2 free men, 1 under the patronage of St. Etheldreda's, the other under the patronage of Harold; 10 acres. ½ plough.
Value 2s.
Gerald [holds this] from Roger.

23 In GRUNDISBURGH Ralph [holds] 20 acres. They belong to Newton. (They are) in the assessment.

24 In 'FINLESFORD' 6 acres.
Meadow, 1 acre.
They belong to Newton in another Hundred.
Ralph holds this.

25 In OTLEY 4 acres. They belong to Stonham (Aspal).
(They are) in the assessment.
Miles *de Belefol* holds this.

COLNEIS Hundred

26 In KIRTON 2 acres.
Value 4d.

LOES Hundred

27 In WOODBRIDGE 1 free man under the patronage of Alwin; 11 acres.
Meadow, ½ acre.
Value 27d.

.XXXVIIII. ⁊TERRE. R. FRIS ILgeri. Colenesse . h̄. In burg. I. lib homo Godricus. com̄. cuidā com. horoldi xvi ac̄ terræ. II borđ. dim̄. car̄.
dim̄ ac̄ p̃ti. ual. III. fot. 7 in tremelaia. II. ac̄. 7. IIII. đ. ual.
⁊In morestona. I. lib hō. c̄omđ Brifmer. IIII. ac̄. XII. đ. ual.
⁊In faltenham. XXVI. ac̄. ten̄ idē. Bri. t. r. e. p̄ man̄. Tc̄. I. car̄. 7. I.
runc̄. &. IIII. an̄. &. XL. oūs. modo int̄ totū nichil. Tc̄ ual. x.
fot. modo. v. fot. hic Brictmarus habuit plures terras. & quedā

424 a

pars fuit libata ex parte regis ingelrico. Et alie partes. Randulfo
fri ilgeri. & tertia pars Radulfo pinello. 7 in ista tertia parte fuit
ista fup̃ dicta terra delibata Rađ fic ipfe dicit & idē pib& h̄. testi
moni. quod ipfe fuit faifitus inpmis. f7 utrū ex parte regis nec n̄
fuiff& faifitus illud ignorant. & dicunt etiā. quod ista terrā. R.
calūpniaū fup̃ radulfū. & uice coms. Rog denominauit illis consti
tutū t̄p. m. ut ambo adfuiffent. Ranulfo ad ueniente⸵ de fuit Radulfus. & idcirco diiudicauer hoēs hundreti. Rannulfū eē. faifitum.
qui modo ten&. f& Rađ pinel negat qđ n̄ fuit fummonit de eo
placito. ⁊Immo testuna. I. liba femina. Vlueua. com̄đ. Bric. x. ac̄.
Tc̄ dim̄ car̄. modo. null. & ual. II. fot.

LANDS OF RANULF BROTHER OF ILGER

COLNEIS Hundred

1 In BURGH 1 free man, Godric, under the patronage of someone under the patronage of Harold; 16 acres of land.
2 smallholders.
½ plough. Meadow, ½ acre.
Value 3s.
In TRIMLEY (St. Martin) 2 acres.
Value 4d.

2 In MORSTON 1 free man under the patronage of Brictmer; 4 acres.
Value 12d.

3 In FALKENHAM the same Brictmer held 26 acres before 1066 as a manor. Then 1 plough;
1 cob, 4 cattle, 40 sheep; now nothing at all.
Value then 10s; now 5s.
This Brictmer had several lands, and a part was delivered on the King's behalf to Engelric; other parts (were delivered) to Ranulf the brother of Ilger; and a third part (was delivered) to Ralph Pinel. The above-mentioned land was delivered in that third part to Ralph, so he himself says, and he also produces the testimony of the Hundred that he was at first in possession of it; but whether he was put in possession on the King's behalf or not they do not know. They say also that Ranulf claimed that land against Ralph, and Roger the Sheriff specified to them a set time that they should both be present; (although) Ranulf came, Ralph was absent and therefore the men of the Hundred judged that Ranulf should be in possession. He now holds (it), but Ralph Pinel denies that he was summoned concerning that assembly.

424 a

4 In MORSTON 1 free woman, Wulfeva, under the patronage of Brictmer; 10 acres. Then ½ plough, now none.
Value 2s.

*In halmelega . 1 . lib hõ brictmar . cõmd dim . Briht . & aliã medietat
Sc̃a Edeldrede . t . r . e . modo ten& . R . de rege p libatione ad fuũ
Dominiũ . fed abbas dicit qd ipfe deb& de eo tenere medietatẽ . xx . 11 .
ac : m̃ . nuł . 7 . 1 . bord . 1 . ac̃ p̃ti . 7 . 1 . ferũ . 7 uał . 1111 . foł . In ead . 1 . lib hõ
Vlwardus . cõmd . Godrici . t . r . e . xx . ac̃ . terræ . & . 11 . bord . & . 1 . car
dim ac̃ p̃ti . & uał . 1111 . foł . Adhuc in ead . 1 . lib hõ . harduuinus
cuidã cõmd . N . 7 . d . com . Edrici . t . r . e . v . ac̃ træ . & dim car.
dim ac̃ p̃ti . & uał . xii . d . In ead . 1 . lib hõ Brihtric . cõmd dim . Brih
mar 7 dim . Stanmar . t . r . e . ix . ac̃ 7 dim car . dim ac̃ prati . 7 uał . 111 . foł.
æcclia . viii . ac̃ . & uał . 11 . foł.
Ii totũ ten . R . fr ilgeri p libatione regis . 7 Willmus denomore
de eo sc̃a edeld . focã.

*H . DE CARLA forda . In merlefham tenet Ædwoldus . t . r . e .

. 11 . car terræ . & dim . p mañ . Semp . x . uill . & x . bord . Tc̃ . 11 . ferũ . Semp
in dñio . 11 . car . & houm . Tc̃ . v . car . modo . 1111 . xii . a p̃ti . modo . 1 . moł .
filua ad xvi . porc . Tc̃ . 111 . runc . modo . v . Tc̃ xx . 1111 . añ modo . xx . Tc̃
xl . porc . modo xxvii . Tc̃ . ccc . oũs . modo . cc . xii . Tc̃ xvi . cap . Tc̃ . vi .
uafa apũ . modo . xii . Tc̃ uał . xl . foł . modo fimilit . & ht . in longo . 1 . lg̃
& v . qr in lato . & de gelto . vi . d . In ead . 1 . æcclia . de xxx . vi . ac̃ . & uał . 111 .
foł . & . 1 . lib hõ Godric nom xvi . ac̃ . & . 1 . bord . & dim car . 7 . 1 . ac̃ p̃ti .
& uał & . 11 . foł .

5 In HEMLEY 1 free man, Brictmer, half under the patronage of Brict and the other half (under that) of St. Etheldreda's before 1066. Now Ranulf holds from the King by a delivery, for his lordship, but the Abbot (of Ely) says that he ought to hold a half from him; 22 acres. Then 1 plough, now none.
    1 smallholder.
    Meadow, 1 acre; 1 slave.
Value 4s.
In the same (Hemley) 1 free man, Wulfward, under the patronage of Godric before 1066; 20 acres of land.
    2 smallholders.
    1 plough. Meadow, ½ acre.
Value 4s.
Also in the same (Hemley) 1 free man Hardwin, [half] under the patronage of N. and half under the patronage of Edric before 1066; 5 acres of land. ½ plough.
    Meadow, ½ acre.
Value 12d.
In the same (Hemley) 1 free man, Brictric, half under the patronage of Brictmer and half (under that) of Stanmer before 1066; 9 acres. ½ plough.
    Meadow, ½ acre.
Value 3s.
    A church, 8 acres; value 2s.
Ranulf brother of Ilger holds the whole of this through the King's delivery, and William of Bosc [holds it] from him.
    St. Etheldreda's (has) the jurisdiction.

Hundred of CARLFORD
6 In MARTLESHAM Edwold [held] before 1066; 2½ carucates of land as a manor.   424 b
    Always 10 villagers; 10 smallholders. Then 2 slaves.
    Always 2 ploughs in lordship. Then 5 men's ploughs, now 4.
    Meadow, 12 acres; now 1 mill; woodland for 16 pigs. Then 3 cobs, now 5; then 24 cattle, now 20; then 40 pigs, now 27; then 300 sheep, now 212; then 16 goats; then 6 beehives, now 12.
Value then 40s; now the same.
It has 1 league in length and 5 furlongs in width; 6d in tax.
In the same (Martlesham) 1 church with 36 acres; value 3s.
Also 1 free man, Godric by name; 16 acres.
    1 smallholder;
    ½ plough. Meadow, 1 acre.
Value 2s.

⁊In Waldinga felda teñ Brihtmar lib̄ hō.t.r.e.1.car̄ terræ ꝑ mañ.
7.1.borđ.Tc̄.11.car̄.m̊.1.&.1.mot.Tc̄.1.runc̄.Tc̄.c.oūs.m̊ xxvii.Tc̄ ual
xx.fot.modo.x.7 h̄t in longo.vi.qr̄.7 in lat.iii.7 de gelto.v.deñ.
In ead.v.lib̄i hōes cōmdati.Brihmari.dim.7 dim.fuæ matri.xl.ac̄.7
.1.car̄.7 ual.iiii.fot

⁊In Preftetuna.x.lib̄i hoes.cōmdati.dim Brihmari 7 dim.Quengeu&
mat ei.un ex his fuit cōmdat dim.sc̄e.Æ.1.car̄ tr̄æ.m̊.ix.borđ.fub
eis.Tc̄.iiii.car̄.modo.11.1.ac̄ p̄ti.Tc̄ ual xx.fot.modo.x.7 h̄t.vi.qr̄
in longo.7 iii.in lato.7 de gelto.vi.đ.

⁊In hafpelega.v.lib̄i hōes cōmdati eidē.Brichmari.ficuti alii.1.car̄ tr̄e
&.v.borđ.7 iii.car̄.11.ac̄ p̄ti.Tc̄ ual.xxx.fot.modo.xx.1.ex iftis fuit
dim hō.Edrici 7 dim hō Normanni.11.ex his fuer̄ cōmdati.Quengeu&
t.r.e.& h̄t in longo.vi.qr̄; in lato.iii.&.v.đ.in gelt.

⁊nnebrunna.xvi.lib̄i hōes.com.Briɱmari.& quengeu&.t.r.e.
7.11.dim cōmd.sc̄æ.Æ.de.1.car̄ terræ.7 xl.ac̄.7 fub eis.xiiii.borđ.
Tc̄.iiii.car̄.modo.iii.1.ac̄.& đ p̄ti.Tc̄ ual xl.fot.m̊.xx.fot.&h̄t

.1.æcclia.xii.ac̄.& ual xvi.đ.& fuit normanni tefte hu̅ɍd.7 h̄t in
longo.vi.qr̄.&.v.in lato.& de gelto vii.đ & obol.

⁊In Kingeflanda.1.car̄ terræ guafta tr̄a & ual.11.fot.& h̄t in longo.iiii.
qr̄.7.iii.in lat.7 de gelto.v.đ.hoc totū teñ.W.de nemore.de.R.fr̄e
ilgeri.

7 In WALDRINGFIELD Brictmer, a free man, held before 1066; 1 carucate of land as a manor.
>   1 smallholder.
>   Then 2 ploughs, now 1.
>   1 mill. Then 1 cob; then 100 sheep, now 27.
>   Value then 20s; now 10[s].
>   It has 6 furlongs in length and 3 in width; 5d in tax.

In the same (Waldringfield) 5 free men half under the patronage of Brictmer and half under his mother's; 40 acres. 1 plough.
Value 4s.

8 In PRESTON 10 free men half under the patronage of Brictmer and half (under that) of Queneva his mother, and one of these was half under the patronage of St. Etheldreda's; 1 carucate of land.
>   Now 9 smallholders under them.
>   Then 4 ploughs, now 2. Meadow, 1 acre.
>   Value then 20s; now 10[s].
>   It has 6 furlongs in length and 3 in width; 6d in tax.

9 In HASPLEY 5 free men under the patronage of the same Brictmer, as the others; 1 carucate of land.
>   5 smallholders.
>   3 ploughs. Meadow, 2 acres.
>   Value then 30s; now 20[s].
>   1 of the (free men) was half Edric's man and half Norman's man, (and) 2 of them were under the patronage of Queneva before 1066.
>   It has 6 furlongs in length and 3 in width; 5d in tax.

10 In NEWBOURN 16 free men under the patronage of Brictmer and Queneva before 1066, and 2 half (free men) under the patronage of St. Etheldreda's, with 1 carucate of land and 40 acres.
>   Under them, 14 smallholders.
>   Then 4 ploughs, now 3. Meadow, 1½ acres.
>   Value then 40s; now 20[s].
>   1 church, 12 acres; value 16d. It was Norman's, as the Hundred testifies.
>   It has 6 furlongs in length and 5 in width; 7½d in tax.

425 a

11 In KINGSLAND 1 carucate of land. The land (is) waste.
>   Value 2s.
>   It has 4 furlongs in length and 3 in width; 5d in tax.

W(illiam) of Bosc holds the whole of this from Ranulf brother of Ilger.

/ In Aluredeftuna. tenuit. Durand lib hō. antec Ro. mal&. t. r. e.
. I. car terræ. 7 LXXX. ac. m̃ ten& Iuo. de. R. frē Ilgeri p man. Semp. VII.
uitt. 7. III. borđ. Tc in dn̄io. II. car. m̃. I. femp hom. III. car. IIII. ac p̃ti.
&. I. molin̄. 7 III. an̄. 7 L. oūs. I. æcclia de XII. ac. & ual. XII. đ. Tc ual. IIII.
lib. modo LX. fot. 7 ħt in longo. VI. qr. &. IIII. in lato. &. X. đ de gelto.
& in Gepefwiz. I. manfura. uacua. 7 alta hofpitata. 7 reddit. VIII. đ.
/ In hafpelega. VII. ac. 7 ſt in p̄tio de almelega. In edulueftuna. IX. ac. & ual
II. fot. In bulges. I. uitt. Vluric. IIII. ac. & ual. VIII. đ.

/ BABENBERGA. DVO. H̃. In Walingafella ten& uluricus teinn⁹
reg. e. I. car. terræ. modo ten̄ Ran̄ p man ex dono reḡ. W. cū foca & faca
femp. I. uitt. 7. III. borđ. Tc & p⁹. I. car. m̃. II. inť oīns 7. IIII. ac p̃ti. Sēp
. II. an̄. Tc XII. porc. modo XVI. Tc XX. oūs. modo. XXX. Tc 7 p⁹ ual. XXX.
fot. modo. XL.

/ SANFORT. H̃. Branham tenuit Aluric⁹ de Wenhou. II. car træ
Tc 7 p⁹. IIII. uitt. m̃. II. Tc. I. borđ. modo. VIII. Tc. II. feru. modo. I. Tc
7 p. II. car in dn̄io. m̃. I. sēp. I. car hom. filu. XII. porc. V. ac p̃ti. 7. I.
falina. 7. I. mot. Tc. I. runc. femp. XII. an̄. 7 XXIIII. porc. 7 LX. oūs. 7 ual
XL. fot. Aluric⁹ focaʰ fub aroldo. Roḡ. de Ranulf.

12 In *ALUREDESTUNA* Durand, a free man, Ro(bert) Malet's predecessor, held before 1066; 1 carucate of land and 80 acres. Now Ivo holds (it) from Ranulf brother of Ilger as a manor.
    Always 7 villagers; 3 smallholders.
    Then 2 ploughs in lordship, now 1; always 3 men's ploughs.
    Meadow, 4 acres; 1 mill. 3 cattle, 50 sheep.
    1 church with 12 acres; value 12d.
    Value then £4; now 60s.
    It has 6 furlongs in length and 4 in width; 10d in tax.
    Also in IPSWICH 1 empty dwelling and another inhabited.
    It pays 8d.

13 In HASPLEY 7 acres.
They are in the assessment of Hemley.

14 In *EDULUESTUNA* 9 acres.
Value 2s.

15 In BOULGE 1 villager, Wulfric; 4 acres.
Value 8d.

  BABERGH Two Hundreds
16 In WALDINGFIELD Wulfric, a thane of King Edward's, [held] 1 carucate of land. Now Ranulf holds (it) as a manor by King William's gift, with full jurisdiction.
    Always 1 villager; 3 smallholders.
    Then and later 1 plough between them all, now 2.
    Meadow, 4 acres. Always 2 cattle. Then 12 pigs, now 16; then 20 sheep, now 30.
    Value then and later 30s; now 40[s].

  SAMFORD Hundred
17 Aelfric of *Wenhou* held BRANTHAM; 2 carucates of land.
    Then and later 4 villagers, now 2; then 1 smallholder, now 8; then 2 slaves, now 1.
    Then and later 2 ploughs in lordship, now 1; always 1 men's plough.
    Woodland, 12 pigs; meadow, 5 acres; 1 salt-house; 1 mill. Then 1 cob. Always 12 cattle, 24 pigs, 60 sheep.
    Value 40s.
    Aelfric (had) the jurisdiction under Harold.
    Roger [holds this] from Ranulf.

.XL. *TERROTBTI FILII CORBVTIONIS. TINGOV. H.*

Brode ten̄ Ricardus quā tenuit Saiardus lib̄ hō. fub ſc̄o edmundo. t. r. e. in foca ſc̄i edmund fed non poterat uendere dim̄ car̄ tr̄æ
&. I. car̄. 7. I. ac̄ 7 dim̄ p̄ti. Tc̄ uat̄. x. fot̄. m̄. xv.

BAbga duo. H̄. Somerledetuna ten̄. Roḡ. quā tenuit ſtaRker
ſub gloſo rege. e. p̄ man̄. I. car̄ terræ in foca ſc̄i. edmund. Semp. II
bord. Tc̄. IIII. feru. m̄. I. Tc̄ & p̄. II. car̄ in d̄nio. modo. I. 7 III. ac̄
7 dim̄ p̄ti. modo. x. an̄. Tc̄ xv. porc̄. modo. VIII. Tc̄ LX. oūs. modo
. L. modo. v. cap̄. Tc̄ & p̄ uat̄. xxx. fot̄. modo xL.

SANFORT. H̄. & dim̄ Wenham tenuit Auti tenn̄. t. r. e.
p̄ man̄. III. car̄ terræ. Tc̄ IX. uitt̄. P̄ 7 modo. VI. Tc̄ 7 p̄. IIII. bord.
m̄. XIIII. femp. I. feru. Tc̄ 7 p̄. II. car̄ in d̄nio. modo dim̄. Tc̄
. v. car̄ hom̄. P̄. IIII. modo. III. XI. ac̄ p̄ti. Tc̄ filu de. x. porc̄.
femp. I. molin̄. Ecclia. de. xx. ac̄. libæ tr̄æ. femp dim̄ car̄. Tc̄. II.
runc̄. 7 IIII. an̄. & xx. porc̄. modo nichil. p̄t xx. III. oūs. Tc̄
& p̄ uat̄ vi. lib̄. m̄. c. fot̄. Auti habuit focā fup fuū dominiū.
7 foca de Wittis erat in bcolt. *Girardus* ten̄ de h̄ manerio.
xxx. ac̄. & uat̄. v. fot̄ 7 ſt̄ in eod̄ p̄tio.

In Wenham ten̄ Godvin. lib̄ homo. x. ac̄. & ē additus huic
manerio. & uat̄. II. fot̄. Soca in bcolt. h̄t XII. qr̄ in longo. 7 VI. in
lat̄. &. II. fot̄ de gelto.

H̄. DE CARLEFORD. In barcheſtuna ten̄ Depekin. lib̄ hō. cō
md heroldi. I. car̄ terræ p̄ man̄. Tc̄. VI. bord. m̄. IIII. Tc̄. in d̄nio
. I. car̄. modo nulla. Tc̄ hom̄. VII. car̄. modo nulla. v. ac̄ p̄ti. 7 VI. oūs.

Tc̄ uat̄. xx. fot̄. modo xII. 7 h̄t in longo. VI. qr̄. 7. IIII. in lato. 7 de-
gelto. III. d̄.

LANDS OF ROBERT SON OF CORBUCION

THINGOE Hundred
1 Richard holds BROCKLEY. Saegard, a free man, held it under St. Edmund's before 1066; in the jurisdiction of St. Edmund's, but he could not sell; ½ carucate of land. 1 plough.
Meadow, 1½ acres.
Value then 10s; now 15[s].

BABERGH Two Hundreds
2 Roger holds SOMERTON. Starker held it under the glorious King Edward as a manor; 1 carucate of land; in the jurisdiction of St. Edmund's.
Always 2 smallholders. Then 4 slaves, now 1.
Then and later 2 ploughs in lordship, now 1.
Meadow, 3½ acres. Now 10 cattle; then 15 pigs, now 8; then 60 sheep, now 50; now 5 goats.
Value then and later 30s; now 40[s].

SAMFORD Hundred and a Half
3 Auti, a thane, held WENHAM before 1066 as a manor; 3 carucates of land.
Then 9 villagers, later and now 6; then and later 4 smallholders, now 14; always 1 slave.
Then and later 2 ploughs in lordship, now ½; then 5 men's ploughs, later 4, now 3.
Meadow, 11 acres; woodland then at 10 pigs; always 1 mill.
A church with 20 acres of free land. Always ½ plough.
Then 2 cobs, 4 cattle, 20 pigs; now nothing except for 23 sheep.
Value then and later £6; now 100s.
Auti had jurisdiction over his lordship; jurisdiction over the villagers was in (East) Bergholt.
Gerard holds 30 acres of this manor.
Value 5s; they are in the same assessment.
In WENHAM Godwin, a free man, held 10 acres; it has been added to this manor.
Value 2s.
The jurisdiction is in (East) Bergholt.
It has 12 furlongs in length and 6 in width; 2s in tax.

Hundred of CARLFORD
4 In BARKESTONE Tepekin, a free man under the patronage of Harold, held 1 carucate of land as a manor.
Then 6 smallholders, now 4.
Then 1 plough in lordship, now none; then 7 men's ploughs, now none.
Meadow, 5 acres. 6 sheep.
Value then 20s; now 12[s].
It has 6 furlongs in length and 4 in width; 3d in tax.

⁊ DIM. H̃ DE COSFORT. In Watefeldā . I . foć . s̄ći eadmūd
. c . āc . ⁊ Tc̄ . I . car̓ . ꝑ dim̃ . modo . nulla ⁊ ual . x . fol . berardus . hō
Abbis ten& de abbæ.

⁊ SANFORT . H̃ . Torintunā tenuit Aluin⁹ lib hō . Stigandi
. t . r . e . II . car̓ terræ . ꝑ man̄ . Tc̄ & p̓⁹ . vi . uilt . modo . IIII . Tc̄ & p̓⁹ . II . bord̓ .
m̊ . v . Tc̄ . II . feru̓ . p̓⁹ & m̊ . I . femp . II . car̓ in dn̄io . Tc̄ & p̓⁹ . III . car̓ hom̄ .
m̊ . II . xx . āc . p̊ti . femp . I . molin̄ . Ecc̄lia . L . āc . libe t̃ræ . m̊ . I . runc̓ .
⁊ . vi . an̄ . Tc̄ . IIII . porc̓ . modo . xxx . ⁊ xx . oūs . ⁊ xxx . cap̓ . sēp ual
. L . fol . Idē focā habuit fub ftigando . hr̄ . vi . qr̄ in longo . ⁊ IIII . in
lato . & . v . d̄ de gelto . Gifardus ten̄ de Robto.

* ⁊ TRE Galteri diaconi . DIM̃ . H̃ . de cosfort . Bileftunā in dn̄io   . XLI .
tenuit Edid̓ . regina . t . r . e . ꝑ man̄ . vi . car̓ t̃ræ . femp . XIIII . uilt .
⁊ . vi . bord̓ . ⁊ viii . feru̓ . & . III . car̓ in dominio . ⁊ . III . car̓ hom̄ . xx . āc
p̊ti . Silua de . x . porc̓ . ⁊ . III . runc̓ . & . x . an̄ . ⁊ xl . porc̓ . ⁊ lxxx . oūs
Ecc̄lia xl . āc . ⁊ . I . car̓ . ⁊ . I . āc p̊ti . Tc̄ ual . viii . lib . modo . x . fed reddit
. xii . hr̄ . I . lḡ in longo . & dim̃ in lato . & . v . den de gelto.

⁊ Claindune . H̃ . Suinlandā tenuit Regina . Edid̓ . t . r . e . II .
car̓ terræ . ⁊ xl āc . ꝑ man̄ . femp vi . uilti . & . vi . bord̓ . & . I . feru̓ .
& . II . car̓ in dominio . & . III . car̓ hom̄ . IIII . āc p̊ti . filua . vi . porc̓ .
Ecc̄lia . de . v . āc . & . I . runc̓ . & . viii . an̄ . ⁊ xviiii . porc̓ Tc̄ lx . oūs .

modo . c . Tc̄ ual . L . fol . modo . lxx . hr̄ . vi . qr̄ in longo . & . IIII . in lat̓ .
⁊ xx . d̄ . de gl . Galt̓ in dn̄io . Regina focā.

Half-Hundred of COSFORD

5 In WHATFIELD 1 Freeman of St. Edmund's; 100 acres. Then 1 plough, later ½, now none.
Value 10s.
Berard, a man of the Abbot's, holds (this) from the Abbot.

SAMFORD Hundred

6 Alwin, a free man of Stigand's, held THORINGTON before 1066; 2 carucates of land as a manor.
Then and later 6 villagers, now 4; then and later 2 smallholders, now 5; then 2 slaves, later and now 1.
Always 2 ploughs in lordship. Then and later 3 men's ploughs, now 2.
Meadow, 20 acres; always 1 mill.
A church, 50 acres of free land.
Now 1 cob, 6 cattle. Then 4 pigs, now 30; 20 sheep; 30 goats.
Value always 50s.
He also had the jurisdiction under Stigand. It has 6 furlongs in length and 4 in width; 5d in tax.
Gifard holds (this) from Robert.

41   LANDS OF WALTER THE DEACON

Half-Hundred of COSFORD

1 Queen Edith held BILDESTON in lordship before 1066 as a manor; 6 carucates of land.
Always 14 villagers; 6 smallholders; 8 slaves;
3 ploughs in lordship; 3 men's ploughs.
Meadow, 20 acres; woodland at 10 pigs. 3 cobs, 10 cattle, 40 pigs, 80 sheep.
A church, 40 acres. 1 plough. Meadow, 1 acre.
Value then £8; now [£] 10, but it pays [£] 12.
It has 1 league in length and ½ in width; 5d in tax.

CLAYDON Hundred

2 Queen Edith held SWILLAND before 1066; 2 carucates of land and 40 acres as a manor.
Always 6 villagers; 6 smallholders; 1 slave;
2 ploughs in lordship; 3 men's ploughs.
Meadow, 4 acres; woodland, 6 pigs.
A church with 5 acres.
1 cob, 8 cattle, 19 pigs; then 60 sheep, now 100.
Value then 50s; now 70[s].
It has 6 furlongs in length and 4 in width; 20d in tax.
Walter [holds this] in lordship.
The Queen (had) the jurisdiction.

426 b

⁋ In Turoluestuna . I . lib hō xvi . ac̄ 7 iiii . borđ . femp dim̃ car̃ . & . I . ac̄ p̃ti . 7 ual . II . fol . 7 viii . đ . dim̃ æcclia . v . ac̄

⁋ In Westrefelda tenuit Almar͗ lib hō . xxx . ac̄ . 7 iiii . borđ . femp . I . car . & . II . ac̄ p̃ti . & ual . viii . fol . Turstin͗ de Galtero de feudo tedrici . rex 7 . c . focā

⁋ In Acrehā . II . libi hões . Suen͗ & Leuinus . L . ac̄ . 7 ual . v . fol . Turstin͗ de Galtero . 7 b̃nardus . de eođ feudo .

⁋ In Westrefelda . III . libi hões xxviii . ac̄ . 7 tc̄ . dim̃ car̃ . 7 ual xxx . vi . đ Bernard͗ . 7 almar͗ . ten& . Rex 7 Coms̃ focā . In eađ . lib hō vi . ac̄ . 7 ual& xii . đ . de eođ feudo . Normannus ten& Soca Reg̃ 7 comitis . ⁋ HERTESMARA . H̃ . Bachetunam . i dn̄io Leuuin͗ lib hō . heroldi . t . r . e . III . car̃ terræ . 7 xl ac̄ . Tc̄ xvii . uilli . modo . viii . Tc̄ . III . borđ . modo . xii . Tc̄ . II . feru̇ . modo . I . Semp in dn̄io . II . car̃ . Tc̄ hom̃ . III . car̃ . modo . II . vi . ac̄ p̃ti . filu̇ ad . c . porc̃ . Tc̄ . I . x . runc̃ . modo . viii . Semp . viii . añ . Tc̄ lx . porc̃ . modo . xl . Tc̄ xvi . ous̃ . modo . . c . Tc̄ . xl . cap͗ . modo . xxxvi . Tc̄ ual . viii . lib . modo . ix . lib . 7 x . fol . . I . æcclia xxiiii . ac̄ 7 ual . III . fol . 7 . xl . libi hões com̃đ . Leuuino . t . r . e . lxx . ac̄ terræ . 7 . I . borđ . Tc̄ . III . car̃ . modo . II . I . ac̄ p̃ti . Tc̄ ual . xx . fol . modo . iiii . lib . 7 . x . fol . Rex & com̃s focā . 7 h̃t i longo . I . lg̃ . 7 . in lato . iiii . qr̃ . & de gelto . vi . đ .

3 In THURLESTON 1 free man; 16 acres.
    4 smallholders.
    Always ½ plough. Meadow, 1 acre.
  Value 2s 8d.
    ½ church, 5 acres.

4 In WESTERFIELD Aelmer, a free man, held 30 acres.
    4 smallholders.
    Always 1 plough. Meadow, 2 acres.
  Value 8s.
    Thurstan [holds this] from Walter, from Theodoric's Holding.
    The King and the Earl (have) the jurisdiction.

5 In AKENHAM 2 free men, Swein and Leofwin; 50 acres.
  Value 5s.
    Thurstan [holds this] from Walter; and Bernard; from the same Holding.

6 In WESTERFIELD 3 free men; 28 acres. Then ½ plough.
  Value 36d.
    Bernard and Aelmer hold (this).
    The King and the Earl (have) the jurisdiction.
  In the same (Westerfield) a free man; 6 acres.
  Value 12d.
    (It is part) of the same Holding. Norman holds (it).
    The jurisdiction (is) the King's and the Earl's.

HARTISMERE Hundred
7 [Walter holds] BACTON in lordship; Leofwin, a free man of Harold's, before 1066; 3 carucates of land and 40 acres.
    Then 17 villagers, now 8; then 3 smallholders, now 12; then 2 slaves, now 1.
    Always 2 ploughs in lordship. Then 3 men's ploughs, now 2.
    Meadow, 6 acres; woodland for 100 pigs. Then 9 cobs, now 8; always 8 cattle. Then 60 pigs, now 40; then 16 sheep, now 100; then 40 goats, now 36.
  1 church, 24 acres; value 3s.
  Value then £8; now £9 10s.
  And 40 free men under the patronage of Leofwin before 1066; 80 acres of land.
    1 smallholder.
    Then 3 ploughs, now 2. Meadow, 1 acre.
  Value then 20s; now £4 10s.
    The King and the Earl (have) the jurisdiction. It has 1 league in length and 4 furlongs in width; 6d in tax.

ꝶIn caldecota.xix.ac̄.de dn̄io de bachetuna.7 ual.iii.ſol.7 iii.đ.7
ħt in longo.ix.qr̄.7 in lato.ii.7.v.perce.7 de gelto.vi.đ.
ꝶIn Weſtorp.briɢtricus liƀ hō com̄.vi.ac̄.7 ual.xii.đ.

427 a

ꝶBABENĒGA.Dvo.H̄.Mellinga ten̄ Galter in dominio
quā tenuit Leuuin de bagatona ten.reḡ.e.p̄ man̄.ii.cař terræ
m̄ ten̄ Galt.& eſt de feudo thederici fris ſui Semp.vi.uiłti.&.vi.
borđ.7.iiii.ſeru.Semp ii.cař in dn̄io.Tc̄ & p̄.iii cař hom̄.m̄.i.
7 vi.ac̄ p̄ti.Silu de.vi.porc.&.i.mol.Semp.ii.eq.7 vi.an̄.modo.
vii.7 xxii.porc.Tc̄.xl.ous.modo.l.Tc̄.xii.cap̄.modo xvi.Tc̄
7 p̄ ual.iiii.liƀ.modo.vi.liƀ.ħt vi.qr̄ in longo.7 iiii.in lato.7 de-
gelto.vii.đ.Eccłia.de xv.ac̄ liƀe terræ.Sup x.ac̄ q̄s ħt.i.liƀ
hō qđ potat uende ħt ſc̄s.e.ſoc 7 ſacā 7 ual.ii.ſol.
ꝶStov.H̄.In dagaworda Wiłłm ten̄.i.liƀ hō de q̄ teri antec̄
de barthetona habuit dim comđ tant.& gut mundus antec̄
hugon̄ de monte forti alta medietat.& poſ ſine licēncia eoȝ
uende.terrā ſuā.7 ħt lx.ac̄.&.i.borđ.Tc̄ & p.i.car.7 dim.m̄
ii.bou.Silua x.porc.&.iii.ac̄ p̄ti.
ꝶIn Weledana xv.ac̄.de tr̄a eiđ liƀ hōis.7 ii.ac̄ p̄ti.Tc̄ 7 p̄
tot ual xx.ſol.modo.v.hauc tr̄a teoderic Ātc̄ Wałti diaconi
ſine liƀatore teſte ħ.Rex & com̄s ſocā 7 ſacā.
ꝶIn Waīdena.i.liƀ hō in ſoca ħ.v.ac̄.& ual.xii.đ.
ꝶDIM.ħ.de gepeſwiz.In burgo ħt Galt.v.domos.7 iii.
manſuras uacuas q̄s ten̄.Regina.t.r.e.7 redđt cſuetđn̄e
7 ual xx.đ.

8 In *CALDECOTA* 19 acres of the lordship of Bacton.
Value 3s 3d.
It has 9 furlongs in length and 2 (furlongs) and 5 perches in width; 6d in tax.

9 In WESTHORPE Brictric, a free man under patronage; 6 acres.
Value 12d.

BABERGH Two Hundreds

10 Walter holds MILDEN in lordship. Leofwin of Bacton, a thane of King Edward's, held it as a manor; 2 carucates of land. Now Walter holds (it) and it belongs to the Holding of his brother Theodoric.
Always 6 villagers; 6 smallholders; 4 slaves.
Always 2 ploughs in lordship. Then and later 3 men's ploughs, now 1.
Meadow, 6 acres; woodland at 6 pigs; 1 mill. Always 2 horses. Then 6 cattle, now 7; 22 pigs; then 40 sheep, now 50; then 12 goats, now 16.
Value then and later £4; now £6.
It has 6 furlongs in length and 4 in width; 7d in tax.
A church with 15 acres of free land.
Over 10 acres which 1 free man has (and) which he could sell, St. Edmund's has full jurisdiction; value 2s.

427 a

STOW Hundred

11 William holds in DAGWORTH; 1 free man over whom Teri the predecessor of .... of *Barthetona* had only half the patronage and Guthmund, Hugh de Montfort's predecessor, (had) the other half, and he could sell his land without their permission. He has 60 acres.
1 smallholder.
Then and later 1½ ploughs, now 2 oxen.
Woodland, 10 pigs; meadow, 3 acres.
In *WELEDANA* 15 acres of the land of the same free man.
Meadow, 2 acres.
Value of the whole, then and later 20s; now 5[s].
Theodoric, Walter the Deacon's predecessor, had this land without a deliverer, as the Hundred testifies.
The King and the Earl (have) full jurisdiction.

12 In WETHERDEN 1 free man in the jurisdiction of the Hundred; 5 acres.
Value 12d.

Half-Hundred of IPSWICH

13 In the Borough (of IPSWICH) Walter has 5 houses and 3 empty dwellings which the Queen held before 1066. They pay the customary due.
Value 20d.

426 b, 427 a

ꝟCLAINDVNE. H̃. Henleie tenuit Vluric lib̃ hõ
.I. cař terre. 7 LXX. ac̃. ꝑ mañ. t. r. e. Tc̃. II. borđ. modo. VI.
Tc̃ 7 ṕ. II. cař in dominio. modo. I. femṕ. I. cař hom̃. IIII. ac̃ p̃ti.

Tc̃. III. runć. Tc̃. II. añ. m̃. III. Tc̃ x. porć. modo. II. Tc̃ XL. oũs
modo XLIIII. Ecc̃lia de VIII. ac̃. Tc̃ ual. XL. fol. 7 m̃. XLVIII. Roḡ.
de Galtero. Rex & com̃s foc̃a. In ead com̃đ. VI. libi hoes. XXXVI.
ac̃. Tc̃ & ṕ. I. cař. & dim̃. modo. I. cař. Tc̃ ual. VI. fol. 7. VIII. đ. m̃
VII. fol. Id. Roḡ. Rex & com̃s foc̃a. In ead. I. lib hõ nõe Suenus,
tenuit. XL. ac̃. ꝑ mañ. t. r. e. femp. I. cař. &. I. borđ. Tc̃ ual.
x. fol m̃ XVIII. Galt̃ teñ. in dñio ht. I. lḡ in longo. & dim̃
in lato. 7 xx đ. de gelto. Rex & com̃s foc̃a.
ꝟIn Bruntuna tenuit Leuuiñ teiññ. t. r. e. I. cař terræ
& XL. ac̃. ꝑ mañ. femp. IX. borđ. 7. II. feru. Tc̃ & ṕ. II. cař.
modo. I. Tc̃ & ṕ. II. cař hom̃. modo. I. v. ac̃ p̃ti. Tc̃. I. runć.
Tc̃ xx. porc̃. modo. x. Tc̃ xx oũs. modo XVI. Tc̃ ual. XL. fol.
modo. XXX. Rob̃ de Galtro. Rex & com̃s foc̃a.
ꝟIn Acheh̃a. IIII. libi hoes. de XXX. II. ac̃ terræ. Tc̃. I. cař. 7 ual
. V. fol. Roḡ de galtero. Rex & com̃s foc̃a.

CLAYDON Hundred
14 Wulfric, a free man, held HENLEY; 1 carucate of land and 70 acres as a manor before 1066.
    Then 2 smallholders, now 6.
    Then and later 2 ploughs in lordship, now 1; always 1 men's plough.
    Meadow, 4 acres. Then 3 cobs; then 2 cattle, now 3; then 10 pigs, now 2; then 40 sheep, now 44.   427 b
    A church with 8 acres.
Value then 40s; now 48[s].
    Roger [holds this] from Walter.
    The King and the Earl (have) the jurisdiction.
In the same (Henley) 6 free men under patronage; 36 acres. Then and later 1½ ploughs, now 1 plough.
Value then 6s 8d; now 7s.
    Roger also [holds this].
    The King and the Earl (have) the jurisdiction.
In the same (Henley) 1 free man, Swein by name, held 40 acres as a manor before 1066. Always 1 plough;
    1 smallholder.
Value then 10s; now 18[s].
    Walter holds (this) in lordship.
    It has 1 league in length and ½ in width; 20d in tax. The King and the Earl (have) the jurisdiction.

15 In *BRUNTUNA* Leofwin, a thane, held 1 carucate of land and 40 acres before 1066 as a manor.
    Always 9 smallholders; 2 slaves.
    Then and later 2 ploughs, now 1; then and later 2 men's ploughs, now 1.
    Meadow, 5 acres. Then 1 cob; then 20 pigs, now 10; then 20 sheep, now 16.
Value then 40s; now 30[s].
    Robert [holds this] from Walter.
    The King and the Earl (have) the jurisdiction.

16 In AKENHAM 4 free men, with 32 acres of land. Then 1 plough.
Value 5s.
    Roger [holds this] from Walter.
    The King and the Earl (have) the jurisdiction.

V̄ · H̃ · DE CARLEFORDA.

V̄ In Witdeſhā tenĕ Leuuin⁹ lib̃ hō . t . r . e . iii . car̃ tr̃e . Semp̃ . x . uiłł . & . iiii . borđ . 7 vi ſeru̅ . m̃ . v . femp . iii . car̃ in dominio . & hom̃ . iiii . car̃ . x . ac̃ p̃ti . & . iii . runc̃ . & viii . añ . & lxviii . porc̃ . 7 c . lxxx . oũs . & xxx . cap̃ . 7 vii . uaſa apũ . Tc̃ ual lx ſoł . m̃ xii . lib . & ht i longo . viii . qr̃ . & . iiii . ī lat̃ . & v . đ in glt̃ . V̄ In fineſforda in d̃nio . xxvi . libi hoes . i . car̃ tr̃æ c̃omđti anteceſſori . Walt . s̃ca . Æ . foca . Tc̃ int̃ eos . iii . car̃ . m̃ . ii . iiii . ac̃ p̃ti.

7 ual . xl . ſoł . 7 ht ĩ lōg . x . qr̃ . 7 . iii . in lato . 7 . x . đ . de gito . V̄ In otelega ĩ d̃nio . vi ac̃ 7 ual xii . đ.

.XLII. V̄ Tr̃Æ TEHELLI DE HERION . B̃ ab ENBERGA . ii . H̃ .   ★

Ilelega tenĕ ulwardus lib̃ hō ſubſtigando . t . r . e . p̃ man̄ . iii . car̃ tr̃æ . Sep̃ . v . borđ . 7 . ii . ſer̃ . femp . ii . car̃ in d̃nio . 7 . iii . ac̃ p̃ti . & . i . mel . & . ii . eq̃ . in halla . & . vi . añ . 7 xx . porc̃ . & . c . oũs . Tc̃ ual . xl . ſoł . p̃ 7 m̃ . lxxx . ſoł . ht dim̃ lg̃ in longo . 7 iiii . qr̃ in lato . 7 de gelto . iii . đ . 7 obol ;

428 a

V̄ RISEBRVGE . H̃ . Hauerhellā . tenuit Clareboldus . t . r . e . p̃ man̄ . ii . car̃ terræ & dim̃ . Tc̃ & p̃ vi . uiłł . modo . i . Tc̃ & p̃ . iiii . borđ . modo . x . femp . x . ſeru̅ . Tc̃ & p̃ 7 femp . ii . car̃ in dominio . Tc̃ & p̃ . i . car̃ . hom̃ . modo dim̃ . Silua de xx . porc̃ . vi . ac̃ p̃ti . Tc̃ia pars mercati in eo ; x . borđ . æcclie . v . ac̃ . Man̄ ual & xl . ſoł . 7 mercatũ xiii . ſoł . 7 . iiii . đ . ht . i . lg̃ in longo . 7 dim̃ in lato . & . vi . đ . de gelto; Alii ibi tenent ;

Hundred of CARLFORD

17 In WITNESHAM Leofwin, a free man, held before 1066; 3 carucates of land.
 Always 10 villagers; 4 smallholders. [Then] 6 slaves, now 5.
 Always 3 ploughs in lordship; 4 men's ploughs.
 Meadow, 10 acres. 3 cobs, 8 cattle, 68 pigs, 180 sheep, 30 goats, 7 beehives.
 Value then 60s; now £12.
 It has 8 furlongs in length and 4 in width; 5d in tax.

18 In 'FINESFORDA' in lordship; 26 free men under the patronage of Walter's predecessor; 1 carucate of land. St. Etheldreda's (has) the jurisdiction. Then between them 3 ploughs, now 2.
 Meadow, 4 acres.
 Value 40s.
 It has 10 furlongs in length and 3 in width; 10d in tax.

19 In OTLEY, in lordship, 6 acres.
 Value 12d.

42   LANDS OF TIHEL OF HELLÉAN

BABERGH Two Hundreds

1 Wulfward, a free man under Stigand, held ELEIGH before 1066 as a manor; 3 carucates of land.
 Always 5 smallholders; 2 slaves.
 Always 2 ploughs in lordship.
 Meadow, 3 acres; 1 mill. 2 horses at the hall, 6 cattle, 20 pigs, 100 sheep.
 Value then 40s; later and now 80s.
 It has ½ league in length and 4 furlongs in width; 3½d in tax.

RISBRIDGE Hundred   428 a

2 Clarenbold held HAVERHILL before 1066 as a manor; 2½ carucates of land.
 Then and later 6 villagers, now 1; then and later 4 smallholders, now 10; always 10 slaves.
 Then and later and always 2 ploughs in lordship; then and later 1 men's plough, now ½.
 Woodland at 20 pigs; meadow, 6 acres; the third part of a market, in it 10 smallholders.
 5 acres, belonging to the church.
 Value of the manor 40s; (value) of the market 13s 4d.
 It has 1 league in length and ½ in width; 6d in tax. Others hold there.

TRÆ RADVLFI DE LIMESI. *BABENBERGA. DUO. H̃.* :XLIII.

Hoketona ten& huthtradus sub heroldo . t . r . e . p mañ . II . car⁊
terræ cū soca . Semp . I . uiłł . & . II . borđ . & . v . seru⁊ . Tc̄ . III . car⁊ in
dominio p̊ 7 modo . IIII . Semp dim⁊ car̊ hom⁊ . Silua . de . xx . porc̊ .
7 . x . ac̄ p̊ti . Semp . I . æqus in halla . Tc̄ . III . añ . modo . nułł.

Finesteda ten& iđ uthtret . t . r . e . p . I . car⁊ terræ . modo ten&
Rađ p b̄wita in hoketona . ab etgaro antecessore suo . Sēp
. I . car⁊ in dominio . Hoketona Tc̄ uał . IIII . łib̄ . modo . c . soł . 7 fine
steda tc̄ & p̊ uał . xx . soł . modo . xxx . sed ē . de . c . solidis . Totū
ht̄ . VIII . q̊r in longo . & . IIII . in lato . & de gelto . IIII . đ .

Rana uadisc teñ Normannus cū soca 7 saca sub rege . e .
p mañ . II . car⁊ træ . Ecc̄lia . de xxx . ac̄ libæ⁊ træ . Semp . v . uiłł .
7 . VIII . borđ . 7 VII . seru⁊ . Tc̄ . II . car⁊ in dñio . p̊ 7 m̊ . IIII . Sēp . III.

428 b

car⁊ hom⁊ . & . I . moliñ . & . x . ac̄ p̊ti . Tc̄ . III . añ⁊ . modo XXIIII . Tc̄
XL . ou̅s . modo . c . x . Tc̄ xxx . porc̄ . m̊ . L . Huic mañ ptin& . I . b̄wita
Rodenhā de . II . car⁊ træ . Tc̄ . v . uiłł . 7 p̊ 7 m̊ . III . Tc̄ . IIII . borđ . p̊
7 m̊ . XIII . Tc̄ 7 p̊ ⁊ II . seru⁊ . modo . I . Tc̄ . II . car⁊ in dominio . p̊ & modo .
. I . 7 . I . car⁊ 7 dim⁊ . hom⁊ . Tc̄ dim⁊ moł . p̊ 7 m̊ nułł . Ecc̄lia de xx . ac̄ .
libæ⁊ træ . Tc̄ 7 p̊ uał totū . c . soł . modo . x . łib̄ . Rana uadis . ht̄ dim⁊
lg̊ in lōngo . 7 . IIII . q̊r in lato & de gelto . x . đ . Kodehā ht̄
                                    7 vi . q̊r . in loñ . 7 . III . in lat̄ . 7 . IIII . đ . 7
                                    obot de . gelto.

Neuuetona teñ iđ uthtret sub heroldo . cū soca & saca p mañ .
. II . car⁊ terræ . Semp . III . uiłł . Tc̄ VII . borđ . p̊ 7 modo xx . Tc̄ . IIII .
seru⁊ . p̊ 7 modo . I . Semp . II . car⁊ in dominio . Tc̄ & p̊ . II . car⁊ . hom⁊ .
modo . II . & dim⁊ . Silua . de . vi . porc̊ . 7 . IIII . ac̄ p̊ti . Æcc̄lia de
xxx . ac̄ libe⁊ træ . Tc̄ . I . eq̊ . m̊ nułł . Tc̄ . III . añ . modo . VIII . Tc̄ XVII porc̊ .

428 a. b

LANDS OF RALPH OF LIMÉSY

BABERGH Two Hundreds
1 Uhtred [held] HOUGHTON under Harold before 1066 as a manor; 2 carucates of land, with the jurisdiction.
   Always 1 villager; 2 smallholders; 5 slaves.
   Then 3 ploughs in lordship, later and now 4; always ½ men's plough.
   Woodland at 20 pigs; meadow, 10 acres. Always 1 horse at the hall. Then 3 cattle, now none.
Uhtred also [held] FENSTEAD before 1066 for 1 carucate of land. Now Ralph holds (it) as an outlier in (the lands of) Houghton. [Uhtred held it] from Edgar, his predecessor. Always 1 plough in lordship. Value of Houghton then £4; now 100s. Value of Fenstead then and later 20s; now 30[s], but it is (part) of the 100s.
   The whole has 8 furlongs in length and 4 in width; 4d in tax.

2 Norman held CAVENDISH, with full jurisdiction, under King Edward; as a manor, 2 carucates of land.
   A church with 30 acres of free land.
   Always 5 villagers; 8 smallholders; 7 slaves.
   Then 2 ploughs in lordship, later and now 4; always 3 men's ploughs.
   1 mill; meadow, 10 acres. Then 3 cattle, now 24; then 40 sheep, now 110; then 30 pigs, now 50.
To this manor belongs 1 outlier, CODDENHAM, with 2 carucates of land.
   Then 5 villagers, later and now 3; then 4 smallholders, later and now 13; then and later 2 slaves, now 1.
   Then 2 ploughs in lordship, later and now 1; 1½ men's ploughs.
   Then ½ mill, later and now none.
   A church with 20 acres of free land.
Value of the whole then and later 100s; now £10.
   Cavendish has ½ league in length and 4 furlongs in width; 10d in tax. Coddenham has 6 furlongs in length and 3 in width; [3]½d in tax.

3 Uhtred also held NEWTON under Harold, with full jurisdiction; as a manor, 2 carucates of land.
   Always 3 villagers. Then 7 smallholders, later and now 20; then 4 slaves, later and now 1.
   Always 2 ploughs in lordship. Then and later 2 men's ploughs, now 2½.
   Woodland at 6 pigs; meadow, 4 acres.
   A church with 30 acres of free land.
   Then 1 horse, now none; then 3 cattle, now 8; then 17 pigs,

modo.xx.Tc̄ lx.oūs.m̄.c.iii.Tc̄.xvii.cap̄.modo.xxx.v.di.m̄ æcclia
de.viii.ac̄ libæ terræ.In ead.i.lib̄ hō.dim̄ uthtredi & dimidi sc̄i
E.c̄om̄d ſ7 tot in ſoca sc̄i.e.Et pot̄at uende ſine licencia.& h̄t
xx.ac̄.Totū tc̄ ual̄.xl.ſol̄.p̄ 7 modo lx.h̄t dim̄ lḡ in longo.7
iiii.q̄r in lato.Et de gelto.vi.d̄.& obol̄.

In Cornierda.i.lib̄ hō.Wiſgari.c̄om̄dation̄ tantū.& ſoca de.i.
car̄ terræ.Semp.v.bord.Sep̄.i.car̄ in dn̄io.7 vi.ac̄ p̄ti.Silua.
de.iiii.porc̄.Semp.v.an̄.Tc̄.x.porc̄.modo xx.Tc̄.xxx.oūs.m̄
lx.Semp ual̄.xx.ſol̄.h̄t dim̄ lḡ in longo 7 dim̄ in lato.& de gelto
.iii.d̄ & obolū.

Biscopes H̄.Bedinga ſ.lda ten̄ Aluric̄ lib̄ hō heroldi
.p man̄.t.r.e.lxxxx.ii.ac̄.Tc̄.ii.bord.modo.iiii.ſemp̄.i.car̄ in dn̄io.

429 a

7.i.car̄ houm̄.ſilua.de.x.porc̄.7.i.ac̄ p̄ti.ſemp.xii.porc̄.7
xx.oūs.Qrta pars eccliæ.vi.ac̄.Tc̄ ual̄.xxx.ſol̄.m̄.xvi.7.viii.d̄.
In ead.vi.lib̄i hōes ex oīb3 aluric̄ c̄m̄d p̄t de dimidio.q̄ fuit ſub ante
c̄ Rob̄ mal̄& c̄om̄d tant̄.& h̄nt.xxx.v.ac̄.&.i.ac̄.p̄ti.ſemp.i.car̄.
& ual̄.xl.d̄.

H̄.de losa.Framelingaham ten̄ Brictmar̄ lib̄ hō.heroldi
.t.r.e.l.ac̄.tr̄æ.p man̄.Sep̄.iii.bord.7.i.ſeru̅.7 in dn̄io.i.car̄.& hom̄
dim̄.car̄.Tc̄ ual̄ & ſemp.xv.ſol̄.

Hertesmera.H̄.Cranlea.ten̄.Aluricus.lib̄ hō.c.ac̄.p
man̄.t.r.e.ſemp.x.bord.&.i.car̄ in dn̄io.7.i.car̄ hom̄,Silua
vi.porc̄.7 ual̄.xx.ſol̄.Aluric̄ habuit dim̄ ſocā.7 rex aliā medietat̄.

now 20; then 60 sheep, now 103; then 17 goats, now 35.
½ church with 8 acres of free land.
In the same (Newton) 1 free man, half under the patronage of Uhtred and half (under that) of St. Edmund's but wholly in the jurisdiction of St. Edmund's; he could sell without permission. He has 20 acres.
Value of the whole then 40s; later and now 60[s].
It has ½ league in length and 4 furlongs in width; 6½d in tax.

4 In CORNARD 1 free man of Withgar's, under patronage only and jurisdiction, with 1 carucate of land.
    Always 5 smallholders.
    Always 1 plough in lordship.
    Meadow, 6 acres; woodland at 4 pigs. Always 5 cattle. Then 10 pigs, now 20; then 30 sheep, now 60.
Value always 20s.
It has ½ league in length and ½ in width; 3½d in tax.

BISHOP'S Hundred
5 Aelfric, a free man of Harold's, held BEDINGFIELD as a manor before 1066; 92 acres.
    Then 2 smallholders, now 4.
    Always 1 plough in lordship; 1 men's plough.
    Woodland at 10 pigs; meadow, 1 acre. Always 12 pigs, 20 sheep.
    The fourth part of a church, 6 acres.
Value then 30s; now 16[s] 8d.
In the same (Bedingfield) 6 free men; over all of them, Aelfric had patronage, except over half of one who, for patronage only, was under Robert Malet's predecessor. They have 35 acres.
    Meadow, 1 acre.
    Always 1 plough.
Value 40d.

429 a

Hundred of LOES
6 Brictmer, a free man of Harold's, held FRAMLINGHAM before 1066; 50 acres of land as a manor.
    Always 3 smallholders; 1 slave;
    1 plough in lordship; ½ men's plough.
Value then and always 15s.

HARTISMERE Hundred
7 Aelfric, a free man, held CRANLEY; 100 acres as a manor before 1066.
    Always 10 smallholders;
    1 plough in lordship; 1 men's plough. Woodland, 6 pigs.
Value 20s.
    Aelfric had half the jurisdiction, the King (had) the other half.

F̄ In haftelea . II . lib̄ hŏes . cóm̄d . x . ac̄ . 7 ual . xx . d̄.
F̄ In Acolt . I . lib̄ hŏ . cóm̄d . vIII . ac̄ 7 ual xvI . d̄ . Totū teñ Rad in dn̄io.
Rex & com̄s focā . In ead . I . lib̄ hŏ com abb̄i de s̄co edmundo . II . ac̄.
& ual . IIII . d̄ . Rex & com̄s focam ;

* F̄ TERRÆ ROBERTI DE TODENIO. *RISEBRVGE* . H̃. .XLIIII.
Bradeleia . tenuit Olfus teinnus p̄ mañ . t . r . e . m̊ . Rog̃ . in dn̄io
teñ . vII . car̕ terræ . femp . xIIII . uilt . 7 xII . bord̄ . & . vI . feru̕ . & . III . car̕
in dominio . 7 vII . car̕ hom̊ . & xIII . ac̄ p̊ti . filua . porc̕ . femp . I.
runc̕ . Tc̄ xII . añ . M̊ xvIII . Tc̄ Lx . porc̕ . modo . L . III . Tc̄ . xx . ou̇s.

429 b

M̊ LxIII . 7 vII . cap̄ . & . I . uafa apū . Ecclia . de . xv . ac̄ . libæ træ . Tc̄ ual
. vI . lib̄ . modo . vIII . ħt . I . lg̃ in longo . 7 vII . qr̕ in lat̕ . 7 vI . d̄ de gelto.
F̄ *BISCOPES* . H̃ . Seilam tenuit cū foca Olfus . t . r . e . p̄ mañ . II . car̕.
& dim̕ træ . Tc̄ vIII . uilt . modo . III . Tc̄ xII . bord̄ . modo . xIII . modo
. I . feru̕ . femp . III . car̕ in dominio . Tc̄ & p̊ . xII . car̕ hom̊ . m̊ . IIII . Silu̇
c . L . porc̕ . vIII . ac̄ . p̊ti . femp . I . mol . Tc̄ . II . runc̕ . modo . I . Tc̄ . vIII . añ.
modo . II . Tc̄ Lxxx . porc̕ . m̊ . xL , IIII . m̊ . vII . ou̇s . & . III . cap̄ . & . I . uas
apū . Tc̄ ual . c . fol . 7 modo fimilit . In ead . v . libi hŏes . ante c̄ . com
xxx . ac̄ . Tc̄ . I . car̕ . modo . dim̕ . & . I . ac̄ . p̊ti . & . ual . v . fol . Ecclia . de.
xvI . ac̄ . & ual . II . fol . In longo . I . lg̃ . & . vIII . qr̕ in lat̕ . & . vII . d̄ . & . ob̕ol
de geldo . foca in hox mañ . ep̄i.

8 In HESTLEY 2 free men under patronage; 10 acres.
Value 20d.

9 In OCCOLD 1 free man under patronage; 8 acres.
Value 16d.
 Ralph holds the whole of this in lordship.
 The King and the Earl (have) the jurisdiction.
In the same (Occold) 1 free man under the patronage of the Abbot of St. Edmund's; 2 acres.
Value 4d.
 The King and the Earl (have) the jurisdiction.

44   LANDS OF ROBERT OF TOSNY

RISBRIDGE Hundred
1 Ulf, a thane, held BRADLEY as a manor before 1066; now [Robert] holds (it) in lordship; 7 carucates of land.
 Always 14 villagers; 12 smallholders; 6 slaves;
 3 ploughs in lordship; 7 men's ploughs.
 Meadow, 13 acres; woodland, 500 pigs. Always 1 cob. Then 12 cattle, now 18; then 60 pigs, now 53; then 20 sheep, now 63; 7 goats; 1 beehive. 429 b
 A church with 15 acres of free land.
 Value then £6; now [£] 8.
 It has 1 league in length and 7 furlongs in width; 6d in tax.

BISHOP'S Hundred
2 Ulf held SYLEHAM, with the jurisdiction, before 1066; as a manor, 2½ carucates of land.
 Then 8 villagers, now 3; then 12 smallholders, now 13; now 1 slave.
 Always 3 ploughs in lordship. Then and later 12 men's ploughs, now 4.
 Woodland, 150 pigs; meadow, 8 acres; always 1 mill. Then 2 cobs, now 1; then 8 cattle, now 2; then 80 pigs, now 44. Now 7 sheep, 3 goats, 1 beehive.
Value then 100s; now the same.
In the same (Syleham) 5 free men under the patronage of [his] predecessor; 30 acres. Then 1 plough, now ½.
 Meadow, 1 acre.
Value 5s.
 A church with 16 acres; value 2s.
 (It has) 1 league in length and 8 furlongs in width; 7½d in tax.
The jurisdiction (is) in the Bishop's manor of Hoxne.

⁊ BLIDIGGA. H̃. Mealla tẽn mannig lib hõ ꝑ mañ. 7 modo
ħt Rodbt in dñio. III. car tr̃æ. femp VIII. uiłł. femp. XII. borđ. femp
III. feru. femp. II. car in dñio. III. car hom̃. filua. ad. c. porc. v. ac
pti. tc. I. mol. modo. null. femp. II. runc. VII. an̅. XXX. porc. XVI.
oũs. Tc ual. L. fol. modo. LX. 7 ħt. X. qr in longũ. &. VII. in lat.
& reddit. II. đ. de geldo.

⁊ Gokesford teñ mannig ꝑ mañ. m̃ teñ. R. iñ dñio. v. car errǽ
Tc XII. uiłł. modo. IX. Tc. II. borđ. m̃. nul. femp. I. feru. femp
. II. car in dñio. 7 hom̃. III. Silu. ad. XXX. porc. XX. ac pti. femp
. I. runc. VII. an̅. XXX. porc. 7 tc ual XL. fol. modo. LX. 7 ħt. X.
qr in longo. 7 VII. in lat. III. đ. de gelto;

430 a

* ⁊ TERRA WALTERI GIFART; PERREHAM. .XLV.

DIM̃. H̃. In blacheffala. I. lib. Codricus. dimidi fub comdat
ante ceffori mal&. & dim abbi. de eli. X. ac. & ual. XX. đ. Rađ
de Langhetot teñ. Soca abbis.

⁊ PLVMESGATA. H̃. Gliemham. teñ. Starlinc. CLXXX.
ac. ꝑ mañ. t. r. e. dimidi comdat Abbi de eli & dimidi. Wiłłmo
mal&. & inde faifitus fuit femp XI. borđ. &. II. car. in dñio.
&. I. car hom̃. &. I. ac pti. femp. II. runc. Tc XVI. por. modo
XXVI. Tc XXX. oũs. modo. L. Tc ual XL. fol M. LX. 7 ſt additi
* XXIIII. libi hoes comd. c. ac. femp. III. car & ual. XL. fol.
ħt. I. lg̃. in longo & dim in lato. & XX đ. de gelto.

⁊ In Straffort. teñ. idẽ. I. car terræ. ꝑ mañ. t. r. e. femp. v. borđ.

BLYTHING Hundred

3 Manni, a free man, held MELLS as a manor; now Robert has (it) in lordship; 3 carucates of land.
> Always 8 villagers; always 12 smallholders; always 3 slaves.
> Always 2 ploughs in lordship; 3 men's ploughs.
> Woodland for 100 pigs; meadow, 5 acres; then 1 mill, now none. Always 2 cobs, 7 cattle, 30 pigs, 16 sheep.
> Value then 50s; now 60[s].
> It has 10 furlongs in length and 7 in width; it pays 2d in tax.

4 Manni held YOXFORD as a manor; now Robert holds (it) in lordship; 5 carucates of land.
> Then 12 villagers, now 9; then 2 smallholders, now none; always 1 slave.
> Always 2 ploughs in lordship; 3 men's [ploughs].
> Woodland for 30 pigs; meadow, 20 acres. Always 1 cob, 7 cattle, 30 pigs.
> Value then 40s; now 60[s].
> It has 10 furlongs in length and 7 in width; 3d in tax.

45   LAND OF WALTER GIFFARD

PARHAM Half-Hundred

1 In BLAXHALL 1 free [man], Godric, half under the sub-patronage of Malet's predecessor and half (under that) of the Abbot of Ely; 10 acres.
> Value 20d.
> Ralph of Lanquetot holds (this).
> The jurisdiction (is) the Abbot's.

PLOMESGATE Hundred

2 Starling held (Great) GLEMHAM; 180 acres as a manor before 1066; (he was) half under the patronage of the Abbot of Ely and half (under that) of William Malet (who) was in possession of it.
> Always 11 smallholders;
> 2 ploughs in lordship; 1 men's plough.
> Meadow, 1 acre. Always 2 cobs. Then 16 pigs, now 26; then 30 sheep, now 50.
> Value then 40s; now 60[s].
> 24 free men under patronage were added; 100 acres. Always 3 ploughs.
> Value 40s.
> It has 1 league in length and ½ in width; 20d in tax.

3 In STRATFORD (St. Andrew) the same man held 1 carucate of land as a manor before 1066.
> Always 5 smallholders;

&. I. car̉ in dn̄io. 7 dim car̉ hom̄. &. IIII. ac̄ p̃ti. &. I. mol̉. 7 ual
XL. fol̉. In ead XIII. libi hoes. 7 dim. com̄d. femp. LX. ac̄. 7. IIII.
&. I. car̉. &. dim. 7 ual. VII. fol. Totū ten&. Rad. de Langhetot.
Soca abbis de eli.

430 b

.XLVI. TERRE COMITISSE. DE ALBAMARLA. BABENbga
duo. H̃. In Simplinga ten̄ Vluric tenn̉. reg̃. e. p man̄. V. car. terræ.
M̊ ten̄ comitiſſa. de albamarla. Tc̄. V. uil̉t. modo. III. Tc̄ & p̃. IIII. bod̉r.
modo. X. femp. VI. feru̯. Tc̄ & p̃. III. car̉. in dn̄io. modo. II. Semp. III.
car̉ hom̄. Silu̯ VIII. porc̃. &. X. ac̄ p̃ti. Sep. I. eq̃. Tc̄ XIIII. an̄.
m̊. VI. Tc̄ XL. porc̃. modo. XXIIII. Tc̄. c. XX. ou̅s. modo. c. Ecc̃lia. de
XXX. ac̄. In ead. V. libi hoes uluric com̄d 7 foca 7 faca. sc̄i. e. t. r. e.
modo ht comitiſſa. I. car terre. &. I. bord. &. I. feru̯. Sep. II. car̉.
&. II. ac̄ p̃ti. Tc̄ & femp ual. IX. lib. ht. I. lg̃ in longo. 7 dim in lato.
& de gelto. V. d.

Scerdatra ten̄ id. ulricus. t. r. e. p man̄. I. car terræ. Semp. I. uilt
&. III. bord. &. III. fer. Tc̄. II. car̉. in dn̄io. modo. nult. Semp. I. car̉ hōum.
7. III. ac̄ p̃ti. Semp ual. LX. fol. ht. IIII. qr̄ in longo. 7. II. in lato.
& de gelto. II. d. & obol.

SANFORT. H̃. 7 dim. Belefteda tenuit Aluric̉ de Wein-
hou. III. car̉ terræ. 7 XL. ac̄. p man̄. femp. XII. uilt. 7. III. bord. Tc̄
. V. feru̯. m̊. I. Tc̄. II. car̉ in dominio. m̊. I. Tc̄. VIII. car̉. P 7 m̊. V. 7. VI.
ac̄ p̃ti. Tc̄ filua. de XXX. porc̃. m̊. XX. Ecc̃lia. de XXX. IIII. ac̄ libe
terræ. modo XXVII. porc̃. 7 XXX. V. ou̅s. Tc̄ ual VIII. lib. modo. VI.

1 plough in lordship; ½ men's plough.
Meadow, 4 acres; 1 mill.
Value 40s.
In the same (Stratford St. Andrew) 13 free men and a half, under patronage; always 60 acres and 4; 1½ ploughs.
Value 7s.
>Ralph of Lanquetot holds the whole.
>The jurisdiction (is) the Abbot of Ely's.

46   LANDS OF THE COUNTESS OF AUMÂLE

BABERGH Two Hundreds

1 In SHIMPLING Wulfric, a thane of King Edward's, held 5 carucates of land as a manor. Now the Countess of Aumâle holds (it).
>Then 5 villagers, now 3; then and later 4 smallholders, now 10; always 6 slaves.
>Then and later 3 ploughs in lordship, now 2; always 3 men's ploughs.
>Woodland, 8 pigs; meadow, 10 acres. Always 1 horse. Then 14 cattle, now 6; then 40 pigs, now 24; then 120 sheep, now 100.
>A church with 30 acres.

In the same (Shimpling) 5 free men; Wulfric (had) the patronage and St. Edmund's (had) full jurisdiction before 1066; now the Countess has (them); 1 carucate of land.
>1 smallholder; 1 slave.
>Always 2 ploughs. Meadow, 2 acres.

Value then and always £9.
>It has 1 league in length and ½ in width; 5d in tax.

2 Wulfric also held CHADACRE before 1066 as a manor; 1 carucate of land.
>Always 1 villager; 3 smallholders; [2] slaves.
>Then 2 ploughs in lordship, now 1; always 1 men's plough.
>Meadow, 3 acres.

Value always 60s.
>It has 4 furlongs in length and 2 in width; 2½d in tax.

SAMFORD Hundred and a Half

3 Aelfric of *Weinhou* held BELSTEAD; 3 carucates of land and 40 acres as a manor.
>Always 12 villagers; 3 smallholders. Then 5 slaves, now 1.
>Then 2 ploughs in lordship, now 1; then 8 [men's] ploughs, later and now 5.
>Meadow, 6 acres; woodland then at 30 pigs, now 20.
>A church with 34 acres of free land.
>Now 27 pigs, 35 sheep.

Value then £8; now [£]6.

Idē Aluricus focā.ħt.ɪ.lḡ in longo.&.ɪɪɪ.qr̄.in lato.7 de gelto
.vɪɪ.đ. ∕Hercheſtedā.teñ.Edeua.faira.vɪɪ.car̄ t̄ræ ꝑ mañ.t.r.e
ſemꝑ.xvɪɪ.uiłł.7 vɪɪɪ.borđ.Tc̄.ɪ.ſeru̅.Tc̄.ɪɪɪ.car̄.in dominio.P̄ 7 m̄
.ɪɪ.ſemper.v.car̄ hom̄.vɪɪɪ.ac̄ p̄ti.filua.xxx.porc̄.7.ɪ.moł.Ec
clia xxɪɪɪɪ.ac̄.&.ɪɪɪɪ.an̄.7 xxɪɪɪɪ.porc̄.7 xl.ou̅s.7 xxvɪɪ.cap̄.

431 a

Tc̄ uał.x.liƀ.modo xɪɪɪɪ.ħt.ɪ.leḡ in longo.7 dimiđ in lat̄.7
xɪɪɪɪ.đ.de gelto;
∕Gutthulues fordā ten&.Edeua.t.r.e.ɪɪ.car̄ terræ ꝑ mañ.
ſemꝑ.ɪ.uiłł &.vɪ.borđ.Tc̄.ɪɪ.car̄ hominu̅.m̄.ɪ.7.ɪɪɪ.car̄ poſ-
ſent reſtaurari.vɪɪɪ.ac̄ p̄ti.Tc̄ filua.xx.porc̄.Tc̄.ɪ.molin̄.Tcia
pars æccłiæ.vɪɪɪ.ac̄.& uał.ɪɪɪ.liƀ.ħt.vɪɪɪ.qr̄ in longo.7.ɪɪɪ.in lato.
&.v.đ de gelto.Edeua focā.

HVnđ.De coleneſſe.In helmelea.ɪ.uiłł.de.ɪx.ac̄.& uał.xx.đ.
& ꝑtin& ad cloptuna.

HVnđ de carleforda.In clopetuna tenuit Burric̄ liƀ ho̅.Radulfi
ſtalra.t.r.e.ɪ.car̄ terræ.& xx.ac̄ ꝑ mañ.Semp.xɪ.borđ.7
in dn̄io.ɪɪ.car̄.Tc̄ hom̄.ɪɪ.car̄.modo.ɪ.ɪɪɪɪ.ac̄ p̄ti.7 x.porc̄
7 xxx.v.ou̅s.Semꝑ uał.xl.soł.In ead.vɪ.ac̄.qs ſeruat & ten&
Vluin̄ pƀr.& uał.xɪɪ.đ.

∕In burg.ɪɪ.liƀi homines.ɪ.com̄dation.S.e.7 ali com̄.R.comiti
de xxxvɪ.ac̄.7.ɪɪ.borđ.Tc̄.car̄.modo dim̄.ɪɪ.ac̄ p̄ti.7 uał.vɪ.soł.
∕In cloptuna.xɪɪ.liƀi hoes 7 dim̄ com̄dati.Burrici.t.r.e.lxxxxɪɪ.
ac̄.&.ɪɪ.borđ.Tc̄.ɪɪɪ.car̄.modo.ɪɪ.ɪ.ac̄ p̄ti.7 uał.xvɪ.soł.7.ɪɪɪɪ.đ.

Aelfric also (had) the jurisdiction. It has 1 league in length and 3 furlongs in width; 7d in tax.

4 Edeva the Fair held HARKSTEAD; 7 carucates of land as a manor before 1066.
 Always 17 villagers; 8 smallholders. Then 1 slave.
 Then 3 ploughs in lordship, later and now 2; always 5 men's ploughs.
 Meadow, 8 acres; woodland, 30 pigs; 1 mill.
 A church, 24 acres.
 4 cattle, 24 pigs, 40 sheep, 27 goats.
 Value then £10; now [£] 14.
 It has 1 league in length and ½ in width; 14d in tax.

431 a

5 Edeva [held] GUSFORD before 1066; 2 carucates of land as a manor.
 Always 1 villager; 6 smallholders.
 Then 2 men's ploughs, now 1; 3 ploughs could be restored.
 Meadow, 8 acres; woodland, then 20 pigs; then 1 mill.
 The third part of a church, 8 acres.
 Value £3.
 It has 8 furlongs in length and 3 in width; 5d in tax. Edeva (had) the jurisdiction.

Hundred of COLNEIS
6 In HEMLEY 1 villager, with 9 acres.
 Value 20d.
 It belongs to Clopton.

Hundred of CARLFORD
7 In CLOPTON Burgric, a free man of Ralph the Constable's, held before 1066; 1 carucate of land and 20 acres as a manor.
 Always 11 smallholders;
 2 ploughs in lordship. Then 2 men's ploughs, now 1.
 Meadow, 4 acres. 10 pigs, 35 sheep.
Value always 40s.
In the same (Clopton) 6 acres which Wulfwin the priest looks after and holds.
Value 12d.

8 In BURGH 2 free men; 1 under the patronage of St. Etheldreda's, the other under the patronage of Earl R(alph); with 36 acres.
 2 smallholders.
 Then 2 ploughs, now ½. Meadow, 2 acres.
 Value 6s.

9 In CLOPTON 12 free men and a half under the patronage of Burgric before 1066; 92 acres.
 2 smallholders.
 Then 3 ploughs, now 2. Meadow, 1 acre.
 Value 16s 4d.

HVnd. DE WILEFORD. In depebes. III. libi hoes. com. Edrici
grim xx. ac. I. ac p̃ti. Tc. I. car. 7 uat. III. fot. I. æcclia. VIII. ac. 7
uat. XVI. deñ. In bulges. I. lib hõ dim ac. & uat. II. d.

HVnd. De Loſa. In mungadena. V. ac. 7 in caresfella. III. ac.
& uat. XII. d.

431 b

.XLVII. H̃. DE COLONESE. TR̃Æ WILL̃ de arcis. In helmele. I. bord. ★
. V. ac. 7 ptinent ad cloptuna. 7 in precio.

H̃. DE CARLEFord. In cloptuna. teñ Ædmund pbr. lib hõ. S. Æ.
. t. r. e. I. car terræ. 7 xx. II. ac. p mañ. &. I. uitt. &. VII. bord. Tc in dñio
III. car. modo. I. Tc hom. I. car. modo dim. IIII. ac p̃ti. modo. I. runc.
Tc. IIII. añ. Tc xl porc. Tc xxx. oũs. modo inť totũ nichil. Tc uat
xxx. fot. modo. x. h ten& Bernard de sco Audoeno. de W.

HVnd. DE LOSA Branteſtuna. tenuit Ædmundus pbr
comd. S. Æ. t. r. e. 7 terrã q̃ cepit. cũ uxore ei. de branteſtuna
& de cloptuna. miſit in ecclia concedente muliere. tali conuentione qd non potuit uendere nec dare. de æcclia. LX. ac. terræ p mañ
&. V. bord. &. II. ſeru. 7 in dñio. I. car. 7 houm. I. car. V. ac p̃ti. ſilu
ad VI. porc. Addite ſt huic manerio. LXXX. ac. terræ p mañ. t. r. e.
Tc. IIII. bord. m̃. XII. bord. modo inť eos. I. car. Silua ad VIII. porc.
7. IIII. ac p̃ti. 7. I. moliñ. modo. I. runc. 7 xx. porc. 7 XVI. oũs. 7 xxx.
cap̃. 7 III. uaſa apũ. Tc uat totũ ſimul. c. fot. modo. LX. fot.
h ht Wittm. p. I. mañ. ſed. t. r. e. erant duo. I. æcclia. XII. ac. 7 uat
. II. fot. 7 ht in longo. I. leuga. & in lato. III. qr. 7 de gelto. V. d. & obot.

Hundred of WILFORD

10 In DEBACH 3 free men under the patronage of Edric Grim; 20 acres.
   Meadow, 1 acre.
   Then 1 plough.
   Value 3s.
   1 church, 8 acres; value 16d.

11 In BOULGE 1 free man; ½ acre.
   Value 2d.

Hundred of LOES

12 In MONEWDEN 5 acres and in CHARSFIELD 3 acres.
   Value 12d.

47   LANDS OF WILLIAM OF ARQUES

Hundred of COLNEIS

1 In HEMLEY 1 smallholder; 5 acres. They belong to Clopton.
   (It is) in the assessment.

Hundred of CARLFORD

2 In CLOPTON Edmund the priest, a free man of St. Etheldreda's, held before 1066; 1 carucate of land and 22 acres as a manor.
   1 villager; 7 smallholders.
   Then 3 ploughs in lordship, now 1; then 1 men's plough, now ½.
   Meadow, 4 acres. Now 1 cob. Then 4 cattle, then 40 pigs, then 30 sheep; now nothing at all.
   Value then 30s; now 10[s].
   Bernard of St. Ouen holds this from William.

Hundred of LOES

3 Edmund the priest, under the patronage of St. Etheldreda's, held BRANDESTON before 1066; and the land which he received with his wife, (parts) of Brandeston and Clopton, he gave up to the Church with his wife's consent by such an agreement that he could not sell or grant (it) away from the Church; 60 acres of land as a manor.
   5 smallholders; 2 slaves.
   1 plough in lordship; 1 men's plough.
   Meadow, 5 acres; woodland for 6 pigs.
   80 acres of land, (held) as a manor before 1066, were added to this manor.
   Then 4 smallholders, now 12 smallholders.
   Now 1 plough between them.
   Woodland for 8 pigs; meadow, 4 acres; 1 mill. Now 1 cob, 20 pigs, 16 sheep, 30 goats, 3 beehives.
   Value of the whole together then 100s; now 60s.
   William has this as 1 manor, but before 1066 there were two.
   1 church, 12 acres; value 2s.
   It has 1 league in length and 3 furlongs in width; 5½d in tax.

Terra Drogonis de Bevreria. Hvnd. de blidinga. .XLVIII.

Sudretunā. tenuit. Rada lib hō de heroldo . ıı . car̄ terræ . ᵱ man̄
M̊ ten& franc̄ de drogone . Tc̄ & p̄ ׃ xvı . bord̄ . modo xıx | ſep.ıı.
Tc̄ & p̄ ׃ ı . car̄ in dn̄io . m̊ . ıı . ſemp . ııı . car̄ hom̄ . 7 . ıı . ac̄ p̄ti . ſilua
de . c . porc̄ . Eccl̄ia . de . v . ac̄ . & . ı . run̄ . & . modo . ı . an̄ . Tc̄ . xıı . porc̄ .
modo xxıııı . 7 xxv . oūs . ſemp xl . ſol . ħt . ı . lḡ in longo . & dim̄ in-
lato . 7 . ı . d̄ . 7 . ııı . ferdiḡ . de gelto . Rada ante ceſſor drogonis
habuit ſocā & ſacā . huic manerio addidit hainfridus de s̄co b̄tino
. ı . lib̄u de . xıı . ac̄ . de q̄ habuit ſuus anteceſſor c̄md̄ . t . r . e . ſemp
. ı . bord̄ . & dim̄ . car̄ . & ual . ıı . ſol .

Terre hugonis de Grentemeſnil . Dim̄ . H̄ . De crosfort . .XLVIIII.

Leiham ten& Alfnod de heroldo . t . r . e . ᵱ man̄ . ııı . car̄ terræ
ſemp . ıııı . uill . & . vıı . bord̄ . Tc̄ . v . ſeru . modo . vı . ſemp . ıı . car̄ in dn̄io .
& . ıı . car̄ hom̄ . 7 xı . ac̄ p̄ti . 7 . ı . runc̄ . & . xv . an̄ . 7 xv . porc̄ . & . c .
oūs . 7 xıx . cap̄ . Tc̄ ual lxx . ſol . modo . c . ħt dim̄ lḡ in longo &
dim̄ in lat̄ . & . ıııı . d̄ de gelto . & obol . S̄ . e . ſocā .

Terræ . Rad̄ . de felgeris . Eſtuteſtuna . tenuit Vlſi lib hō .L.

com̄d̄ . Guerti . ıı . car̄ terræ ᵱ man̄ . t . r . e . Semp . ıııı . uill . &
ıııı . bord̄ . Tc̄ in dn̄io . ıı . car̄ . M̊ . ı . Sep̄ hom̄ . ı . car̄ . vı . ac̄ p̄ti . Tc̄ . ıı . an̄ .
M̊ . ı . Tc̄ . v . porc̄ . Tc̄ ual lx . ſol . m̊ . xl . ſol . & . ııı . lib̄i hoēs com̄ . Vlſi
xıı . ac̄ . & ual . ıı . ſol . Rex & coms ſoc̄ .
In frondeſtuna . vı . ac̄ . & ual . xıı . d̄ .

48 LAND OF DROGO OF BEUVRIÈRE

Hundred of BLYTHING

1 Rada, a free man, held SOTHERTON from Harold; 2 carucates of land as a manor. Now Frank holds (it) from Drogo.
  Then and later 16 smallholders, now 19; always 2 slaves.
  Then and later 1 plough in lordship, now 2; always 3 men's ploughs.
  Meadow, 2 acres; woodland at 100 pigs.
  A church with 5 acres.
  1 cob; now 1 cattle; then 12 pigs, now 34; 25 sheep.
  Value always 40s.
    It has 1 league in length and ½ in width; 1¾d in tax. Rada, Drogo's predecessor, had full jurisdiction.
    To this manor Humphrey of St. Bertins added 1 free [man] with 12 acres, over whom his predecessor had patronage before 1066.
      Always 1 smallholder;
      ½ plough.
    Value 2s.

49 LANDS OF HUGH OF GRANDMESNIL

Half-Hundred of COSFORD

1 Alfnoth [held] LAYHAM from Harold before 1066 as a manor; 3 carucates of land.
  Always 4 villagers; 7 smallholders. Then 5 slaves, now 6.
  Always 2 ploughs in lordship; 2 men's ploughs.
  Meadow, 11 acres. 1 cob, 15 cattle, 15 pigs, 100 sheep, 19 goats.
  Value then 70s; now 100[s].
    It has ½ league in length and ½ in width; 4½d in tax. St. E(dmund's has) the jurisdiction.

50 LANDS OF RALPH OF FOUGÈRES

[Hundred of HARTISMERE]

1 Wulfsi, a free man under the patronage of Gyrth, held STUSTON; 2 carucates of land as a manor before 1066.
  Always 4 villagers; 4 smallholders.
  Then 2 ploughs in lordship, now 1; always 1 men's plough.
  Meadow, 6 acres. Then 2 cattle, now 1; then 5 pigs.
  Value then 60s; now 40s.
  3 free men under the patronage of Wulfsi; 12 acres.
  Value 2s.
    The King and the Earl (have) the jurisdiction.

2 In THRANDESTON 6 acres.
  Value 12d.

.LI. **TERRA GALTERI DE SCO WALERICO.** *Stov. H̄.* ★

In Cratinga teñ Aluric lib hō t.r.e. edrici ant Rotbti. mal. comd tant Rotbt tenuit f7 p̄ fuit defaitus. 1. car. & dim trae &. 11. uilt. 7 IX. bord. Semp. 11. car & dim in dñio. Tc. 1. car. hom. p̄ & modo dim. Tc filua XL porc. m. nult. 7.1. mol. 7 VI. ac pti. & dim æcclia. x. ac libae trae. 7.v. añ. 7 IX. oūs. 7. XII. porc. 7 ual .c. fol. In ead teñ Galt. 1. lib hō. Tholi comd. x. ac. 7 dim. Tc 7 p̄ 7 m̄ dim car. 7 ual. III. fol.

BOSEMERA. H̄. In Cratinga. 1. lib hō .LX. ac. t. r. e. comdat ante ceffori Robti mal& & pat ei inde faifitus fuit femp. IIII. uilt. 7 dim car h̄ iac& in Cratingis in hund de Stou & in p̄tio. In ead. IIII. libi hoes cm. VII. ac jn Vledana. 1. lib hō. comd. IIII. ac. & ual. II. fol. Rex & coms focā.

LAND OF WALTER OF ST. VALÉRY

STOW Hundred

1 In CREETING (St. Peter) Aelfric held; before 1066 (he was) a free man of Edric, Robert Malet's predecessor, under patronage only. Robert held but later was dispossessed; 1½ carucates of land.
    2 villagers; 9 smallholders.
    Always 2½ ploughs in lordship; then 1 men's plough, later and now ½.
    Woodland, then 40 pigs, now none; 1 mill; meadow, 6 acres.
    ½ church, 10 acres of free land.
    6 cattle, 9 sheep, 12 pigs.
Value 100s.
In the same (Creeting St. Peter) Walter holds; 1 free man under the patronage of Toli; 10½ acres. Then and later and now ½ plough.
Value 3s.

BOSMERE Hundred

2 In CREETING 1 free man; 60 acres before 1066. (He was) under the patronage of Robert Malet's predecessor; his father was in possession of it.
    Always 4 villagers;
    ½ plough.
    This belongs to Creeting (St. Peter) in the Hundred of Stow.
(It is) in the assessment.
In the same (Creeting) 4 free men under patronage, 7 acres; in 'OLDEN' 1 free man under patronage, 4 acres.
Value 2s.
    The King and the Earl (have) the jurisdiction.

H̄vndret. De carleforda. Terre vmfridi camera-
rii. In oteleia tenuit. Lefleda. liƀa femina. com̄'.e. ante c̄'. R.
mal&. i. car' terræ. 7 dim'. Semp. iii. uilł. 7 x. bord. Tc̄ in dn̄io.
. ii. car' modo. i. & dim'. Tc̄ hom'. iii. car'. modo. ii. Silua ad xx. porc'.
. ii. ac̄. p̄ti. femp. ii. runc. Tc̄. v. an̄. Tc̄ xl. porc'. 7 modo fimilit̄. Sēp
. c. oūs. 7 xx. v. cap̄. & vi. uafa apū. Tc̄ ual. c. fol. m̄. vi. liƀ. Wilł.
mal& fuit faifitus. die q᷈ obiit. 7 p̄t. R. tefte hund. In ead ten̄
Luftwin. com̄'. e. t. r'. e. dim'. car' terræ ꝑ man̄. Sēp. i. uilł. &
iiii. bord. Tc̄. i. car'. modo. i. 7 đ in dn̄io. Semp hom'. i. car'. ii. ac̄ p̄ti.
Silua ad. v. porc'. Tc̄ ual xx. fol. m̄. xxx. In ead xvi. liƀi hōes 7 dim'.
com̄đ Leflede. lxix. ac̄. Tc̄. iii. car'. 7 modo. Tc̄ ual. xx. fol m̄. xxx.
fol. i. æcclia. de. xx. ac̄. 7 ual. iiii. fol. ex h̄ toto erat. Wilłm̄ Mal&
faifitus die q᷈ obiit. 7 R. p̄t. 7 Rex 7 Com̄s foca. In ead ten̄
Amundus. i. liƀ hō. Brithwoldus. com̄'. e. reginæ. xxx. ac̄.
7. i. uilł. 7. iiii. bord. Tc̄. i. car' modo. i. &. dim'. i. ac̄ p̄ti.
Silu ad. x. porc'. Tc̄ ual. viii. fol modo. x.

⁊ In Cloptuna. xx. ac̄. &. i. bord. 7. ual. v. fol. h̄ ten̄ Amund.
de Winfrido.

⁊ In oteleia. vi. liƀi hōes. com̄đ Brihtuuoldi. xxvii. ac̄. tr̄æ
Tc̄. ii. car'. m̄. i. Tc̄. ual. x. fol. 7 modo fimilit̄.

⁊ In burg. i. liƀ hō. com̄đ eid dim 7 dim'. sēa. Æ. xxiiii. ac̄.
& dim' car'. 7 dim' ac̄ p̄ti. 7 ual. x. fol

. lii .

52 LANDS OF HUMPHREY THE CHAMBERLAIN

Hundred of CARLFORD

1 In OTLEY Aelfled, a free woman under the patronage of E(dric), Robert Malet's predecessor; 1½ carucates of land.
   Always 3 villagers; 10 smallholders.
   Then 2 ploughs in lordship, now 1½; then 3 men's ploughs, now 2.
   Woodland for 20 pigs; meadow, 2 acres. Always 2 cobs. Then 5 cattle; then 40 pigs, now the same; always 100 sheep, 25 goats, 6 beehives.
Value then 100s; now £6.
   William Malet was in possession on the day he died; later Robert (was in possession), as the Hundred testifies.
In the same (Otley) Lustwin, under the patronage of E(dric) before 1066, held ½ carucate of land as a manor.
   Always 1 villager; 4 smallholders.
   Then 1 plough in lordship, now 1½; always 1 men's plough.
   Meadow, 2 acres; woodland for 5 pigs.
Value then 20s; now 30[s].
In the same (Otley) 16 free men and a half under the patronage of Leofled; 69 acres. Then 3 ploughs, and now (the same).
Value then 20s; now 30s.
   1 church with 20 acres; value 4s.
   William Malet was in possession of the whole of this on the day he died, and later Robert (was in possession).
   The King and the Earl (have) the jurisdiction.
In the same (Otley) Amund holds; 1 free man, Brictwold, under the patronage of Queen Edith; 30 acres.
   1 villager; 4 smallholders.
   Then 1 plough, now 1½.
   Meadow, 1 acre; woodland for 10 pigs.
Value then 8s; now 10[s].

2 In CLOPTON 20 acres.
   1 smallholder.
   Value 5s.
   Amund holds this from Humphrey.

3 In OTLEY 6 free men under the patronage of Brictwold; 27 acres of land. Then 2 ploughs, now 1.
   Value then 10s; now the same.

4 In BURGH 1 free man, half under the patronage of the same man and half (under that) of St. Etheldreda's; 24 acres. ½ plough.
   Meadow, ½ acre.
   Value 10s.

HVNDRET DE LOSA. Gretingahā ^{Amund' ten&} tenuit BrihtWaldus comd. regiñ.

433 b

LXXX.III. ac̄. p̄ mañ. Tc̄ & modo. I. uitt. &. I. bord. &. I. seru.
& in dn̄io. I. car. & hom d. car. IIII. ac̄ p̄ti. I. æcclia. VIII. ac̄.
7 uat. XVI. den. Semp III. runc. &. III. añ. 7 XXIIII. porc.
& XL. ous. 7 XX. V. cap. 7. IIII. uasa apū. Tc̄ uat. XX. sot. m̄.
XXX. In eadē. VIII. libi hoes integros. 7. IIII. dim. comd. eid.
LXVI. ac̄ træ. Tc̄. II. car. modo. I. 7 dim. I. ac̄ p̄ti. Tc̄ uat. XX. sot.
Modo. XXXI. sot.

HVNDRET^{de}. *BOSEMERA*. In assa tenuit Aluuinus
lib hō. IIII. ac̄. Tc̄ uat XVI. d. modo. VIII. In oteleia hunfrid
ten& in dn̄io. I. lib hm̄. III. uirg. & uat. III. d. In ead. I. liba
femina. Listeua. I. ac̄. & ual&. II. d.

In brictices haga est silua q̄ poterant pasci XVI. porc
t. r. e. modo IIII. & Amundus ten& de hunfrido 7 iacet
in gratinge ham.

Claindune. *HV*Ndret. Elminghehā tenuit Grimolf
lib homo comdat regine. C. XX. ac̄ træ & iac& in dn̄io
de oteleia. semp. I. uitt. &. V. bord. 7. I. car hominū. III.
ac̄ p̄ti. Silu. L. porc. & ē in p̄tio de oteleia In ead in dn̄io
XI. libi hoes comdati sub ante cessore p̄t duo q̄ fuerant
comdati brictuoldo. t. r. e. LXVIII. ac̄. t. r. e. semper
II. car. 7 uat. XX. sot. In ead ten lib homo Brictu
oldus. XL. ac̄. t. r. e. semp. II. uitti. 7. III. bord
semp. II. car. III. ac̄ | 7 uat. XX. sot. Amund
ten& de hunfrido. Rex 7 Com̄s soci.

Hundred of LOES

5 Amund holds CRETINGHAM; Brictwold held (it) under the patronage of the Queen; 83 acres as a manor. 433 b
    Then and now 1 villager, 1 smallholder, 1 slave;
    1 plough in lordship; ½ men's plough.
    Meadow, 4 acres.
    1 church, 8 acres; value 16d.
    Always 3 cobs, 3 cattle, 24 pigs, 40 sheep, 25 goats, 4 beehives.
Value then 20s; now 30[s].
In the same (Cretingham) 8 whole and 4 half free men under the patronage of the same man; 66 acres of land. Then 2 ploughs, now 1½.
    Meadow, 1 acre.
Value then 20s; now 31s.

Hundred of BOSMERE

6 In ASH(BOCKING) Alwin, a free man, held 4 acres.
Value then 16d; now 8[d].

7 In OTLEY Humphrey holds in lordship 1 free man; 3 poles (of land).
Value 3d.
In the same (Otley) 1 free woman, Licteva; 1 acre.
Value 2d.

8 In BRICTICESHAGA there is woodland in which 16 pigs could be pastured before 1066, now 4. Amund holds (it) from Humphrey. It belongs to Cretingham.

CLAYDON Hundred

9 Grimwulf, a free man under the patronage of the Queen, held HELMINGHAM; 120 acres. It belongs to the lordship of Otley.
    Always 1 villager; 5 smallholders;
    1 men's plough.
    Meadow, 3 acres; woodland, 50 pigs.
It is in the assessment of Otley.
In the same (Helmingham) in lordship 11 free men, under patronage under (his) predecessor, except for two who were under the patronage of Brictwold before 1066; 68 acres before 1066. Always 2 ploughs.
Value 20s.
In the same (Helmingham) a free man, Brictwold, held 40 acres before 1066.
    Always 2 villagers; 3 smallholders.
    Always 2 ploughs. Meadow, 3 acres.
Value 20s.
    Anund holds (this) from Humphrey.
    The King and the Earl (have) the jurisdiction.

In Affefelda . II . libi homs . IIII . ac & ual . VIII . d . Soca abbis.
In bermefdena . tenuit . II . lib hoes Anant . LXX . ac t . r . e.
femp . I . bord . Tc . I . car . II . ac pti . Tc ual xx . fol . modo xxx.
Hunfrid in dnio Rex & Coms foca Et . I . lib ho addit . IIII.
ac . & ual . II . fol.

TERRÆ EVDONIS FILII SPIRVIC. *LACFORDA H.* .L.III.

In ecclingaham Moruant ten& de eudone qua tenuit
Anant lib ho fub sca aldreda . t . r . e . p man . II . car terræ
fed n poterat uende . m ten& eudo fili fpiruic ab henfrido
ante ceffore fuo . f7 foca & faca . sci . e . Tc 7 p . VII . uilt . m
VI . 7 . VI . bord . & . I . feru . Semp . II . car in dnio . 7 . I . car hom .
& . V . ac pti . 7 . I . molin . modo . LXXX . IIII . ous . Tc ual IIII .
lib . modo . LX . fol.

BoSemera . h . Wledana ten Siric lib ho . t . r . e . p man
modo Wil . LXX . ac . femp . II . bord . Tc . II . car . modo . I . 7 d . &.
. II . ac pti . Tc . II . runc . modo XVI . porc . 7 XXVIII . ous . 7 ual
XX . fol . In ead . XIII . libi hoes de duob3 habuit ante ceffor.
Rogi . comdtion XL . ac . & . I . car . 7 ual x . fol . Rex . & coms
foca . ht . I . lg in longo . & . III . qr in lat . & . x . d . de gelto.
Alii ibi tenent;

10 In ASHFIELD 2 free men; 4 acres.
　　Value 8d.
　　　The jurisdiction (is) the Abbot's.

11 In *BERMESDENA* Anund held 2 free men in patronage; [60] acres before 1066.
　　　Always 1 smallholder.
　　　Then 1 plough. Meadow, 2 acres.
　　Value then 20s; now 30[s].
　　　Humphrey [holds this] in lordship.
　　　The King and the Earl (have) the jurisdiction.
　　1 free man has been added; 4 acres.
　　Value 2s.

53　　LANDS OF EUDO SON OF SPIRWIC

LACKFORD Hundred

1 In ICKLINGHAM Morvant holds from Eudo what Anund, a free man, held under St. Etheldreda's before 1066 as a manor; 2 carucates of land. But he could not sell. Now Eudo son of Spirwic holds (it); from Heinfrid, his predecessor. But the full jurisdiction (is) St. Edmund's.
　　　Then and later 7 villagers, now 6; 6 smallholders; 1 slave.
　　　Always 2 ploughs in lordship; 1 men's plough.
　　　Meadow, 5 acres; 1 mill. Now 84 sheep.
　　Value then £4; now 60s.

BOSMERE Hundred

2 Siric, a free man, held 'OLDEN' before 1066 as a manor; now William [holds it]; 70 acres.
　　　Always 2 smallholders.
　　　Then 2 ploughs, now 1½.
　　　Meadow, 2 acres. Then 2 cobs; now 16 pigs, 28 sheep.
　　Value 20s.
　　In the same ('Olden') 13 free men; Roger's predecessor had patronage over two of them; 40 acres. 1 plough.
　　Value 10s.
　　　The King and the Earl (have) the jurisdiction. It has 1 league in length and 3 furlongs in width; 10d in tax. Others hold there.

Betesfort teñ Iarnagot quā tenuit Kerinc lib hō. t. r. e.
.I. car terræ. 7 xx. ac. p man. modo Jarnagod. & semp. v. bord.
& . I. seru. Tc. II. car in dñio. modo. I ; & d car hom. vi. ac pti. tc
silu LX. porc; modo. x. Tc. II. runc. modo. xx. porc. 7. xi. ous.
7 xii. cap. 7 ual xxv. sol. In eade. III. libi hoes. xx. ac. de duobus
d ecclia. xx. ac.
habuit suus ante c comd. semp dim car. & ual. v. sol. Rex
& coms soca.

In Codenham. Siric lib hō. v. ac. 7 ual. x. d. Soca regis.

HVnd. de Wanne forda. Flixtuna teñ Gosfridu quā
tenuit. Offa. lib hō. com. Stigando. t. r. e. II. car terræ. p man.
Tc xvi. uill. modo. x. Tc. xi. bord. modo. xIIII. Semp. II. seru.
& in dñio. II. car. Tc hom. XIII. car 7 dim. modo. IX. 7 dim.
Semp. I. runc. & . II. an. 7. vi. porc. 7 xxvi. ous. xii. ac pti.
silu ad xx. porc. dim mol. Tc ual. xL. sol. modo Lx. dim ecclia
x. ac. 7 ual xvi. d. In ead. II. libi hoes. comd eid. xxx. ac. Semp
. III. bord. 7 dim. 7. II. car & dim. silu. ad. II. porc. III. ac. 7 dim.
pti. Tc ual. vii. sol. modo. x. 7 viii. d. 7 ht in longo. I. lg. 7 dim
in lato. 7 de gelto xx. d.

HERTES MARA. H. West torp tenuit Vlricus haganæ
ide. G. ten &
.I. car terre. p man. t. r. e. Semp. I. bord. & . I. seru. 7 in dñio.
.I. car 7 dim silua ad xii. porc. vi. ac pti. 7. III. runc. 7. II. an.

3 Iarnagot holds BATTISFORD; Cynric, a free man, held it before 1066; 434 b
1 carucate of land and 20 acres as a manor. Now Iarnagot (holds it).
> Always 5 smallholders; 1 slave.
> Then 2 ploughs in lordship, now 1; ½ men's plough.
> Meadow, 6 acres; woodland, then 60 pigs, now 10. Then 2 cobs; now 20 pigs, 11 sheep, 12 goats.
> ½ church, 20 acres.

Value 25s.
> In the same (Battisford) 3 free men; 20 acres. His predecessor had patronage over two (free men). Always ½ plough.

Value 5s.
> The King and the Earl (have) the jurisdiction.

4 In CODDENHAM Siric, a free man; in lordship, 5 acres.

Value 10d.
> The jurisdiction (is) the King's.

Hundred of WANGFORD

5 Geoffrey holds FLIXTON; Offa, a free man under the patronage of Stigand, held it before 1066; 2 carucates of land as a manor.
> Then 16 villagers, now 10; then 11 smallholders, now 14. Always 2 slaves;
> 2 ploughs in lordship. Then 13½ men's ploughs, now 9½.
> Always 1 cob, 2 cattle, 6 pigs, 26 sheep. Meadow, 12 acres; woodland for 20 pigs; ½ mill.

Value then 40s; now 60[s].
> ½ church, 10 acres; value 16d.

In the same (Flixton) 2 free men under the patronage of the same man; 30 acres.
> Always 3 smallholders and a half;
> 2½ ploughs.
> Woodland for 2 pigs; meadow, 3½ acres.

Value then 7s; now 10[s] 8d.
> It has 1 league in length and ½ in width; 20d in tax.

HARTISMERE Hundred

6 Geoffrey also holds WESTHORPE; Wulfric Hagni held (it); 1 carucate of land as a manor before 1066.
> Always 1 smallholder; 1 slave;
> 1½ ploughs in lordship.
> Woodland for 12 pigs; meadow, 6 acres. 3 cobs, 2 cattle,

7 xxx.I.porc̷.7.L.oūs.7 xv.cap̷.7.y.uafa apū.Tc̄ ual xx.fot.
modo xxx.7 xv.libi hoēs.com̷.Vlurici.xxx.iii.ac̄.Semp.i.
car̷.filua ad.ii.porc̷.ii.ac̄ p̷ti.7 ual.x.fot.Sup h̃ manerium

435 a

habuit Sc̄s eadmundus.t.r.e.Soc̄ 7 Sacā 7 com̷d.7 non potuit uende nec dare ab ecclia.7 ex xv.libis hōib; 7 fup Vlnoht
habuit.com̷.Ante ceffor.R.mal.tefte hund.7 n̄ potuit uende
nee dare de eo.terrā fuā;

*f*DIM̷.H̃.De cosfort.In Weces hā.i.lib hō.de quo abbas de eli
habuit com̷ 7 focā.t.r.e.i.car̷ terræ.7.iii.bord.&.i.car̷.&.iii.ac̄ p̷ti.
7 ual xx.fot.Sc̄s.E.vi.forisfacturas Iarnacotus ten&.

TERRÆ WILLI.DE WATE VILLA. RISEBRVGE.H̃. .LIIII
Ligatā ten̄ Stori̥.p̧ mān̄.t.r.e.iiii.car̷ terræ.7 lx.ac̄.Semp̧
ix.uilt.7 xii.bord̷.7.i.feru̷.&.ii.car̷ in dn̄io.Tc̄.iii.car̷ hom̷.m̷.
ii.x.ac̄ p̷ti.filua de.xv.porc̷.femp.i.runc̷.m̷.v.an̄.7 xxv.porc̷.
Tc̄ xxx.iii.oūs modo.c.xl.7 xiii.cap̷.Tc̄ ual.lxxx.fot.7 m̷ fimil.
ht.i.leuga in longo.&.viii.qr̷ in lato.7 xiii.d̷.& obot.de gelto.Alii
ibi tenent;

TINGOho.H̃.Haragraua ten̄ Aluiet.i.liba femina.t.r.e.fub
sc̄o edmundo & n̄ poterat uende.iiii.car̷ træ.Tc̄ & p̧.vi.uilli.
modo.viii.Tc̄ 7 p̧.iiii.bord̷.modo.vii.Tc̄.iiii.feru̷.modo.ii.Sep̧
.ii.car̷ in dn̄io.Tc̄ 7 p̧.iiii.car̷ hom̷.m̷.iii.Tc̄.i.eq̷.m̷.mult.
Tc̄.ii.an̄.modo.viii.Tc̄.v.porc̷.modo.xl.m̷.c.oūs.&.iiii.ac̄
p̷ti.Silu de.xvi.porc̷.Ecclia.xii.ac̄ libæ træ.Tc̄ 7 femp ual.iiii.lib.

435 b

Ht viii.qr̷ in longo.&.v.in lato.& de gelto.vii.d̷.

31 pigs, 50 sheep, 15 goats, 5 beehives.
Value then 20s; now 30[s].
15 free men under the patronage of Wulfric; 33 acres. Always 1 plough.
Woodland for 2 pigs; meadow, 2 acres.
Value 10s.
Over this manor before 1066 St. Edmund's had full jurisdiction and patronage. He could not sell or grant (it) away from the Church. R(obert) Malet's predecessor had patronage over the 15 free men and over Wulfnoth, as the Hundred testifies; he could not sell or grant his land away from him.

435 a

Half-Hundred of COSFORD

7 In WATTISHAM 1 free man over whom the Abbot of Ely had patronage and jurisdiction before 1066; 1 carucate of land.
3 smallholders.
1 plough. Meadow, 3 acres.
Value 20s.
St. Edmund's (has) the 6 forfeitures.
Iarnagot holds (this).

54   LANDS OF WILLIAM OF VATTEVILLE

RISBRIDGE Hundred

1 Stori held LIDGATE as a manor before 1066; 4 carucates of land and 60 acres.
Always 9 villagers; 12 smallholders; 1 slave;
2 ploughs in lordship. Then 3 men's ploughs, now 2. Meadow, 10 acres; woodland at 15 pigs. Always 1 cob. Now 5 cattle, 25 pigs; then 33 sheep, now 140; 13 goats.
Value then 80s; now the same.
It has 1 league in length and 8 furlongs in width; 13½d in tax.
Others hold there.

THINGOE Hundred

2 Aelfgyth, 1 free woman, held HARGRAVE before 1066, under St. Edmund's; she could not sell; 4 carucates of land.
Then and later 6 villagers, now 8; then and later 4 smallholders, now 7; then 4 slaves, now 2.
Always 2 ploughs in lordship; then and later 4 men's ploughs, now 3.
Then 1 horse, now none; then 2 cattle, now 8; then 5 pigs, now 40; now 100 sheep. Meadow, 4 acres; woodland at 16 pigs.
A church, 12 acres of free land.
Value then and always £4.
It has 8 furlongs in length and 5 in width; 7d in tax.

435 b

Lacheforda . H̄ . Bertunna teñ Alued . I . lib̃ hō . v . car̃ terre . & hanc
terrā teñ . W . de regina . modo teñ alwewe de rege . Tc̄ . x . uill.
modo . vii . modo . v . borđ . Tc̄ . ix seru̇ . Tc̄ . iiii . car̃ . in dominio . m̄
. i . Semp . iii . car̃ hom̃ . ii . piscar̃ . ii . ac̄ p̃ti . Tc̄ . i . runc̃ . & modo
ii . eq̇ . Tc̄ . x . añ . modo . v . Tc̄ . cc . oūs . modo . iii . Tc̄ xl . porc̃ . modo
iii . Tc̄ ual viii . lib̃ . & p̃ . vi . lib̃ . modo . xxx . fol . 7 ḣt . i . lḡ . in long̃
7 dim̄ in lato . 7 de gelto xx . đ . Soca 7 saca . sc̃s . edmund.

.LV. **TERRA JOH̄IS FILII WALERAMI.** B*Abenb̃*ga duo . H̄ ★
In bura teñ Vluric̃ fili bric̃trici . t . r . e . ii . car̃ trᷓ sub rege . e .
Tc̄ . vii . seru̇ . 7 . i . fab̃ . modo . iiii . seru̇ . 7 modo . ii . borđ . Semp . ii . car̃
in dn̄io . Silua de xl porc̃ . 7 . iiii . ac̄ p̃ti . modo . i . mol̃ . m̄ . ii .
eq̇ . 7 . ii . añ . Tc̄ lx . oūs . m̄ . c . xl . Tc̄ xl . porc̃ . modo . xx . m̄ . xxxv .
cap̃ . Tc̄ ual . lx . fol . modo . xl . In ead̃ teñ tosti lib̃ hō sub rege .
. e . i . car̃ terrᷓ . Tc̄ . i . uill . modo null . 7 m̄ . ii . borđ . 7 . i . ser̃ . Sep̃
. i . car̃ . Silua de . x . porc̃ . & . ii . ac̄ p̃ti . Tc̄ xl . porc̃ . m̄ xx . 7 xx .
oūs . modo . xv . cap̃ . 7 ual . xx . fol . In ead . ii . libi hōes heroldi .
& poterant uende . & h̄nt ḷx . ac̄ . & . i . car̃ . & ual . v . fol . & fuer̃
libati ad p̃ficiendū mañ.

★ **TERRA HVNFRIDI FILII ALBBICI.** S*TOV* . H̄ . de escan- .LVI.
gio normannie . In anehus . x . libi hōes Ketelli . com̃d tantū
lx ac̄ . trᷓ . & . i . borđ . Tc̄ . ii . car̃ . p̃ & modo . i . & iii . ac̄ p̃ti . 7
ual x . fol . Rex & com̃s soc̃.

LACKFORD Hundred

3 Alfgeat, 1 free man, held BARTON (Mills); 5 carucates of land. William held this land from the Queen; now Aelfeva holds (it) from the King.
    Then 10 villagers, now 8; now 5 smallholders; then 9 slaves.
    Then 4 ploughs in lordship, now 1; always 3 men's ploughs.
    2 fisheries; meadow, 2 acres. Then 1 cob, now 2 horses; then 10 cattle, now 5; then 200 sheep, now 3; then 40 pigs, now 3.
Value then £8; later £6; now 30s.
    It has 1 league in length and ½ in width; 20d in tax. The full jurisdiction (is) St. Edmund's.

55   LAND OF JOHN SON OF WALERAN

BABERGH Two Hundreds

1 In BURES Wulfric son of Brictric held before 1066 under King Edward; 2 carucates of land.
    Then 7 slaves and 1 smith, now 4 slaves; now 2 smallholders. Always 2 ploughs in lordship.
    Woodland at 40 pigs; meadow, 4 acres; now 1 mill. Now 2 horses, 2 cattle. Then 60 sheep, now 140; then 40 pigs, now 20; now 35 goats.
Value then 60s; now 40[s].
In the same (Bures) Tosti, a free man under King Edward, held 1 carucate of land.
    Then 1 villager, now none. Now 2 smallholders; 1 slave. Always 1 plough.
    Woodland at 10 pigs; meadow, 2 acres. Then 40 pigs, now 20; 20 sheep; now 15 goats.
Value 20s.
In the same (Bures) 2 free men of Harold's; they could sell. They have 60 acres. 1 plough.
Value 5s.
    They were delivered to make up the manor.

56   LAND OF HUMPHREY SON OF AUBREY

STOW Hundred

1 (Part) of an exchange in Normandy; in ONEHOUSE 10 free men under the patronage only of Ketel; 60 acres of land.
    1 smallholder.
    Then 2 ploughs, later and now 1. Meadow, 3 acres.
Value 10s.
    The King and the Earl (have) the jurisdiction.

✓ BOSEMERA. H̄. In Codenham xi. libi hões. lxxx. ac
. ii. min⁹. Tc. ii. car. modo. i. 7 đ. & ii. ac p̃ti.
✓ In Vledana. v. libi hões de. xx. ac. semp dim car.
✓ In hauungestuna. iii. libi. hões. ix. ac. 7 totū ual&. xxx. sol.
Rex & cõms soca. In Cadenham. viii. ac. Aluric⁹ lib homo
t. r. e. in eodẽ p̃tio.
✓ Claindune. H̄. In codenhā. i. lib hõ. iiii. ac. & ual. viii. đ.
soca regis. 7. c. De molino de belingesfort vii. sol. &. iiii. dẽn.
✓ In Eusfort. h̄. In nordfolc.

★ TERRA Hubti de monte canesio. Hertes mera. hund̄. .LVII.
Wiuertestunā ten Leuuin⁹ calu⁹. t. r. e. i. car terræ p man̄.
Tc. iiii. bord. m̄. iii. Tc ii. car in dn̄io. Post. i. m̄. i. 7 dimidia
7 dim car hom. 7. iii. ac p̃ti. Tc Silu. xl. porc. modo. xx.
Æcclia. xvi. ac. 7 dim. car. semp. i. runc. 7. iii. an. 7 xii.
cap. &. x. porc. 7 semp ual. xxx. sol. In ead. vi. libi hões
cõmdati. Leuuino. xxxvii. ac. semp. i. car. & ual&. x. sol.

436 b
Hoc ten& totū Ricardus de hubto. Rex & cõms soca. hr̄. i. lḡ
in longo. 7 iiii. qr & dim in lato. &. viii. đ. de gelto.

BOSMERE Hundred

2 In CODDENHAM 11 free men; 80 acres less 2. Then 2 ploughs, now 1½. Meadow, 2 acres.

3 In 'OLDEN' 5 free men with 20 acres. Always ½ plough.

4 In HEMINGSTONE 3 free men; 9 acres.
Value of the whole 30s.
The King and the Earl (have) the jurisdiction.

5 In CODDENHAM 8 acres; Aelfric a free man before 1066. (It is) in the same assessment.

CLAYDON Hundred

6 In CODDENHAM 1 free man; 4 acres.
Value 8d.
The jurisdiction (is) the King's and the Earl's.
From the mill of Billingford 7s 4d.
In EYNSFORD Hundred in Norfolk

57   LAND OF HUBERT OF MONT-CANISY

HARTISMERE Hundred

1 Leofwin the Bald held WYVERSTONE before 1066; 1 carucate of land as a manor.
Then 4 smallholders, now 3.
Then 2 ploughs in lordship, later 1, now 1½; ½ men's plough.
Meadow, 3 acres; woodland, then 40 pigs, now 20.
A church, 16 acres. ½ plough.
Always 1 cob, 3 cattle, 12 goats, 10 pigs.
Value always 30s.
In the same (Wyverstone) 6 free men under the patronage of Leofwin; 37 acres. Always 1 plough.
Value 10s.
Richard holds the whole of this from Hubert.   436 b
The King and the Earl (have) the jurisdiction.
It has 1 league in length and 4½ furlongs in width; 8d in tax.

.LVIII. **TERRA . GONDWINI** Camerarii . Sanfort . H̃ . & dim̃.   ★

Hecham . tenuit Affeman . lib̃ hõ . com̃dat Roḃto filio Wi-
marce . ꝑ man̄ . I . cař terræ . femp . I . uiłł . & Tc̃ . III . borđ . p̃ 7 m̃
. II . Tc̃ . II . cař in dn̄io . P̃ nichil . m̃ . I . cař . Tc̃ . I . cař hom̃ . P̃ 7 m̃
dim̃ . VII . ac̃ p̃ti . filua . X . porc̃ . femp . I . molin̄ . Pars æccłiæ . de .
. II . ac̃ . m̃ . III . an̄ . 7 VIII . porc̃ . 7 . VI . oũs . 7 VIII . cap̃ . 7 tc̃ uał
xxx . foł . modo . xx . f̧ fuit ad firmã ꝑ xxx . foł . h̃t . VIII . qr̃
in longo . & . VI . in łat̃ . 7 XII . đ . de gelto . Alii ibi ten& . Soca in
ƀcolt.

.LIX. **TERRE SAISSELINI** . *BRADEMERA . HVND̄* .   ★

Torp ten& Acolfus . t . r . e . teinn̄ . ꝑ man̄ . I . cař . třæ . femp . II .
borđ . Tc̃ 7 P̃ . II . cař in dn̄io . m̃ . I . 7 dim̃ cař hom̃ . VI . ac̃ . p̃ti . Semp .
. I . molin̄ . Semp . II . an̄ . Tc̃ . X . porc̃ . modo . XVI . femp . xxx . oũs .
7 IIII . lib̃i hões . de qƀȝ habuit fuũ ante c̃ com̃d . t . r . e . 7 h̃nt . XIII .
ac̃ . 7 dim̃ . cař . 7 uał . xx . foł . Sapeftuna ten̄ . Godman . teinn̄

437 a

t . r . e . dim̃ . cař . třæ . femp . II . borđ . 7 . I . cař in dn̄io . V . ac̃ p̃ti .
femp . I . molin̄ . 7 . II . an̄ . Tc̃ . III . porc̃ . m̃ . V̄ . Tc̃ xx . oũs . modo
xxxIII . femp uał . xv . foł . In eađ . VIII . lib̃i hões com̃đ . xx . IIII .
ac̃ . 7 uał . III . foł . Sc̃s eadmundus de h̃ 7 de toto hund̄ foc̃ 7 facã ;

58 LAND OF GUNDWIN THE CHAMBERLAIN

SAMFORD Hundred and a Half
1 Aescman, a free man under the patronage of Robert son of Wymarc, held HIGHAM before 1066; 1 carucate of land as a manor.
    Always 1 villager. Then 3 smallholders, later and now 2.
    Then 2 ploughs in lordship, later nothing, now 1 plough; then
        1 men's plough, later and now ½.
    Meadow, 7 acres; woodland, 10 pigs; always 1 mill.
    Part of a church, with 2 acres.
    Now 3 cattle, 8 pigs, 6 sheep, 8 goats.
    Value then 30s; now 20[s]; but it was at a revenue for 30s.
    It has 8 furlongs in length and 6 in width; 12d in tax. Others hold there.
    The jurisdiction (is) in (East) Bergholt.

59 LANDS OF SASSELIN

BRADMERE Hundred
1 Acwulf, a thane, [held] (Ixworth) THORPE before 1066; 1 carucate of land as a manor.
    Always 2 smallholders.
    Then and later 2 ploughs in lordship, now 1; ½ men's plough.
    Meadow, 6 acres; always 1 mill. Always 2 cattle. Then 10 pigs, now 16; always 30 sheep.
    4 free men over whom his predecessor had patronage before 1066.
    They have 13 acres. ½ plough.
    Value 20s.

2 Godman, a thane, held SAPISTONE before 1066; ½ carucate of land.
    Always 2 smallholders;
    1 plough in lordship.
    Meadow, 5 acres. Always 1 mill; 2 cattle. Then 3 pigs, now 5; then 20 sheep, now 33.
    Value always 15s.
    In the same (Sapistone) 8 free men under patronage; 24 acres.
    Value 3s.
    St. Edmund's (has) full jurisdiction over this and over the whole Hundred.

437 a

* **T**ERRA ROBERTI DE VERLI. *BL*Ackebrune. H̃. .LX.
I Weſtunā tenuit Alsi lib hō.t.r.e. p mañ.1.car̋ terræ.7.1.borď
7.11.ſeru̇.Tc̄.11.car̋ in dominio. P̊ nichil.modo.1.ſemp.dim̋
car̋ hom̋.111.ac̄.p̋ti.ſemp.1.moliñ.modo.1.runc̋.7.11.an̋.7 v111.
porc̋.7.L.oūs.7.v1.libi hőes̋ cm̋ď.c.111.ac̄.Tc̄.11.car̋.m̃.1.
7.1.ac̄.p̋ti.Ecct́ia.x11.ac̄.7 dim̋.car̋. H̃ mañ ual& ſemp
xxv.ſot.7 Libi hōes.v.ſot.

* **T**ERRA. RADVLFI PINEL. In Reinduna ten& .LXI.
.11.libi.hőes.Erniet̋.7 Aluort.xL.ac̄.ſemp.dim̋ car̋.&.1.borď.
7 uat.x.ſot hanc tr̃a tenuit Raď de dono regis ſed ex ea ſeruiū.
Goſfriď de magna uilla. Soca in b̃colt.

V DIMID̃. H̃. DE COSFORT. Laſham. ten̄ briċthmarus
t.r.e.xL.ac̄.ſemp.1.borď.7.1.ſeru̇.7.1.car̋.7 uat.x.ſot; sc̄s.eď.ſoca;

.LXII. **T**ERRA ISAC̋. *BOSEMERA*. H̃. Offetunā.ten̄ Siric̋ *
lib hō.t.r.e.c.ac̄. p mañ.ſemp.11.borď.7 tc̄.1.car̋.modo dim̋.
Ecct́ia.v11.ac̄.7 dim̋.Tc̄ uat.xx.ſot.modo xxx.Rex & com̃s.
ſocam.

437 b

60   LAND OF ROBERT OF VERLY

BLACKBOURN Hundred

1 Alsi, a free man, held (Market) WESTON before 1066; as a manor,
   1 carucate of land.
   1 smallholder; 2 slaves.
   Then 2 ploughs in lordship, later nothing, now 1; always ½ men's plough.
   Meadow, 3 acres; always 1 mill. Now 1 cob, 2 cattle, 8 pigs, 50 sheep.
   6 free men under patronage; 103 acres. Then 2 ploughs, now 1.
   Meadow, 1 acre.
   A church, 12 acres. ½ plough.
   Value of this manor always 25s; (value) of the free men 5s.

61   LAND OF RALPH PINEL

[SAMFORD Hundred and a Half]

1 In RAYDON Erngeat and Alward, 2 free men, [held] 40 acres.
   Always ½ plough;
   1 smallholder.
   Value 10s.
   Ralph held this land by the King's gift but from it he gave service to Geoffrey de Mandeville.
   The jurisdiction (is) in (East) Bergholt.

Half-Hundred of COSFORD

2 Brictmer held LAYHAM before 1066; 40 acres.
   Always 1 smallholder; 1 slave;
   1 plough.
   Value 10s.
   St. Edmund's (has) the jurisdiction.

62   LAND OF ISAAC   437 b

BOSMERE Hundred

1 Siric, a free man, held OFFTON before 1066; 100 acres as a manor.
   Always 2 smallholders.
   Then 1 plough, now ½.
   A church, 7½ acres.
   Value then 20s; now 30[s].
   The King and the Earl (have) the jurisdiction.

★ ★ ℣In Sumerſham teñ Vluuin⁹ libomo . LX . ac̄ . trǣ . p̄ mañ . . t . r . e.
Tc̄ . I . car̕ . Tc̄ ual̕ xx . ſol̕ . modo . xx . Rex & com̄s ſocā . In ead̄ . Coleman . lib̄ homo . v . ac̄ . & ual̕ . xx . d̄ . Rex & com̄s ſocā.
℣In hamingeſtuna . IIII . ac̄ . de dn̄io . & ual̕ . VIII . d̄ . In ead̄
. I . lib̄ hō dim̕ ac̄ . & ual̕ . I . d̄ . Rex . 7 com̄s ſocā.
Claindune . H̃ . Hamingeſtunā tenuit . Leutic⁹ lib̄ hō . t̕.
r̕ . e . I . car̕ trǣ . p̄ mañ . ſemp . II . bord̄ . Tc̄ . II . car̕ . m̊ . I . & . IIII .
ac̄ . p̄ti . Silua . II . porc̄ . ſemp . I . runc̄ . Tc̄ . II . añ . m̊ . I . Tc̄ . XI .
oūs . modo . XX . Tc̄ . XIII . porc̄ ⸝ m̊ . XX . Tc̄ . VII . cap̄ . Tc̄ ual̕ . XX .
ſol̕ . modo . XXV . VIII . d̄ min̕ . In ead̄ . III . libi . hoēs . XXIIII . ac̄ .
Tc̄ 7 p̄ . I . car̕ . m̊ dim̕ . 7 ual̕ . V . ſol̕ . Rex 7 Com̄s ſocā.

HERTESMERA . H̃ . Thorham tenuit Leuricus
com̄dat briſtrico p̄poſito s̄co eadmundi . t . r . e . I . car̕ terrǣ
p̄ mañ . ſemp . II . bord̄ . Tc̄ . II . car̕ . P̄ dim̕ . m̊ . I . II . ac̄ p̄ti .
Tc̄ ſilua . de XXX . porc̄ ⸝ m̊ . XX . Semp . II . runc̄ . 7 quarta
pars æcclię . III . ac̄ . 7 dim̕ . Tc̄ ual̕ . XXX . ſol̕ . modo XX . De hac
tr̄a habuit Abbas . tres partes ſochę . 7 Rex quartā . In eadē
. III . libi hoēs . IIII . ac̄ . 7 dim̕ . & . ual̕ . VIII . d̄ . h̄t VIII . qr̄ in longo
7 . VIII . in lato . 7 VIII . d̄ & obolū de gelto.

Hvnd̄ . de CLAINDVNE . In henleie . XVI . ac̄ . libe tr̄ę

p̄tinentes in hamingeſtuna . & in p̄tio.

2 In SOMERSHAM Wulfwin, a free man, held 60 acres of land as a manor before 1066. Then 1 plough.
Value then 20s; now 20[s].
The King and the Earl (have) the jurisdiction.
In the same (Somersham) Coleman, a free man; 5 acres.
Value 20d.
The King and the Earl (have) the jurisdiction.

3 In HEMINGSTONE 4 acres in lordship.
Value 8d.
In the same (Hemingstone) 1 free man; ½ acre.
Value 1d.
The King and the Earl (have) the jurisdiction.

CLAYDON Hundred
4 Leofric, a free man, held HEMINGSTONE before 1066; 1 carucate of land as a manor.
Always 2 smallholders.
Then 2 ploughs, now 1.
Meadow, 4 acres; woodland, 2 pigs. Always 1 cob. Then 2 cattle, now 1; then 11 sheep, now 20; then 13 pigs, now 20; then 7 goats.
Value then 20s; now 25[s] less 8d.
In the same (Hemingstone) 3 free men; 24 acres. Then and later 1 plough, now ½.
Value 5s.
The King and the Earl (have) the jurisdiction.

HARTISMERE Hundred
5 Leofric, under the patronage of Brictric the reeve of St. Edmund's, held THORNHAM (Magna) before 1066; 1 carucate of land as a manor.
Always 2 smallholders.
Then 2 ploughs, later ½, now 1.
Meadow, 2 acres; woodland then at 30 pigs, now 20. Always 2 cobs.
The fourth part of a church, 3½ acres.
Value then 30s; now 20[s].
Over this land, the Abbot had three parts of the jurisdiction, and the King (had) the fourth (part).
In the same (Thornham Magna) 3 free men; 4½ acres.
Value 8d.
It has 8 furlongs in length and 8 in width; 8½d in tax.

Hundred of CLAYDON
6 In HENLEY 16 acres of free land belonging to Hemingstone. 438 a
(They are) in the assessment.

437 b, 438 a

HVṆ DE COSFORT. In Redles. dim car̃ terræ. ten&. I. soc̃
ſtigango. Tc̃ & p̃. I. car̃. modo nult. 7. I. ac̃ p̃ti. 7 ual&. XVIII. ſot.
In hac terra iacebant. XIIII. ac̃ ſiluæ q̃s. W. de burnoluilla. inde
abſtulit. & m̃. ten&.

TERRA NORMANNI VICECOMITIS. Dim̃. h̃. de gepeſwiz. .LXIII.

In burgo h̃t normannus. II. burgenſes. unũ in uadimonio. contra
eundẽ. & alterũ p debito. ſed Rex h̃t ſuas conſuetudines.

✱ TERRA Iuichel p̃bri. *BOSEMERA*. H̃. In ſtanhã ten& .LXIIII.

Aluricus lib̃ h̃o Edrici ante ceſſoris Robti mal&. LXXXX. ac̃
p man̄. 7 inde fuit ſaiſitus. Rob. ſemp. VI. bord. &. I. ſeru. &. I. car̃
& dim̃ in dominio. & dim̃ car̃ hom̃. 7. II. ac̃ p̃ti. ſilua. X. porc̃.
&. VII. añ. Tc̃. I. porc̃. modo. V. Tc̃. VIII. oũs. modo. XL. &. V. lib̃i
hões. XX. IIII. ac̃. & dim'̃ car'̃. & tc̃ ual. XX. ſot. m̃ XXXV. In ead
.Æccſia. XVI. ac̃. & dim' car'̃.
. I. lib̃ h̃o. XXIIII. ac̃. Tc̃. I. car̃. & ual. V. ſot. Rex & Cõms ſoc̃.
h̃t. I. leuga in longo. 7. III. qr in lato. Alii. ibi tenent. &. VII. d. &
obolũ de gelto.

In Stanham. I. æccl̃ia. XX. ac̃. q̃s ibi deder̃. IX lib̃i hões p animab; ſuis.
BISOPES. H̃. In horan. I. car̃. t̃ræ. ten̄ Algar̃. t. r. e. lib̃ h̃o
ſtigandi. 7 II. alii. un̄ h̃o Almari ẽpi. 7 al̄ h̃o Edrici de laxafelda

Hundred of COSFORD

7 In *REDLES* ½ carucate of land; 1 Freeman, belonging to Stigand, [held it]. Then and later 1 plough, now none.
    Meadow, 1 acre.
    Value 18s.
    To this land belonged 14 acres of woodland which W(illiam) of Bourneville took away from there and now holds.

63   LAND OF NORMAN THE SHERIFF

Half-Hundred of IPSWICH

1 In the Borough (of IPSWICH) Norman has 2 burgesses, one in pledge to him, the other for a debt; but the King has his customary dues.

64   LAND OF JUDICAEL THE PRIEST

BOSMERE Hundred

1 In STONHAM Aelfric, a free man of Edric, Robert Malet's predecessor, [held] 90 acres as a manor. Robert was in possession of it.
    Always 6 smallholders; 1 slave;
    1½ ploughs in lordship; ½ men's plough.
    Meadow, 2 acres; woodland, 10 pigs. 7 cattle; then 1 pig, now 15; then 8 sheep, now 40.
    5 free men; 24 acres; ½ plough.
    A church, 16 acres. ½ plough.
    Value then 20s; now 35[s].
    In the same (Stonham) 1 free man; 24 acres. Then 1 plough.
    Value 5s.
    The King and the Earl (have) the jurisdiction.
    It has 1 league in length and 3 furlongs in width. Others hold there. 7½d in tax.

2 In STONHAM 1 church; 20 acres which 9 free men granted there for their souls.

BISHOP'S Hundred

3 In HORHAM 1 carucate of land; Algar, a free man of Stigand's, and 2 others, one a man of Bishop Aelmer's and the other a man of Edric of Laxfield's, held (it) before 1066.

438 b

 Semṕ vii . borḋ . 7 . 1 . ferú . 7 . 1 . car in dñio . Silua . xxiiii . porć . & 14.
 ać p̃ti . & . 1 . car hoḿ . Tć . ii . runć . Tć . viii . añ . femp xxiiii . porć .
 Tć xxiiii . oús . 7 . 1 . uas . apū . 7 iiii . libi hoes . xx . iiii . ać . q̇s reclamat .
 delibatione . Tć diḿ car . m̊ . ii . boús . Ecclia de . xx . ii . ać & ual
 xxii . d . Semṕ ual . xx fol . Soca in hoxa eṕi .

. LXV .   **TERRE** GIRoldi marefchalchi . RiSebruge . H̃ . Damar-
 deftunā . teñ Coḿs Algar̉ p̣ bereuuita in bademundesfelda .
 t . r . e . ii . car terræ . femṕ . iiii . uilĺ . & . 1 . borḋ . 7 . iii . ferú . 7 ii . car in
 dñio . Tć ual . lx . fol . modo . lxx . femṕ . i . runć . Tć . ii . añ . modo .
 xv . 7 xxiiii . porć . 7 . xl . iiii . oús .

. LXVI .   **TERRÆ** RobTI . BLVNDI . Brademere . Hvnd . Gifwor-
 tham . teñ Achỉ p̣ mañ . t . r . e . iii . car terræ . femṕ . ii . borḋ . Tć
 . v . ferú . m̊ . ii . femp . iii . car in dñio . & . 1 . mol . 7 xx . ać p̃ti . Tć . ii .
 runć . modo . i . Seṕ . v . añ . Tć . xl . porć . modo . xx . ii . Tć . viii . oús .
 modo lxxxx . ii . 7 iii . arpenni uineæ . & uñ parć . Tć ual . lxxx .
 fol . modo . vi . lib . In eadē . xxv . libi hoes . coḿ . ii . car . & dim̉ terræ .
 Tć . v . car . modo . iiii . & dim . & . iiii . ać p̃ti . femp ual . xx . fol De toto
 . H̃ . scs eadḿ . fać & focá . In eadē . v . libi hoes . coḿ . i . car terræ . 7 lxxx .
 ać . Tć . v . car . m̊ . ii . 7 . iii . ać p̃ti . Tć ual . xxx . fol modo xx .
 Æcclia lxxx . ać libæ terre . 7 . i . car . & . 1 . ać p̃ti . 7 ual . v . fol . Totū

439 a

 ht . ii . lg in longo . & . vi . qr̉ in lat . 7 xxii . d & . iii . ferding . de geldo .

Always 7 smallholders; 1 slave;
1 plough in lordship. Woodland, 24 pigs; meadow, 2 acres;
1 men's plough.
Then 2 cobs; then 8 cattle; always 24 pigs. Then 24 sheep.
1 beehive.
4 free men, 24 acres, whom he claims by a delivery. Then ½ plough; now 2 oxen.
A church with 22 acres; value 22d.
Value always 22s.
The jurisdiction (is) in the Bishop's (manor of) Hoxne.

65 LANDS OF GERALD MARSHAL

RISBRIDGE Hundred
1 Earl Algar held DENSTON as an outlier in (the lands of) Badmondisfield before 1066; 2 carucates of land.
Always 4 villagers; 1 smallholder; 3 slaves;
2 ploughs in lordship.
Value then 60s; now 70[s].
Always 1 cob. Then 2 cattle, now 15; 24 pigs; 44 sheep.

66 LANDS OF ROBERT BLUNT

BRADMERE Hundred
1 Aki held IXWORTH as a manor before 1066; 3 carucates of land.
Always 2 smallholders. Then 5 slaves, now 2.
Always 3 ploughs in lordship.
1 mill; meadow, 2 acres. Then 2 cobs, now 1; always 5 cattle.
Then 40 pigs, now 22; then 8 sheep, now 92. 3 *arpents* of vines; 1 park.
Value then 80s; now £6.
In the same (Ixworth) 25 free men under patronage; 2½ carucates of land. Then 5 ploughs, now 4½.
Meadow, 4 acres.
Value always 20s.
St. Edmund's (has) full jurisdiction over the whole Hundred.
In the same (Ixworth) 5 free men under patronage; 1 carucate of land and 80 acres. Then 5 ploughs, now 2.
Meadow, 3 acres.
Value then 30s; now 20[s].
A church, 80 acres of free land. 1 plough. Meadow, 1 acre. Value 5s.
The whole has 2 leagues in length and 6 furlongs in width; 22¾d in tax.

⁋ Walſam . t . r . e . teñ Achi⁹ . ꝑ man̄ . ɪɪ . car̄ t̄ræ . ſemp . ɪɪɪɪ . bord̄.
Tc̄ . ɪɪ . car̄ in dn̄io . modo . ɪɪɪ . 7 dim̄ . car̄ hom̄ . & . v . ac̄ p̄ti . ſilua . xx.
porc̄ . ſēp . ɪ . runc̄ . Tc̄ . ɪɪɪ . an̄ . m̄ . ɪ . Tc̄ . xl . porc̄ . m̄ . xx . ɪx . Tc̄ . v . ous̄.
modo . xxx . Tc̄ ual̄ . xl . ſol̄ . m̄ . lx . In eadē . xx . libi hoes . com̄d̄ . ɪ . car̄ t̄ræ
ſemp . ɪɪ . car̄ . & . ɪɪ . ac̄ p̄ti . ſilua . x . porc̄ . Tc̄ ual̄ . x . ſol̄ . modo xx . In ead̄
. ɪɪɪ . libi hoes 7 dim̄ . ɪ . car̄ terræ . Tc̄ 7 p̄ . ɪɪɪ . car̄ . 7 dim̄ . modo . ɪɪ . 7 . ɪɪ.
ac̄ & dim̄ p̄ti . Silua de . ɪɪɪɪ . porc̄ . ſemp ual̄ . xx . ſol̄ . Eccl̄ia dimidia.
x . ac̄ . & . ɪ . ac̄ p̄ti . & ual̄ vɪɪɪ . d̄ . ħt . ɪɪ . leuḡ in longo . & . vɪ . qr̄ in lato.
& xvɪɪ . d̄ de gelto . Alii ibi tenent.

⁋ Eaſcefeld̄a teñ Achi⁹ . ꝑ man̄ . t . r . e . ɪɪɪ . car̄ . t̄ræ . ſemp . ɪx . bord̄.
Tc̄ . ɪɪɪɪ . car̄ in dominio . modo . ɪɪɪ . & xɪɪ . ac̄ p̄ti . ſilua . lx . porc̄.
ſemper . ɪɪ . runc̄ . & . ɪɪ . an̄ . Tc̄ lx . porc̄ . modo . xv . Tc̄ xxv . ous̄.
modo . x . 7 . x . uaſa apu̅ . ſemp ual̄ . lx . ſol̄ . In eadē . xɪɪɪɪ . libi
hoes . com̄d̄ . lxxx . ac̄ . ſemp . ɪ . car̄ . & . ɪɪɪɪ . ac̄ . p̄ti . ſilua . ɪɪɪɪ . porc̄.
7 ual̄ . vɪɪɪ . ſol̄ . In eadē . ɪ . lib̄ . ho̅ Chetel . ɪ . lib̄ ho̅ . ɪ . car̄ terræ
ꝑ man̄ . ſemp . ɪɪ . bord̄ . 7 . ɪɪ . feru̅ . 7 . ɪɪ . car̄ in dn̄io . 7 . ɪɪɪɪ . ac̄ p̄ti.
ſilua xx . porc̄ . 7 . ɪɪɪ . libi hoes . ſub eo xxɪɪ . ac̄ . 7 dim̄ . car̄ . ſemp.
ɪɪ . runc̄ . Tc̄ . ɪɪɪɪ . an̄ . Tc̄ . xxɪɪɪɪ . porc̄ . modo . xxɪɪɪ . Tc̄ . xxɪɪ . ous̄.
M . c . Tc̄ xl . cap̄ . modo . xɪɪ . ſemp ual̄ & . xxx . ſol̄ . ex ħ habuit antec̄.
Rob̄ti . cm̄d̄ . Willm̄ ten & de Rob̄to . In ead̄ . ɪɪɪ . lib̄ hoes . com̄d̄ . ɪ . car̄

66

2 Aki held WALSHAM (le Willows) before 1066; as a manor, 2 carucates of land.
  Always 4 smallholders.
  Then 2 ploughs in lordship, now 3; ½ men's plough.
  Meadow, 5 acres; woodland, 20 pigs. Always 1 cob. Then 3 cattle, now 1; then 40 pigs, now 29; then 5 sheep, now 30.
  Value then 40s; now 60[s].
  In the same (Walsham le Willows) 20 free men under patronage; 1 carucate of land. Always 2 ploughs.
  Meadow, 2 acres; woodland, 10 pigs.
  Value then 10s; now 20[s].
  In the same (Walsham le Willows) 3 free men and a half; 1 carucate of land. Then and later 3½ ploughs, now 2.
  Meadow, 2½ acres; woodland at 4 pigs.
  Value always 20s.
  ½ church, 10 acres. Meadow, 1 acre. Value 8d.
  It has 2 leagues in length and 6 furlongs in width; 17d in tax.
  Others hold there.

3 Aki held (Great) ASHFIELD as a manor before 1066; 3 carucates of land.
  Always 9 smallholders.
  Then 4 ploughs in lordship, now 3.
  Meadow, 12 acres; woodland, 60 pigs. Always 2 cobs, 2 cattle. Then 60 pigs, now 15; then 25 sheep, now 10; 10 beehives.
  Value always 60s.
  In the same (Great Ashfield) 14 free men under patronage; 80 acres. Always 1 plough.
  Meadow, 4 acres; woodland, 4 pigs.
  Value 8s.
  In the same (Great Ashfield) 1 free man, Ketel; 1 carucate of land as a manor.
  Always 2 smallholders; 2 slaves;
  2 ploughs in lordship.
  Meadow, 4 acres; woodland, 20 pigs.
  3 free men under him; 22 acres. ½ plough.
  Always 2 cobs. Then 4 cattle; then 24 pigs, now 23; then 32 sheep, now 100; then 40 goats, now 12.
  Value always 30s.
  Robert's predecessor had this under patronage, William holds (it) from Robert.
  In the same (Great Ashfield) 3 free men under patronage; 1 carucate

terræ . 7 . LX . ac̄ . 7 . I . borđ . femp . III . cař . 7 . IIII . ac̄ p̃ti . filua de . IIII . porc̃ . 7 femp ual& . xxx . fol . h̃ tenent . II . milĩtes . Æcc̃lia . IX . ac̄;

439 b

Hr̃ . XI . qr̃ in longo . 7 . XI . in lato . & . V . den̄ . & obolū de gelto . Alii
⁄Wicā ten& Aki⁹ . t . r . e . p mañ . I . cař terræ Tc̄ . III . borđ ⁄ibi tenēt .
Tc̄ III . ferŭ . modo . II . femp . II . cař in dn̄io . 7 . III . ac̄ p̃ti . filŭ
X . porc̃ . Tc̄ . I . runc̃ . modo . II . femp . I . añ . Tc̄ . XII . porc̃ . m̃ xx .
III . Tc̄ . xx . v . oūs . modo . xxxvIII . femp ual . xxx . fol . & . v
liƀi hões . & dim̄ . cōmd . I . cař tr̃æ . femp . II . borđ . 7 fub eĩs . II . liƀi
hões . IIII . ac̄ . femp . II . cař . & . VI . ac̄ p̃ti . 7 q̃rta pars mol . Tc̄ ual
xx . fol . modo . XIII .
⁄In Sapeftuna . II . liƀi hões regis . e . xvIII . ac̄ . 7 ual . III . fol .
Langham ten̄ haret lib̃ hō de q̃ ses eadmund . habuit cm-
t . r . e . III . cař terræ . Tc̄ . I . uiff . femp . III . borđ . 7 . III . ferŭ .
Tc̄ 7 p⁹ . III . cař in dn̄io . modo . II . Tc̄ dim̄ cař hom̃ . XII . ac̄
p̃ti . filua . VI . porc̃ . Tc̄ . VII . runc̃ . modo . I . Tc̄ . VIII . añ . m̃ . II .
Tc̄ xxx . porc̃ . modo xvI . Tc̄ . c̃ . XL . oūs . m̃ . XII . Tc̄ ual . LXXX .
fol . modo . LX . In ead . II . liƀi hões . cōmd . xx . ac̄ . Tc̄ dim̄ . carř .
modo . II . bou . 7 ual . III . fol . ht . VII . qr̃ in longo . 7 VI . in lato .
& . x . đ in gelt .
⁄In hepworda . dim̄ lib̃ homo . xL . ac̄ . 7 . I . borđ . 7 femp dim̄
cař & dim̄ ac̃ p̃ti . 7 ual x . fol .
⁄In Wica . I . lib̃ hō cōmd . Lx . ac̄ . & . I . borđ . femp . I . cař .
7 ual& . x . fol .

439 a, b

of land and 60 acres.
> 1 smallholder.
> Always 3 ploughs.
> Meadow, 3 acres; woodland at 4 pigs.
>
> Value always 30s.
>> 2 men-at-arms hold (this).
>> A church, 9 acres.
>>
>> It has 11 furlongs in length and 11 in width; 5½d in tax. Others hold there.

439 b

4 Aki [held] WYKEN before 1066; as a manor, 1 carucate of land.
> Then 3 smallholders; then 3 slaves, now 2.
> Always 2 ploughs in lordship.
> Meadow, 3 acres; woodland, 10 pigs. Then 1 cob, now 2; always 1 cattle. Then 12 pigs, now 23; then 25 sheep, now 38.
>
> Value always 30s.
> 5 free men and a half, under patronage; 1 carucate of land.
>> Always 2 smallholders.
>
> Under them, 2 free men; 4 acres.
>> Always 2 ploughs.
>> Meadow, 6 acres; the fourth part of a mill.
>
> Value then 20s; now 13[s].

5 In SAPISTON 2 free men of King Edward's; 18 acres.
> Value 3s.

6 Haret, a free man over whom St. Edmund's had patronage before 1066, held LANGHAM; 3 carucates of land.
> Then 1 villager. Always 3 smallholders; 3 slaves.
> Then and later 3 ploughs in lordship, now 2; then ½ men's plough.
> Meadow, 12 acres; woodland, 6 pigs. Then 7 cobs, now 1; then 8 cattle, now 2; then 30 pigs, now 16; then 140 sheep, now 12.
>
> Value then 80s; now 60[s].
> In the same (Langham) 2 free men under patronage; 20 acres. Then ½ plough, now 2 oxen.
>
> Value 3s.
>> It has 7 furlongs in length and 6 in width; 10d in tax.

7 In HEPWORTH a half free men; 40 acres.
> 1 smallholder.
> Always ½ plough. Meadow, ½ acre.
>
> Value 10s.

8 In WYKEN 1 free man under patronage; 60 acres.
> 1 smallholder.
> Always 1 plough.
>
> Value 10s.

⁊In Icſeẁrda.I.liƀ hō xl.aē ſemp.I.car⁷
⁊ ual&.v.ſot Ex his oībȝ liƀis hoībȝ ┊regē ad Waraṅt Sc̄s
eadmund.de toto ſocā ⁊ ſacā.

440 a

⁊In Icſewrda.tenuit Ketel liƀ hō.cc.aē.ꝑ man̄.ſemp
ii.bord.&.ii.ſeru⁷.&.ii.car⁷ in dn̄io.⁊ vi.aē p̄ti.&.i.mot.
& ſub eo.vi.liƀi hoes.xxix.aē.Tc̄.ii.car.modo.i.ſemp ual&
lx.ſot.Ex h̄ habuit Angar⁹.ſtalra c̄omd.t.r.e.Rad.fr̄ Roƀ
erat ſaiſitus quando fuit mortuus ⁊ Roƀ.recp̄it de rege.

⁊Dimid⁷.H̄.de Cosfort.In Watefella.v.liƀi hoes de uno
habuit ſc̄s.e.c̄omd ⁊ de oībȝ ſocā.antec̄ Roƀti nec c̄md⁷.& h̄nt
lx.aē.Tc̄.ii.car.modo.i.ſemp uat.vi.ſot.modo xx.In ead
.iiii.liƀi hoes lxiii.aē.Tc̄.ii.car modo.dim⁷.⁊ uat.x.ſot.⁊.viii.d.
Blidinga.h̄ In Weſtledeſtuna.xxvii.aē.⁊ dim⁷ ⁊ꝑ eſcanḡ.
ten& Brunar⁹ pƀr.T.R.E.ſemp dim car⁷.⁊ uat.iiii.ſot.

⁊Herteſmera.H̄.In Giſilmcham.xxx.aē de dn̄io de Waleſam
qd̄ tenuit Achi.&.i.aē p̄ti.⁊ uat.vi.ſot.⁊ viii.d.In ead.iii.liƀi
hoes c̄omd.Achio⁹ Alger⁹.Godric.Goduuin⁹.liii.aē.&.i.liƀ hō
ſub eis.i.aē.Tc̄ & p.ii.car.modo.dim⁷.&.i.aē p̄ti.ſilu xxiiii.
porc⁷.& uat xvi.ſot.Sup ii⁹ˢ.feminas iſtoȝ⁷ hominu⁷ habuit
Abbas ſc̄i edmund.dim⁷ c̄omd⁷.⁊ dim⁷ ſoc⁷

Herteſmara.H̄.In Weſttorp.iiii.liƀi hoes com Achi.t.
t.e.iiii.aē.⁊ dim⁷ ⁊ uat.xvi.d.In finingahā.ii.aē.de dn̄io
de Walſā.

9 In IXWORTH 1 free man; 40 acres. Always 1 plough.
Value 5s.
Concerning all these free men he calls the King as warrantor. St. Edmund's (has) full jurisdiction over the whole.

10 In IXWORTH Ketel, a free man, held 200 acres as a manor.   440 a
Always 2 smallholders; 2 slaves;
2 ploughs in lordship.
Meadow, 6 acres; 1 mill.
Under him, 6 free men; 29 acres. Then 2 ploughs, now 1.
Value always 60s.
Over this, Asgar the Constable had patronage before 1066. Ralph, Robert's brother, was in possession when he died. Robert acquired (it) from the King.

Half-Hundred of COSFORD

11 In WHATFIELD 5 free men; St. Edmund's had patronage over one, and jurisdiction over all; and Robert's predecessor (did) not (have) patronage. They have 60 acres. Then 2 ploughs, now 1.
Value always 6s; now 20[s].
In the same (Whatfield) 4 free men; 63 acres. Then 2 ploughs, now ½.
Value 10s 8d.
(It is) by exchange.

BLYTHING Hundred

12 In WESTLETON 27½ acres. Brunmer the priest [held it] before 1066.
Always ½ plough.
Value 4s.

HARTISMERE Hundred

13 In GISLINGHAM 30 acres of the lordship of Walsham (le Willows) which Aki held.
Meadow, 1 acre.
Value 6s 8d.
In the same (Gislingham) 3 free men under the patronage of Aki; Algar, Godric, Godwin; 53 acres. 1 free man under them; 1 acre.
Then and later 2 ploughs, now ½.
Meadow, 1 acre; woodland, 24 pigs.
Value 16s.
Over 2 of the wives of these (free) men, the Abbot of St. Edmund's had half the patronage and half the jurisdiction.

HARTISMERE Hundred

14 In WESTHORPE 4 free men under the patronage of Aki before 1066; 4½ acres.
Value 16d.

15 In FINNINGHAM 2 acres of the lordship of Walsham (le Willows).

⁊ In Wiuertheſtuna . ɪɪ . liɓi hões . com̃d Achi . t . r . e . xxx . aċ
T̄c dim̃ . cař . ſilua ad ɪɪ . porċ . dim̃ aċ p̃ti . 7 ual . v . ſoł . hoc teñ
. R . ouethel . de . R . blond; ⁊ STOV . H̃ . In eſcefella . iac& . ɪ . borđ
de . ɪɪɪ . aċ . 7 ređđ . xɪɪ . đ.

440 b

. LXVII. **TERRA HERVEJ BITVRICENS** . STOV . H̃ . In Tornei ten&
Euen de erueo . ɪ . cař terræ . quã tenuit briċtriċ blac ſub witgaro
anteċ Ricardi de clara . & non poť uendere ſine licencia eius.
modo ten& herueus ex dono regis . T̄c . vɪ . borđ . p̃ 7 modo . ɪɪɪ . T̄c .
ɪɪ . cař . p̃ nułł . & modo . ɪ . cař . & . ɪɪɪɪ . aċ p̃ti . T̄c . ɪɪ . cař hom̃ . p̃ &
modo nulla . T̄c ual xxx . ſoł . modo xlvɪɪ . ſoł . Rex & com̃s ſocam.

⁊ Boſemera . H̃ . Hamingeſtunã teñ Rainaldus de herueho . quã
tenuit . Vlmarus liɓ hõ com̃datus tant . Edrico . t . r . e . anteceſſori
Roɓti mal& . c . aċ tr̃æ ꝑ man̄ . ſem̃p . vɪ . borđ . & . ɪ . cař in dominio.
T̄c . ɪ . cař hom̃ . modo dim̃ & . ɪɪ . aċ p̃ti . & . ɪ . liɓ hõ . ɪɪɪɪ . aċ . Totũ ual
xx . ſoł . Rex & com̃s ſocã . Ex hac terra fuit ſaiſitus . Wiłł . mal& ea die
qua fuit mortuus 7 p̃ea Roɓ mal& filꝯ ei.

16 In WYVERSTONE 2 free men under the patronage of Aki before 1066; 30 acres. Then ½ plough.
Woodland for 2 pigs; meadow, ½ acre.
Value 5s.
R. Oudkell holds this from Robert Blunt.

STOW Hundred
17 In (Great) ASHFIELD belongs 1 smallholder, with 3 acres.
He pays 12d.

67 LAND OF HERVEY OF BOURGES

STOW Hundred
1 In THORNEY Euen holds from Hervey 1 carucate of land. Brictric Black held it under Withgar, Richard of Clare's predecessor; he could not sell without his permission. Now Hervey holds (it) by the King's gift.
Then 6 smallholders, later and now 3.
Then 2 ploughs, later none, now 1 plough. Meadow, 4 acres.
Then 2 men's ploughs, later and now none.
Value then 30s; now 47s.
The King and the Earl (have) the jurisdiction.

BOSMERE Hundred
2 Reginald holds HEMINGSTONE from Hervey. Wulfmer, a free man under the patronage before 1066 only of Edric, Robert Malet's predecessor, held it; 100 acres as a manor.
Always 6 smallholders;
1 plough in lordship. Then 1 men's plough, now ½. Meadow, 2 acres.
1 free man; 4 acres.
Value of the whole 20s.
The King and the Earl (have) the jurisdiction.
William Malet was in possession of this land on the day he died; later on Robert Malet, his son, (was in possession).

CLAINDVNE . H̃. Pettehaga tenuit briētuolt in dñio . I . car̃ terræ & . xxx . ac̃ . p mañ . t . r . e Anteceſſor . Roḃ mal& . comdatione habuit Sep̃ . v . borđ . Tc̃ . II . car̃ in dñio . P̃ & modo . I . III . ac̃ p̃ti . femp . I . runc̃ . Tc̃ . III . añ . modo . I . Tc̃ . XIIII . porc̃ . modo . VIII . Tc̃ . XXX . II . oũs . m̃ xx . Tc̃ uaĺ LX . fot . modo . XL . In eadẽ . v . liḃi homines . comd . XVIII . ac̃ . Tc̃ . II . car̃ . modo . I . Ecctia . de . II . ac̃ . & dim̃ . & uat . v . fot . hoc fuit ad firmã . p . III . liḃ . & xv . fot . fed hões inde fuer̃ confufi . & modo app̃-

441 a
tiatũ ẽ . XLV . fot . Ht̃ . I . lg̃ in longo . & . III . qr in lato . ỹ . x . đ . de gelto. Abbas de eli dimidiã focã & anteceſſor comitis hugonis dimiđiã. In Affefelda . Godmañ . liḃ hõ comdtus t . r . e . Roḃti mal& p mañ . xxx . ac̃ . 7 . I . borđ . 7 . tc̃ . I . car̃ P̃ . nichil . modo dim̃ car̃ . Ecctia . IIII . ac̃ . 7 . uat . x . fot . Rannulfus teñ . Soca aḃḃis . & hante ceſſoris hugonis . Ex his duoḃ3 maneriis fuit faifitus Wittm mal& die fui obitus . In ead . I . liḃ hõ . II . ac̃ . & ual& . IIII . đ . Soca aḃḃis. Perreham dim̃ ħ . Brutge ten& Edricus . comdatus Edrico Ante ceſſori . R . mal& . c . xx . ac̃ p mañ . Tc̃ . II . car̃ . p . I . modo dim̃ . 7 IIII . ac̃ p̃ti . femp . I . moliñ . & qrta pars ecctiæ . de . VI . ac̃.

CLAYDON Hundred

3 Brictwold held PETTAUGH in lordship; 1 carucate of land and 30 acres as a manor before 1066. Robert Malet's predecessor had the patronage.
> Always 5 smallholders.
> Then 2 ploughs in lordship; later and now 1.
> Meadow, 3 acres. Always 1 cob. Then 3 cattle, now 1; then 14 pigs, now 8; then 32 sheep, now 20.

Value then 60s; now 40[s].
In the same (Pettaugh) 5 free men under patronage; 18 acres. Then 2 ploughs, now 1.
> A church with 2½ acres; value 5s.

This was at a revenue for £3 15s, but the men were thereby ruined and now it is assessed at 45s.
> It has 1 league in length and 4 furlongs in width; 10d in tax. The Abbot of Ely (had) half the jurisdiction, and Earl Hugh's predecessor (had) half.

441 a

4 In ASHFIELD Godman, a free man under the patronage of Robert Malet before 1066; as a manor, 30 acres.
> 1 smallholder.
> Then 1 plough, later nothing, now ½ plough.
> A church, 4 acres.

Value 10s.
> Ranulf holds (this).
> The jurisdiction (belonged to) the Abbot and to (Earl) Hugh's predecessor.
> William Malet was in possession of these two manors on the day of his death.

In the same (Ashfield) 1 free man; 2 acres.
Value 4d.
> The jurisdiction (is) the Abbot's.

PARHAM Half-Hundred

5 Edric, under the patronage of Edric, R(obert) Malet's predecessor [held] BRUTGE; 120 acres as a manor. Then 2 ploughs, later 1, now ½.
> Meadow, 4 acres; always 1 mill.
> The fourth part of a church with 6 acres.

440 b, 441 a

VIII . porc̄ . Tc̄ ual . XL . fol . modo . XX . Abbas de eli foca . 7 Garner⁹
ten& de herueo . In ead . VIII . libi hoēs . additi . XX . ac̄ . Tc̄ . I . car̓
p̓ dim̓ . modo . nichil . 7 ual& XL . den̄ . de dimidio hui⁹ fræ herueus
conciliatus abƀi . & p̓⁹ eā de rege tenuit . Ƕt . VIII . qr̄ in longo
7 VI in lato . & XL . d̄ . de gelto.

⁋In beurefhā . ten̄ Aluric⁹ liƀ hō in foca & com̓d abƀis de eli
LX . ac̄ . ꝑ man̄ . Tc̄ . I . car̓ . III . ac̄ p̓ti . Tc̄ ual . XX . fol . P̓⁹ & modo . V.
⁋In ead . II . libi hoēs com̓dati fup̓dicto . alurico . X . ac̄ . Tc̄ dim̓ . car̓
p̓⁹ 7 m̂ nichil . & ual . II . fol . Id Garner⁹ ten& de herueo . 7 jpfe ē
c̄ciliatus abƀi ex hoc꞉ fup̓dicto . m̂ .

BISCOPES . HVNDRET . In Cipbenhala in dn̄io . I . liƀ
hō heroldi . LX . ac̄ . t . r . e . 7 femp . II . uiƚƚ . 7 . II . car̓ . & . II . ac̄ p̓ti . filua
XXX . porc̄ . Tc̄ ual . X . fol . modo . XX . Ƕ tenuit . W . fili⁹ gorham.
⁋In Coleftuna . I . liƀ hō . com̄d . Edrici . XXX . ac̄ . 7 . III . bord . & dim̓ . car̓.

441 b

Tc̄ ual& . X . fol . modo XX . & ꝑtin& ad cranesfordā . Ƕ ten& War-
nari⁹ . de her̓

HVND̄ de colenefse . In Kelebroc ten̄ Kenoldus de herueu
. I . liƀ hm̓ Vluricū . com̓d . fce Æ . XIIII . ac̄ . dim̓ car̓ . dim̓ moƚ.
. I . ac̄ p̓ti . & . II . bord . Tc̄ ual . V . fol . modo . IX . fol.

8 pigs.
Value then 40s; now 20[s].
The Abbot of Ely (has) the jurisdiction.
Warner holds (this) from Hervey.
In the same (*Brutge*) 8 free men were added; 20 acres. Then 1 plough, later ½, now nothing.
Value 40d.
Concerning half of this land Hervey came to an agreement with the Abbot; later he held it from the King.
It has 8 furlongs in length and 6 in width; 40d in tax.

6 In BEVERSHAM Aelfric, a free man in the jurisdiction and under the patronage of the Abbot of Ely, held 60 acres as a manor. Then 1 plough.
Meadow, 3 acres.
Value then 20s; later and now 5[s].
In the same (Beversham) 2 free men under the patronage of the above-mentioned Aelfric; 10 acres. Then ½ plough, later and now nothing.
Value 2s.
Warner also holds (this) from Hervey, who came to an agreement with the Abbot over this above-mentioned manor.

BISHOP'S Hundred
7 In CHIPPENHALL in lordship; 1 free man of Harold's; 60 acres before 1066.
Always 2 villagers;
2 ploughs.
Meadow, 2 acres; woodland, 30 pigs.
Value then 10s; now 20[s].
W. son of Gorham held this.

8 In COLSTON 1 free man under the patronage of Edric; 30 acres.
3 smallholders.
½ plough.
Value then 10s; now 20[s].
It belongs to Cransford. Warner holds this from Hervey.

441 b

Hundred of COLNEIS
9 In KEMBROKE Cynwold holds from Hervey 1 free man, Wulfric, under the patronage of St. Etheldreda's; 14 acres. ½ plough.
½ mill; meadow, 1 acre.
2 smallholders.
Value then 5s; now 9s.

HVND. de Carleforda. In grundefburg. tenuit Godricus
lib hō.t.r.e.heroldi.i.car terræ.p mañ.Semp.i.uilt.&.
iiii.bord.Semp.i.car in dominio.& hom.i.car.iii.ac
p̄ti.Tc ual xvi.fol.modo fimilit.In eadē.iii.dimidii
libi hōes.com eid.Godwinus Wluinus Leuericus.vii.ac trae.
Tc dim car.modo.nult.Tc ual.ii.fol.modo.xii.d.Adhuc
in eadē in dñio.ii.libi homines Burric.& ailric.comd.Afchilli
hufcarli.t.r.e.v.ac.Tc dim.car.modo.nulla.& ual.x.d.
In eadē in dñio.i.lib hō Brunus.comd.e.ante c.Rob.mal&.xx.
ac.7 has xx.ac.tenebat de.edrico.Tc.i.car modo.dim.ii.ac 7 di-
m p̄ti.Tc ual.v.fol.modo.iiii.fol.

In belinges in dñio.x.libi hōes.Blakemanus.Aluinus.Stanardus
Ana.Vluric.Turbtus.Edric.Godwinus Aleftanus.Anundus.p̄br.
7 de hoc haldena comd.& de aliis.sca Æ.de lxxx.ac &.iiii.ac
terræ.Tc.iiii.car.modo.ii.car.viii.ac p̄ti.Tc ual.xx.fol.m̄ fimil.
In eadē.i.lib hō.Vlmarus fuit hō.haldeni ante cefs.Gaosfridri
de magna uilla.de.c.ac trae in dñio p mañ.& ipfe Vlmarus.
fit fubfe.iii.uilt.Tc ī dñio.ii.car.modo.i.7 hom.i.car.7.iii.ac
p̄ti.Tc.ii.runc.modo.iiii.Tc.iiii.añ.modo.iii.Tc.xvi.porc.

modo.xii.Tc lxxx.ous.modo.lx.Tc ual.xx fol.modo.xl.fol.
.i.Æcclia.xx.ac.7 ual.xl.d.Soca s.æ.

In parua belinges ten Gosfridus.ii.fochemanni.Glademanus
Brihtricus.fup hos habuit Godwinus foca 7 faca 7 confuetudinem
7.i.Leofsi dequo Edric habuit com.illi.ii.foc hab.xxviii.ac.Tc
i.car.m̄.nulla.i.ac.p̄ti.& .ual.ii.fol.7 Leoffi.in dñio.xx.ac.

Hundred of CARLFORD

10 In GRUNDISBURGH Godric, a free man of Harold's, held before 1066; 1 carucate of land as a manor.
>Always 1 villager; 4 smallholders.
>Always 1 plough in lordship; 1 men's plough. Meadow, 3 acres.

Value then 16s; now the same.

In the same (Grundisburgh) 3 half free men under the patronage of the same man; Godwin, Wulfwin, Leofric; 7 acres of land. Then ½ plough, now none.

Value then 2s; now 12d.

Also in the same (Grundisburgh) in lordship; 2 free men, Burgric and Aethelric, under the patronage of Askell, a guard, before 1066; 5 acres. Then ½ plough, now none.

Value 10d.

In the same (Grundisburgh) in lordship; 1 free man, Brown, under the patronage of E(dric), Robert Malet's predecessor; 20 acres. He held these 20 acres from Edric. Then 1 plough, now ½.
>Meadow, 2½ acres.

Value then 5s; now 4s.

11 In (Great) BEALINGS in lordship; 10 free men, Blackman, Alwin, Stanhard, Ani, Wulfric, Thorbert, Edric, Godwin, Alstan, Anund the priest; over the latter, Haldane had patronage, and over the others St. Etheldreda's (had it); with 80 and 4 acres of land. Then 4 ploughs, now 2.
>Meadow, 8 acres.

Value then 20s; now the same.

In the same (Great Bealings) 1 free man, Wulfmer, he was a man belonging to Haldane, Geoffrey de Mandeville's predecessor, with 100 acres of land in lordship as a manor; and Wulfmer himself [had] under him 3 villagers. Then 2 ploughs in lordship, now 1; 1 men's plough.
>Meadow, 3 acres. Then 2 cobs, now 4; then 4 cattle, now 3; then 16 pigs, now 12; then 80 sheep, now 60.

Value then 20s; now 40s.

1 church, 20 acres; value 40d.

St. Etheldreda's (has) the jurisdiction.

12 In LITTLE BEALINGS Geoffrey holds; 2 Freemen, Gladman (and) Brictric, over whom Godwin had full jurisdiction and the customary due, and 1 (Freeman) Leofsi, over whom Edric had patronage. The 2 Freemen had 28 acres.
>Then 1 plough, now none. Meadow, 1 acre.

Value 2s.

Leofsi (had) 20 acres in lordship.

441 b, 442 a

Tc̄. I. car. modo. nulla. III. ac̄ p̃ti. I. molin̄. 7 uał. III. sol. In ead. in dn̄io. II. libi hoes comd. Sc̄a. Æ. t. r. e. Leuric 7 Brihtric. x. ac̄. Semp. dim car. dim ac̄. p̃ti. 7 uał. II. sol. Adhuc in eadem in dn̄io. II. libi hoes. com. eid. Æ. t. r. e. Vlmar. & bondus. IIII. ac̄
★ & ual& VIII. đ. 7 in ead dn̄io. hardekin lib hō comd Durandi hō Edrici dim 7 dim heroldi. III. ac̄. & . uał. VI. đ. 7 ht in longo. VI. qr̄. & . V. in lato. 7 de gelto. VII. den. & obolū.

In nechemara. in dn̄io. I. lib hō. Vlfwin. com Ingulfi huscarli. III. ac̄. & . uał. VI. den̄.

In Riscemara in dn̄io. I. lib hō Brunnuin. comd. Guerti. xxx. ac̄ Semp. I. car. I. ac̄ p̃ti. 7 uał. semp. x. sol. 7 ht VIII. qr in longo & . VII. in lato. 7. XVI. đ de gelto.

In tudeham in dn̄io. IIII. ac̄. 7 st in belinges. & uał. VIII. đ. In ead . I. liba femina Aldeda. comd. E. de laxefella. VI. ac̄. 7 uał. XII. đ.

Then 1 plough, now none. Meadow, 3 acres; 1 mill.
Value 3s.
In the same (Little Bealings) in lordship; 2 free men, Leofric and Brictric, under the patronage of St. Etheldreda's before 1066; 10 acres. Always ½ plough.
Meadow, ½ acre.
Value 2s.
Also in the same (Little Bealings) 2 free men, Wulfmer and Bondi, under the patronage of the same (St.) Etheldreda's before 1066; 4 acres.
Value 8d.
In the same (Little Bealings) [in] lordship; Hardekin, a free man, half under the patronage of Durand, a man of Edric's, and half (under that) of Harold; 3 acres.
Value 6d.
It has 6 furlongs in length and 5 in width; 7½d in tax.

13 In NECHEMARA in lordship; 1 free man, Wulfwin, under the patronage of Ingulf, a guard; 3 acres.
Value 6d.

14 In RUSHMERE (St. Andrew) in lordship; 1 free man, Brunwin, under the patronage of Gyrth; 30 acres. Always 1 plough.
Meadow, 1 acre.
Value always 10s.
It has 8 furlongs in length and 7 in width; 16d in tax.

15 In TUDDENHAM in lordship; 4 acres. They are in (the lands of) Bealings.
Value 8d.
In the same (Tuddenham) 1 free woman, Aldgyth, under the patronage of E(dric) of Laxfield; 6 acres.
Value 12d.

In ead teñ Bernardus de alencun. Lxxx ac̄. quā tenuit Brihtmarus liƀ hō. t. r. e. comdatus Edrici de laxefel ꝑ mañ. Sēp.
vi. borđ. &. i. ſeru. 7. ii. car̄ in dn̄io. 7. iiii. ac̄ p̄ti. Tc̄. m. tunc.
modo null. Tc̄. iii. porc̄. modo. v. Tc̄. xv. oūs. m̄. x. Tc̄. vi. cap̄.

442 b

modo. null. Tc̄ ual. xx. ſol. m̄ ſimiliſ. 7 De h̄ manerio fuit anteceſſor. R. mal& Edric ſaiſitus. t. r. e. 7 W. mal& qndo fuit mortuus.
& n̄ poterat tr̄a ſua dare l̄ uende. alicui. &. v. liƀi hōes com eid Brih-
tmari. xiiii. ac̄. Tc̄. dim. car̄. modo. null. Tc̄ ual. iiii. ſol. modo. iii.
ſol. In ead. ii. liƀi hōes un comd ante c̄. R. fr̄is ilgeri. 7 ali comd. cu-
iuſdā comd. S. E. vii. ac̄. Tc̄ dim car̄. modo. null. 7 ual. xvi. d. &
ht in longo. x. qr̄. &. vi. in lato. 7 xv. d. de gelto. h̄ totū ten& Bernardus de belencun de. hejuehu.

Thiſteldena. i. liƀ hō. frana. comdat. Edrici. t. r. e. xxx. ac̄. tr̄æ.
Sēp. ii. borđ. 7. i. car̄. ii. ac̄ p̄ti. 7 ual. viii. ſol. hoc teñ Renoldus.
de heruehu. ſed W. mal& inde fuit ſaiſitus die qua obiit.

In derneford. xi. liƀi hōes comdati Durandi hō dim. E. t. r. e. 7 dim.
Heroldi. lxxx. ac̄. &. iii. borđ. Tc̄. iiii. car̄. modo. iii. &. ii. ac̄ p̄ti.
Tc̄ ual xl. ſol. modo. xv.

In ingoluestuna. xiii. liƀi hōes. t. r. e. modo. vi. comdti eid. Durandi. i. car̄ terræ. &. iiii. ac̄. Tc̄. v. car̄. modo. i. v. ac̄ p̄ti. & ual. x. ſol.

In ead. i. liƀ hō comd. eid. Durandi. xii. ac̄. & dim. car̄. & ual. xl. d.
& ht. in longo. vi. qr̄. &. v. in lato. &. vii. d. 7 obolū de gelto. hoc ten&
petrus. de paludel. de herueu.

In the same (Tuddenham) Bernard of Alençon holds 80 acres. Brictmer, a free man under the patronage of Edric of Laxfield, held it before 1066 as a manor.
    Always 6 smallholders; 1 slave;
    2 ploughs in lordship.
    Meadow, 4 acres. Then 2 cobs, now none; then 3 pigs, now 5; then 15 sheep, now 10; then 6 goats, now none.   442 b
Value then 20s; now the same.
    Of this manor, R(obert) Malet's predecessor, Edric, was in possession before 1066, and W(illiam) Malet (was in possession) when he died, and he could not grant or sell his land to someone else. 5 free men under the patronage of the same Brictmer; 14 acres.
Then ½ plough, now none.
Value then 4s; now 3s.
In the same (Tuddenham) 2 free men, one under the patronage of the predecessor of R(anulf) brother of Ilger, and the other under the patronage of someone under the patronage of St. Etheldreda's; 7 acres.
Then ½ plough, now none.
Value 16d.
    It has 10 furlongs in length and 6 in width; 15d in tax.
    Bernard of Alençon holds the whole of this from Hervey.

16 THISTLETON; 1 free man, Frani, under the patronage of Edric before 1066; 30 acres of land.
    Always 2 smallholders;
    1 plough. Meadow, 2 acres.
Value 8s.
    Reginald holds this from Hervey, but W(illiam) Malet was in possession of it on the day he died.

17 In DERNEFORD 11 free men under the patronage of Durand (who was) half E(dric)'s man before 1066 and half Harold's; 80 acres.
    3 smallholders.
    Then 4 ploughs, now 3. Meadow, 2 acres.
Value then 40s; now 15[s].

18 In INGOLUESTUNA 13 free men before 1066, now 6, under the patronage of the same Durand; 1 carucate of land and 4 acres. Then 5 ploughs, now 1.
    Meadow, 5 acres.
Value 10s.
In the same (*Ingoluestuna*) 1 free man of the same Durand's; 12 acres. ½ plough.
Value 40d.
    It has 6 furlongs in length and 5 in width; 7½d in tax.
    Peter of Palluel holds this from Hervey.

HVNDRET . DE WILEFORDA. Berdefelda tenuit Suartingʼ.
com ante c̅. Roḃ. mal&. t. r. e. LXXX. ac̅. &. 1. borḋ. Tc̅. 1. car & dim̄.
modo . 1 . Tc̅ . 11 . runc̄ . m̄ . 11 . & . 1 . a̅ . 7 XXVII . ou̅s . Tc̅ ual xx . ſol.
modo . xxx . 7 h̄t in longo . 1 . l̄g . 7 dim q̄r 7 . vi . q̄r in lato . & de gelto
XIII . den̄ . & obolū . In ead XXI . liḃ hoe̅s c̅omd̄ Suartingi . t . r . e . 1 . car̄

443 a

t̅r̅æ . 7 xxII . ac̅ . Tc̅ . IIII . car̄ . modo . III . dim̄ ac̅ p̅ti . Tc̅ ual . xxx . ſol.
modo ſimil. Adhuc in ead . 1 . liḃ ho̅ . c̅omd̄ . cuid̄a c̅omd̄ . ante . c̅. Roḃ
mal& . xII . ac̅ . ſemp . dim̄ . car̄ . & ual . 11 . ſol . Ex hoc erat . Will mal&
ſaiſit die qua obiit.

Ranulfus
In Wikham . ten̄ . 1 . liḃ ho̅ . c̅om Edrici . t . r . e . xxx . irſ . ac̅ . p̅ man̄.
Atserʼ
& . 1 . borḋ . III . ac̅ . p̅ti . Tc̅ . 1 . car̄ . modo . nuł . & . II . libi hoes . ſub ſe . VIII.
ac̅ . Tc̅ dim̄ . car̄ . Tc̅ ual . x . ſol . modo . vi . 7 ex h̄ ſimilit̄.

Arcenbaldus
In ſuttuna . ten& ide atſerʼ . t . r . e . LX . ac̅ . p̅ man̄ . Semp . II . borḋ
Tc̅ & p̅ . 1 . car̄ . m̄ . dim̄ . dim̄ . ac̅ p̅ti . Tc̅ ual . x . ſol . m̄ ſimilit̄ . In ead
ten̄ ide Arcebaldus . 1 . liḃ ho̅ . c̅omd̄ . Edrici . vi . ac̅ . Sep̄ . II . bou̅ . 7
tc̅ ual . II . ſol . m̄ ſimilit̄ ex hoc tatidē . ſimil.

In horapola . ten̄ odo . 1 . liḃ h̅m commendationʼ . S . æ . & dim̄ . Edrici
xvi . ac̅ . & ual& . III . ſol.

Hundred of WILFORD

19 Swarting, under the patronage of Robert Malet's predecessor, held BREDFIELD before 1066; 80 acres.
> 1 smallholder.
> Then 1½ ploughs, now 1.
> Then 2 cobs, now 2; 1 cattle, 27 sheep.
> Value then 20s; now 30[s].
> It has 1 league and ½ furlong in length, and 6 furlongs in width; 13½d in tax.
> In the same (Bredfield) 21 free men under the patronage of Swarting before 1066; 1 carucate of land and 22 acres. Then 4 ploughs, now 3.
> Meadow, ½ acre.
> Value then 30s; now the same.
> Also in the same (Bredfield) 1 free man under the patronage of someone under the patronage of Robert Malet's predecessor; 12 acres. Always ½ plough.
> Value 2s.
> William Malet was in possession of this on the day he died.

443 a

20 In WICKHAM (Market) Ranulf holds; Azor, 1 free man under the patronage of Edric before 1066; 33 acres as a manor.
> 1 smallholder.
> Meadow, 3 acres.
> Then 1 plough, now none.
> 2 free men under him; 8 acres. Then ½ plough.
> Value then 10s; now 6[s].
> Of this, likewise (William Malet was in possession on the day he died).

21 In SUTTON Erchenbald holds; Azor also [held it] before 1066; 60 acres as a manor.
> Always 2 smallholders.
> Then and later 1 plough, now ½. Meadow, ½ acre.
> Value then 10s; now the same.
> In the same (Sutton) Erchenbald also holds; 1 free man under the patronage of Edric; 6 acres. Always 2 oxen.
> Value 2s; now the same.
> Of this, likewise (William Malet was in possession on the day he died).

22 In HARPOLE Odo holds 1 free man [half] under the patronage of St. Etheldreda's and half (under that) of Edric; 16 acres.
> Value 3s.

★ ⸏In bredefella ten̄ petrus . I . lib̄ homo . comd́ation̄e Durandi . de-
offetuna . xii . ac̄ . iii . boū . 7 xxiii . ōus . & ual& . ii . fot. In ead . i . lib̄
homo comd́ation Ailrici deburc . iiii . ac̄ . & ual . viii . d.
⸏In Ludeham dim lib̄ hō comd́ Suartingi . t . r . e xv . ac̄ & ual . ii . fot.
⸏In bulges . i . lib̄ hō . comd́ Edrici . grim̄ . de . v . ptis terræ . & ual& . iiii d
⸏In horepolo . i . lib̄ hō . comd́ation . Edrici . v . ac̄ . & dim ac̄ pti . & ual . xii . d.
HVND . DE LOSA . Martele tenuit . Brihtmarus . comd́
heroldi . t . r . e . p m lxxx . ac̄ Semp . v . bord . & in dn̄io . ii . car . ix . ac̄
pti . 7 . i . runc . 7 . i . an . & . ix . porc . 7 . xvii . ōus . 7 xxx cap̄ . Tc̄ ual . xl .
fot . modo xxx . 7 . x . libi homines . 7 ii . dim comd́ eid̄e . lx . ac̄ .
Semp . ii . car . i . ac̄ & dim pti . & ual . x . fot . i . ex his calūpniat́

443 b

Rob mal& . & hab& . in longo . i . leuga . & dim in lato . & de
gelto . xi . den̄ .
⸏Campeseia tenuer̄ . ii . libi hōes Suartingus , 7 edricus cō
md́ Edrici . de laxefella . lx . ac̄ . træ p man̄ , Semp . iii . uilt .
Semp . ii . car . & . d . car hominū . viii . ac̄ pti . i . molin̄ . & . ii .
runc . & . viii . porc . & xx . ōus . & . iii . ruscas ap̄ . Tc̄ ual . xx . fot .
modo . xxx . & . xii . libi homines . comd́ . eid̄ . xxxviii ac̄ . træ
Tc̄ . ii . car . modo . i . Tc̄ ual viii . fot . modo . x . & ht in longo
vi . qr̄ . & . in lato . iiii . & de gelto . vii . d . Willm̄ mal& fuit
faiatus die q̊ obiit.

23 In BREDFIELD Peter holds 1 free man, the patronage was Durand of Offton's; 12 acres. 3 oxen.
 23 sheep.
Value 3s.
In the same (Bredfield) 1 free man under the patronage of Aethelric of Burgh; 4 acres.
Value 8d.

24 In LOUDHAM a half free man under the patronage of Swarting before 1066; 15 acres.
Value 2s.

25 In BOULGE 1 free man under the patronage of Edric Grim, with 5 perches of land.
Value 4d.

26 In HARPOLE 1 free man under the patronage of Edric; 5 acres.
 Meadow, ½ acre.
Value 12d.

Hundred of LOES ·

27 Brictmer, under the patronage of Harold, held MARTLEY before 1066; as a manor, 80 acres.
 Always 5 smallholders;
 2 ploughs in lordship.
 Meadow, 9 acres. 1 cob, 1 cattle, 9 pigs, 17 sheep, 30 goats.
Value then 40s; now 30[s].
10 free men and 2 half (free men) under the patronage of the same man; 60 acres. Always 2 ploughs.
 Meadow, 1½ acres.
Value 10s.
 Robert Malet claims 1 of these (men).
 It has 1 league in length and ½ in width; 11d in tax.

443 b

28 2 free men, Swarting and Edric, under the patronage of Edric of Laxfield, held CAMPSEY (Ash); 60 acres of land as a manor.
 Always 3 villagers.
 Always 2 ploughs; ½ men's plough.
 Meadow, 8 acres; 1 mill. 2 cobs, 8 pigs, 20 sheep, 2 hives of bees.
Value then 20s; now 30[s].
12 free men under the patronage of the same man; 38 acres of land.
Then 2 ploughs, now 1.
Value then 8s; now 10[s].
 It has 6 furlongs in length and 4 in width; 7d in tax.
 William Malet was in possession on the day he died.

Renlesham ten Godgeua liba femina . com'd . dim' . sca . æ
& dim' . Edrici de laxefella , LX . ac̄ . p man̄ . Tc̄ . II . car̄ . modo . I .
. II . ac̄ p'ti . & . I . uilt . Semp ual xx . fol . & . I . lib ho̅ . & dim' . x . ac̄
com'd eid̄e . & dim . car̄ . in eod' p'tio . H ten& Bernardus . de
Alencun . de herueu . Willm fuit faifitus . die qua obiit . &
ht in longo . I . lḡ . & in lato . dim' & de gelto . XIIII d.

Potesforda ten odonus p man̄ . LXXX . ac̄ p man̄ quā tenuit
Wenningus . comm'd . dim' . S . Æ . & dim' . Edrici . Semp
II . uilt . & . II . bord . & , VI . ac̄ p'ti . Tc̄ . II . car̄ . m̊ . I . I . runc . &
IIII . an . & . X . cap' . Semp ual xx . fol . 7 jn ead̄e . VIII . libi hoes
. III . ex iftis foris fecer̄ fuā terrā cont' abb . ne poftea uidit .
hundret qd eā redimer& . & qrtus fuit ho̅ abb . & ceti quat-
tuor . fuer̄ com'd . Wenningi . xxx . ac̄ . hi om̄s dim' car̄
. I . ac̄ . & dim' p'ti . Semp ual . x . fol . & ht in longo . I . leuga

444 a

& dim' in lato . & de gelto . XI . d . Wilt fuit faiatus die qua obiit
Glereuinges ten Brihtmarus . com'd Edrico . t . r . e . p man̄
XL ac̄ . & . I . bord . & . I . car̄ . III . ac̄ p'ti . I . molin̄ . & . XX . ous . Tc̄ ual
VIII . fol . modo . X . In ead̄e uilla . XVII . libi homs . & dim' . com'd
eid . LX . ac̄ . Tc̄ . II . car̄ . modo . I . I . ac̄ p'ti . Tc̄ ual . XVII . fol . modo . XV .
W . mal& fuit faiatus die qua obiit . & . ht in longo . I . lḡ . & in
lato . dim' . & de gelto . XXII . d . h ten& . Odo . de herueu .

29 Godiva, a free woman, half under the patronage of St. Etheldreda's and half (under that) of Edric of Laxfield, held RENDLESHAM; 60 acres as a manor. Then 2 ploughs, now 1.
    Meadow, 2 acres.
    1 villager.
Value always 20s.
1 free man and a half (free man) under the patronage of the same; 10 acres. ½ plough.
(It is) in the same assessment.
    Bernard of Alençon holds this from Hervey. William (Malet) was in possession on the day he died.
    It has 1 league in length and ½ in width; 14d in tax.

30 Odo holds POTSFORD; as a manor, 80 acres. Wynning, half under the patronage of St. Etheldreda's and half (under that) of Edric, held it.
    Always 2 villagers; 2 smallholders.
    Meadow, 6 acres.
    Then 2 ploughs, now 1.
    1 cob, 4 cattle, 10 goats.
Value always 20s.
In the same (Potsford) 8 free men; 3 of these forfeited their land to the Abbot and later on the Hundred did not see that they should redeem it, and a fourth was the Abbot's man, and the other four were under the patronage of Wynning; 30 acres. All of these [had] ½ plough.
    Meadow, 1½ acres.
Value always 10s.
    It has 1 league in length and ½ in width; 11d in tax.
    William Malet was in possession on the day he died.

31 Brictmer, under the patronage of Edric, held GLEVERING before 1066; as a manor, 40 acres.
    1 smallholder.
    1 plough.
    Meadow, 3 acres; 1 mill. 20 sheep.
Value then 8s; now 10[s].
In the same village 17 free men and a half under the patronage of the same man; 60 acres. Then 2 ploughs, now 1.
    Meadow, 1 acre.
Value then 17s; now 15[s].
    W(illiam) Malet was in possession on the day he died.
    It has 1 league in length and ½ in width; 22d in tax.
    Odo holds this from Hervey.

In delingahou . XL . ac̄ . qud̄ tenuer̄ . III . libī hōes . & ual . VI . fol.
In ead . II libī hōes com̄d̄ dim̄ . Suartingi & dim̄ . Brumani.
XX . ac̄ . Tc̄ dim̄ . car̄ . & ual . III . fol . & ht in longo . I . lḡ . & in lato
III . qr̄ . & de gelto . VII . d̄ & obolū . In ead̄ē . II . dim̄ hōes . com̄ . Edriei
v . ac̄ . & ual . XII . d̄.

PLVMESGATE . H̃ . Cranesforda . ten& . Atſur , com̄d̄ . Edrici
de laxefella . LXXX . ac̄ tr̄æ . p̄ man̄ . Semp . I . bord̄ . Tc̄ . II . car̄
modo . I . I . ac̄ p̄ti . Tc̄ . II . runc̄ . Tc̄ . XXIIII . porc̄ . m̄ . I . 7 XVI . ōus .
Tc̄ XL cap̄ . Tc̄ ual . XX . fol . m̄ XIII . & . IIII . d̄.

TERRE GISLEBERTI BALASTARII . *BIDINGA . H̃ .* .LXVIII.
In eſtuna ten̄ Edricus fili̇ . Wluiat heroldi comiti com̄d̄ . t . r . e
M . G . p̄ man̄ . de rege . II . car̄ terræ . Tc̄ . V . uill . modo . III . Semp
. V . bord̄ . & . I . ſerui . Tc̄ . I . car̄ & dim̄ in dominio . modo nichil.
Semp hom̄ . III . car̄ . filua . ad VIII . porc̄ . III . ac̄ p̄ti . Tc̄ . I . falina

M . nulla . Tc̄ . I . runc̄ . & . III . an̄ . & . II . porc̄ . & LXXX . ōus . m̄ nichil.
Tc̄ ual . XL . fol . modo XX . fol . Rex & com̄s foca̅ . Adhuc in ugge-
cehala . I . uill . Vluricus de XX . ac̄ . & dim̄ car̄ . ~~Rex & com̄s foca̅~~ .
7 In cedeſtan . I . uill oſketellus de XX . ac̄ . & dim̄ car̄ . & in eod̄ p̄tio .
de eſtuna . Id̄ē Giſlebtus . ten& in cedeſtan . I . lib̄ hō Godricus
com̄d̄ eid̄ . de XX . ac̄ . & . II . bord̄ . & dim̄ car̄ . & dim̄ ac̄ p̄ti . filua
ad . VI . porc̄ . & ual . IIII . fol . Et in eſtuna . II . libī homines Godric.
& Oſketel . com̄d̄ eid̄ē . de XX ac̄ . tr̄æ . femp . I . car̄ . & ual . IIII . fol.

32 In DALLINGHOO 40 acres. 3 free men held it.
Value 6s.
In the same (Dallinghoo) 2 free men, half under the patronage of Swarting and half (under that) of Brunman; 20 acres. Then ½ plough. Value 3s.
It has 1 league in length and 3 furlongs in width; 7d in tax.
In the same (Dallinghoo) 2 half [free] men under the patronage of Edric; 5 acres.
Value 12d.

PLOMESGATE Hundred
33 Azor, under the patronage of Edric of Laxfield, [held] CRANSFORD; 80 acres of land as a manor.
> Always 1 smallholder.
> Then 2 ploughs, now 1.
> Meadow, 1 acre. Then 2 cobs; then 24 pigs, now 1; 16 sheep; then 40 goats.

Value then 20s; now 13[s] 4d.

68   LANDS OF GILBERT THE CROSSBOWMAN

BLYTHING Hundred
1 In EASTON (Bavents) Aelfric son of Wulfgeat, under the patronage of Earl Harold, held before 1066; now Gilbert [holds it] as a manor from the King; 2 carucates of land.
> Then 5 villagers, now 3. Always 5 smallholders; 1 slave.
> Then 1½ ploughs in lordship, now nothing; always 3 men's ploughs.
> Woodland for 8 pigs; meadow, 3 acres; then 1 salt-house, now none. Then 1 cob, 3 cattle, 2 pigs, 80 sheep, now nothing.

444 b

Value then 40s; now 20s.
The King and the Earl (have) the jurisdiction.

2 Also in UGGESHALL 1 villager, Wulfric, with 20 acres. ½ plough. And in CHEDISTON 1 villager, Askell, with 20 acres. ½ plough.
(This is) in the same assessment of Easton (Bavents).

3 Gilbert also holds in CHEDISTON; 1 free man, Godric, under the patronage of the same man, with 20 acres.
> 2 smallholders.
> ½ plough.
> Meadow, ½ acre; woodland for 6 pigs.

Value 4s.

4 And in EASTON (Bavents) 2 free men, Godric and Askell, under the patronage of the same man, with 20 acres of land. Always 1 plough.
Value 4s.

Rex & coms̄ focā. Eſtuna hab̄.1.lḡ in longo.& dim̄ in lato.& de-
gelto.vi.d̄.Alii ibi tenent.

HERTESMARA. H̄. Giſlincham ten̄ Alsi lib̄ hō.ii.car̄ t̄ræ
p man̄.&.ii.bord̄.Tc̄ & p.ii.car̄.in dn̄io.modo.i.&.ii.ac̄ p̄ti.
Silua.iiii.porc̄.7 ual̄.xl.ſol.h̄ maneriū fuit uiuente rege.
edwardo de dn̄io abb̄is Lefſtani de ſc̄o edmundo. 7 Lefſtanus abbas
eū ac̄comodauit Alſio & uxori ſuæ tali conuentione qd̄ poſt obitū
eoȝ rehaberet Abbas ſuū maneriū.& unū aliū man̄ Alſi nōe
Euſtuna Rex & Coms̄ focā.In ead̄.viii.libi hōes com̄d̄ Alſio
xvi.ac̄.Tc̄.i.car̄.modo.dim̄.& ſt̄ in ſupiori p̄tio.In ead̄.iii.
libi hōes com̄d̄ ante ceſſori Alb̄ici de uer.vi.ac̄.& ual̄.xii.d̄.Rex
& coms̄ focā.h̄t.i.lḡ in longo.&.vii.qr̄ in lato.& x.d̄.de gelto;

445 a

* **TERRÆ RADVLFI BALISTARII.** *DIMIDIAM. H̄.*   .LXVIIII.
DELVDINGA LAND.Burch tēnuit.Stigandus ep̄s.cū foca
t.r̄.e.iiii.car̄ terræ p man̄.Semp.x.uill̄.&.v.bord̄.Tc̄.ii.ſeru.
modo nulla.Tc̄ in dn̄io.iii.car̄.modo.ii.Tc̄ hom̄.iiii.car̄.modo
.iii.x.ac̄ p̄ti.iii.ſaline.Semp.iii.runc.&.vi.an̄.7 xvii.porc.
&.c.lx.ous̄.i.æcclia.x.ac̄.&.i.ac̄ p̄ti.Tc̄ ual̄.c.ſol.modo.c.&.vi.ſol.
Caldecotan tenuit Bundus com̄d̄.Guerti.t.r.e.i.car̄.terre.
p man̄.Tc̄.i.bord̄.modo.iii.Tc̄.i.car̄.modo.dim̄.Tc̄ ual̄.x.ſol.
modo.viii.

The King and the Earl (have) the jurisdiction.
Easton (Bavents) has 1 league in length and ½ in width; 6d in tax. Others hold there.

HARTISMERE Hundred
5 Alsi, a free man, held GISLINGHAM; 2 carucates of land as a manor.
2 smallholders.
Then and later 2 ploughs in lordship, now 1.
Meadow, 2 acres; woodland, 4 pigs.
Value 40s.
During the reign of King Edward this manor belonged to the lordship of Abbot Leofstan of St. Edmund's. Abbot Leofstan leased it to Alsi and his wife with the agreement that after their death the Abbot should have his manor back and one other manor of Alsi's, Euston by name.
The King and the Earl (have) the jurisdiction.
In the same (Gislingham) 8 free men under the patronage of Alsi; 16 acres. Then 1 plough, now ½.
They are in the above assessment.
In the same (Gislingham) 3 free men under the patronage of Aubrey de Vere's predecessor; 6 acres.
Value 12d.
The King and the Earl (have) the jurisdiction.
It has 1 league in length and 7 furlongs in width; 10d in tax.

69 LANDS OF RALPH THE CROSSBOWMAN

Half-Hundred of LOTHINGLAND
1 Bishop Stigand held BURGH (Castle) with the jurisdiction before 1066; 4 carucates of land as a manor.
Always 10 villagers; 5 smallholders. Then 2 slaves, now none.
Then 3 ploughs in lordship, now 2; then 4 men's ploughs, now 3.
Meadow, 10 acres; 3 salt-houses. Always 3 cobs, 6 cattle, 17 pigs, 160 sheep.
1 church, 10 acres. Meadow, 1 acre.
Value then 100s; now 106s.

2 Bondi, under the patronage of Gyrth, held CALDECOTT before 1066; 1 carucate of land as a manor.
Then 1 smallholder, now 3.
Then 1 plough, now ½.
Value then 10s; now 8[s].

In earetuna . I . lib hō . Ketelus comd . Vlfus . t . r . e . xL.
ac̄ . Tc̄ . I . bord . modo . null . Semp dim car . Sēp ual . IIII . fol.
In fumerledeſtuna . I . lib hō . Aluoldus comd Guerti . xxx ; ac̄ . Tc̄
dim car . modo . null . Silua ad . v . porc . & ual . II . fol.

* **TERRA RAINALDI BRITONIS** q̃ reuocat in elemofina . LXX
regis . *RISEBRVGE . H̃* . Litgatā . tenuer . III . libi homines
p̃ . IIII . car . terræ . Tc̄ . IX . uill . p̃ . VII . m̃ . III . Tc̄ . I . bord . p̃ . IIII . m̃ . VI.
Tc̄ . III . feru . p̃ . I . m̃ . null . Tc̄ & p̃ . III . car . m̃ . I . Tc̄ & p̃ . VII . car . hom.
modo . II . filua . de . x . porc . x . ac̄ p̃ti . Tc̄ . II . porc . m̃ . xxx . femp . VII.
oūs . Tc̄ ual . Lxxx . fol . m̃ Lx ; hanc tr̃a calūpniatur hōes de Wate
uilla ad fuū feudū.

445 b

. **LXXI** . **TERRA . ROBERTI DE STRATFORT .** *SAnfort . H̃*
Boitunā ten . Suenus Suart . t . r . e . I . car terre . pro maner.
Tc̄ . II . bord . modo . VI . Tc̄ . II . car in dominio . femp . I . car hom.
V . ac̄ p̃ti . Tc̄ ual . xL . fol . modo xxx . Soca in bcolt . In eadē
tenuit brixi lib hō . I . car . terræ p̃ man . t . r . e . Tc̄ . I . bord.
modo . II . femp . I . car in dn̄io . & modo . I . runc . & . VI . oūs . &
ual & . xx . fol ht . VII . qr in longo ; & . VI . in lato . 7 xIIII . d de gelto.
Alii ibi tenent foca in bcolt.

3 In CORTON 1 free man, Ketel, under the patronage of Ulf before 1066; 40 acres.
  Then 1 smallholder, now none.
  Always ½ plough.
  Value always 4s.

4 In SOMERLEYTON 1 free man, Alwold, under the patronage of Gyrth; 30 acres. Then ½ plough, now none.
  Woodland for 5 pigs.
  Value 2s.

70 LAND OF REGINALD THE BRETON which he claims as the King's alms

RISBRIDGE Hundred

1 3 free men held LIDGATE as 4 carucates of land.
  Then 9 villagers, later 7, now 3; then 1 smallholder, later 4, now 6; then 3 slaves, later 1, now none.
  Then and later 3 ploughs, now 1; then and later 7 men's ploughs, now 2.
  Woodland at 10 pigs; meadow, 10 acres. Then 2 pigs, now 30; always 7 sheep.
  Value then 80s; now 60[s].
  The men of (William of) Vatteville claim this land for his Holding.

71   LAND OF ROBERT OF STRATFORD

SAMFORD Hundred

1 Swein Swart held BOYNTON before 1066; 1 carucate of land as a manor.
  Then 2 smallholders, now 6.
  Then 2 ploughs in lordship; always 1 men's plough. Meadow, 5 acres.
  Value then 40s; now 30[s].
  The jurisdiction (is) in (East) Bergholt.
  In the same (Boynton) Brictsi, a free man; 1 carucate of land as a manor before 1066.
  Then 1 smallholder, now 2.
  Always 1 plough in lordship.
  Now 1 cob, 6 sheep.
  Value 20s.
  It has 7 furlongs in length and 6 in width; 14d in tax. Others hold there. The jurisdiction (is) in (East) Bergholt.

In belesteda tenuit. Turí LXXX. ac̅ ꝑ ma͠n. ſemp. III. uilt. &
II. bord. Tc̅. I. caȓ. in d͞nio. ſemp. I. caȓ hom̑. & . II. ac̅ p̅ti. & q̊rta
pars eccłiæ. & uał. XXIII. ſoł. ſoca in b̅colt.

.LXXII. TERRA STANARDI. filii alwii. Riſebruge. H̅. In Vueſdana
XXX. ac̅ ten̅ Wiſgar. t. r. e. ſemp. I. bord. 7. I. caȓ. & . II. ac̅ p̅ti.
7 uał XX ſoł.

.LXXIII. TERRA Wlmari. Risebruge. H̅. In Laſham. XXIIII. ac̅
& dim̑. caȓ. & uał. IIII. ſoł. s̅c̅s. e. ſoca. In ead͞e. IX ac̅. ten̅ id͞e
Vlmarus q̊s inuadauit. t. r. Witti de ante ceſſore. Rad̑ pinel
pro. XXI. ſoł & uał XII. d̑. Vicecom̅s Rog̅ habuit de patre
ſuo herref.

446 a

TERRA VAVASORVM. BOSEMERA. H̅.   .LXXIIII.
In hamingeſtuna. I. lib̅ ho̅. de XX ac̅. in ſoca regis. & . V. bord.
ſemp. I. caȓ. & uał. V. ſoł.
In facheduna. III. lib̅i hoes in ſoca regis. XXX. ac̅. ſemp. I. caȓ. &
val & . V. ſoł. In eod̑. H̅. In Beteſfort. ten̅. I. lib̅ ho̅ durandus. XXX.
ac̅. t. r. e. M̅. ſiuuardus in ſoca regis. Tc̅ dim̑ caȓ. modo. II. bou̇.
& . II. ac̅.

2 In BELSTEAD Thuri held 80 acres as a manor.
   Always 3 villagers; 2 smallholders.
   Then 1 plough in lordship; always 1 men's plough. Meadow, 2 acres.
   The fourth part of a church.
   Value 23s.
   The jurisdiction (is) in (East) Bergholt.

72   LAND OF STANHARD SON OF AETHELWY

RISBRIDGE Hundred
1 In OUSDEN 30 acres; Withgar held (it) before 1066.
   Always 1 smallholder;
   1 plough. Meadow, 2 acres.
   Value 20s.

73   LAND OF WULFMER

RISBRIDGE Hundred
1 In *LAFHAM* 24 acres. ½ plough.
   Value 4s.
   St. Edmund's (has) the jurisdiction.
   In the same (*Lafham*) Wulfmer also holds 9 acres which he annexed after 1066 from Ralph Pinel's predecessor for 21s.
   Value 12d.
   Roger the Sheriff had the heriot from his father.

74   LAND OF VAVASSORS

BOSMERE Hundred
1 In HEMINGSTONE 1 free man in the King's jurisdiction, with 20 acres.
   5 smallholders.
   Always 1 plough.
   Value 5s.

2 In *FACHEDUNA* 3 free men in the King's jurisdiction; 30 acres. Always 1 plough.
   Value 5s.

3 In the same Hundred in BATTISFORD 1 free man, Durand, held 30 acres before 1066. Now Siward [holds it], in the King's jurisdiction.
   Then ½ plough, now 2 oxen.
   2 acres.

⁊ In Vledana . IIII . liɓi hões Rabboda . Leuricus . Edric⁹ . Vluric⁹
VIII . ac̄ . 7 ual . XVI . d . iſti sū additi . ad firmā . t . r . Wiłłi . & rog
ē warat̄ inde Vlmaro p̄poſito . qui eos addidit & n̄ p̄tinebāt
&. R . neſciebat qd ēent additi.
ad ullā firmā . In ead . I . liɓ hō . Vlmar⁹ . q̄rtā parte . uni acre
& . ual . II . d . hunc tenuit briētmar . bedel . & dedit uade.
Vlmarus p̄poſitus fide iuſſor . In ead . I . liɓ hō Lewinus . II . ac̄ . &
dim . & ual . VIII . d.
⁊ In hamigeſtuna . I . liɓ hō brictuolt . IIII . ac̄ . & ual . VIII . d.
⁊ In Cratingis . Liɓa femina Aldid dim . ac̄ . & ual . I . d.
⁊ HVND . DE CLAINDVNE . In haminghelanda . I . liɓ -
hō Aluuin Comdatus Guert . XXX . ac̄ . Tc̄ dim . car̄ . & ual . v . ſol.
Vlmar⁹ p̄poſit⁹ adiunxit hunc liɓum homine ad firmā regis
de BRū for . & rog uicecoms ē ei inde warant . & reddit uno q̄q̄ anno . v . ſol . 7 rex & coms ſoca.
⁊ In Turolweſtuna tenuit Rolf . t . r̄ . ē . m̄ . Aluric⁹ fili ei burgenſis
de gipeſwiz . XII . ac̄ . & ual . II . ſol . Rex & coms ſoca . 7 ex hac
fuit ſaiſitus . R . coms quando forisfecit . Ide Aluric⁹ ten& æccłā.

Sc̄i iuliani jn burgo de gipeſwiz . XX . ac̄ . terræ . & ual . XL d . 7 ex hac
eccłia fuit ſaiſitus . R . coms.
⁊ In Claindune . ten . Alric⁹ łiɓ hō . VI . ac̄ . & dim . t . r̄ . ē . modo Idem Aluricus . & ual . XIIII . d . Rex & coms dimidiā ſoca 7 sc̄a Adeldreda
aliā medietate . hanc terrā tenuit ille Aluric⁹ in uadimonio . &
non ht inde warant . Iſti s̄ in manu regis.

4 In 'OLDEN' 4 free men, Radbod, Leofric, Edric, Wulfric; 8 acres.
Value 16d.
   These (free men) were added to the revenue after 1066 and concerning them Roger is guarantor for Wulfmer the reeve who added them. Roger did not know that they had been added. They did not belong to any revenue.
   In the same ('Olden') 1 free man, Wulfmer; the fourth part of 1 acre.
Value 2d.
   Brictmer the beadle held this and gave a pledge. Wulfmer the reeve (is) the surety.
   In the same ('Olden') 1 free man, Leofwin; 2½ acres.
Value 8d.

5 In HEMINGSTONE 1 free man, Brictwold; 3 acres.
Value 8d.

6 In CREETING a free woman, Aldgyth; ½ acre.
Value 1d.

Hundred of CLAYDON

7 In HEMINGSTONE 1 free man, Alwin, under the patronage of Gyrth; 30 acres. Then ½ plough.
Value 5s.
   Wulfmer the reeve added this free man to the King's revenue of Bramford. Roger the Sheriff is guarantor for him concerning it.
   He pays 5s each year.
   The King and the Earl (have) the jurisdiction.

8 In THURLESTON Rolf held before 1066; now his son Aelfric, a burgess of Ipswich [holds it]; 12 acres.
Value 2s.
   The King and the Earl (have) the jurisdiction.
   Earl R(alph) was in possession of this when he forfeited.

9 Aelfric also holds St. Julian's church in the Borough of IPSWICH; 446 b
20 acres of land.
Value 40d.
   Earl R(alph) was in possession of this church.

10 In CLAYDON Alric, a free man, held 6½ acres before 1066. Now Aelfric also [holds it].
Value 14d.
   The King and the Earl (have) half the jurisdiction and St. Etheldreda's (has) the other half. Aelfric held this land in pledge and he does not have a guarantor for it.
   These are in the King's hand.

⁊In Weſtrefelda . vi . libi hoes Aluuinus flint . Aluuinus . Edricus . Vluricus . Aleſtan . int eos . xv . ac . & . i . car . 7 ual xxx . d . Vn ex his noe
flint dedit uad ex h qd dix qd dabāt firmā in Gipeſwiz . & uicecoms derationauit qd mentitus erat . & id uice comes de
eo ē fide iuſſor . Rex 7 coms focā . ⁊xx . d.
⁊In Turolueſtuna . i . lib ho Godwin comdatus Stigand . x . ac 7 ual
⁊In hoc hund ht Rex . xxx . libos hoes . cxlvii . ac 7 dim . & una
æcclia in Widituna . de . x . ac . ſemp . iii . car . & . i . ac pti . & ual&
xl . ſol . & . iiii . d . H ſt eoȝ noa . Aiſtan . Godric Goduuin . Offa.
Rictan . Gadinc . Aluric . Eſtrat Aluric . Touilt . Leuuinus Aluric . Gunequata . Vluric . Tchetel . Godric . Edied . Dirfi.
Brictmer . Leueua . Aluric . Vluric . Normann . Leuuric.
Saxlef . Aluuin . Vluuin . Edric Sigar . hos ten& uice coms in
manu regis . Rex & coms focā.
⁊In Weſtrefelda . ten& ſemp Aluric pbr . xii . ac . & . ii . ac pti.
& ual . iii . ſol . Rex & coms focā.
⁊In Turueſtuna . ii . libi hoes . Vluric . 7 Ormar . vi . ac . & ual
xii . d . Soca Regis . Vice coms ſeruat in manu regis.

447 a
⁊In Codenham . i . pbr frieb . dim ac in elemoſina . & ual . i . d.

⁊Iſti ſunt libi homines de Sudfulc q̇ remanent in manu .LXXV.
regis . BRADEMERA . HVND . In torp . i . lib ho
xxx . ac . t . r . e . Tc & p dim car . modo . ii boues . & ual . ii . ſol.
& . vi . d . hunc tenuit Rob blund putans ēe . de feudo abbis
& ide ho confirmabat ſe Robto eſſe de feudo abbis . ſ7 abbas ex h
non ē ſibi warant . modo tandē recognouit illū non ēe de feudo
Abbis dimiſit eū in manu regis . 7 ex h dedit uadē.

11 In WESTERFIELD 6 free men, Alwin, Flint, Alwin, Edric, Wulfric, Alstan; between them 15 acres. 1 plough.
Value 30d.
    One of them, Flint by name, gave a pledge for what he said that they gave (to) the revenue in Ipswich and the Sheriff proved that he had lied. The same Sheriff is surety concerning it.
    The King and the Earl (have) the jurisdiction.

12 In THURLESTON 1 free man, Godwin, under the patronage of Stigand; 10 acres.
Value 20d.

13 In this Hundred the King has 30 free men; 147½ acres. And a church in WHITTON with 10 acres. Always 3 ploughs.
    Meadow, 1 acre.
Value 40s 4d.
    These are their names: Aethelstan, Godric, Godwin, Offa, Rictan, Goding, Aelfric, Estred, Aelfric, Tovild, Leofwin, Aelfric, Gunvati, Wulfric, Thorkell, Godric, Edith, Dersi, Brictmer, Leofeva, Aelfric, Wulfric, Norman, Leofric, Saxlef, Alwin, Wulfwin, Edric, Sigar. The Sheriff holds these (men) in the King's hand.
    The King and the Earl (have) the jurisdiction.

14 In WESTERFIELD Aelfric the priest has always held 12 acres.
    Meadow, 2 acres.
Value 3s.
    The King and the Earl (have) the jurisdiction.

15 In THURLESTON 2 free men, Wulfric and Ordmer; 6 acres.
Value 12d.
    The jurisdiction (is) the King's.
    The Sheriff looks after (this) in the King's hand.

16 In CODDENHAM 1 priest, Frideb... ; ½ acre as alms.   447 a
Value 1d.

75   THESE ARE THE FREE MEN OF SUFFOLK WHO REMAIN IN THE KING'S HAND

BRADMERE Hundred

1 In (Ixworth) THORPE 1 free man; 30 acres before 1066. Then and later ½ plough, now 2 oxen.
Value 2s 6d.
    Robert Blunt held this (man), thinking he was of the Abbot's Holding, and the man himself confirmed to Robert that he was of the Abbot's Holding. But the Abbot was not his guarantor. Now at last he has recognized that that man is not of the Abbot's Holding and has given him up into the King's hand. He gave a pledge concerning this.

ꝟIn Icſewrda.ɪ.liƀ hō.xɪɪ.ac̄.& ual̄.ɪɪ.fol̄.Sc̄s eadmundus
dim̄ cōmđ.t.r.e.⁊ foca & faca.& ante c̄.Petri de ualoniis dimidiā cōmđ.Hunc tenuit Ricarđ hō Roƀti blundi & dedit uadē
Roƀ non ei warant.

HꝟNĐ.DE BISCOPES; In horan.ɪ.liƀ hō.vɪ.ac̄.& ual̄
xɪɪ.đ.hc̄ tenuit herƀtus blacun in manu regis iuſſu herfaſti
ep̄i ſ⁊ iuchel.pƀr reclamat de dono regis.&.inde faiſitus
fuit.& ſuus antec̄md̄.t.r.e.Soca in hoxa.

ꝟIn Iſteda.ɪ.liƀ hō ⹉ de quo habuit Ailmarus ep̄s.c̄mđ.de.x.
ac̄.⁊.dim̄.⁊ q̄rta pars molini.&.ɪ.borđ.&.tc̄ dim̄ car̄.&
modo.ɪɪ.boū.& ual̄.ɪɪ.fol̄.hoc tenuit.Will.malet.p̄ ea
Roƀ fil̄ꝰ eꝯ ſuus putans c̄e de feudo patris ſui.

447 b

ꝟIn badingafelda.ɪɪ.liƀi hōes q̄ remanent in manu regis
p̄ refpec̄tū placiti.int̄ ep̄m baiocens̄.& matr̄e Roƀti mal&
unus fuit cōmđ.Stigando.& alt̄ dim̄.Leurico.anteceſſori
Roƀti.mal&.& alia medietas Saxo.& h̄nt.xL.ac̄.&.ɪɪɪ.
borđ.femp̄.ɪ.car̄.filua.xx.porc̄.& ual̄.x.fol̄.foca in hoxa.

.LXXVI. INVASIONES SVPER REGEM. RISE
BRVGE. H̃. Ricardus filꝰ Gisleƀti comitis.
In bradeleia.ɪɪɪɪ.liƀi hōes.Vluuinus.Leuricus.Vluuinus.& h̄nt.
xv.ac̄.& q̄rtus bundo.& h̄t.ɪ.car̄ terræ.femp̄.ɪɪ.car̄.&.v.ac̄ p̄ti.
& ual& xxɪɪ.fol̄.&.vɪ.den̄.Ex his n̄q̄ habuit ſuus ante ceſſor
cōmđ.Malus uicinus ten& carrucatā.Sc̄s.e.totā focā.

2 In IXWORTH 1 free man; 12 acres.
Value 2s.
   St. Edmund's (had) half the patronage before 1066 and full jurisdiction, and the predecessor of Peter of Valognes (had) half the patronage.
   Richard, Robert Blunt's man, held him, and gave a pledge. Robert (is) not guarantor for him.

BISHOP'S Hundred
3 In HORHAM 1 free man; 6 acres.
Value 12d.
   Herbert Blacun held him in the King's hand by order of Bishop Erfast, but Judicael the priest claimed him back by the King's gift and was in possession of him and his predecessor had the patronage before 1066.
   The jurisdiction (is) in Hoxne.

4 In INSTEAD 1 free man over whom Bishop Aelmer had patronage, with 10½ acres.
   The fourth part of a mill.
   1 smallholder.
   Then ½ plough, now 2 oxen.
Value 2s.
   William Malet held this; later on Robert his son [held it], thinking it was (part) of his father's Holding.

5 In BEDINGFIELD 2 free men who remain in the King's hand through the adjournment of the lawsuit between the Bishop of Bayeux and Robert Malet's mother. One was under the patronage of Stigand; the other (was) half (under that) of Leofric, Robert Malet's predecessor, and the other half (under that) of Saxi. They have 40 acres.
   3 smallholders.
   Always 1 plough. Woodland, 20 pigs.
Value 10s.
   The jurisdiction (is) in Hoxne.

ANNEXATIONS IN THE KING'S DESPITE
RICHARD SON OF COUNT GILBERT['S ANNEXATIONS]

RISBRIDGE Hundred
1 In BRADLEY 4 free men: Wulfwin, Leofric, and Wulfwin have 15 acres; the fourth, Bondi, has 1 carucate of land. Always 2 ploughs.
   Meadow, 5 acres.
Value 22s 6d.
   His predecessor never had patronage over these (free men).
   Malus Vicinus holds the carucate. St. Edmund's (has) the whole of the jurisdiction.

BABENbga duo . *HVNDRET*. In grotena ten Ricardus
fili.Gisbti . I, lib ho . Rotbti . filii Wimarc comd tantu . LX . ac.
ac terræ . Tc . IIII . bor. modo . I . Tc & p . I . car . m nulla . & . I . ac pti.
Tc & p ual . x . fol . M . xvIII . fol . Hanc inuafit Roger de orbec &
ten& fub ricardo filio gifleƀto . & hoies . Ri . reuocant ad feudum.
Wifgari anteceffori fui . Sed fic hund teftat nuq pertinuit.
nec comd nec foca . ⌠In kaua . nadifc inuafit Aluricus fr Edrici . pdicti
& ho Witgari . medietate terræ fris fui . LX . ac . modo ten&

448 a

Rog de sco germ . ad feudu Ricardi fed nuq pertinuit ad feudu
comd l foca . Semp e ibi . I . uilt . & . I . bord . & . I . ac . pti.
⌠In Cormerda ten& aluric campo . II . libos hoes comdat tntu
in foca sci . e . t . r . e . fed qq rex . Will . aduenit inuafit Wifgarus
ante cuention . Ricardi . q modo ten& . & lint . II . car terræ . &
XL ac . Tc & p . IIII . bord . M . xI . Tc . v . feru . modo . IIII . Tc . III . car
in dominio . Modo . III . int fe 7 hoes . Silua . xxx . por . & . VIII . ac
pti . Tc . III . equi . modo . IIII . an . modo . xxx . porc . modo . c .
x . ous . Ecclia de xv . ac libæ træ . Tc & p ual . xx . fol . modo reddit
vI . liƀ . ht VIII . qr in longo . & . IIII . in lato . & de gelto xxIIII . d
quicuq ibi ten&.
⌠N Saibamus ten Ricardus . I . lib ho Rodbti filii Wimarce comd
7 foca & faca sci . E . f 7 Wifgar ten qndo fe fore fec . M ten Ricardus
fucceffor ei . & ht . I . car terræ . & . III . bord . & . II . feru . Semp . I . car . &
vII . ac pti . Modo . L . ous . & vII . porc 7 ual . xx . fol.
⌠In Kauanadis Aluuoldus . I . lib ho . heroldi comd & foc & faca
T.R.E . 7 pqua Rex . W . aduenit ; modo inuafit . Ricardus & ht
. I . car terræ . Semp . I . car & dim . & . II . ac . pti . & ual . xx . fol.

BABERGH Two Hundreds

2 In GROTON Richard son of (Count) Gilbert holds; 1 free man of Robert son of Wymarc, under patronage only; 60 acres of land.
Then 4 smallholders, now 1.
Then and later 1 plough, now none. Meadow, 1 acre.
Value then and later 10s; now 18s.
Roger of Orbec annexed this and holds (it) under Richard son of (Count) Gilbert. Richard's men claim it for the Holding of Withgar, his predecessor. But, as the Hundred testifies, it never belonged [to the Holding] nor (did) the patronage or the jurisdiction.

3 In CAVENDISH Aelfric brother of Edric, a man of the said Withgar's, annexed a half of his brother's land; 60 acres. Now Roger of St. Germain holds (it) in Richard's Holding, but it never belonged to the Holding, (nor did) the patronage or the jurisdiction.
There has always been 1 villager and 1 smallholder.
Meadow, 1 acre.

448 a

4 In CORNARD before 1066 Aelfric Kemp [held] 2 free men under patronage only, in the jurisdiction of St. Edmund's; but after King William came, Withgar (Richard's) predecessor annexed (them) with the agreement of Richard who now holds (them). They have 2 carucates of land and 40 acres.
Then and later 4 smallholders, now 11; then 5 slaves, now 4.
Then 23 ploughs in lordship; now 3 between himself and the men.
Woodland, 30 pigs; meadow, 8 acres. Then 3 horses; now 4 cattle; now 30 pigs; now 110 sheep.
A church with 15 acres of free land.
Value then and later 20s; now it pays £6.
It has 8 furlongs in length and 4 in width; 24d in tax, whoever holds there.

5 In SAIBAMUS Richard holds; 1 free man of Robert son of Wymarc's under patronage; the full jurisdiction (was) St. Edmund's. Withgar held (him) when he forfeited. Now Richard, his successor, holds (him). He has 1 carucate of land.
3 smallholders; 2 slaves.
Always 1 plough.
Meadow, 7 acres. Now 50 sheep, 7 pigs.
Value 20s.

6 In CAVENDISH Alwold, 1 free man under the patronage and full jurisdiction of Harold before 1066, and after King William came. Now Richard has annexed (him). He has 1 carucate of land. Always 1½ ploughs.
Meadow, 2 acres.
Value 20s.

447 b, 448 a

In eaḋ inuafit Ricardus de clara. libū homꝫ. reḡ. e. fed ante
ceffor fuus nichil oīno in eo habuit. & ħt. I. caṝ. terræ. Tc̄. IIII.
uiłł. p̄⁹ & modo. II. &. VII. borḋ. & tc̄ & p̄⁹ꝫ II. caṝꝫ. modo. I. &
. I. caṝꝫ homꝫ. &. IIII. ac̄ p̄ti. &. modo. I. molin̄. Silua. x. porc̄ꝫ.
& uał. xx. fol.

448 b

HVND. DE BLACBRVNA. In Scantuna. I. liba femina
comꝫḋ. sc̄oꝫ. e. t. r. e. xxx. ac̄. & uał. v. fol.

⁊In gnedaffala. xxx. ac̄ tenꝫ. sc̄s. e. t. r. e. & dim̄ moł. & uał. v. fol
⁊In beordewella manfiones cuida⁹ libi hois.ꝫ sc̄i. e. In eaḋ. dim̄ lib hō
sc̄i. e. VIII. ac̄. & uał xvI. ḋ. In eaḋ. x. ac̄. cuida⁹ libe. S̄. e. ⁊ uał xx
ḋ. hoc totū inuafit. W de partenai fup abbem. & tenꝫ comꝫd uni⁹
lib hoisꝫ

⁊*HVND DE BOSEMERA.* In fumerfam. I. lib hō. Vluricus
noe de xII. ac̄. ⁊ uał. IIII. fol. De hoc fuit faifitus. R. coms qdo
forisfecit. & fuus antec̄ꝫ habuit in nedefteda comꝫdationēꝫ. huic in
uafit Vlmar⁹ p̄pofitus regisꝫ & dedit uadēꝫ. Roḡ bigot. fide iuffor.
& ē in manu regis. Rex & coms foca.

⁊In briefeta. sꝫt. xx. ac̄. que iacent in manerio Witti de othobur
uilla. quod tenuit. Anfchillus. t. r. e. modo tenꝫ eas Botilt que-
da femina. & reuocat hugonē de hofdenc ad warant. fed ipfe
ē in captione regis. & non poteft refponḋe. modo sꝫt in manu
Regis & Vlmarus p̄pofit⁹ eas cuftodit. & uał. v. fol.

7 In the same (Cavendish) Richard of Clare annexed a free man of King Edward's, but his predecessor had nothing at all in relation to him. He has 1 carucate of land.
   Then 4 villagers, later and now 2; 7 smallholders.
   Then and later 2 ploughs, now 1; 1 men's plough.
   Meadow, 4 acres; now 1 mill; woodland, 10 pigs.
Value 20s.

[WILLIAM OF PARTHENAY'S ANNEXATIONS]

Hundred of BLACKBOURN   448 b

8 In STANTON 1 free woman under the patronage of St. Edmund's before 1066; 30 acres.
Value 5s.

9 In KNETTISHALL 30 acres; St. Edmund's held (it) before 1066.
   ½ mill.
Value 5s.

10 In BARDWELL the dwellings of a certain free man of St. Edmund's.

11 In the same (Bardwell) a half free man of St. Edmund's; 8 acres.
Value 16d.

12 In the same (Bardwell) 10 acres of a certain free (woman) of St. Edmund's.
Value 20d.
   William of Parthenay annexed the whole of this in the Abbot's despite and holds patronage over one free man.

[WULFMER THE REEVE'S ANNEXATIONS]

Hundred of BOSMERE

13 In SOMERSHAM 1 free man, Wulfric by name, with 12 acres.
Value 4s.
   Earl R(alph) was in possession of this when he forfeited, and his predecessor had the patronage in Nettlestead. Wulfmer, the King's reeve, annexed this. He gave a pledge; Roger Bigot is surety. (This) is in the King's hand.
   The King and the Earl (have) the jurisdiction.

[HUGH OF HOUDAIN'S ANNEXATION]

14 In BRICETT are 20 acres which belong to the manor of William of Auberville. Askell held (them) before 1066. Now a woman, Botild, holds them and calls Hugh of Houdain as guarantor, but he is in the King's custody and cannot answer. They are now in the King's hand and Wulfmer the reeve has charge of them.
Value 5s.

⨏In Belham. dim͛ eccłia. xii. ac̄ tenuit Regina Edeua. t͛. r͛. e͛.
& qdiu uixit. Poſtea tenuit Witłm de burnoluilla. M e͛ in manu regis & uał. ii. soł. ex h̄ dedit. u̇adē. Turſtin͛ filiͦ Guidonis fide
iuſſor ;
HV̄ND. STOV. In finebga. i. lib̄ hō de quo ante ceſſor Rog͛ medietatē c͛om͛d̄ euſtac. alia͛ medietatē c͛om͛ ⁓& p͛ tenuit Comes
de mauritanio ; ſed Rog͛. tenuit eū q͛ndo relinq͛d terra͛. 7 Rodb̄ arbał

449 a

ſub eo. modo ten&. R. bigot In manu regis. q͛ ad uſq͡ derationaͭ͛
ſit. & ħt. xv. ac̄ trae. Tc̄ dim͛ car͛. modo nichil & uał. iii. soł.
HV̄ND. Blidinga In Wiſeta. manerio comitis Alani. p͛tinebat
. i. lib̄ hō. iiii. ac̄ quæ iacent innorthala. & uał. viii. den͛.
h̄ inuaſ͛ Rob̄ de curtun. hunc tenē. R. c. q͛do forisfecit. ex hoc dedit
uadē. In ead̄. i. lib̄ hō. viii. ac̄. & uał. xvi. d̄. de quo habuiͪt abuit
ante Witłmi de Waŕ c͛om͛d̄. t. r. e. & ħt de ſua tra͛ p͛ eſcag͛.
Iſtas etia͛ inuaſit Rob̄. cū. iiii. ac̄ ſup͛dictis.

⨏In Wggeſſala. ii. libi hóes. Normannus. 7 Kctel de xviii. ac̄. &
dim͛ cař. & uał. iii. soł. h̄ inuaſit bereng͛ hō sc̄i. e. 7 e͛ in midia
regis hic infirmus erat. non potuit uenire ad placitū. m̊do ſunt
in cuſtodia uice comiť.

[WILLIAM OF BOURNEVILLE'S ANNEXATION]

15 In BAYLHAM ½ church, 12 acres. Queen Edith held (it) before 1066 and while she lived. Later on William of Bourneville held (it). Now it is in the King's hand.
Value 2s.
   He gave a pledge concerning this; Thurstan son of Guy (is) surety.

[ROGER (OF AUBERVILLE)'S ANNEXATION]

Hundred of STOW

16 In FINBOROUGH 1 free man over whom Roger's predecessor had half the patronage and Eustace had the other half of the patronage. Later the Count of Mortain held (him); but Roger held him when he gave up the land, and Robert the crossbowman under him. Now Roger Bigot holds him in the King's hand until it is adjudged. He has 15 acres of land. Then ½ plough, now nothing.
Value 3s.

[ROBERT OF COURSON'S ANNEXATIONS]

Hundred (of) BLYTHING

17 In Count Alan's manor of WISSETT 1 free man belonged; 4 acres which belong to Covehithe.
Value 8d.
   Robert of Courson annexed this. Earl R(alph) held this (free man) when he forfeited. He gave a pledge for this.

18 In the same (Wissett) 1 free man; 8 acres.
Value 16d.
   William of Warenne's predecessor had patronage over him before 1066. He has (it as part) of his land by exchange. Robert also annexed these (8 acres) with the above-mentioned 4 acres.

[BERENGAR'S ANNEXATION]

19 In UGGESHALL 2 free men, Norman and Ketel, with 18 acres. ½ plough.
Value 3s.
   Berengar, a man of St. Edmund's, annexed this and is in the King's mercy. He was ill and could not come to the assembly; they are in the Sheriff's charge.

*In Kanauadifc teñ Radulſ de limefi . 1 . liƀ hō heroldi quã tenuit edricus diaconus Qui fuit mortuus cum eo in bello . & fuit liƀa⸗ ta bainardo ꝑ terra . Etgaͣr addidit in ranauadifc ꝑquã bainardus ꝑdidit . modo ten& Raƌ de limefi in dñio halle.

*In Lauen Alƀicus deuer teñ . III . liƀos Vlwini . antec̄ Alƀici de uer c̄omᵈ tantũ in foca . sc̄i . e . 7 h̃nt . L . ac̄ . Tc̄ int̃ oms̃ . II . caſ modo . I . Semp ual . VI . fol.

*In Kodenhã teñ antec̄ Galteri de sc̄o Walerico c̄omᵈdatioñe

449 b

tantũ . II . liƀi hoẽs . modo teñ Roḡ deramis . fed hund nefcit q̃m̃ . Nec fuit aliquis ex parte fua q̓ dicer& q̓modo . & hñt xx . ac̄ . tr̃æ . Tc̄ & pͣ ual& . x . fol . modo nichil.

HERTESMERA . H̃ . In eiam ten& . Roƀ mal& . I . liƀum homem noẽ Suartric . c̄omᵈ haroldo . & in foca eius ꝉ c . & xx . ac̄ . ꝑ mañ . Semp . IIII . borƌ . & . I . car in dñio. & . IIII . ac̄ pͭti . Silua de . XIII . porc̄ . & ual xx . fol.

450 a

DE CALVPNIIS Int̃ eṗm baiocenſe & matr̃e Roƀti malet.

H̃erteſmera . H̃ . In acolt . xx . ac̄ . teñ briƌtere liƀ hoˢ Stigandi. ſep . I . borƌ . 7 ual . XL . ƌ . Hanc tr̃a dedit Stiganƌ matri Roƀti malet. 7 ipfa eaͣ pͣa teñ de regina . m̃ . e .

[RALPH OF LIMÉSY'S ANNEXATION]
[BABERGH Two Hundreds]

20 In CAVENDISH Ralph of Limésy holds; 1 free man of Harold's, Edric the deacon, who died with him in the battle, held it. It was delivered to Baynard as an estate. Edgar added (it) to Cavendish after Baynard lost (it). Ralph of Limésy now holds (it) in lordship.

[AUBREY DE VERE'S ANNEXATION]

21 In LAVENHAM Aubrey de Vere holds 3 free (men) belonging to Wulfwin, Aubrey de Vere's predecessor, under patronage only, in the jurisdiction of St. Edmund's. They have 50 acres. Then 2 ploughs between them all, now 1.
Value always 6s.

[ROGER OF RAMES'S ANNEXATION]

22 In CODDENHAM Walter of St.Valéry's predecessor held 2 free men under patronage only. Now Roger of Rames holds (them), but the Hundred does not know how; nor was there anyone on his behalf who could say how. They have 20 acres of land.
Value then and later 10s; now nothing.

449 b

[ROBERT MALET'S ANNEXATION]
HARTISMERE Hundred

23 In EYE Robert Malet holds 1 free man, Swartrik by name, under the patronage of Harold and in his jurisdiction; 120 acres as a manor.
   Always 4 smallholders;
   1 plough in lordship.
   Meadow, 4 acres; woodland at 13 pigs.
Value 20s.

[77] CONCERNING THE DISPUTES BETWEEN   450 a
      THE BISHOP OF BAYEUX AND ROBERT MALET'S MOTHER

HARTISMERE Hundred

1 In OCCOLD Brictere, a free man of Stigand's, held 20 acres.
   Always 1 smallholder.
Value 40d.
   Stigand gave this land to Robert Malet's mother. Later on she held it from the Queen. Now the Bishop [holds it].

In eadē tenͧ Chericͨ libͬ hō dimͬ ſub cͦmdat
antecͨ Robͬ malet. 7 dimid cͦmdatͨ Saxo antecͨ. Ra. piperelli. xx. acͨ. 7.ıı. bord.
7.ı..carͨ. 7 ual. xL. d̄.

Biſcopes. H̃. In badingefelda tenͬ. Brictere. 7 Chericͦ ſupͬdicti xL. acͨr.
ſupͬdicto m̃. Tncͨ. ı. carͨ. m̃ dim̃. Silua. xL. porcͨ. 7. ı. libͬ hō cͦmdatus
Brictredo. v. acͨ. totu̅ ual xı. ſol. / Herteſmara. H̃. In aſpala. ıııı. libi
hoͬes. De rulf cͨmd. abbi de eli. 7 Turſtan cͦmd. Saxa. 7 Marculf
cͦmd edrici antecͨ. R. malet..7 Grunulf ſubcͦmd antecͨ. R. malet. Lxxxvı. acͨ.
7 vıı. bord. Sepͬ. ııı. carͬ. ıı. acͨ pͬti. Sepͬ ual. xL. ſol. Ex hac tra fuit Witlmͬ
malet ſaiſit. ſicͨ hund teſtatͬ antͬ quaͬ epcͨ baiocͨfis; 7 pea uenit hubͬt de portu.
& deracionau̅ libͬam tram 7 ſaiſiuit epm̃ ex hac tra qͫ libi hoͬes eaͬ tenebant.
7 die q̄ Rad com̃ forisfecͬ. Mat Robͬti inde ſaiſita erat teſte hund̄. 7 uſqͬ
ad placitu̅ de hodiha. m̄. e. in pace reḡ. ſicͨ rex pͬcep it epm̃. 7 matre Robͬti.

**Anno ᴍillesimo octogesimo sexto. ab
incarnatione dn̄i. vigesimo v̊ regni
will̄i facta est ista descriptio. non
solvm p̄ hos tres comitatvs. sed &ĩa
p̄ alios**

2 In the same (Occold) Cynric, a free man, held; (he was) half under the sub-patronage of Robert Malet's predecessor, and half under the patronage of Saxi, Ranulf Peverel's predecessor; 20 acres.
    2 smallholders.
    1 plough.
    Value 40d.

BISHOP'S Hundred

3 In BEDINGFIELD the above-mentioned Brictere and Cynric held 40 acres in the above-mentioned manner. Then 1 plough, now ½.
    Woodland, 40 pigs.
    1 free man under the patronage of Brictere; 5 acres.
    Value of the whole 11s.

HARTISMERE Hundred

4 In ASPALL 4 free men; Derwulf, under the patronage of the Abbot of Ely; Thurstan under the patronage of Saxi; Marculf under the patronage of Edric, R(obert) Malet's predecessor; and Gunnulf under the sub-patronage of R(obert) Malet's predecessor; 86 acres.
    7 smallholders.
    Always 3 ploughs. Meadow, 2 acres.
    Value always 40s.
    William Malet was in possession of this land before the Bishop of Bayeux, as the Hundred testifies. Later on, Hubert of Port came; he proved the land (to be) free and put the Bishop in possession of this land because free men held it. On the day that Earl Ralph forfeited, Robert Malet's mother was in possession of it, as the Hundred testifies, and until the lawsuit at Odiham. Now it is in the King's peace, as the King commanded, between the Bishop and Robert's mother.

THIS SURVEY WAS MADE IN THE ONE THOUSAND AND EIGHTY SIXTH YEAR SINCE THE INCARNATION OF THE LORD, AND IN THE TWENTIETH OF THE REIGN OF WILLIAM, NOT ONLY THROUGH THESE THREE COUNTIES BUT ALSO THROUGH THE OTHERS.

SUFFOLK HOLDINGS
ENTERED ELSEWHERE IN THE SURVEY
The Latin text of these entries is given in the county volumes concerned

In CAMBRIDGESHIRE
EC 1
[1]   LAND OF THE KING   DB 189 b

      In STAPLOE Hundred   189 d

12 In EXNING King William has 13½ hides. Land for 34 ploughs. In lordship 7 ploughs; a further 3 possible.

       35 villagers and 34 smallholders with 24 ploughs.

       7 slaves; 3 mills, 20s and 7,000 eels; meadow for 4 ploughs.

Total value £53; when Godric acquired it £12; before 1066 £56.

    Edeva the Fair held this manor, and in this manor were 7 Freemen, Edeva's men; they could withdraw without her permission, but she had jurisdiction of them herself; each of them found cartage in the King's service, or 8d or a pledge.

EC 2
14   LAND OF COUNT ALAN   DB 193 d

    (In STAPLOE Hundred)   195 c

68 In EXNING Wymarc holds 1½ hides from the Count. Land for 3 ploughs. In lordship 2 ploughs;

       4 villagers have 1 plough;

       8 slaves; 1 mill, 5s 4d; a fishery, 1,200 eels; meadow for 2 ploughs; pasture for the village livestock.

The value is and was 50s; before 1066, 60s.

    Alsi, Edeva's man, held this land; he could withdraw without her permission.

In ESSEX
EE 1
1   LANDS OF THE KING   LDB 1 b

    Hundred of TENDRING   6 a

26 Harold held BRIGHTLINGSEA as a manor, for 10 hides. Now King William (holds it) ...

Then Brightlingsea and Harkstead between them paid 2 nights' provisions; when P(eter) acquired (them) £25; now £22. However, the outlier lies in Suffolk ...

189 b, d, 193 d, 195 c, LDB 1 b, 6 a

E

EE 2
23   LAND OF RICHARD SON OF COUNT GILBERT   LDB 38 b

(Hundred of HINCKFORD)   40 a
27 In SUDBURY 5 burgesses who hold 2 acres.
They with all the above pay £15 6s 6d. The whole is in Richard's lordship.

EE 3
32   LANDS OF ROBERT GERNON   LDB 63 b

(Hundred of TENDRING)   67 b
40 William holds ARDLEIGH from Robert, which Scalpi held as a manor, for ½ hide and 30 acres. It lies (in the lands of) a manor in Suffolk; but it belongs in this Hundred ...   68 a

EE 4
34   LANDS OF RANULF PEVEREL   LDB 71 b

(Hundred of HINCKFORD)   74 a
21 Thorold holds (Great) HENNY from Ranulf which Wulfwin, a free man, held before 1066 as a manor for 2½ hides and 45 acres ...
To this manor belongs 12d of the customary due from Sudbury ...

EE 5
35   LAND OF AUBREY DE VERE   LDB 76 a

Hundred of HINCKFORD   76 b
5 Aubrey holds (Castle) HEDINGHAM in lordship, which Wulfwin held as a manor, for 2 hides ...
Value then £13; now [£] 20.
To this manor are attached 15 burgesses in Sudbury; they are assessed in the £20 ...

EE 6
40   LAND OF JOHN SON OF WALERAN   LDB 84 a

(Hundred of HINCKFORD)
4 Roger holds HENNY from John, which a free man held before 1066 as a manor, for 2½ hides ...
To this manor belongs a customary due of 22½d which is from Sudbury ...   84 b

In NORFOLK

ENf 1

1   **[LAND OF THE KING]**   LDB 109

GUILTCROSS Hundred   120

76 In KNETTISHALL 1 free man, at 30 acres of land. It   120
appertains in Kenninghall.
   2 villagers.
   Meadow, 1 acre. Always ½ mill; ½ plough; 24 acres of land.
The whole is in the valuation of Kenninghall.

ENf 2

4   **LANDS OF COUNT ALAN**   LDB 144

The Half-Hundred of EARSHAM   149

48 In Alburgh 12 acres of land; meadow, ½ acre.
It belongs in Rumburgh.

ENf 3

7   **LANDS OF ROBERT MALET**   LDB 153 b

(DEPWADE Hundred)   156 a

21 In HARDWICK 1 villager, at 5 acres. It is in the valuation of Eye ...

ENf 4

9   **LAND OF ROGER BIGOT**   LDB 173 a

LODDON Hundred   176 b

49 In MUNDHAM Aelfric, a free man under Stigand, held 30 acres of land before 1066 ...
Value always 5s.
   This Aelfric was outlawed and Ulfketel, the King's reeve, had possession of the land in the King's hand; Roger Bigot asked for it from the King and he granted it   177 a
to him. Count Alan claims this because Earl R(alph) held it as part of his manor of Rumburgh; the men of the Hundred heard Ulfketel acknowledge this on one occasion during the year before R(alph) forfeited and likewise on one occasion after he forfeited, that he, Ulfketel, was doing service in Rumburgh, and finally the Hundred heard this same man say that he was doing service to Roger Bigot. Count Alan's men had 10s from there each year except for the last 4 years and this they are willing to prove by any means. Ulfketel holds.

LDB 109 b, 120 a, b, 144 a, 149 b, 153 b, 156 a, 173 a, 176 b, 177 a

ENf 5

42 LANDS OF GILBERT SON OF RICHERE

The Hundred of CLACKCLOSE
1 Aethelgyth held MILDENHALL before 1066.
   Then 2 ploughs, now 1.
   Always 15 villagers; 5 smallholders. Then 4 slaves, now 2.
   Then 2 men's ploughs, now 1. Then 1 cob. Then 16 pigs, now 8. 2 head of cattle. Always 29 sheep; meadow, 10 acres.
   Value then £5; now 4.

NOTES ON THE TEXT AND TRANSLATION

ABBREVIATIONS used in the Notes
AN ... Anglo-Norman.
arr ... *arrondissement*.
Battle 1980 ... *Proceedings of the Battle Conference on Anglo-Norman Studies III, 1980*, ed. R. Allen Brown (Boydell Press, Woodbridge, Suffolk, 1981).
Björkman ... E. Björkman, *Nordische Personennamen in England in Alt- und Frumittelenglischer Zeit* (Halle 1910).
BT ... J. Bosworth and T. N. Toller, *An Anglo-Saxon Dictionary* (Oxford 1882-1898).
DB ... Domesday Book.
DBE ... H. C. Darby, *Domesday England* (Cambridge 1977).
DBS ... P. H. Reaney, *A Dictionary of British Surnames* (2nd edn. by R. M. Wilson, London etc. 1977).
DEPN ... E. Ekwall, *The Concise Oxford Dictionary of English Place-Names* (4th edn., Oxford 1960).
DG ... H. C. Darby and G. R. Versey, *Domesday Gazetteer* (Cambridge 1975).
Ellis ... Sir H. Ellis, *A General Introduction to Domesday Book* (2 vols. 1833, reprinted 1971).
Exon ... Exon. Domesday Book.
Farrer ... W. Farrer, *Honors and Knights' Fees* (3 vols. London and Manchester 1923-1925).
FB ... *The Feudal Book of Abbot Baldwin*, see Appendix II; references are to pages in FD.
FD ... D. C. Douglas (ed.), *Feudal Documents from the Abbey of Bury St. Edmunds* (London 1932).
von Feilitzen 1939 ... O. von Feilitzen, 'Notes on Old English bynames', *Namn och Bygd* xxvii (1939), 116-130.
von Feilitzen 1945 ... idem, 'Some unrecorded Old and Middle English personal names', *Namn och Bygd* xxxiii (1945), 69-98.
von Feilitzen 1963 ... idem, 'Some Continental Germanic personal names in England', in *Early English and Norse Studies presented to Hugh Smith*, edd. Á. Brown, P. Foote (London 1963), 46-61.
von Feilitzen 1976 ... idem, 'The personal names and bynames of the Winton Domesday', *Winchester in the Early Middle Ages*, ed. M. Biddle (*Winchester Studies* i, Oxford 1976), 143-229.
Fellows Jensen ... G. Fellows Jensen, *Scandinavian Personal Names in Lincolnshire and Yorkshire* (Copenhagen 1968).
Forssner ... T. Forssner, *Continental-Germanic Personal Names in England in Old and Middle English Times* (Uppsala 1916).
Förstemann ... E. Förstemann, *Altdeutsches Namenbuch*, Band 1, *Personennamen* (2nd edn., Bonn 1900).
GDB ... Great Domesday Book.
Harmer, *ASWrits* ... F. E. Harmer, *Anglo-Saxon Writs* (Manchester 1952).
Hart ECEE ... C. R. Hart, *The Early Charters of Eastern England* (Leicester 1966).
HRH ... D. Knowles, C. N. L. Brooke, V. C. M. London (eds.), *The Heads of Religious Houses: England and Wales 940-1216* (Cambridge 1972).
ICC ... The Cambridgeshire Inquiry, *Inquisitio Comitatus Cantabrigiensis*, quoted from the same edition as IE, below; on it see further, Cambridgeshire, Introduction.
IE, IEAL, IEBrev, IENV ... For these texts see Appendix I; references are to pages in N.E.S.A. Hamilton (ed.), *Inquisitio Comitatus Cantabrigiensis* (London 1876); in the notes below, page numbers are not repeated when they are the same as those in the first reference in a particular LDB section.
J.M.D. ... Professor John McN. Dodgson, *in litteris*.
Lat ... Latin.
Latham ... R. E. Latham (ed.), *Revised Medieval Latin Word-List from British and Irish Sources* (London, 1965).
LDB ... Little Domesday Book.
LibEl ... E. O. Blake (ed.), *Liber Eliensis* (Camden Society, 3rd series, xcii, 1962).
Loyd ... C. T. Clay and D. C. Douglas (eds.), *The Origins of Some Anglo-Norman Families, by the late Lewis C. Loyd* (*Harleian Society* ciii, Leeds 1951).
MDB ... V. H. Galbraith, *The Making of Domesday Book* (Oxford 1961).
ME ... Middle English.
MLat ... Medieval Latin.
ModE ... Modern English.
MRH ... D. Knowles and R. N. Hadcock, *Medieval Religious Houses: England and Wales* (Revised edn., London 1971).
MS ... Manuscript.
NFr ... Norman French.
OBret ... Old Breton.
ODan ... Old Danish.

OE ... Old English.
OEB ... G. Tengvik, *Old English Bynames* (*Nomina Germanica* iv, Uppsala 1938).
OFr ... Old French.
OG ... Old German.
OLG ... Old Low German.
ON ... Old Norse.
OS ... Old Saxon.
O.S. ... Ordnance Survey.
OScand ... Old Scandinavian.
OSw ... Old Swedish.
OWScand ... Old West Scandinavian.
PNDB ... O. von Feilitzen, *The Pre-Conquest Personal Names of Domesday Book* (*Nomina Germanica* iii, Uppsala 1937).
Regesta i ... H. W. C. Davis (ed.), *Regesta Regum Anglo-Normannorum 1066-1154*, i, *1066-1100* (Oxford 1913).
Robertson, *AS Charters* ... A. J. Robertson (ed.), *Anglo-Saxon Charters* (Cambridge 1939).
Rom ... Romance.
Round FE ... J. H. Round, *Feudal England* (London 1895).
Sawyer ... P. H. Sawyer, *Anglo-Saxon Charters: An Annotated List and Bibliography* (*Royal Historical Society*, 1968).
Scand ... Scandinavian.
VCH ... *The Victoria History of the County of Suffolk*, i, ed. W. Page (London 1911), with Domesday translation adapted from that by Lord J. Hervey (Bury St. Edmunds 1888-1891).
VCH Cambridgeshire i ... *The Victoria History of the County of Cambridgeshire and the Isle of Ely*, i, ed. L. F. Salzman (London 1938).
Whitelock, *AS Wills* ... D. Whitelock (ed.), *Anglo-Saxon Wills* (Cambridge 1930).

The Editor is grateful to Miss Philippa Brown for a preliminary collation of the Suffolk text to FB and IE; and to the Suffolk County Record Office, Ipswich, for the use of maps of administrative divisions.

The text of the Domesday Survey for Suffolk is contained in Little Domesday Book (now preserved, with the larger volume, at the Public Record Office, London). The manuscript was written, by more than one scribe, on either side of leaves, or folios, of parchment (sheep-skin) measuring about 11 by 8 inches (28 by 20 cms). On each side, or page, is a single column, making two to each folio. The folios were numbered in the 17th century, and the two columns of each are here lettered a, b. Red ink was used to distinguish some chapter headings and most Hundred headings. Deletion was marked by putting a line (in the ink of the text) through incorrect words. The running title on the recto of folios was usually an abbreviatd form of the name of the Landholder whom the chapter concerned; the running title on the verso was an abbreviation of the county name.

SUFFOLK. *SVDFULC, -FVLCH, SVT(H)FVLC.* Abbreviated in the running title as $\overline{SVD}F$, $SV\overline{D}F$, $SVD\overline{F}$.

References to text in other DB counties are to the Chapter and Section of the editions in this series. The Anglo-Saxon letter 'ash' is rendered *AE, ae*; the letter 'eth' by *th*.

L - 1

GENERAL NOTES

L   LANDHOLDERS. See also folios 292a and 372a for partial lists of landholders which were used by the copyists as a running guide to the order of chapters before the full Suffolk list was constructed. The partial list on folio 372a was subsequently deleted. Similar partial lists occur in the Essex section of LDB on folios 9a and 17a. The presence of these partial lists in the MS reflects the way in which the county returns were put together from booklets relating to each of the major landholders.

1,1-60   LAND ... BELONGING TO THE REALM. *Terra regis de regione*; a similar phrase is used in 31,44 (referring to the same royal manor of Thorney). Swaffham in Norfolk (4,1) is also said to have belonged *ad regionem*. Round FE 119 dismissed the use of *de regione* as a copying error for *(de) regno*, but this is unlikely with the Swaffham example. It is more likely that *regio* is used as an alternative word for *Regnum*, 'realm, kingdom', which occurs with apparently similar usage in the heading before 1,120-121 below and in Norfolk 1,71; *regnum* is also used in connection with the King's lordship land in Devon in a heading in Exon., folio 83a.

1,1   ROGER BIGOT. The Sheriff, see 7 and note.
          THORNEY. In Stowmarket.
          KING EDWARD. The Confessor, died 5 January 1066.
          ALWAYS. *Se(m)p(er)*; before 1066 and still in 1086.
          THEN. *T(u)nc*; before 1066.
          LATER ON. *Postea*; sometime between 1066 and 1086.
          NOW NONE, BUT BEFORE 1066. MS *Regis.eW.*; Farley adds the abbreviation mark.
          LATER. *P(ost)*; sometime between 1066 and 1086.
          NOW 19. In the MS there is an erasure between *x* and *ix*, perhaps of an ampersand.
          HUGH DE MONTFORT ... CLAIMS. See 31,44.
          23 ACRES. In the MS there is an erasure between *xx* and *.iii.* Cf. the 25 acres mentioned in 31,44.
          £15. The records of the Domesday Survey used the English currency system which lasted for a thousand years until 1971. The pound contained 20 shillings, each of 12 pence, abbreviated respectively as L(ibrae), s(olidi), d(enarii). Note however that, in common with other medieval records, the Domesday manuscripts frequently have instances where quantities of pence have not been converted into shillings, and quantities of shillings have not been converted into pounds. Sometimes a number of pennies was expressed in *orae* rather than shillings, see 1,94 note.
          [£] 40 BLANCHED. A sample of coin was melted as a test for the presence of alloy or baser metal. Money could also be said to be blanched when, without a test by fire, a standard deduction from the face value was made to allow for alloying or clipping.
          LEAGUE. Generally reckoned as a mile and a half.
          15D IN TAX. That is, a sum of 15d in tax when the Hundred in which the manor lay was liable for £1.
          HUGH DE MONTFORT. Cf. 31,44;53.
          COUNT ROBERT. Of Mortain, see 2 and note.
          ROGER OF AUBERVILLE. Cf. 29,1 where 6 Freemen belonging to this manor are mentioned.
          FRODO. Possibly the brother of Abbot Baldwin of St. Edmund's, see *12* and note.
          ROGER OF POITOU. Cf. 8,51;54.

1,2   BRAMFORD. See also 1,7.
          VALUE THEN £ ... In the MS there is an erasure before *lib*; and *ual* has been corrected from *ual&* by subpuncting, although this is not shown by Farley.
          BY WEIGHT. *ad pensu(m)*; that is the coins were weighed (although apparently not assayed) rather than being accepted at face value. This was to counteract any payment in coins which had been clipped.

1,5   'OLDEN'. Lost in Coddenham, see VCH 419,n.2.
          AND A HALF. Half-shares in the rights over free men *(liberi homines)* or Freemen *(sochemanni)* are frequently found in the Suffolk and Norfolk folios of LDB.

1,6   BISHOP OF BAYEUX. For his lands in Stonham, see 16,15;22.

1,7   THIS ENTRY. Repeated at 74,7 under the lands of vavassors.
          HEMINGSTONE. Here and at 62,4;6 and 74,7 assigned to Claydon Hundred, but elsewhere in the neighbouring Hundred of Bosmere. Both here and at 74,7 the form *haminghelanda* is used instead of *hami(n)gestuna*, showing alternation of OE *land* and *tun*, both with the meaning of 'estate'.

GYRTH. Probably Gyrth, Earl of East Anglia from 1057. He was the brother of King Harold and was killed at the Battle of Hastings. In LDB *comes* appears frequently to have been omitted before his name.
WULFMER THE REEVE. See 73 and note.
BRAMFORD. See 1,2.
IS GUARANTOR FOR HIM. *e(st) ei Warant*; Wulfmer the reeve names his superior, the Sheriff, as having given him official authority to alter a fiscal arrangement.

1,8 DISS. Now in Norfolk, but apparently partly in Suffolk in 1086.
24 SMALLHOLDERS. In the MS *x* has been erased between *xx* and *iiij*.
2 SLAVES. *ii.* altered from *.i.* in MS.
JURISDICTION OF ONE AND A HALF HUNDREDS. Cf. Norfolk 1,50-51 where reference is made to the jurisdiction of the Half-Hundred of Diss, belonging to Diss in Suffolk.
HALF A DAY('S SUPPLY) OF HONEY. Enough honey to meet the needs of the King and his companions were they to stay at this royal manor for half a day. Honey was used for wax as well as for food and in the preparation of mead and medicines, see DBE 277-279. Reckoning of amounts of renders in terms of so many days' provisions is found on several royal manors in 1086.

1,9 ANUND. LDB *Anand(us)*. ODan, OSw *Anund*, PNDB 161-162.
3 FREE [MEN]. LDB *lib̃ i.* is in error for *lib̃i*.

1,10 EASTON (BAVENTS). Below (at 68,1;4) in Blything Hundred, as was Blythburgh (see 1,12).
EARL R(ALPH). Either Earl Ralph the Constable (died 1069/70) or his son Earl Ralph Wader (forfeited 1075).
R(OBERT) MALET. Sheriff of Suffolk at some time between 1066 and 1086. See 6 and note.

1,11 W(ILLIAM) OF BOURNEVILLE. One of Roger Bigot's subtenants, see 7,56 note.
1,12 3 OXEN. That is, land for 3 oxen, meaning land for three-eighths of a plough.
THE FOURTH PENNY FROM THE DUES. That is, one quarter of them.
RISEBURC. Unidentified, but perhaps a fortified market-site within the manor of Blythburgh. DBE 285 suggests that the enclosure was a sea-weir but this is less likely.
HERRINGS. An important part of the medieval diet. For a map of herring renders in 1086, see DBE 286.
OSBERN MALE. The Latin byname *masculus* corresponds to OFr *masle* or *masculin*, 'male', OEB 351-352. He may be identical with Osbert Male in 34,6. Alternation between the forms *Osbernus* and *Osbertus* in references to a single individual is not unusual in medieval records.

1,13 FREE MAN. LDB *home* is in error for *hom̃*.
1,14 PREDECESSOR. Each of the 1086 landholders was deemed to be the legal successor of one or more 1066 landholders, each of whom was termed his *antecessor*.
1,17 (HUGH) DE MONTFORT. See 31 and note.
1,21 CHURCH. LDB *eccl̃e* is in error for *eccl̃a*.
1,22 R(OBERT) OF VAUX. See 6,84 note.
1,23 3½ [CARUCATES]. LDB *carant̃* is here in error for *carucat̃*, 'carucate'. Cf. following.
4 [PLOUGHS]. LDB *carant̃* is here in error for *caruce*, 'ploughs'. Cf. preceding.
VALUE THEN 60S. In the MS *uat* has been altered by erasure from *uab&*; cf. *hab&* on the following line.
4 OF THESE 12. A total of 13 are detailed here.

1,25 KISLEA. Unidentified, DG 104.
1,29 BECHETUNA. The same as *BEKETUNA* at 31,26. In Lothing Hundred. Unidentified, DG 390.
ALL THESE. The free men in 1,23-30.

1,30 AELFRIC. Probably the Reeve mentioned in 1,17.
THIS CUSTOMARY DUE. In the MS *hoc* has been untidily altered to *hanc*, with another *hanc.* interlined.

1,31 OSFERTH. In the MS *Osfert(us)* has been altered from *Osfee-*.
EDRIC OF LAXFIELD. See 6,305 and note.
1,32 GORLESTON. Now in Norfolk.
1,33 ALWAYS 10 SMALLHOLDERS ... NOW 3. Repeated in error in LDB. The copyist's eye was misled by two successive sentences beginning *se(m)p(er)* at the turning of the page.
11 PIGS. LDB *.x.* with *.i.* interlined.
1,34 HELD. LDB *tenuit* interlined, with two vertical dots used as a *signe de renvoi*.

	[IN LORDSHIP]. LDB omits *in dominio*.
1,35	[MEN'S] PLOUGHS. LDB omits *hominum*.
1,40	VALUE ... WHOLE OF THIS. This refers to 1,32-35;37-40. The 2 carucates which it excludes are those assessed in 1,36.
	THIS HALF-HUNDRED. Of Lothingland, cf. 1,32.
	FURLONG. 220 yards or one eighth of a mile.
1,43	[IN] BECCLES. LDB *Abecles* is probably a copyist's error for *In becles* as in 1,39.
	IN THE ASSESSMENT. Translating *cu(m) p(re)tio*; cf. *in p(re)tio* in 1,42.
1,47	THEN 3 PLOUGHS IN LORDSHIP, NOW 2. In the MS a third minim has been erased after *ii*.
1,51	HOPTON. Farley prints *ho.tuna* for MS *hovtuna*, in which -v- has been written over another letter (?*c*).
	4 OXEN. LDB *arm* may stand for arm(enta), 'cattle for ploughing', unless it is a copyist's error for *anim(alia)*.
	THEN 3 PLOUGHS. In the MS *tař* is in error for *cař*.
1,52	WOODLAND FOR 5 PIGS. In the MS *v* has been written over *x* which has been erased.
1,57	'NEWTON'. Lost in the sea east of Corton; VCH 423, n.10.
1,59	90 ACRES. In the MS *LXXX* has been altered to *LXXXX*.
1,60	ALL THESE MEN. Probably all those in 1,44-60.
	ALRIC THE REEVE. LDB *Alric(us)* may here stand for OE *Aelfric*. This may be the same reeve who is mentioned in 1,17 in a similar context.
	H(UGH) OF HOUDAIN. One of Roger Bigot's subtenants, see 7,60 and note.
	£50. This seems a huge increase, and may imply that Hugh of Houdain misused some authority delegated to him by Roger Bigot.
	THE MEN. The jurors, either of the Hundred or of the vill. Their evidence was recorded by the Commissioners in cases of dispute.
1,61-95	EARL RALPH. Of East Anglia. He is given the byname Wader in Cambridgeshire (19,4) and was the son of Earl Ralph the Constable (see 1,101 note). He forfeited his lands after taking part in a rebellion in 1075 and died in exile. His byname may be from a place-name, see OEB 119.
	GODRIC THE STEWARD. See *13* and note.
1,61	EDEVA THE RICH. Also called 'the Fair'. Probably the same as Countess Edeva in 4,17. She held extensive lands and patronage in Cambridgeshire, Hertfordshire, Norfolk and Suffolk before 1066.
1,62	ST. EDMUND'S. See *14* and note.
1,64	STOW HUNDRED. In the MS the *T* of *STOV* has been altered from *O*.
	EDITH. Probably 'the Rich', as in 1,63.
1,65	BELONGS IN. In the MS there is an erasure (? of two letters) after *p(er)tinɢ*, and *i(n)* is squeezed in at the beginning of the next line.
1,67	EDEVA THE FAIR. See 1,61 note.
	POLE. Translating *uirga*.
1,68	LANGHEDENA. Also at 7,66. 8,62;64 (*Langedana*). 29,10. 38,9. Unidentified, DG 404. Consistently assigned to Bosmere Hundred.
1,70	7S [8]D. Farley prints *iiii* in error for *viii* of MS.
1,71	60 ACRES. In the MS there is an erasure before the *L*, and *X* is interlined. The copyist may at first have written *XL*.
1,73	OVER ALL OF THEM. The free men in 1,68-73.
1,74	CODDENHAM. Near Needham Market. Here and at 8,77 and 56,6 it is assigned to Claydon Hundred, but elsewhere to the neighbouring Hundred of Bosmere.
1,75	THEN 24 SHEEP. The dots in Farley represent a rubbed area of the MS. No text appears to be lost.
	AS A PREMIUM. In the MS *gersuma* has been altered from *gersume*.
1,76-77	BURGHARD. Called 'of Mendlesham' in 14,152.
1,77	ALWIN. Perhaps Alwin 'of Mendlesham' in 31,51.
	THE ABBOT. Of St. Edmund's, see 14,146.
	TO THIS MANOR. LDB *huc* is in error for *huic*.
	PERCHES. The perch is a measure of length, usually reckoned as 5½ yards.
1,87	ALL THIS. Referring to 1,83-87.
1,88	ABBOT OF ST. EDMUND'S. Norton is not referred to in chapter *14*.
	50 LEAGUES. LDB *L* is probably in error for *i*.

	THIS MANOR. In the MS *monarium* has been altered to *monerium*, in error for *manerium*. Farley shows the *e* as suprascript but in the MS the *a* is merely altered to *e* by the addition of an extra loop.
1,90	VILLAGERS. LDB *Witti* is in error for *uill(an)i*.
	MEADOW, 3 ACRES. In the MS there is an erasure after *.iii.*
	IT HAS 1 LEAGUE. LDB has an otiose letter *E* at the beginning of the line.
1,92	REDENHALL. In Norfolk.
	JURISDICTION ... HOXNE. The Bishop of Thetford's manor (18,1). Bishop's Hundred was renamed after it by 1191.
1,93	THORMOD OF PARHAM. See 1,75.
1,94	*ORA*. Literally an ounce, in Scandinavia a monetary unit and coin still in use; in the Domesday records valued at 16 (assayed) or 20 (unassayed) pence, see S. Harvey, 'Royal revenue and Domesday terminology', *Economic History Review*, 2nd series, xx (1967), 221-228.
1,96	PETER OF VALOGNES. Sheriff of Essex and Hertfordshire in 1086, see 37 and note. Here acting as Sheriff of Essex.
	HAROLD. Earl of Wessex (1053-), King 1066. For his landholding, see Ann Williams, 'Land and power in the eleventh-century: the estates of Harold Godwineson', *Battle 1980*, 171-187. He is rarely given the title *comes* in LDB and never that of *rex*. Most of the instances of the name Harold in Suffolk probably refer to him.
	BRIGHTLINGSEA. See Essex 1,26.
1,97-99	EARL MORCAR'S MOTHER. Aelfeva, wife of Earl Algar (see 8,33 note). She is named in 16,10. Morcar became Earl of Northumbria in 1065. He survived the Conquest but joined revolts against King William and was imprisoned first in Normandy and later at Winchester. He was still alive in 1087, and was freed by King William on his deathbed only to be imprisoned again by King William Rufus.
	WILLIAM THE CHAMBERLAIN. Perhaps the same as the tenant of Westminster Abbey in North Ockendon, Essex 6,10.
	OTTO THE GOLDSMITH. He held Gestingthorpe in Essex (81,1) which had formerly been held by Earl Algar. He was also holding Shalford and Finchingfield in the same county (1,11-12) on behalf of the King, both of which had been held by Earl Algar. In Colchester (Essex B3j) he had 3 houses which Countess Aelfeva used to hold. Before 1066 he married Leofgifu the widow of a citizen of London. He was the tenant of St. Edmund's Abbey at Hawstead (14,13). On him, and his son Otto, see FD cxxxix-cxli.
1,97	SUDBURY. In 1086 a detached part of Thingoe Hundred. Later in Babergh Hundred.
	BURGESSES ... AT THE HALL. LDB *in d(omi)nio* deleted before *halle*. 'At the hall' has the same meaning in LDB as 'in lordship'.
	ST. GREGORY'S CHURCH. This was the recipient of a bequest of Waldingfield in 1000 x 1002; Whitelock, *ASWills* no. 15, Sawyer no. 1486, Hart ECEE no. 64.
1,99	VALUE ... WHOLE. Of 1,98-99.
1,100-106	AELFRIC WAND. The byname is from OE *wand*, 'mole', OEB 367. Not necessarily the same man as at Essex 25,24:26.
1,100	HAROLD. As 1,96 note.
1,101	EARL RALPH THE CONSTABLE. Earl of East Anglia from before March 1068. Father of Earl Ralph Wader (see 1,61-95 note). Died 1069/70. LDB *stalra* is from OE *st(e)allere*, 'staller, King's marshal', sometimes represented by Latin *constabularius*; OEB 270-271.
	AFTER 1066. In the MS *T(empore). R(egis). Will(el)mi).* has been altered from *T(empore). R(egis). E(dwardi).*
	[PARK] LDB *porc(us)* is in error for *parc(us)*. Cf. DBE 201-203. See also 6,83 note.
1,102	TO THIS MANOR ... The remainder of this entry probably refers to East Bergholt rather than to Shotley.
	MALET. This could refer to both or either of Robert Malet (6) and his father William Malet.
	ROBERT SON OF WYMARC. Father of Swein of Essex, see 27 and note.
1,103	HUNDRED AND A HALF. Of Samford.
	OF GYRTH'S. In the MS the letter before *uert*, presumably *G*, has been smudged; Farley prints *.uert.*
	AS A PREMIUM. LDB has an abbreviation mark, presumably to read as *gersu(m)ma*.
	AS MUCH [THENCE]. Farley *m̊* is in error for *in* of MS, for *iñ(de)*.
	AELFRIC THE REEVE ... THIS AELFRIC. The latter is probably Aelfric Wand, but not necessarily the former.

DOES NOT REMAIN ... WHAT MAKES THAT PROFIT. The second negative of the Latin text is not translated.
TAX OF 8D. Farley shows by means of dots an erasure in the MS after *gelt*.
1,105 AUBREY DE VERE. See *35* and note.
1 FREEMAN. At *Canepetuna*, see 35,4.
ALDHAM. See 35,6.
1,106 *CANAPPETUNAM*. The same as *CANEPETUNA* at 35,4 and *CANAPETUNA* at 3,80. Unidentified, DG 393. Consistently assigned to Samford Hundred.
CHATTISHAM. Not elsewhere mentioned in LDB. Some text may have been omitted here.
1,107-119 STIGAND. Consecrated Bishop of Winchester in 1047, he held that See with the Archbishopric of Canterbury from 1052 until he was deposed in 1070. Died 1072.
WILLIAM OF NOYERS. Probably from Noyers (Calvados), rather than Noyers (Eure), OEB 103. He was a tenant of the Bishop of Thetford, see 19,17.
1,107 20 ACRES. In the MS there is an erasure (? of *x*) after *xx*.
PLOUGH, NOW ½. In the MS there is an erasure after *dimid'*.
1 COB. *.i.r.* MS; Farley adds the abbreviation mark.
UNDER HIM. LDB *sub se* is in error for *sub eo*, referring to Thurstan.
1,108 COVEHITHE. Formerly 'North Hales'.
ALL THIS. Probably meaning 1,107-108.
1,110 ... CARUCATE. LDB omits the numeral.
6 VILLAGERS ... 15 PIGS. In the MS between lines 18 and 19 of folio 288a and in the right margin several words have been erased.
2 BROTHERS. LDB *fr(atr)is* is in error for *fr(atr)es*; in the MS it has been altered from *fr(atr)i*.
EARL H(UGH). See *4* and note.
60 ACRES. See 4,25.
10 ACRES. 1 PLOUGH IN LORDSHIP. In the MS an ampersand has been erased after *car(uca)*.
1 MEN'S PLOUGH. LDB has an otiose numeral *.i.* after *ho(min)u(m)* and an extra point before it.
1,111 PAT. The same personal name occurs in Cheshire 27,2 but is of obscure origin; PNDB 343.
ALFGER. LDB *Alfger(us)* may represent ON *Álfgeirr* rather than OE Aelfgar; PNDB 173.
1,112 SMALLHOLDERS' PLOUGH. LDB *bordarii* (genitive singular) is in error for *bordariorum* (genitive plural); it is a variant of the usual *hominum*.
1,115 KING EDWARD GAVE ... ST. EDMUND'S. Mildenhall was granted by Edward the Confessor to St. Edmund's in 1043 x 1044; Harmer, *ASWrits* no. 9, Sawyer no. 1069, Hart *ECEE* no. 106. It appears to have been leased to Archbishop Stigand and taken back into royal hands by King William.
THEN ... 30 VILLAGERS. In the MS there is an erasure after *xxx*; probably of *p(ost)* which, with the tironian nota for *et* (7), was subsequently inserted before the numeral.
FISHERIES. LDB *piscat'* is for *piscat(iones)*, replacing the more usual *piscina* or *piscaria*. For various types of fisheries in 1086, see DBE 279-286.
WILD MARES. LDB *eque siluatice*, literally 'woodland mares'.
11¼D IN TAX. In the MS there is an erasure before *ferdingu(m)*.
BRAMFORD. Elsewhere in Bosmere Hundred, but placed here in the Hundred of Samford, probably because of its association with East Bergholt (1,100).
HAROLD. As 1,96 note.
BISHOP ERFAST. See 19,1-2 note.
1,120-121 BELONGING ... REALM. See 1,1 note.
PICOT. Probably the Sheriff of Cambridgeshire.
TRIBUTE. Translating *censu(m)*.
1,121 ALGAR. Earl Algar, see 65,1.
1,122a-122g ROGER BIGOT. See 1,1-60 note.
1,122a-122b THE QUEEN. Edith, wife of Edward the Confessor and daughter of Earl Godwin of Wessex.
1,122a THIRD PART. Cf. 3,55 and reference there to the 'third penny'.
1,122b GRANGE. Earl Gyrth also held a grange in Ipswich before 1066, see 3,55.
1,122c POOR BURGESSES. Cf. the 'poor men' in Dunwich (6,84).

1 - 2

	APART FROM ... HEADS. A similar poll-tax was levied at Colchester, see Essex B3b,d,m.
1,122d	ALWULF. LDB *Alnulfus* is in error for *Aluulfus*, see Forssner 23, s.n. *Alnoldus*. The corrected form would represent OE *Aelfwulf*.
	CULLING. The name also occurs among the burgesses of Colchester, Essex B3a. It probably represents either the OE pers. n. *Colling*, also found as a byname (OEB 141-142, von Feilitzen 1976, 153) or ON *Kullungr*, PNDB 307.
	TUMBI. Perhaps ODan *Tumbi*, a short form of *Thurmoth, Thurmund*, see PNDB 388.
1,122f	FEAST OF ST. JOHN. Probably 24 June, the Nativity of St. John the Baptist, rather than 29 August the Decollation.
	COUNT ALAN. See *3* and note.
	EARL RALPH. See 1,61-95 note.
	IVO TALLBOYS. The byname is from OFr *tailgebosc*, 'cut wood', OEB 388. He was the brother of Ralph Tallboys, Sheriff of Bedfordshire. He commanded the siege of Hereward the Wake at Ely in 1069. He was later Steward to King William Rufus and died about 1115.
	AS (ITS) DELIVERER. That is, to bear witness that he had delivered ownership, on the King's behalf, to Count Alan.
	AESCHERE ... GODRIC ... 1 ACRE. This text is interlined in the MS, as shown by Farley, but appears to have been inserted a few lines too early.
	AESCHERE. An OE pers. n. *AEschere*, see von Feilitzen 1945, 72 and 73 n.1.
1,122g	SESTERS. Usually 4, but sometimes 5 to 6 gallons, see R.E. Zupko, *A Dictionary of English weights and measures from Anglo-Saxon times to the nineteenth century* (Univ. of Wisconsin Press, 1968), 155.
	TO THE PREBENDARIES. For their food, cf. Essex B 6 (Colchester).
	NOW IT PAYS. LDB repeats *modo reddit* in error.
2	ROBERT COUNT OF MORTAIN. A half-brother of King William, and younger brother of Odo, Bishop of Bayeux (*16*).
2,1	ST. ETHELDREDA'S. See *21*.
	ALWAYS 1½ PLOUGHS. IE (142) adds 'in lordship'.
2,2	JURISDICTION. IE (142), 'full jurisdiction'.
2,3	1 OX. That is, one eighth of a ploughteam of 8 oxen.
2,5	ALL THIS. Perhaps referring to 2,1-5.
	COUNT BRIAN. Brother of Count Alan of Brittany (*3*).
2,7	NIGEL [HELD]. Farley prints *ten..t* for what in the MS is probably intended to be *tenuit*, although some erasure has taken place. If he is the same Nigel as in 2,8 the past tense appears appropriate.
2,8	CHURCH OF STOW(MARKET). Also at 34,6.
	TO THE MANOR. LDB *man(us)* is in error for *man(erio)*.
	IN THE CHURCH OF COMBS. In the MS *ta(m)bas* is in error for *ca(m)bas*; Farley silently corrects.
2,9-10	ST. MARY'S OF GRESTAIN. The Benedictine Abbey in Normandy founded by Count Robert's father, Duke Robert I.
2,9	7 CATTLE. In the MS *vii* has been altered from *vi*.
2,10	HARDWIN, THE EARL'S BROTHER. The Earl referred to is probably Ralph (cf. 7,67) the Constable.
2,11	COUNT ... IN LORDSHIP. The two dots in the MS before *in*, shown by Farley, are probably an anticipation of those either side of the following numeral.
	VALUE [10]D. Farley prints *cx.d̄.* but in the MS the *c* is an erroneous anticipation of the bowl of *d* that follows the numeral.
2,12	ANUND. Added above the line in LDB.
	[HELD IT]. Cf. below.
	BELONGING TO THE CHURCH. Translating *Eccl(esi)ae*.
2,14	HELD. LDB *tenenuit* is in error for *tenuit*.
2,15	WHATFIELD. MS *gaWatefelda*; Farley *goWatefelda* in error. The place-name form should be taken as *Watefelda*, with the *ga-* of the MS being an unerased false start with Norman *g* for *w*.
2,16	2 FREE MEN ... PATRONAGE (OF) ST. ETHELDREDA'S. IE (144) adds, 'in full jurisdiction'.
	18 ACRES. IE (144) and IEAL (189), '14'.
	IN TAX. In the MS *degelt(o)* altered from *det-*.
2,18	THORPE. In Trimley, VCH 432, n.20a.

2,19   'ALSTON'. Lost in Trimley, VCH 432, n.21. Also at 7,96;101;113.
        NORMAN. LDB *normandNi* is in error for *normanni*. From OE *northmann*, originally
        designating a Scandinavian, especially a Norwegian, but by 1066 functioning as a pers. n.;
        PNDB 331-332.
2,20   EUDO. Son of Nigel, as 2,16.
        ALL THIS. 2,17-20.
Folio 292a, foot. A partial list of landholders (*3-4*) occurs here. This was a running guide to the
contents of the quire which begins with this leaf. It should have been deleted after use like the one at
folio 372a, below. See further, note to List of Landholders, above.
3   COUNT ALAN. Of Brittany. He was the son-in-law of King William. His name is OBret
        Alan.
3,1   MANNI SWART. LDB *Mannius Suart*, from ODan *Manni* (PNDB 324) and the OWScand
        byname *suartr, suarti*, 'black' (OEB 338). For his son Ulf, see 6,109 and note.
        1 [PLOUGH] WITH THE VILLAGERS. The formula is that found in ICC and IE, see
        Cambridgeshire, Introduction.
        WESTON (COLVILLE). See Cambridgeshire 14,80 and note; and ESf.
3,2   IN THE ASSESSMENT OF RUMBURGH. The main entry for Rumburgh was omitted
        from LDB however. Cf. 3,105 and ENf2;4.
        STONE (STREET). LDB places this in Bradmere Hundred. Geographically it is in
        Blything Hundred (as was RUMBURGH) and has been so mapped.
3,3   MEN'S PLOUGHS. In the MS the first *c* of *car(uce)* has been altered from *a*.
        PIGS. LDB *pors*.
        THE KING ... JURISDICTION. Misplaced in LDB in the middle of, rather than after, the
        value. It may perhaps have been interlined in an exemplar MS.
        3¾D IN TAX. LDB has *ser* in error for *fer(dingi)*, 'farthings'.
3,4   THIS ASSESSMENT. In the MS *Hoe* is in error for *Hoc*; Farley corrects.
3,5   16 SMALLHOLDERS. LDB *vxvi*, with an erroneous anticipation of the *v*.
3,7   (IT IS) ... JURISDICTION. Referring to 3,5-7 and the assessment of Bramfield
        mentioned in 3,4.
3,8   THORPE. In Blything Hundred. Near Heveningham, VCH 432, n.23. DG 413 places it in
        Aldingham (*recte* Aldringham), but that is in Bishop's Hundred. Cf. 7,16 note.
        WAS DELIVERED [TO HIM]. That is, the Count was put in lawful possession of him
        and the land. Cf. Bedfordshire 56,2 *quae sibi lib(er)ata fuit*.
3,9   8 CATTLE. In the MS *viii* has been altered from *vii*.
        MAYNARD. OG *Maganhard, Mainard*, Forssner 181.
3,10   R(ALPH) THE CONSTABLE. Earl Ralph. LDB *Stabra* is in error for *Stalra*. See 1,101
        note.
        60 PIGS. In the MS the *L* of the numeral is written over an erased *x*.
3,13   IT IS ALL ... MANOR. That is, the 14 free men in 3,10 and the items in 3,11-13 are
        included in the assessment of Wissett in 3,10.
        THE COUNT ... LENGTH ... TAX. These details refer to the whole manor of Wissett.
3,14   IN THIS CHURCH ... 12 MONKS. The Priory of Rumburgh, founded by Bishop Aelmer
        and Abbot Thurstan of St. Benedict of Holme, see MRH 74. See also 3,105.
        £20. See 3,10.
3,15   WRABETUNA. In Blything Hundred (also at 6,91;99;108. 7,11;28). Unidentified, DG 417;
        but referred to *temp.* Henry II (VCH 433, n.24).
        HAMO OF VALOGNES. Probably from Valognes (La Manche). The LDB form *deuellenis*
        may be compared to *de walenus* in 14,78 as a spelling for Peter of Valognes; cf. OEB 117.
3,16   COVEHITHE. As 1,108 note.
3,17   BEFORE 1066; [20] ACRES. In the MS *xxx* has been altered to *xx* by erasure; Farley
        prints *xxx* in error.
        VALUE ALWAYS 4S. In the MS there is an erasure after *uat*.
3,20   (EARL) SOHAM. Identified DG 397.
3,21   IN CAPEL (ST. ANDREW). IE (147) and IEAL (185). 'In CAMPSEY (Ash)'.
        EDRIC GRIM. The byname is OE *grimm*, 'fierce, savage', OEB 346-347.
3,24-27 EDRIC. Grim (IE 147).
3,26   IEAL (185) adds, '3 free men, 15 acres'.
3,27   26 ACRES. IEAL (185), 16.
3,28   'LITTLE' CHARSFIELD. LDB *parua ceresfella*.
3,29   E(DRIC). Grim (IE 147).
3,31   AETHELWOLD THE PRIEST. IE (148) and IEAL (185), '1 free man'.
        50 ACRES. IEAL (185, in error), 1.
        THEN 1 PLOUGH. IE 'Then 2 ploughs in lordship'.
        ALL THIS. 3,21-31.

3,32	1 FREE MAN. IE (147) adds, 'of St. Etheldreda's' but omits the mention of patronage.
3,33	IN BOULGE. IE (147) and IEAL (185), 'in (Little) BEALINGS'.
	2 FREE MEN. IE adds, 'of St. Etheldreda's' but omits the patronage.
	THEY ... ASSESSMENT. Referring to 3,32-33.
3,34	EDRIC GRIM. IE (146) adds, 'a free man'.
	VALUE OF THE HEAD OF THE MANOR. That is, of the core. The total value, with the outliers, is given at 3,44.
	6 FREEMEN. IE adds, 'under the patronage of Edric Grim'.
	36 ACRES. IEAL (185), 30.
	2 FREE MEN ... ST. ETHELDREDA'S. In the MS an ampersand has been erased before *Eldre*.
3,35	12 FREE MEN AND A HALF. IEAL (185), 12.
3,36	ST. ETHELDREDA'S. In the MS *El* is written over an erasure.
	THE THREE OTHERS. IE (153), referring to these only, '15 acres. Value 3s.'
	1 CARUCATE. IEAL (185), 3.
3,39	5 WHOLE ... FREE MEN. IE (147) and IEAL (185), 6.
	W(ILLIAM) MALET. In the MS there is an erasure after *W*.
	WHEN HE DIED. Probably 1069 x 1071.
	34 ACRES. IE, 20.
3,40	AND A HALF. IE (147) and IEAL (185) omits.
	34 ACRES. IE, 30; IEAL, 4.
	EARL R(ALPH). Wader. He forfeited in 1075, see 1,61-95 note.
3,41	*BRODERTUNA*. Also at 6,278. Unidentified DG 392. In Loes Hundred.
	7 FREE MEN. IEAL (185), 6.
	HALF UNDER THE PATRONAGE ... LAXFIELD. IE (147), 'under the patronage of Edric Grim'.
	FORFEITED. In the MS *fec(it)* has been altered to *forisfec(it)*. He forfeited in 1075, see 1,61-95 note.
3,42	4½ ACRES. IE (147) and IEAL (185), 3.
3,44	8 ACRES. IE (147) and IEAL (185), 7.
	VALUE ... MANOR NOW £23 11S. IE, 'Value of the whole, £18. A church with 29 acres' IEAL, '11 churches, 29 acres'. The manor referred to is that of Kettleburgh, including 3,34-45.
3,45	ASSESSMENT. See preceding note.
3,46	ST. EDMUND'S. In the MS *.E.* altered to *.E.tmundi*, with two otiose abbreviation marks. IE (148), 'St. Etheldreda's'. IE uses the present tense here (*tenet*).
	(EARL) SOHAM. As 3,20 note.
	VALUE ... NOW £18 13S 4D. IE, 'Value £18'.
3,47	24 ACRES. IEAL (185), 23.
3,48	A HALF FREE MAN. IE (148) and IEAL (185), '1 free man'.
	THEY ... ASSESSMENT. Referring to 3,47-48.
3,49	2 VILLAGERS ... 50 ACRES. IE (148) adds 'under the patronage of Edric Grim'.
	50 ACRES. IEAL (185, in error), 1.
3,50	2 FREE MEN. IE (148) and IEAL (185), 1.
3,52	5 FREE MEN. Farley *libi* is in error for *lib̄i* of the MS.
	ALL THIS ... KETTLEBURGH. Referring to 3,51-52.
3,53	WULFRIC. In the MS *Vlurici* has been altered from *Vlul-*.
3,54	BLUNDESTON. The LDB form *dunstuna* is corrupt.
3,55	TOWN OF IPSWICH. LDB *Gespeswiz* is in error for *Gepeswiz*.
	GRANGE. For another grange here, see 1,122b.
	THIRD PENNY. A third share in the profits of jurisdiction, traditionally the perquisite of the local Earl. Cf. 1,122a;g.
3,56	GAUTI. LDB *Gouti*, from ON *Gauti*, ODan *Góti*; see PNDB 258, n.4 where this holder of the name is tentatively identified as *Gouti* in Whitelock *ASWills* no. 31 (and p. 136), Sawyer no. 1531, of A.D. 1043 x 1045. That man was associated however with Norfolk rather than Suffolk.
	ERLAND. In the MS *halanalt* has been altered from *halant*. The same man occurs as *harlenat* in 3,62. Both forms seem ultimately to derive from OG *Erland*, Förstemann 773 (J.M.D). Cf. Forssner 142, s.n. *Halanant*.
	ONLY THE PATRONAGE. LDB repeats *tantu(m)* in error.
	£7 10S. LDB *libi* is in error for *lib̄*, anticipating the 'free men'.

3

3,57	NARDRED. Possibly an OG name, but perhaps *Nardred(us)* is in error for *Hardred(us)* from OE *Heardred*; Forssner 193. THE JURISDICTION. IE (143), 'full jurisdiction and patronage from him'. HE WAS IN POSSESSION. Probably referring to Count Alan. (EARL) R(ALPH). Wader. See 1,61-95 note.
3,59	ABOVE LAND ... HUMPHREY HOLDS ... FORFEITED. This appears to refer to part of Nettlestead in 3,56 and to be misplaced here. BETWEEN WOODLAND AND OPEN LAND. Translating *int(er) silua(m) & planu(m)* which, however, probably stands for the OE formula *on wudu and on feld*, that is, it includes both sorts of terrain. WARENGAR. OG *Weringer*, Forssner 246. The LDB form has NFr *G-* for *W-*. Warengar also held from Roger Bigot in Essex (43,1-2). HE HELD (IT) LIKEWISE. Perhaps the subject of this is Count Alan, as in 3,57. (EARL) RALPH. Wader. See 1,61-95 note.
3,61	BARN. An ON byname, 'child', PNDB 192; cf. OEB 237. RALPH THE CONSTABLE BEFORE 1066. LDB *Radulf(us)* is in error for *Radulfo*, due to misreading of final *-o* as the abbreviation mark for *-us*.
3,62	ERLAND. See 3,56 note. NETTLESTEAD. 3,56. THIS ENTRY. IEAL (185) adds '3 free men; 50 acres'.
3,63	BEFORE 1066. In the MS, the text from *t.r.e.* (line 7) to the foot of folio 295a is in a different colour of ink to the preceding text on the page. 20 ACRES. In the MS *xx* has been altered from *xxx* by erasure.
3,64	SAME (THURLESTON). Although Westerfield is the last place named, the reference is back to the name at the beginning of the entry.
3,65	27 ACRES. In the MS *xxvii* has been altered from *xxvi*.
3,67	ERMENGOT. LDB *Ermiot*. The name is probably OG *Ermingaud*, *Ermengaut*, see Forssner 81.
3,68-69	EDEVA. Probably 'the Fair', cf. 3,67.
3,69	BERIA. Unidentified, DG 390.
3,70-71	FULCRIC. LDB *Furic*, representing OG *Fulcric* (PNDB 256-257) with AN loss of *l*.
3,71-74	EDEVA. As 3,68-69 note.
3,71	FULCRIC ... COUNT. This statement is out of place after the jurisdiction and is preceded by a paragraph marker, but seems to refer to Bentley.
3,73	TWO [MANORS]. Those in 3,72-73.
3,74	THEN 5 COBS. Farley adds the abbreviation mark above *r(uncini)*, which is not in the MS. IN LENGTH ... IN WIDTH. LDB *in longe, in latitudo* are in error for *in longo, in latitudine*. IN TAX. In the MS *get* has been altered (? from *gersumma*).
3,75	BEFORE 1066. In the MS *euardi* has been altered from *euau-*. Farley prints as *euaRdi*.
3,76-77	EDEVA. As 3,68-69 note.
3,76	THURSTAN. In the MS a word (? *tainus*, 'thane') has been erased after the pers. n.
3,79-80	LDB *Suuart*, probably in error for *Siuuart*, *Siuuard(us)* from OE *Sigeweard* or ODan *Sigwarth*. Cf. PNDB 378.
3,80	*CANAPETUNA*. See 1,106 note. ABOVE ASSESSMENT. Of Hintlesham in 3,79.
3,81	EDEVA. As 3,68-69 note.
3,83	SAME ASSESSMENT. Of Brantham in 3,82.
3,84	EDEVA. As 3,68-69 note.
3,86	PARHAM HALF-HUNDRED. The abbreviated form in LDB stands for *P(ER)REHAM*, cf. 1,75 etc. MALET. As 1,102 note.
3,88-89	HAMO. Perhaps 'of Valognes", cf. 3,87.
3,89	BROTHER. LDB *Brotho*, from ON *Bróthir*, ODan *Brothir*; PNDB 208.
3,91	[HELD]. LDB *ten&* is in error for *tenuit*. EDHILD. A FREE MAN. The name is OE *Ēadhild* (feminine), PNDB 232. The description of her as *lib(er) h(om)o* is not unusual since this was a description of status, not of gender, which could be applied to either male or female.
3,92	BLAXHALL. In the MS *ii* has been erased after this place-name. It was probably written in anticipation of *iiii* further along the line.
3,93	3 FREE MEN. IE (148) adds, 'under him'.
3,94	SHEEP, NOW 170. In the MS *clxx* has been altered from *clxxx* by erasure.

3,95	IN LORDSHIP, 8 FREE MEN ... ABBOT OF ELY. Cf. IE (149), 'In the same village 3 free men under the patronage of Edric Grim; 60 acres. And 6 other (free men) under the patronage of St. Etheldreda's'. Cf. also IEAL 186, which assigns 1 carucate of land to the 6 (free) men. 8 FREE MEN. In the MS in d(omi)nio has been erased after .viii. ABOVE-MENTIONED EDRIC. Grim, see 3,95. IE (149) adds, '1 free man'. HUNEPOT. According to PNDB 296, the pers. n. may be OG *Hunbod but could also be OE Huna/ON Húni with an added byname pot (bot?). The byname may be either OE *Pott with a meaning 'plump' or 'stupid' (OEB 329-330) or OE *But(t) 'cut off, truncated, short' (OEB 295-296), if Hunebot at 8,16 is the same name. [4 ACRES]. In the MS .iiii. is written above x which has been erased. Farley prints both numerals. 1 LEAGUE. There is an erasure in the MS before i.
3,96	(LITTLE) GLEMHAM. LDB Thieue gliemha(m). The affix may be OE thīfe, 'stolen', cf. BT 1058, s.v. þīfe-feoh.
3,98	85 ACRES. In the MS all except Lx is written over an erasure and is followed by xvi erased. Cf. note on 91 ACRES, below. LATER AND NOW 1; ALWAYS. In the MS p(ost) 7 m(odo) .i. se(m)p(er) is written over an erasure. 2 MEN'S PLOUGHS. In the MS there is an erasure after ho(m inu)m. 91 ACRES. In the MS all except lx is written over an erasure and is followed by an erased numeral. Cf. note on 85 ACRES, above. VALUE ... 60S. In the MS there is an erasure before lx. HIS FATHER. William Malet. 60 ACRES. IEAL (186), 10. ALWAYS 7 SMALLHOLDERS. In the MS vii has been altered from vi.
3,99	OSTULA. A derivative of OG Ost-, Forssner 201, PNDB 340.
3,100	THIS ENTRY. Cf. IE (149), '2 free men under the patronage of St. Etheldreda's, with 20 acres. Count Alan holds this.' Also IEAL (186), '3 free men; 20 acres'.
3,101	TUTFLED. LDB Tutflet. The second element of this feminine pers. n. is OE -flǣd but the first is obscure; PNDB 389. MAGNI. LDB magna, perhaps from ON, ODan Magni (PNDB 323), but possibly from ODan Manni, OSw Manne (PNDB 324). HIS FATHER ... POSSESSION. William Malet. In the MS there is an erasure after fuit, probably the words ant(e)c(essori) malet which were subsequently interlined in a different place.
3,102	WACRA. Perhaps a byname meaning 'watchful, vigilant', either from OE *Wacra or from ON *Vakri; PNDB 407. HAMO ... ALL THIS. 3,99-102.
3,105	CHURCH OF RUMBURGH. See 3,14 note.
4	EARL HUGH. Hugh of Avranches, created Earl of Chester in 1071.
4,2-3	MANUUIC Also at 6,19 and 16,32 (MANEWIC); all in Claydon Hundred. Unidentified, DG 405.
4,3	WAILOLF. LDB Wailolf(us), IE (146) Waiolf(us), probably from OG *Wadalulf, see PNDB 408. UNDER ... PATRONAGE ... ABBOT OF ELY. IE (146) adds, 'in the jurisdiction'.
4,4	YRIC. LDB Iric(us) is explained by PNDB (299-300) as an OE form for ON *Eyríkr.
4,6-7	THORPE (HALL). In Ashfield.
4,6	HUGH ... HOLDS ALL THIS. 4,1-6.
4,10	SKULI. LDB Scula; ON Skúli, ODan Skuli, OSw Skule, see PNDB 366. Note that in the Nottinghamshire volume (10,23;52. 30,28) the spelling Escul for this name was incorrectly interpreted as Aswulf.
4,11	... CARUCATE. LDB omits the numeral.
4,13	; ALWAYS ...; Farley prints a curled dash before se(m)p(er), representing what in the MS is a cross-bar to a capital T which was never completed. This was probably an anticipation of T in T(u)nc on the line below. The word se(m)p(er) also seems to be otiose, probably anticipating its occurrence further along the line. BIGOT OF LOGES. From Loges (Calvados), OEB 95. Note that the first reference given in OEB is not however to Bigot but to Gerwy of Loges, see Gloucestershire 76,1. For the byname Bigot, see 7 note, with reference to Roger Bigot. Bigot of Loges may be identical with Roger Bigot, or with a relative of his, since Roger's son held land at Loges in 1133, see Loyd 14-15.

	7½D IN TAX. Farley *gelt(o)* is in error for *get* of MS.
	THROUGH HIS (OWN) POSSESSION. Translating *p(er) sua(m) sesina(m)* and referring to a public ceremony in which lawful possession had been transferred to Count Alan.
4,14	R(OBERT) OF COURSON. Cf. 7,8. He came from Courson (Calvados), OEB 85.
4,15	MUNULF. The name is either OSw or OG, see PNDB 331.
	FROM HIM. From Munulf.
	BRUNWIN. MS *Brunwin(us)* altered from *Buin Win(us)*, Farley *BRunWin(us)*.
	MUNULF'S. LDB *Munolf* is in error for *Munolfi*.
	ASMOTH. LDB *Esmoda*. The name is ODan, see PNDB 168.
	TOLI THE SHERIFF. Of Suffolk and Norfolk under Edward the Confessor, see Harmer, *ASWrits* nos. 20, 25, 61; Sawyer nos. 1080, 1085, 1109; Hart ECEE nos. 115, 119, 135. See Norfolk 1,229 etc.
	BRICTMER, R(OBERT) MALET'S REEVE. Perhaps the same as Brictmer the Beadle in 74,4.
	INGOLD. This represents an Anglo-Scandinavian form of ON *Ingialdr*, ODan *Ingeld*, OSw *Ing(i)aeld*; PNDB 297-298.
	WALTER OF CAEN. From Caen (Calvados), OEB 79.
	WALTER OF DOL. From Dol or Dol-de-Bretagne (Ille-et-Villaine), OEB 86. He was exiled in 1075.
4.17	BURGH. In the MS *burh* has been altered from *burc*.
	COUNTESS EDEVA. Probably the same as Edeva the Rich or Fair. See 1,61 note.
4,18	[HALF]. LDB omits *dim̃*.
4,19	5 CARUCATES ... BEFORE 1066. In the MS *t.r.e.* has been erased but is still partially visible. Farley retains it.
	ALWAYS 3 CATTLE. In the MS there is an erasure after *an(imalia)*, as shown by Farley's gaps on this line and the next.
	40 ACRES AS 1 MANOR. In the MS *m(anerio)* is interlined above a blotted attempt at alteration which precedes an erasure.
	SUMMERLED. LDB *Sumerlet*, from ON *Sumarlithr*; PNDB 377-378.
	FOURTH PART OF 1 MILL. In the MS there is an erasure after *mol(endini)*, probably of *T(u)nc*, anticipating the next line.
4,20	WARIN SON OF BURNIN. LDB *Warin(us) filius Burñ*; below (4,29) -*burnnini*. The forename is OG *Warin*, Forssner 246-247; this perhaps makes less likely the suggestion (OEB 176) that the patronym is OE *Byrnwine*. Cf. also Burnin in 4,32.
4,24	THERE COULD BE ... LDB omits the numeral.
4,25	MANOR WHICH THE KING HOLDS. That at 1,110.
	... WHOLE OF THIS. For the name, see 4,20 note.
4,29	WARIN SON OF BURNIN ... WHOLE OF THIS. For the name, see 4,20 note. This sentence probably refers to 4,21-29.
4,30	MUNDRED ... HELD. In the MS *q(uod)* is squeezed between *mundret(us)* and *ten(uit)* as an insertion, probably made at the same time as the overline insertion of *ten&*.
	MUNDRED. Apparently OE *Mundrǣd*, PNDB 331. He may also have held the City of Chester and other lands from Earl Hugh in Cheshire (C24. 1,22;34. 2,13. 26,3). Note that the translated form in the Cheshire volume should read Mundred not Mundret.
	ALWAYS 1 COB. In the MS *ea* has been erased before *r(uncinus)*. Farley shows the erasure by the use of dots, but no text seems to be missing.
4,31	CROSCROFT. Unidentified, DG 396.
	SOTTERLEY ... TAX. Misplaced ere in 4,31 rather than in 4,30.
4,32	W. THE CONSTABLE. Not found elsewhere in LDB.
	EARL R(ALPH). Wader, see 1,61-95 note.
	HELD IT. LDB *qua(m)* either stands as a pronoun for *terra* or is in error for *que(m)* referring to the free man.
	BURNIN. Apparently the same name as that which formed the patronym of Warin in 4,20;29. It might refer to Warin's father, but could also be a short form for Warin son of Burnin himself.
4,33	HETHEBURGAFELLA. The same as HATHEBURGFELDA in 31,24. In Wangford Hundred. Unidentified, DG 400.
4,36	RODENHALA. Also at 31,28. In Lothing Hundred. Unidentified, DG 409.
	R(ALPH) BAYNARD. See *33* and note.
4,39	FREE [MEN]. LDB *lib(er)os* has been corrected from *lib(er)is*.
	HUGH ... HOLDS THE WHOLE OF THIS. 4,36-39.

4,41	SAME MAN. Probably Gyrth of 4,40.
	[16] ACRES. MS *xvi*; Farley prints *xv* in error.
4,42	R(OGER) BIGOT. In the MS the name is added in the inner margin.
	UNDER ... AELMER AND. In the MS there is an erasure from 7 to the end of the line.
	6 WHOLE FREE MEN. LDB *integros lib(er)os* is in error for *integri lib(er)i*.
	IN THE SAME ... 1 FREE MAN. The numeral has been inserted between *eade(m)* and *lib(er)*.
	1 VILLAGER. LDB *uill(an)i* is in error for *uill(an)us*.
	ETHEREG. Unidentified, DG 397.
	[ST.] ETHELDREDA'S. LDB *soca* is in error for *sancta*.
5	COUNT EUSTACE. Of Boulogne, brother-in-law of King Edward.
5,2	JURISDICTION. IE (141), 'full jurisdiction'.
	60 ACRES. IEAL (189), 40.
	ALDRED. LDB *heldret*, from OE *Ealdrǣd*; cf. PNDB 241-242.
	7 ACRES. IEAL, 6.
5,3-5	ENGELRIC. The predecessor of Count Eustace in many of his lands, particularly in Essex (chapter 20). The founder of St. Martin le Grand in London. See also 14,101 note.
5,4	(LITTLE) FINBOROUGH. Identified, VCH 444, n.51.
5,5	BUXHALL. FD no. 9 is a writ 1066 x 1087 of King William which orders that the men of Frodo in Buxhall taken away by Count Eustace's men are to be returned to the Abbot of St. Edmund's.
5,6	WITH 4 ACRES; 24 ... In the MS *de iiii acr(is)*. *7 xxiiii* has been written over an erasure; *ac.* follows but has been erased.
	RALPH OF MARCY. From Marcy (La Manche), OEB 97.
5,7	*STANFELDA*. Unidentified, DG 410.
	HATO. OG *Hatho, Hatto* ; Förstemann 790 (J.M.D.).
5,8	SAME ASSESSMENT. That in 5,7.
6	ROBERT MALET. Sheriff of Suffolk at same time between 1066 and 1086. The son of William Malet and member of a family which came from Graville-Ste-Honorine (Seine-Inf.), see Loyd 56. His extensive Holding, mainly in Suffolk, was later known as the Honour of Eye (cf. 6,191). The byname is OFr *malet*, a diminutive of *mal* 'evil', OEB 350-351. The main predecessor of William and Robert was Edric of Laxfield (6,305 and note). For Robert's mother, see 6,76-77 note.
6,1	WINTER MILL. *Mol(endinum) hyemal(e)*, a mill on a winterbourne, where the flow of water in summer was insufficient to turn the wheel.
6,2	THE COUNT. Presumably an error for Robert Malet. The scribe was no doubt affected by the three preceding comital chapters.
	PLOUGHS ... AND BETWEEN THE MEN. The meaning is probably 'a further 2 ploughs between the men'.
	THE SAME 3 FREE MEN. Translating *.iii. ide(m) lib(er)i ho(min)es*, but this may be in error for *in eade(m) .iii. lib(er)i ho(min)es*.
6,3	ROBERT OF GLANVILLE. From Glanville (Calvados), OEB 89-90.
6,4	PREDECESSOR. Farley shows an erasure in the MS after *antec(essor)* by the use of four dots.
	CUSTOMARY DUES. In the MS *consuetudins* has been altered from *consuetudine(m)*.
6,5	DAM. *excluse* (genitive singular) from *exclusa*. Probably a fish-weir.
6,7	'OLDEN'. As 1,5 note.
6,10-11	WILLIAM GOULAFRE. LDB *gulaf(f)ra*; the byname is OFr *goulafre, gouliafre*, 'glutton', OEB 347.
6,11	ABBOT. Of Ely. Cf. 21,31. In the present chapter, all unspecified references to 'the Abbot' refer to Ely.
	30 ACRES ... IN ANOTHER HUNDRED. The precise significance is not apparent. Debenham (in Claydon Hundred) bordered on Bosmere, Hartismere, and Loes Hundreds.
	IN THE SAME ... 11 FREE MEN ... In the MS thre is an erasure after *xi*.
	SAXI, RANULF PEVEREL'S PREDECESSOR. Cf. 34,12.
6,12	THORPE (HALL). In Ashfield.
6,18	CHURCH OF ST. MARY. For the rest of it, see 16,28 and 34,12.
	TO ANSWER FOR. Translating *ad defendu(m)* and preserving the ambiguity of the Latin. This may refer to a fiscal liability on the part of Robert, or to a duty to maintain this proportion of the church. The contemporary cross in the left-hand margin of the MS (not shown by Farley) may have been meant to draw attention to this ambiguity.

	CHURCH OF ST. ANDREW. For the rest of it, see 16,28.
6,19	MANUUIC. As 4,2-3 note.
6,20	UNDER PATRONAGE. In the MS there is an erasure after *co(m)m(en)d(ati)*.
6,21-22	JURISDICTION ... SAME WAY. Divided between the Abbot and Earl Hugh, as in 6,20.
6,21;23	THORPE (HALL). In Ashfield.
6,23	TIGIER. LDB *Tiger(us)*; OFr *Tigier* from OG *Thiodger*, Forssner 234. The source of the surname *Tigar*, according to DBS 349.
6,25	THORPE (HALL). In Ashfield.
6,27	HUBERT HOLDS (THIS). This probably includes 6,26 too.
6,28	BRUTGE. Also at 67,5. In Parham Hundred. Unidentified, DG 393.
	WALTER DE RISBOIL. Below (6,284), *de Risbou*. His place of origin is unidentified.
6,30	121 ACRES. These no doubt represent the land held by the 22 free men but were misplaced in LDB.
	GILBERT OF WISSANT. From Wissant (Pas-de-Calais), OEB 120-121.
	WILLIAM OF ÉMALLEVILLE. LDB *de malauill'*, below (6,33) *desmala uill'*. From Émalleville (Eure), OEB 114-115, Loyd 40.
6,32	NIUETUNA. Unidentified, DG 407.
	[PLOUGH]. LDB omits *car(uca)*.
	[ACRES]. LDB omits *ac(re)*.
6,33-34	Cf. IE (151), 'a half free man under the patronage of St. Etheldreda's; 10 acres. ½ plough. Value 3s. Also 1 free man; 12 acres. Value 2s. Another (free man); 2 acres. Value 4d.'
6,34	OF HIS PREDECESSOR. That is, of Robert Malet's predecessor.
6,41-42	CHELETUNA, CHILETUNA. The same as KELETUNA in 6,288. In Plomesgate Hundred. Unidentified, DG 394. Cf. VCH 447, n. 55 for a possible later reference.
6,43	OF THIS MANOR. Referring to *Chiletuna* in 6,42.
6,44	90 ACRES. In the MS the numeral and the 'acres' are written on either side of a hole (now repaired) in the parchment of folio 308a. See also 6,46 note.
6,45	OF HIS PREDECESSOR. As 6,34 note.
6,46	ROBERT OF CLAVILLE. From Claville-en-Caux (Seine-Inf.), Loyd 29; cf. OEB 82.
	VALUE THEN 10S. In the MS on folio 308b *ual(uit)*. and *x. sol(idos)* are written on either side of the same hole which affects 6,44 on the other side of the leaf.
	ROBERT SON OF FULCRED. The patronym is more probably OG **Fulcrad* than OE *Folcrǣd*; cf. Forssner 98-99.
	AETHELWY. LDB *Ailwi*; OE *Aethelwīg*, PNDB 189.
	HARDWIN. LDB *haruin(us)*; OG *Hardwin*, PNDB 286-287, Forssner 143.
6,48	5 SMALLHOLDERS. Misplaced in LDB among the ploughs.
	ALWIN. It is not certain whether this is the name of the free man, or of the half free man.
6,49	ROBERT ... LIKEWISE. 'Likewise' may refer to the jurisdiction, belonging to the Abbot as in 6,48.
	LEOFRIC. Perhaps the name of one of the free men. As *Leuric(us)* is in the nominative it cannot (unless there is an error here) be associated with *co(m)mend(ati)*.
6,51	ALWYNN. LDB *Aluuem* is in error for *Aluuen*, from late OE *Alwynn* (feminine), PNDB 160-161.
	FREE MAN. See note to 3,91 *sub* EDHILD.
6,54	UNDER PATRONAGE; 1½ ACRES. In the MS there is an erasure after *c(om)m(en)d(atus)*, perhaps of *xx*.
6,55	BADINGHAM. LDB *hadincha(m)* is in error for *b-*, cf. 6,306.
6,57	FROM ROBERT. Malet.
	ROBERT BLUNT. Cf. 66,16.
6,59	SAME ASSESSMENT. Of Westhorpe in 6,58.
6,61	PENNIES. Translating *nu(m)mos*.
	VALUE OF THE WHOLE OF THIS, 21S. It is not clear to what this refers.
6,62	4 COBS, 6 CATTLE. In the MS *7 .iiii. r(uncini). 7 vi. an(imalia)* is written over an erasure.
	RICKINGHALL. LDB *kikingahala* is in error for *R-*.
	ST. E(DMUND'S). Cf. 14,46.
6,63	WILLIAM SHIELD. LDB *scutet*. The byname is from OFr **Escuet*, equivalent to Lat. *scutatus*, 'equipped with a shield', OEB 372. A man of this name was one of King William's cooks, see *Regesta* i, no. 270 and Wiltshire 2,4 etc.
6,66	[HELD]. LDB *ten&* is in error for *tenuit*.
6,67	WILLIAM OF CAEN. Perhaps in error for Walter of Caen, cf. 6,5 etc.

6,69	CARLTON. At 3,94 this was assigned to Plomesgate Hundred, but the present entry appears to belong to Bishop's Hundred through its association with the neighbouring Kelsale, a detached part of Bishop's Hundred.
6,70;74	ALDRINGHAM. This was subsequently in Blything Hundred but seems in 1086 to have been a detached part of Bishop's Hundred.
6,76-77	LAND OF ROBERT MALET'S MOTHER. Robert's mother, the widow of William Malet, held several estates in Suffolk in 1086. She was in dispute with the Bishop of Bayeux concerning some of them, see 77.
	OF THE QUEEN'S HOLDING. Robert's mother held other estates from this Holding in Suffolk (6,209;229-230. 77,1). In Norfolk (7,14) she held Burston which was said to be *ex dono regine*.
6,78	BLYTHING HUNDRED. IN DARSHAM. In the MS the *H*' was originally placed after *dersa(m)* but was subsequently erased and another one interlined above *Blidinga*.
6,79	EDRIC WAS OUTLAWED. Edric of Laxfield is meant here.
	A WRIT AND A SEAL. Probably a sealed writ rather than two separate items.
6,80	HUNTINGFIELD. Farley uses dots before and after *huntingafelda* to indicate erasures in the MS. The erasure after the name was of *H*' (cf. 6,78 note).
	IDLE CATTLE. Translating *an(imalia) otiosa*. Cattle not used in ploughing.
6,81	1 MANOR. LDB *man* has an otiose abbreviation mark.
6,82	(IN) HUNTINGFIELD. LDB *huntingafelde* may represent an OE dative (locative) case, rather than a Latin genitive. Cf. *in huntingafelda* with reference to the 40 acres, below.
	TO THIS MANOR. Of Linsted, in 6,81.
6,83	[PARK]. LDB *porcu(m)* in error for *parcu(m)*. See 1,101 note.
	CHURCHES. LDB *aeccl(esi)a* is in error for *aeccl(esi)ae*.
6,84	THE SEA ... (CARUCATE). Half the arable has been washed away by the sea, apparently since 1066. LDB *alia* is in error for *alia(m)*.
	POOR MEN. Cf. the 'poor burgesses' of Ipswich in 1,122c.
	ROBERT OF VAUX. OEB 117 was unable to locate the particular place from which Robert was named, due to the frequency of the place-name occurrence in France.
	GILBERT BLUNT. For the byname see note on Robert Blunt (66).
6,85	LEAGUES IN WIDTH. In the MS an attempt has been made to alter *liug* (? to *leug*), but the result is not very clear; *lat(itudine)* is written over an erasure.
6,89a	ORA. As 1,94 note.
6,89b	CORPORAL PUNISHMENT. Mutilation, if not hanging.
6,90	60 AND 13 SHEEP. Perhaps in error for '60 [cattle *or* pigs] and 13 sheep', if a word has been omitted from LDB, but perhaps a total of 73 sheep is intended.
6,91	UURABRETUNA. As 3,15 note *sub WRABET UNA*.
	ASMOTH. LDB *amod*; ODan *Asmoth*, PNDB 168.
6,92	... PIGS. 1 PLOUGH. MEADOW ... The plough is misplaced among the resources.
6,94	WALTER SON OF RICHERE. The patronym is OG; Forssner 214-215.
	THEN 1 PLOUGH. In the MS (folio 313a) the words *T(u)nc.i.* are separated from *car(uca)* by a hole in the parchment (later repaired). Cf. 6,100 note.
6,96	IN WESTLETON. The solitary capital *I* at the end of the preceding line probably represents a false start in the writing of *In*.
6,97	EDRIC ... UNDER THE PATRONAGE OF EDRIC. The subordinate Edric is probably the same as the one in 6,78-79 who was under the patronage of Edric of Laxfield.
6,98	ABOVE-MENTIONED STANWIN. See 6,92.
	WALTER OF CAEN. In the MS *Galteri(us) de* and *cadomo* are separated by a hole in the parchment.
	TALK. LDB *Talcha*; a byname possibly related to OE **tealcian*, 'to talk', PNDB 382.
6,99	WARABETUNA. As 3,15 note *sub WRABETUNA*.
6,100	HOPPETUNA. The same as OPITUNA (7,29). In Blything Hundred. Unidentified, DG 402.
	MEADOW, 2 ACRES and 18 ACRES. In the MS (folio 313b) the last two lines of this page begin further to the right than the preceding ones, because of the hole in the parchment which also affects 6,94 on the other side of the leaf.
6,106	OSFERTH. His land formed part of the Holding of Peter who became a 'feudal man' of Abbot Baldwin of St. Edmund's 1066 x 1087, see FD xc-xci and no. 168.
	IN THE ASSESSMENT. The *o* of *p(re)tio* is written suprascript in the MS, as in Farley, because of a hole in the parchment.
6,108	WRABBATUNA. As 3,15 note *sub WRABETUNA*.
6,109	SWART HOGA. The fore-name is ON *Svartr*, ODan, OSw *Swart*, PNDB 379. The byname is OE *hoga*, 'careful, prudent', OEB 347.

	ULF SON OF MANNI SWART. Apparently the same as Ulf son of 'Mannig Sparcingesone' mentioned in British Library, Additional MS 14847, folio 24, as having given Chippenhall to St. Edmund's Abbey (cf. 14,105); see VCH 504 n.132 and Hart ECEE no. 368. For his father, see 3,1 note.
6,110	WULFMER. Apparently the same as Wulfmer the priest, whose land formed part of the same Holding as that of Osferth in 6,106 note.
	'STRUOSTUNA'. The same as 'STRUUSTUNA' 7,88; 'STRUESTUNA' 7,103;105. A lost place in Kirton, DG 412.
	GLEMAN. LDB *Gleman(us)*; OE **Glīwmann*, associated with OE *glīwmann, glēomann*, 'minstrel, jester', ModE *gleeman*, PNDB 262.
	CARLEWUDA. Unidentified, DG 394.
	HOPEWELLA. Unidentified, DG 402. The suggestion OEB 45, that it may be Hopewell, Derbyshire, is very unlikely.
	KYLUERTESTUNA. The same as *KULUERTESTUNA* (7,118) and *CULUERDESTUNA* (31,11), all in Colneis Hundred. It is formally (and perhaps actually) identical with Kilverstone in Norfolk (*Culuer(s)testuna*), part of which (Norfolk 7,3) was held by Robert Malet in 1086 after someone called Edric. DG 404,396 does not identify.
	MODGEVA. OE **Mōdgifu*, PNDB 328.
	BERNARD ... HALF FREE MAN. The three lines *Bernard(us) ... dim(idius) lib(er) h(om)o* inset by Farley are thus in the MS to avoid a hole (later repaired) in the parchment.
	R(OBERT) OF CLAVILLE. For the byname, see 6,46 note. LDB *de clauilla* has an otiose abbreviation mark, probably due to confusion with *de glauilla* which occurs as a form for Robert of Glanville's name (6,157;291 etc).
6,111	'MYCELEGATA'. Also at 7,110. Lost, in Trimley; DG 406.
6,112	UNFRID SON OF ROBERT. LDB *ymfrid(us)*, below at 6,122 *Vmfrid(us)*; OG *Unfrid, Unfred, Umfred*, Forssner 236. Here taken to be distinct, because of the name-forms, from Humphrey at 6,125.
	THE QUEEN. Edith, as 1,122a-122b note.
	A CUSTOMARY DUE. LDB *consuetudo* (nominative singular) may be in error for the accusative singular *consuetudinem*; if so, Robert also had this.
6,113	*NECCHEMARA*. The same as [*NECKEMARA*] at 32,25 and *NECHEMARA* at 67,13. All in Carlford Hundred. Unidentified, DG 406.
6,114	3 FREE MEN; 3. The second numeral is probably otiose here.
	ROBERT ... FULL JURISDICTION. LDB *soca & saca* is in error for *soca(m) & saca(m)*.
	OSLAC. His land formed part of the same Holding as that of Osferth in 6,106 note.
6,115	THE SMALLEST WALDRINGFIELD. LDB *minima Waldringafelda*.
6,117	*HOPESTUNA*. The same as *HOBBESTUNA* in 32,30. In Carlford Hundred. Unidentified, DG 402.
	ST. ETHELDREDA'S. In the MS *A* has been altered from *E*.
6,118	LUSTWIN. OE *Lustwine*, PNDB 322.
	JURISDICTION. LDB *soca* is in error for *soca(m)*.
	THEY DWELL. But LDB *manent* may be in error for *manebant*, 'they dwelt'.
6,120	ANOTHER FREE MAN. In the MS *alius* has been altered from *aliud*; Farley prints as *aliuS*.
6,122	UNFRID SON OF ROBERT. See 6,112 note.
	HOLDS ALL THIS. Referring to 6,113-122.
6,125	AS 1 MANOR. HUMPHREY HOLDS. In the MS between *M(anerio)* and *& ten&* an interlined insertion of text has been erased. The insertion seems to have duplicated the text on the following two lines from *T(u)nc to .iiii. ac(re)*.
	UNDER HIM. LDB *sub se* is in error for *sub eo*.
6,127	GILBERT OF COLEVILLE. From Coleville (Seine-Inf.), Loyd 30. Cf. OEB 83.
6,130	ARKELL. LDB *Archillus*; ON *Arnkell*, ODan *Arnketil*, PNDB 163.
6,132	WALTER SON OF GRIP HELD ALL THIS. The patronym is OWScand *Grípr*, ODan *Grip*; OEB 185. LDB *tenuit* is probably in error for *ten&*. The statement refers to 6,130-132.
6,133	GILBERT BLUNT ... FROM. In LDB *blon.de.* is corrected to *blvnd(us). de*.
6,134	G(ILBERT). Blunt, as 6,133.
6,136	THORPE. In Aldringham, DG 413.
6,137	DENNINGTON. Farley *dinguiet* is in error for MS *dingiuet*, an abbreviated form for *dingiuetuna, -tona* (cf. 6,264;266-269;289).
6,138	FREE MEN. In the MS *lib(er)os* has been altered from *lib(er)i*.
6,141	MEADOW, 1 ACRE. LDB repeats this in error.
6,142	*CLE'PHAM*. Unidentified, DG 395. The LDB form may be for *CLEMPHAM*.

6,143	12 FREE MEN. As 6,138 note.
6,144	*BURGESGATA*. Unidentified, DG 393.
6,145	*BURCH*. Unidentified, DG 393.
6,146	*INGOLUESTUNA*. Unidentified, DG 403. In Plomesgate Hundred. Perhaps distinct from the place of the same name in Carlford Hundred (21,65 etc).
6,147	*PRESTETUNA*. Unidentified, DG 408.
	[ACRE]. LDB omits *acr(a)*.
6,148	FISHERY. LDB *piscat* is for *piscat(io)*. See 1,115 note.
	7D IN TAX. *p(er) totu(m) hundret* deleted in LDB after *.vii. d(enarii).*; *p(er) totu(m) Hund(ret)* was subsequently added on the next line after *soca(m)*.
6,150	1 ACRE. In the MS there is an erasure after *acr(is)*.
6,151	'LANEBURH'. The same as 'LANEBURC' at 6,173-174. Lost in Sutton, DG 404.
6,153	'TURSTANESTUNA'. Also at 11,2 ('THUR-') and 26,19 ('TOR-'). Lost in Bromeswell, DG 414.
6,154	THEY ARE ALL ... HOLLESLEY. That is 6,150-154.
6,155	LEOFSTAN. His land formed part of the same Holding as that of Osferth in 6,106 note. Apparently identical with Leofstan in 16,26.
6,156	'CULESLEA' Lost in Alderton, DG 396.
6,160	R(OBERT) OF GLANVILLE ... WHOLE OF THIS. Referring to 6,158-160.
6,164	12 ACRES. IE (162), '12 acres of the lordship (of St. Etheldreda's)'.
6,165	GODWIN. The other half of his patronage belonged to St. Etheldreda's, IE (162). He is called Godwin 'of Sutton' in 6,169.
	9 FREE MEN ... 1 FREE MAN. IE, '10 free men in the jurisdiction and patronage of St. Etheldreda's'.
6,167	ACRES. In the MS *acr(e)* has been altered from *ar-*.
6,168	WALTER ... ROBERT MALET. This sentence was added later to this entry in the MS.
6,169	6S 2D. IE (162), 7s 2d.
	MAYNARD. LDB *Menard(us)*; from OG *Maganhard, Mainard*, Forssner 181.
	CLAIMS. LDB *calu(m)piat(ur)* is in error for *calu(m)pniat(ur)*. In the MS the *p* has been altered from *n*.
	EARL R(ALPH). Wader, see 1,61-95 note.
	GODWIN OF SUTTON. Named from Sutton (6,165).
6,171	FREEMAN. MS *socmanū*, for *soc(he)manv(m)*. Farley prints the abbreviation for *-us* above the *c* in error.
	AEDI. The form may represent an otherwise unrecorded OE *Ēadig*, PNDB 171-172.
6,172	HUMPHREY SON OF R. Cf. Humphrey son of Rodric in 26,1.
	... POSSIBLE. LDB omits the numeral.
6,173-174	'LANEBURC'. See 6,151 note.
	VALUE [12]D. Farley *xx* is in error for *xii* of MS.
	WALTER ... (THIS). *in d(omi)nio* 'in lordship' deleted in LDB after *ten&*.
6,176	'HALGESTOU'. Lost in Shottisham, DG 400.
6,177	MALET. Robert Malet.
6,179-180	FREE MEN. As 6,138 note.
6,179	CHARSFIELD. Here and at 31,18 assigned to Wilford Hundred, but elsewhere in the neighbouring Hundred of Loes.
	TO THE CHURCH. LDB *Ecl(es)iae* is in error for *Eccl-*. In the MS a capital *I* has been erased beneath *E-*.
6,181	WULFWIN. Farley *Wlfuim*, although in the MS the final letter seems to be intended as *n* (followed by a partially erased otiose stroke).
6,183	FREE MEN. As 6,138 note.
6,187	[OF LAND]. LDB omits *t(er)rae*.
	1 PLOUGH, NOW 2. *nulla* 'none' deleted in LDB, *.ii.* interlined.
6,189	MEADOW ... ½ PLOUGH. The items are out of their usual order in LDB.
6,190	FREE MEN. As 6,138 note.
6,191	ROBERT ... IN LORDSHIP. In the MS there is an erasure after *d(omi)nio*.
	FISHERY. LDB *piscatio*. See 1,115 note.
	WALTER THE CROSSBOWMAN. MS *arbat̄* with a single vertical stroke above the *r*, as in Farley. Perhaps an attempt to change the word to *Albat̄*, for AN *alblaster*, instead of Latin *arbalistarius*; cf. OEB 234-235.
	THAT IS, WHAT THE BISHOP ... HAD. Interlined in LDB as an explanatory gloss; *habeb(er)e* is in error for *habuisse*.

	THEN 4½ PLOUGHS. In the MS *7* has been erased after *T(u)nc*.
	DYNECHAIE. This form is corrupt. J.M.D. suggests that it may be a misreading of *Dyrechaie*, standing for ODan *Thyri* with the byname *kai* 'left-handed'.
	SWARTRIK. LDB *suartric(us)*, from ON **Svartríkr*; PNDB 380.
6,193	SMERT. Of uncertain origin according to PNDB 367; but perhaps LDB *Smert* is for *Siuert* from OE *Sigefrith* (cf. 7,77 and PNDB 360).
	WYNSTAN. LDB *Pinstan*, with *P-* in error for the Anglo-Saxon letter wynn; PNDB 429.
6,194	STUBHARD. LDB *Stubart*. The second element is OE *-heard* or OG *-hard*; the first element may be OE *stubb*, 'stub, stump' but is not certain, see PNDB 376-377.
	[AND]. LDB omits *7*.
6,195	MELLIS. The abbreviation mark in LDB, on the first *l*, is otiose.
	[MAN]. LDB omits *h(om)o*.
	FULCARD. The name is OG, PNDB 256.
6,196	YAXLEY. *Lacheleia* in Farley is in error for *l-* in the MS. Cf. 6,229 note.
6,199	IN THORNHAM PARVA. LDB *In paruo thornha(m)*.
6,200	THORNHAM MAGNA. LDB *Marthorham, Martonham* (6,214); *Mar-* represents OE *māra*, 'greater', DEPN 467.
6,201	[HOLDS THIS] LDB omits *ten&*.
6,202	ALWARD. LDB *AWart, Alwart*; late OE *Alweard*, PNDB 155-157.
6,203	[HOLDS THIS]. As 6,201 note.
6,205	3S. In LDB *.vi.d(enarios)* has been deleted and *.iii. sol(idos)* interlined, along with the first line of 6,206 which had previously been omitted.
6,207	FRESSINGFIELD. Geographically this is in Bishop's Hundred, although the previous Hundred rubric is that of Hartismere. It has been mapped in Bishop's Hundred. Cf. following note.
6,208	KNETTISHALL. Elsewhere this is placed in Blackbourn Hundred. Here both the previous and the subsequent Hundred rubric relates to Hartismere Hundred, suggesting that some intervening rubrics have been omitted from LDB. Cf. preceding note.
6,212	CALDECOTA. Probably identical with *KALDECOTES* 14,136; *CALDECOTA* 14,149; *CALDECOTEN* 31,37; *CALDECOTAN* 31,39; and *CALDECOTA* 41,8. Although the name is of a common type, all these entries are assigned to Hartismere Hundred. Unidentified, DG 393.
	WALTER OF DOL ... FORFEITED. He was exiled in 1075. For the byname, see 4,15 note.
6,213	WULFEVA HAS THE JURISDICTION. LDB *hab&* may be in error for *habuit*, 'had', but Wulfeva was alive in 1075 (see 6,212 and preceding note).
6,214	THORNHAM MAGNA. See 6,200 note.
6,215	BRUNGAR. LDB *brungart*; OE *Brūngār*, PNDB 209.
	WALTER OF DOL ... FORFEITED. In LDB *fecit fecit* has been deleted and *.forisfecit*. interlined. See also 6,212 note.
	16 SHEEP. In the MS *v* has been erased before *xvi*.
6,216	ALSI NEPHEW OF EARL R(ALPH). Cf. 8,50 for the full name-form. Reference is probably to Earl Ralph the Constable.
	RINGWULF. LDB *Ringulf(us)*; OE *Hringwulf*, PNDB 293.
	BESI. Possibly from ODan *Bǿsi*, OSw *Bǿse*; PNDB 201.
	AUBREY DE VERE. Cf. 35,7-8.
	SORCBES. According to PNDB 368, a corrupt form of a name with Scand. *Svart-* as first element. Perhaps an Anglo-Scandinavian formation **Svart-thiofr* (J.M.D.).
	VALUE 12D. In the MS *ual* has been erased above *ual(&)*.
	CHIPPING. LDB *Chipinc*; OE *Cypping*, PNDB 221-222.
6,217	TEIT. ON *Teitr*, ODan, OSw *Tet*; PNDB 382.
6,218	IN THORNHAM PARVA. LDB *In paruo thornham*.
	14 ACRES. In the MS *xiiij* has been altered from *xiii*.
6,222	9D IN TAX. In the MS there is an erasure before *ix*.
6,223	3 MEN'S PLOUGHS. In the MS the first letter of *ho(minu)m* has been altered (? from *e*).
	[THEN] 200 PIGS. LDB omits *t(u)nc*.
6,226	BRICTMER BUBBA. The byname is probably an original OE nickname *Bubba*, denoting someone of a thickset stature, see OEB 296.
6,229	YAXLEY. As 6,196 note.
	HAGRIS. Possibly as Scand. byname, **Há-Gríss*, 'the tall *Gríss*'; PNDB 282.
	ROBERT'S MOTHER ... FROM THE QUEEN'S HOLDING. Referring to 6,209-229.

6,232	BEDINGFIELD. Here assigned to Hartismere Hundred, but elsewhere in the neighbouring Bishop's Hundred.
6,234	BROMESWELL. In the MS *brumeswella* has been altered from *bui-*.
6,238	GODRIC OF PEYTON. See 27,13.
6,242	EDRIC. LDB *edic* is in error for *edric(i)*.
6,247	14 FREE MEN. These appear to have been divided equally between Morewin and St. Etheldreda's, see IE (163) 'Under him, 7 free men with 20 acres. Meadow, 5 acres. Then 1 plough, now ½. Value 10s.'
6,250	['HUNDESTHOFT']. LDB *hundesthost* in error. The same as *HUNDESTUF* 21,82. The second element is ON *topt*, ODan. late OE *toft*, 'a house-plot'. Lost in Sutton, DG 402. FREE MEN. As 6,138 note.
6,254	SUTTON. LDB *stituna* is in error for *suttuna*.
6,256	[2] ACRES. Farley *viii* in error. In the MS *viii* has been altered to *ii* by erasure. VALUE 4D. The vertical line in Farley after the value is in error for *I* in the MS, being a false start for *In* of the following line.
6,261	FREE MAN. In the MS the first letter of *lib(eru)m* has been altered from *h-*.
6,264	EDRIC OF LAXFIELD. LDB *Edrici* is in error for *Edric(us)*. AND 14. Presumably 14 acres not included in the outlier. [PLOUGH]. LDB omits *car(uca)*. ASSESSMENT OF THE (PLACE) ABOVE. That is, of Dennington. FREEWOMAN. Translating LDB *soc(he)femina*. IEVA. Standing for OE *Gi(e)fu, *Geofu; PNDB 260. THORKELL. His land formed part of the same Holding as that of Osferth in 6,106 note.
6,265	WILLIAM ALSO HOLDS. Apparently in error for Walter (of Caen), cf. 6,264.
6,266-267	IN LORDSHIP. LDB *in d(omi)niu(m)* is in error for *in d(omi)nio*. See also 6,267 note.
6,267	HACHESTON. LDB *h& cetuna*, that is *h(et)cetuna*, is in error for *heccetuna*, from OE *Haecci* and *tūn*, see DEPN 209. AND 28. That is, 28 acres in some way separate from the 60 there. HE HOLDS (THIS) IN LORDSHIP. In the MS the words *& ten(et) i(n) d(omi)niu(m)* were added slightly later. See also 6,266-267 note.
6,270	SAME ASSESSMENT. Of Dennington, as in 6,269.
6,271	ALWAYS 1 PLOUGH. VALUE ... HUNA. This is an addition in the right-hand margin, much closer in to the main text than is shown in Farley. VALUE 7 ... LDB omits the unit of currency, probably shillings. TIGIER HOLDS IT. In LDB *q(uo)d ten& tiger(us)* was interlined at the same time as the addition was made in the right-hand margin. WOODBROWN. LDB *Vdebrun*, OE *Wudu-Brūn*, possibly 'Brūn who lives in the wood'; PNDB 417. THIS ENTRY. Cf. IE (151). 'In KENTON 1 free man, Edric, under the patronage of St. E(theldreda's); 30 acres. Value 5s. R(obert) Malet holds him, and R(oger) Bigot.' Also IEAL (183), in the Holding of Hamo of Saint-Clair, 'but Robert Malet had a half of the man'. Hamo, from Saint-Clair-sur-Elle (Manche), Loyd 88, is not named in LDB or IE, but occurs in IEAL.
6,274	CLACHESTORP. Also at 6,284. In Loes Hundred. Unidentified, DG 394.
6,276	[VALUE]. LDB omits *valuit*.
6,277	POSSEFELDA. Unidentified, DG 408.
6,278	BRODERTUNA. See 3,41 note.
6,283	THEN AND NOW 1 PLOUGH. The last line of folio 326b is inset in the MS, as shown by Farley, because of an irregularly shaped leaf.
6,284	CLACHESTORP. See 6,274 note. WALTER *DE RISBOU*. See 6,28 note.
6,287	IN WIDTH. In the MS *in longo* has been corrected to *in lato*.
6,288	KELETUNA. The same as *CHELETUNA, CHILETUNA*, see 6,41-42 note.
6,291	AND 17. That is, 17 acres.
6,295	HUNDRED [OF]. LDB omits *de*. THICCHEBROM. Unidentified, DG 412. Cf. VCH 466, n.78 for a later reference.
6,297	ICHEBURNA. Unidentified, DG 402.
6,301	WALTER OF CAEN. In the MS *Galter(us)*, altered from *W-*. 3 SMALLHOLDERS. MEADOW, 4 ACRES. In the MS there is an erasure between *bor(darii)* and *.iiii.*.

6,303	DENNINGTON. LDB *Binneuetuna(m)* is in error for *Dinueue-*. [FURLONGS]. LDB omits *q(ua)r(entinas)*.
6,304	17 SMALLHOLDERS. In the MS *xvii* has been written over an erasure.
6,305-306	EDRIC. Of Laxfield (cf. 6,305). Predecessor of Robert (and William) Malet in many entries in Suffolk and Norfolk. He was also known as Edric *Cecus*, 'the blind' (=Edric Blind, Wiltshire 67,53), see FD xc-xcii and no. 168.
6,305	VILLAGERS, LATER 8, NOW 6. In the MS *m(odo)* has been repeated in error; Farley prints it only once. Also, *vi* has been altered from *iji*.
	THEN 4 PLOUGHS. *semp(er)*, 'always' deleted in LDB before *.iiii*.
	LOERNIC. The LDB form is corrupt. It may perhaps be for *Leouric* FROM OE *Lēofric*, or from OG *Wenric*, Förstemann 1616 (J.M.D.).
6,306	IN LENGTH. In the MS *in lo(n)g(o)* has been altered from *in la-*.
	[£]10. LDB *sol(idis)* is in error for *lib(ris)*, see above.
	EDRIC HAS FULL JURISDICTION. LDB *hab&* may be in error for *habuit*, 'had', but Edric does appear to have been alive in 1086, see 6,305-306 note.
6,308	WINGFIELD. Cf. 21,45. The spelling *Wineb(er)ga* appears to represent an alternative second element for the place called *Wighefelda* in 19,8.
	WALTER HOLDS. In the MS *ten&* has been altered from *tet-*.
6,309	4 SMALLHOLDERS. In LDB *.7.i.ser(uus)*, 'and 1 slave', has been deleted after *bor(darii)*.
6,310	IT HAS ... IN TAX. The measurements and tax probably refer to Horham (6,309) in whose assessment Wilby was counted.
6,311	10 PLOUGHS. LDB repeats 7 in error before *x*.
6,313	[MEN'S] PLOUGHS. LDB omits *ho(minu)m*.
6,314	VALUE 10S. This may be the value of the 1 free man held by Walter, but may also be otiose here.
6,318	(WALTER SON OF GRIP) ALSO (HOLDS). In LDB *ide(m)* is interlined.
6,319	1 FREE MAN. In the MS *lib(er)* has been altered to *lib(eru)m*.
	VALUE 22S 8D. In the MS there is an erasure of three or four words after this value. The first two words erased may be *Rainald(us) pr(esbiter)*. Cf. perhaps the priest mentioned in 6,319 as being in sub-patronage.
7	ROGER BIGOT. The ancestor of the Bigots, Earls of Norfolk. He came from a family with only a small amount of land in Calvados, Loyd 14-15. He was Sheriff of Suffolk and Norfolk in 1086, see 1,1-60;122 etc. His byname was OFr and meant 'bigot', OEB 342. He may possibly be the same as Bigot of Loges, see 4,13 note.
7,1	STANHARD. See following note. Cf. Stanhard son of Aethelwy (72).
	AETHELWY OF THETFORD. LDB *Ailwius*, for OE *AEthelwīg*. He was the father of Stanhard, the 1086 undertenant, and may have been Sheriff of Norfolk before 1066, see PNDB 189-190 n. 11.
	WILD MARES. As 1,115 note.
	160 SHEEP. In the MS there is an erasure (probably of *p*) after *.c.lx*.
7,2	[HAD]. LDB *hab&* is in error for *habuit*.
	... OF HOUDAIN. Probably Houdain (Pas-de-Calais), but cf. also Houdeng-au-Bosc (Seine-Inf.) and Houdain (Nord); OEB 92-93. Cf. Hugh of Houdain (7,60 etc.)
7,3	(VALUE OF) THE OTHER MANOR. That is, value now of the manor formerly held by Wulfeva.
7,4	AITARD. The Rom. form of OG *Eidhart*, see Forssner 17-18. Note that the name given as Aethelhard in Cheshire 9,17 should also read Aitard.
	AITARD ALSO HOLDS HIM. LDB *qua(m)* is in error for *que(m)*. In the MS *ten&* has been altered from *p(er)tin&*.
	AITARD ALSO HOLDS HIM. LDB *qua(m)* for *que(m)* as above.
	AFTER THE KING ARRIVED. After 1066. Aelmer was deposed in 1070.
7,6	... PLOUGH AND A HALF. LDB omits the numeral.
7,7	PADDA. A byname from late OE *pad(d)e* or ON *padda*, 'toad, frog'; PNDB 343.
7,9	G(ODRIC) THE STEWARD. Cf. 13,3.
7,10	[MEN'S] PLOUGHS. LDB *boū* is in error for *hoū ho(min)u(m)*.
7,11	WARABETUNA. See 3,15 note *sub* WRABETUNA.
	ROGER BIGOT. In the MS *Rog(ero)* has been altered from *Rob(erto)*.
	[SLAVE]. LDB *acī* is in error for *ser*.
7,12	COVEHITHE. Formerly 'North Hales'.
7,15	WILLIAM MALET ... DIED. Probably 1069 x 1071.
	LEDMAN. Perhaps more likely OE *Lēodmann* than OG *Liudman*; PNDB 309.
	STANHARD. LDB *Stauhart* is in error for *Stanhart*.

	BAYNARD. Both Ralph Baynard and his nephew William occur in LDB Suffolk; Ralph and Geoffrey in LDB Essex; Ralph and possibly Roger in LDB Norfolk.
	GOUTI. LDB *Couta*. See 3,56 note.
7,16	THORPE. The same place as at 7,26. Lost, near Heveningham, in Blything Hundred. DG 413 seems incorrect in placing these two entries (and 3,8) under Thorpe (in Aldingham, *recte* Aldringham) which is in Plomesgate Hundred.
	WILLIAM MALET, HIS FATHER. LDB 7 between *malet* and *pat(er)* is otiose.
7,17	HIS FATHER. William Malet.
	HOLDS THE WHOLE OF THIS. 7,16-17.
7,18	YOXFORD. Farley *Lokesfort* is in error for *Iokesfort* of the MS.
	HUGH OF CORBON. From Corbon (Calvados), Loyd 32, OEB 83-84.
7,19	ALI. LDB *ala*, probably from ON *Áli*, ODan *Ali*, OSw *Ale* but possibly from ON *Alli*; PNDB 146.
	ROBERT OF TOSNY. See 44 note. In the MS *malet* has been erased after *rob(er)ti*.
	80 ACRES AND 10. And 10 acres.
	EARL R(ALPH). Wader. See 1,61-95 note.
7,21	OUTLIER. LDB *bereuuite* is in error for *bereuuita*.
7,23	FREE MEN. The words *lib(er)i ho(min)es* are written both in the main text and in the left-hand margin. The marginal instance is perhaps not strictly contemporary; there is an offlay of ink from it in the MS on to the facing page. Cf. 7,55;77;136 notes. The entries governed by the sub-heading may extend to 7,54.
7,25	COVEHITHE. Formerly 'North Hales'.
	W(ILLIAM) OF WARENNE. Cf. 26,15.
7,26	THORPE. See 7,16 note.
	R(OBERT) MALET ... DUNWICH. Cf. 6,84.
	IN THE SAME ASSESSMENT. Translating *ad ide(m) p(re)tium*.
7,28	UURABETUNA. See 3,15 note *sub WRABETUNA*.
	MANSON. LDB *mansunu*, OE **Mansunu*; PNDB 325.
7,29	OPITUNA. See 6,100 note *sub HOPPETUNA*.
	PLOUGH; NOW 1. It is unclear to whom the plough belonged in 1086.
	½ CHURCH ... ½ ACRE. The ½ acre may have been of meadow, if LDB has omitted *p(ra)ti*.
7,32	;3 WERE. LDB *s(ed) 7* seems otiose here and is not translated.
7,34	SAME ASSESSMENT. Of Kelsale.
7,36	LEOFRIC COBBE. Probably 'Toli's man' referred to above before the details of population and ploughs which interrupt the text here. The byname is OE **Cobba*, probably signifying a man of stout stature; OEB 305-306.
	AETHELWARD ALSO HAD HALF THE PATRONAGE. LDB *ei(us)de(m) ageluuard(us) dimidi(us)* is in error for *ide(m) ageluuard(us) dimidia(m)*.
	BRUNMAN BEARD. LDB *Brumanbeard*; PNDB 210.
	BRUNNER. LDB *brimari* (genitive) is in error for *brunari*, from OE **Brūnmǣr*; cf. PNDB 210, which omits this form.
	IN THE MANOR OF KELSALE. In the MS there is an erasure after *man(erio)*.
7,37	AKILE SUFFERING. LDB *akile sufreint*. The fore-name is a variant of ODan *Aki*, OSw *Ake* which occurs in ICC as *Achillus* (see Cambridgeshire 17,5 note); cf. also *Akeli* (Cambridgeshire 37,1 note) and PNDB 142. The byname appears to be OFr *soufrant*, *suffrant*, '(long-) suffering', OEB 356.
	WHOEVER HOLDS LAND THERE. In the MS *ten'* has been corrected from *tenuit*. The significance of the phrase is not apparent.
7,39	[SHE WAS]. LDB ÷, the abbreviation for *est* appears in error here for *fuit*.
7,43	ASSESSMENT OF 20S. That is, of Willingham in 7,42.
7,44	OF THE WHOLE OF THIS. LDB *De hoc totu(m)* is in error for *De hoc toto*.
	EARL R(ALPH). Wader, see 1,61-95 note.
7,47	[HE WAS]. LDB omits *fuit*.
7,48	GODWIN. Probably the son of Toki, as in 7,47.
7,49	REVENUE [FOR] 40S. LDB omits *pro*.
7,51	FREE MAN, GODWIN. In the MS *lib(er)u(m) h(o)m(inem)* has been altered from *lib(er) h(o)m(o)*. Farley prints the *m* of *h(o)m(inem)* as a capital although it was not intended as such;
	in the MS it has been altered from *o*.
	30[S]. In the MS 7 has been erased after .xxx.
7,52	THEY ARE ASSESSED. LDB *s(u)nt p(re)tiati*; the use of the masculine plural form implies that both Wulfsi and the acres are meant.

7,53	*WIMUNDAHALA.* Also at 31,29. In Lothing Hundred. Unidentified, DG 416.
7,54	ALI. As 7,19 note.
7,55	OF THE HOLDING. *de Feudo* in the right-hand margin of LDB, perhaps not strictly contemporary with the main text; there is an offlay of ink from the two words in the MS on to the facing page. The words may be intended to mark the end of the part of this chapter governed by the words 'FREE MEN' before 7,23. Cf. 7,23;77;136 notes. MEADOW, 5 ACRES. In the MS the numeral has been altered from *ij*. FOR THE COMPLETION OF BAYLHAM. Tranlating *ad p(er)ficiendu(m) belha(m)*. Perhaps to make up for a deficiency in value there. ANOTHER HUNDRED. Bosmere Hundred. NEITHER A WRIT NOR A DELIVERER. No written or oral message had been received by the men of the Hundred from the King to give royal authority to Roger's acquisition of this.
7,56	WILLIAM OF BOURNEVILLE. From Bourneville (Eure), OEB 78.
7,57	BATTISFORD. The abbreviation mark in Farley above the *f* of the place-name is above the *o* in the MS. It is however otiose and is probably a copying error in LDB. It may in fact have been the lower part of a semi-colon in the exemplar text after *Will(elmus)* in the line above. VALUE [THEN]. LDB *7 ual(uit)* is in error for *T(u)nc ual(uit)*.
7,58	½ CHURCH, 12 ACRES. Cf. 76,14.
7,59	LEOFRIC HOBBESON. The patronym is OE **Hobba*, a byname which probably denoted either a stout or a stupid person; OEB 157-158.
7,60	HUGH OF HOUDAIN. He also held from Roger Bigot in Essex (43,6). For the byname, see 7,2 note. VILLAGERS. Farley prints *nitt* in error for *uill* of the MS. THEN 2 PLOUGHS ... NOW NONE. Probably in lordship. THEN ½ PLOUGH, NOW 1. Probably belonging to the 'men'. 40 SHEEP. Farley prints *LXL* for MS *XL* altered from *LX* by the deletion of *L* before the *X* and the addition of another *L* after it. 10 FREE MEN. In the MS *lib(er)j* has been altered from *lib(er)os*. Farley prints *libs* in error. [WERE] UNDER THE PATRONAGE OF. LDB *fuit com(men)datus* is in error for *fuerunt com(men)dati*.
7,62	HUGH OF HOUDAIN HOLDS (THIS). *Hugo de hosdenc ten&*. The same words were originally written at the beginning of this entry but were then deleted.
7,64	ROGER OF RAMES. See *38*. In Essex (43,1) he also claimed land against Warengar. Cf. 7,68. THESE FREE MEN. LDB *lib(er)oos* is in error for *lib(er)os*.
7,65	3 FREE MEN. Only 2 of them, Wulfbold and Leofstan are named.
7,66	*LANGHEDENA.* See 1,68 note. WHO HAD. Translating *h(abe)ns*. For the use of the present participle with a past continuous sense, cf. the reference to Wailolf in 7,67 where the time described is stated to be before 1066. HE ALSO HOLDS. Warengar, as 7,65.
7,67	WIGULF. LDB *Wicolf(us)* from ON *Vigúlfr*, ODan *Wighulf*, OSw *Vigholf*; PNDB 404-405. WAILOLF. LDB *Wailoff(us)* is in error for *Wailolf(us)*. The origin of the name is uncertain, unless it is OG **Wadalulf*, see PNDB 408.
7,68	FARMAN. LDB *Farmann(us)* from ON *Farmann*, ODan, OSw *Farman*; PNDB 250. ROGER OF RAMES. As 7,64 note.
7,71	THANE OF KING EDWARD'S. In the MS there is an erasure after *e*, probably of the letter *w*. KNODISHALL ... ANOTHER HUNDRED. In Blything Hundred. PEASENHALL ... ANOTHER HUNDRED. In Blything Hundred. [PLOUGHS]. LDB omits *car(uce)*. JURISDICTION ... THE ABBOT'S. Of Ely. Plomesgate Hundred was one of the 5½ Hundreds belonging to St. Etheldreda's.
7,72	*BECCLINGA.* Unidentified, DG 390. RANULF ... IN LORDSHIP. *Ran(ulfus)* may be an error in LDB for *Rog(erus)*.
7,73	RALPH OF TOURLEVILLE. From Tourleville (La Manche), OEB 116.
7,75	HARTISMERE HUNDRED. A false start (*Her*) on the Hundred-name was made in LDB on the previous line, before it was realised that, as the name of the Hundred, it should stand at the beginning of a line. 40 SHEEP. *por(ci)* deleted in LDB and *ou(es)* interlined.

	80 ACRES AND 16. 16 acres.
	1 FREE MAN, AELFRIC. In the MS *lib(er)u(m) h(omine)m* has been altered from *lib(er) h(om)o*.
	OF THIS FREE (MAN). In the MS *lib(er)i* has been altered from *lib(er)*.
7,76	[BELONGS]. LDB omits a verb such as *pertinet*.
	15 FREE MEN. In the MS *xv* is written over an erasure and is followed by *iii* erased.
7,77	FREE MEN. *lib(er)i ho(min)es* is written in the left-hand margin in LDB, perhaps not strictly contemporary with the text. Cf. 7,23;55;96;136 notes.
	SHEARMAN. LDB *Sereman(us)*, a byname from OE *scēarmann*, 'one who shears woollen cloth'; PNDB 355-356.
	SWEETMAN. LDB *Suetman(us)* from OE *Swētmann*; PNDB 381-382.
	AELFRIC STICKSTAG. LDB *stikestac* is probably an imperative nickname 'stick/stab stag'; OEB 387-388.
	SIFRITH. LDB *Siuert(us)* from OE *Sigefrith*; PNDB 360.
	13 FREE MEN. 14 men are named as being 'Roger Bigot's free men', 13 were probably taken over from Norman but one of them, Aelfric Stickstag, is stated below to have been half Edric's.
7,78	PASTURE COMMON TO ... THE HUNDRED. At present unidentified.
7,79	'MAISTANA'. Lost in Trimley, DG 405.
	ALWAYS 3 PLOUGHS. In the MS *acˀ* was written first in error for *carˀ* and the *a-* was then erased to leave *cˀ*. Farley shows the erasure by means of a dot. Cf. 7,138 note.
	MAN OF EDRIC. LDB *Edric(us)* is in error for *Edrici*.
7,80	LUNDEN. The origin of the name is obscure according to PNDB 322. Probably an OScand name, ON *Lundinn*, ODan *Lunden* (J.M.D.). Cf. Lundi, Essex B3a.
	THEY BELONG TO WALTON. Either the smallholders or the free men.
7,82	MOREGRIM. Possibly an Anglo-Scandinavian byname *Mōr-Grímr*, 'Grímr on the moor'; PNDB 328-329.
7,83	'TURSTANESTUNA'. In Colneis Hundred. Lost in Trimley, DG 414.
7,84	OTTI. ODan *Otti*, OSw *Otte*; PNDB 342.
7,85	'PLUMGEARD'. LDB *p̄lu(m)geard*, with an otiose abbreviation mark over the *p*. The same place as at 21,51. Lost in Trimley, DG 408 (s.n. *Plugeard*). For a later reference, see VCH 477 n.94.
	BEFORE 1066, 2 PLOUGHS. Unusually, LDB here uses *t.r.e.* instead of *T(u)nc*.
7,86	RALPH OF TOURLEVILLE'S. LDB *Radulfi(us)* is in error for *Radulfi*. For the byname, see 7,73 note.
7,88	'STRUUSTUNA'. See 6,110 note.
7,89	'GUTHESTUNA'. Lost in Kirton, DG 400.
7,92	SPRETMAN. LDB *Spretman(us)* from OE *Sprēotmann*; PNDB 370.
7,93	'LEOFSTANESTUNA'. Also at 7,106;111. Lost in Trimley, DG 404. Cf. Leofstan, one of the free men here, after whom the place might have been named. For a later reference, see VCH 478 n.96.
	STANFLED. LDB *Stanfleda* from OE *Stānflǣd* (feminine); PNDB 371.
7,96	'ALSTON'. See 2,19 note.
	ALL OF THESE ... FREE MEN OF ROGER BIGOT. Those in 7,77;79-96; cf. the heading before 7,77.
7,98	OF THIS SWETING. In the MS *sueting* has been corrected from *suetingu(m)*.
7,99	HERMAN. LDB *Heremann(us)* from OG *Her(e)man*; PNDB 290, Forssner 149-150.
7,101	'ALSTON'. See 2,19 note.
7,102	PATRONAGE OF ALNOTH. LDB *Alnot(us)* is in error for *Alnoti*.
7,103	'STRUESTUNA'. See 6,110 note.
	THORILD. LDB *Durilda* from ON *Thórhildr*, ODan *Thorild*; PNDB 393.
7,104	KETEL UVA. LDB *Keteluua* from ON *Ketill*, ODan *Ketil*, OSw *Kaetil* with the addition of a byname, possibly ON *úfi*, 'ruffled, rough, hostile'; PNDB 304-305.
7,105	'STRUESTUNA'. See 6,110 note.
	HUSTEMAN. LDB *Husteman(us)*, possibly a form for OE *Ūhtmann*; PNDB 297.
7,106	'LEOFSTANESTUNA'. See 7,93 note.
	BURGRIC. The LDB form *Burric(us)* may have been due to misreading of the combination of letters -*rgr*- in insular minuscule script as -*rr*-.
7,109	LANGFER. The same name as *Langfere* at 32,2 below and *Lancfer* Huntingdonshire 19,13, *Langfer* Northamptonshire 3,1. Probably a byname from OE *lang-fēre*, *lang-fǣre*, 'long-lasting, enduring, old' (J.M.D.).

SEGAR. LDB *Fegar(us)* with a misreading of insular minuscule *s* as *f* (>*F*); OE **Sǣgār*, PNDB 352-353.

7,110 'MYCELEGATA'. See 6,111 note.
REGIFER. LDB *Regifer(us)*, possibly OG *Ragifred* or *Re(g)infrid*; PNDB 348.

7,111 'LEOFSTANESTUNA'. See 7,93 note.
THEODORIC. LDB *Teoddrrc(us)* is corrupt. OG *Theodric*; PNDB 383-384, Forssner 231-233. Cf. 8,56 note.

7,112 HILDFERTH. LDB *Hildeuert* from OE *Hildefrith*; PNDB 291.
UNDER THE PATRONAGE OF NORMAN. Perhaps referring only to Goda and Hildferth, since Derstan is treated separately. However, Derstan may have been under the sub-patronage of Wulfmer.

7,113 'ALSTON'. See 2,19 note.

7,114 EDRIC. Of Laxfield, cf. 6,128.

7,115 WILLIAM OF BOSC. LDB *de silua* here but below *de Nemore* (7,134.39,11), *de Nomore* (39,5). For the vernacular form *de Bosc* see Essex 37,17 and OEB 73-74. The place is unidentified, being a common name in Normandy. Cf. William *de More* in 16,1 and note.
10 FREE MEN. Only 9 are named in LDB.

7,117 WHITE. LDB *Whita* from OE *Hwīta*; PNDB 297.

7,118 *KULUERTESTUNA*. See 6,110 note.

7,119 ALSO ... 1 FREE MAN. In the MS *i* has been altered from *ii*.
WHOLE OF THIS. 7,118-119.

7,120 'OXELANDA'. Lost in Trimley, DG 407.

7,121 14 FREE MEN. 15 are named.
[73] ACRES. Farley prints *LXIII* in error for *LXXIII* of the MS.
WHOLE OF THIS. 7,120-121.
THIS LAND ASSESSED. LDB *pretiata* is in error for *pretiata(m)*.

7,122 WHOLE OF THIS LAND. This probably refers to the land and men formerly held by Norman (7,77;79-122).
EXCEPT ... WALTON. 7,76.

7,123 THORVOLD. LDB *Turnold(us)* is a scribal misreading for *Turuold(us)* from ON *Thorvaldr*; PNDB 397.

7,125 THURSTAN SON OF GUY. The spelling of the fore-name, *Sturstan(us)*, is corrupt in LDB. In the MS there is an erasure of two letters in the patronym between *Wid* and *donis*.

7,133 BRICTMER. LDB *Brihtmar(us)* is in error for *Brictmaru(m)*.
30 ACRES. IEAL (188), 35.
5 FREE MEN ... 16 ACRES. IE (152) and IEAL (183), '5 free men under him; 16 acres'.
EARL R(ALPH) ... W(ILLIAM) MALET ... POSSESSION. In the MS the text is arranged around a hole in the parchment which also affects 7,139 on the other side of the leaf. Earl Ralph Wader is meant here.
THURSTAN HOLDS ... FROM ROGER BIGOT. IE (152), 'Roger Bigot holds these (free men) under the Bishop of Bayeux'. Cf. IEAL (183) in the Holding of Hamo of Saint-Clair (see 6,271 note).

7,136 FREE MEN OF ROGER BIGOT. The words *lib(er)i ho(min)es* are repeated in the right-hand margin. They are perhaps not strictly contemporary with the main text, cf. 7,23 note.
2 (UNDER THAT OF) THE ABBOT OF ELY. IE (151) adds 'Value 5s.'

7,137 EDHILD. LDB *Edilt* from OE *Ēadhild* (feminine); PNDB 232.

7,138 1½ [PLOUGHS]. LDB *acr̃* is in error for *car̃*, cf. 7,79 note.

7,139 This section is affected by the hole in the parchment mentioned in 7,133 note.

7,143 UNDER ... PATRONAGE OF NORMAN. LDB *normann(us)* is in error for *normanno*.
LEOFRIC SNIPE. The byname is probably from the OE or ON antecedent of ME *snipe*, perhaps describing a thin man, see OEB 366.

7,144 MALET. Here Robert Malet is meant.

7,145 5½S. That is 5s 6d.

7,147 SWEFLING. LDB *suest lingua* is in error for *sueftlinga*.

7,148 3 WERE. LDB *suere* in error for *fuere*.
GODRIC. LDB *Gadric* is in error for *Godric*.

7,151. IN (GREAT) GLEMHAM ... JURISDICTION. In the MS there is an erasure of text between lines 4 and 5 of folio 345b.

Folio 345b, line 6. The Hundred-rubric shown by Farley after 7,151 also occurs thus in the MS. It is not part of Chapter 7 however, being a false start for the first Hundred-rubric in Chapter 8.

8   ROGER OF POITOU. A younger son of Roger of Montgomery, Earl of Shrewsbury. He appears to have forfeited his lands in Lancashire, Derbyshire, Nottinghamshire, Norfolk and Suffolk (see 8,46) by 1086, possibly for supporting King William's rebellious son Robert of Normandy.
8,1   BEFORE THIS ENTRY. IE (149) has an additional entry, 'In PRESTON Roger of Poitou holds a half free man, Leofsi, under the patronage of St. Etheldreda's; 12 acres'. Cf. also IEAL (187), '1 free man; 12 acres'.
        80 ACRES. IEAL, 70.
        THEN 2 PLOUGHS IN LORDSHIP, NOW 3. IE, 'always 2 ploughs in lordship'. Cf. also IEAL.
        THEN 2 MEN'S PLOUGHS, NOW 1. IEAL, '2 belonging to the men'.
        COBS, NOW 1. In the MS *i* has been altered from *ii*.
8,2   THEN 1 PLOUGH, NOW NONE. IE (149), '1 plough in lordship'. IEAL (187), '2 ploughs in lordship'.
8,4   LICTWIN. LDB *Lihtwin(us)* from OE *Lēohtwine*; PNDB 319.
        68 ACRES. IE (149) and IEAL (187), 80.
        50 ACRES. IEAL (in error), 1.
        THEN 3 PLOUGHS, NOW 2. IEAL, '3 ploughs'.
8,5   5 FREE MEN. IE (149) and IEAL (187), 4.
        21 [ACRES]. LDB has *car* in error for *ac*, cf. 7,79;138 notes. IE (149) and IEAL (187), '21 acres'.
8,6   20 ACRES. IE (149) and IEAL (187), 30. IE adds, 'In the same village the men of Roger of Poitou annexed 8 acres of the lordship. These belong to Kingston.' Cf. also IEAL.
        1½ ACRES. Repeated in error in LDB at the turning of the page.
        AETHELRIC OF BURGH. Probably named from Burgh in Carlford Hundred, cf. 32,28.
        2 FREE MEN, 1 UNDER ... ST. ETHELDREDA'S. Cf. IE, '1 free man under the patronage of St. Ethedreda's; 30 acres. 3 smallholders. 1 plough. Meadow, 1 acre. Value 5s.' Cf. also IEAL.
        1 FREE MAN OF ST. ETHELDREDA'S. Named in IE as Brictnoth.
8,7   MEADOW, 4 ACRES. Misplaced in LDB amongst the ploughs.
        ROGER SON OF ARNOLD HOLDS (THIS). Added slightly later than the main text in LDB. Cf. Roger son of Arnulf in 8,8.
8,8   ALWIN, A FREE MAN. IE (150) calls him a 'Freeman'.
        [WITH] 16 ACRES. LDB *dxvi* is in error, probably for *de xvi*. IEAL (187), 18.
        1 [FREE MAN] ... BROWN. LDB omits *lib(er)*. IE, '1 free man, Brown, under the patronage of St. Etheldreda's; 6 acres. Value 12d.' Cf. also IEAL.
        1 FREE MAN GIVEN TO ST. ETHELDREDA'S. 'Given', *dat(us)* is an alternative expression for 'under the patronage of', *commendatus*. See IE, '1 free man, Grimbold, under the patronage of St. Etheldreda's'. Cf. also IEAL, '2 free men, one with 16 acres, the other 8'.
        9½ ACRES. IE, 9. In the MS of LDB *7 di(midia)* is squeezed in between *.ix. ac(re)*. and the *dim(idia)* belonging to 'Meadow, ½ acre', probably having at first been omitted.
        ROGER SON OF ARNULF. Cf. Roger son of Arnold in 8,7.
8,9   8S. IE (150) adds, 'and a half'. That is, 6d.
        1 FREE MAN AND A HALF. In the MS *7* has been squeezed in between *.i.* and *dim(idius)*.
        1 FREE MAN ... 50 ACRES. IE names him as Edwy.
        VALUE ... NOW 11[S]. IE, 'Value 10s'.
8,10   MEADOW, 1 ACRE. IEAL (187), 2.
        VALUE ... NOW 7 [S]. IE (150), '2s' or '3s' in the different MSS.
8,11   PLOUGHS ... POSSIBLE. LDB omits the numeral.
8,12   1 UNDER ... ST. ETHELDREDA'S. IE (150) names him as Aelfric and assigns him '8 acres. Value 8d'. Cf. also IEAL (187).
        1 AND A HALF ... GRIMWULF. Perhaps they were under his sub-patronage.
8,14   GRENEWIC. Unidentified, DG 399.
8,15   BURNT ALBERT HOLDS THIS. 8,14-15. LDB *Alb(er)t(us) cremat(us)*, the byname being from Latin *cremare* 'to burn'.
8,16   HUNEBOT. See 3,95 note.
8,17   ROGER SON OF ARNOLD. LDB *AErloldi* stands for *AErnoldi* but has been the subject of AN dissimilation of *l* and *n*.
        VALUE THEN 8S; NOW THE SAME. IE (151), 'Value 10s'.
        1 FREE MAN OF ST. ETHELDREDA'S. IE names him as Godric.
        26 ACRES. IEAL (187), 27.

8,19	FREE [MEN]. LDB omits *homines*.
8,20	1 CARUCATE OF LAND AND 40 ACRES. IEAL (187) omits the carucate.
8,21	MEN'S [PLOUGH]. LDB omits *car(uca)*.
	1 FREE WOMAN. IE (152) and IEAL (182) adds 'under him, under the patronage of St. Etheldreda's'.
8,22	IN MONDEWDEN. IE (152) and IEAL (188) suggests that this entry relates to Kettleburgh.
	BEFORE 1066 14 FREE MEN AND A HALF, NOW 10. IE and IEAL 'there are 14 free men'.
	THEN 4 PLOUGHS, NOW 2. IEAL, '4 ploughs'.
	HUMPHREY THE CHAMBERLAIN. The byname is Latin *ca(m)barari(us)*.
	ERTALD. From the Rom. form *Hertald* of OG *Hardolt*, Forssner 143-144.
8,23	1 FREE MAN. IE (152) names him as Brictwold and adds, 'Edric; 16 acres. Value 30d.' Edric is credited with 15 acres in MSS B, C of IE; and with 20 acres in IEAL (188). IE places both these free men under Kettleburgh.
8,25	32 ACRES. In IE (152) and IEAL (188) the 4 free men are credited with 8 acres.
8,29	*CATESFELLA*. Unidentified, DG 394.
8,30	THRANDESTON. Elsewhere in Hartismere Hundred. It is possible that the rubric before 8,31 has been placed one entry too late.
8,32	LATER ..., NOW. Either a numeral or *7* has been omitted from LDB.
8,33	EARL ALGAR. Of East Anglia 1051-52, 1053-57; of Mercia 1057-62. He was probably dead by 1066, see Harmer, *ASWrits* 546-547. For his wife Aelfeva, mother of Earl Morcar, see 1,97-99 note.
	2 PLOUGHS IN LORDSHIP. In the MS there is an erasure after *car(uce)*.
8,35	VALUE THEN £6; NOW [£]4. In the MS *h(om)o* has been erased after *lib̃*. The scribe at first misconstrued *lib̃* as *lib(er)* 'free' rather than *lib(ras)* 'pounds'.
	NORMAN SON OF TANCRED. LDB *tauredi* is in error for *tanredi*. The patronym is OG *Thancrad, Tancrad* in the Norman form *Tancred*; Forssner 227-228.
	RICHARD. Son of Count Gilbert, see *25*.
	THE 6 FORFEITURES. Certain profits of justice which were usually reserved to the King, but which were sometimes granted as a special privilege.
8,37	SELL. LDB *uend(er)ae* is in error for *uend(er)e*.
8,40	THEN ½ PLOUGH. LDB *T(un)c 7 dim(idia) car(uca)*; either *7* is otiose, or *post*, 'later' has been omitted.
8,45	OF THESE. LDB *histis* is in error for *istis*.
8,46	WHEN R(OGER) LEFT (IT). When Roger of Poitou forfeited, see *8* note.
	NORMAN ... CAVENDISH. Cf. 43,2.
	JURISDICTION OF WITHGAR. *saca* here stands as an alternative to *soca*; cf. Norfolk, Technical Terms.
8,47	RICHARD. As 8,35 note.
8,49	LEOFWIN CROC. He was also one of Roger of Poitou's predecessors in Essex (46,2). The byname is probably ON *krókr*, 'hook'; OEB 308. See also DBS, s.n. *Crook*. LDB *Leswin(us)* is in error for *Lefwin(us)*, due to confusion between *s* and *f* in insular minuscule script.
8,50	ALSI NEPHEW OF EARL RALPH. Probably Earl Ralph the Constable (see 1,101 note).
8,51	A DELIVERER. Anyone who had royal authority to transfer possession.
	GERALD. Perhaps Raymond Gerald, cf. 8,55.
8,55	WILLIAM OF WARENNE ... TUNSTALL. See 26,6.
	CHURCH, WITH 5 ACRES. *iiii* deleted in LDB, *v* interlined.
8,56	THEODORIC. LDB *Tednc(us)* is in error for *Tedric(us)*. Cf. 7,111 note.
	GODMAN. Cf. IE (144), '1 free man of St. Etheldreda's, Godman, with full jurisdiction and patronage, with 6 acres'.
8,59	ONE OF THESE. IE (144) names him as Algar.
	HERVEY OF BOURGES. Cf. 67,2.
	FINN, RICHARD'S PREDECESSOR. Finn the Dane, predecessor of Richard son of Count Gilbert (*25*). His widow Wulfeva was a landholder in Essex (*84*).
8,62	*LANGHEDENA*. See 1,68 note.
8,63	C(OUNT) G(ILBERT). Farley prints *C*... with a suprascript *G*. There is no erasure in the MS, which reads *C.G.* with another *G* suprascript. The *G* on the line was altered from *a*, rather unclearly, and the suprascript *G* was added to clarify the reading.
8,64	*LANGEDANA*. See 1,68 note.
	GINNI. Farley *Ghim(us)* is in error for *Ghini(us)* of the MS. From ODan *Ginni*, PNDB 261.

8,66	60 ACRES. IEAL (187), 40.
	GOSBERT. From OG *Gausbert*, etc.; Forssner 124.
8,68	ABBOT. Of Ely, see IE (146).
8,77	CODDENHAM. See 1,74 note.
8,81	NORDBERIA. Unidentified, DG 407.
	IN THE SAME ... Cf. IE (148), '50 free men who belong to Sudbourne, with 290½ acres. From them, the Abbot had full jurisdiction and patronage before 1066. 2 of these, Aelfric and Edwin, could not sell or grant their land'. Cf. also IEAL (187), which associates the men with Barham.
	UNDER THE PATRONAGE. LDB repeats *& c(om)m(en)datione* in error.
9	WILLIAM OF ÉCOUIS. From Écouis (Eure), Loyd 39-40, OEB 114.
9,1	BRUNARD. The name is OG; Förstemann 340.
9,2	HUARD OF VERNON. From Vernon (Eure), Loyd 110, OEB 119. The fore-name is an OFr form of OG *Hugihard*, Forssner 154-155.
	(MARKET) WESTON. LDB omits the abbreviation mark from above the final letter of *Westuna*, which should be in the accusative case.
	10 FREEMEN. In the MS *soč* has been altered from *soci*.
9,3	ROBERT OF VAUX. Cf. 7,24.
9,4	5 ... 'acres' has perhaps been omitted from LDB here.
	THIS ENTRY appears to have been written on a different occasion to 9,1-3.
10	HERMER OF FERRERS. From Ferrières-St.-Hilaire (Eure), OEB 88. The fore-name is OG *Her(e)mar*, Forssner 151.
10,1	[MEN'S]. LDB omits *ho(minu)m*.
11	RALPH OF BEAUFOUR. From Beaufour (Calvados), OEB 71.
11,2	'THURSTANESTUNA'. See 6,153 note.
11,4	RICHARD OF SAINT-CLAIR. Perhaps from Saint-Clair (La Manche), but cf. also Saint-Clair-sur-l'Elle (La Manche), Saint-Clair-sur-les-Monts (Seine-Inf.) and Saint-Clair-D'Arcy (Eure); Saint-Clair (Seine-et-Oise) is less likely. See OEB 112-113.
	MODGEVA. LDB *Modgeua* from OE *Mōdgifu*; PNDB 328.
	[ACRES]. LDB omits *acr(e)*.
12	FRODO THE ABBOT'S BROTHER. Brother of Abbot Baldwin of St. Edmund's (14,26 note). He also held land in Essex (56) where, however, in the Index of Persons he is wrongly described as brother of the Abbot of Ely. His fore-name is OG, Forssner 96.
12,1	MEADOW, 4 ACRES. In the MS *iiij* has been altered from *iii*.
12,2	6 FREE MEN. IE (142), 7.
	PLOUGHS, NOW 1. IE suggests that there are still 3.
12,3	VALUE. LDB omits *ual(uit)*.
12,5	SIWARD OF MALDON. The predecessor of Ranulf Peverel in Essex (34,9 etc.) and Suffolk (34,1-2 below, etc.). Named from his tenure of Maldon in Essex (34,12).
12,6	NOW FRODO HOLDS (IT). In the MS there is an erasure after *ten̄*.
	HORSES. LDB *eq(uus)* is in error for *equi*.
	1½D IN TAX. Expressed in LDB as 'three halfpennies', *.iii. ob(oli)*.
13	GODRIC THE STEWARD. He held lands in Suffolk (1,61-95) and at Great Sampford in Essex (1,30) on the King's behalf. In the heading to the present chapter, *GODRICI* has been altered in the MS from *GODRID-*.
13,2	EDWIN ... CHURCH, 12 ACRES. Edwin bequeathed 4 acres of land to the church at Blyford in the mid-11th century, see Whitelock, *ASWills* no. 33, Sawyer no. 1516, Hart ECEE no. 94.
13,3	OTHULF. LDB *Odulf(us)* from ON *Authúlfr*, ODan *Øthulf*, OSw *Ødhulf*; PNDB 170.
13,4	UUARLE. Unidentified, DG 414. For a later reference, see VCH 491 n. 122.
13,6	IN LORDSHIP. In the MS the words *i(n) d(omi)nio* are written in the margin and may not be strictly contemporary with the main text.

Folio 356b. Most of the remainder of the Suffolk LDB text was written by a different scribe from that in the preceding chapters. His form of both minuscule and capital *e* has a distinctive downward stroke to complete the middle bar/ tongue of the letter. His abbreviated form for *tunc* is *t(un)c* rather than *t(u)nc* as used by the preceding scribe.

14	ST. EDMUND'S. Literally, 'St. Edmund' (see 14,167 note). The Abbey of Bury St. Edmunds, Suffolk. For a list of the food rents due from the Abbey's estates in Suffolk before 1066, see Robertson, *ASCharters* no. 104, Hart ECEE no. 108.
14,1	ALL ... AT FOLD. That is, they are subject to fold-rights (see Technical Terms).
	1 FREE MAN WITH [½] CARUCATE. LDB *deď* stands for *de d(imidia)*, cf. FB i (3). FB ii (24), '60 acres'.

13 - 14

    1 SLAVE. FB ii (24), 2.
    HE COULD GRANT ... THE LAND. LDB *t(er)re* is in error for *t(er)ram*.
14,2 COULD NOT GRANT OR SELL. The insular abbreviation for *uel* 'or' is used here in LDB.
    ANOTHER HOLDS THERE. But LDB may have *ali(us)* here in error for *alii*.
14,3 9 SLAVES. LDB *serr* is in error for *seru(i)*.
    6 FREE MEN ... 4 SMALLHOLDERS. Cf. FB ii (24), 'at HAWSTEAD Ralph holds 1½ carucates; 2 smallholders'. For the 30 acres and 4 smallholders which Ralph does not hold, cf. the preceding paragraph in LDB. VALUE ALWAYS 60S. In the MS there is an erasure after *sol(idos)*.
14,5-6 CHEVINGTON and SAXHAM. FB i (4) adds that these were among the manors formerly held by Brictwulf son of Leofmer. After Brictwulf's death King William granted his manors to Abbot Baldwin of St. Edmunds (see 14,26 note) to be granted out in return for military service. Baldwin retained Chevington and Saxham however in the church's lordship, since they were closest to Bury.
14,7 1 LEAGUE IN LENGTH. In the MS there is an erasure after *long*.
14,9 COULD NOT GRANT OR SELL THE LAND. LDB *t(er)rae* is in error for *t(er)ram* or *t(er)ras*.
14,10 ICKWORTH. LDB *KKewortha(m)* is probably a misreading of *Icke-*.
14,11 ALBERT AND FULCHER ... 8 SMALLHOLDERS. FB ii (16) 'Albert holds from St. (Edmund's) 1 carucate; 1 villager, 3 smallholders'. FB ii (17) 'Fulcher holds from St. (Edmund's) 1½ carucates of land; 7 villagers, 5 smallholders'.
    FULCHER. Of Mesnières (Seine-Inf.), cf. Loyd 63. On him, see FD lxxxiv and n.4.
    GRANT AND SELL THE LAND. LDB *t(er)re* is in error for *t(er)ram* or *t(er)ras*.
    [PERMISSION]. LDB omits *lic(entia)*.
    OTHERS HOLD THERE. In the MS *Alii* has been altered by erasure.
14,12 6 SMALLHOLDERS. FB ii (17), '2 smallholders and a half'.
    BETWEEN THEM ALL. In the MS *o(mn)es* has been altered from *ho(min)es*.
14,13 HAWSTEAD. See also 14,3 note.
    OTTO. LDB *Odo*. Otto the Goldsmith (senior), see FD cxxxix-cxl and above 1,97-99 note. A gift by Otto and his wife of land at Hawstead to St. Edmund's Abbey was confirmed by King Henry I 1102 x 1105, see FD no. 20. This was probably the former land of Otto's which was granted by Abbots Baldwin and Robert for the rebuilding of the Abbey, see FD nos. 104, 106.
    CLERIC, ALBOLD. Probably the same as Albold the priest who witnessed FD no. 104, relating to Otto's former land. Perhaps identical with Ailbold the priest in 14,39.
    AGENET. LDB *Agenetus*. Probably a derivative in *-et*, from either the Scand. pers. n. *Haghni, Hagne* etc.(PNDB 282) or OG *Hagan*. (J.M.D.).
14,14 BROCKLEY and THEOBALD ... Cf. FB ii (18), 'Theobald the cleric holds from St. (Edmund's) 1 carucate of land; 1 villager, 3 smallholders, 3 slaves'.
    3 FREEMEN. In the MS *lib(er)os* has been altered from *lib(er)i*.
    MEADOW, 5 ACRES. In the MS *v* hs been altered from *xv*.
    STILL BELONGED TO. In the MS there is an erasure after *rem*.
14,15 WARIN HAS. In the MS *hAb&* has been altered from *Ab-* (? the beginning of *Abbas*).
    SELL THE LAND. LDB *t(er)rae* is in error for *t(er)ram*.
14,16 HENRY HAS FROM THE ABBOT ... 4 SMALLHOLDERS. FB ii (19) 'at REDE and at *UUILMUNDESTUN* Henry holds from St. (Edmund's) ½ carucate of land; 1 smallholder'. Cf. *WIMUNDESTUNA* at 25,18;105.
    SELL THE LAND. As 14,15 note.
    BERARD HOLDS ... 50 ACRES. FB ii (20), 'at REDE Berard holds from St. (Edmund's) 1 carucate of land; 3 smallholders; 1 free (man) with 20 acres'. Berard is OG or OFr, see Forssner 282, addendum.
    7 FREE MEN. In the MS *lib(er)os* has been altered from *lib(er)i*.
14,17 WESTLEY. See also 25,27 note.
    PETERS HOLDS 1 ... ABBOT. 5 SMALLHOLDERS. FB ii (19), 'At HORRINGER and WESTLEY Peter brother of Burghard holds from St. (Edmund's) 1 carucate of land; 3 smallholders'.
    SELL THE LAND. As 14,15 note.
14,18 THEY COULD GRANT. In LDB *pot*, for *pot(uerunt)*, has been altered from *potuit*.
    SELL THE LAND. As 14,15 note.
14,19 WANGFORD and WULFWARD. Wulfward of Wangford became the man of King Henry I in 1100 x 1107, see FD no. 26. He appears to have died by November 1120, see FD no. 38.

14

14,20	ELVEDEN. FB ii (17) states that Wulfward (of Wangford) 'holds'. SELL THE LAND. As 14,15 note.
14,21	FRODO. The Abbot's brother, see *12*. This was one of the manors formerly held by Brictwulf son of Leofmer (see 14,5-6 note) which Abbot Baldwin granted to his brother, see FB i (4-5). 9 FREE MEN. FB ii (23), '9 free (men) and a half'.
14,22	FULCHER HOLDS. FB ii (21), 'At (Great) LIVERMERE and at (Great) SNAREHILL (Norfolk 14,10) Fulcher the Breton holds 1 carucate of land; 3 smallholders'. FREE MEN. In the MS *lib(er)os* has been altered from *lib(er)i*.
14,23	OF THIS LAND. In the MS *t(er)ra* has been altered from *t(er)re*. 37 VILLAGERS. FB ii (5), 17. SMALLHOLDERS, NOW 10. FB, 30. [BEE] HIVES. LDB omits *apium*.
14,24	WINTER MILL. See 6,1 note. 80 AND 18 SHEEP. That is, fourscore and 18. 4 MEN HOLD. Only 3 are named here, but cf. FB ii (21), 'At COCKFIELD Gamilo holds from St. (Edmund's) 9 acres'. BERARD (HOLDS) 3 CARUCATES. FB ii (20, '(Berard) holds 1 carucate of land. 6 smallholders; 12 free (men) with 90 acres; 4 smallholders'. JAMES. LDB *Iames*, a very early occurrence in England of the OFr form of Latin *Iacobus*. Cf. DBS, s.n. *James*. COLEMAN. LDB *Goleman(us)* from OG *Coloman, Colman*; Forssner 55-56. BELONGED TO ST. (EDMUND'S). LDB *ei* is in error for *er(ant)*, cf. 14,27 etc.
14,25	1½ CARUCATES. The symbol in Farley between *&* and *d(imidia)* does not represent anything in the MS and appears to be a typographical error. WINTER MILL. See 6,1 note. [BUT] ST. EDMUND'S. LDB *r* (=*r(egis)*, cf. 14,29) is in error for *s(ed)*.
14,26	ARNULF. The name is interlined in LDB but appears to be the Abbey's 1086 tenant, as in 14,27. 3 FREEMEN ... LAND. FB ii (20) adds, '8 free men with 60 acres'.
14,27	ARNULF. In FB ii (20) he 'holds 3 carucates of land; 1 free (man) with 15 acres'.
14,28	FRODO. As 14,21 note. OTHERS HOLD THERE. LDB *ten&* is in error for *tenent*.
14,29	VALUE BEFORE 1066. LDB repeats *reg(is)* in error after *.t.r.e.* 6 [ORA]. LDB *bor* in error for *or*. For the *ora*, see 1,94 note. If it were here worth 16d, then the value given would equal 96d. Such a value for 50 acres would be roughly proportionate to the 16d for 8 acres in 14,30.
14,30	3 FREEMEN. FB i (5), 4. [BUT]. LDB *7* is in error for *s7* (=*s(ed)*).
14,32	ADELUND. LDB *Aelons*. See 14,36 note. ALWAYS 3 VILLAGERS ... SMALLHOLDERS, NOW 10. Misplaced in LDB, amongst the resources. VALUE ... NOW [£]2½. That is, £2 10s.
14,35	RALPH HOLDS ... SMALLHOLDERS. FB ii (18), Ralph the Fat (*Crassus*) holds ½ carucate of land and 40 acres; 5 smallholders'.
14,36	ADELUND ... 23 ACRES. FB ii (21), 'Adelo holds from St. (Edmund's) 1 carucate of land; 12 villagers, 2 slaves; 11 free (men)with 23 acres'. ADELUND. [LDB here *Aelons* (also in 14,32), but below at 14,58 *Adeludel*' and at 14,98 *Adelund*'] is from OG *Adalland*, Förstemann 174. The FB form is from OG *Adelo*, Förstemann 159, apparently used as an alternative name for the same man (J.M.D.).
14,37	1 FREE MAN ... SMALLHOLDERS. FB ii (18), Ralph the Fat (*Crassus*) 'holds 60 acres; 3 smallholders'. FULL JURISDICTION AND PATRONAGE OVER THEM ALL ... WRITS AND SEAL. These documents have not survived but were no doubt sealed writs of Edward the Confessor, cf. Hart ECEE no. 96. They related to the free men in 14,35-37.
14,38	60 ACRES ...; 60 ACRES ... FB ii (16), '1 carucate of land'. 2 VILLAGERS; 1 VILLAGER. FB, 2. 3 SMALLHOLDERS; 1 SMALLHOLDER. FB, 6.
14,39	AILBOLD THE PRIEST. Perhaps the same as Albold, a cleric, in 14,13. The name-forms, here *Ailboldus* and at 14,13 *Alboldus*, are probably both from OG *Ailbald, Aglebald*, Förstemann 29 (J.M.D.). King Henry I granted the land at Stonham formerly of Ailbold the priest, with service, to St. Edmund's 1100 x 1107, see FD no. 25.

	ENGELRIC. Probably the same as Engelric ('the priest' in FB) mentioned in 14,101 as one of the King's barons to whom the Abbot was in pledge. See 14,101 note. WHEN THE ENGLISH BOUGHT BACK THEIR LANDS. Some Englishmen who survived the Norman Conquest, and who could afford to, appear to have been allowed to buy back some of their lands. Cf. 14,101 and note.
14,42	10 VILLAGERS; 19 SMALLHOLDERS. FB i (9), '9 villagers, 15 smallholders'. 24 FREE MEN ... 80 ACRES. FB, '23 free (men) with 50 acres of land; 12 smallholders; 1 Freeman with 30 acres of land'.
14,44	12 FREE MEN AND 1 FREEMAN ... 30 ACRES. FB i (9), '14 free (men) with ½ carucate of land'.
14,45	4 CARUCATES ... 11 VILLAGERS ... 17 SMALLHOLDERS. FB i (10), '6 carucates of land; 1 villager; 19 smallholders'. 6 PIGS. In the MS *vi* has been altered from *xvi*. 29 FREE MEN. FB, 'Freemen'. 2 CARUCATES OF LAND LESS 12 ACRES. FB, '2 carucates of land'.
14,46	RICKINGHALL (SUPERIOR). Farley prints *Rachingehala* in error for *Richingehala* of the MS. FB i (9) has *Uprichingehale*. 14 FREE MEN ... 80 ACRES. FB, '9 free (men) with 50 acres of land'.
14,47	ST. EDMUND'S. In the MS there is an erasure (of about 3 letters) after *s(an)c(tu)s*.
14,48	THEDWESTRY HUNDRED. In the MS there is an erasure of two-thirds of a line of writing (ending *de s(an)c(t)o eadm(undo)*) before the name of the Hundred. 5 SMALLHOLDERS. FB i (5), 2. 7O FREE MEN. FB, 'Freemen'. 5 CARUCATES. In the MS *ii* has been erased before *v*. BELONG TO THE FOLD. See 14,1 note.
14,49	PAKENHAM. An estate here had been granted to St. Edmund's by King Edward 1044 x 1047 and had formerly belonged to one Osgot, see Harmer, *ASWrits* no. 14, Sawyer no. 1074, Hart ECEE no. 111. This Osgot may perhaps have been identical with the free man who leased ½ carucate for life from the Abbot, mentioned in this entry in LDB and in FB i (5-6). 31 FREE MEN. FB i (5), 'Freemen'.
14,50	10 FREE MEN. FB i (6), 'Freemen'.
14,51	90 FREE MEN. In the MS *LXXX* has been altered from *LXXX*. FB i (6), 'Freemen'.
14,52	3 FREE MEN. FB i (6), 'Freemen'. THIS ENTRY. FB ii (20), 'At BRADFIELD Arnulf holds from St. (Edmund's) 1 carucate of land; 6 smallholders; 2 free (men) with 15 acres'.
14,53	PETER. The Steward (*Dapifer*), FB ii (18); he is said to hold '60 acres; 6 smallholders'. OF THESE CARUCATES. LDB *histis* is in error for *istis*. 2 VILLAGERS (AND) 2 SMALLHOLDERS. FB, '1 villager, 10 smallholders, 1 Freeman and a half'. The number of smallholders in FB probably includes those whom Peter held at Culford, see 14,70 and note. HALL ... IN ANOTHER HUNDRED. Probably at Culford (in Bradmere Hundred), see 14,70.
14,54	RICHARD HOLDS ... ABBOT. FB ii (24) 'Richard the Bald (*Caluus*) holds 1½ carucates 'of land from St. (Edmund's)'. 8 FREE MEN. LDB *lib(er)i* is in error for *lib(er)os*. VALUE OF THE WHOLE SUB-HOLDING. Translating *medietaĺ om(n)e ual(et)*; *medietaĺ* would appear to stand for *medietat(um)* and to refer to Richard's mesne-tenure. Cf. 14,78 note. A CHURCH. The church at Thurston was confirmed to one Osward by Abbot Baldwin 1065 x 1098 and had previously been given to Osward's father, Aelfric the priest, by Abbot Leofstan, see FD no. 103. VALUE ... ALWAYS £1½. That is, £1 10s.
14,55-57	THESE ENTRIES. A large part of the text covered by these entries was added to LDB after the preceding and following entries, but by the same scribe. Part of 14,55 and all of 14,56 are squeezed untidily into the main text-block, while 14,57 is written in the left-hand margin with a transposition sign directing it to its proper place after 14,56.
14,55	HALL ... IN ANOTHER HUNDRED. Woolpit is near the boundary between Thedwestry and Blackbourn Hundreds. 17 VILLAGERS. FB i (6), 18. ... IN LORDSHIP. The number of lordship ploughs seems to have been omitted from LDB.

	JURISDICTION. Hart ECEE no. 103 (1042 x 1065) is a lost charter of Edward the Confessor which referred to Woolpit as being *de socagio*.
	IN WIDTH. LDB repeats *in* in error.
14,56	1 CARUCATE OF LAND. LDB *.i. car(ucata) in t(er)rae*; the word *in* is otiose and is probably a repetition of the last word of the previous line.
	6 SMALLHOLDERS. FB i (6), 11.
14,57	½ CARUCATE. FB ii (20), '60 acres'.
	ON HIM. Translating *sup(er) eu(m)*; that is, 'charge imposed on him'. This seems to be the value of a mesne-tenure here, cf. 14,54;78. A similar sub-value is given in 14,59;62.
14,58	ADELUND ... LAND. FB ii (21), '2 carucates of land; 3 smallholders'.
	ADELUND. See 14,36 note.
	... STILL BELONGED. Some text is missing from LDB here, giving details of the rights reserved to St. Edmund's.
14,59	RORIC ... ABBOT. FB ii (18) adds, '8 villagers; 4 smallholders; 5 slaves'. Forssner 219 takes the name to be OG *(H)Rodric*; note that the FB form is *Rerius* however.
	FALC ... ½ CARUCATE. FB ii (19-20), '60 acres of land; 4 smallholders; a half Freeman with 2 acres of land'. For the name, cf. Forssner 87 s.n. *Falco* and n.1.
	[ON] THEM. LDB *sub* seems to be in error for *sup(er)*, cf. 14,57;62 and notes.
	54S. VCH 499 is probably incorrect in taking *sot* to be an error for *soc* from *sochemanni*.
	SELL THEIR LANDS. *t(er)ras suas* was added in the margin in LDB, with a line to indicate
	its correct position in the text.
14,61	IN RATTLESDEN. The *I* of *In* has been omitted from LDB.
	[HE HAS]. LDB *h(abe)nt* is in error for *h(abe)t*.
	THIS ENTRY. Cf. FB ii (18), 'At RATTLESDEN Peter the Steward (*Dapifer*) holds from St. (Edmund's) 60 acres; 6 smallholders'.
14,62	ON HIM. As 14,57 note.
	20 ACRES. FB ii (24), 30.
	[VALUE]. LDB omits *ualuit*.
14,63	6 FREE MEN. In the MS *lib(er)os* has been altered from *lib(er)i*.
	THIS ENTRY. FB ii (21) adds, 'At AMPTON and TIMWORTH Saer holds from St. (Edmund's) 80 acres; 2 smallholders; 12 Freemen with 12 acres'.
14,64	1 PLOUGH; VALUE 20S. In the MS there is an erasure before *uat*, possibly *xx*.
	AS ALMS. LDB *elemosine* is in error for *elemosina*.
	7D IN TAX. In the MS there is an erasure before *.vii*.
	THIS ENTRY. See 14,63 note.
14,65	BEFORE 1066. LDB *.T.r.* is in error for *T.r.e.*
	FRODO. As 14,21 note.
14,66	WARIN. LDB *Gaurincus* is from the Rom. form (*Gaurin*) of OG *Warin*; Forssner 246-247.
	HOLDS 80 ACRES. FB ii (19), 'holds 1 carucate of land; 2 smallholders'.
14,68	(GREAT) LIVERMERE. Elsewhere placed in Lackford Hundred. The present entry, including 5 carucates, is the largest one however and the place is therefore mapped below in Thedwestry Hundred.
	10 FREE MEN WITH 1 CARUCATE; 12 FREE MEN WITH 2 CARUCATES; 1 FREE MAN ... WITH 2 CARUCATES. FB i (6), '23 free men with 3 carucates of land'.
	12 FREE MAN. In the MS *lib(er)os* has been altered from *lib(er)i*.
	IN THE SAME. LDB *Iead(em)* is in error for *In ead(em)*.
	1 FREE MAN. In the MS *lib(er)u(m)* has been altered from *lib(er)*.
	WERNO OF POIX. Probably from Poix (Somme), OEB 105. The fore-name (LDB *Guernoni*, dative) is from OG *Werino*, *Werno*; Forssner 251.
	HE GAVE THE LAND BACK. Between 1066 and April 1070 King William I granted the service from Livermere, until then held by Werno, to St. Edmund's, see FD no. 2.
	THIS ENTRY. FB ii (22) adds, 'At (Great) LIVERMERE Hubert the Breton holds from St. (Edmund's) 2 carucates of land; 2 villagers; 4 smallholders; 2 slaves. In the same place, Reginald his brother holds 1½ carucates; 3 smallholders; 23 free men with 1½ carucates of land'. Reginald may be identical with Reginald the Breton (*70*).
14,69	WULFWY. Farley prints *Wlfiuus* in error for *Wlfuius* of the MS.
14,70	PETER. The Steward (*Dapifer*), FB ii (18) where the number of smallholders at Culford is not given, although they are probably included in the total for Fornham (St. Genevieve), see 14,53 and note.
	[IN LORDSHIP]. LDB omits *in dominio*.
14,71	17D IN TAX. In the MS *xvii* has been altered from *xiiii*.
	THIS ENTRY. FB ii (19) adds that Odard 'holds 2 carucates of land; 8 smallholders; 14 free (men) with 60 acres of land'.

14,72	7 FREE MEN. LDB *lib(er)os* is in error for *lib(er)i*.
	THIS ENTRY. FB ii (19) adds that in Stanton Burcard holds '3 free (men) with 31½ acres' and in Bardwell '5 free (men) and a half with 60 acres'.
14,73	[HELD]. LDB *ten&* is in error for *tenuit*.
	ANOTHER HOLDS THERE. As 14,2 note.
14,75	THESE (FREEMEN) ... PATRONAGE AND JURISDICTION. LDB repeats 'patronage' in error after 'jurisdiction'.
	WHICH BELONG. LDB *p(er)tin&* (sing.) is in error for *p(er)tinent* (plural).
	OTHERS HOLD. LDB *tenet* is in error for *tenent*.
14,76	CONEY WESTON. This was granted to St. Edmund's 1051 x 1057, see Harmer, *ASWrits* no. 20, Sawyer no. 1080, Hart ECEE no. 115.
	[OF LAND]. LDB omits *terrae*.
	VILLAGERS; NOW AND ALWAYS 3 SMALLHOLDERS. However the ampersand (&) might perhaps be an error in LDB for the number of villagers 'now'.
14,77	14 FREE MEN. FB i (7), 'Freemen', *sochemannos* (accusative).
14,78	FULCHER ... ABBOT. FB ii (17), Fulcher holds '80 acres of land and 10; 4 free (men) with 36 acres of land'.
	AS A WHOLE SUB-HOLDING. Translating *de omñe medietaĺ*. Cf. 14,54 and note. The abbreviation-sign above *omne* appears to be otiose.
	PETER OF VALOGNES. See 37 and note.
	30 ACRES. FB ii (24), 'a half free (man) with 30 acres'.
14,79	OF THIS LAND, RORIC ... 1 CARUCATE. FB ii (19), 'At WATTISFIELD and at HEPWORTH he holds 1 carucate of land; 3 smallholders; 3 free (men) with 8 acres of land'.
	OTHERS HAVE [LAND] THERE. Translating *Alii ibi h(abe)nt*.
14,80	FULCHER ... ½ CARUCATE. FB ii (17), he 'holds 60 acres of land; 4 smallholders'.
	ANOTHER HOLDS THERE. As 14,2 note.
14,81-82	BURCARD. Because of the context, LDB *bucardus* is taken to be from OG *Burghard*, *Burcard* (Forssner 53-54), rather than OE *Burgheard* (PNDB 211-212).
14,81	FREE MEN ... 3. FB ii (19), 'Freemen', *sochemannos* (accusative).
	PETER OF VALOGNES ... 3 CARUCATES. Cf. FB ii (23), 'he holds 1 carucate of land; 10 villagers; 4 smallholders'. In LDB *& dim(idia)* has been deleted after *car(ucatis)*.
14,82	BARDWELL. The hyphen in the name-form in Farley represents a horizontal line in the MS correcting *beordewella* from two words to one.
	PETER OF VALOGNES HOLDS 10. FB ii (24), '10 free (men) and a half'.
	34¼D IN TAX. In the MS there is an erasure before the numeral.
	THIS ENTRY. FB ii (18) adds that at Bardwell Fulcher 'holds 60 acres of land; 1 smallholder'. FB ii (19) adds that Burcard 'holds from St. (Edmund's) 3 carucates of land; 3 smallholders; 2 slaves'. See also 14,72 note.
14,83	PETER OF VALOGNES ... 4 WITH 80 ACRES. FB ii (23), 'he holds 6 free (men) with 80 acres and 9 acres'.
14,85	FREE [LAND]. LDB omits *terrae*.
	PETER HOLDS 1 CARUCATE. FB ii (23), 'Peter of Valognes holds from St. (Edmund's) 1 carucate of land; 2 villagers; 2 free (men) with 70 acres; 9 free (men) with 60 acres'.
14,86	24 FREE MEN. FB i (8), 14.
14,87	7 FREE MEN. FB i (8), 6.
	STILL BELONG. LDB *remanet* (sing.) is in error for *remanent* (plural).
	WALTER HOLDS ... LAND. FB ii (20), 'Walter nephew of Peter the cleric holds from St. (Edmund's) 1½ carucates of land; 2 smallholders; 1 free (man) with 3 acres'.
	3 FREE MEN. LDB *lib(er)i* is in error for *lib(er)os*.
14,89	FULCHER HOLDS 80 ACRES. FB ii (17), '1 carucate of land'.
14,90	THIS ENTRY. Cf. FB ii (17), Fulcher 'holds 80 acres of land; 2 smallholders; 8 free (men) with 40 acres'.
14,91	2 FREE MEN. LDB *lib(er)os* is in error for *lib(er)i*.
14,92	WITH 3 CARUCATES OF LAND. In the MS there is an erasure after *car(ucatis)*, possibly of *acŕ*.
	STILL BELONG. LDB *reman&* is in error for *remanent*.
	ROBERT BLUNT ... LAND. FB ii (22) 'he holds 1½ carucates of land; 2 smallholders; 10 free (men) with 80 acres; over another 10 (free men) 3 carrying-services; a church with 8 acres; also the jurisdiction of the aforesaid villages (of Walsham le Willows and Great Ashfield)'.

14

14,93	ODARD ... 17 FREE MEN ... ACRES. FB ii (19), 'Odard holds from St. (Edmund's) 1 carucate of land; 5 smallholders; 13 free (men) with ½ carucate of land'. The fore-name Odard (LDB *Odar(us)*) represents the Rom. form of OG *Authart, Othard*; Forssner 194. ANOTHER HOLDS THERE. As 14,2 note.
14,95	4 SMALLHOLDERS. FB i (8), 3. [VALUE]. LDB omits *uat̂*. BURCARD ... 6 FREE MEN ... LAND. FB ii (19), Burcard 'holds 1 carucate of land; 4 smallholders and a half; 4 free (men) with 80 acres of land'. For Burcard, see 14,81-82 note. 6 FREE MEN. LDB has *lib(er)is* in error for *lib(er)os*.
14,96	PETER ... SMALLHOLDERS. FB ii (23), Peter of Valognes 'holds 1 carucate of land; 2 half free (men) with 45 acres; 8 villagers; 3 smallholders'. FREE MEN. LDB *lib(er)i* is in error for *lib(er)os*.
14,97	PETER. FB ii (24), of Valognes. 60 ACRES OF LAND. FB adds, '1 villager'.
14,98	ADELUND ... LAND. FB ii (21), 'he holds 1 carucate of land; 5 smallholders; 1 free (man) with 1 acre'. For Adelund, see 14,36 note. FREE MEN. As 14,96 note. [VALUE]. As 14,95 note. ANOTHER HOLDS THERE. As 14,2 note.
14,99	FULCHER ... SMALLHOLDERS. FB ii (18), Fulcher 'holds 60 acres of land; 8 smallholders'.
14,100	ROBERT BLUNT. In the MS *RodbErt(us)* has been altered from *Rod bl-*. 5 MEN. FB ii (21), '5 free (men)'.
14,101	9 FREE MEN. In the MS *lib(er)os* has been altered from *lib(er)i*. 1 FREE MAN. LDB *lib(er) h(om)o* is in error for *lib(er)u(m) ho(min)em*. PUT THIS LAND IN PLEDGE TO. FB i (8), 'bought this land back from'. Cf. 14,39 and note. BISHOP W(ILLIAM). Of Thetford (*18*). ENGELRIC. The priest, FB. Probably he of 14,39 and to be identified with the royal official in Essex (1,19;24;27), where he is shown to be identical with the predecessor of Count Eustace, see above 5,3-5 note. THIS ENTRY. Cf. FB ii (22), Robert Blunt 'holds 1 carucate of land; 7 free (men) and 2 half (free men) with 60 acres; a church with 12 acres.
14,102	[IT HAS]. LDB omits *Habet*. 10D IN TAX. In the MS there is an erasure before the numeral.
14,105	CHIPPENHALL. Given to St. Edmund's by Ulf son of Manni Swart, see 6,109 note.
14,106	FRODO. FB ii (23) adds, 'the Abbot's brother'. See *12* and note. MENDHAM. This manor was given to Frodo by Abbot Baldwin in exchange for one of the manors formerly held by Brictwulf son of Leofmer (see 14,5-6 note); FB i (4, 10). ABBOT. Baldwin, FB i (10). 19 ACRES OF LAND. FB i (10), 30. THIS ENTRY. FB ii (23) combines the details of population and land with those given in another entry for Mendham, in Norfolk (14,19), which was also held by Frodo from Abbot Baldwin.
14,107	[HOLDS]. LDB omits *ten̂*.
14,108	BEFORE 1066. In LDB *reg(is)* is otiose after *TR.e*. 13 SMALLHOLDERS. FB i (9), 14.
14,109	BEFORE 1066. LDB *.t.r.e.r.* with an otiose *r*. THEN AND NOW, ALWAYS. *t(un)c 7 m(odo)* in LDB is probably intended to be replaced by *se(m)p(er)*, but was not erased. IN TAX. See 14,110 first note.
14,110	MEADOW, 6 ACRES. The words *de.g̃.* after *.vi.* belong to the last sentence of 14,109. They were added to the MS later than the writing of the first line of 14,110. BERARD ... LAND. FB ii (21), 'he holds 1½ carucates of land'.
14,111-114	BEFORE 1066. As 14,109 note.
14,111	NOW 50[S]. In the MS there is an erasure after the numeral. BERARD ... FREE MEN. FB ii (21), 'he holds 1 carucate of land and 12 acres; 3 smallholders'. The 12 acres may perhaps be included in 14,112 which also relates to Whatfield.

	IN THE SAME ASSESSMENT. In the MS the words *i(n) eod(em) p(re)tio* were added in the margin. OTHERS HOLD. LDB *ten&* is in error for *tenent*.
14,112	FERTHING OF ALDHAM. FB i (9), 'Aldham'. The Ferthing (OE *feorthing*, 'a fourth part') represented a sub-division of the Hundred in E. Anglia into quarters, see O. S. Anderson, *The English Hundred-Names*, Lund 1934, xviii and note 5. THEY HAVE 1½ CARUCATES. In LDB *vi* has been deleted before *h(abe)nt*. VALUE OF THEIR LAND. Farley prints *uale7* in error for *ual7* of the MS. BERARD ... 40 ACRES. Cf. note to 14,111 (with regard to Whatfield).
14,113	IN LINDSEY. LDB *n* is in error for *In*. WHOEVER HOLDS THERE. This phrase is probably misplaced in LDB and should come after the details of tax.
14,114	KETTLEBASTON. Farley prints *bitel-* in error. In the MS the first letter is a *k* altered from *l*. The place-name form is thus *kitelbeornastuna*. GAMAS ... CARUCATE. FB ii (21), 'At MANTON he holds 1½ carucates of land; 3 villagers; 2 smallholders'. The fore-name is obscure but may represent a scribal error for *Gamar* < Rom. *Guaimar* < OG *Weimar*, cf. Forssner 100.
14,115	BEFORE 1066. *re* in LDB after *.t.r.e.* is otiose. ARNULF ... 30 ACRES. FB ii (20), 'At BRETTENHAM he holds 20 acres; 3 villagers'.
14,116	... [HOLDS]. LDB omits details of the holder, presumably St. Edmund's.
14,117	IN WALDRINGFIELD QUENEVA HELD. FB i (11), 'At WALDRINGFIELD 1 free (man)'. The fore-name (LDB *Quengeua*) is from OE **Cwengifu*, PNDB 220. She was the mother of Brictmer in 39,7-10. ABBOT. Baldwin, FB.
14,118	AND A HALF. *& dim* in LDB; this appears otiose, unless it refers to a half free man not under the patronage of St. Edmund's. It does not appear in FB i (11).
14,119	DURAND. The cleric, of St. Edmund's and of Abbot Baldwin's, FB i (11). Cf. also FB ii (24). FREE MEN. LDB *lib(er)i* is in error for *lib(er)os*.
14,120	... MEN'S PLOUGHS. LDB omits both *car* and the numeral. HERRINGS. As 1,12 note.
14,121	BISHOP W(ILLIAM). Of Thetford (*18*).
14,122	10 ACRES. FB i (10), 20.
14,123	19 ACRES. FB ii (22), 16. THIS ENTRY. See 14,151 note.
14,126	14 FREE MEN. FB i (10), 10.
14,129	IN OAKLEY ... HARTISMERE HUNDRED. *In ACLE* appears to have been written in error in LDB before the Hundred rubric, anticipating the following line and necessitating the use of the preposition *DE*. 1 FREE MAN ... 90 ACRES ... 10 FREE MEN; 30 ACRES. FB i (10), '11 free (men) with 1 carucate of land'.
14,130	5 FREE MEN ... 44½ ACRES. FB i (10), '4 free (men) with 30 acres of land'.
14,131	11 FREE MEN ... 68 ACRES. FB i (10), '6 free (men) with ½ carucate of land'. ST. EDMUND'S. LDB *s(an)c(tu)s* is in error for *s(an)c(t)i*.
14,132	8 FREE MEN ... 60 ACRES. FB i (10), '6 free (men) with ½ carucate of land'.
14,133	LIKEWISE. That is, in the jurisdiction and under the patronage of the Abbot, as in 14,132.
14,134	6 FREE MEN ... 75 ACRES. See 14,151 note.
14,135	1 VILLAGER. FB i (10), '1 free (man)'.
14,136	KALDECOTES. See 6,212 note. THEY ALL ... DUES. Probably referring to the men in 14,129-136, all in Hartismere Hundred as was Rickinghall (Superior).
14,137-138	THESE ENTRIES. Cf. FB i (10), 'At OAKLEY and at STUSTON 16 free (men) with 1 carucate of land and 50 acres; 12 smallholders. Jocelyn, a man of Frodo's, holds this from St. Edmund's and Abbot Baldwin'.
14,138	LEOFSIDU. LDB *Leuseda* from OE *Lēofsidu*; PNDB 315 note 3. 4 PIGS. In the MS *iiij* has been altered from *iii*.
14,139	ANSELM. A man of Frodo's, FB i (10). Radfrid, FB ii (17). ABBOT. Baldwin. FB i (10). 6 SMALLHOLDERS. FB i (10), 5. FB ii (17), 7. 12 FREE MEN AND A HALF; 42 ACRES. FB i (10), '13 free (men) and a half with 41 acres of land'. FB ii (17), '14 Freemen and a half with 45 acres of land'.

14 - 16

14,141-
142 [ST.] LDB omits *sancti*.
14,145 CHIPPENHALL. Here placed in Hartismere Hundred, but elsewhere in Bishop's Hundred.
14,146 BURGHARD. Of Mendlesham, see 14,152 and 1,76-77.
ROBERT FARTHING. LDB *fardenc*. The byname may be a patronymic from ON *Farthegn*, ODan *Farthin*, but may also be from OE *feorthing*, 'a fourth part', 'a farthing'. See OEB 217; DBS 124.
WALTER OF DOL ... FORFEITED. See 4,15 note.
14,149 CALDECOTA. See 6,212 note.
14,151 THIS ENTRY and 14,123;134. FB i (10) combines the entries and states, 'At WYVERSTONE 9 free (men) and a half with 110 acres of land. Of these (free men), Richard Houerel holds 5 and a half from St. Edmund's and Abbot Baldwin'. The byname Houerel may perhaps be an OFr derivative from **houer* 'one who makes or uses hoes', cf. A. Dauzat, *Dictionnaire étymologique des noms de familles et prénoms de France*, Paris 1951, s.nn. *Houel, Hoyau, Houyer* (J.M.D.).
14,152 BURGHARD OF MENDLESHAM. See 1,76.
14,155 75 [ACRES]. LDB *car* is in error for *acr*, cf. FB i (8).
14,156 95 ACRES. FB i (8), 25.
14,157 8 FREE MEN. FB i (8), 9.
14,162 THIS ENTRY. Misplaced in LDB, before rather than after 14,163.
TRACT OF LAND. Translating *diuisio*.
14,163 FOR THE SUPPLIES OF THE MONKS. This was one of the manors whose revenue paid for the food of the monks.
SEA-WEIR. LDB *heie maris* (genitive), a device for off-shore fishing, here apparently for herring. See further, DBE 285-286.
14,164 GODWIN. FB i (11), '1 free (man)'.
UGGESHALL. Cf. also *Huggingehale*, FB ii (16), where 'Berengar holds from St. (Edmund's) 2 carucates of land; 1 villager; 12 smallholders; 2 free (men) and 2 half (free men) with 50 acres of land'. See also 76,19.
ST. EDMUND'S ... JURISDICTION. LDB has an otiose abbreviation mark above *socam*; *s(an)c(t)i* is in error for *s(an)c(tu)s*.
1 FREE MAN AND A HALF. FB i (11), '1 Freeman and a half'.
14,166 IN UFFORD. LDB *Iuffeforda* is in error for *In uffeforda*.
14,167 ST. EDMUND ... KING AND MARTYR. The King of the East Angles who was killed by the Vikings in 870 and who was the patron saint of Bury.
CERTAIN (AMOUNT OF) AID. Translating *aliq(ui)d adiutorii*. It is uncertain whether *adiutorium* should be taken to be similar to the later *auxilium*, 'aid', owed by the royal Boroughs to the King.
AND YET IT IS THE SAME NOW. LDB *si* is in error, perhaps for *etsi*, 'and yet'.
CHRISTIAN PEOPLE. In the MS *pop(u)lo* has been altered from *põl*.
THIS ENTRY. There is no mention here of the mint, although the Abbot's moneyers are referred to in documents of Edward the Confessor (Harmer, *ASWrits* no. 25; Sawyer no. 1085; Hart ECEE no. 119), William I (FD no. 5), and William II (FD no. 14).
Folio 372a, foot. A (deleted) partial list of landholders (*15-16, 18-19*), similar to that at folio 292a, above. This occurs on the first folio of quire 48 in LDB. It gives the names of four of the five landholders in this quire (omitting *17*, Ramsey Abbey). See further, note to List of Landholders, above.
15 ARCHBISHOP LANFRANC. Of Canterbury, 1070-89.
THE MONKS' SUPPLIES. That is, the monks of Holy Trinity, Canterbury, see 15,2-3 note.
STIGAND. Archbishop of Canterbury, see 1,107-119 note.
15,2-3 HOLY TRINITY. More usually known as Christ Church, Canterbury.
15,2 3 FREEMEN DWELL. In LDB *manent* has been altered from *m(odo)* but the superscript *o* has not been erased.
15,3 JOHN NEPHEW OF WALERAN. A landholder in Essex (*65*) and distinct from John son of Waleran (*55* below; and Essex *40*).
15,4 1 FREE MAN. LDB *lib(er)u(m) ho(min)em* is in error for *lib(er) h(om)o*.
16 BISHOP OF BAYEUX. Odo, half-brother of King William and elder brother of Count Robert of Mortain (*2*). He was Earl of Kent 1066/67 to 1082, 1087 to 1088. He acted as 'regent' during some of King William's absences abroad but was imprisoned 1082-87. During his imprisonment his lands were maintained as a unit and appear so in the Domesday Survey.

16,1	TIHEL. Cf. Tihel of Helléan 16,9. HIS PREDECESSOR. That is, the Bishop's. THE 6 FORFEITURES. As 8,35 note.
16,3	BEORN ... 50 ACRES. IE (151) adds, 'which he could not sell'. IEAL (183), in the Holding of Hamo of Saint-Clair (see 6,271 last note). Cf. also IEAL (188), among the lands which Roger Bigot annexed from St. Etheldreda's, '1 free man; 1 acre of land. Meadow, 4 acres'. W. DE MORE. OEB 47 suggests that the byname is from an unidentified place named from OE mōr, 'moor'. Another possibility however is that de More is in error for de Nemore, de Nomore and that this refers to William of Bosc (see 7,115 note). EARL R(ALPH). Wader, see 1,61-95 note. THREE MANORS. The one at Seckford (16,2) and the two at Little Bealings (16,3).
16,4	1 FREE MAN ... ST. E(THELDREDA'S). IE (146) and IEAL (182), 'Young Leofwin'. RALPH OF SAVENAY. From Savenay (Calvados), Loyd 95. Cf. OEB 114. NOW ½. IE, 'now 1'. THIS ENTRY. IEAL (182), in the Holding of Hamo of Saint-Clair (see 6,271 last note). Cf. IEAL (188), amongst the lands which Roger Bigot annexed from St. Etheldreda's, '6 free men; 32 acres. 1 plough'.
16,5	15 ACRES. IE (146) and IEAL (182), 16. IEAL (188), 12. FREE MAN. LDB lib(er)u(m) ho(min)em might seem to be in error for lib(er) h(om)o, unless it is to be taken that he also was held by R(oger) Bigot, as in 16,4. Cf. IE and IEAL (188). ½ ACRE. IE, 3 or 4 in the different MSS. IEAL (182,188), 4. THIS ENTRY. IEAL (182) in the Holding of Hamo of Saint-Clair (see 6,271 last note). Cf. IE (146) and IEAL (188) amongst, the lands which Roger Bigot annexed from St. Etheldreda's.
16,6	IN CHARSFIELD ... THE ABBOT. Cf. IE (152), '3 free men half under the patronage of St. E(theldreda's) and 5 free men under the patronage of St. Etheldreda's; 3 carucates of land'. Cf. also IEAL (188), '8 free men; 3 carucates of land', amongst the lands which Roger Bigot annexed from St. Etheldreda's; and IEAL (183), '8 Freemen with 3 carucates of land', in the Holding of Hamo of Saint-Clair (see 6,271 last note). 2 FREEMEN ... 7 ACRES. IE (152) and IEAL (183) names them as Leofric and Alfwold and IE (152) adds, 'who could not sell their land'. Cf. also IEAL (188), amongst the lands which Roger Bigot annexed from St. Etheldreda's, 'in BLAXHALL 2 free men'. 1 FREE MAN. LDB lib(er)u(m) ho(min)em is in error for lib(er) h(om)o. MARCULF. This represents either ODan Markulf or OG Marculf; PNDB 325, Forssner 287.
16,7	BALKI. LDB Balchi. Ths name is ON, PNDB 192.
16,8	4 ... ST. E(THELDREDA'S). IE (152) and IEAL (183) names them as Godric, Wulfric, Huscarl, and Sprotwulf. IEAL (183), in the Holding of Hamo of Saint-Clair (see 6,271 last note). Cf. IEAL (188), amongst Roger Bigot's annexations from St Etheldreda's. Huscarl in IE and IEAL is here used as a pers. n. (PNDB 296-297); see 67,10 for its use as a descriptive occupational term ('guard'). TIHEL OF HELLÉAN. See 42 and note. AELFEVA MOTHER OF EARL MORCAR. See 1,97-99 note. RALPH OF COURBÉPINE. From Courbépine (Eure), OEB 85.
16,11	WILLIAM OF BOUVILLE. Probably from Bouville (Seine-Inf.), OEB 78-79. He was the son of Saxwalo of Bouville, see 32,31.
16,12	ALSI. This represents late OE Alsige, PNDB 151-152. WARENGAR. From OG Weringer, Forssner 246. Possibly the same man who held lands from Roger Bigot in Essex (43,1-2).
16,13	RODEHAM. Unidentified, DG 409.
16,15	ROBERT MALET ... HIS FATHER. William Malet. [IN POSSESSION OF]. LDB omits saisitus. [THE EARL]. LDB omits comes. SPERUN. PNDB 369-370 suggests that this is a byname from OFr esperun, 'spur'.
16,16	'OLDEN'. See 1,5 note. ROGER OF RAMES. See 38 and note. He was also in dispute over land held by Roger Bigot's sub-tenant Warengar in Essex (43,1). THORMAR. LDB Thurmero (ablative) from ODan, OSw Thormar; PNDB 395. WAR(ENGAR). See note on Roger of Rames above.
16,18	AILBERN. LDB Ailb(er)nus, from OG Egilbern, Ailbern; PNDB 141.
16,19	PACHETUNA. Unidentified, DG 407.

16,20	HAROLD ... 30 ACRES. IEAL (188), among Roger Bigot's annexations from St. Etheldreda's. IE (144), he is 'in the full jurisdiction' of the Abbot. MEADOW, 2 ACRES. IE, 1 acre.
16,21	'OLDEN'. As 1,5 note.
16,22	60 ACRES. The cross in Farley above *LX* is also in the MS. It probably marks a place where an insertion was to be made, but none was added. Cf. the interlineation in the previous entry. ALWOLD. LDB *Aluol*, from late OE *Alweald*; PNDB 154-155.
16,24	ROGER. Probably Roger Bigot as in 16,23.
16,25	MALET. Robert Malet.
16,26	HELMINGHAM. LDB *Hm-* is in error for *Helm-*. LEOFSTAN. His land formed part of the same Holding as that of Osferth in 6,106 note. He was apparently identical with Leofstan in 6,155. ... OF FREE LAND. LDB omits the number of acres.
16,27	IN THE JURISDICTION. IE (145), 'in the full jurisdiction'. MEADOW, 2 ACRES; ... As shown by Farley, two-thirds of a line of writing has been erased in the MS. THIS ENTRY. IE adds, 'R(oger) Bigot now holds from him [the Bishop of Bayeux]'. Cf. also IEAL (188). IEAL (182), listed in the Holding of Hamo of Saint-Clair (see 6,271 last note).
16,28	40 ACRES. IEAL (188), 41. THIS ENTRY. IEAL (182), in the Holding of Hamo of Saint-Clair. Cf. IE (145-146) and IEAL (188), amongst Roger Bigot's annexations from St. Etheldreda's.
16,29	IN ULVERSTON ... 8 ACRES. IEAL (182), in the Holding of Hamo of Saint-Clair. Cf. IE (145-146) and IEAL (188), amongst Roger Bigot's annexations from St. Etheldreda's.
16,30	WILLIAM MALET. In the MS there is an erasure after *malet*. AELFRIC THE PRIEST ... IEAL (182) lists this and the following free men in this entry under the Holding of Hamo of Saint-Clair. Cf. IE (145-146) and IEAL (188), where they are listed amongst Roger Bigot's annexations from St. Etheldreda's. IEAL (188) omits one of the free men with 40 acres. PATRONAGE (ARE). In the MS there is an erasure after *co(m)m(en)datio*, probably of *ne*, cf. the line below. YOUNG LEOFWIN. The byname (LDB *cilt*) is from OE *cīld*, 'child, young', OEB 243-245.
16,31	½ ACRE. IEAL (188), 4 acres. THIS ENTRY. IEAL (182), in the Holding of Hamo of Saint-Clair. IE (145-146) and IEAL (188), amongst Roger Bigot's annexations from St. Etheldreda's. BEFORE THIS ENTRY. IE (145), 'In DEBENHAM 1 free man, Brictric, with 40 acres'. IEAL (182), in the Holding of Hamo of Saint-Clair. Cf. IE (145-146) and IEAL (188), amongst Roger Bigot's annexations from St. Etheldreda's.
16,32	*MANEWIC*. See 4,2-3 note on *MANUUIC*. WOODBROWN. LDB *W de brun*, but cf. 16,14. From OE **Wudu-Brūn*, PNDB 417. OEB 391 erroneously interprets the LDB form as Willelmus *de Brun*, standing for *le Brun*. 27 ACRES. IEAL (188), 28. THIS ENTRY. IEAL (182), in the Holding of Hamo of Saint-Clair. IE (145-146) and IEAL (188), amongst Roger Bigot's annexations from St. Etheldreda's.
16,33	IN WINSTON. IE (145) includes the additional entry, 'In WINSTON 1 free man with 25 acres'. Also in IEAL (182,188). 21 FREE MEN. IEAL (182), '21 Freemen'; in the Holding of Hamo of Saint-Clair. '21 free men' IE (146) and IEAL (188), amongst Roger Bigot's annexations from St. Etheldreda's. (EARL) RALPH. Wader, see 1,61-95 note. MALET. Robert Malet.
16,34	SNARING. LDB *Suarin(us)*, with *u* in error for *n*. The name is either a derivative of ON *Snari, Snara*, or is OG *Snaring*; PNDB 367. NORMAN. The Sheriff (63). HUBERT OF PORT. He is also mentioned as a royal official in 77,4. Cf. also Essex 32,29 and 83,2. He took his name from Port-en-Bessin (Calvados), OEB 108, Loyd 79-80. His main holding was at Mapledurwell (Hampshire 24,1). THE KING'S BARONS. Probably a reference to the Domesday Commissioners themselves. THIS ENTRY. IEAL (182), in the Holding of Hamo of Saint-Clair. IE (146) and IEAL (188), amongst Roger Bigot's annexations from St. Etheldreda's.

16,35	AND 1 MILL, NOW ½. Either ½ mill or ½ plough could be meant here. JURISDICTION ... EXCEPT OVER HIS HOUSE. LDB *Saca* may here be in error for *Soca*, but cf. Norfolk, Technical Terms.
16,38	MALET. Robert Malet.
16,40	TUNEMAN. OE *Tūnmann*, literally 'villager', but here used as a fore-name; PNDB 388-389. THEN 7 VILLAGERS. The 7 before *vii* is otiose in LDB. 4D [IN TAX]. LDB omits *de gelto*.
16,41	1 LEAGUE IN LENGTH. *in long(itudine)* repeated in error in LDB and deleted. SMERI. Perhaps from ON *Smiǫri*, see PNDB 367. AELFRIC KEMP. The byname is either OE *cempa* 'warrior' or a derivative of OWScand *kampr*, 'moustache'; OEB 243. [1] FREE MAN. In the MS *.i. lib(er) h(om)o*; Farley omits the numeral.
16,43	BELENEI. Unidentified, DG 390. ALWOLD. LDB *Alnold*, with *n* in error for *u*. From late OE *Alweald*, PNDB 154-155. ALFILDESTUNA. Also at 36,5. In Samford Hundred and a Half. Unidentified, DG 389 (which has *Als-* in error for *Alf-*).
16,47	TOFT. Also at 25,73. In Samford Hundred and a Half. Unidentified, DG 413.
17	ST. BENEDICT'S OF RAMSEY. The Benedictine Abbey at Ramsey, Huntingdonshire. In the MS there is a letter *f* in the left margin next to the chapter number, not shown by Farley. Similar marginalia occur *passim* against chapter numbers in both GDB and LDB. Their significance has not yet been fully ascertained. Cf. R. Welldon Finn, *Domesday Studies: The Eastern Counties*, London, 1967, 61-62.
18	WILLIAM, BISHOP OF THETFORD. William of Beaufour, a royal clerk, nominated Bishop of Thetford 25 December 1085. The date of his consecration is not recorded. He died, or resigned, before 27 January 1091. THETFORD. The East Anglian See had been moved from (North) Elmham in 1071 or early in 1072. It moved again, to Norwich, 1094 x 1095.
18,1	BISHOP AELMER. Consecrated Bishop of Elmham after August 1047. Deposed *c*.11 April 1070. He was the brother of Archbishop Stigand of Canterbury (see 1,107-119 note). ROBERT (MALET). Son of William Malet, see 6. CHURCH ... EPISCOPAL SEE. The church at Hoxne was the Suffolk centre of the East Anglian Bishopric before 1066. The Norfolk centre was then at (North) Elmham (see *18*, second note). Bequests to the community at Hoxne were made in 942 x 951 (Whitelock, *ASWills* no. 1; Sawyer no. 1526; Hart ECEE no. 49) and 1035 x 1040 (Whitelock, *ASWills* no. 26; Sawyer no. 1489; Hart ECEE no. 88).
18,4	10 MEN'S PLOUGHS. In LDB *omniu(m)* has been deleted before *ho(m)i(n)u(m)*. NOW IT PAYS. LDB *reddid(it)* is in error for *redd(it)*. FERTHING. See 14,112 note. JURISDICTION ... EXCEPT OVER BISHOP STIGAND'S MEN. In the MS the words *saca(m) p(re)t(er) ho(min)es Stigan-* have been written over an erasure. HAD A WRIT. This has not survived, see Hart ECEE no. 120. THAT HE HIMSELF. In the MS there is an erasure before *ipse*. HIS MEN. LDB *sui* is in error for *suos*.
18,6	CHURCH OF HOXNE. That is, the Bishopric, see 18,1 note. VCH 516 erroneously places this entry in the following chapter. The heading to Chapter 19 is placed however against the second entry on folio 379b (here designated 19,1).
19	THE BISHOP OF THETFORD'S HOLDING. This chapter includes the lands acquired by Bishop Aelmer himself, distinct from those anciently belonging to the See listed in *18*. See also 18,6 note.
19,1-10	[BISHOP'S HUNDRED]. The Hundred rubric is omitted from LDB.
19,1-3	AELMER. Bishop Aelmer, see 18,1 note.
19,1-2	ERFAST. Consecrated Bishop of Elmham in 1070. He moved the See to Thetford in 1070 or early in 1072.
19,2	[MEN'S] PLOUGHS. LDB omits *hominum*. CHURCH. The minster and a hide of land at Mendham were granted to the church there in 942 x 951 (Whitelock, *ASWills* no. 1; Sawyer no. 1526; Hart ECEE no. 49). The same document also refers to the community at Mendham church. See also following note. LISTED IN NORFOLK. Translating *in breuiata in norfolc*. Mendham straddled the county boundary in 1086; see Norfolk 10,32 for another 43 acres of church land there.
19,9	CHICKERING. LDB *Cicheling* altered to *Ciccheling*.
19,14	NOW IT PAYS [x3]. As 18,4 note.

19,15	BISHOP STIGAND. Bishop Aelmer's brother, see 18,1 note. NOW IT PAYS 10[S] 8D. LDB *reddit* is in error for *redd(it)*. NOW IT PAYS 31[S] 4D. LDB *reddidit* is in error for *reddit*.
19,16	(SOUTH) ELMHAM. LDB *Almea(m)* altered to *Almeha(m)*. INGVAR. LDB *In Wari* (genitive), where it was apparently mistaken for a place-name. From ODan, OSw *Ingvar*; PNDB 298-299. 1 COB ... 30 GOATS. Misplaced in LDB, among the ploughs, rather than after the woodland. VALUE THEN ... S. LDB omits the numeral.
19,17	WILLIAM OF NOYERS. See 1,107-119 note.
19,18	HAD PATRONAGE. LDB *habuit* is in error for *habuerunt*.
19,19	OTHERI. LDB *Othem(us)* is in error for *Otheri(us)*. From OG *Otheri*, *Authari*, Förstemann 195 (J.M.D.).
19,21	[OF LOTHINGLAND]. LDB omits the name.
20	BISHOP OF ROCHESTER. Bishop Gundulf, 1077-1108. In the MS there is a letter *f* in the right margin next to the chapter number, not shown by Farley; see *17* note.
20,1	ORTHI. Possibly OSw, see PNDB 338. FRECKENHAM. Sawyer no. 349, Hart ECEE no. 48, is a spurious charter of King Alfred granting Freckenham to the Bishop of Rochester. It may have been forged to back up the Bishop's claim to the estate which was the subject of dispute after 1066. LANFRANC. Archbishop of Canterbury, see *15* note. EARL RALPH. Wader, see 1,61-95 note.
21	ST. ETHELDREDA'S. Ely Abbey. For a list of food rents from its Suffolk (and other) manors, see LibEl 152-153.
21,1	MEN'S PLOUGHS, NOW 3. IE (153), 6. IEBrev (171), 6 or 5 in the different MSS. IENV (175), 15. MEADOW, 16 ACRES. IE, adds '2 beehives'. THEN [AND] NOW. LDB omits 7. VALUE ALWAYS £10. IE, 'Value then £8; now [£]10'. HUMPHREY. Son of Rodric, see 26,1. 16 FURLONGS. IE, '1 league and 4 furlongs'.
21,2	FALC. Probably he of 14,59. ABBEY ... IN THE KING'S HAND. Probably during the vacancy in the Abbey, 1075/6-1082, see HRH 45.
21,3	SMALLHOLDERS, NOW 7. IE (154) and IEBrev (172), 8. MEN'S PLOUGHS, NOW 1. IEBrev and IENV (175), 2. HORSES. IE, 'cobs'.
21,4	THE FULL JURISDICTION. IE (154) adds, 'and patronage'. VALUE 4S. IEAL (182), '5s'. THIS ENTRY. IEAL, stated to be held by Henry, the Abbot of St. Edmund's man.
21,5	4 SMALLHOLDERS. IE (154) adds, 'and 1 in WANGFORD'. MEADOW, [3] ACRES. Farley omits *7.iii.* which is present in the MS. IE, 4; it adds,'½ mill' and 'always 2 cobs'. 2 ASSES. The only two mentioned in Domesday Suffolk.
21,6	5 SMALLHOLDERS. IE (154), 4. FISHERIES. An annual gift to Ely of 4000 eels from Lakenheath was confirmed by King Cnut in 1021 x 1023, according to Sawyer no. 980, Hart ECEE no. 86. HORSES. IE 'cobs'. 20D IN TAX. IE, '10d'.
21,7	UNDLEY. LDB *Lundale* is in error for *Und-*. 3 SMALLHOLDERS. IE (154), 'Always 5 smallholders'. 2 PLOUGHS. IE, 1. HORSE. IE, 'COB'. 24 CATTLE. IE, 23. THIS ENTRY. IEAL (181), Norman is stated to hold this manor from the lordship.
21,8	JURISDICTION. IE (155), 'full jurisdiction'.
21,9	IN (GREAT) LIVERMERE. IE (154) adds, 'and in WANGFORD'. IN THE JURISDICTION OF ST. EDMUND'S. IE, 'now under the patronage and in the full jurisdiction of St. Edmund's'.
21,10	18 SMALLHOLDERS. IE (155) and IEBrev (172), 16. 7 MEN'S PLOUGHS. IE and IEBrev, 8.

	HORSES. IE, 'cobs'.
	8 CATTLE. IE, 18.
	1 FREEMAN ... 8 ACRES. IE adds, 'Value 12d.'.
21,11	HORSES. IE (155), 'cobs'.
	VALUE 5S. IE, '3s'.
	[FREEMAN]. LDB *soca* is in error for *soć*.
21,12	NOT SELL. IE (157) adds, 'or grant'.
21,13	10 ACRES OF FORFEITED LAND. IE (157) '10 acres of land. He could not sell his land'.
21,14	ROGER OF AUBERVILLE. Cf. 29,1.
	34 ACRES OF LAND. IE (157) adds, 'which they could not sell. ½ plough'.
	VALUE 4S. IE, '5s'.
21,15	THEN 1 SLAVE. IE (158) adds, 'now none'.
	4D IN A TAX OF 20S. Stoke paid 4d when a tax of 20s was levied on the Half-Hundred of Ipswich.
21,16	MEN'S PLOUGHS, NOW 15. IENV (175), 6.
	A CHURCH ... 2 PLOUGHS. IE (157), '1 plough'.
	ARPENTS. A French measure of uncertain and probably variable size, usually applied to vineyards in the Domesday records, but sometimes to meadow and woodland. See Wiltshire 12,4 note. In the MS there is an erasure after *arpen*, probably of *7i*.
	IN LORDSHIP, 11 COBS. IE, 'and 1 part of BOSMERE. Always 11 cobs'.
	AFTER 1066. LDB *.t.r.e. Will(elm)i* is in error for *.t.r. Will(elm)i*.
	THE ABBOT ... FOR £20. IE, '(Value) now £20'.
	THIS ENTRY. Cf. IEAL (181) which states that Sictric holds 1 carucate of land in Barking from the lordship.
21,17	FREE MEN. LDB *lib(eri) lib(er)i ho(min)es* with an erroneous repetition of 'free'.
	1 CARUCATE. IEAL (178), 2.
	JURISDICTION. IE, 'full jurisdiction'.
	BISHOP OF ST. LÔ. Also at 29,9. IE, 'Bishop of Coutances'.
21,18	ROGER. IE (157), Roger Bigot.
21,19	JURISDICTION. As 21,17 note.
	ROGER OF AUBERVILLE. Cf. 29,9.
21,21	1 FREEMAN ... 12 ACRES. IE (158) adds, 'Value 8s'.
21,22	**JURISDICTION.** IE (158), 'full jurisdiction'.
21,23	THIS ENTRY. IE adds 'This belongs to Barham'.
	'OLDEN'. As 1,5 note.
21,25	KING AND EARL ... JURISDICTION. IE (159), 'in the jurisdiction of the King'.
21,26	LICTEVA. LDB *Listeua*, from OE **Lēohtgifu*; PNDB 319.
	BARHAM. According to LibEl 166 (Hart ECEE no. 116), Earl Algar (see 8,33 note) granted Barham to the Abbot of Ely 1051 x 1057.
	AS A MANOR. IE (159) adds, 'in lordship'.
	PLOUGHS IN LORDSHIP, NOW 1. IEBrev (172), 2.
	16 ACRES. IE adds, 'of free land'.
	17 SHEEP. In the MS *xvij* has been altered from *xvi*. IE, 27 or 28, in the different MSS.
	ALWAYS 1 PLOUGH. IE adds, 'Meadow, 2 acres'.
	THEN 1 PLOUGH, NOW ½. IE, 'Always 1 plough'.
	THEN 1 SMALLHOLDER, NOW 2. IE, '3 smallholders'.
21,27	IN SHARPSTONE. Farley prints *Escarletuna* in error for *Escarlestuna* of the MS. IE (159) 'In the same village (of Barham)'. IEAL (181), 'In Barham'.
21,28	PLOUGHS IN LORDSHIP, NOW 1. IEBrev (172), 2.
21,29	ASERET. Probably from ON *Asrøthr*; PNDB 169.
	25 ACRES. IE (159-160) adds, 'He could not sell his land'.
	UNDER PATRONAGE. IE (160) adds, 'only'.
21,30	THORKELL ... 20 ACRES. IEAL (179), '1 free man with 21 (acres)'.
	OF HUGH'S PREDECESSOR. IE (160), 'of the Earl'.
21,31	A HALF FREE MAN. IEAL (178), '1 free man'.
21,32	VALUE 8D. IE (160), '10d' or '9d' in the different MSS.
21,35	WALTER. IE (161), 'Walter the Deacon'.
21,36	IN BLAXHALL. IE (165) adds, 'St. Etheldreda's holds in lordship'.
	½ PLOUGH. IE, 1.
	THIS ENTRY. Cf. perhaps also IEAL (180) where it is stated that Hervey of Bourges holds in Blaxhall, '5 free men with 16 acres'.

21,38	SMALLHOLDERS, NOW 21. IE (165) and IEBrev (172), 22.
	THEN 2 SLAVES. IE adds, 'now not'.
	PLOUGHS IN LORDSHIP, NOW 1. IEBrev, 3.
	MEN'S PLOUGHS, NOW 6. IE and IEBrev, 5.
	THEN 1 COB, NOW 2. IE, 'Always 2 cobs'.
	VALUE ALWAYS £7. IE, 'Value then £6; now £7', or 'now £8' in the different MSS. See also 21,104 note.
21,39	2 COBS. IE (166), 'Always 2 cobs at the hall'.
	UNDER PATRONAGE. IE adds, 'of St. Etheldreda's'.
21,40-41	6 FORFEITURES. See 8,35 note.
21,40	FRODO ... FROM THE ABBOT. IEAL (181) states that he held this from the lordship and identifies him as Abbot (Baldwin's) brother (12).
	THEN 20 SHEEP. IE (155) adds, 'now none'.
21,42	VILLAGERS, NOW 36. IEBrev (172), 26.
	PLOUGHS IN LORDSHIP, NOW 3. IEBrev, 4.
	VALUE THEN £20. IE (156), '£16'.
21,43	MEN'S PLOUGHS, NOW 1. IEBrev (172) and IENV (175), 2.
	2 COBS. IE (156) adds, 'always'.
	CHURCH, 7 ACRES. IE, 8.
21,44	60 ACRES. IEAL (178) adds, 'of thaneland'. That is, leasehold land.
	123 ACRES. In the MS there is an erasure before the numeral. IEAL (187), '1 hide and 24 acres from the lordship'.
21,45	2 CARUCATES. IEAL (178), 3.
	7 SMALLHOLDERS. IE (156), 8.
	[BEE]HIVES. LDB here uses the MLat word *rusca* (Latham 414) rather than the usual *vasa*.
	ROBERT MALET. LDB *Male&* is in error for *Mal&*.
	HOLDS (IT). IE adds, 'from the Abbot'.
	JURISDICTION. IE uses *saca* instead of LDB's *soca*. See Norfolk, Technical Terms.
21,47	ALNETERNE. Unidentified, DG 389 (*Alnet'ne*).
	TO THIS MANOR BELONG. LDB *p(er)tinet* is in error for *p(er)tinent*.
	80 BURGESSES. IE (158), 'men'.
	[ON] 14 ACRES. Farley prints *iii* in error for *in* of the MS.
	IN THE SAME (*ALNETERNE*). IE, 'To this manor'.
	WHO DWELL ... BOSMERE. IE omits.
	FULL JURISDICTION. IE adds, 'and patronage'.
	THIS ENTRY. IEAL (181) states that Sictric holds this from the lordship.
21,48-50	UNDER THE PATRONAGE. IE (158) adds, 'and in the full jurisdiction'.
21,50	H(ERVEY) OF BERRY. LDB *berruari(us)*. See 67 and note.
21,51	'PLUMGEARD'. See 7,85 note.
	OF (ST.) ETHELDREDA'S. IE, 'under the patronage and in the full jurisdiction of St. Etheldreda's'.
	H(ERVEY). IE, Hervey Bedruel (*bebruel, beruel*). See 67 and note.
21,52	1 FREE MAN. IEAL (178), 2.
	OF (ST.) ETHELDREDA'S. IE (159), as 21,51 note.
	7 ACRES. IEAL (178), 12.
	2 OXEN. IE adds, 'always'.
	ST. ETHELDREDA'S ... TO IT. IE omits this sentence but states instead, 'Over the whole Hundred of Colneis, St. Etheldreda's has full jurisdiction. Value 40s.'.
	JURISDICTION OF THE 5½ HUNDREDS. The Hundreds of Carlford, Colneis, Loes, Plomesgate and Wilford, and the Half-Hundred of Parham.
21,53	2 CARUCATES. So in the MS, but he O.S. Facsimile reads *i*.
	NOW 8 SMALHOLDERS. IE (160) and IEBrev (172), 7.
21,54	HE DWELLS. *& manet* repeated in error in LDB, and the first instance then deleted.
	4¼D IN TAX. IE (160), '4d.'.
21,55	**6 CATTLE.** IE (160), 5.
	HERVEY OF BERRY. Farley *de beruari(us)*, with *de beruari* written next and then deleted. In the MS the first *de* is also deleted, but Farley does not show this. See 67 and note.
21,56	THIS ENTRY. Cf. IE (163), 'Hervey Bedruel holds 3 half free men under the patronage of St. Etheldreda's. Value 3s.' For Hervey, see 67 note. Cf. also IEAL (179), '2 free men with 18 acres'.

21,57	HASKETON. LDB *hascetuna* altered to *haschetuna*. VALUE 4S. IE (163), '2s'.
21,58	1 FREE MAN, WULFMER. Cf. IE (163), Hervey Bedruel holds him. See *67* note. 5 FREE MEN UNDER HIM. IE adds, 'with with 20 acres'. THIS ENTRY. Cf. also IEAL (180), '6 free men with 80 acres'.
21,60	15 ACRES. IE (163) and IEAL (180), 20.
21,61	VALUE 8D. IE (163), '10d'.
21,62	20 ACRES. IE (163), 25. VALUE ... NOW 6[S]. IE, 'Value 5s'. THIS ENTRY. Cf. also IEAL (180), '6 free men; 1 carucate of land'.
21,63	HERVEY OF BERRY. IE (164), Hervey Bedruel. See *67* note.
21,64	*KALLETUNA*. IE (164), *carletuna*. Unidentified, DG 403. 8 FREE MEN. IE, 7. In LDB *lib(er)os* has been altered from *lib(er)i*. ISAAC [HOLDS THIS]. In LDB *homo ten&* has been deleted before *Isaac*.
21,65	*INGOLUESTUNA*. Also at 32,26 and 67,18; all in Carlford Hundred. Unidentified, DG 403.
21,66	1 FREE WOMAN. IEAL (179), '1 free man'. 1 FREE MAN. IE (163) adds, 'under her'. WITH 10 ACRES. IE, 'with 1 acre'.
21,69	VALUE 10S. IE (163) adds, 'St. Etheldreda's holds this in its lordship', referring to 21,66-69. Cf. however IEAL (179) where 21,66-68 are stated to be held by Hervey of Bourges.
21,70	'FINESFORD'. Also at 29,14 and ('FINLESFORDA') 32,31 and ('FINLESFORD') 38,24 and ('FINESFORDA') 41,18; all in Carlford Hundred. Lost, in Witnesham, DG 398. LEOFEVA. Farley prints *keueua* in error for *Leueua* of the MS. Cf. PNDB 312, note 2. 40 ACRES. IE (164) and IEAL (179). '1 carucate of land'.
21,71	9 FREE MEN ... 1 FREE MAN ... ST. ETHELDREDA'S. IE (162), '10 free men ... in the jurisdiction and under the patronage of St. Etheldreda's'. MEADOW, ½ ACRE. IE, '1 acre'. THIS ENTRY. Cf. IEAL (178), '10 free men with 1 carucate and 12 acres'.
21,73	1 FREE MAN AND A HALF [FREE MAN]. IEAL (178), '2 free men'.
21,75	3 WHOLE FREE MEN ... 3 HALF [FREE MEN] ... FOURTH PART OF 1 FREE MAN. IE (162) omits the 'fourth part' and adds, 'in the jurisdiction and under the patronage of St. Etheldreda's'. IEAL (178), '4 free men and a half [free man]'. VALUE 6S 2D. IE, '7s 2d'.
21,76	UNDER THE PATRONAGE. IE (162) adds, 'with full jurisdiction'.
21,77	12 ACRES. IE (162) and IEAL (179) adds, 'of lordship (land)'.
21,78	UNDER THE PATRONAGE. IE (162) adds, 'in the jurisdiction'. 33 ACRES. IE (162) and IEAL (179), 37.
21,79	IN BREDFIELD. IEAL (179), 'in BAWDSEY'. THE ABBOT ... PATRONAGE. IE (162) adds that they were in the jurisdiction of St. Etheldreda's. ROBERT MALET HOLDS. IE also, referring to entries 21,71-79.
21,80	AS A MANOR. IE (161) adds, 'before 1066'. MEN'S PLOUGHS, NOW 3½. IEBrev (172), 4 or 5, in the different MSS. 1 COB. IE adds, 'Always' and '1 cattle'. 1 MILL. Misplaced in LDB, among the livestock. [IT HAS] BEEN COUNTED. IE adds, 'in Melton'. 1 LEAGUE IN LENGTH. LDB repeats *.i. l(eu)g(am)* in error. 9[½] FURLONGS. LDB *de dim̄* is in error for *7 dim̄*.
21,81	1 FREE MAN. IE (161) adds, 'always under the patronage of the Abbot'.
21,82	'HUNDESTUF'. See 6,250 note.
21,83	WITH 10 ACRES. In LDB *x* has been altered from *xvi*. 1 CHURCH ... OF LAND. IE (161), '1 church ... of free land'. THIS ... ABBOT'S LORDSHIP. LDB *EHoc* is in error for *Hoc*. IN THE SAME VILLAGE ... 70 FREE MEN. IEAL (179), 'In MELTON 70 Freemen'. In the MS *lib(er)os* has been altered from *lib(er)i*. ALL CUSTOMARY DUES. IE adds, 'before 1066'. 45 [WITH] 2 CARUCATES. LDB omits *de*. Cf. IE. IN THE SAME (BROMESWELL) 4 FREE MEN. IEAL (179), 'in the same (MELTON)'. UNDER THE PATRONAGE ... ABBOT. IE adds that the Abbot had full jurisdiction.
21,84	3 FREE MEN. IEAL (179), 4. UNDER THE PATRONAGE. IE (161) adds, 'in the jurisdiction'.

	76 ACRES. IE, 71.
	WITH 5 ACRES. IE adds, '2 smallholders'.
21,85	WHICH ... HELD. LDB *qte* is in error for *q(ue) ten(uit)*.
	WHOLE OF THIS. Probably referring to 21,84-85.
21,86-88	UNDER THE PATRONAGE. IE (162), as 21,84 note.
21,86	THEN 2 PLOUGHS, NOW ½. IE, 'Then 2 ploughs, and now'.
21,87	HERVEY. IE (162), Hervey Bedruel (*bebruel*); see *67* note.
21,88	FREE MEN. In the MS *lib(er)os* has been altered from *lib(er)i*.
	4 ACRES. IE (162) and IEAL (179), 12.
21,89	1 ACRE. IE (162) and IEAL (178) adds, 'of lordship (land)'.
21,90	THEN 4 SMALLHOLDERS, NOW 2. IE (162), '4 smallholders'.
	IN THE SAME ... ST. ETHELDREDA'S. IE (162-163), 'Also 11 free men. In the same village under the patronage of St. Etheldreda's.
21,91	UNDER THE PATRONAGE. IE (163), as 21,84 note.
	20 ACRES ... 1 PLOUGH. IE, '60 acres. 1 smallholder. Always 1 plough' and adds, 'Value 10s'.
	MEADOW, 2½ ACRES. IE, '5 acres'.
21,92	HALF 2 FREE MEN. IEAL (179), '1 free man'. IE (163) adds, 'under the patronage of St. Etheldreda's'.
	13½ ACRES. IE (163) and IEAL (179), 12.
	VALUE 20D. IE, 'Value 2s' and adds, 'R(obert) Malet holds this' referring to 21,88-92.
21,93	1 FREE MAN. IE (164), 'St. Etheldreda's holds 1 free man in its lordship, under patronage'.
21,94	A HALF FREE MAN. IE (164), 'R(obert) Malet holds from the Abbot a half free man, Bondi, under the patronage of St. Etheldreda's' and adds, 'Meadow, 1 acre'. IEAL (179), '1 free man'.
	VALUE 3S. IE, '5s'.
21,95	PLOUGHS IN LORDSHIP, NOW 2. IEBrev (172), 3.
	WILLIAM OF BOUVILLE. LDB *debu uilla*. See 16,11 note.
	IT ... ADJUDGED. LDB *.i.* is probably in error for *7*.
	HIS LORD. LDB *dominiu(m)* is in error for *dominu(m)*.
	AS GUARANTOR. Translating *ad tutore(m)*. William names his lord, Geoffrey de Mandeville, as the person from whom he had received the carucate.
	VALUE 16D. IE (164), '12d' and adds, 'The whole of this is in the lordship of St. Etheldreda's'.
21,98	1 VILLAGER. In the MS *uilla(nus)* has been altered from *uilla*.
21,99	PLOUGHS, NOW 1. MEADOW, [1] ACRE. LDB *car(uce). modo .i. ac(ra) p(ra)ti*, omitting one instance of the numeral *.i.* Cf. IE (164).
21,100	7 FREE MEN BEFORE 1066, NOW 2. IE (165) and IEAL (180), '7 free men'.
	THEN 1 PLOUGH. IE adds, 'now none'.
	VALUE ... NOW 5[S]. IE adds, 'Hervey Bedruel holds this from the Abbot', referring to entries 21,96-100. For Hervey, see *67* note.
	1 FREE MAN. IE, 'a half free man, Aelmer, under the patronage of St. Etheldreda's'. IEAL (179), 'a half free man'.
	16½ ACRES. IE, and IEAL (179), 15.
21,101-102	A HALF FREE MAN. IE (165) adds, 'under the patronage of St. Etheldreda's'.
21,102	RENDLESHAM. LDB *reslesha(m)* altered to *renslesha(m)*.
21,103	2 SMALLHOLDERS. IE (165) adds, 'of St. Etheldreda's'.
21,104	1 FREE MAN ... ANOTHER. IE (165), '2 free men under the patronage of St. Etheldreda's'.
	VALUE 3S. IE adds, 'St. Etheldreda's holds these in its lordship', referring to 21,101-104 and to 21,38.
22	BISHOP OF EVREUX. Evreux (Eure). In the left margin of the MS, not shown by Farley, is the letter *f*, next to the chapter number. See *17* note.
22,1	'UDEHAM'. Lost, in Sutton, DG 414.
22,2	50 ACRES. IE (146) and IEAL (189), 60; IEAL (188), 40.
	THIS ENTRY. IE adds before this entry, 'In WICKHAM (Market) 1 free man, Thorkell, under the patronage of St. Etheldreda's, with 20 acres'. IEAL (189) adds that Roger Bigot holds Wickham (Market) and Campsey (Ash) from the Bishop. Cf. also IEAL (188) where these two entries are included amongst the lands which Roger Bigot annexed from St. Etheldreda's.

23	ABBOT OF BERNAY. The Benedictine Abbey of Bernay (Eure). In the right margin of the MS, not shown by Farley, is the letter *f*, next to the chapter number. See *17* note.
23,1	ASSESSED ... IN ANOTHER HUNDRED. Probably with 23,2 in Bosmere Hundred. HARDWIN. Cf. 2,10.
23,2	CREETING (ST. MARY). As VCH 526.
23,4	1 VIRGATE. A quarter of a carucate is probably meant here.
23,6	'OLDEN'. As 1,5 note.
24	ABBEY OF CHATTERIS. The Benedictine Abbey of the B.V.M. at Chatteris, Cambs., founded 1007 x 1016 by Ednoth, successively Abbot of Ramsey and Bishop of Dorchester, see LibEl 141. See also Cambridgeshire (*11*) and Hertfordshire (*12*). In the right margin of the MS, not shown by Farley, is the letter *f*, next to the chapter number. See *17* note.
	CHATTERIS. The two dots printed by Farley in the middle of the name-form represent a black blot in the MS. In Cambridgeshire (*11*) and Hertfordshire (*12*) the name is spelt *Cetriz, Cietriz*; above, in the List of Landholders, *ceterith*. The form beneath the blot here may have been *CETERIHT*.
24,1	ST. MARY'S. Literally, 'St. Mary'.
	1 PLOUGH. LDB *ăcaŕ* is in error for *caŕ*.
25	RICHARD SON OF COUNT GILBERT. In Kent (11,1) he was called Richard of Tonbridge, while in Suffolk (67,1. 76,6) he occurs as Richard of Clare (cf. 25,1); the places named being his important residences in the two counties. He was the son of Count Gilbert of Brionne. For the origin and distribution of his Holding, see R. Mortimer, 'The Beginnings of the Honour of Clare', *Battle 1980*, 119-141.
25,1	AELFRIC. Son of Withgar. His own son was also called Withgar, see below. On Aelfric, see Robertson, *ASCharters* 425.
	ARPENTS. See 21,16 note.
	ST. JOHN'S. The collegiate church at Clare, founded by Aelfric *c*.1045, MRH 423.
	LEDMER THE PRIEST. See also Essex (23,4).
	CHARTER. This has not survived, see Hart ECEE 110.
	ABBOT LEOFSTAN. Of St. Edmund's, 1044-1065.
	WITHGAR. Richard's predecessor in most of his East Anglian estates, see Mortimer, 'Honour of Clare', 128-129 (see *25* note).
25,3	SHEEP ... NOW 960. In the MS *m(od)o. dccclx.* was added in the margin.
	TAX IN TWO HUNDREDS. That is, Risbridge Hundred and Lackford Hundred (cf. 25,35-36; 39-41).
	ROBERT HOLDS THIS. Interlined in LDB, and taken to refer to 25,3 rather than 25,4 (as in VCH 527), since statements of the 1086 tenant usually occur at the end rather than at the beginning of entries in Suffolk.
25,6	[THEN] 10 CATTLE. LDB has *&* in error for *T(un)c*.
	WILLIAM PECHE. LDB *peccatu(m)*, equivalent to OFr *peche*, 'sin'; OEB 353. He also held from Richard in Essex (23,4).
25,7	WILLIAM HURANT HOLDS THIS. The statement is misplaced among the resources, rather than after the value, cf. 25,11-12. the byname is OFr *Hurand, -ant*, 'hairy, shaggy-haired'; OEB 318.
25,8	ALWAYS 2 VILLAGERS. LDB has an otiose *&* after *semp(er)*.
25,11	ROGER HOLDS (THIS). The statement is misplaced in LDB, see 25,7 note.
25,12	HAMO HOLDS (THIS). As preceding note.
25,17	THESE FREEMEN. Those in 25,4-17.
	6 FORFEITURES. See 8,35 note.
25,18	*WIMUNDESTUNA*. Also at 25,105. In Risbridge Hundred. Unidentified, DG 416. Cf. 14,16 first note.
	65 ACRES. In the MS *LXV* has been altered from *LV*.
25,19	FINN. The Dane, see 8,59 note.
	3 SMALLHOLDERS. In the MS *bor* has been altered from *boū*.
	THEN 3 COBS. In the MS there is an erasure before *rúnc*, which has an otiose abbreviation-mark above *u*.
	6 FORFEITURES. See 8,35 note.
25,20	AETHELWARD SON OF BELL. LDB *filius belli*. The patronym may be OE **Bell*, see OEB 173.
25,22	ROBERT BLUNT. See *66* and note.
25,24	FATHIR. LDB *fader* from ODan *Fathir*, OSw *Fadhir*; PNDB 250.
	WALTER THE DEACON. See *41* and note.

25,27	WESTLEY 3 FREE MEN. Richard's son Gilbert granted 2 free men here to St. Edmund's 1090 x 1098, see FD no. 170.
	6 FORFEITURES. See 8,35 note.
25,30	JURISDICTION. LDB has *saca* for *soca*, cf. Norfolk, Technical Terms.
25,35-36;39-41	DESNING. See 25,3.
25,36	FISHERIES. See 21,6 note.
	THESE 2 LANDS. That is, 25,35-36.
25,37	RICHARD'S SAME PREDECESSOR. Withgar. The meaning of the deleted word *comine* is not apparent.
25,42	WITHGAR [HELD]. LDB *ten&* is in error for *tenuit*.
25,44	CORESFELLA. Unidentified, DG 395.
25,46	ELINANT. The name is OG, Forssner 66-67. He also held from Richard in Essex (23,5).
25,47	CAVENDISH. LDB *Ranauadisc* is in error for *Kauan-*. Cf. 28,4 note on CAVENHAM; also 43,2 and note.
	ROGER OF ST. GERMAIN. From St. Germain-la-Campagne (Eure), Loyd 94. Cf. OEB 113.
25,49	2 PLOUGHS. Misplaced in LDB, after instead of before the meadow.
25,51	FINN. In the MS there is an erasure after *find*. The Dane, see 8,59 note.
25,52	ST. PETER'S. See also 1,122f and 25,60;62. Cf. 25,54 note.
	[MEN'S] PLOUGHS. LDB omits *hominum*.
	ROGER THE SHERIFF. Roger Bigot (7), cf. 1,122.
	KING'S MANOR OF BRAMFORD. 1,2 in Roger Bigot's custody.
	13 BURGESSES ... OVER 4 ... OVER 12. The numbers do not add up.
	HONOUR. A number of estates administered together.
25,53	THE ABBOT CLAIMS ½ CARUCATE. Apparently the Abbot of Ely, cf. IE (143), 'In BADLEY (Richard son of Count Gilbert) holds 70 acres of the Abbey's lordship which belong in (the lands of) Barking'. Cf. also IEAL (187).
	26 FREE MEN ... AFTER 1066. In the MS *t.r. Will(el)mi .xx.vi. lib(er)i ho(min)es* altered from *t.r.e. xx.vi. uill(an)i*.
25,54	ASSESSMENT OF £15. Probably that of St. Peter's, Ipswich, in 25,52.
25,55	GERMUND. The name is either ON or OG, see Forssner 108. He also held from Richard in Essex (23,15. 90,53).
25,56	ROGER. Of Orbec, see below. From Orbec (Calvados), Loyd 75, OEB 104.
	ROGER OF RAMES. Cf. 38,8.
	RANULF PEVEREL. Cf. 34,8.
	HE CLAIMS BACK. That is, Richard claims back as Finn's successor.
25,57	*RIGNESETA*. Unidentified, DG 409. Ringsett, VCH 531.
	HARDEKIN. LDB *Hardechinus*, from OG **Hardekin*; PNDB 286.
	GODRIC ... [HELD] ... BEFORE 1066. LDB *tenet* is in error for *tenuit*.
25,58	*FACHEDUNA*. Also at 74,2. In Bosmere Hundred. Unidentified, DG 398.
	1 FREE MAN ... [HELD] ... BEFORE 1066. LDB *ten&* is in error for *tenuit*.
25,59	YRIC. As 4,4 note.
	EDRIC ... [HELD] ... BEFORE 1066. LDB *ten&* is in error for *tenuit*.
	A FREEMAN WITH 12 ACRES. IE (143) adds, 'with every customary due'.
	WHO COULD NOT WITHDRAW. In LDB *potuit* has been altered to *pot*. IE has *pot(er)at*.
	OSBERN OF WANCHY. Possibly from Wanchy-Capval (Seine-Inf.), OEB 119.
25,60	UNDER THE PATRONAGE OF AELFRIC FATHER OF WITHGAR. The word *comdato* is otiose.
	WALDWIN. The name is OG, PNDB 408.
	BISHOP ERFAST. Of Thetford. See 19,1-2 note.
25,60;62	ST. PETER'S, IPSWICH. See 25,52.
25,62	ABOVE-MENTIONED £15. In 25,52.
	OTHERS HOLD THERE. LDB *tenet* is in error for *tenent*.
25,63	PLOUGHS IN LORDSHIP. The second instance is probably in error in LDB for 'men's ploughs'.
25,64	CEOLWOLD. LDB *Celeolt* from *Cēolweald*; PNDB 214.
25,65	TORP. In Samford Hundred and a Half. Unidentified, DG 413.
25,66	*PURTEPYT*. Unidentified, DG 408.
25,67	HUN. The name may be OE *Hūn* rather than either OE *Hūna* or ON *Húni*, ODan *Huni*, OSw *Hune*; PNDB 295.
25,69	*EDUINESTUNA*. Also at 36,14. In Samford Hundred and a Half. Unidentified, DG 397.

25,70	3 FREE MEN. In the MS *lib(er)os* has been altered from *lib(er)i*.
25,71	AELFRIC STARLING. The byname is OWScand *stari*, 'starling'; OEB 366.
25,73	TOFT. See 16,47 note.
	ASGAR THE CONSTABLE. LDB *stalre*, the same description as was given to Earl Ralph (see 1,101 note). See also 32,1 note.
25,74	RICHARD HOLDS THE WHOLE OF THIS. Referring to 25,67-74.
25,75	HONOUR. See 25,52 note.
25,76	ROGER OF ABENON. From Abenon (Calvados), Loyd 1, OEB 66.
25,78-102	Cf. 25,102 where the end of this group of entries is specified.
Heading	6 FORFEITURES. See 8,35 note.
25,78	EDRIC SPUD. LDB *spuda* from OE **Spudda*, probably denoting 'a short, thick-set person'; OEB 336.
25,79	BRICTRIC BLACK. LDB *blacus*, probably from OE *blaec*, 'black, dark', rather *blāc*, 'bright, pale'; OEB 292-293.
	[HELD]. LDB *ten&* is in error for *tenuit*.
	FRODO, THE ABBOT'S BROTHER. See *12* note.
	2 FREE MEN. LDB repeats *ii. lib(er)i ho(min)es* in error.
25,82	FRIDEBERN. LDB *Fredeb(er)nus*, from OG *Fridebern, Frithu-, Frethubern*; PNDB 253-254.
	[HELD]. As 25,79 note.
25,83	HANCHET. LDB *haningehaec*. DG 400, *Haningehest* is in error.
25,84	FREE MAN, LEOFWARU. LDB *Leuiara*, from OE *Lēofwaru* (fem.); PNDB 316. Here, as often in LDB, *liber homo* is used as a technical term without reference to gender.
	GODARD. LDB *Godart(us)*, from OFr *Godard*, see Forssner 120 s.n. **Godehard*.
	WILARD. From OG *Willihard, Wilhart*; cf. Forssner 255.
25,87	LOTHER. LDB *Loher(us)*, from OG *Lother, Lothar (Hlodochar)*, Förstemann 852-853 (J.M.D.).
25,89	AINUAR. Farley prints *Ajuuar* in error for *Alnuar* of the MS. PNDB 142 suggests that the LDB form is a misreading of *Aimar*, from OE *Aethelmāer*. Another possibility is that it is a misreading of *Aluuar*, from OE *Aelfwaru*.
	WILLIAM PERET. The byname probably stands for OFr *Per(r)ot*, a diminutive of the forename *Perre*, 'Peter'; OEB 224.
25,91	ROC. Probably from OE **Hrōc*, but perhaps ON *Hrókr*; PNDB 294.
25,92	69 ACRES. In the MS *Lx.viiij* has been altered from *Lx.viii*.
25,93	29 ACRES. In the MS *xxviiij* has been altered from *xxviii*.
25,102	4½S. That is, 4s 6d.
	ALL THESE (FREE MEN) ... SAID ABOVE. See 25,78-102 HEADING.
25,104	EDEVA. Probably Edeva the Fair, but cf. also Edith 1,90.
	(EARL) RALPH. Wader, see 1,61-95 note.
	WIDARD. From OG *Withard, Witard*; Forssner 253.
25,105	WIMUNDESTUNA. See 25,18 note.
	THAT HE COULD NOT GRANT. LDB *poterat* altered from *poterant* by subpuncting.
25,107	LINDSEY. Farley prints *halesheia* in error for *balesheia* of the MS. Cf. 14,113 *blalsega*.
25,108	HIS PREDECESSOR. Richard's predecessor.
25,111	6 FORFEITURES. See 8,35 note.
25,112	RANULF PEVEREL ... LOOSE. Cf. 34,5.
26	WILLIAM OF WARENNE. From Varenne near Bellencombre (Seine-Inf.), Loyd 111-112. He was created Earl of Surrey shortly after 16 April 1088, and died 24 June 1088.
26,1-3	IN EXCHANGE (FOR) LEWES. William appears to have acquired lands in Suffolk, Norfolk and Essex to compensate for estates he had lost in Sussex from his Rape of Lewes. See L. F. Salzman, 'The Rapes of Sussex', *Sussex Archaeological Collections* lxxii (1931), 25-26 and J. F. A. Mason, 'The Rapes of Sussex and the Norman Conquest', ibid. cii (1964), 80-87.
26,1	2 FREE MEN ... 40 ACRES ... 60 (ACRES). IEAL (184), '4 score acres of land'.
	ONE OF THEM. In the MS the words *un(us) eor(um)* have been written over an erasure.
	COULD SELL. LDB *poterat* altered from *poterant* by subpuncting.
	HUMPHREY SON OF RODRIC. The patronym is OG *Hrodric*; OEB 196. See also 21,1.
	AND JURISDICTION. In the MS *sa* has been erased before 7 *soca*.
26,3-4	NICHOLAS. He held Kennett, Cambridgeshire (18,8) from William and was a juror in Staploe Hundred there (Appendix A). In Suffolk, he also held from William at Herringswell (26,4) and Tunstall (26,6). See Farrer iii. 342.

26,4-5	[HELD]. LDB *ten&* is in error for *tenuit*.
26,4	TOKI. William's predecessor in Cambridgeshire (18,1;3;5-8), a thane of King Edward's.
	FREDERICK. Called William's brother in Cambridgeshire (18,7) but apparently his brother-in-law, see L. C. Loyd, 'The origin of the family of Warenne', *Yorkshire Archaeological Journal* xxxi (1934), 111-113. He was killed in 1070.
26,5	MUNULF. LDB *monulfus*, from either OSw or OG *Munulf*; PNDB 331.
	AND 20 ACRES. In the MS *xx* has been altered from *xxx*.
	IN EXCHANGE (FOR) LEWES. See 26,1-3 note.
26,6	NICHOLAS. See 26,3-4 note.
26,7	FREE MAN. In the MS *h(o)m(inem)* has been altered from *h(om)o*.
26,8	HUGH SON OF GOLD. LDB *goldae* may be from either OE *Golda* (masc.) or *Golde* (fem.); OEB 184-185.
	BOSTEN. LDB *Bosteinn(us)*. The name is OSw; PNDB 207.
26,9 Heading	FREDERICK. See 26,4 note.
26,9	HUGH OF WANCHY. From Wanchy (Seine-Inf.), Loyd 111. Cf. OEB 119.
	TOKI. See 26,4 note.
	3 CARUCATES. In the MS *iij* has been altered from *ii*.
26,11	HUGH. Probably Hugh of Wanchy, cf. 26,9.
	TOKI. See 26,4 note.
26,12a-12d	THESE ENTRIES describe a large but fragmented unit of land in 1066, held by William and his subtenants in 1086. The unit's measurements and fiscal liability are given at the end of 26,12d.
26,12a	ROBERT OF PIERREPONT. From Pierrepont (Seine-Inf.), Loyd 78. Cf. OEB 106.
	THORKELL. Called 'of Wrentham' in 26,12d.
	BLYTHBURGH. The *H* (for 'Hundred') after the place-name is otiose in LDB.
26,12b	WILLIAM SON OF REGINALD. He also held at Covehithe (26,15). On him, see Farrer iii. 327.
	IN THE SAME VILLAGE ... DWELT. In the MS there is an erasure after *villa*.
	HE ALSO HOLDS IT. Probably referring to William son of Reginald, but perhaps to the free man.
	UNDER HIM ... 2 FREE MEN. In the MS *lib(er)os* has been altered from *lib(er)i*.
	AELFRIC OF SANFORD. LDB *de sanford* may be from Samford Hundred and a Half (Suffolk) or from one of the Sampfords in Essex or from a lost OE name *sandford.
	[1]½ CARUCATES. LDB omits the numeral.
26,12c	GODFREY OF PIERREPONT. See 26,12a note on ROBERT OF PIERREPONT.
26,13	RANULF ... HELD. LDB *teñ*, here apparently for *ten(uit)*; cf. following note.
	WILLIAM ... HOLDS. LDB *teñ*, here apparently for *ten(et)*. The following words *in d(omi)nio* are deleted in LDB.
	HALF A PRIEST. That is, half of the rights over him.
	OF ROBERT ... OF ROBERT. The second instance is probably an erroneous repetition in LDB.
26,14	IDLE CATTLE. LDB *an(imalia) otiosa*; that is, not used for ploughing.
	ROBERT MALET CLAIMS LIKE THE OTHER. Presumably referring back to 26,13.
26,15	COVEHITHE. Formerly 'North Hales'.
	[1]½ PLOUGHS. LDB omits the numeral.
	PLOUGHS, NOW 1. *modo* was written twice in LDB, but then the first instance was deleted.
26,16 Heading	HUNDRED OF CARLFORD. LDB *EARLAFORDA* is in error for *CARLAFORDA*.
	AETHELRIC. LDB *Alricus*. Called Aethelric of Burgh (from the manor in this entry) in 8,6;9 etc.
26,17	ROBERT. Of Glanville (see 6,3 note); Farrer iii. 424.
26,19	'TORSTANESTUNA'. See 11,2 note.
27	SWEIN OF ESSEX. Sheriff of Essex until at least 1075, in succession to his father Robert son of Wymarc. See further, Essex (*24* and note).
27,3	ROBERT. Son of Wymarc, see preceding note.
	[HELD]. LDB *tenet* is in error for *tenuit*.
	CHURCH. A religious community existed here in the 10th and early 11th centuries (MRH 483). It received bequests of lands from Ealdorman Aelfgar and his daughters in Whitelock, *AS Wills* nos. 2,14-15; Sawyer nos. 1483, 1494, 1486. These bequests included Withermarsh, Polstead, Stratford St. Mary and Freston; cf. 27,4-5;9;12.

27 - 30

27,5	4 CARUCATES. *car(ucate)* was repeated in error in LDB, then the first instance was deleted.
	MEADOW, 31 ACRES. In LDB *xxx* has been interlined above *.i.*
27,6	IN LENGTH. LDB *lango* altered from *lato*; for *longo*.
27,7	HAD SEEN. LDB *uidissed* is in error for *uidisset*.
27,8	ROBERT. Son of Wymarc, see *27* note.
	HE HAS LOST ... HE HAS. The subject here is Swein. He still retained rights over the property of the dead burgesses.
27,9	ROBERT. There are two men of this name in this entry. The first is Swein's father; the second is the 1086 subtenant, who is called Robert of Stratford in his own chapter (*71*).
27,10-12	ROBERT. Son of Wymarc, see *27* note.
27,10	[HELD] ... BEFORE 1066. LDB *ten&* is in error for *tenuit*.
27,13	GODRIC. Called 'of Peyton' (from the manor in the present entry) in 6,238.
	1 LEAGUE. Farley prints *leugā* in error for what in the MS is *leuga* altered from *leugu*.
28	EUDO THE STEWARD. The youngest son of Hubert of Ryes (Calvados; Loyd 40). Steward to King William. In the chapter-heading in LDB *EEVDONIS* is in error for *EVDONIS*.
28,1b	CHAMBERLAIN'S HALL. LDB *coclesworda*; DG 394.
	THEN AND LATER 5 PLOUGHS. In LDB *T(un)c 7 p(ost) .v. car(uce)* was repeated in error, then the first instance deleted.
28,2	6 FREEMEN. IEAL (187), 7.
	[WHO] COULD NOT. LDB *q(uo)d* is in error for *q(ui)*.
	LISOIS. Of Moutiers. He probably took his name from Moutiers-Hubert (Calvados), cf. OEB 102. See also Essex (25,5 and note).
	EUDO HELD ... WITH FULL JURISDICTION. IE (142), 'Eudo held them and holds with full jurisdiction'.
	4 SMALLHOLDERS. IE adds, 'under them'.
	FISHERIES. See 21,6 note.
28,4	CAVENHAM. LDB *Ranauaha(m)* is in error for *Kauana-*. DG 394 *Kanaua-* is in error. Cf. 25,47 note on CAVENDISH.
28,6	PIROT. The LDB form may be in error for *Picot*. See Essex (25,11 and note), Cambridgeshire (25,1-2 and note) which suggest that this is Picot the Sheriff of Cambridgeshire.
	THIS ENTRY. Cf. IE (153), 'In North Glemham 1 free man, Wulfric son of Hugh (*Hugo sune*, *hugesune*), under the patronage of St. Etheldreda's; 1½ carucates of land. Eudo the Steward holds this'. Cf. also IEAL (187), '1 free man with 1 carucate (of land)'.
28,7	1 SLAVE. In the MS there is an erasure after *ser*.
29	ROGER OF AUBERVILLE. Perhaps from Auberville-la-Renaut (Seine-Inf.); OEB 104-105. For his brother William, see *30*.
29,1	CARRYING-SERVICE. *Summagium*, the service of carriage by pack-animals, often commuted to a money payment. Parallel to *avera* in Cambridgeshire, etc.
	GUTHMUND. Brother of Abbot Wulfric of Ely, see 31,8 note.
	RICHARD'S PREDECESSOR. That of Richard son of Count Gilbert (*25*).
29,3	[HELD]. LDB *ten&* is in error for *tenuit*.
	PILEBERGA. Unidentified, DG 408.
29,4	WILGRIP. LDB *Wilgripus*, from ODan *Vilgrip*; PNDB 405.
29,6	ELLA. Unidentified, DG 397.
29,7	LEOFRIC HOBBESON. The patronym is OE *Hobba*, a nickname meaning a lumpish or a stupid person; OEB 157-158. See also 30,3.
29,8	GODRIC OF RINGSHALL, WILLIAM OF AUBERVILLE'S PREDECESSOR. William, Roger's brother, held lands at Ringshall (30,2-3), but a Godric is not named there.
29,9	BISHOP OF ST. LÔ. Also at 21,17.
29,10	LANGHEDANA. See 1,68 note.
29,11	TEPEKIN. LDB here *Tepechinus*, below (29,14) *Tepekin* and (40,4) *Depekin*. An OLG diminutive in *-kin*, perhaps added to a hypocoristic form of OS *Thiadbald*, *-bern*, etc.; PNDB 383.
29,12	15D IN TAX. In LDB *den(arii)* was written twice in error and the first instance then deleted.
29,14	'FINESFORD'. See 21,70 note.
	TEPEKIN. See 29,11 note.
30	WILLIAM BROTHER OF ROGER OF AUBERVILLE. For his brother, and the byname, see *29* and note. In the right margin of the MS, not shown by Farley, is the letter *f*, next to the chapter number; see *17* note.

30,1	RINGSHALL. See also Godric of Ringshall in 29,8.
	THEN 2 PLOUGHS, NOW ½. Misplaced in LDB, among the population details.
30,2-3	[HELD]. LDB *ten&* is in error for *tenuit*.
	LEOFRIC HOBBESON. See 29,7 note.
	HUGH OF HOUDAIN. See 7,60 note.
31	HUGH DE MONTFORT. From Montfort-sur-Risle (Eure); OEB 101, Loyd 68.
31,1	THIS ENTRY. LDB does not give a value.
31,2	EARL HUGH. Cf. 4,11.
31,3	ROGER OF CANDOS. From Candos (Eure, arr. Pont-Audemer), Loyd 26-27. Cf. OEB 81.
31,4-6	HE ALSO HOLDS. Roger of Candos, as 31,3.
31,4	HORHAM. Farley prints *borant* in error for *horant* of the MS.
31,7	7½S. That is, 7s 6d.
31,8-14	GUTHMUND. The brother of Abbot Wulfric of Ely. For the lands leased to him by his brother 1045 x 1066 (including Nacton, Great Livermere, and Occold, Suffolk; here 31,8;13a;40;60), see LibEl 166-167, 424-425. See also Essex 27,14 note.
31,8	23 SHEEP. 12 or 22 in the different MSS of IE (143).
	VALUE ... 70S. IE, 'Value £4'.
31,9	[*BRIHTOLUESTUNA*]. Farley prints *brihtoluestana* in error for *-tuna* of the MS. The place is also mentioned in 31,14. Unidentified, DG 392.
	AND 20 ACRES. IEAL (186), 'Meadow, 20 acres'.
	4 SMALLHOLDERS. IE (143), 3.
	PLOUGHS, NOW 5. MEADOW, 2 ACRES. In the MS there is an erasure before *.ii.* and *.v.* is interlined.
	6 ACRES. IE adds, 'of free land'. IEAL, 'with 5 acres of meadow'.
31,11	*CULUERDESTUNA*. See 6,110 note on *KYLUERTESTUNA*.
	THEN 2 PLOUGHS, NOW 1. IEAL (186), '2 carucates of land'.
	IT HAS 3 FURLONGS ... IN TAX. IE (144) gives these details as part of the entry equivalent to 31,12.
31,12	*ISTEUERTONA*. Unidentified, DG 403.
	VALUE. IE (143) adds, 'of all these free men'.
	JURISDICTION. IE, 'full jurisidiction and patronage'.
	WHOLE OF THIS LAND. Referring to 31,8-12; cf. IE (143-144).
	THIS ENTRY. Cf. IEAL (186), '6 free men; 2 carucates (of land) and 28 acres. Meadow, 1 acre. Always 4 ploughs in lordship'.
31,13	LURK. LDB *Lurc*, from ON *Lurkr*; a byname from the word for a cudgel, PNDB 322.
	PATRONAGE OF N. Perhaps for 'Norman', cf. elsewhere in Suffolk. In LDB *ei(us)d(em)* has been deleted before *.N.*.
31,13a	NACTON. See 31,8.
	THE HUNDRED. IE (144) adds, 'and the Shire'.
31,15	1 FREE MAN. IE (150), Stanhard.
	HALF UNDER ... ST. ETHELDREDA'S AND HALF ... EDRIC GRIM. IE, 'under the patronage of St. Etheldreda's'.
	19 ACRES. IE, 16. IEAL (186), 6.
	VALUE 4S 9D. IE, '4s'.
31,16	1 FREE MAN. IEAL (186), '2 free men'.
	VALUE 8D. IE (150), '6d'.
31,17	THIS ENTRY. Cf. IE (150), '2 free men under the patronage of St Etheldreda's; 14 acres. Value 2½s.' Cf. also IEAL (186).
31,18-19	THESE ENTRIES. IEAL (186) adds, 'Also in CHARSFIELD 1 free man; 6 acres. In the same (Charsfield) 2 Freemen; 8 acres of land'.
31,18	CHARSFIELD. See 6,179 note.
	10 FREE MEN ... ST. ETHELDREDA'S. IE (151), '11 free men ... 1 wholly, the others half under the patronage of St. Etheldreda's'. IEAL (186), '9 free men'.
	VALUE ... NOW 22S 8D. IE, 'Value 20s.'
31,19	2 FREE MEN ... HUGH DE MONTFORT'S PREDECESSOR ... OVER 1. IE (151), '1 free man and a half under the patronage of St. Etheldreda's'. IEAL (186), '1 free man'.
31,21	IN LORDSHIP. In LDB *ten̄* is deleted before *in d(omi)niu(m)*.
	30S 30D. That is, 32s 6d.
31,24	*HATHEBURGFELDA*. Altered from *athe-* in LDB. See 4,33 note.
31,26	*BEKETUNA*. See 1,29 note.
	1500 HERRINGS. Expressed in LDB as '1 thousand and a half herrings'.
31,28	*RODENHALA*. See 4,36 note.

	ASLAC. LDB *Aslacus*, from ON *Áslákr*, ODan, OSw *Aslak*; PNDB 168.
	WHOLE ... IN LORDSHIP. Referring to 31,27-28.
31,29	*WIMUNDAHALA*. See 7,53 note.
	500 HERRINGS. Expressed in LDB as 'half a thousand herrings'.
31,31	*HORNES*. Unidentified, DG 402.
	[BEFORE 1066]. LDB *t(empore). r(egis)*, omitting the name of the King.
31,34	WHOLE ... IN LORDSHIP. Referring to 31,29-34.
	WALTER OF [DOL]. LDB *de doai*, 'of Douai' is in error here, cf. 4,15 etc. Walter of Douai was still holding in 1086, see Essex (*52*), etc.
31,36	VALUE 4S. In the MS *7.v.* has been erased after *sol(idos)*.
31,37	*CALDECOTEN*. See 6,212 note.
31,38	GUTHMUND. See 31,8-14 note.
31,39	*CALDECOTAN*. See 6,212 note.
31,40-43	GUTHMUND. See 31,8-14 note.
31,40	HUGH OF *BEUERDA*. The place is unidentified.
	HOLDS. In LDB *ten&* has been repeated in error, then the second instance deleted.
	ALWAYS 4 VILLAGERS. IE (142), 'Always 3 villagers'.
	HORSE. IE, 'cob'.
	[THEN] 160 SHEEP. LDB omits *T(un)c*.
	VALUE ... 40S. IE, 'Value always 40s'.
31,42	146 SHEEP. In LDB *.cxlvi.* is interlined above *Lxxxxvi* which is deleted.
	PESSERERA. Obscure, but possibly an erroneous form of the OFr byname **Paisforiere*, 'pasture meadow', OEB 386 (J.M.D.).
31,43	GUTHMUND, HUGH'S PREDECESSOR, HELD. In LDB *tenuit* has been altered (needlessly) to *ten̄*. *Ante c̄u* is in error for *Antecessor*.
31,44	KING'S MANOR OF THORNEY. See 1,1.
	BELONGING TO THE REALM. See 1-60 note.
	BY A DELIVERY. Translating *ex lib(er)atione*; by a lawful transfer of possession.
	[IN LENGTH]. LDB omits *in longo*.
31,45-46	GUTHMUND. See 31,8 note.
31,45	17 FREE MEN ... UNDER PATRONAGE ONLY. In the MS *xvii* has been altered from *xviii*. The last letter of *com̄a* has been written over an erasure.
31,46	*ERUESTUNA*. Unidentified, DG 397.
	HUGH'S PREDECESSOR. In the MS there is an erasure after *antec(essoris)*.
31,47	*TORPE*. In Stow Hundred. Unidentified, DG 414.
	[OF HUGH'S] PREDECESSOR. LDB omits *hugonis*. Probably meaning Guthmund, as in 31,46 and 31,48.
	JURISDICTION. LDB uses *sac(a)* here for *soc(a)*, cf. Norfolk, Technical Terms.
31,48	*VLTUNA*. Unidentified, DG 414.
	GUTHMUND'S. See 31,8 note.
31,49	*TORSTUNA*. Unidentified, DG 414.
	BY A DELIVERY. As 31,44 note.
	KING'S MANOR OF THORNEY. See 1,1.
	... AND THE JURISDICTION. the meaning of *c̄*, the final word of folio 409a is not apparent, but it might be in error for *c̄*, standing for *c(onsuetudines)*, 'the customary dues'.
31,50	*BREME*. In this entry LDB has both *breme* and *bremere* as spellings of OE **Brēme*, the second instance having an inorganic AN *re*; PNDB 207.
	IN THE BATTLE OF HASTINGS. LDB *in bello hastingensi*; one of the few references to the battle in the Domesday records.
	MEADOW, 1½ ACRES. Farley prints *T(un)c* in error for *7* of the MS.
	WILLIAM SON OF GROSS. The patronym is a nickname from OFr *gross(e)*, 'big, stout'; OEB 185-186.
31,51	ALWIN OF MENDLESHAM. Perhaps identical with Alwin in 1,77.
	[HELD]. LDB *ten&* is in error for *tenuit*.
31,53	MANOR ... OF THE KING. See 1,1.
	RALPH THE CONSTABLE. See 1,101 note.
	RALPH, HIS SON. Earl Ralph Wader, see 1,61-95 note.
	DELIVERER. Someone who had the power to deliver possession of the land.
	TO THIS MANOR ... 10D IN TAX. In the MS this part of the entry is written on either side of a large hole in the centre of the leaf.
	ST. AUGUSTINE'S. Ipswich, mentioned in 1,122d, rather than Canterbury.

31 - 32

31,57	THIS ENTRY is also written in the MS on either side of the hole which affects 31,56. The only reflection of this arrangement given by Farley is the hyphen in the place-name, which also occurs in the MS.
31,60	GUTHMUND. See 31,8 note.
	WULFRIC, THE ABBOT OF ELY. ?1044 x 1045 - ?1066, HRH 45.
	THEN 2 SLAVES. IE (153) adds, 'now none'.
	THEN AND LATER 2 PLOUGHS IN LORDSHIP, NOW 1. IEAL (186), '2 ploughs in lordship'.
	THEN 2 MEN'S PLOUGHS, LATER AND NOW 1½. IEAL, '2 ploughs belonging to the men'.
	JURISDICTION OVER THE WHOLE. IE adds, 'under the Abbot'.
32	GEOFFREY DE MANDEVILLE. From Manneville (Seine-Inf.), Loyd 57; cf. OEB 96.
32,1	ASGAR. The Constable (see 25,73 note). Geoffrey's predecessor in a number of counties. On him, see Harmer, *ASWrits* 560-561 (s.n. Esgar, the staller); Ellis ii. 43.
	VALUE ... 40S. In LDB *xxx.v.* has been deleted and *.xl.* interlined.
32,2	LANGFER. See 7,109 note.
32,3-5	ASGAR. As 32,1 note.
32,4	[HELD]. LDB has *ten&* in error for *tenuit*.
32,6	RAINALM. LDB *Rainelmus*, from *Rainalm* the Rom. form of OG *Raginhelm*; Forssner 210.
	STUTTON. LDB *Scottuna(m)*. DG (412), omits this form.
	2 [CARUCATES]. LDB omits *car(ucate)*.
	SLAVES, NOW ... LDB omits either 7 before *modo*, or a numeral after it.
32,8	ASGAR. As 32,1 note.
32,9	UNDER THE PATRONAGE. LDB *co(m)m(en)datus* is in error for *co(m)m(en)data*, since the subject is female.
32,13	W(ILLIAM) SON OF SAXWALO. The same as William of Bouville, cf. 32,31. For the OG patronym, see OEB 197.
32,14	1 FREE MAN. IE (151), named as Ceolric (*Gelric(us)*, see PNDB 214), and stated there to be one of the 6 free men of the previous sub-entry in LDB.
	1 PLOUGH. IE and IEAL (186), 1½.
32,15	WILLIAM. Son of Saxwalo, as 32,13.
	HOLDS THIS. Probably referring to 32,14-15.
32,16	[HELD]. LDB *ten&* is in error for *tenuit*.
32,18	WICHEDIS. Unidentified, DG 416.
32,19	[HELD]. As 32,16 note.
	ASGAR'S. That of Asgar the Constable, see 32,1.
	1 MARK OF SILVER. 13s 4d.
32,20	COVEHITHE. Formerly 'North Hales'.
32,21	THORPE. In Dallinghoo, DG 413.
	[HELD]. As 32,16 note.
32,23	AETHELRIC OF BURGH. See 32,28 note.
32,25	[*NECKEMARA*]. Farley prints *net-* in error for *nec-* of the MS. See 6,113 note.
32,26	*INGOLUESTUNA*. See 21,65 note. Cf. perhaps IE (145), 'In *GULUESTEHAM*, a half free woman, Mawa (*Maua*), with 20 acres, in the jurisdiction and under the patronage of St. Etheldreda's'.
32,27	OF HALDANE'S. LDB *halden*, uninflected. Cf. 32,22-24;26;28-30 for the use of a similar uninflected form for the genitive case.
32,28	AETHELRIC OF BURGH. Here *Alric*, but above (32,23) *Eilrici* (genitive). See 8,6 note.
	BRICTWOLD MUFFLE. The byname is from OFr *mo(u)fle*, 'a winter glove'; OEB 371.
	THIS ENTRY. Cf. IE (145), 'In BURGH 1 free man, Brictwold, half under the patronage and in the jurisdiction of St. Etheldreda's, with 40 acres'. Cf. also IEAL (186).
32,29	THE THIRD ... ST. ETHELDREDA'S. Cf. IE (145), 'In CULPHO 1 free man, Brictnoth, in the jurisdiction and under the patronage of St. Etheldreda's; 16 acres' or, in another MS, 'with 6 acres'. Cf. also IEAL (186), '1 free man; 6 acres'.
32,30	*HOBBESTUNA*. IE (145), *Hopestuna*. See 6,117 note *sub HOPESTUNA*.
	IN THE SAME ... 1 FREEMAN. IE adds, 'who could not sell his land'.
	TOPI. The name is ODan; PNDB 386.
	15 ACRES. IEAL (186), 16.
32,31	'FINLESFORDA'. See 21,70 note *sub* 'FINESFORD'.
	WHOLE OF THIS. Probably 32,21-31.
	WHOLE OF THE JURISDICTION. In LDB *p(er)* is otiose.

33	RALPH BAYNARD. Sheriff of Essex at a date between 1066 and 1086, see Essex *33*. Castle Baynard in London was named after him. The patronym is OG *Beinhard, Beinhart*; OEB 213, Forssner 40-41.
33,1-3	6 FORFEITURES. See 8,35 note.
33,1	AETHELGYTH. LDB *Ailad*; PNDB 183-184.
33,2	WE HAVE SEEN THE WRIT. A rare use of the first person (plural) in LDB, *uidimus breue(m)*. NORIGOLD. LDB *Noriolt*, from OG *Norigaud*; Forssner 193. RICHERE. LDB *Ricer(us)*, from OG *Richer(e)*, OFr *Rich(i)er*; Forssner 214-215.
33,3-4	[HELD]. LDB *ten&* is in error for *tenuit*.
33,4-8	BLYTHING HUNDRED. LDB *BIDINGA* is in error for *BLIDINGA*.
33,4	THEN [3] COBS. Farley prints *ii* in error for *iii* of the MS. 3 FURLONGS IN LENGTH. In the MS the first two minims of *iii* are joined and the second one is elongated, perhaps intended as an alteration to *vi*.
33,6	[HELD]. As 33,3-4 note. THE KING ... 6 FORFEITURES. In LDB *soca(m)* has been deleted after *Com(e)s*. For the 6 forfeitures, see 8,35 note.
33,7	ANBOLD. LDB *ābold(us)*. Probably from OG *Aganbold*; Förstemann 38 (J.M.D.). 6 FORFEITURES. See 8,35 note.
33,9-10	BLYTHING HUNDRED. The Hundred rubric is otiose here.
33,9	IN THIS MANOR. LDB *In huic* is in error for either *In hoc* or *Huic*.
33,10	WOODLAND FOR 250 PIGS. Expressed in LDB as 'woodland for two and a half hundred pigs'. [VALUE]. LDB omits *ual&* after *semp(er)*. FREEMEN. Translating *franci ho(min)es*. FREE(MAN). Translating *francus*. [HELD]. As 33,3-4 note.
33,13	BAYNARD. In the MS *hainardus* in error for *bainardus*. Farley silently corrects.
34	RANULF PEVEREL. The byname is from OFr *peurel*, Latin *piperellus* 'pepper'; OEB 326.
34,1-2	SIWARD OF MALDON. See 12,5 note.
32,2	ACTON. LDB *ARetona* is in error for *Aketona* and *Aratona* for *Acatona*. RANULF ACQUIRED FOR LAND. Probably 'in exchange for land'. HONILEGA. Unidentified, DG 402.
34,3-4	SIWARD. Of Maldon, cf. 34,1-2.
34,3	REMAINING IN THE JURISDICTION. LDB *remanentēs* with an otiose abbreviation mark, having been altered from *remanente(m)*.
34,4	WARIN. LDB *Garinus*, from the OFr form of OG *Warin*; Forssner 246-247.
34,5	OVER 1 CARUCATE. LDB *dei* is in error for *de.i*. HOLY TRINITY IN CANTERBURY. See 15,2-3 note.
34,6	KETEL. His estate at Onehouse is referred to in his will, 1052 x 1066 (Whitelock, *AS Wills* no. 34, Sawyer no. 1519, Hart ECEE no. 118). On him see Whitelock, *AS Wills* 201-202. See also Norfolk (32,2-5) and below 37,6 note. OSBERT MALE. Cf. Osbern Male 1,12 and note. CHURCH OF STOW(MARKET). Cf. 2,8.
34,7	FROM [RANULF]. Farley prints *Radulfo* in error for *Ranulfo* of the MS.
34,8	AND 4 ACRES. See 25,56. WHAT LEOFSTAN HELD. In LDB *.i. lib(er) h(om)o* has been deleted before *qu(o)d*. In the MS *qu(o)d* has been altered from *que(m)*. NOW 2 OXEN. In LDB *bou(es)* is interlined above *car(uce) hom(inum)* which has been deleted.
34,9	A PART. In LDB *Queda(m)* was written twice in error, then the first instance deleted.
34,12	SAXI ... PATRONAGE OF THE ABBOT. Cf. IE (145), 'In DEBENHAM 1 free man, Saxi, [held] before 1066; 1 carucate of land as a manor. In the jurisdiction and under the patronage of St. Etheldreda's'. Cf. also IEAL (189). 8 ACRES. See 6,11 where '6 acres' and '2 acres' are treated as separate units both previously held by Saxi and by the Malets' predecessor. ALWAYS 2 PLOUGHS IN LORDSHIP. Repeated in LDB. The first instance was probably misplaced and should have been deleted when the phrase was interlined above its correct place. [THEN] 40 PIGS. LDB omits *T(un)c*.
34,15	BUT [ANOTHER] POSSIBLE. LDB omits a word here, perhaps *alia*.

	CHURCH, 15 ACRES FROM FOUR LORDSHIPS. LDB ... *de quattuor dominationib(us)*. Presumably meaning that the church had been founded to serve four estates and had been endowed with land from each.
	THIS ENTRY. IE (150-151), 'In the same (Clopton) a half free man ... under the patronage of St. Etheldreda's; 1 carucate of land and 30 acres, and 12 acres in *CAISNEID* ... Value 25s'. Cf. also IEAL (189), 'In Clopton 1 carucate and 30 acres. In *CAISNED* 12 acres as a manor. 3 ploughs in lordship; 2 [ploughs] belonging to the men'. *Caisne(i)d* is probably lost in Clopton.
34,17	TUSEMERA. Unidentified, DG 414.
	AS HIS WAGES. Translating *p(ro) suis solidatis*.
35	AUBREY DE VERE. From Ver (La Manche), Loyd 110; cf. OEB 118.
35,1	ARPENT. See 21,16 note.
35,3	FERMEUS. Obscure, unless it represents a scribal error for Latin *seruiens* (J.M.D.).
	RALPH TALLBOYS AND FINN. Both appear to have been dead by 1086. Ralph's wife occurs in Cambridgeshire (*42*) and Bedfordshire (*55*). Finn's wife occurs in Essex (*84*).
	DELIVERER. See 31,53 note.
	REEVE. Probably the Hundred-reeve.
35,4	CANEPETUNA. See 1,106 note.
35,5	[MEN'S] PLOUGHS. LDB omits *hominum* in error.
	... CHURCHES. LDB omits the numeral.
	ADELELM. LDB *Adelalm(us)*, from OG *Adalhelm, Adel(h)elm*; cf. Forssner 8, PNDB 184.
35,6	IN ALDHAM. LDB *Ialelham* is in error for *I(n) aldham*.
35,7	MILD. LDB *Milda*, from OE **Milde*; PNDB 328.
	9 FREE MEN. Only 8 are named in LDB.
	BESI. LDB *Beso*; a Scand. name of uncertain etymology, see PNDB 201.
	BOTI. LDB *Botius*, from ON *Bóti*, OSw *Bote*; PNDB 207.
	LEOFWIN BENNE. The byname is probably a patronym from OE *Bynna*; OEB 289.
	FULCARD THE HALF (FREE MAN). LDB *Furcardus* has AN -*r*- for -*l*-; PNDB 256.
	MENLEVA. LDB *Menleua*, probably from OG *Meginliuba, Meginlioba*; PNDB 327.
35,8	LEOFCWEN. LDB *Lefquena*, from OE *Lēofcwēn*, PNDB 311.
	AUBREY. In the MS there is an erasure after *alb(er)ico*.
36	ROBERT GERNON. The byname is from OFr *grenon*, 'moustache'; OEB 314-315.
36,1-2	SCALPI, A THANE. The name is ON *Skálpi*, PNDB 365. Probably referring to the same man as the Guard (*huscarl*) of that name mentioned in Essex (30,16) as having died after 1066 in outlawry in Yorkshire. The present Scalpi is definitely the same as he in Essex 32,40 who held at Ardleigh before William (*de Alno*), see below EE 3.
	THESE ENTRIES. See EE 3 note.
36,1	OF HAROLD'S. Of Earl Harold's, cf. Essex 30,16.
	CHURCHFORD. LDB here *Cercesfort*, and 36,16 *Ciresfort*. Unidentified in DG (394).
	WILLIAM DE ALNO. The place from which he took his name is so far unidentified, see OEB 67-68; DBS 94, s.n. *Dando*. He also held from Robert in Essex (32,40).
36,2-7	WILLIAM. *De Alno*, as 36,1.
36,3	MAWA. LDB *Mauua*. Of obscure etymology, perhaps related to OE *māwian* 'to mow' or *mǣw* 'sea-gull'; PNDB 325.
36,4	ST. BENEDICT'S OF RAMSEY. See *17* note.
	MANESFORT. Unidentified, DG 405.
36,5	ALFILDESTUNA. See 16,45 note.
36,6	TURCHETLESTUNA. Unidentified, DG 414.
36,7	IN THE SAME WAY. As in 36,6.
36,8	[HELD]. LDB *ten&* is in error for *tenuit*.
36,10	EDNOTH. LDB *AEtnod*, from OE *Ēadnōth*; PNDB 233.
36,11	TELA. Obscure, see PNDB 382.
36,14	EDUINESTUNA. See 25,69 note.
	SPIETA. Perhaps ON *Spióti*, OSw *Spiute*; PNDB 370.
36,16	CHURCHFORD. See 36,1 note.
36,17	HE ALSO HOLDS. That is, William *de Alno*.
37	PETER OF VALOGNES. From Valognes (La Manche), OEB 117. Sheriff of Essex and Hertfordshire in 1086. In the MS there is a letter *f* in the left margin next to the chapter number, not shown by Farley; see *17* note.
37,1	[VALUE]. LDB omits *ual&*.
37,5	2 MEN'S OXEN. Misplaced in LDB; it should have been placed before the meadow.
	FOR LAND. Probably meaning 'in exchange for land'.

37,6	AUTI. LDB *Alti(us)*, from ODan *Auti*; PNDB 169.
	KETEL. He bequeathed his estate at Rushford to his priest Aelfric, 1052 x 1066, in his will mentioned in 34,6 note.
38	ROGER OF RAMES. From Rames (Seine-Inf.), Loyd 84. Note that some earlier volumes in the present series followed OEB 109 in stating that he came from Raismes (Nord); they should be corrected to follow Loyd.
38,2	*LINHOU*. Unidentified, DG 404.
	[HELD]. LDB *ten&* is in error for *tenuit*.
38,6	MILES. Probably *de Belefol*, cf. 38,25.
38,8	BRICETT. See also 25,56.
38,9	*LANGHEDANA*. See 1,68 note.
	MAN. In the MS *h(omine)m* has been altered from *h(om)o*.
	VALUE 18D. In the MS *xviii* has been altered from *xiii*.
38,10	THEY ... ASSESSED. In LDB *ual* has been deleted before *app(re)ciate*.
38,11	[UNDER ... PATRONAGE OF] GYRTH. The name *Guert* is interlined in LDB, having probably at first been omitted during copying. The word *commendatus* has also been omitted and would probably have followed *Gotwin(us)*.
	SUNWIN. LDB *Sunwin(us)*, from either OE **Sun(n)wine* or OG **Sunwin*; PNDB 378.
38,13	TUDDENHAM. Here placed in Claydon Hundred, but elsewhere in the neighbouring Hundred of Carlford. Cf. 38,15.
38,14	1 POLE. Translating *uirga*.
38,15	WHICH BELONG. LDB *quē* has an otiose abbreviation mark.
	CHURCH OF TUDDENHAM. Cf. 38,13 note.
38,19-20	MILES. Probably *de Belefol*, cf. 38,25.
38,20	AELFRIC AND BOTI, FREE MEN. LDB repeats *boti* in error after *ho(min)es*.
38,21	HAROLD. Earl Harold, see 1,100.
38,22-23	[HOLDS]. LDB omits *ten&* in error.
38,22	FREE MAN, AELFRIC. In the MS *h(omine)m* has been altered from *h(om)o*; *Aluric(us)* should have been altered to *Aluricum* but was not. Farley prints *Aluric(us)* of the MS.
	UNDER ... PATRONAGE ... FROM THE ABBOT (OF ELY). IE (151), 'under the patronage of St. Etheldreda's'.
	MEADOW, 2 ACRES. IE (151), 1 or 3 in the different MSS. IEAL (189), 4.
	1 UNDER ... ST. ETHELDREDA'S. IE names him as Edric and assigns to him '8 acres. Value 20d'. Cf. also IEAL.
38,24	'FINLESFORD'. See 21,70 note.
38,25	STONHAM (ASPAL). LDB *estuna*. DG 397 identifies this as Easton Bavents, but cf. 38,6-7;19, with two of which Miles (*de Belefol*) appears to be associated.
	MILES *DE BELEFOL*. His place of origin is unidentified.
39	RANULF BROTHER OF ILGER. Ranulf appears consistently in GDB and LDB as 'brother of Ilger', although in IE (149) he is called 'son of Ilger'. The name Ilger is from OG *Hilger*, see OEB 187.
39,1	16 ACRES. In the MS *xvi* has been altered from *xv*.
	2 SMALLHOLDERS. In the MS *ii* has been altered from *i*.
39,3	ROGER THE SHERIFF. Roger Bigot (7.
	A SET TIME. LDB *constitutu(m) t(em)p.m*, in error for *-t(em)pus* (neuter accusative sing.). In
	the MS *u* has been erased between *p* and *m* of the second word.
39,5	BRICT. Perhaps from OE *Beorht*, but possibly an abbreviated form of Brictmer, cf. 39,4. See PNDB 193.
	THE ABBOT (OF ELY) ... OUGHT TO HOLD. The half free man claimed by the Abbot may be the one at an unnamed place in IE (144), 'Ranulf brother of Ilger holds a half free man with 11 acres in the full jurisdiction and under the patronage of St. Etheldreda's. Value 2s.' In another MS, '9 acres'.
	[HALF]. In the MS *d(imidius)* has been erased before *cui(us)da(m)*, but should have been retained in preference to the latter.
	N. Probably Norman as in 39,9.
	STANMER. In the MS there is an erasure after *Stanmar*.
	VALUE 3S. In the MS this extends into the margin and was perhaps omitted at first.
	WILLIAM OF BOSC. LDB *de Nomore*; see 7,115 note.
39,6	[HELD]. LDB *tenet* is in error for *tenuit*.
	36 ACRES. In the MS *xxx.vi* has been altered from *xxx.iii*.
39,8-10	QUENEVA. See 14,117 note. Farley prints *Quengeu&* in error, with & standing for the Anglo-Saxon letter 'ash' of the MS. PNDB 220 and n. 2 is thus incorrect.

39,10	2 HALF (FREE MEN). IE (149) names them as Thorkell and Goda. IEAL (189), '3 free men'.
	VALUE ... 20[S]. In LDB *& h(abe)t* is deleted after the value. It probably represents an erroneous anticipation of the last sentence of this entry.
39,11	W(ILLIAM) OF BOSC. LDB *de Nemore*; see 7,115 note.
	WHOLE OF THIS. Referring to 39,6-11.
39,12	*ALUREDESTUNA*. Unidentified, DG 389.
39,14	*EDULUESTUNA*. Unidentified, DG 397.
39,15	BOULGE. Here placed in Carlford Hundred, but elsewhere in the neighbouring Hundred of Wilford.
39,16	[HELD]. LDB *ten&* is in error for *tenuit*.
39,17	AELFRIC OF *WENHOU*. Also below at 46,3 (of *Weinhou*). His place of origin is unidentified.
40	ROBERT SON OF CORBUCION. Also a landholder in Essex (*40*) and Norfolk (*35*). His patronym is perhaps OFr *Corbucion* from Vulgar Latin *Corbutio*, an extended form of Latin *corvus*, 'raven'; OEB 178-179. In the MS there is a letter *f* in the left margin next to the chapter number, not shown by Farley; see *17* note.
40,1	BROCKLEY. Farley prints *Brode* in error for *Brocle* of the MS.
	SAEGARD. LDB *Saiardus*, from OE *Sǣgeard*; PNDB 353.
40,3	OVER THE VILLAGERS. LDB *de Wittis* is in error for *de uill(an)is*.
40,4	TEPEKIN. See 29,11 note.
40,5	FROM THE ABBOT. The LDB form is in error for *abb(at)e*.
40,6	GIFARD. He also held from Robert in Norfolk (35,3;16-17). The name is OG; Forssner 113-114.
41	WALTER THE DEACON. Also a landholder in Essex (*42*). In the MS there is a letter *n̄* in the right margin next to the chapter number, not shown by Farley; see *17* note.
41,4	THEODORIC'S HOLDING. That of Theodoric the predecessor and brother of Walter. Also in Essex (42,1).
41,5-6	SAME HOLDING. Theodoric's, as in 41,4.
41,6	BERNARD AND AELMER HOLD. However, the verb in LDB is singular. The meaning is probably rather that Aelmer *held* (cf. 41,4) and Bernard *holds*.
41,7	LEOFWIN. Probably Leofwin of Bacton, see 41,10 note.
	3 CARUCATES. In the MS the *c* of *car(ucate)* has been written over a minim; *iii* has thus been altered from *iiii*.
41,8	*CALDECOTA*. See 6,212 note.
41,10	LEOFWIN OF BACTON. Here described as a thane, but probably the same man as the Leofwin, free man, in 41,7 at Bacton. Probably also the same as Young Leofwin in Essex 42,4 (cf. also 42,2;6).
41,11	TERI. LDB *Teri(us)*, possibly from OFr *Tier(r)i*, *Terri* from OG *Theodric* or perhaps ODan *Thyri*; PNDB 383.
	... OF *BARTHETONA*. The place is unidentified, unless it is a corrupt form of *Bachetona*, from Bacton; cf. Leofwin of Bacton in 41,10.
	GUTHMUND. See 31,8-14 note.
	WELEDANA. Unidentified, DG 415.
41,15	*BRUNTUNA*. Unidentified, DG 392.
41,17-19	THESE ENTRIES are additions to this chapter, written by the same scribe but in a compressed manner. They were squeezed into the space which had been left between chapters *41* and *42*. In order to keep to the same text in each line as the MS, Farley increased his line-length here.
41,17	[THEN]. LDB omits *T(un)c*.
41,18	**'FINESFORDA'.** See 21,70 note.
42	TIHEL OF HELLÉAN. Also called Tihel the Breton. From Helléan (Morbihan); OEB 91. His byname has been fossilised in Helions Bumpstead (Essex 38,4) which he held in 1086. In the MS there is a letter *f* in the left margin next to the chapter number, not shown by Farley; see *17* note.
42,2	CLARENBOLD. LDB *Clareboldus*, from OG *Clare(n)bald*; Forssner 54-55.
43	RALPH OF LIMÉSY. From Limésy (Seine-Inf.), Loyd 54, OEB 95. In the right margin of the MS are the letters *f* and *r* next to the chapter number, not shown by Farley; see *17* note.
43,1	[HELD]. LDB *ten&* is in error for *tenuit*.
	EDGAR, HIS PREDECESSOR. That is, Ralph's predecessor.

43,2	CAVENDISH. LDB *Rana uadisc, Rana uadis* are in error for *Kauanadisc, Kauanadis*. Cf. 25,47 and note. 10D IN TAX. CODDENHAM. In the MS *.x.ď. Kode...* is written over an erasure. [3]½D IN TAX. Farley prints *iiii* in error for *iii* of the MS.
43,9	RALPH HOLDS THE WHOLE ... LORDSHIP. This sentence may be misplaced in LDB. It was perhaps intended to stand at the end of this entry and to refer to 43,1-9.
44	ROBERT OF TOSNY. From Tosny (Eure), Loyd 99, OEB 116. In the MS there are the letters *f* and *r* in the right margin next to the chapter number, not shown by Farley; see *17* note.
44,1	[ROBERT]. LDB *Rog(erus)* is in error for *Rob(ertus)*.
44,2	BISHOP'S MANOR OF HOXNE. See 18,1.
44,4	MEN'S [PLOUGHS]. LDB omits *car(ucate)*.
45	WALTER GIFFARD. Walter's father was a cousin of King William. Walter succeeded him before 1085 and was later created Earl of Buckingham, probably after 1093. The byname is either a patronym from OG *Gifard* or is a hereditary nickname from OFr *giffard* 'the chubby-cheeked one'; OEB 219-220. In the MS there is a letter *f* in the right margin next to the chapter number, not shown by Farley; see *17* note.
45,1	1 FREE [MAN]. LDB *lib(er)*. IEAL (186), '1 Freeman'. RALPH OF LANQUETOT. From Lanquetot (Seine-Inf.), Loyd 53, OEB 94.
45,2	180 ACRES. IE (153), '1½ carucates'. THIS ENTRY. In the MS (folio 430a, lines 10-11) there is a contemporary note in the right margin: *q(ua)t(er) xx ac(re) 7 Lxx*, 'fourscore acres and 70'. Farley omits.
45,3	RALPH ... HOLDS THE WHOLE. Probably referring to 45,2-3.
46	COUNTESS OF AUMÂLE. King William's sister. In the left margin of the MS are the letters *f* and *r* next to the chapter number, not shown by Farley; see *17* note.
46,1	4 SMALLHOLDERS. LDB *bođr* is in error for *borđ.*
46,2	[2] SLAVES. Farley prints *iii* in error for *ii* of the MS. PLOUGHS IN LORDSHIP, NOW 1. The interlined numeral *.i.* in LDB is here taken to be a correction for *null(a)* which should have been deleted.
46,3	AELFRIC OF *WEINHOU*. See 39,17 note. [MEN'S] PLOUGHS. LDB omits *hominum*.
46,4	EDEVA THE FAIR. In the MS *faira* has been altered from *feira*.
46,5	EDEVA. Probably the Fair, as 46,4. [HELD]. LDB *ten&* is in error for *tenuit*.
46,8	1 UNDER ... ST. ETHELDREDA'S. IE (150), '1 free man under the patronage of St. Etheldreda's; 16 acres. 2 smallholders. Meadow, 1 acre. Value 32d.' Cf. IEAL (189).
46,10	UNDER ... EDRIC GRIM. IE (148), 'under the patronage of St. Etheldreda's'. THIS ENTRY. IE adds, 'The Countess of Aumâle has 1 of these (free men)'. Cf. IEAL (185), where the three free men are stated to be held by Count Alan, and (189) where the meadow is said to be held by the Countess of Aumâle.
47	WILLIAM OF ARQUES. Probably from Arques (Pas-de-Calais), OEB 68-69. In the MS there are the letters *f* and *r* in the left margin next to the chapter number, not shown by Farley; see *17* note.
47,2	AND 22 ACRES ... 1 VILLAGER. IE (150), 'and 10 acres. He could not sell or grant it. 1 villager; 12 acres'. THEN 1 MEN'S PLOUGH, NOW ½. IE, 'Then 2 ploughs belonging to the men, now 1'. BERNARD OF ST. OUEN. From St.-Ouen-sous-Bailli (Seine-Inf.), Loyd 91, OEB 112.
47,3	GAVE UP TO THE CHURCH. IE (152), 'gave to St. Etheldreda's'. WOODLAND FOR 6 PIGS. After this, IE adds, 'Value 20s'.
48	DROGO OF BEUVRIÈRE. From La Beuvrière (Pas-de-Calais), OEB 73. In the MS there is a letter *f* in the right margin next to the chapter number, not shown by Farley; see *17* note.
48,1	RADA. Perhaps OE **Hrada* from *hraed*, 'quick, alert' or ON *Hrathi*, ODan *Rathi*; PNDB 344. FRANK. LDB *franc(us)* could be translated as 'a Frenchman', but cf. Norfolk (8,137) where 'a certain man of Drogo of Beuvrière, Frank by name' occurs. The name is OG *Franco*; Forssner 92.
49	HUGH OF GRANDMESNIL. From Le Grand-Mesnil (Calvados), Loyd 47, OEB 90. In the MS there is a letter *f* in the right margin next to the chapter number, not shown by Farley; see *17* note.
49,1	[HELD]. LDB *ten&* is in error for *tenuit*.

50	RALPH OF FOUGÈRES. From Fougères (Ille-et-Villaine), OEB 88-89. In the MS there is a letter *f* in the right margin next to the chapter number, not shown by Farley; see *17* note.
50,1	[HUNDRED OF HARTISMERE]. The rubric is omitted in LDB.
51	WALTER OF ST. VALÉRY. From St. Valéry-sur-Somme (Somme), OEB 114. In the left margin of the MS next to the chapter number are the letters *f* and *r*, not shown by Farley; see *17* note.
51,2	HIS FATHER. William Malet, father of Robert.
	'OLDEN'. See 1,5 note.
	THIS ENTRY. In the MS this is followed by an erasure of two and a half lines of writing.
52	HUMPHREY THE CHAMBERLAIN. In the right margin of the MS next to the chapter number is a letter *ñ*, not shown by Farley; see *17* note.
52,1-2	AMUND. LDB *Amund(us)*, from OSw *Aghmund*, cf. PNDB 141.
52,1	IN POSSESSION ... DIED; LATER. In the MS *saisitus* has been altered from *saiatus*.
52,2	FROM HUMPHREY. LDB *Winfrido* is in error for *Vmfrido*.

Folio 433a, the bottom corner of this folio is irregular in shape and affects the line-length of the text in part of 52,5.

52,5	8 WHOLE ... FREE MEN. LDB *lib(er)i ho(min)es integros* is in error; all three words should be in the nominative case.
52,7	LICTEVA. LDB *Listeua*, from OE *Lēohtgifu*; PNDB 319.

Folio 433b, the last four lines of the text of 52,8 are affected by the same irregular ity in the shape of the folio that affected 52,5.

52,8	BRICTICESHAGA. Unidentified, DG 392.
52,11	BERMESDENA. Unidentified, DG 390. For a later reference to the place, see VCH 568, n. 351.
	IN PATRONAGE. This is probably the meaning of the interlineation *7 i(n) cuñ*.
	[60] ACRES. Farley prints *LXX* in error. In the MS the second *X* has been erased.
53	EUDO SON OF SPIRWIC. Also a landholder in Lincolnshire and Norfolk (*29*). The patronym was taken to be OG in OEB 198, but may be Breton, see von Feilitzen 1939, 126. In the right margin of the MS next to the chapter number are the letters *f* and *r*, not shown by Farley; see *17* note.
53,1	MORVANT. He also held from Eudo in Norfolk (29,7). The personal-name (here *Moruant*, in Norfolk *Moruā*) has as first element the OE theme *Mor-* discussed in PNDB 328-329, but the second element is obscure (J.M.D.).
	HEINFRID. Also Eudo's predecessor in Norfolk (29,8). The name is OG *Heim-*, *Heinfrid*; Forssner 144-145.
	1 SLAVE. IE (142), '5 slaves'.
	MEADOW, 5 ACRES. IE, 'Meadow, 3 acres'.
53,2	'OLDEN'. See 1,5 note.
	ROGER. Perhaps Roger of Poitou, cf. 8,61.
53,3	IARNAGOT. LDB *Iarnagot(us)*, *Iarnagod* and (53,7) *Iarnacotus*. An Anglo-Scand. personal-name *Iarnagot* (J.M.D.).
	CYNRIC. LDB *Kerinc* is in error for *Kenric*, from OE *Cynerīc*; PNDB 220-221, Forssner 171.
53,6	WULFRIC HAGNI. The byname (LDB *hagana*) is a patronym from ODan *Hag(h)ni*; PNDB
	282, Fellows Jensen 122. Cf. OEB 221,186.
	WULFNOTH. Probably in error in LDB for Wulfric.
53,7	VALUE 20S. IE (142), 'Value 15s'.
	6 FORFEITURES. See 8,35 note.
	IARNAGOT. See 53,3 note.
54	WILLIAM OF VATTEVILLE. Probably from Vatteville (Seine-Inf.) but perhaps from Vatteville (Eure); OEB 120. In the right margin of the MS next to the chapter number is a letter *f*, not shown by Farley; see *17* note.
54,1	LIDGATE. William's men also claimed another estate here, see 70,1.
54,2	AELFGYTH. LDB *Aluiet*, from OE *AElfgyth*; PNDB 174.
54,3	ALFGEAT. LDB *Alued(us)*, from OE *AElfgeat*; PNDB 173.
	AELFEVA. LDB *alwewe*, from OE *AElfgifu*; cf. PNDB 173-174.
	ST. EDMUND'S. LDB *s(an)c(tu)s* is in error for *s(an)c(t)i*.
55	JOHN SON OF WALERAN. Also a landholder in Essex (*40*) and Cambridgeshire (*35*). In the left margin of the MS next to the chapter number is a letter *f*, not shown by Farley; see *17* note.
55,1	2 CARUCATES. In the MS *ii* has been altered from *iii*.
	1 SMITH. The only one mentioned in Domesday Suffolk.

56	HUMPHREY SON OF AUBREY. Also a landholder in Norfolk (*39*). In the right margin of the MS next to the chapter number is a letter *f*, not shown by Farley; see *17* note.
56,3	'OLDEN'. See 1,5 note.
56,4	VALUE ... JURISDICTION. Referring to 56,2-4.
56,6	CODDENHAM. See 1,74 note.
	MILL OF BILLINGFORD ... NORFOLK. Humphrey held Billingford in Eynsford Hundred in Norfolk (39,2), where the mill is listed but this value is not given. Although the present entry suggests that the mill was counted as part of Coddenham, it may be that it has simply been misplaced in Suffolk rather than in Humphrey's Norfolk chapter. Cf. Norfolk (ESf 7).
57	HUBERT OF MONT-CANISY. From Mont-Canisy (Calvados), OEB 100. In the right margin of the MS next to the chapter number is a letter *f*, not shown by Farley; see *17* note.
58	GUNDWIN THE CHAMBERLAIN. Perhaps the same as Gundwin in Essex (*80*) and Gundwin the keeper of the granaries (Wiltshire 68,29). The name is OG *Gund(e)win*; Forssner 135. In the left margin of the MS next to the chapter number is a letter *f*, not shown by Farley; see *17* note.
58,1	AESCMAN. LDB *Asseman(us)*, from OE *AEscmann*, possibly here a byname meaning 'sailor'; PNDB 182.
	OTHERS HOLD. LDB *ten&* is in error for *tenent*.
59	SASSELIN. Also a landholder in Essex (*57*). The name is a diminutive of OG *Saxo*; Forssner 223. In the left margin of the MS next to the chapter number is a letter *f*, not shown by Farley; see *17* note.
59,1	[HELD]. LDB *ten&* is in error for *tenuit*.
60	ROBERT OF VERLY. From Verly (Aisne), OEB 118. Also a landholder in Norfolk (*38*). In Essex (32,14-15;37;45) he held under Robert Gernon and gave his name to Virley (LDB *Salcota(m)*; 32,15). In the right margin of the MS next to the chapter number is a letter *f*, not shown by Farley; see *17* note.
60,1	WESTON. Before the name in LDB there is an otiose letter *I*. The scribe probably began writing *In* but stopped when he realised that *Westuna(m)* was the direct object of *tenuit* and not governed by a preposition.
61	RALPH PINEL. Also a landholder in Essex (*77*). The byname is OFr *pinel*, a diminutive of *pin*, 'a pine tree'; OEB 369. In the right margin of the MS next to the chapter number is a letter *f*, not shown by Farley; see *17* note.
61,1	[SAMFORD HUNDRED AND A HALF]. LDB omits the Hundred-heading.
	[HELD]. LDB *ten&* is in error for *tenuerunt*.
	GEOFFREY DE MANDEVILLE. Cf. 32,4;8.
62	ISAAC. Also a landholder in Norfolk (*47*). In the left margin of the MS next to the chapter number is a letter *f*, not shown by Farley; see *17* note.
62,2	WULFWIN, A FREE MAN. Farley prints *libomo* in error for *lihomo* of the MS (standing for *li(ber) homo*).
	MANOR BEFORE 1066. Farley prints an extra point between *man(erio)* and *.t.r.e.*, not present in the MS.
62,4	HEMINGSTONE. See 1,7 note.
62,5	OF ST. EDMUND'S. LDB *s(an)c(t)o* is in error for *s(an)c(t)i*.
62,6	HEMINGSTONE. See 1,7 note.
62,7	REDLES. Unidentified, DG 408.
	[HELD IT]. LDB *ten&* is in error for *tenuit*.
63	NORMAN THE SHERIFF. He also occurs in entries associated with two other Sheriffs of Suffolk, Robert Malet and Roger Bigot (6,91;290 and 7,36) and probably held the office before them.
64	JUDICAEL THE PRIEST. Also a landholder in Norfolk (*44*). His forename is OBret; PNDB 301, DBS 195 s.n. *Jekyll*. In the right margin of the MS next to the chapter number is a letter *f*, not shown by Farley; see *17* note.
64,1	[HELD]. LDB *ten&* is in error for *tenuit*.
64,3	7 SMALLHOLDERS. In the MS *vii* has been altered from *iii*.
	BISHOP'S (MANOR OF) HOXNE. See 18,1.
65	GERALD MARSHAL. In the left margin of the MS next to the chapter number is a letter *f*, not shown by Farley; see *17* note.
65,1	BADMONDISFIELD. See 1,121.
66	ROBERT BLUNT. Sheriff of Norfolk in 1086. His byname here is from OFr *blund*, *blond*, 'blonde, fair'; OEB 294. In Wiltshire (*60*) he has the Latin byname *flavus*, 'yellow, blonde'

	(OEB 313); in Northamptonshire (33) the Latin byname *albus*, 'white' (OEB 293); and in Norfolk (1,231. 26,3) the OFr byname *blanchart*, 'whitish' (OEB 293).
66,1	ARPENTS. See 21,16 note.
66,3	1 FREE MAN, KETEL. In LDB *.i. lib(er) h(om)o* was repeated in error after *Chetel*, then deleted. THEN 32 SHEEP. In the MS the interlined *x* touches the first *x* of *xxii* and is much easier to recognize as an emendation of the numeral than the way it appears in Farley. THIS ENTRY. FB ii (22), 'At (Great) ASHFIELD (Robert Blunt) holds 3 carrying-services (*aueres*) from 9 men'.
66,4	[HELD]. LDB *ten&* is in error for *tenuit*. THIS ENTRY. FB ii (22), 'At WYKEN (Robert Blunt) holds full jurisdiction over those who dwell on the King's land'.
66,6	HARET. The second element is OE *-rāed*, but the first is obscure; PNDB 287. ST. EDMUND'S HAD. In the MS there is an erasure after *eadmund(us)*.
66,9	ALL THESE FREE MEN. Probably those in 66,5-9.
66,12	BRUNMER. LDB *Brunar(us)*, from OE *Brūnmāer*; PNDB 210. [HELD IT]. LDB *ten&* is in error for *tenuit*.
66,13	WALSHAM ... AKI. See 66,2.
66,15	WALSHAM (LE WILLOWS). See 66,2.
66,16	WYVERSTONE ... AKI. Cf. 6,57. R. OUDKELL. LDB *Ouethel*. The byname is from the Anglo-Scand. masc. personal-name *Authketill*, *Authkell*, see Fellows Jensen 39 (J.M.D.).
66,17	(GREAT) ASHFIELD. Here placed in Stow Hundred which borders Blackbourn and Bradmere Hundreds to which it is assigned in 14,93 and 66,3.
67	HERVEY OF BOURGES. His byname *bict-*, *bituricensis*, *bituriensis* probably refers to Bourges (Cher); he also occurs as Hervey of Berry (*berruarius*, equivalent to OFr *berruier*, *beruier*, *barruier*), the province in central France in which Bourges is situated; see OEB 132. He also occurs in IE (158, 162, 165 etc) as Hervey Bedruel (*bebruel*, *bedruel*, *beruel*, *bredruel*); this byname was taken by OEB (132 n.1) to be an obscure local byname but is rather to be explained as an AN version of OFr *berruier*, 'of Berry' as above.
67,1	EUEN. The name-form may represent *Euen(d)* from the OScand. masc. personal-name *Eyvindr* (Björkman 36), but might also be the OE fem. personal-name *Eawynn* (von Feilitzen 1945, 79) (J.M.D.).
67,1	RICHARD OF CLARE'S PREDECESSOR. That of Richard son of Count Gilbert, see 25 note.
67,3	ROBERT MALET'S PREDECESSOR. Probably Edric, as 67,2.
67,4	1 FREE MAN. IE (146) adds, 'in the jurisdiction and under the patronage of St. Etheldreda's'.
67,5	[HELD]. LDB *ten&* is in error for *tenuit*. BRUTGE. See 6,28 note. WARNER. LDB *Garner(us)*, from the OFr form of OG *Warinhari*; Forssner 247-248. THIS ENTRY. Cf. IE (165), 'In *BRUGGE* 1 free woman under the patronage of St. Etheldreda's, with 80 acres as a manor. Then 1 plough, now ½. Meadow, 2 acres; ½ mill. Value then 20s; now 10[s]'. Cf. also IEAL (180).
67,6	THEN 1 PLOUGH. IE (165) adds, 'now not'. UNDER ... AELFRIC. IE, 'under the patronage of St. Etheldreda's'. WARNER ... ABBOT. IE, 'Hervey Bedruel holds this from the Abbot', referring to 67,6 and to the entry in 67,5 note.
67,7	W. SON OF GORHAM. The patronym may be OBret *Goron*; OEB 185.
67,9	UNDER ... ST. ETHELDREDA'S. IE (144) adds, 'in full jurisdiction'. VALUE ... NOW 9S. IE, 'Value 10s'.
67,10	4 SMALLHOLDERS. In the MS the first minim of *iiii* is written over an erasure. A GUARD. LDB *huscarli* (genitive) is here used as a descriptive term, probably denoting a trained soldier. For *Huscarl* used as a name, see 16,8 note.
67,11	10 FREE MEN ... [HAD IT]. IE (144), '9 free men over whom St. Etheldreda's had full jurisdiction and patronage'; eight of the LDB names are then given, excluding Wulfric and Edric. ANI. LDB *Ana*, from ODan *Ani*; PNDB 161. 80 AND 4 ACRES. In LDB *ac(ris)* has been deleted between *LXXX*. and *&*. For the 4 acres, cf. 67,15 and note. WULFMER ... [HAD]. LDB *h(abe)t* is in error for *habuit*.

67,12	LEOFRIC AND BRICTRIC; and WULFMER AND BONDI. IE (144) adds 'over these the Abbot has full jurisdiction and patronage'.
	[IN] LORDSHIP. In the MS *in ead(em) in d(omi)nio*. Farley omits the second *in*.
	HARDEKIN. See 25,57 note.
67,13	NECHEMARA. See 6,113 note.
	A GUARD. As 67,10 note.
67,15	4 ACRES ... BEALINGS. Cf. the 4 acres in 67,11 (Great Bealings) which is kept separate from the 80 acres therein.
	BERNARD OF ALENÇON. From Alençon (Orne); OEB 67. Cf. below.
	HE COULD NOT GRANT ... SOMEONE ELSE. The subject here is Edric.
	THE OTHER UNDER ... SOMEONE UNDER ... ST. ETHELDREDA'S. Cf. IE (145), '1 free man over whom the Abbot has full jurisdiction and patronage.'
	BERNARD OF ALENÇON. In the MS *de belencún*; Farley prints *de belencun*. The LDB form is in error for *de alencun*, as above.
67,16	FRANI. LDB *frana*, from ON *Fráni*; PNDB 252.
	REGINALD. LDB *Renoldus*, from *Rainald* the Rom. form of OG *Raginald*; Forssner 208.
67,17	DERNEFORD. Unidentified, DG 396.
67,18	INGOLUESTUNA. See 21,65 note.
	PETER OF PALLUEL. LDB *de paludel*. From either Palluel (Pas-de-Calais) or Paluel (Seine-Inf.); OEB 105.
67,20-21	AZOR. LDB *Atser(us)*, from ODan, OSw *Azur*; PNDB 170-171.
	(WILLIAM MALET ... DIED). As in 67,19.
67,21	ERCHENBALD. LDB *Arce(n)baldus*, from OG *Ercanbald*, Rom. *Archembald*; Forssner 76.
	[HELD IT]. LDB *ten&* is in error for *tenuit*.
	OF THIS, LIKEWISE. In LDB *totide(m)* has been deleted after *ex hoc*.
67,22	FREE MAN. In the MS *h(omine)m* has been corrected from *h(om)o*.
	[HALF] UNDER THE PATRONAGE. LDB omits the first *dim(idium)*.
	THIS ENTRY. Cf. IE (146), '1 free man, *Wenelin(c)g*, half under the patronage of the Abbot, with 8 acres'. The name *Wenelin(c)g* is probably a patronymic derived from OG *Wenilo*; PNDB 411.
67,23	1 FREE MAN. In the MS *hom(ine)m* has been altered from *homo*. Farley prints as *homǒ*.
67,25	PERCHES. In the MS *p(erti)cis* has been altered from *p(erti)cas*.
67,27	17 SHEEP. In the MS *xvii* has been altered from *xiiii*.
67,28	ALWAYS 2 PLOUGHS. Presumably in lordship.
	HIVES. The MLat term *rusca* is used here instead of the more usual *vas*.
67,29	UNDER THE PATRONAGE OF THE SAME. Either of Godiva or of Edric of Laxfield.
	1 FREE MAN AND A HALF. IE (148), '2 free men'. Cf. also IEAL (180).
67,30	ODO. LDB here *Odonus*, below (67,31) *Odo*. From OG *Odo*; Forssner 198-199. The first form appears to have a diminutive ending (perhaps it stands for *Odoinus*, with a Rom. suffix *-in*, cf. OEB 192).
	AS A MANOR. The scribe repeated *p(ro) man(erio)* in LDB then deleted the second instance.
	WYNNING. LDB *Wenningus*, from OE *Wynning*; PNDB 428. IE (148) calls him '1 free man'.
	8 FREE MEN. IE, '8 free men and a half'.
	THEY SHOULD REDEEM. LDB *redimer&* is in error for *redimerent*. IE has the correct form.
67,31	ODO. See 67,30 note.
67,32	HELD IT. In the MS *qu(o)d* has been altered from *qui*.
67,33	[HELD]. LDB *ten&* is in error for *tenuit*.
68	GILBERT THE CROSSBOWMAN. He also held land in Norfolk (52). Note that MLat *balistarius* has usually been translated as 'Gunner' in the present series but 'crossbowman' is more accurate and is preferred here. In the right margin of the MS next to the chapter number is a letter *f*, not shown by Farley; see *17* note.
68,1-4	BLYTHING HUNDRED. LDB *BIDINGA* is in error for *BLIDINGA*.
68,1	AELFRIC SON OF WULFGEAT. LDB has here *Elricus* but he appears to be the same as *Aluricus* at 16,2-3; see PNDB 180 and n.2.
68,2	WULFRIC ... ½ PLOUGH. In LDB the words *Rex & com(e)s soca(m)* have been deleted after *car(uca)*.
68,3-4	PATRONAGE OF THE SAME MAN. Earl Harold, as in 68,1.
68,5	DURING THE REIGN OF KING EDWARD. Translating *uiuente rege.edwardo*, an alternative to *t.r.e.*

	EUSTON. Cf. 14,98.
	AUBREY DE VERE'S PREDECESSOR. Probably Wulfwin, cf. 35,7-8 and 35,1-2;5-6.
69	RALPH THE CROSSBOWMAN. He also held land in Norfolk (*53*). For the byname see *68* note. In the right margin of the MS near the chapter number is a letter *R*, not shown by Farley; see *17* note.
69,1	BISHOP STIGAND. See 1,107-119 note.
69,3	CORTON. LDB *earetuna*, in error for *caretuna*.
70	REGINALD THE BRETON. The byname is MLat *Brito*, 'Breton'; OEB 133. In the right margin of the MS next to the chapter number is a letter *f*, not shown by Farley; see *17* note.
70,1	(WILLIAM OF) VATTEVILLE. Cf. 54,1.
	CLAIM. LDB *calu(m)pniatur* (sing.) is in error for *calu(m)pniantur* (plural).
71	ROBERT OF STRATFORD. From Stratford St. Mary (in Samford Hundred), which he held from Swein of Essex, see 27,9; cf. OEB 51.
71,1	SWEIN SWART. The byname is OWScand *Suartr*, *Suarti*, 'black'; OEB 338.
72	STANHARD SON OF AETHELWY. Possibly the same as Stanhard in Essex (*87*). Cf. also Stanhard son of Aethelwy of Thetford (7,1).
73	WULFMER. Probably the same as Wulfmer the (King's) reeve in 1,7 and 74,4;7 and 76,13-14.
73,1	LAFHAM. Unidentified, DG 404.
	HERIOT. A payment due at the time of death from a warrior to his lord, representing the return of his military equipment.
	HIS FATHER. Wulfmer's father.
74	VAVASSORS. Undertenants. The obsolete term is retained here because of its rarity in the Domesday records. It has been observed only here, in Buckinghamshire (12,30) and on the Isle of Wight (Hampshire IOW 7,15).
74,2	FACHEDUNA. See 25,58 note.
74,3	2 ACRES. Probably of meadow, if *prati* has been omitted.
74,4	'OLDEN'. As 1,5 note.
	RADBOD. LDB *Rabboda*, from OG *Radbodo*, *Rabbodo*; PNDB 344, Forssner 205.
	ROGER. Bigot, the Sheriff, see *7* and note.
	WULFMER THE REEVE. See *73* and note.
	BRICTMER THE BEADLE. The byname *bedel* is from OE *bydel*, Lat. *bedellus*, 'beadle'; OEB 240. He may perhaps be the same as Brictmer, Robert Malet's reeve, who is mentioned in 4,15, since Robert Malet was Sheriff at one point, see *6* note.
74,7	THIS ENTRY. This duplicates 1,7 under the King's lands.
74,8-9	EARL R(ALPH). Wader, see 1,61-95 note.
74,10	THESE ... KING'S HAND. Referring to 74,8-10.
74,11	FLINT. A byname from OE *flint*, 'flint, rock'; PNDB 251.
74,13	30 FREE MEN ... NAMES. Only 29 are named.
	RICTAN. Of obscure origin. Perhaps a misreading.
	ESTRED. LDB *Estrat*, from OE *Ēastrǣd*; cf. PNDB 244.
	TOVILD. LDB *Touilt*, from ON *Tófa-Hildr*, 'Hildr the daughter of Tófi'; cf. PNDB 384 and Essex 90,72.
	GUNVATI. LDB *Gunequata*, from ON *Gunnhvati*, cf. PNDB 277.
	DERSI. LDB *Dirsi*, from OE *Dēorsige*.
	SAXLEF. From OG *Sahsleib*, see von Feilitzen 1963, 57; (J.M.D.).
74,16	FRIDEB... LDB *Frieb'*. This abbreviated form could represent OG *Fridebern*/*Fridebert* or OE *Frithubeorht*.
75	FREE MEN ... IN THE KING'S HAND. These free men and their lands seem to have been the subject of disputes, some of them as yet unresolved.
75,1	THE ABBOT. Of St. Edmund's, cf. 14,100.
75,3	HERBERT BLACUN. The byname is a patronym from OE *blaechūn*; OEB 214.
	BISHOP ERFAST. See 19,1-2 note.
	JUDICAEL THE PRIEST. Cf. 64,3.
75,4	BISHOP AELMER. See 18,1 note.
75,5	2 FREE MEN ... ROBERT MALET'S MOTHER. Probably Brictere and Cynric of 77,3.
76	ANNEXATIONS. For similar chapters, see Essex *90* and Norfolk *66*. The entries represent instances of the unlawful occupation of lands, brought to light by the Domesday Survey. They are grouped according to the landholder responsible for the annexation.
76,1-7	RICHARD SON OF COUNT GILBERT. See *25* and note.

76,1 BRADLEY. Cf. 25,92.
MALUS VICINUS. A Lat. byname meaning 'bad neighbour', equivalent to OFr *mauveysin* which is the base of the medieval surname *Malveysyn, Mauueysin, Mauvesyn*, etc. which appears in the reigns of Henry III and Edward III in W. Rye, *A calendar of the Feet of Fines for Suffolk* (Ipswich, 1900), 47, 71, 196, 223 (sometimes printed therein as -nn-).

76,2 GROTON. Cf. 25,50.
ROBERT SON OF WYMARC. As 1,102 note.
ROGER OF ORBEC. As 25,56 note.

76,3 CAVENDISH. Cf. 25,47.
SAID WITHGAR. In LDB *p(re)dicti* is misplaced after *Edrici* rather than after *Witgari*.
ROGER OF ST. GERMAIN. As 25,47 note.

76,4 CORNARD. CF. 25,43.
AELFRIC KEMP. As 16,41 note.
[HELD]. LDB *ten&* is in error for *tenuit*.
(RICHARD'S) PREDECESSOR ... AGREEMENT OF RICHARD. LDB *ante c(on)uention(e) .Ricardi* stands for *ante(c essor) c(on)uention(e) .Ricardi*, with *Ricardi* written only once although being governed by both of the preceding words. Cf. *ante* for *ante(cessor)* in 76,18.

76,5 SAIBAMUS. Unidentified, DG 409.

76,6-7 CAVENDISH. Cf. 25,47.

76,8-12 WILLIAM OF PARTHENAY. From Parthenay (Deux-Sèvres) or possibly Parthenay-de-Bretagne (Ille-et-Vilaine); OEB 105.

76,8 STANTON. Cf. 14,72.

76,9 KNETTISHALL. Cf. 14,99.

76,10-12 BARDWELL. Cf. 14,82.

76,12 WHOLE OF THIS ... ABBOT'S DESPITE. Referring to 76,8-12 all of which was taken away from St. Edmund's.

76,13 WULFMER, THE KING'S REEVE. See 73 and note.

76,14 BRICETT ... 20 ACRES. See also 30,3.
BOTILD. From ON *Bóthildr*, ODan,OSw *Bothild*, cf. PNDB 207.

76,15 BAYLHAM ... WILLIAM OF BOURNEVILLE. Cf. 7,58 where '½ church, 12 acres' is entered.

76,16 ROGER (OF AUBERVILLE). Cf. 29,1.
EUSTACE. Count Eustace, cf. 5,4.
COUNT OF MORTAIN. Robert, see 2 and note.
HE GAVE UP. LDB *relinq(ui)d* is in error for *relinq(ui)t*.
ROBERT THE CROSSBOWMAN. LDB *arbal(istarius)*; OEB 234-235. He was a minor landholder in Norfolk (54).

76,17-18 ROBERT OF COURSON. See 7,6-7 note.
COVEHITHE. As 1,108 note.
COUNT ALAN ... WISSETT. Cf. 3,10.
EARL R(ALPH). Wader, the son of (Earl) R(alph) the Constable in 3,10. See 1,61-95 note.

76,18 WILLIAM OF WARENNE. See 26 and note.

76,19 UGGESHALL ... BERENGAR. Cf. 14,164 note.

76,20 RALPH OF LIMÉSY. See 43 and note.
[BABERGH TWO HUNDREDS]. Omitted here before Cavendish, Lavenham and Coddenham.
CAVENDISH. Cf. 43,2.
IN THE BATTLE. Of Hastings, 1066.
BAYNARD. Perhaps Ralph Baynard (33), or his nephew William (33,10).
EDGAR. Probably Ralph's predecessor in 43,1.
IN LORDSHIP. Translating *in d(omi)nio halle*.

76,21 AUBREY DE VERE. See 35 and note.
LAVENHAM ... WULFWIN. Cf. 35,1.

76,22 ROGER OF RAMES. See 38 and note.
CODDENHAM. Cf. 38,5.
WALTER OF ST. VALÉRY. See 51 and note.
FREE MEN. LDB *lib(er)i* is in error for *lib(er)os*.
ON HIS BEHALF. In the MS *sua* has been altered from *suę*.

76,23 ROBERT MALET. See 6 and note.
THIS ENTRY. This largely duplicates the last part of 6;191.

[77]	DISPUTES ... This chapter is not included in the List of Landholders in the MS, although it has been inserted there in the present edition, see folio 281a. It is written by one of the scribes of LDB and is contemporary with the rest of the Suffolk text. The dispute is also mentioned in 75,5. BISHOP OF BAYEUX. See *16* and note. ROBERT MALET'S MOTHER. See 6,76-77 note.
77,1-2	OCCOLD. Cf. 6,193.
77,1	BRICTERE. From OE *Beorhthere*; PNDB 194.
77,3	BEDINGFIELD ... 40 ACRES. Cf. 75,5. IN THE ABOVE-MENTIONED MANNER. Translating *sup(ra)dicto m(odo)*.
77,4	ASPALL. Cf. 6,201 and 16,48. THURSTAN. One of the free men belonging to the Holding held by Peter from Abbot Baldwin of St. Edmund's after 1066, see FD xci and no. 168. MARCULF. Either ODan *Markulf* or OG *Marculf*; PNDB 325. GUNNULF. LDB *Grunulf(us)*, from ON *Gúnnulfr*, ODan, OSw *Gunnulf*, see PNDB 278. He also belonged to the same Holding as Thurstan, above. WILLIAM MALET. Robert Malet's father. HUBERT OF PORT. One of the King's officials, see 16,34 and note. ODIHAM. A royal manor in Hampshire (1,1) and the centre of a Hundred there. It is within 5 miles of Mapledurwell (Hampshire 24,1), the main holding of Hubert of Port, see preceding note.
COLO- PHON	THIS SURVEY ... THE OTHERS. Written in red ink at the end of the text of LDB, which included the Domesday Survey for Essex, Norfolk and Suffolk, the three counties referred to here. See further, MDB 180-185.
EC1-	
EC2	EXNING. In Cambridgeshire until the 12th century (VCH Cambridgeshire i. 340, n.3).
EC2	WYMARC. Count Alan's steward *(dapifer)*, ICC (4).
EE1	HARKSTEAD. See 1,96 above.
EE2	WITH ALL THE ABOVE. Referring to several Freemen described in Essex 23,16-26.
EE3	MANOR IN SUFFOLK. Probably either Churchford (36,1) or Stutton (36,2). Both were held in succession by Scalpi and William *de Alno*, the latter from Robert Gernon.
ENf4	EARL R(ALPH). Wader, see above 1,61-95 note.

THE HUNDREDS AND HALF-HUNDREDS

Most of the twenty-five Suffolk Hundreds and Half-Hundreds named in 1086 survived without much change into the 19th century. Some are termed alternatively 'Hundred' or 'Half-Hundred' in LDB and later medieval records and there appears to have been little actual difference in legal status between the two terms in the post-Conquest period – a small Hundred might occasionally be called a Half-Hundred , that was all. In the same way, the Hundred and a Half of Samford was sometimes termed just a Hundred (see 3,67. 39,17. 40,6. etc.). The double Hundred of Babergh is rather more consistently described as two Hundreds, but not always (in 6,1 it is treated as a single Hundred, for example) . All were centres of the same type of Hundredal jurisdiction, whatever their physical size or fiscal capacity.

There is no evidence that the double Hundred of Babergh was formed by the union of two originally separate smaller Hundreds. Several such fusions of Hundreds or Half-Hundreds did occur in Suffolk, however, in the medieval period. The Hundreds of Blackbourn and Bradmere were already intermingled by 1086 and had become the double Hundred of Blackbourn by 1182. Bosmere and Claydon Hundreds were joined together after 1086; later on, by the 13th century, a third part of Claydon Hundred became the separate Half-Hundred of Thredling (the name itself meaning 'third part', from OE *thridling*). The Half-Hundred of Parham was subsumed into the Hundred of Plomesgate after 1086, and the latter was termed a Hundred and a Half by 1240. Even as late as 1763, the two Half-Hundred s of Mutford (called Lothing in 1086) and Lothingland were united to form a single Hundred .

Other changes to the list of Suffolk Hundreds made after 1086 include the name-change of Bishop's Hundred to Hoxne Hundred (by 1191); and the addition of the Half-Hundred of Exning (by 1199), after the transference of the parish from Cambridgeshire.

Some of the Hundreds or Half-Hundreds included detached parts in 1086. Claydon Hundred was then in three separate sections (hence Thredling Half-Hundred, mention ed above), while Parham was in two parts. Sudbury was a detached part of Thingoe Hundred. Kelsale (and probably Aldringham and part of Carlton, see 6,69-70 notes) was an outlier of Bishop's Hundred. Kenton, Woodbridge, Butley, and Gedgrave were outliers of the Hundred of Loes.

The unit known as a Ferthing (from OE *feorthing* 'a fourth part') is mentioned twice in LDB Suffolk, in connection with those of Aldham (14,112) and South Elmham (18,4), see 14,112 note.

A group of eight and a half Hundreds in the west of the county formed the Liberty of the Abbey of Bury St. Edmunds in the medieval period. Although it is reputed to have been granted by Edward the Confessor, it is not specifically mentioned in the Domesday Survey. The Liberty included the Hundreds of Blackbourn, Bradmere, Lackford, Risbridge, Thedwestry, and Thingoe; the double Hundred of Babergh; and the Half-Hundred of Cosford. A further five and a half Hundreds in the south-east of the county belonged to the Abbey of Ely. These were the Hundreds of Carlford, Colneis, Loes, Plomesgate, and Wilford; and the Half-Hundred of Parham.

There is no absolute consistency in the order in which the Hundredal units occur within chapters in LDB Suffolk. The following series occur in more than one chapter, however: (i) Thedwestry, Thingoe, Lackford, Babergh, Stow, Ipswich, Bosmere, Claydon, Samford; (ii) Risbridge, Cosford, Bishop's, Blything, Colneis, Carlford, Wilford, Loes; (iii) Parham, Plomesgate, Hartismere; (iv) Wangford, Lothing, Lothingland. Only the last of these makes obvious geographical sense. The others probably reflect an order in which material was copied into LDB or into a previous draft, rather than any conventional ordering of the Suffolk Hundredal units. Some Hundredal rubrics may have been omitted from chapter *6* (see 6,207-208 notes). Such omissions are rare in the Suffolk folios but others do occur (before 50,1 and 61,1 for example) .

For further information about, and medieval references to, the Suffolk Hundreds and Half-Hundreds, see O. S. Anderson, *The English Hundred-Names* (Lund 1934) 83-98.

THE COUNTY BOUNDARY

The county of Suffolk has its origin as the southern division (or *folc*) of the Kingdom of the East Angles, divided from the northern division (Norfolk) by the rivers of the Little Ouse and the Waveney. To the south it is divided from Essex by the River Stour. Its western boundary against Cambridgeshire was formerly the River Kennet, but part of it was moved westwards to include Exning in the 12th century. There is evidence in the Domesday Survey of some tenurial association with estates in Norfolk (Alburgh, Diss, Gillingham, Gorleston, Hardwick, Kenninghall, Mundham, Redenhall, and Yarmouth); Cambridgeshire (Weston Colville); and Essex (Ardleigh, Brightlingsea, Bures [Essex 23,16 note], Castle Hedingham, Great and Little Henny, Moze, and Nayland [Essex 24,57 note]).

The parish of Ballingdon cum Brundon was transferred from Essex to the Borough of Sudbury in Suffolk in 1832 and 1835 (*The Place-Names of Essex* ed. P. H. Reaney, *English Place-Name Society* xii, Cambridge 1935, 407n.); for its Domesday entries see the Essex volume.

APPENDIX I

THE ELY INQUIRY
Inquisitio Eliensis (IE)

The Ely Inquiry, usually referred to as IE, is a collection of material relating to holdings of Ely Abbey in Cambridgeshire, Essex, Hertfordshire, Huntingdonshire, Norfolk, and Suffolk whose source appears to have been drafts (now lost) of the returns for three different circuits of the DB Survey. It was put together, for the benefit of Ely Abbey, very soon after 1086, but survives only in three manuscripts written in the second half of the 12th century — British Library, Cotton Tiberius A.vi, folios 38-70 (MS A; this manuscript also contains the sole surviving text of the *Inquisitio Comitatus Cantabrigiensis*, ICC, for an account of which, see the Cambridgeshire volume, Introduction); Trinity College Cambridge 0.2.41, pages 161-274 (MS B) and 0.2.1, folios 177v-213 (MS C). Of these three manuscripts, B and C are derived from a common source, while A is a copy of B. Although B is now thought to be the most reliable of them, IE was reproduced in record type in 1816 by Sir Henry Ellis from A (see DB 4, pp. 495-528). N.E.S.A. Hamilton also used A as the base text for his edition of IE in 1876 (pages 97-168 of his *Inquisitio Comitatus Cantabrigiensis*), but also gave variant readings from B and C in footnotes.[1] Footnotes to the Victoria County History translation of LDB Suffolk also supply items of extra information from IE, translated from Hamilton's edition (*The Victoria History of the County of Suffolk*, i (1911), 419-582).

For Suffolk, IE (Hamilton 141-166; and summaries at 122) supplies details of the Ely Abbey holdings in the county (cf. above, Chapter *21*) and of other pieces of land and rights claimed by the Abbey. The order of entries is largely on a Hundredal basis but is not always the same as that in LDB. The IE text does not include all the information to be found in LDB, nor are its statistics always identical, but it does have some material not to be found in LDB. Hamilton also edited some other documents, subsidiary to IE, which are dependent on, or relevant to, the DB Survey. The *Inquisitio Eliensis* Breviate (IEBrev; Hamilton 168-173) gives summaries of the numbers of ploughs and people in each of the Abbey's holdings, and the *Nomina Villarum* (IENV; Hamilton 174-175) lists the numbers of ploughs held by the villagers therein. These are followed by lists of holdings alienated from the Abbey's possession (IEAL; Hamilton 175-189) and an account of an inquiry into the Abbey's losses held between 1071 and 1075 (Hamilton 192-195). In the notes to the present volume, quotations from IE and its related documents have only been given where information occurs which is different from, or extra to, that in LDB.

For further comments on IE, see R. Welldon Finn, 'The Inquisitio Eliensis reconsidered', *English Historical Review* lxxv (1960), 385-409. For the Ely Abbey claims, see E. Miller, 'The Ely land pleas in the reign of William I', *English Historical Review* lxii (1947), 438-456 and *Liber Eliensis*, ed. E. O. Blake, 426-432. See also the Introduction to the Cambridgeshire volume for a sample of text from IE.

---

[1] Note that in the Cambridgeshire volume, Introduction, The Ely Inquiry, it is wrongly stated that Ellis and Hamilton edited IE from MS C and that Hamilton collated it to MSS A and B. The true situation is as stated in the present Appendix.

APPENDIX II

THE FEUDAL BOOK OF ABBOT BALDWIN OF [BURY] ST. EDMUNDS (FB)

FB is a survey of holdings in Suffolk, Norfolk, and Essex which belonged to the Abbey of [Bury] St. Edmunds (cf. Chapter *14*, above). The fullest surviving version of it forms part of the late 12th-century section of the Black Book of the Abbey, now Cambridge University Library, Mm. 4.19 (folios 124-143v), but its name associates its origin with the time of Abbot Baldwin (1065-1098). Part of FB is also included in the 14th-century Bury register, now Cambridge University Library, Ee. 3.60 (folios 178v foll.); this part was edited by Lord Francis Hervey in *The Pinchbeck Register* (Brighton, 1925) i, 410 foll. The fullest modern edition of FB is that by D. C. Douglas in FD, *Feudal Documents from the Abbey of Bury St. Edmunds* (London, 1932), 3-44, with an introduction, xlvi-lxvii. If in fact it was the work of Abbot Baldwin, FB dates from between 9 September 1087 and (?)29 December 1097, the respective dates of death of William I (see below) and of Abbot Baldwin.[1] However, R. Lennard in *Rural England: 1086-1135* (Oxford, 1959), 359 has disputed the connection with Abbot Baldwin and has suggested a terminal date of March 1119. FB contains three sections:

FB i; folios 124-131v, FD 3-15. A survey of the Abbey's lordship manors in Norfolk and Suffolk and of the lands which the Abbey's tenants held there when King William caused 'the survey of the whole of England' to be made and also on the day of his death. Within each Hundred in the Suffolk portion the individual entries are largely given in the same order as in LDB, but the Hundreds themselves are in a different order, those in FB beginning with the eight-and-a-half Hundreds of St. Edmund's in the west of the county. A number of places are omitted from FB and there are frequent differences between the statistics given in FB and in LDB.

FB ii; folios 132-134v, FD 15-24. A survey of the lands of the Abbey's *feudati homines* in Norfolk, Suffolk, and Essex (two entries only), arranged by tenants rather than by Hundred. In the Suffolk section not all the sub-tenancies given in LDB are included and there are a number of discrepancies.

FB iii; folios 135-143v, FD 25-44. A list of the holdings and rents or tax-liability of named peasants, relating only to thirty-one places in the Suffolk Hundreds of Thedwestry and Blackbourn and the Half-Hundred of Cosford.

In the notes to the present volume, reference to FB has only been made where information occurs which is different from, or extra to, that in LDB.

---

[1] Douglas, FD xlviii-xlix, dates between 7 September 1087 and 4 January 1098. For the date of Abbot Baldwin's death, see *The Heads of Religious Houses: England & Wales 940-1216*, edd. D. Knowles, C. N. L. Brooke, V. London (Cambridge, 1972), 32.

INDEX OF PERSONS

Familiar modern spellings are given where they exist. Unfamiliar names are usually given in an approximate late 11th century form, avoiding variants that were already obsolescent or pedantic. Spellings that mislead the modern eye are avoided where possible (thus Leofled, not Leofflaed). While an attempt has been made to differentiate individuals with the same name, there remain several individuals who cannot be so differentiated. Readers are therefore advised that a group of references given under a single name (e.g. Edric) do not necessarily refer to the same individual; where the same name occurs more than once in a single entry and could refer to different individuals, the possible number of different individuals is shown in brackets after the entry reference. In general, notes on either personal names or individuals have been placed under the first reference listed in this index.

References are to persons named in the translation of LDB or to those identified in the notes from additional information contained in IE, FB or FD. All names or name-forms which are supplied from IE, FB or FD are printed in italics; to avoid confusion with this extra material, all unidentified place-names (e.g. Carlewuda) which occur as part of personal-names are printed in this index in roman type although they are in italics in the translation. The chapter-numbers of listed landholders are also here printed in italics, as are references to entries governed by a sub-heading (e.g. 1,61-95; but not those added in the translation of Chapter 76).

Acwulf	12,1. 59,1
Adelelm	35,5;7-8
Adelo	14,36 note
Adelund	14,32;36;58;98
Aedi	6,171
Aelfeva mother of Earl Morcar	16,10
(Aelfeva) mother of Earl Morcar	*1,97-99* and note
Aelfeva	7,36;38-39. 21,50. 84,3
Aelfgyth	54,2
Aelfled	6,38;57;211. 8,31;53;55-56. 33,12. 52,1
Aelfric brother of Edric	76,3
Aelfric father of Withgar, see Aelfric son of Withgar	
Aelfric Kemp	16,41. 28,7. 38,2. 76,4
Aelfric of Hopewella	6,110
Aelfric of Sanford	26,12b
Aelfric of Weinhou, Wenhou	39,17. 46,3
Aelfric son of Bondi	7,37
Aelfric son of Brown	16,11
Aelfric son of Rolf, burgess of Ipswich	74,8-10
Aelfric son of (? Edwin) the smith in Carlewuda	6,110
Aelfric son (and father) of Withgar	25,1;60
Aelfric son of Wulfgeat	16,2-3. 68,1
Aelfric Starling	25,71
Aelfric Stickstag	7,77
Aelfric the deacon	38,22
Aelfric the priest	2,17. 3,64;74-78. 16,30. 74,14
Aelfric the reeve of the Abbot (of St. Edmund's)	14,152
Aelfric the reeve	1,17;30 and note;60 note;103
Aelfric Wand	*1,100-106*
Aelfric, a thane of King (Edward's)	3,88
Aelfric	1,102. 2,20. 3,66;94;100. 4,11;13;19;21;40. 5,7. 6,40;57;90;110;116;191-192;309-310. 7,40;48-49;66;75;79;104;108;118;121;134; 137. 8,6;55. 9,1-2. 14,41;44;49. 16,15-16; 20(×2);35;38;41(×2);42. 19,18. 21,23;63. 23,2-3. 25,60(×2);64-65. 26,13-14. 31,20; 56. 36,5;12-13. 38,11;20. 43,5;7. 51,1. 56,5. 64,1. 67,6. 74,13(×4). ENf4
Aelfric	notes to 8,12;81

Aelfwin brother of Goda	7,37
Bishop Aelmer (of Elmham)	2,3–5. 3,96. 6,311. 7,4. 8,42. 18,1;4;6. 19,11; 14–16;18;20. 64,3. 75,4
(Bishop) Aelmer (of Elmham)	19,1–3;9;13–14;17
Aelmer the King's reeve	8,60
Aelmer the priest	1,56
Aelmer	1,73–74. 3,95. 4,42. 6,9;92;209;239. 7,79; 80(X2);83;101;104;121. 8,61. 13,3. 16,20. 21,90. 32,23. 38,6. 41,4;6.
Aelmer	21,100 note
Aeschere	1,123f
Aescman	58,1
Aethelgyth	33,1;13. ENf5
Aethelric of Burgh	8,6;9. 32,23;28. 67,23
Aethelric (of Burgh)	26,16
Aethelric	1,18. 6,112. 14,38. 16,18;26;31. 26,17;18;20. 67,10
Aethelric, wife of	14,38
Aethelsi	1,19
Aethelstan	1,19;55. 4,1;18. 16,7;26. 74,13
Aethelward son of Bell	25,20
Aethelward the King's reeve	7,18;36
Aethelward	7,5
Aethelwin	8,65
Aethelwold the priest	3,31
Aethelwold	6,123
Aethelwy of Thetford (?Sheriff of Norfolk)	7,1 and note
Aethelwy	6,46
Aethelwy, see Stanhard	
Agenet	14,13
Ailbern	16,18. 25,68;85
Ailbold the priest	14,13 note;39
Ainuar	25,89
Aitard	7,4
Aki	6,57;85. 66,1–4;13–14;16
Akile Suffering	7,37
Count Alan (of Brittany)	3 and note. 1,123f. 4,13. 13,3. 26,12a;12d;15. 76,17. EC2. ENf2;4. Also folio 291a
Count Alan (of Brittany)	46,10 note
Count Alan, see Wymarc	
Alan	37,5
Burnt Albert	8,15
Albert	8,13;56–58. 14,11
Albold, a cleric	14,13;39 note
Aldred	5,2
Aldgyth	67,15. 74,6
Aldwin	7,60
Aldwulf	7,80;82;107–109
Alfgeat	1,102. 6,216. 16,35. 25,73. 29,6. 54,3
Alfger	1,111
Alfheah	4,15. 14,43
Alfhere, see Godwin	
Alfnoth	49,1
Alfred	32,4. 36,8
Alfsi	6,191. EC2
Alfwold	16,6 note
Earl Algar	8,33. 12,4. 16,9. 25,58;77. 38,1. 65,1
(Earl) Algar	1,121 and note
Algar the priest	8,75
Algar	6,106;197. 7,18;71;118;124. 8,62. 12,5. 16,36. 19,12. 21,55–56. 27,10. 28,3. 64,3. 66,13
Algar	8,59 note

Algar, see Godwin	
Ali	7,19;54
Alnoth	6,32(×2);100;196. 7,36;102. 16,30
Alric the reeve	1,60
Alric	1,44-45. 74,10
Alsi nephew of Earl Ralph	8,50
Alsi nephew of Earl R(alph)	6,216;233
Alsi	5,3. 16,12. 21,28;34. 60,1. 68,5
Alsi, wife of	68,5
Alsi, see Godwin	
Alstan	6,191;228. 37,1;4. 67,11. 74,11
Alward	6,202. 61,1
Alwin of Mendlesham	1,77 note. 31,51
Alwin the priest	1,13-14. 16,30
Alwin	1,7;77;110. 3,9. 6,38;48;57;207;211;296. 7,23;85;111;136. 8,8. 16,34;41. 19,14;16. 23,5. 25,73;83-84;90. 33,8. 35,7(×2). 36,5. 38,6;10;27. 40,6. 52,6. 67,11. 74,7;11(×2);13
Alwin, wife of	6,57
Alwold the priest	16,22
Alwold	8,68. 16,45. 69,4. 76,6
Alwulf the priest	1,122d
Alwy	4,22. 12,6. 19,16
Alwynn	6,51
Amund	52,1-2;5;8-9
Anbold	33,7
Andrew	8,11
Ani	67,11
Anselm	14,139
Ansgot	3,67;84
Ansketel the priest, Roger Bigot's chaplain	7,36
Ansketel	7,13. 38,8
Anund the priest	67,11
Anund	1,9. 2,12. 3,32-33;46-48. 7,15. 13,7. 52,11. 53,1
Arkell	6,130
Arnold	8,9. 38,14;16
Arnold, see Roger	
Arnulf	8,10. 14,26-27;35;62;115. 27,12
Arnulf	14,52 note
Artald	8,55
Aseret	21,29
Asgar the Constable	25,73. 66,10
Asgar (the Constable)	32,1;3-5;8;19
Asgar	6,217
Askell the priest	4,14
Askell, a guard	67,10
Askell, a villager	68,2
Askell	7,37;109;143. 19,15. 25,53. 30,3. 68,4. 76,14
Aslac	31,28
Asmoth	4,15. 6,91
Asmoth, see Brictmer	
Aubrey de Vere	*35*. 1,105. 6,216;227. 68,5. 76,21. EE5
Aubrey, see Humphrey, Walter	
Countess of Aumâle	*46*
Auti, a thane	37,6. 40,3
Auti	37,7
Azor	67,20-21;33
Bald, see Leofwin, Richard	
Abbot Baldwin (of St. Edmund's)	14,26;167. 18,4
Abbot Baldwin (of St. Edmund's)	notes to 14,5-6;21;28;65;106-107;137-139;151
Abbot Baldwin (of St. Edmund's), see Durand, Frodo	
Balki	16,7;26
Barn	3,61

Barthetona, see penultimate entry	
Baynard	7,15. 76,20
Baynard, see Ralph, William	
Beard, see Brunman	
Bedruel, see Hervey	
Bell, see Aethelward	
Benne, see Leofwin	
Beorn	16,3
Berard	14,16;24;57;110-112. 40,5
Berengar	14,38. 76,19
Berengar	14,164 note
Bernard of Alençon	67,15;29
Bernard of London	6,110
Bernard of St. Ouen	47,2
Bernard	7,102. 41,5-6
Berner the crossbowman	21,11
Besi	6,216. 35,7
Bigot of Loges	4,13
Bigot, see Roger	
Black, see Brictric	
Blackman	6,93-94;112. 7,36;76;99;111;120-121. 16,26. 67,11
Blackman, wife of	6,93
Blackson	6,32. 7,60;146. 16,35
Blackwin	7,60. 25,79. 34,4
Blacun, see Herbert	
Blunt, see Gilbert, Robert	
Bondi the smith	7,37
Bondi	6,253. 7,29;121. 19,16. 25,56;103. 67,12. 69,2. 76,1
Bondi	21,94 note
Bondi, see Aelfric	
Bosten	26,8
Boti	2,11. 7,33. 35,7. 38,20
Botild	76,14
Breme	31,50
Count Brian	2,5-6;9
(Count) Brian	2,7;13
Brian, see Ralph	
Brict	39,5
Brictere	77,1;3
Brictfled	6,62
Brictman	8,6
Brictmer Bubba	6,226
Brictmer son of Asmoth	4,15
Brictmer the beadle	74,4
Brictmer the reeve of Robert Malet	4,15
Brictmer the reeve of St. Edmund's	62,5
Brictmer	3,65;101. 6,11;173;201;209;215;271. 7,98;115; 121;133;140;145. 8,65. 21,39. 22,2. 32,8. 35,7. 38,16. 39,5;7-9. 39,2-4;10. 43,6. 61,2. 67,15;27;31. 74,13
Brictmer, see Queneva	
Brictnoth	2,20. 6,46;264. 7,80;120. 8,2. 19,17
Brictnoth	notes to 8,6. 32,29
Brictric Black	25,79. 67,1
Brictric	2,17. 7,80;87;95;106;108;117;137. 8,1;6. 25,105. 32,28. 39,5. 41,9. 67,12(×2)
Brictric	16,31 note
Brictric, see Wulfric	
Brictsi	71,1
Brictwold Muffle	32,28
Brictwold son of Leofmer	notes to 14,5-6;21;28;65;106
Brictwold	6,10;271. 16,16;36. 52,1;3-5;9. 67,3. 74,5

Brictwold	8,23 note
Brother	1,53. 3,89
Brown the reeve of Ipswich	7,63–66
Brown	1,119. 8,8. 16,43. 67,10
Brown, see Aelfric, Leofwin	
Brunard	9,1
Brungar	6,215. 7,62. 16,35. 27,7
Brunloc	14,152
Brunman Beard	7,36
Brunman of Burgh	6,110
Brunman	7,108. 67,32
Brunmer the priest	66,12
Brunmer	2,18. 7,36;109;111
Brunwin	4,15. 16,23. 35,4. 67,14
Bubba, see Brictmer	
Burcard	
Burcard	14,72 note
Burghard of Mendlesham	14,152
Burghard (of Mendlesham)	1,76-77. 14,46 and notes
Burghard	1,83-84;86;95. 4,12;24;26;28-31;33;35;38-39. 6,215. 7,42-43. 16,15;26. 31,21-24;26-30; 32-33;35-36
Burghard, see Peter	
Burgric	3,100. 7,79;106. 16,43. 46,7;9. 67,10
Burnin	4,32
Burnin, see Warin	
Burnt, see Albert	
Canute	28,3–4
Ceolric	32,14 note
Ceolwold	25,64
Chipping	6,216
Clarenbold	42,2
Cobbe, see Leofric	
Coleman	6,216. 7,77;80. 14,24. 35,7. 62,2
Corbucion, see Robert	
Crawa	25,78
Croc, see Leofwin	
Culling, a burgess of Ipswich	1,122d
Cus	6,44. 7,37
Cynric	3,57. 4,15. 7,99. 53,3. 77,2-3
Cynwold	67,9
Dering	7,118
Dersi	74,13
Derstan	7,112
Derwulf	21,39. 77,4
Dot	3,100. 29,3
Drogo of Beuvrière	*48*
Drogo	19,12
Durand of Offton	67,23
Durand *the cleric, of St. Edmund's and of Abbot Baldwin*	14,119 and note
Durand	6,128. 7,84;111;118;121. 14,77;119. 16,25. 39,12. 67,12;17-18. 74,3
Dynechaie	6,191
E.	8,11
Countess Edeva	4,17
Edeva the Fair, the Rich	1,61;63;67;73. 3,67. 31,54. 46,4. EC1
Edeva (the Fair, the Rich)	1,64. 3,68-69;71-74;76-77;81;84. 25,104. 46,5. EC2
Edgar	43,1. 76,20
Edhild	3,91. 7,137
Queen Edith	1,122a-122b. 6,26. 25,56. 37,2. 41,1-2. 52,1. 76,15
Queen (Edith)	6,112 and note

Edith	1,88–90. 74,13
Edmer, a thane	8,33
Edmer	6,8
King Edmund	14,167
Edmund the priest	47,2-3
Edmund the priest, wife of	47,3
Edmund	3,70–71. 25,67
Ednoth	7,85. 16,37. 36,10
Edred	8,58
Edric Grim	3,21–23;28;34–42;50–52;89;94–95. 8,26. 31,15. 34,15. 46,10. 67,25
Edric *Grim*	3,24–27;29 and notes
Edric Grim	3,49 note
Edric of Laxfield	1,31. 3,34;39;41. 6,28;58;62;79–80;83–84;110; 114;128–129;135;148;260;264;272-273;295; 303-304. 7,23;36. 8,29. 14,68. 16,6;15;25. 19,16. 31,20;27. 64,2. 67,15;28–29;33
Edric (of Laxfield)	6,305-306. 7,114 and notes
Edric son of Ingold	4,15
Edric Spud	25,78
Edric the deacon	76,20
Edric the King's reeve	6,217
Edric	1,50;111;123f. 2,16. 3,45;95;98;101. 4,15; 18(×2). 6,3;5–6;10;11;14–16;32–34;36–37;42; 44–46;48;57;60–61;64–65;67–69;78–79;82; 87;90;92–95;97(×3);102;106;110–111;115– 118;123;126–127;130;132-133;135–141;149- 150;153;156;159;161–162;164–165;170–172; 174–180;183–184;187–190;191(×2);192–196; 198;201–202;205;236–239;242;245–249;251; 253–254;257;261–262;264–271;276–278;280– 289;293;296;308;311. 7,13;15;38;56;58;76– 77;79(×2);90;98;105;111;121;123;125; 131;142(×2);143;145–146;151. 8,8;25;30. 16,14;16;24;26–30;33;38;43. 21,67;90. 22,3. 25,59;87. 26,12a;12d;13;15. 29,4. 30,2. 31,16–18;27. 32,1. 35,7. 38,4;6. 39,5;9. 51,1. 64,1. 67,2;5(×2);8;11–12;15–16;20–22;26; 28;30–32. 74,4;11;13. 77,4
E(dric)	6,119–120;122;124;134;143;151-152;154-155; 157;173;197;199–200;203;238;240–241;243– 244;252;255–256;290–292. 52,1. 67,10;17
Edric	notes to 8,23. 38,22
Edric, wife of	6,57
Edric, see Aelfric	
Edward	4,4. 7,109
Edwin the priest	8,81
Edwin the smith in Carlewuda	6,110
(? Edwin) the smith in Carlewuda, see Aelfric	
Edwin	3,72–73;83;86. 7,18. 8,58. 13,2;7. 21,51. 25,70. 32,8
Edwold	8,11–12. 39,6
Edwold, wife of	8,11
Edwy	16,41;47
Edwy	8,9 note
Elinant	25,46
Engelric *the priest*	14,101 and note
Engelric	5,3–5. 14,39;107. 39,3
Erchenbald	67,21
Bishop Erfast (of Thetford)	1,119. 25,60. 75,3
(Bishop) Erfast (of Thetford)	19,1–2
Eric	21,22
Erland	3,56;62

Ermengot	3,67
Erngeat	7,83. 61,1
Ernwulf	6,32
Ertald	8,22
Estmund	1,102
Estred	74,13
Eudo son of Nigel	2,16
Eudo (son of Nigel)	2,20
Eudo son of Spirwic	53. 6,210
Eudo the Steward	*28*. 16,41. 29,11
Euen	67,1
Count Eustace	*5*
(Count) Eustace	76,16
Fair, see Edeva	
Falc	14,59. 21,2
Farman	7,68. 21,75
Farthing, see Robert	
Fat, see Ralph	
Fathir	25,24
Fermeus	35,3
Finn (the Dane)	8,59 and note. 25,19;51-53;56-57;59;61;63; 72;75;77. 35,3
Flint	74,11
Frani	67,16
Frank	48,1
Frederick	26,4;9
Frewin	7,121
Frideb..., a priest	74,16
Fridebern	25,82. 32,6
Frodo brother of Abbot (Baldwin of St. Edmund's)	*12*. 25,79
Frodo *brother of Abbot (Baldwin of St. Edmund's)*	14,21;28;65;106. 21,40 and notes
Frodo brother of Abbot (Baldwin of St. Edmund's)	notes to 14,137-139
Frodo	1,1. 2,7. 7,56. 14,33;68;86. 6,195. 35,7(×2)
Fulcard	
Fulcher *the Breton*	14,22 and note
Fulcher *of Mesnières*	14,11;78;80;89-90;99
Fulcher	14,82 note
Fulcred	1,10. 6,83;92;95-96;289. 25,9;90
Fulcred, see Robert	
Fulcric	3,70-71
Fulk	30,1;3
Gamas	14,114
Gamilo	14,24 note
Gauti	3,56. 7,15
Geoffrey de Mandeville	*32*. 8,4. 61,1. 67,11
G(eoffrey) de Mandeville	6,112. 21,58;95
Geoffrey son of Hamo	25,86
Geoffrey	25,57. 53,5-6. 67,12
Gerald Marshal	*65*
Gerald	8,51. 25,105. 38,14;22-23
Gerald, see Raymond	
Gerard	40,3
Germund	25,55
Gernon, see Robert	
Gifard	40,6
Giffard, see Walter	
Bishop Gilbert of Evreux	*22*
Count Gilbert, see Richard	
Gilbert Blunt	6,84-88;105;133;254
G(ilbert Blunt)	6,134 and note
Gilbert of Coleville	6,127;180;236;272

Gilbert of Wissant	6,30;143;239;244;281;286–287
Gilbert son of Richere	ENf5
Gilbert the crossbowman	*68*
Gilbert the priest	32,4
Gilbert	6,19–21;29–30;34–37;40;52;83;92;100;279; 283. 25,8;78. 29,8. 31,38
Ginni	8,64
Gladman	67,12
Gleman of Levington	6,110
Goda brother of Aelfwin	7,37
Goda of 'Struostuna'	6,110
Goda	7,22;75;80;82;105;108-109;110(X2);112. 16,29. 25,81
Goda	39,10 note
Godard	25,84
Godfrey of Pierrepont	26,12c;14
Godhere	8,4
Goding	3,73. 7,89(×2). 16,35. 74,13
Godiva	7,90. 11,4. 25,33. 67,29
Godman, a thane	59,2
Godman	2,17. 3,68. 6,65–66. 7,90;117;119. 8,56. 25,55. 29,4. 67,4
Godmer	3,59
Godric Long	7,77
Godric of Peyton	6,238
Godric (of Peyton)	27,13 and note
Godric of Ringshall	29,8
Godric son of Herebold	6,108
Godric the priest	6,128. 7,114
Godric the smith	7,76
Godric the Steward	*13. 1,61–95.* 14,146
G(odric) the Steward	7,9
Godric	1,19;111;123e-123f. 2,17. 3,95. 4,2. 6,36;84; 159;176–177;186;191;193;202;234;245. 7,8–9;24;57;77(×3);80(×3);85;91;97–98; 108–109;117–118;120–121;148(×2). 8,3;81. 11,1-3. 13,6. 16,23;26;36. 21,52. 25,57;67; 69–70;75. 32,26. 35,7(X2). 39,1;5-6. 45,1. 66,13. 67,10. 68,3-4. 74,13(×2). EC1
Godric	notes to 8,17. 16,8
Godstan	16,43
Godwin of Sutton	6,169
Godwin (of Sutton)	6,165-168
Godwin son of Alfhere	6,1–2;112–114
Godwin son of Algar	7,36
Godwin son of Alsi	6,26–27
Godwin son of Toki	7,22;47–48
Godwin the priest	7,122. 38,11
Godwin, a thane of King Edward's	28,1a
Godwin, a thane	33,3
Godwin	1,49;53. 2,17;19. 3,82. 6,12;116;120; 191;307. 7,14;51;82;92;98. 8,63. 14,164. 16,35;44. 21,39;71. 25,60;79;86. 35,7. 38,8; 11. 40,3. 66,13. 67,10-12. 74,12-13
Godwy	16,22;28–29. 25,57. 30,1
Gold, see Hugh	
Gorham, see W.	
Gosbert	8,66;69–70
Goulafre, see William	
Grim	7,56;87;89. 14,123. 36,6–7
Grim, see Edric	
Grimbold	8,8 note
Grimwulf	4,4. 8,12. 52,9
Grip, see Walter	

Gross, see William	
Gundwin the Chamberlain	58
Gunner	7,17;117
Gunnulf	7,42. 77,4
Gunvati	74,13
Guthmund brother of Abbot Wulfric of Ely, a thane	31,60
Guthmund brother of Abbot Wulfric of Ely, a thane	29,1. 31,8-14;38;40-43;45-46;?47;48. 41,11
Guy, see Thurstan	
Earl Gyrth	1,23;101-102;122a. 3,55
Gyrth	1,7;18-19;32;34;44-49;51;103. 3,19. 4,20; 34-35;37;40;41 and note. 6,13;125. 7,40; 47;75. 8,14-15. 16,35. 19,18. 21,30;62. 25,67;71. 31,25;31;34. 36,6. 38,11. 50,1. 67,14. 69,2;4. 74,7
Hagni, see Wulfric	
Hagris	6,229
Hakon	1,18;47
Haldane	4,16. 6,112;118;165. 7,40;50. 8,4;6. 26,12b; 12d. 32,2;9;11-16;19;21-31. 67,11
Hamo of Saint-Clair	notes to 6,271. 7,133. 16,3-6;8;27-34
Hamo of Valognes	3,15;87
Hamo	3,88-89;94;98;102 and note. 25,12
Hamo, see Geoffrey	
Hardekin	25,57. 67,12
Harding	7,25. 29,9
Hardwin brother of Earl Ralph	7,67
Hardwin brother of Earl (Ralph)	2,10 and note
Hardwin	6,46. 9,1-2. 21,16. 23,1. 39,5
Haret	66,6
Earl Harold	68,1;3-4 note
(Earl) Harold	1,96;100;102;119. 36,1 and note. 38,21 and note. EE1
Harold	2,16;19-20. 4,16. 6,17;92;191;226. 7,13;57; 73;102;119;122;147. 8,3;7;11;31;48;55-56. 16,2;20;40. 20,1. 25,60. 27,13. 29,11. 31,20. 32,14;16. 36,3;5-7;15. 38,22. 39,1;17. 40,4. 41,7. 43,1;3;5-6. 48,1. 49,1. 55,1. 67,7; 10;12;27. 76,6;20;23
Harthacanute	7,85
Hato	5,7
Heinfrid	53,1
Henry	14,16
Henry	21,4 note
Herbert Blacun	75,3
Herbert	6,191
Herebold, see Godric	
Hereward	6,108
Herewold	14,152
Herman	6,106;289
Hermer of Ferrers	7,99
Hervey Bedruel (= of Berry, of Bourges)	10
Hervey of Berry, of Bourges	notes to 67. 21,56;58;63;87;100. 67,6
Hervey	67. 8,59. 21,50-51;55;63;85;96. 32,28
Hilary	21,29-30;83;86-87. 31,36;42
Hildferth	16,3
Hobbeson, see Leofric	7,112
Hoga, see Swart	
Houdain, see final entry	
Houerel, see Richard	

Howard	1,111
Huard of Vernon	9,2–3
Hubert of Mont-Canisy	57. 6,190;260
Hubert of Port	16,34. 77,4
Hubert the Breton	14,68 note
Hubert the Breton, see Reginald	
Hubert	6,1;27 and note;30;53;57-58;62;109;196;235; 248-249;260;280;299;302
Earl Hugh	4. 6,19–20;21–22 note. 16,34. 31,2;34. 67,3. Also folio 291a
(Earl) Hugh	1,110. 67,4
Hugh of Beuerda	31,40
Hugh de Montfort	*31.* 1,1. 2,6. 29,1. 36,6. 41,11
(Hugh) de Montfort	1,17
Hugh de Montfort	36,7 note
Hugh of Corbon	7,18;38;75
Hugh of Grandmesnil	*49*
Hugh of Houdain	7,2 note;60;62;103–105. 30,3. 76,14
H(ugh) of Houdain	1,60
Hugh of Wanchy	26,9
Hugh son of Gold	26,8
Hugh son of Norman	4,6;35;39 and note
Hugh	6,67. 7,75. 9,2. 21,30. 26,11. 30,1
Hugh, see Wulfric	
Humphrey of St. Bertin's	48,1
Humphrey son of Aubrey	*56.* 34,9
Humphrey son of R.	6,172
Humphrey son of Rodric	6,172 note. 26,1
Humphrey (son of Rodric)	21,1 and note
Humphrey the Chamberlain	*52.* 8,22
Humphrey	3,56;59;69. 6,13;17;125;175;261–263;295; 311–315;319. 14,114. 21,1. 26,5;7. 52,2
Hun	25,67
Huna	3,99. 6,39;45;48;251;271. 7,117
Hunebot	8,16
Hunepot	3,95
Hurant, see William	
Huscarl	16,8 note
Husteman	7,105
Iarnagot	53,3;7
Ieva	6,264
Ilger, see Ranulf	
Ingold, see Edric	
Ingulf, a guard	67,13
Ingvar, a thane	19,16
Isaac	*62.* 7,4. 8,67. 21,64
Ivo Tallboys	1,123f
Ivo	39,12
James	14,24
Jocelyn	6,19. 14,138. 21,1
Jocelyn	14,137 note
John nephew of Waleran	15,3
John son of Waleran	*55.* EE6
John	14,63
Judicael the priest	*64.* 75,3
Kemp, see Aelfric	
Ketel Uva	7,104
Ketel, a thane of King Edward's	34,6
Ketel, a thane	37,6
Ketel	7,49. 56,1. 66,10;13. 69,3. 76,19
Archbishop Lanfranc (of Canterbury)	*15.* Also folio 372a
(Archbishop) Lanfranc (of Canterbury)	20,1 and note
Langabein	7,22
Langfer	7,109. 32,2

Ledman	7,15
Ledmer the priest	25,1
Ledmer	5,6. 16,36
Leofcild	7,60;62. 29,2
Leofcwen	35,8
Leofeva	15,3. 16,20;48. 21,70. 32,9. 74,13
Leofgeat	7,76. 25,34;80
Leofled	1,123f. 7,111. 52,1
Leofmer, see Brictwold	
Leofred	38,18
Leofric Cobbe	7,36
Leofric Cook	6,107
Leofric Hobbeson	7,59. 29,7. 30,3
Leofric of Hemley	6,110
Leofric Snipe	7,143
Leofric the deacon	7,31
Leofric, a thane	5,1
Leofric	1,11;58. 3,95(×2). 4,15. 6,8;49;58;116;209; 227. 7,15;56;77;80(×2);82;86;94;97-98;101; 108;111;117-118;138-139;143. 8,56(×2);63. 12,4. 14,128. 16,15;24. 21,49;69. 25,70;74; 77;103. 29,8. 34,9. 35,7. 62,4-5. 67,10;12. 74,4;13. 75,5. 76,1
Leofric	16,6 note
Leofsi	6,92;193. 67,12
Leofsi	8,1 note
Leofsidu	14,138
Leofson	7,59;90. 29,1. 38,16
Abbot Leofstan of St. Edmund's	25,1. 68,5
Leofstan of Falkenham	6,110
Leofstan of Loes	29,1
Leofstan the priest	1,122d. 7,40
Leofstan	2,19. 6,111;155;202. 7,41;65;76;87;89;93;98; 110;121. 8,57. 16,26. 25,72. 34,5;8;14. 35,8
Leofwaru	25,84
Young Leofwin	16,30
Young Leofwin	16,4 note
Leofwin Benne	35,7
Leofwin Croc	8,49
Leofwin of Bacton, a thane of King Edward's	6,212;217. 41,10;?11 note
Leofwin (of Bacton)	41,7 and note
Leofwin son of Brown	6,110
Leofwin son of Ringwulf	6,216
Leofwin the Bald	57,1
Leofwin, a thane of King Edward's	8,32
Leofwin, a thane	41,15
Leofwin	6,3;191;209(×2). 7,15;56;76. 8,60. 16,15-16; 24;33;38. 25,103. 26,6. 41,5;17. 74,4;13
Leofwold	8,68
Licteva	21,25. 52,6
Lictwin	8,4
Lisois (of Moutiers)	28,2 and note
Loernic	6,305-306;308;310
Lother	25,87
Lunden	7,80
Lurk	31,13
Lustwin	6,118;184. 7,56. 8,12;66. 52,1
Lustwin, wife of	6,118
Magni	3,101
Male, see Osbern, Osbert	
Malet	1,102. 3,86;89. 4,42. 6,11;33;38-39;46-47;49; 57;211;217-218. 7,71;136;140;144-145;148. 16,16;30. 28,6. 45,1
Malet, see Robert, William	

Malus Vicinus	76,1
Mann	1,102
Manni Swart	3,1;3
Manni Swart, see Ulf	
Manni	7,19;54. 44,3-4
Manson	7,28;76;84;86
Manstan	7,58
Marculf	16,6. 77,4
Mawa, a free man	36,3
Mawa, a half free woman	32,26 note
Maynard	3,9. 6,169
Menleva	35,7
Mild	35,7
Miles de Belefol	38,25
Miles (de Belefol)	38,6;19-20 and notes
Modgeva of Colcarr	6,110
Modgeva	11,4
Earl Morcar, see Aelfeva	
Morcar	7,77
Moregrim	7,82;89
Morewin	6,247. 21,37;91
Morvant	53,1
Muffle, see Brictwold	
Munding	7,58
Mundret	4,30-31
Munulf the priest	26,5
Munulf	4,15;42
N.	31,13. 39,5
Nardred	3,57
Nicholas	26,3-4;6
Nigel, a servant of Count Robert (of Mortain)'s	2,8
Nigel	2,7
Nigel, see Eudo	
Norigold	33,2
Norman son of Tancred	8,35;46-47;49
Norman the Sheriff	*63*. 6,91;290. 7,36
Norman (the Sheriff)	16,34 and note
Norman, a thane	7,18
Norman	2,19. 3,61. 6,28;84;135;258. 7,3;10-12;28;30; 32;37-39;70;76-77;79-80;96;112;114;126-128;136-143. 8,46;51. 14,1;41. 21,105. 25,23. 31,13. 39,9-10. 41,6. 43,3. 74,13. 76,19
N(orman)	7,81-90;92-94;97-101;103-111;113;115;117-121;129;132
Norman, see Hugh	
Odard	14,93
Odard	14,71 note
Odo	3,68. 67,22;30-31
Offa	53,5. 74,13
Ordgar in Kyluertestuna	6,110
Ordgar the reeve of the Abbot (of St. Edmund's)	14,152
Ordmer	12,3. 74,15
Ordric	6,210. 7,92. 31,58. 35,7
Orthi, a thane	20,1
Osbern Male	1,12
Osbern Male, cf. Osbert Male	
Osbern of Wanchy	25,59
Osbern	3,61;97. 6,46. 25,65-66;75;79. 28,5
Osbert Male	34,6
Osbert Male, cf. Osbern Male	
Osbert	7,120-121. 13,3
Osferth	1,31. 6,106. 7,85;91
Osgeat	7,143
Osgot	7,108. 16,17;36

Oslac, a thane	31,3
Oslac	3,91. 4,7. 6,114
Osmund	3,100. 6,186;238. 7,36. 10,1
Ostula	3,99
Oswulf	7,76. 21,39
Otheri	19,19
Othulf	13,3
Otti	7,84
Otto the Goldsmith	*1,97-99*
Otto (the Goldsmith)	14,13 and note
Oudkell, see R.	
Padda	7,7
Pat	1,111
Payne	25,81-82;84
Peche, see William	
Peret, see William	
Pesserera	31,42
Peter *brother of Burghard*	14,17 and note
Peter of Palluel	67,18
Peter of Valognes (Sheriff of Essex and Herts.)	*37* and note. *1,96.* 14,78;81-83. 75,2
P(eter of Valognes, Sheriff of Essex and Herts.)	EE1 and note
Peter *of Valognes, Sheriff of Essex and Herts.*	14,85;96-97 and notes
Peter *the Steward*	14,53;61;70 and notes
Peter, a cleric	14,13
Peter the cleric, see Walter	
Peter	14,17;36;53;61. 67,23
Peverel, see Ranulf	
Picot (? Sheriff of Cambridgeshire)	*1,120-121.* 28,6 note
Pinel, see Ralph	
Pirot	28,6
Queneva mother of Brictmer	39,8-10
Queneva (mother of Brictmer)	14,117 and note
(Queneva) mother of Brictmer	39,7 and note
R., see Humphrey	
R. Oudkell	66,16
Rada	48,1
Radbod	74,4
Radfrid	14,139 note
Rainalm	32,6
Earl Ralph the Constable	1,101
(Earl) Ralph the Constable	3,15;61;98-100. 4,14. 14,101. 31,53. 46,7
(Earl) R(alph) the Constable	3,10;17-18. 13,6. 32,10
Earl Ralph (Wader)	*1,61-95* and note. 1,123f. 3,56. 20,1. 77,4
(Earl) Ralph (Wader)	3,59. 16,33. 25,104. 31,53 and notes
Earl R(alph Wader)	3,40-41. 4,32. 6,169. 7,19;44;133. 16,3. 46,8. 74,8-9. 76,13;17. ENf4 and notes
(Earl) R(alph Wader)	3,57 and note
Earl R(alph)	1,10. 3,1. 46,8
Earl Ralph, see Alsi, Hardwin	
Earl R(alph), see Alsi	
Ralph Baynard	*33*
R(alph) Baynard	4,36
Ralph Baynard, see William Baynard	
Ralph brother of Robert Blunt	66,10
Ralph of Beaufour	*11*
Ralph of Courbépine	16,10
Ralph of Fougères	*50*
Ralph of Lanquetot	45,1;3 and note
Ralph of Limésy	*43.* 8,46. 76,20
Ralph of Marcy	5,6
Ralph of Savenay	16,4;6-8;13;23-24;30;34-35;48. 21,39. 34,7; 10;12;17
Ralph of Tourleville	7,73;86;98
R(alph of Tourleville)	7,99-101

Ralph Pinel	*61*. 39,3. 73,1
Ralph son of Brian	34,8
Ralph son of (Earl) Ralph the Constable (= Earl Ralph Wader)	31,53
Ralph Tallboys	35,3
Ralph the crossbowman	69
Ralph *the Fat*	14,35 and note
Ralph the Fat	14,37 note
Ralph	3,79. 4,32. 6,177–178. 7,145–148. 14,3;35;53. 25,88. 31,42. 38,16;23
Ranulf brother of Ilger	39
R(anulf) brother of Ilger	67,15
Ranulf nephew of William of Warenne	26,13
Ranulf Peverel	*34*. 6,11. 7,64–65. 16,20–22;26;33. 25,56. 77,2. EE4
R(anulf) Peverel	21,39. 25,112.
(Ranulf) Peverel	16,23;30. 38,11
Ranulf son of Walter	7,20;124
R(anulf) son of Walter	7,21
Ranulf	6,39. 7,71–72. 33,6. 67,4;20
Raven	6,193. 7,100–101
Raymond Gerald	8,51 note;55;63
Regifer	7,110
Reginald brother of Hubert the Breton	14,68 note
Reginald the Breton	*70*. 14,68 note
Reginald	67,2;16
Reginald, see William	
Rich, see Edeva	
Richard *Houerel*	14,151 and note
Richard of Clare, son of Count Gilbert	*25*. 16,15. 21,44. 33,1. 67,1. 76,1–7. EE2
Richard (of Clare), son of C(ount) G(ilbert)	8,63
Richard (of Clare, son of Count Gilbert)	8,35;47;59. 29,1 and notes
Richard of Saint-Clair	11,4
Richard *the Bald*	14,54 and note
Richard	6,304. 14,151. 31,42. 40,1. 57,1. 75,2
Richere	33,2
Richere, see Gilbert, Walter	
Rictan	74,13
Ringwulf	6,216
Ringwulf, see Leofwin	
Count Robert of Mortain	2
Count Robert (of Mortain)	1,1 and note
Count (Robert) of Mortain	21,1. 31,48. 76,16 and notes
Count Robert (of Mortain), see Nigel	
Robert Blunt	*66*. 6,57. 14,92;100–101;123. 25,22. 75,1–2
Robert Blunt, see Ralph	
Robert Farthing	14,146
Robert Gernon	*36*. EE3
Robert Malet, Sheriff of Suffolk, son of William Malet	*6*. 1,103;105. 3,94–95. 4,15. 7,11;15–16;138–140;143. 8,42. 16,14–15;29. 19,9. 20,31. 21,16;45–46;75. 26,12d;13–14. 31,15. 32,1. 34,12. 38,6. 43,5. 51,1–2. 64,1. 67,2–4;10; 19;27. 75,4–5. 76,23. 77,2. ENf3
Ro(bert) Malet (as above)	21,71;79;85;100. 39,12
R(obert) Malet (as above)	1,10;14. 2,17–18;20. 3,28;41. 7,6;13;17;21; 26;30;33;36;75;79. 8,8. 16,26. 21,48;65;74; 88. 32,28. 34,15. 52,1. 53,6. 67,5;15. 77,4
(Robert) Malet (as above)	3,98-102. 6,177. 7,144. 16,25;33 and note; 38 and note
Robert (Malet, as above)	18,1 and note
Robert Malet (as above)	notes to 21,92;94
Robert Malet (as above), mother of	*77*. 6,76–77. 6,8;11;156;161;176;191;193–195;199–201;209;216;229 and note;230; 232;251;253;271;311. 34,13. 75,5

Robert Malet, see Brictmer, William Malet	
Robert of Blythburgh	7,5. 33,8
Robert of Claville	6,46
R(obert) of Claville	6,110
Robert of Courson	7,6–7;23;51. 76,17–18
R(obert) of Courson	4,14. 7,8
Robert of Glanville	6,3;5;51;54;157;291;308–309
R(obert) of Glanville	6,124;160 and note;179;181. 26,16;19
Robert (of Glanville)	26,17 and note;20
Robert of Pierrepont	26,12a
Robert of Stratford	*71*
Robert (of Stratford)	27,9 and note
Robert of Tosny	*44.* 7,19
Robert of Vaux	6,84. 7,14–15;19. 9,3
R(obert) of Vaux	1,22. 7,17;24;40;44–45;49–50;54
Robert of Verly	*60*
Robert son of Corbucion	*40*
Robert son of Fulcred	6,46–49
Robert son of Wymarc (Sheriff of Essex), father of Swein (Sheriff of Essex)	1,102. 3,70. 25,49;76. 27,7. 58,1. 76,2;5
Robert (son of Wymarc, as above)	27,3–6;8–12
Robert the crossbowman	76,16
Robert	6,50;55;306. 14,14;62;64. 25,3;78. 31,42. 41,15
Robert, see Unfrid	
Roc	25,91
Rodric, see Humphrey	
Roger Bigot, the Sheriff (of Suffolk)	*7. 1,1–60;122.* 1,103;105;123f–123g. 3,57;59. 4,9;13 note. 6,46;73. 16,12-14;16–17;23;30; 34;40;48. 21,17;44–45;49;52. 25,52. 39,3. 73,1. 74,7. 76,13. ENf4
Roger (Bigot, as above)	16,24. 74,4 and notes
Ro(ger) Bigot (as above)	14,117. 16,3–4;6;8;15;35;37;46
R(oger) Bigot (as above)	2,17. 4,15;32;42. 6,69;91;177. 16,2. 21,83
Roger *Bigot*	21,18 and note
Roger Bigot	notes to 6,271. 16,5;20;27–29;31–33. 22,2
Roger Bigot, see Ansketel	
Roger of Abenon	25,76
Roger of Auberville	*29.* 1,1. 21,14;19;26
Roger (of Auberville)	76,16 and note
Roger of Auberville, see William	
Roger of Candos	31,3;20;53;56;60
(Roger of Candos)	31,4–6 and note
Roger of Orbec	25,56. 76,2
Roger of Poitou	*8.* 1,1. 53,2 note
Roger of Rames	*38.* 7,64;68. 8,63. 25,56;59. 76,22
Ro(ger) of Rames	16,16
Roger of Rames, daughter of	38,9;11
Roger of St. Germain	25,47. 76,3
Roger son of Arnold	8,7–8;17
Roger	8,6. 25,11;56;63–64;78;80. 26,4. 39,18. 40,2. 41,14;16. 53,2. EE6
Rolf	74,8
Rolf, see Aelfric	
Roric	14,59;79
Saegard	40,1
Saer	14,63 note
Sasselin	*59*
Saxi	6,11. 7,64. 16,8;13;16;20–23;26;28;30–31;33. 34,12–13;17. 38,11;22. 75,5. 77,2;4
Saxlef	74,13
Saxwalo of Bouville, see William	
Saxwin	31,35
Scalpi, a thane	36,1–2

Scalpi	16,35. 36,8;16. EE3
Segar	7,109
Sewin	7,102;111
Shearman	7,77
Shield, see William	
Sictric	6,19
Sictric	notes to 21,16;47
Sifrith	7,77
Sigar	74,13
Siric	1,51. 6,186;218–221. 7,121. 8,6. 16,43. 38,21. 53,2;4. 62,1
Siward of Maldon, a thane	12,5. 34,1–4
Siward	3,79-80. 16,39. 74,3
Siwold	7,92;117
Skuli, a thane of King Edward's	4,10
Smeri	16,41
Smert	6,193
Snaring the priest	16,34
Snipe, see Leofric	
Sorcbes	6,216
Sparrowhawk	3,95. 6,45. 37,2
Sperun	16,15
Spieta	36,14
Spirwic, see Eudo	
Spretman	7,92
Sprot	7,77
Sprotwulf	1,18;55
Sprotwulf	16,8 note
Spud, see Edric	
Stanfled	7,93
Stanhard son of Aethelwy	72
Stanhard	6,194;200. 7,1;15. 35,7. 67,11
Stanhard	31,15 note
Stanmer	7,76;87. 39,5
Stanwin	3,61. 6,17;92;98;172. 7,13
Starker	40,2
Starling	3,98. 45,2–3
Starling, see Aelfric	
Stein	3,94
Stickstag, see Aelfric	
(Archbishop) Stigand (of Canterbury), Bishop (of Winchester)	*1,107–119*. 6,93. 15,1;3. 18,4. 19,15. 32,16. 69,1
Stigand	3,79. 6,76–77;213;219–223;225. 7,4;51;60;75;124. 8,44;47. 16,35. 19,1;16–17;21. 32,20. 38,16. 40,6. 42,1. 53,5. 62,7. 64,3. 74,12. 75,5. 77,1. ENf4
Stori	54,1
Strangwulf	25,67
Stubhard	6,194
Suffering, see Akile	
Summerled	4,19
Suneman	7,86
Sunwin	38,11
Swart Hoga	6,109
Swart, see Manni, Swein	
Swarting	6,106. 28,5. 67,19;24;28;32
Swartling	7,37
Swartrik	6,191. 76,23
Sweetman	7,77;80
Swein Swart	71,1
Swein (the Sheriff) of Essex	27
Swein	6,159;177. 7,77. 41,5;14
Sweting	7,98
Talk	6,98

Tallboys, see Ivo, Ralph	
Tancred, see Norman	
Teit	6,217
Tela	36,11
Tepekin	29,11;14. 40,4
Teri	41,11
Theobald *the cleric*	14,14 and note
Theodoric brother of Walter the deacon	41,4;5 note;10–11
Theodoric	7,111. 8,56
Thorbern the priest	38,11
Thorbern	6,22. 7,96;101
Thorbert	67,11
Thored	3,54. 4,36. 13,5. 33,4;6–7;9–11
Thorgar	1,51
Thorgils	35,3
Thorild	7,103
Thorkell of Wrentham	26,12d
Thorkell, a thane	34,7
Thorkell	1,123f. 6,116;223;264. 7,36. 21,29–30;62. 26,12a. 74,13
Thorkell	notes to 22,2. 39,10
Thormar	16,16
Thormod of Parham	1,93
Thormod	1,75. 22,1;3
Thorold	7,97. 31,41. 34,15. EE4
Thorvold	7,123
Thurgot	16,46
Thuri of Kyluertestuna	6,110
Thuri, a thane of King Edward's	25,61;63
Thuri	16,30. 25,67. 71,2
Thurstan son of Guy	7,122;125;133. 76,15
Thurstan	1,107. 3,74–78. 41,4–5. 77,4
Tigier	6,23;127;271
Tihel of Helléan	42. 16,9
Tihel	16,1
Toki	7,80. 26,4;9;11. 35,3
Toki, see Godwin	
Toli the Sheriff (of Suffolk)	4,15. 7,31;67. 31,53
Toli	6,106. 7,29;36. 27,11. 51,1
Topi	32,30
Tosti	55,1
Tovi, a free man	29,9
Tovi, a thane	29,12
Tovild	74,13
Trumwin	30,1. 36,9
Tulf	7,148
Tumbi	1,122d
Tuneman	16,40
Tutfled	3,101
Uhtred	3,96. 43,1;3
Ulf of Mutford	7,41
Ulf son of Manni Swart	6,109
Ulf the priest	4,13
Ulf, a thane	19,2. 44,1–2
Ulf	1,19;48;55. 3,93;98;103. 7,15;27;37;136;141. 8,34;42. 32,5. 69,3
Ulfketel the King's reeve	ENf4
Ulfketel	1,53. 4,19. 6,272;274–275. 7,25;27;41;119
Unfrid son of Robert	6,112;122 and note;172 note
Uva, see Ketel	
Viking	7,108. 16,22;26
W. de More	16,3
W. son of Gorham	67,7
W. the Constable	4,32

Wacra	3,102
Wader, see Earl Ralph	
Wailolf	4,3. 7,67
Waldwin	25,60. 29,7
Waleran	32,16
Waleran, see John (×2)	
Walter de Risboil/Risbou	6,28;284–285
Walter Giffard	*45*
Walter *nephew of Peter the cleric*	14,87 and note
Walter of Caen	4,15. 6,5;7;67 note;90,98-99;103;143;191; 245;247;301;316. 25,61
W(alter) of Caen	6,93;162;165;264;265 note
Walter (of Caen)	6,168–170
Walter of Dol	4,15. 6,212;215. 14,146. 16,34. 31,34
Walter of Douai	31,34 note
Walter of St. Valéry	*51.* 76,22
Walter son of Aubrey	6,2;32;80;183;292
W(alter) son of Aubrey	6,189
Walter son of Grip	6,132 and note;308;311;317–318
Walter son of Richere	6,94
Walter the crossbowman	6,191;238
Walter the deacon	*41.* 25,24
Walter *the deacon*	21,35 and note
Walter the deacon, see Theodoric	
Walter	6,12; 44–45;81;90;129;173;191;202–204;305–306;308;311;314. 14,23;87. 21,35. 33,2
Walter, see Ranulf	
Wand, see Aelfric	
Warengar	3,59. 7,63–65;66 note;67–68. 16,12;38–39. 38,5;21
War(engar)	16,16–17
Warin son of Burnin	4,20-21;29 and note. 6,296
Warin	6,64;304. 14,15;66. 34,4
Warner	67,5–6;8
Wenelincg, Weneling	67,22 note
Werno of Poix	14,68
White	7,117
Widard	25,104
Wigmer	26,10
Wigulf	7,67–68. 8,56. 38,4
Wihtmer	2,7. 7,84;106–107;108(×3);109–110;112–114
Wihtred the priest	1,52
Wihtric of Carlewuda	6,110
Wihtric	1,102. 7,61;76;83;119–120. 16,20
Wilard	25,84
Wilgrip	29,4
Bishop W(illiam) of Thetford	*18*
Bishop W(illiam of Thetford)	14,101;121
William Baynard, nephew of Ralph Baynard	33,10
William de Alno	36,1-7;16–17
William *de Alno*	EE3 and note
William Goulafre	6,10–11;14;25;65–66;138–141;206
W(illiam) Goulafre	6,271;293
William Hurant	25,7
William Malet, father of Robert Malet	3,94–95;100. 4,42. 6,11. 7,8;15–16;36;138–140;143;148. 16,6;30. 19,6. 26,14. 28,6. 31,20. 45,2. 52,1. 67,2;4;19;28;30. 75,4. 77,4
W(illiam) Malet (as above)	3,39–40. 6,93;159. 7,26;33;131;133. 8,42. 18,1 67,15–16;31
William (Malet, as above)	3,99;144;146. 38,6. 67,29
(William Malet, as above)	notes to 3,98;101. 7,17. 16,15. 51,2. Also 67, 20–21
William of Arques	*47.* 6,192. 31,20
William of Auberville, brother of Roger of Auberville	*30.* 29,8. 76,14

William of Bosc	7,115-116;134. 16,3 note. 39,5
W(illiam) of Bosc	39,11
William of Bourneville	7,56-59;117;121 and note. 76,15
W(illiam) of Bourneville	1,11. 7,119 and note. 62,7
William of Bouville, son of Saxwalo of Bouville	16,11. 32,1-2;19;31 and note
W(illiam) of Bouville (as above)	21,95. 32,13
W(illiam) of Ecouis	21,27
William (of Bouville, as above)	32,15 and note
William of Çaen	6,67
William of Écouis	*9*. 21,21
William of Émalleville	6,30;33
William of Noyers	*1,107-119*. 19,17
William of Parthenay	76,8-12
William of Vatteville	*54*
(William of) Vatteville	70,1
William of Warenne	*26*. 8,55. 76,18
W(illiam) of Warenne	7,25. 21,1
William of Warenne, see Ranulf	
William Peche	25,6;91
William Peret	25,89
William Shield	6,63. 7,75
William son of Gross	31,50
William son of Reginald	26,12b;15
William the Chamberlain	*1,97-99*
William	3,57. 4,19. 6,250;265. 19,16. 29,7;9. 41,11. 53,2. 66,3
Withgar son of Aelfric	25,1;60
Withgar	*25,78-102*. 7,121. 8,35;46-47;59;63;66. 16,11; 38. 25,2-3;17 note;19;25;27-35;37-38;40-49; 52;55-56. 29,1. 32,1. 43,4. 67,1. 72,1. 76,2-5
Withgar, see Aelfric	
Woodbrown	6,271. 16,14;32
Wulfbold	7,65;79;111. 29,10
Wulfbold, see Wulfheah	
Wulfeva	3,102. 6,209;212-216;218;222-225;227-230; 232. 7,3. 39,4
Wulfeva, son of	6,212
Wulfgar	25,48
Wulfgeat	6,13;15;125. 16,35. 21,48. 35,7
Wulfgeat, see Aelfric	
Wulfhard	7,121
Wulfheah father of Wulfbold	7,76(×2);79;99-100
Wulfhere	2,17
Wulfled	25,78
Wulfmer the (King's) reeve	*73* note. 1,7. 74,4;7. 76,13-14
Wulfmer *the priest*	6,110
Wulfmer, a thane	8,44;48;55
Wulfmer	*73*. 1,110. 2,11. 3,59;95(×2). 6,49;64;211. 7,16;26;61;76-77;85;89;98. 8,20-24. 13,3. 16,35. 21,58. 25,10;58;60;77;84. 35,7-8. 67,2; 11-12. 74,4
Wulfmer, father of	73,1
Wulfnoth	1,55;102. 2,6;9-10;13. 6,121. 7,71;76;140. 53,6
Wulfred	8,55
Abbot Wulfric of Ely, brother of Guthmund	31,60
Wulfric brother of Wulfsi	1,110
Wulfric Hagni	53,6
Wulfric son of Brictric	55,1
Wulfric *son of Hugh*	28,6 and note
Wulfric the deacon	7,36
Wulfric, a thane of King Edward's	8,46. 39,16. 46,1-2
Wulfric, a thane	8,36-37;55

Wulfric, a villager	68,2
Wulfric	2,16. 3,53;64;92. 6,81;130;191(×2);210;214. 7,58;73;76;79;88;104(×2);111;113;117;147. 8,7;19;29. 9,3. 14,43;150. 15,4. 16,20;22;40. 25,19;59. 26,12a. 28,6. 30,1. 31,57. 32,11. 38,2. 41,14. 67,9;11. 74,4;11;13(×2);15. 76,13
Wulfric	16,8 note
Wulfsi brother of Wulfric	1,110
Wulfsi	1,16;19;23;36;46;60;111. 4,20-23. 7,6;15;24; 50;52. 31,33. 36,9. 50,1
Wulfsi, two brothers of	7,24
Wulfstan	3,81
Wulfward	7,98;118. 8,47. 14,12;19;39. 29,5. 39,5. 42,1
Wulfward	14,20 note
Wulfwaru	5,8. 35,7
Wulfwin the priest	1,122d. 6,124;181. 46,7
Wulfwin, a thane of King Edward's	35,1-2. 68,5 note
Wulfwin	2,17. 6,211;216;227. 7,92;96. 8,55. 16,41. 25,103. 35,5-6. 62,2. 67,10;13. 74,13. 76,1(×2);21. EE4-EE5
Wulfwy, man-at-arms of St. Edmund's	14,69
Wulfwy	7,121. 16,18
Wymarc, *Count Alan's steward*	EC2 and note
Wymarc, see Robert	
Wynning	67,30
Wynstan	6,193
Yric	4,4. 25,59
... of Barthetona	41,11
... of Houdain	7,2

CHURCHES AND CLERGY

Alnesbourn (St. Andrew's)	8,13
Bayeux, Bishop	*16. 77.* 1,6. 75,5. Also folio 372a
Bernai, Abbot	*23*
Blyford	13,2 and note
Blythburgh	7,5
[**Bury**] **St. Edmund's**	*14. 25,78-102.* 1,62;115. 2,1;3-5;15. 3,2;46. 4,10. 6,62;209.299-302. 7,1;2. 8,32;35;45-47. 9,2. 10,1. 11,4. 12,1-2;4;6. 15,3. 16,1;33. 18,4. 19,12. 20,1. 21,2;9;40-41. 25,17;19;22; 25;27;33-34;40;103;111-112. 26,2-4. 27,1;3; 7. 28,1b;4. 29,12-13. 31,2;40. 33,1-3;12-13. 34,1;14. 35,6-7. 37,6 and note. 38,2. 40,1-2; 5. 41,10. 43,3. 46,1. 49,1. 53,1;6-7. 54,2-3. 59,2. 61,2. 66,1;6;9;11. 73,1. 75,2. 76,1;4-5; 9-12;19;21
Abbot	1,77;88. 6,57;210-211;214-215. 8,55. 9,2. 12,6. 14,1-4;8;11-12;14-19;22-24;27;32-33; 36-39;41-46;49;52-54;59;61-64;66;68-70; 72-73;77-78;82;90;96-101;104;106;117; 119-120;122-123;125-128;130;132;133 note; 134;136-137;139;143;146;148;153;167. 15,4. 16,16. 27,7. 30,1. 40,5. 43,9. 62,5. 66,13. 75,1 and note. 76,12 and note. See also Baldwin, Leofstan
Abbot	21,4 note
cleric	see Durand
monks	14,163;167
reeves	see Aelfric, Brictmer, Brictric, Ordgar
Archbishop	see Lanfranc, Stigand

Canterbury	(Holy Trinity)	*15*. 34,5
	monks	*15*
Chatteris	(St. Mary's)	24
Clare	(St. John's)	25,1
Combs		2,10
Coutances, Bishop		21,17 note
Debenham	(St. Andrew's)	6,18. 16,28
	(St. Mary's)	6,18. 16,28. 34,12
Elmham, Bishop		see Aelmer and 18,1 note
Ely	(St. Etheldreda's)	*21*. 2,1–2;16;20. 3,27;31;34;36. 4,42. 5,2. 6, 114;116–118;148–149;239;247;251; 258;265. 7,55;122 and note;133. 8,1–2;4–6;8–10;12;17; 20;25;27;46. 12,2. 14,40. 16,3–4;6;8;13;28. 22,2–3. 25,59. 26,1;3;5. 28,2. 31,12–13;15–19; 40. 32,14;26;29–30;31 and note. 34,4;15. 38,22. 39,5;8;10. 41,18. 45,1–3. 46,8. 47,2–3. 52,4. 53,1. 67,9;11–12;15;22;29–30. 74,10
	(*St. Etheldreda's*)	notes to 3,32-33;46,98;100. 6,33–34;164-165; 271. 8,1;21. 16,5;31. 46,10
	Abbot	1,75. 3,57;62;86;89;92–95;97–103. 4,1;3–4;6; 8 and note. 6,11-12;14-15;17;19-20;21-22 and note;23;25;28–30;32–37;39;41;43–49;51–56. 7,15;56;58;61;67;71–72;136–146;148;151. 8,56–57;59;63;66;68;80–82. 16,3;6;20;22; 27;29–34;38–39;48. 21,12;16–19;21–22;25–31;36–37;40;45–46;49–52;64–65;75;79–80; 82–85. 25,53 and note;112. 28,6. 29,9. 32,1. 34,12;16. 38,3;22. 39,5. 52,10. 53,7. 67,3–6; 30. 77,4. See also Wulfric
Evreux, Bishop		*22*. See also Gilbert
Eye	(St. Peter's)	6,191
Flixton	(St. Michael's)	19,21
Grestain	(St. Mary's)	2,9–10
Ipswich	(Holy Trinity)	1,122d
	(St. Augustine's)	1,122d. 31,56
	(St. George's)	38,3
	(St. Julian's)	74,9
	(St. Laurence's)	1,122f
	(St. Mary's)	1,122d
	(St. Michael's)	1,122d
	(St. Peter's)	1,122f. 25,52;54 note;60;62
	(St. Stephen's)	1,122f
Ramsey	(St. Benedict's)	*17*. 36,4
Rochester, Bishop		*20*
Rumburgh		3,14 note;105
St. Lô, Bishop		21,17. 29,9
Stowmarket		2,8. 34,6
Sudbury	(St. Gregory)	1,97
Thetford, Bishop		*18–19*. 6,70–72;76–77;308;311. 8,42. 31,3;5–6. 44,2. 64,3. See also Erfast, William, and folio 372a
Thurleston	(St. Botolph's)	1,122e
Tuddenham		38,15
Winchester, Bishop		see Stigand
chaplain, to Roger Bigot		Ansketel the priest
cleric		Albold, Durand, Peter, Theobald
deacon		Aelfric, Edric, Leofric, Walter, Wulfric

priest Aelfric, Aelmer, Aethelwold, Ailbold, Algar, Alwin, Alwold, Alwulf, Ansketel, Anund, Askell, Brunmer, Edmund, Edwin, Engelric, Frideb..., Gilbert, Godric, Godwin, Judicael, Ledmer, Leofstan, Munulf, Snaring, Thorbern, Ulf, Wihtred, Wulfmer, Wulfwin

SECULAR TITLES AND OCCUPATIONAL NAMES

Beadle (*bedel*) ... Brictmer. **Burgess** (*burgensis*), of Ipswich ... Aelfric son of Rolf, Culling. **Chamberlain** (*cambararius, camerarius*) ... Gundwin, Humphrey, William. **Constable** (*cunestabla, stalra, stalre*) ... Asgar, Earl Ralph, W. **Cook** (*cocc̄*) ... Leofric. **Count** (*comes*) ... Alan, Brian, Eustace, Gilbert, Robert. **Countess** (*comitissa*) ... Aumâle, Edeva. **Crossbowman** (*arbalastarius, balastarius, balistarius*) ... Berner, Gilbert, Ralph, Robert, Walter. **Earl** (*comes*) ... Algar, Gyrth, Harold, Hugh, Morcar, Ralph the Constable, Ralph Wader. **free men** ... **in the King's hand** (*liberi homines ... in manu regis*) ... 75. **Goldsmith** (*aurifex*) ... Otto. **Guard** (*huscarlus*) ... Askell, Ingulf. **King's reeve** (*prepositus regis*) ... Aelmer, Aethelward, Edric, Ulfketel, Wulfmer. **Man-at-arms** (*miles*) ... Wulfwy. **Marshal** (*mareschalchus*) ... Gerald. **Queen** (*regina*) ... Edith, and 6,76-77;209;229 and note;230. 7,14-15;63. 41,13. 52,5;9. 54,3. 77,1. **Reeve of Ipswich** (*prepositus de Gypeswiz*) ... Brown. **Reeve** (*prepositus*) ... Aelfric (X2), Alric, Brictmer (X2), Brictric, Ordgar. **Servant** (*seruiens*) ... Nigel, and 35,3 note. **Sheriff** (*vicecomes*) ... Aethelwy of Thetford (?), Norman, Peter of Valognes, Picot (?) Robert Malet, Robert son of Wymarc, Roger Bigot, Swein, Toli. **Smith** (*faber*) ... Bondi, Edwin, Godric. **Steward** (*dapifer*) ... Eudo, Godric, Peter, Wymarc. **Thane of King Edward's** ... Aelfric, Godwin, Ketel, Leofwin of Bacton, Leofwin, Skuli, Thuri, Wulfric, Wulfwin. **Thane** (*tegnus, teignus, teinnus, teinus, tennus, tenus*) ... Auti, Edmer, Godman, Godwin, Guthmund, Ingvar, Ketel, Leofric, Leofwin, Norman, Orthi, Oslac, Scalpi, Siward of Maldon, Thorkell, Tovi, Ulf, Wulfmer, Wulfric. **Vavassors** (*vavasores*) ... 74. **Villager** (*villanus*) ... Askell, Wulfric. **Young** (*cilt*) ... Leofwin.

INDEX OF PLACES

The name of each place is followed by (i) the abbreviated name of its Hundred and its location on the Map in this volume (Suffolk places only); (ii) its National Grid reference; (iii) chapter and section references in LDB Suffolk, or a reference to a note in the present volume which identifies the place. Bracketed chapter and section references denote mention in sections dealing with a different place. Unless otherwise stated, the identifications of DG and the spellings of the Ordnance Survey are followed for places in Suffolk; of OEB for places abroad. Inverted commas denote lost places (that is, those whose former site is known); italic print denotes unidentifiable places. Places whose names have changed since 1086 are entered under their present name. The National Grid reference system is explained on all Ordnance Survey maps, and in the Automobile Association Handbooks; the figures reading from left to right are given before those reading from bottom to top of the map. Places whose grid references are shown within round brackets do not appear on 1-inch or 1:50,000 maps. Where LDB does not differentiate between what are now two or more distinct settlements (e.g. Creeting All Saints, St. Mary, and St. Olave), separate sets of Grid references are given, but the chapter and section references are combined. The Suffolk Hundreds and Half-Hundreds are Babergh (Ba), Bishop's (Bi), Blackbourn and Bradmere (BB denotes places assigned to both Hundreds; *BB those always assigned to Blackbourn Hundred; †BB those always assigned to Bradmere Hundred), Blything (Bly), Bosmere (Bo), Carlford (Ca), Claydon (Cd), Colneis (Cn), Cosford (Co), Hartismere (H), Ipswich (I), Lackford (La), Loes (Ls), Lothing (Lt), Lothingland (Ltl), Parham (Pa), Plomesgate (Pl), Risbridge (R), Samford (Sa), Stow (St), Thedwestry (Td), Thingoe (Tg), Wangford (Wa), Wilford (Wi); the town of Bury St. Edmunds is marked by the letter B. The places in each Hundred or Half-Hundred are listed after the present index, immediately before the Map. References to Ballingdon cum Brundon, in Suffolk only since 1832 and 1835, should be sought in the Essex volume.

	Map	Grid	Text
Acton	Ba	TL 89 45	34,2
Akenham	Cd	TM 14 48	1,117. 8,68;71. 38,11. 14,5;16
Akethorpe	Ltl	(TM 54 93)	1,56
Alburgh (Norfolk)	—	TM 27 87	ENf2
Aldeburgh	Pl	TM 46 56	6,130. 21,105
Alderton	Wi	TM 34 41	6,152;159;162;164;240. 21,77
Aldham	Co	TM 04 44	14,112. 35,6. (1,105)
Aldringham	Bi	TM 44 60	6,70;74
Alfildestuna	Sa	unidentified	16,45. 36,5
Alnesbourn	Ca	TM 19 40	8,13
Alneterne	Bly	unidentified	21,47
'Alston'	Cn	(TM 26 34)	2,19. 7,96;101;113
Aluredestuna	Ca	unidentified	39,12
Ampton	Td	TL 86 71	14,64
Ardleigh (Essex)	—	TM 05 29	EE3
Ash	Ls	TM 33 55	6,282;290
Ashbocking	Bo	TM 16 54	1,73. 21,25. 25,59. 52,6
Ashfield	Cd	TM 21 62	3,65. 4,6. 6,20;22. 16,29; 34. 21,32. 52,10. 67,4
Great Ashfield	BB	TL 99 67	14,93. 66,3;17. 14,*92 note*
Ash Street	Co	TM 01 46	2,14
Aspall	H	TM 16 64	6,201;206;221. 16,48. 34,18. 77,4
Assington	Ba	TL 93 38	34,3
Aveley	Ba	TL 94 39	27,7
Bacton	H	TM 05 67	41,7. (41,8)
Bacton, see also Leofwin			
Badingham	Bi	TM 30 68	6,306. (6,55)
Badley	Bo	TM 06 55	1,70. 21,20. 25,53
Badmondisfield	R	TL 74 57	1,121. (65,1)

	Map	*Grid*	*Text*
Bardwell	*BB	TL 94 73	14,72 *note*;82. 25,21. 76,10-12
Barham	Cd	TM 13 50	6,10. 8,66;78;*81 note*; 21, 26;*27 note*. (21,*22 note*;24)
Barkestone	Ca	TM 27 46	40,4
Barking	Bo	TM 07 53	21,16;18. (21,14;20. 25,*53 note*)
Barnby	Lt	TM 47 89	1,30. 4,39
Barnham	BB	TL 86 79	4,10. 7,1. 14,89. 26,8. 31,1
Barningham	BB	TL 96 76	10,1. 14,81. 37,4
Barrow	Tg	TL 76 64	1,120
Barsham	Wa	TM 39 89	6,296. 7,40;45. 18,5. 19,18
Barthetona, see Persons Index, penultimate entry			
Great Barton	Td	TL 86 67	14,48
Barton Mills	La	TL 71 73	25,33;38. 54,3
Battisford	Bo	TM 05 54	7,57. 31,56. 53,3. 74,3. (2,11)
Bawdsey	Wi	TM 34 40	6,154;157;161. 11,1. 21,76; *79 note*;80
Baylham	Bo	TM 10 51	7,58;61;63;65. 76,15. (7,55)
Great Bealings	Ca	TM 23 48	6,121. 67,11. (67,15)
Little Bealings	Ca	TM 22 48	3,*33 note*. 16,3. 21,59. 31,16. 67,12
Beccles	Wa	TM 42 90	1,39;40;43. 14,120
Becclinga	Pl	unidentified	7,72
Bechetuna, see *Beketuna*			
Bedfield	Bi	TM 22 66	6,307
Bedingfield	Bi	TM 17 68	6,68;75-77;232;319. 14,104. 19,10. 31,5-6. 43,5. 75,5. 77,3. (6,12)
Beketuna, Bechetuna	Lt	unidentified	1,29. 31,26
Belenei	Sa	unidentified	16,43
Belstead	Sa	TM 12 41	6,26. 16,42. 32,5. 35,3. 46,3. 71,2
Belton	Ltl	TG 48 02	1,35;59
Benacre	Bly	TM 51 84	14,165
Benhall	Pl	TM 37 61	3,101. 6,47;53-54. 7,140; 149-150
Bentley	Sa	TM 11 38	1,101;103-104. 3,71;75
East Bergholt	Sa	TM 07 34	1,100;*102 note*;103-105. (1,101;119. 3,68;70;80-82. 5,6-8. 16,35-37;41;46-47. 25,65-67;69-70;72-73; 75;77. 28,5. 32,5;8. 35,3-4. 38,21. 40,3-4. 58,1. 61,1. 71,1-2)
Beria	Sa	unidentified	3,69
Bermesdena	Cd	unidentified	52,11
Beuerda, see Hugh			
Beversham	Pa	TM 35 58	67,6
Beyton	Td	TL 93 62	31,54
Bildeston	Co	TL 99 49	41,1
Billingford (Norfolk)	—	TG 01 20	(56,6)
Bing	Wi	TM 28 53	6,187;245
Bixley	Ca	TM 20 44	3,17. 21,68. 31,14
Great Blakenham	Bo	TM 11 50	1,3;67. 8,57. 9,1
Little Blakenham	Bo	TM 10 48	29,5. (21,21)
Blaxhall	Pa	TM 35 56	3,87;89;92. 6,29;33-34;37; 39;41. 7,136. 8,80. 16,*6 note*. 21,36. 45,1
Blundeston	Ltl	TM 51 97	3,54. 7,54
Blyford	Bly	TM 42 76	13,2
Blythburgh	Bly	TM 45 75	1,12. (1,10. 6,82;89b-89c. 7,5. 26,12a. 33,10)

	Map	Grid	Text
Blythburgh, see also Robert			
Bosmere	Bo	TM 09 54	21,47. (21,*16 note*)
Boulge	Wi	TM 25 52	3,33. 6,181;244. 8,18. 26,17. 32,11. 39,15. 46,11. 67,25
Boxted	Ba	TL 82 50	8,46
Boynton	Sa	TM 09 37	3,81. 16,44. 25,72. 71,1
Boyton	Pl	TM 37 47	6,132;134;138;140
Boyton	R	TL 71 44	25,16;88–89
Boyton	Wi	TM 37 47	6,172
Bradfield [Combust, St. Clare, and St. George]	Td	(TL 89 57 (TL 90 57 (TL 90 59	2,3. 14,52;59
[Great and Little] Bradley	R	(TL 67 53 (TL 68 52	14,157. 25,92;103. 44,1. 76,1
Braiseworth	H	TM 13 71	6,198;205;225–226;228
Bramfield	Bly	TM 39 73	3,3. (3,4;3,7 *note*)
Bramford	Bo	TM 12 46	1,2;119. 25,52. (1,7. 74,7)
Brampton	Bly	TM 43 81	1,107. 7,7. 33,4
Brandeston	Ba	TL 91 46	16,10
Brandeston	Ls	TM 24 60	21,96. 47,3
Brandon	La	TL 78 86	21,5. 28,2
Brantham	Sa	TM 11 34	3,73;82;85. 6,27. 16,43. 36,3;7;11. 39,17. (3,*83 note*)
Bredfield	Wi	TM 26 52	3,27;31. 6,169;182;246;258. 7,129. 21,75;79;84–85;87. 25,23. 26,20. 67,19;23
Brettenham	Co	TL 96 53	2,13. 14,115. 25,109
[Great and Little] Bricett	Bo	(TM 03 50 (TM 05 49	25,56. 29,8. 30,3. 34,8. 38,8. 76,14
Bricticeshaga	Bo	unidentified	52,8
Bridge	Bly	TM 47 70	7,6. (7,52)
Brightlingsea (Essex)	—	TM 07 18	EE1. (1,96)
Brightwell	Ca	TM 24 43	21,54
Brihtoluestuna	Cn	unidentified	31,9. (31,14)
Brockford	H	TM 12 65	14,47
Brockley	R	TL 72 47	25,14
Brockley	Tg	TL 82 55	8,45. 14,14. 40,1
Brodertuna	Ls	unidentified	3,41. 6,278
Brome	H	TM 14 76	1,9. 6,63–64;203. 7,75. 11,5. 14,141. 19,20
Bromeswell	Wi	TM 30 50	3,23;53. 6,168;180;185;190. 6,235;249. 21,74;83;86;88
Browston	Ltl	TG 49 01	1,53
Bruisyard	Pl	TM 32 66	3,98. 7,73;145
Bruntuna	Cd	unidentified	41,15
Brutge	Pa	unidentified	6,28. 67,5
Bucklesham	Cn	TM 24 42	2,16. 21,61
Bulcamp	Bly	TM 43 76	7,19. 13,5
Bungay	Wa	TM 33 89	1,110–111. 4,19;25. (1,108 and note)
Burch	Pl	unidentified	6,145
Bures	Ba	TL 90 34	14,30. 25,42. 38,1. 55,1
Burgate	Cn	TM 29 36	7,77;108
Burgate	H	TM 08 75	35,5;7
Burgesgata	Pl	unidentified	6,144
Burgh	Ca	TM 23 51	3,20. 4,17. 6,119;123–124. 8,10. 21,67. 26,16. 31,15. 32,22;28. 46,8. 52,4
Burgh	Cn	TM 29 34	7,80. 39,1
Burgh, see also Aethelric, Brunman			
Burgh Castle	Ltl	TG 47 04	69,1
Burstall	Sa	TM 09 44	16,18;35. 25,71;77. 34,7

		Map	*Grid*	*Text*
	Bury St. Edmund's	B	TL 85 64	14,167
	Butley	Ls	TM 36 51	3,40;50. 6,292. 8,25
	Buxhall	St	TM 00 57	5,5. 7,55. 8,49. 12,7. 21,13. 26,5
	Caisne(i)d (IE)	—	unidentified	34,*15 note*
	Caldecota(n), -coten, Kaldecotes	H	unidentified	6,212. 14,136;149. 31,37;39. 41,8
	Caldecott	Ltl	TG 47 01	69,2
	Campsey Ash	Ls	TM 32 55	3,*21 note*;38. 6,279;288. 22,2. 67,28
	Canap(p)etuna, Canepetuna	Sa	unidentified	1,106. 3,80. 35,4
	Candlet	Cn	TM 29 36	7,95
	Capel St. Andrew	Wi	TM 37 48	3,21. 6,150;166;183. 7,126. 21,72;79
	Carlewuda, see Aelfric son of (?Edwin) the smith, Edwin the smith, Wihtric			
	Carlton	Pl	TM 38 64	3,94. 6,69. (3,49;*50 note*)
	Carlton Colville	Lt	TM 51 90	4,38. 31,32
	Catesfella	Wa	unidentified	8,29
	Cavendish	Ba	TL 80 46	25,47. 43,2. 76,3;6–7;20. (8,46)
	Cavenham	La	TL 76 69	25,35. 28,4
	Chadacre	Ba	TL 85 52	46,2
	Chamberlain's Hall	La	TL 74 77	28,1b
	Charsfield	Ls	TM 25 56	3,26;28 'Little';36. 6,179. 7,133. 16,6. 21,78;104. 31,18–19. 32,9. 46,12. (16,5)
	Chattisham	Sa	TM 09 42	1,106
	Chedburgh	R	TL 79 57	21,40
	Chediston	Bly	TM 35 77	3,13. 7,14–15. 68,2–3
	Cheletuna, see *Keletuna*			
	Chelsworth	Co	TL 98 47	14,109
	Chevington	Tg	TL 78 60	14,5
	Chickering	Bi	TM 20 76	6,318. 8,40. 19,7;9
	Chilbourne	R	(TL 72 48)	1,91. 25,86
	Chiletuna, see *Keletuna*			
	Chillesford	Pl	TM 38 52	3,93
	Chilton	Ba	TL 88 42	6,2
	Chilton	St	TM 04 59	21,12. 31,49
	Chippenhall	Bi	TM 28 75	6,311. 14,105;145. 67,7
	Churchford	Sa	TM 08 38	36,1. (36,16)
	Clachestorp	Ls	unidentified	6,274;284
	Clare	R	TL 76 45	25,1
	Clare, see also Richard			
	Claydon	Cd	TM 13 49	74,10. (8,54)
	Cle'pham	Pl	unidentified	6,142
	Clopton	Ca	TM 22 52	6,127. 8,7. 31,17. 34,15. 46,7;9. 47,2. 52,2. (8,43. 34,16. 46,6. 47,1)
	Clopton	R	TL 76 54	21,41. 25,5–5a;80;91. 26,11
	Cockfield	Ba	TL 90 54	14,24
	Coddenham	Ba	TL 95 39	43,2. 76,22
	Coddenham	Bo	TM 13 54	1,74. 3,60. 6,6. 7,67;69. 8,63;77. 16,20. 21,24. 34,9. 38,5;10;17;20. 53,4. 56,2; 5–6. 74,16
	Colcarr, see *Modgeva*			
	Colston	Bi	TM 31 67	67,8
	Combs	St	TM 04 56	2,6. (2,8)
	Coney Weston	*BB	TL 95 77	14,76. (14,78;80–81;84)
	Cookley	Bly	TM 34 75	7,24. 9,3
	Coresfella	Ba	unidentified	25,44
	[Great and Little] Cornard	Ba	(TL 88 40 (TL 90 39	1,98. 14,29. 25,43. 43,4. 76,4. (1,99)

	Map	Grid	Text
Corton	Ltl	TM 54 97	1,45. 69,3
Cotton	H	TM 07 66	1,77;79;84;95. 6,61;217. 14,135;148. 25,24. 31,35
South Cove	Bly	TM 49 80	3,12. 6,97
Covehithe [formerly 'North Hales']	Bly	TM 52 81	1,108. 3,16. 7,12;25. 26,15. 32,20. (76,14)
Cowlinge	R	TL 71 54	3,1
Cranley	H	TM 16 72	43,7
Cransford	Pl	TM 31 64	3,103. 6,44;52;55;128;137. 7,142. 67,33. (67,8)
Cratfield	Bly	TM 31 74	33,10
Creeting [All Saints, St. Mary, and St. Olave]	Bo	(TM 08 56 (TM 09 56 (TM 09 57	2,10. 6,5. 16,17. 23,2;4. 26,7. 51,2. 74,6. (23,1)
Creeting St. Peter	St	TM 08 57	2,9. 6,3. 8,53. 16,11. 23,1. 32,1. 51,1. (8,52. 51,2)
Cretingham	Ls	TM 22 60	3,47. 4,18. 16,7. 21,98. 31,20. 52,5. (52,8)
Croscroft	Wa	unidentified	4,31
Crowfield	Bo	TM 14 57	16,14. 38,4
'Culeslea'	Wi	(TM 33 43)	6,156
Culford	†BB	TL 83 70	14,70. (14,*53 note*;88)
Culpho	Ca	TM 21 49	8,1;3;5. 32,29
Culuerdestuna, see *Kul-, Kyluertestuna*			
Dagworth	St	TM 04 61	31,43-44;50;52. 41,11
Dalham	R	TL 72 61	25,6
Dallinghoo	Ls	TM 26 54	3,42;48. 6,265;291. 8,26. 21,99;101. 67,32
Darmsden	Bo	TM 09 53	1,71. 3,57. 21,17. 31,57
Darsham	Bly	TM 42 69	1,13. 3,7. 6,78;94-95;101. 7,36;50
Debach	Wi	TM 24 54	3,30. 7,125. 8,19. 16,5. 26,18. 32,10. 34,16. 46,10
Debenham	Cd	TM 17 63	6,11;15-16;18;28;31. 21,31. 34,12. (16,33;48)
Denham	Bi	TM 18 74	1,114. 6,71. 7,4. 19,3
Denham	R	TL 75 61	25,7
Dennington	Bi	TM 28 66	6,303. (6,137;255;257;264; 266-269;*270 note*;289)
Denston	R	TL 76 52	25,4;5a. 65,1
Depden	R	TL 77 56	25,79. 26,9
Derneford	Ca	unidentified	67,17
Desning	R	TL 73 63	25,3. (25,35-36;39-41)
Diss (Norfolk)	H	TM 11 80	1,8. (1,11)
Dodnash	Sa	TM 10 36	3,72
Santon Downham	La	TL 81 87	14,21. 21,8
Drinkstone	Td	TL 95 61	2,1. 14,56. 21,3
Dunningworth	Pl	TM 38 57	7,149
Dunwich	Bly	TM 47 70	6,84;89. 7,6;26. 21,47
Easton	Ls	TM 28 58	6,270. 8,23
Easton Bavents	Bly	TM 51 78	1,10. 68,1;4. (68,3)
Eduinestuna	Sa	unidentified	25,69. 36,14
Eduluestuna	Ca	unidentified	39,14
Edwardstone	Ba	TL 94 42	6,1
[Brent and Monks] Eleigh	Ba	(TL 94 48 (TL 96 47	14,27. 15,5. 16,9. 25,45. 42,1
Ella	Bo	unidentified	29,6
Ellough	Wa	TM 44 86	1,37. 7,44;46
South Elmham [All Saints, St. Cross, St. James, St. Margaret,	Wa	(TM 34 82 (TM 29 84 (TM 32 81	3,105. 6,298. 13,6. 19,14;16. (18,4)

	Map	Grid	Text
South Elmham (cont'd.)			
St. Michael, St. Nicholas,		(TM 31 83	
and St. Peter]	Wa	(TM 34 83	
		(TM 32 82	
		(TM 33 84	
Elmsett	Co	TM 05 46	29,12
Elmswell	*BB	TL 98 63	14,73
Elveden	La	TL 82 79	5,3. 14,20. 25,34. 26,3
Ely (Cambridgeshire)	—	TL 54 80	(25,36)
Eriswell	La	TL 72 78	28,1
Eruestuna	St	unidentified	31,46
Erwarton	Sa	TM 22 34	25,63;68
Ethereg	?Ls	unidentified	4,42
Euston	*BB	TL 89 78	14,98. (68,5)
Exning (formerly Cambridgeshire)	—	TL 62 65	EC1–EC2
Eye	H	TM 14 73	6,191. 76,23. ENf3. (6,71; 204. 18,1)
Eynsford Hundred (Norfolk)	—	—	(56,6)
Facheduna	Bo	unidentified	25,58. 74,2
Great Fakenham	BB	TL 89 76	14,96. 37,1
Little Fakenham	*BB	TL 91 76	14,97
Falkenham	Cn	TM 29 39	7,76;86;98. 39,3
Falkenham, see also Leofstan			
Farley	R	TL 73 53	25,13
Farnham	Pl	TM 36 59	6,50;135. 7,139
Felsham	Td	TL 94 57	14,58
Fenstead	Ba	TL 80 50	43,1
[Great and Little] Finborough	St	(TM 01 57	1,64. 5,4. 21,14. 29,1. 76,16
		(TM 01 54	
'Finesford(a)', 'Finlesford(a)'	Ca	(TM 18 49)	21,70. 29,14. 32,31. 38,24. 41,18
Finningham	H	TM 06 69	6,59;209;231. 14,131;135. 66,15
Flempton	Tg	TL 81 69	14,12
Flixton	Ltl	TM 51 95	1,47;50. 19,21
Flixton	Wa	TM 31 87	19,15;17. 53,5
Flowton	Bo	TM 08 46	7,62. 25,55. 29,4
Fordley	Bly	TM 42 66	6,79;88;106. 7,30;34
Fornham All Saints	Td	TL 83 67	14,9
Fornham St. Genevieve	Td	TL 83 68	14,53
Fornham St. Martin	Tg	TL 85 66	14,50
Foxhall	Ca	TM 22 43	21,60
Framlingham	Ls	TM 28 63	4,42. 6,264;266;289. 19,11. 43,6. (4,12)
Framsden	Cd	TM 20 59	4,1
Freckenham	La	TL 66 71	20,1
Fressingfield	Bi	TM 26 77	6,207 and note
Freston	Sa	TM 17 39	25,76. 27,12
Fritton	Ltl	TG 47 00	1,49;58
Frostenden	Bly	TM 47 81	33,6
Gapton	Ltl	TG 51 05	1,36;55
Gedding	Td	TL 95 58	14,60. 26,2
Gedgrave	Ls	TM 40 48	3,49;51. 6,275;286. 7,132
Gillingham (Norfolk)	—	TM 41 92	1,38
Gisleham	Lt	TM 51 88	4,37. 31,30. (1,23)
Gislingham	H	TM 07 71	1,11;87. 6,194;216;233. 14,44. 31,38. 35,7–8. 66,13. 68,5
Great Glemham	Pl	TM 33 61	3,95;102. 6,45;49–51;56. 7,144;151. 8,82. 14,41. 28,6. 45,2
Little Glemham	Pl	TM 34 58	3,96
Glemsford	Ba	TL 83 48	21,10. 34,4
Glevering	Ls	TM 29 57	67,31

	Map	Grid	Text
Gorleston (Norfolk)	Ltl	TG 52 04	1,32;42;54. (1,41)
Grenewic	Ca	unidentified	8,14
Grimston Hall	Cn	TM 26 36	2,20. 7,99
Groton	Ba	TL 95 41	1,99. 14,25. 25,50. 76,2
Grundisburgh	Ca	TM 22 51	4,16. 6,122. 8,2;6. 21,55–56. 32,23. 38,23. 67,10
Gulpher	Cn	TM 30 36	7,81
Guluesteham (IE)	–	–	32,*26 note*
Gusford	Sa	TM 14 42	46,5
'Guthestuna'	Cn	(TM 29 40)	7,89
Hacheston	Ls	TM 31 58	1,94. 3,37. 6,267;283. 14,118
Hadleigh	Co	TM 02 42	15,2
'North Hales', see Covehithe			
Halesworth	Bly	TM 38 77	3,11. 4,13. 7,17
'Halgestou'	Wi	(TM 31 43)	6,176
Hanchet	R	TL 64 45	25,83
Hardwick (Norfolk)	–	TM 22 90	ENf3
Hargrave	Tg	TL 76 60	54,2
Harkstead	Sa	TM 19 35	1,96. 36,13. 46,4. EE1
Harleston	St	TM 03 60	14,36
Harpole	Wi	TM 29 56	3,32;44. 6,251;253;259. 7,124. 21,92;94. 67,22;26
Hartest	Ba	TL 83 52	21,11. 25,48
Hasketon	Ca	TM 25 50	6,118;126. 8,8;12. 21,57. 32,24
Haspley	Ca	(TM 28 41)	14,117. 39,9;13
Hastings (Sussex)	–	TQ 80 09	(31,50)
Hatheburgfelda, Hetheburgafella	Wa	unidentified	4,33. 31,24
Haughley	St	TM 02 62	31,42
Haverhill	R	TL 67 45	14,160. 16,1. 25,82;95;102. 42,2
Hawkedon	R	TL 79 52	8,34. 25,8–9;90;101
Hawstead	Tg	TL 85 59	14,*3 note*;13. 25,30
Castle Hedingham (Essex)	–	TL 78 35	EE5
Helmingham	Cd	TM 19 57	2,12. 4,8. 8,74. 16,25–26. 25,61. 38,18. 52,9
Hemingstone	Bo	TM 14 53	1,7. 3,58. 6,8. 7,68. 8,59–60; 65;67. 16,23. 21,21–22. 56,4. 62,3–4. 67,2. 74,1;5;7. (3,62. 62,6)
Hemley	Cn	TM 28 42	7,91. 8,43. 39,5. 46,6. 47,1. (39,13)
Hemley, see also Leofric			
Hengrave	Tg	TL 82 68	14,8. (14,12)
Henham	Bly	TM 44 78	33,8
Henley	Cd	TM 15 51	6,17. 8,72;79. 21,33. 29,11. 41,14. 62,6
[Great and Little] Henny (Essex)	–	(TL 86 37 (TL 86 38	EE4;EE6
Henstead	Bly	TM 48 86	26,12c
Hepworth	BB	TL 98 74	14,78;79 *note*. 66,7
Herringfleet	Ltl	TM 47 97	1,60
Herringswell	La	TL 71 69	14,18. 25,40. 26,4
Hessett	Td	TL 93 61	12,2. 14,57
Hestley	H	TM 14 68	43,8
Hetheburgafella, see *Hatheburgfella*			
Heveningham	Bly	TM 33 72	7,13;27
Higham	Sa	TM 03 35	5,6. 16,43. 25,75. 38,21. 58,1
Hinderclay	*BB	TM 02 76	14,74
Hintlesham	Sa	TM 08 43	1,118. 3,79;*80 note*
Hinton	Bly	TM 43 72	7,5
Hitcham	Co	TL 98 51	21,42;44. 25,20;106

	Map	Grid	Text
Hobbestuna, see *Hopestuna*			
Holbrook	Sa	TM 17 36	3,68
Hollesley	Wi	TM 35 44	6,148;160. (6,149;154 and note;156–157; 256;294)
Holton	Bly	TM 40 77	6,102. 7,9;23. 13,3
Holton St. Mary	Sa	TM 05 36	32,3
Homersfield	Wa	TM 28 85	18,4. 19,13
Honilega	Ba	unidentified	34,2
Honington	*BB	TL 91 74	14,85
Hoo	Ls	TM 25 59	21,95
Hoo	Wi	TM 29 49	6,158. 21,81
Hopestuna, Hobbestuna	Ca	unidentified	6,117. 32,30
Hopewella, see *Aelfric*			
Hoppetuna, Opituna	Bly	unidentified	6,100. 7,29
Hopton	*BB	TL 99 79	14,80
Hopton	Ltl	TG 52 00	1,51
Horham	Bi	TM 21 72	6,309;316–317. 14,161. 19,4; 6. 31,4. 64,2. 75,3. (7,4)
Hornes	Lt	unidentified	31,31
Horringer	Tg	TL 82 62	14,2;*17 note*. 25,29
Horswold	Bo	TM 14 56	21,19. 29,9
Houghton	Ba	TL 78 46	43,1
Hoxne	Bi	TM 18 77	18,1. (1,92;114. 6,70;308; 311–313. 8,36–37;42. 14,161. 18,6. 21,45–46. 44,2. 64,3. 75,3;5)
Huggingehale (FB)	–	–	14,*164 note*
'Hundesthoft', -'tuf'	Wi	(TM 32 48)	6,250. 21,82
Hundon	R	TL 73 48	25,2;12
Hunston	*BB	TL 97 68	1,89. 14,95
Huntingfield	Bly	TM 33 74	6,80;82
Icheburna	Wa	unidentified	6,297
Icklingham	La	TL 77 72	1,115. 34,1. 53,1
Ickworth	Tg	TL 81 61	14,10
Ilketshall [St. Andrew, St. John, St. Lawrence, and St. Margaret]	Wa	(TM 37 87 (TM 36 87 (TM 36 86 (TM 34 85	4,20;22–24;26;28;32. 13,7
Ingham	†BB	TL 85 70	8,32. 14,69. (14,64)
Ingoluestuna	Ca	unidentified	21,65. 32,26. 67,18
Ingoluestuna	Pl	unidentified	6,146
Instead	Bi	TM 23 80	75,4
Ipswich	I	TM 16 44	1,116;122a–122d;122f–122g. 3,55. 6,4. 16,47. 25,52. 27,8. 31,55. 32,7. 38,3. 39,12. 41,13. 63,1. 74,9. (3,63. 25,60;62. 74,11)
Ipswich, see also Aelfric son of Rolf, Brown, Culling			
Isleton	Ca	TM 21 43	21,66. 32,27
Isteuertona	Cn	unidentified	31,12
Ixworth	BB	TL 93 70	14,100. 66,1;9–10. 75,2
Kaldecotes, see *Caldecota(n)*			
Kalletuna	Co	unidentified	21,64
Kalweton	Sa	TM 24 34	3,78
Kedington	R	TL 70 47	14,158. 25,15;94. 33,1
Keletuna, Cheletuna, Chiletuna	Pl	unidentified	6,42. (6,41;*43 note*;288)
Kelsale	Bi	TM 38 65	6,73. 7,3. (6,69. 7,34–36;72; 74;132)
Kembroke	Cn	TM 26 41	7,92;121. 21,52. 67,9
Kenninghall (Norfolk)	–	TM 04 85	ENf1
Kenton	Ls	TM 19 65	6,271. 14,119. 16,8. (6,11)
Kentwell	Ba	TL 86 47	12,5

	Map	Grid	Text
Kersey	Co	TM 00 43	24,1. 25,108
Kesgrave	Ca	TM 21 45	6,114
Kessingland	Lt	TM 52 86	1,31. 4,35. 31,27
Kettlebaston	Co	TL 96 50	14,114
Kettleburgh	Ls	TM 26 60	3,34. 6,261;269. 8,21;22-23 notes. (3,31 and note; 45 note;52 and note;53 note;95)
?Kilverstone (Norfolk), see *Kul-, Kyluertestuna*			
Kingsland	Ca	TM 23 54	39,11
Kingston	Ca	TM 26 47	21,53. (8,6 note)
Kirkley	Lt	TM 52 91	1,28. 31,33. (1,23)
Kirkton	Sa	TM 23 35	25,67
Kirton	Cn	TM 28 39	7,87;114. 38,26
Kislea	Lt	unidentified	1,25
Knettishall	*BB	TL 97 80	6,208. 14,99. 76,9. ENf1
Knodishall	Bly	TM 42 61	7,21;33;71
Kul-, Kyluertestuna, Culuerdestuna	Cn	?Kilverstone (Norfolk)	7,118. 31,11
Kul-, Kyluertestuna, see also Ordgar, Thuri			
Lackford	Tg	TL 79 70	14,7. (14,12;71)
Lafham	R	unidentified	73,1
Lakenheath	La	TL 71 82	21,6. 25,36. 28,2. (21,7)
'Laneburc', '-burh'	Wi	(TM 32 46)	6,151;173–174
Langer	Cn	TM 28 32	7,100;102
Langham	BB	TL 98 69	14,94. 66,6
Lang(h)edana, -dena	Bo	unidentified	1,68. 7,66. 8,62;64. 29,10. 38,9
Lavenham	Ba	TL 91 49	12,6. 35,1. 76,21
Lawshall	Ba	TL 86 54	17,1
Laxfield	Bi	TM 29 72	6,305
Laxfield, see also Edric			
Layham	Co	TM 03 40	1,109. 14,110. 28,7. 36,15. 49,1. 61,2
Leiston	Bly	TM 43 62	6,83. (6,69–70;106;136)
'Leofstanestuna'	Cn	(TM 25 39)	7,93;106;111
Letheringham	Ls	TM 26 58	8,24. 21,97. 32,14
Levington	Cn	TM 23 39	7,94;117. 31,10
Levington, see also Gleman			
Lewes (Sussex)	—	TQ 41 10	(26,3;5)
Lidgate	R	TL 72 58	54,1. 70,1
Linburne	Wa	TM 28 84	14,121
Lindsey	Co	TL 97 44	14,113. 25,107
Linhou	Ba	unidentified	38,2
Linstead [Magna and Parva]	Bly	(TM 31 76 (TM 33 77	6,81;104. (6,82 note)
Littlecross	Wi	TM 29 46	6,163
Great Livermere	Td	TL 88 71	14,22;68. 21,9. 31,40
Little Livermere	*BB	TL 87 72	14,87
Loes, see Leofstan			
London, see Bernard			
Loose	Co	TM 00 53	34,5. (25,112)
Loudham	Wi	TM 30 54	3,25. 6,188–189;237;247; 257. 7,123;127. 21,91. 22,3. 67,24
Lound	Ltl	TM 50 98	1,34;44;46
Lowestoft	Ltl	TM 55 93	1,33
'Maistana'	Cn	(TM 31 37)	7,79
Maldon (Essex), see Siward			
Manesfort	Sa	unidentified	36,4
Man(e)uuic, Manewic	Cd	unidentified	4,2-3. 6,19. 16,32
Manston	Tg	TL 83 56	14,15. 25,31. 27,2
Manton	Co	TL 97 53	14,114. 34,2

	Map	Grid	Text
Marlesford	Ls	TM 32 58	1,93-94. 3,43. 6,276. 14,118
Martlesham	Ca	TM 26 46	39,6
Martley	Ls	TM 28 58	3,35;52. 6,293. 8,28. 67,27
Long Melford	Ba	TL 86 46	14,23
Mellis	H	TM 10 74	6,195;227. 14,140. 35,7
Mells	Bly	TM 40 76	44,3
Melton	Wi	TM 28 50	3,24. 6,175. 8,17. 21,80; 83 note;93. 32,13
Mendham	Bi	TM 26 82	6,72;313. 8,37;42. 13,1. 14,106. 19,2
Mendlesham	H	TM 10 65	1,65;76. (1,66;77-80;82;85; 87. 8,55. 14,146)
Mendlesham, see also Alwin, Burghard			
Mettingham	Wa	TM 36 89	4,21;23
Mickfield	Bo	TM 13 61	14,38. 34,10
Middleton	Bly	TM 43 67	3,6. 4,15. 6,86. 7,31;39. 26,13
Milden	Ba	TL 95 46	14,34. 41,10
Mildenhall	La	TL 71 74	1,115. 25,39. ENf5
Minsmere	Bly	TM 46 65	6,107. 7,32
Monewden	Ls	TM 23 58	6,262. 8,20;22;28. 21,104. 46,12
Morston	Cn	TM 25 38	2,17. 7,90;115. 21,48. 39,2;4
Moulton	R	TL 69 64	15,1
Moze (Essex)	—	TM 20 26	(32,7)
Mundham (Norfolk)	—	TM 32 98	ENf4
Mutford	Lt	TM 48 88	1,23;24. (7,46)
Mutford, see also Ulf			
'Mycelegata'	Cn	(TM 26 38)	6,111. 7,110
Nacton	Cn	TM 21 39	31,8;13a. (31,55)
Nayland	Ba	TL 97 34	27,6
Nec(c)hemara, Neckemara	Ca	unidentified	6,113. 32,25. 67,13
Nedging	Co	TL 99 48	21,43
Nettlestead	Bo	TM 08 49	3,56. (3,59 note;62. 76,13)
Newbourn	Ca	TM 27 43	8,15. 14,117. 39,10. (21,54)
Newton	Ba	TL 91 41	14,32. 43,3
Newton	Cd	TM 19 51	38,16. (38,23-24)
'Newton'	Ltl	(TM 54 98)	1,57
Old Newton	St	TM 05 62	8,50. 16,12. 23,3;5. 31,51. (31,35)
Niuetuna	Pa	unidentified	6,32
Nordberia	Pl	unidentified	8,81
Normandy	—	—	(56,1)
Norton	*BB	TL 96 66	1,88. (1,61-64;67;73)
Norton	Cn	TM 25 38	7,84;107;122
Nowton	Tg	TL 86 60	14,4
Oakley	H	TM 15 77	6,65. 7,75. 14,129;137-138. 19,12
Occold	H	TM 15 70	1,82. 6,193;224. 14,144. 31,60. 43,9. 77,1-2. (31,6)
Odiham (Hampshire)	—	SU 74 51	(77,4)
Offton	Bo	TM 06 49	1,69. 7,60. 29,7. 62,1
Offton, see also Durand			
'Olden'	Bo	(TM 12 56)	1,5. 6,7. 8,61. 16,16;21. 21,23. 23,6. 51,2. 53,2. 56,3. 74,4
Onehouse	St	TM 01 59	2,7. 14,37. 34,6. 56,1
Opituna, see *Hoppetuna*			
Otley	Ca	TM 20 54	8,11. 38,25. 41,19. 52,1;3;7. (52,9)
Ousden	R	TL 73 59	5,1. 72,1
'Oxelanda'	Cn	(TM 32 36)	7,120

	Map	Grid	Text
Pachetuna	Bo	unidentified	16,19
Pakefield	Lt	TM 53 88	1,27. 4,41. (1,23)
Pakenham	Td	TL 92 67	14,49
Palgrave	H	TM 11 78	14,45
Pannington	Sa	TM 14 40	3,76. 27,10
Parham	Pa	TM 30 60	1,75. 3,88;90. 4,9. 6,32;35. (1,94)
Parham, see Thormod			
Peasenhall	Bly	TM 35 69	6,92;103. 7,10;20;72. (7,12)
Pettaugh	Cd	TM 16 59	16,39. 21,30. 67,3
Peyton	Wi	TM 31 41	27,13
Peyton, see also Godric			
Pileberga	Bo	unidentified	29,3
Playford	Ca	TM 21 48	6,112
'Plumgeard'	Cn	(TM 28 36)	7,85. 21,51
Polstead	Ba	TL 98 38	27,5
Poslingford	R	TL 76 48	14,154. 25,87;98. 33,2
Possefelda	Ls	unidentified	6,277
Potsford	Ls	TM 29 57	67,30
Prestetuna	Pl	unidentified	6,147
Preston	Ba	TL 94 50	8,47. 14,26
Preston	Ca	TM 24 46	8,*1 note*. 39,8
Purtepyt	Sa	unidentified	25,66
Ramsholt	Wi	TM 30 42	6,177. 11,3
Rattlesden	Td	TL 97 59	2,2. 5,2. 14,61. 21,1-2. 25,26. 26,1
Raydon	Sa	TM 04 38	5,8. 16,37;41. 25,74. 28,5. 32,4;8. 61,1
Rede	Tg	TL 80 55	14,16. 21,4. 25,32. 27,1
Redenhall (Norfolk)	—	TM 26 84	(1,92)
Redgrave	H	TM 05 78	14,42
Redisham	Wa	TM 40 84	7,51
Redles	Co	unidentified	62,7
Redlingfield	H	TM 18 70	6,192
Rendham	Pl	TM 34 64	3,99. 6,43. 7,135;141;146;148
Rendlesham	Ls	TM 32 52	3,39. 6,268;270;272;281. 7,131. 21,102. 67,29
Reydon	Bly	TM 49 78	33,4
Rickinghall Inferior	*BB	TM 03 75	6,302. 14,75. (14,79)
Rickinghall Superior	H	TM 04 75	6,62. 14,46. 35,7. (14,136 and note)
Rigneseta	Bo	unidentified	25,57
Ringsfield	Wa	TM 40 88	1,16;20. 4,29. 7,41. (1,17)
Ringshall	Bo	TM 04 52	2,11. 7,56. 30,1-2
Ringshall, see also Godric			
Risby	Tg	TL 80 66	8,44. 14,1. (14,12)
Riseburc	?Bly	unidentified	1,12
Rishangles	H	TM 16 68	6,222
Rodeham	St	unidentified	16,13
Rodenhala	Lt	unidentified	4,36. 31,28
Rougham	Td	TL 91 62	14,51. (14,57;67)
Rumburgh	Bly	TM 34 81	ENf2;ENf4. (3,2;105)
Rushbrooke	Co	TL 94 52	14,115. 25,110
Rushbrooke	Td	TL 89 61	14,67
Rushford	†BB	TL 92 81	37,6
Rushmere	Lt	TM 49 87	1,23;26. 4,40. 31,34. (1,24)
Rushmere	Pl	TM 42 59	6,139
Rushmere St. Andrew	Ca	TM 19 46	1,15. 3,17;19. 6,116;125. 8,16. 21,62;69. 67,14. (6,13)
Saibamus	Ba	unidentified	76,5
Sanford, see Aelfric			
Sapiston	BB	TL 92 74	14,83. 37,3. 59,2. 66,5
[Great and Little] Saxham	Tg	(TL 78 62 (TL 79 63	1,63. 14,6;11. 25,28

	Map	Grid	Text
Saxmundham	Pl	TM 38 62	7,70–71;74. (7,20–21)
Saxtead	Bi	TM 26 65	4,12
Seckford	Ca	TM 25 48	16,2
Semer	Co	TL 99 46	14,108
Shadingfield	Wa	TM 43 83	1,112. 7,47;52. 32,16. 33,11
Sharpstone	Cd	(TM 12 51)	1,72. 3,62. 16,24;27. 21,27;35
Shelland	St	TL 99 59	25,51
Shelley	Sa	TM 03 38	1,100;104
Shimpling	Ba	TL 85 51	33,13. 46,1
Shipmeadow	Wa	TM 38 89	4,23;27. 7,48
Shotley	Sa	TM 23 36	1,102–104. 25,64
Shottisham	Wi	TM 32 44	6,167;186;238. 21,73;89
Sibton	Bly	TM 36 69	3,9. 6,90;93
Snape	Pl	TM 39 59	6,129;133
Sogenhoe	Wi	TM 28 52	6,242
Earl Soham	Ls	TM 23 63	3,46. 6,285. 31,59. (3,20;33 and note;48 and note)
Monk Soham	Bi	TM 21 65	14,102. 21,46. 31,3
Somerleyton	Ltl	TM 49 97	1,41;48;52. 69,4
Somersham	Bo	TM 09 48	1,4. 7,59. 29,2. 62,2. 76,13. (29,6)
Somerton	Ba	TL 81 53	14,28;33. 40,2
Sotherton	Bly	TM 44 79	48,1
Sotterley	Wa	TM 45 85	4,30–31
Southwold	Bly	TM 50 76	14,162–163
Stanfelda	Sa	unidentified	5,7. (5,*8 note*)
Stanningfield	Td	TL 87 56	2,5. 14,66. 33,12
Stansfield	R	TL 78 52	14,155. 25,11;78
Stanstead	Ba	TL 84 49	31,41
Stanton	*BB	TL 96 73	6,301. 14,72. 76,8. (14,78)
Staverton	Ls	TM 35 50	6,260;273;280. (6,31;187;235)
Sternfield	Pl	TM 39 61	3,97. 6,131;141. 7,138;143
Stoke	I	TM 16 43	21,15
Stoke Ash	H	TM 11 70	1,86. 6,213;220. 14,122;125; 146
Stoke by Clare	R	TL 74 43	25,17;97
Stoke by Nayland	Ba	TL 98 36	27,3
Stokerland	Wi	TM 32 48	6,236
Stone Street	Bly	TM 38 82	3,2
Stone Street	Co	TM 01 43	25,112
[Earl and Little] Stonham	Bo	(TM 10 58 (TM 11 60	1,6;66. 3,59. 6,9. 7,64. 8,52; 55;63. 14,39. 16,15;22. 25,54. 34,11. 64,1–2. (7,63. 8,54)
Stonham Aspal	Bo	TM 13 59	38,6–7;19. (38,25)
Stoven	Bly	TM 44 81	7,22. 31,7
West Stow	†BB	TL 81 70	14,71
Stowlangtoft	*BB	TL 95 68	14,77. 25,22
Stowmarket	St	TM 04 58	2,8. (34,6)
Stradbroke	Bi	TM 23 73	6,308. 8,39
Stradishall	R	TL 74 52	25,100
Stratford, see Robert			
Stratford St. Andrew	Pl	TM 35 60	6,48. 45,3
Stratford St. Mary	Sa	TM 05 34	27,9
Stratton	Cn	TM 24 38	6,110. 7,119
Strickland	Bly	TM 38 69	1,14. 6,87;98. 7,35;37
'Struestuna', 'Struustuna'	Cn	(TM 25 40)	7,88;103;105
'Struostuna', see Goda			
Stuston	H	TM 13 77	14,137. 50,1
Stutton	Sa	TM 16 34	3,83. 32,6. 36,2;10
Sudbourne	Pl	TM 41 53	6,143. 21,38. (8,25. 21,37; *82 note*)

	Map	Grid	Text
Sudbury	Tg	TL 87 41	1,97. EE2;EE4–EE6
Sutton	Wi	TM 30 46	3,22. 6,149;155;165;170; 178;184;248;252;254. 21,71. 67,21
Sutton, see also Godwin			
Swefling	Pl	TM 34 63	3,100;104. 6,46. 7,147
Swilland	Cd	TM 18 52	41,2
Syleham	Bi	TM 20 78	19,1. 44,2
Tannington	Bi	TM 24 67	6,304
Tattingstone	Sa	TM 13 37	16,46. 36,9;12
Theberton	Bly	TM 43 65	6,109
Thelnetham	*BB	TM 01 78	6,300. 12,1. 14,90
Thetford, see Aethelwy			
Thicchebrom	Wa	unidentified	6,295
Thistleton	Ca	TM 23 52	8,9. 21,58. 67,16
Thorington	Bly	TM 42 74	3,5. 7,38. 26,14. 32,19
Thorington	Sa	TM 01 35	40,6
Thorndon	H	TM 14 69	6,223. 14,128;143
Thorney	St	(TM 05 58)	1,1. 8,51;54. 31,53. 67,1. (1,65. 29,1. 31,44;49)
Thornham Magna	H	TM 10 71	1,81. 6,200;214–215. 14,127; 130;147. 35,7. 62,5
Thornham Parva	H	TM 10 72	6,199;218
Thorpe	Cn	TM 25 37	2,18. 7,104;116
Thorpe	Bly	(TM 34 73)	3,8. 7,16;26
Thorpe	Ca	(TM 27 55)	32,21
Thorpe	Pl	(TM 45 60)	6,136
Thorpe Hall	Cd	TM 20 62	4,6–7. 6,12;21;23;25. 14,40. 21,34
Thorpe Morieux	Co	TL 94 53	8,35. 14,115–116
Ixworth Thorpe	BB	TL 91 72	9,2. 14,91;101. 37,2. 59,1. 75,1
Thorpe, cf. also *Torp*, *Torpe*			
'Thorstanestuna', see 'Turstanestuna'			
Thrandeston	H	TM 11 76	6,66–67;202;204. 8,30. 14,139;150. 18,6. 19,19. 35,7. 50,2
Thurleston	Cd	TM 15 48	1,122e. 3,64;66. 8,69–70;75. 9,4. 25,60;62. 41,3. 74,8; 12;15
[Great and Little] Thurlow	R	(TL 68 50 (TL 67 51	1,90. 14,156. 25,93;104
'Thurstanestuna', see 'Turstanestuna'			
Thurston	R	TL 79 51	8,33
Thurston	Td	TL 92 65	1,62. 14,54
Timworth	Td	TL 86 69	14,63. 25,25
Toft	Sa	unidentified	16,47. 25,73
Toppesfield	Co	TM 02 41	15,3–4
Torp	Sa	unidentified	25,65
Torpe	St	unidentified	31,47
'Torstanestuna', see 'Turstanestuna'			
Torstuna	St	unidentified	31,49
Tostock	Td	TL 96 63	1,61. 14,65
Trimley [St. Martin, and St. Mary]	Cn	TM 27 37	7,97;112. 21,49. 39,1
Troston	*BB	TL 90 72	14,86
Tuddenham	Ca	TM 19 48	3,18. 6,120. 8,4. 21,63. 38,13; 22. 67,15. (38,15)
Tuddenham	La	TL 73 71	12,4. 25,37. 28,3
Tunstall	Bo	TM 08 49	8,58. 26,6. (8,55)
Tunstall	Pa	TM 36 55	6,36
Turchetlestuna	Sa	unidentified	36,6
'Turstanestuna'	Cn	(TM 28 38)	7,83

	Map	Grid	Text
'Turstanestuna', 'Thor-', 'Thur-', 'Tor-'	Wi	(TM 30 50)	6,153. 11,2. 26,19
Tusemera	H	unidentified	34,17
Ubbeston	Bly	TM 32 72	33,9
'Udeham'	Wi	(TM 30 44)	22,1
Ufford	Wi	TM 29 52	6,239;243;255. 7,127. 14,166. 21,90
Uggeshall	Bly	TM 45 80	4,14. 7,8. 14,164. 68,2. 76,19
Ultuna	St	unidentified	31,48
Ulverston	Cd	TM 14 63	16,29–30;38. 34,13. (34,10; 18)
Undley	La	TL 69 81	21,7
Wadgate	Cn	TM 29 33	7,82;109
[Great and Little] Waldingfield	Ba	(TL 91 43 (TL 92 45	8,48. 14,31. 25,46;49. 34,2. 35,2. 39,16
Waldringfield	Ca	TM 28 44	6,115. 14,117. 39,7
Walpole	Bly	TM 36 74	3,4
Walsham le Willows	BB	TL 99 71	6,299. 14,92. 66,2. (66,13;15)
Walton	Cn	TM 29 39	7,76. 21,50. 31,13. (7,81;122)
Wangford	Bly	TM 46 79	33,7
Wangford	La	TL 75 83	14,19. 21,5 *note*;9 *note*. 25,41
Wantisden	Pa	TM 36 53	3,86;91. 6,30–31;38;40. 7,137. 8,80. 21,37
Warabetuna, see *Wrabetuna*			
UUarle	Bly	unidentified	13,4
Wattisfield	BB	TM 01 74	4,11. 14,79. 31,2
Wattisham	Co	TM 00 51	25,19. 53,7
Weinhou, see Aelfric			
Weledana	St	unidentified	41,11
[Great and Little] Welnetham	Td	(TL 87 59 (TL 88 60	2,4. 14,62
[Great and Little] Wenham	Sa	(TM 07 38 (TM 08 39	3,67;84. 16,36;40. 40,3–4
Wenhaston	Bly	TM 42 75	3,5
Wenhou, see Aelfric			
Westerfield	Cd	TM 17 47	3,61;63–64. 6,13;24. 8,73;76. 21,29. 31,58. 32,2. 38,12;14. 14,4;6. 74,11;14
Westhorpe	H	TM 04 69	6,58;60;210. 14,132;142. 37,7. 41,9. 53,6. 66,14. (6,59 *note*)
Westleton	Bly	TM 44 69	6,85;96;105. 66,12
Westley	Tg	TL 82 64	14,17. 25,27
Weston	Wa	TM 42 87	1,18;21;113. 7,43;49. 31,22. 32,17. (7,53)
Weston Colville (Cambridgeshire)	—	TL 61 53	(3,1)
Market Weston	*BB	TL 99 78	9,2. 14,84. 60,1
Wetherden	St	TM 00 62	14,35. 31,45. 41,12
Wetheringsett	H	TM 12 66	1,80. 6,234. 14,124;153. 21,39
Weybread	Bi	TM 24 80	1,92. 6,312;314–315. 8,37–38;41. 14,107. 18,2
Whatfield	Co	TM 02 46	2,15. 7,2. 14,111–112. 25,111. 29,13. 34,14. 40,5. 66,11
Whepstead	Tg	TL 83 58	14,3
Wherstead	Sa	TM 16 40	3,70;77. 27,11
Whittingham	Bi	TM 27 78	8,36
Whitton	Cd	TM 13 47	74,13
Wichedis	Wa	unidentified	32,18
Wickham Market	Wi	TM 30 55	3,29. 6,241;251. 7,130. 16,4. 22,2 *note*. 32,12. 67,20
Wickham Skeith	H	TM 09 69	1,78;85. 6,230. 8,31. 14,126; 152

	Map	*Grid*	*Text*
Wickhambrook	R	TL 75 54	25,99
Wilby	Bi	TM 24 72	6,310. 18,3. 19,5;7
Wilford	Wi	TM 29 50	6,171;256. 7,128
Willingham	Wa	TM 45 86	1,37. 7,42. 31,21;23. (7,43)
Willisham	Bo	TM 07 50	8,56
UUilmundestun (FB)	—	unidentified	14,*16 note*
Wimundahala	Lt	unidentified	7,53. 31,29
Wimundestuna	R	unidentified	14,*16 note*. 25,18;105
Wingfield	Bi	TM 22 76	6,308. 19,8. 21,45
Winston	Cd	TM 18 61	4,4–5. 6,14. 16,33. 21,28
Wissett	Bly	TM 36 79	3,10;*13 note*;14. 76,17. (3,16)
Withermarsh	Ba	TM 00 37	27,4
Withersdale	Bi	TM 28 80	(6,104)
Withersfield	R	TL 65 47	25,84;96. 26,10
Witnesham	Ca	TM 17 50	41,17
Wixoe	R	TL 71 42	33,3
Woodbridge	Ls	TM 27 49	3,45. 6,263;287;294. 7,134. 8,27. 21,100;103. 32,15. 38,27
Woolpit	Td	TL 97 62	14,55
Woolverstone	Sa	TM 18 38	3,74. 36,8
Wordwell	*BB	TL 82 72	14,88
Worlingham	Wa	TM 44 89	1,19;22. 4,34. 14,121. 31,25
Worlington	La	TL 69 73	12,3
Worlingworth	Bi	TM 23 68	14,103
Wortham	H	TM 08 77	6,197;219. 11,4. 14,43. 35,7. (11,5)
Wrabetuna, Warabetuna, UUrab(r)etuna, Wrabbatuna	Bly	unidentified	3,15. 6,91;99;108. 7,11;28
[Great and Little] Wratting	R	(TL 68 48 (TL 69 47	14,159. 25,10;81;85
Wrentham	Bly	TM 48 82	26,12
Wrentham, see also Thorkell			
Wyken	†BB	TL 96 71	37,5. 66,4;8
Wyverstone	H	TM 04 67	1,83. 6,57;211. 14,123;134; 151. 31,36. 57,1. 66,16
Yarmouth (Norfolk)	—	TG 52 07	(1,32. 14,162)
Yaxley	H	TM 12 73	6,196;229. 18,6;19
Yoxford	Bly	TM 39 68	7,18. 44,4

Places not named
7,78. 25,70. 36,15;17. 38,15. EE3

Places not in Suffolk
References are to entries in the Indices of Persons and Places. The names of Churches and Clergy are starred.

Elsewhere in Britain
CAMBRIDGESHIRE ... Chatteris*. Ely*, and Places Index. Exning. ?Sheriff, see Picot. Weston Colville. ESSEX ... Ardleigh. Brightlingsea. Castle Hedingham. Great and Little Henny. Maldon, see Siward. Moze. Sheriff, see Peter of Valognes, Robert son of Wymarc, Swein of Essex. HAMPSHIRE ... Odiham. Winchester*. HERTFORDSHIRE ... Sheriff, see Peter of Valognes. HUNTINGDONSHIRE ... Ramsey*. KENT ... Canterbury*. Rochester*. LONDON ... see Bernard. NORFOLK ... Alburgh. Billingford. Diss. Eynsford Hundred. Gillingham. Gorleston. Hardwick. Kenninghall. ?Kilverstone. Mundham. Redenhall. Thetford*, and see Aethelwy. Yarmouth. SUSSEX ... Hastings. Lewes.

Outside Britain
More precise details as to location are given in the Notes.
Abenon ... Roger. Alençon ... Bernard. Alno ... William. Arques ... William. Auberville ... Roger, William. Aumâle ... Countess. Bayeux*. Beaufour ... Ralph. Belefol ... Miles. Bernai*. Berry ... Hervey. Beuvrière ... Drogo. Bosc ... William. Bourges ... Hervey. Bourneville ... William. Bouville ... Saxwalo, William. Brittany ... Count Alan, Fulcher the Breton, Hubert the Breton, Reginald the Breton. Caen ... Walter, William. Candos ... Roger. Claville ... Robert. Coleville ... Gilbert. Corbon ... Hugh. Courbepine ... Ralph. Courson ... Robert. Coutances*. Dol ... Walter. Douai ... Walter. Ecouis ... William. Emalleville ... William. Evreux*. Ferrers ... Hermer. Fougeres ... Ralph. Glanville ... Robert. Grandmesnil ... Hugh. Grestain*. Hellean ... Tihel. Houdain ... Hugh, see also final entry in Persons Index. Lanquetot ... Ralph. Limesy ... Ralph. Loges ... Bigot. Mandeville ... Geoffrey. Marcy ... Ralph. Mesnieres ... Fulcher. Mont-Canisy ... Hubert. Montfort ... Hugh. More ... W. Mortain ... Count Robert. Moutiers ... Lisois. Normandy ... 56,1. Noyers ... William. Orbec ... Roger. Palluel ... Peter. Parthenay ... William. Pierrepont ... Godfrey, Robert. Poitou ... Roger. Poix ... Werno. Port ... Hubert. Rames ... Roger. Risboil, Risbou ... Walter. St. Bertin's ... Humphrey. Saint-Clair ... Hamo, Richard. St. Germain ... Roger. St. Lo. St. Ouen ... Bernard. St. Valery ... Walter. Savenay ... Ralph. Tosny ... Robert. Tourleville ... Ralph. Valognes ... Hamo, Peter. Vatteville ... William. Vaux ... Robert. Vere ... Aubrey. Vernon ... Huard. ?Wader ... Ralph. Wanchy ... Hugh, Osbern. Warenne ... William. Wissant ... Gilbert.

MAPS AND MAP KEYS

The County Boundary is marked by thick lines, dotted for the modern boundary; Hundred boundaries are marked by thin lines, broken where uncertain.

The letters of National Grid 10-kilometre squares are shown on the map border. Each four-figure square covers one square kilometre (5/8ths of a square mile).

SUFFOLK HUNDREDS AND HALF-HUNDREDS (WEST)

Babergh (Ba)
20 Acton
29 Assington
27 Ayeley
8 Boxted
18 Brandeston
33 Bures
16 Cavendish
4 Chadacre
22 Chilton
2 Cockfield
28 Coddenham
Coresfella
26 Great and Little Cornard
23 Edwardstone
13 Brent and Monks Eleigh
7 Fenstead
12 Glemsford
25 Groton
5 Hartest
Honilega
15 Houghton
14 Kentwell
11 Lavenham
1 Lawshall
Linhou
17 Long Melford
19 Milden
34 Nayland
24 Newton
30 Polstead
9 Preston
Saibamus
6 Shimpling
3 Somerton
10 Stanstead
32 Stoke by Nayland
21 Great and Little Waldingfield
31 Withermarsh

Blackbourn and Bradmere
(BB: in both Hundreds.
*BB: in Blackbourn.
†BB: in Bradmere)
33 Great Ashfield
18 *Bardwell
3 Barnham
11 Barningham
8 *Coney Weston
27 †Culford
35 *Elmswell

5 *Euston
9 Great Fakenham
10 *Little Fakenham
16 Hepworth
12 *Hinderclay
14 *Honington
4 *Hopton
32 *Hunston
28 †Ingham
29 Ixworth
2 *Knettishall
30 Langham
21 *Little Livermere
34 *Norton
13 *Rickinghall Inferior
1 †Rushford
15 Sapiston
19 *Stanton
26 †West Stow
31 *Stowlangtoft
7 *Thelnetham
23 Ixworth Thorpe
22 *Troston
25 Walsham le Willows
17 Wattisfield
6 *Market Weston
20 *Wordwell
24 †Wyken

Bury (B)
B Bury St. Edmund's

Cosford (Co)
17 Aldham
13 Ash Street
9 Bildeston
2 Brettenham
11 Chelsworth
15 Elmsett
20 Hadleigh
6 Hitcham
Kalletuna
18 Kersey
8 Kettlebaston
22 Layham
16 Lindsey
4 Loose
3 Manton
10 Nedging
Redles
5 Rushbrooke
12 Semer

19 Stone Street
1 Thorpe Morieux
21 Toppesfield
7 Wattisham
14 Whatfield

Lackford (La)
12 Barton Mills
2 Brandon
6 Cavenham
9 Chamberlain's Hall
1 Santon Downham
7 Elveden
8 Eriswell
15 Freckenham
16 Herringswell
13 Icklingham
4 Lakenheath
10 Mildenhall
14 Tuddenham
5 Undley
3 Wangford
11 Worlington

Risbridge (R)
7 Badmondisfield
31 Boyton
13 Great and Little Bradley
27 Brockley
8 Chedburgh
22 Chilbourne
30 Clare
12 Clopton
10 Cowlinge
3 Dalham
4 Denham
16 Denston
9 Depden
2 Desning
14 Farley
28 Hanchet
29 Haverhill
18 Hawkedon
23 Hundon
26 Kedington
Lafham
6 Lidgate
1 Moulton
5 Ousden
24 Poslingford
17 Stansfield
32 Stoke by Clare
15 Stradishall

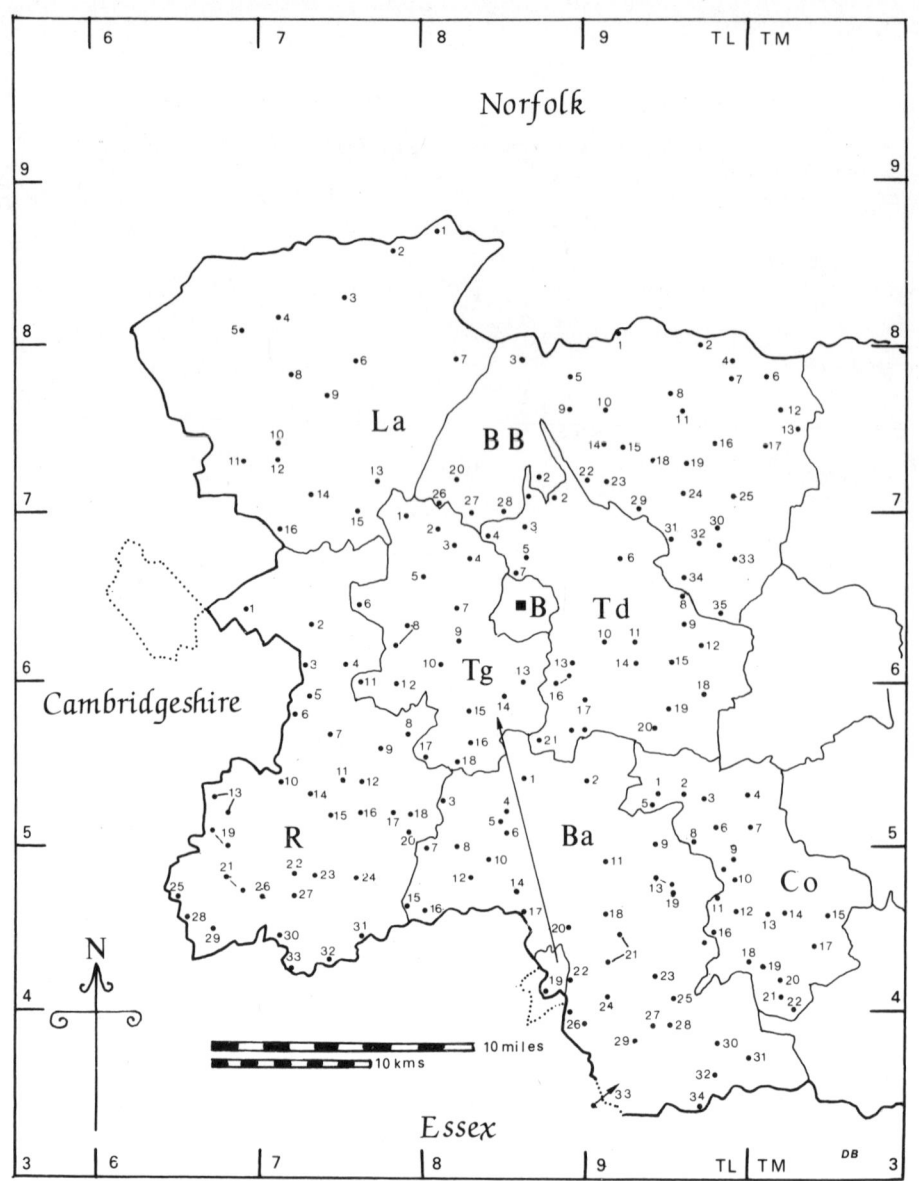

HUNDREDS AND HALF-HUNDREDS (WEST)

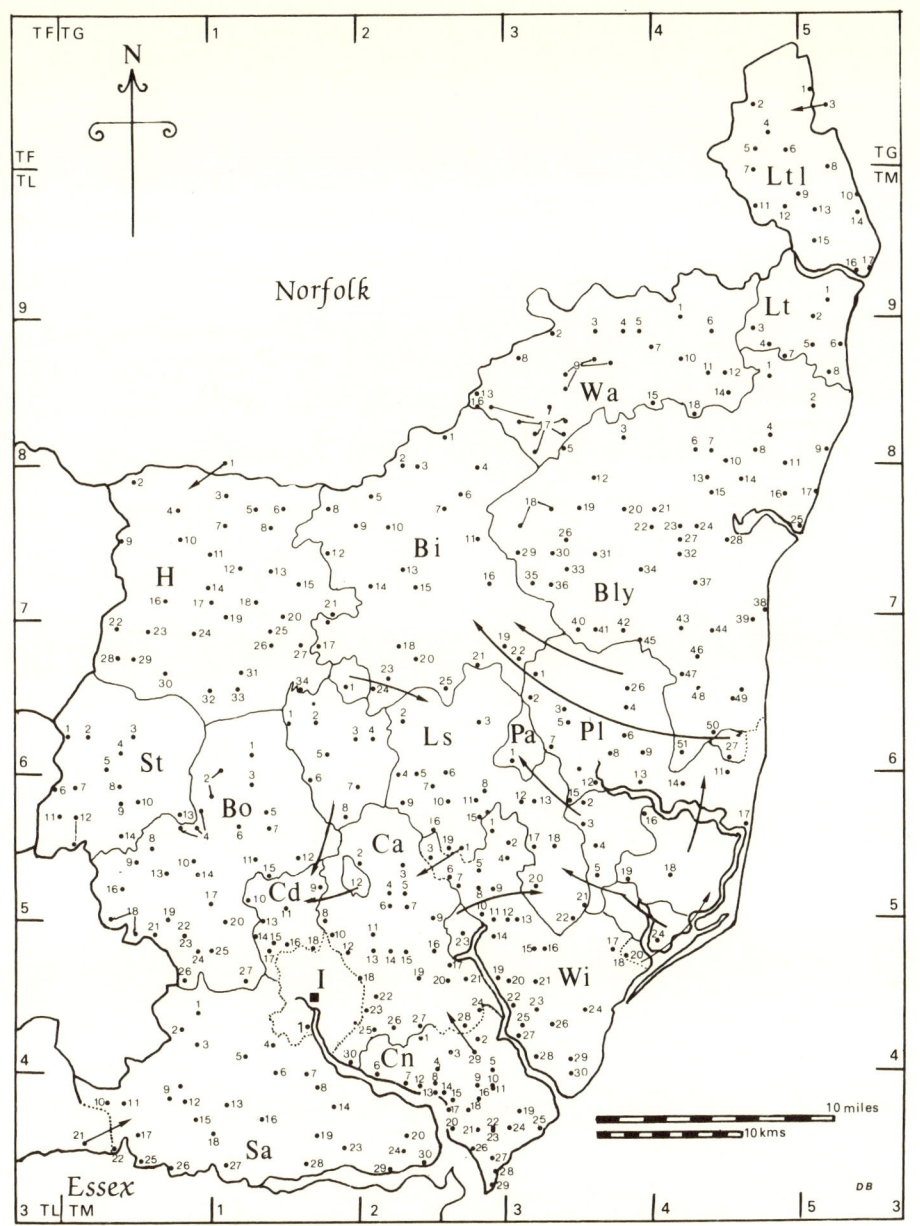

HUNDREDS AND HALF-HUNDREDS (EAST)

19 Great and Little Thurlow
20 Thurston
11 Wickhambrook
   Wimundestuna
25 Withersfield
33 Wixoe
21 Great and Little Wratting

Thedwestry (Td)
1 Ampton
5 Great Barton
11 Beyton
17 Bradfield Combust,
   St. Clare, and St. George
15 Drinkstone
20 Felsham
4 Fornham St. Genevieve
7 Fornham St. Martin

19 Gedding
14 Hessett
2 Great Livermere
6 Pakenham
18 Rattlesden
10 Rougham
13 Rushbrooke
21 Stanningfield
8 Thurston
3 Timworth
9 Tostock
16 Great and Little Welnetham
12 Woolpit

Thingoe (Tg)
6 Barrow
18 Brockley

12 Chevington
2 Flempton
4 Fornham All Saints
11 Hargrave
14 Hawstead
3 Hengrave
9 Horringer
10 Ickworth
1 Lackford
16 Manston
13 Nowton
17 Rede
5 Risby
8 Great and Little Saxham
19 Sudbury
7 Westley
15 Whepstead

SUFFOLK HUNDREDS AND HALF-HUNDREDS (EAST)

Bishop's (Bi)
27 Aldringham
19 Badingham
23 Bedfield
17 Bedingfield
9 Chickering
11 Chippenhall
22 Colston
12 Denham
21 Dennington
7 Fressingfield
14 Horham
8 Hoxne
2 Instead
26 Kelsale
16 Laxfield
1 Mendham
25 Saxtead
24 Monk Soham
13 Stradbroke
5 Syleham
20 Tannington
3 Weybread
6 Whittingham
15 Wilby
10 Wingfield
4 Withersdale
18 Worlingworth

Blything (Bly)
Alneterne
2 Benacre
23 Blyford
28 Blythburgh
34 Bramfield
6 Brampton
39 Bridge
24 Bulcamp
19 Chediston
26 Cookley
11 South Cove
9 Covehithe

29 Cratfield
43 Darsham
38 Dunwich
17 Easton Bavents
47 Fordley
8 Frostenden
20 Halesworth
15 Henham
1 Henstead
36 Heveningham
37 Hinton
21 Holton
   Hoppetuna, Opituna
30 Huntingfield
51 Knodishall
50 Leiston
18 Linstead Magna and Parva
22 Mells
46 Middleton
49 Minsmere
40 Peasenhall
16 Reydon
   ?*Riseburc*
5 Rumburgh
41 Sibton
13 Sotherton
25 Southwold
3 Stone Street
7 Stoven
42 Strickland
48 Theberton
32 Thorington
33 'Thorpe'
35 Ubbeston
10 Uggeshall
31 Walpole
14 Wangford
   UUarle
27 Wenhaston
44 Westleton
12 Wissett

Wrabetuna, Warabetuna,
   UUrab(r)etuna,
   Wrabbatuna
4 Wrentham
45 Yoxford

Bosmere (Bo)
12 Ashbocking
8 Badley
13 Barking
9 Battisford
17 Baylham
20 Great Blakenham
25 Little Blakenham
10 Bosmere
27 Bramford
18 Great and Little Bricett
   Bricticeshaga
11 Coddenham
4 Creeting All Saints,
   St. Mary, and St. Olave
5 Crowfield
14 Darmsden
   Ella
   Facheduna
26 Flowton
15 Hemingstone
7 Horswold
   Lang(h)edana, -dena
1 Mickfield
21 Nettlestead
23 Offton
6 'Olden'
   Pachetuna
   Pilebergа
   Rigneseta
16 Ringshall
24 Somersham
2 Earl and Little Stonham
3 Stonham Aspal
22 Tunstall
19 Willisham

Carlford (Ca)
30 Alnesbourn
  Aluredestuna
21 Barkestone
15 Great Bealings
14 Little Bealings
23 Bixley
27 Brightwell
7 Burgh
4 Clopton
11 Culpho
  Derneford
  Eduluestuna
10 'Finesford(a)',
  'Finlesford(a)'
26 Foxhall
  Grenewic
6 Grundisburgh
9 Hasketon
29 Haspley
  Hopestuna, Hobbestuna
  Ingoluestuna
25 Isleton
22 Kesgrave
3 Kingsland
17 Kingston
20 Martlesham
  Nec(c)hemara, Neckemara
28 Newbourn
2 Otley
13 Playford
19 Preston
18 Rushmere St. Andrew
16 Seckford
5 Thistleton
1 'Thorpe'
12 Tuddenham
24 Waldringfield
8 Witnesham

Claydon (Cd)
15 Akenham
4 Ashfield
13 Barham
  Bermesdena
  Bruntuna
14 Claydon
2 Debenham
7 Framsden
8 Helmingham
10 Henley
  Man(e)uuic, Manewic
11 Newton
6 Pettaugh
12 Sharpstone
9 Swilland
3 Thorpe Hall
16 Thurleston
1 Ulverston
17 Westerfield
18 Whitton
5 Winston

Colneis (Cn)
26 'Alston'
  Brihtoluestuna
1 Bucklesham
22 Burgate
27 Burgh
23 Candlet
10 Falkenham
20 Grimston Hall
24 Gulpher
5 'Guthestuna'
2 Hemley
  Isteuertona
3 Kembroke
9 Kirton
  Kul-, Kyluertestuna,
  Culuerdestuna
29 Langer
8 'Leofstanestuna'
7 Levington
19 'Maistana'
14 Morston
15 'Mycelegata'
6 Nacton
13 Norton
25 'Oxelanda'
21 'Plumgeard'
12 Stratton
4 'Struestuna', 'Struustuna'
17 Thorpe
18 Trimley St. Martin and
  St. Mary
16 'Turstanestuna'
28 Wadgate
11 Walton

Hartismere (H)
34 Aspall
29 Bacton
18 Braiseworth
33 Brockford
8 Brome
10 Burgate
  Caldecota(n), -coten,
  Kaldecotes
30 Cotton
15 Cranley
1 Diss (Norfolk)
13 Eye
23 Finningham
16 Gislingham
26 Hestley
11 Mellis
32 Mendlesham
6 Oakley
20 Occold
3 Palgrave
2 Redgrave
21 Redlingfield
9 Rickinghall Superior
27 Rishangles
19 Stoke Ash
5 Stuston

25 Thorndon
17 Thornham Magna
14 Thornham Parva
7 Thrandeston
  Tusemera
22 Westhorpe
31 Wetheringsett
24 Wickham Skeith
4 Wortham
28 Wyverstone
12 Yaxley

Ipswich (I)
1 Ipswich
1 Stoke

Loes (Ls)
18 Ash
5 Brandeston
  Brodertuna
21 Butley
17 Campsey Ash
16 Charsfield
  Clachestorp
4 Cretingham
19 Dallinghoo
11 Easton
  ?Ethereg
3 Framlingham
24 Gedgrave
14 Glevering
12 Hacheston
7 Hoo
1 Kenton
6 Kettleburgh
10 Letheringham
13 Marlesford
8 Martley
9 Monewdon
  Possefelda
15 Potsford
20 Rendlesham
2 Earl Soham
22 Staverton
23 Woodbridge

Lothing (Lt)
3 Barnby
  Beketuna, Bechetuna
2 Carlton Colville
5 Gisleham
  Hornes
8 Kessingland
1 Kirkley
  Kislea
4 Mutford
6 Pakefield
  Rodenhala
7 Rushmere
  Wimundahala

Lothingland (Ltl)
16 Akethorpe
4 Belton
13 Blundeston
6 Browston
2 Burgh Castle
5 Caldecott
14 Corton
15 Flixton
7 Fritton
1 Gapton
3 Gorleston (Norfolk)
11 Herringfleet
8 Hopton
9 Lound
17 Lowestoft
10 'Newton'
12 Somerleyton

Parham (Pa)
2 Beversham
3 Blaxhall
  Brutge
  Niuetuna
1 Parham
4 Tunstall
5 Wantisden

Plomesgate (Pl)
17 Aldeburgh
  Becclinga
8 Benhall
20 Boyton
1 Bruisyard
  Burch
  Burgesgata
4 Carlton
19 Chillesford
  Cle'pham
2 Cransford
16 Dunningworth
12 Farnham
7 Great Glemham
15 Little Glemham
  Ingoluestuna
  Keletuna, Cheletuna,
  Chiletuna
  Nordberia
  Prestetuna
3 Rendham
14 Rushmere
6 Saxmundham
13 Snape
9 Sternfield
10 Stratford St. Andrew
18 Sudbourne
5 Swefling
11 'Thorpe'

Samford (Sa)
Alfildestuna
Belenei
5 Belstead

13 Bentley
26 East Bergholt
  Beria
15 Boynton
27 Brantham
1 Burstall
  Canap(p)etuna,
  Canepetuna
3 Chattisham
12 Churchford
18 Dodnash
  Eduinestuna
29 Erwarton
8 Freston
4 Gusford
23 Harkstead
22 Higham
2 Hintlesham
19 Holbrook
17 Holton St. Mary
30 Kalweton
24 Kirkton
  Manesfort
6 Pannington
  Purtepyt
11 Raydon
10 Shelley
20 Shotley
  Stanfelda
25 Stratford St. Mary
28 Stutton
16 Tattingstone
21 Thorington
  Toft
  Torp
  Turchetlestuna
9 Great and Little Wenham
7 Wherstead
14 Woolverstone

Stow (St)
11 Buxhall
8 Chilton
14 Combs
13 Creeting St. Peter
4 Dagworth
  Eruestuna
12 Great and Little Finborough
5 Harleston
2 Haughley
3 Old Newton
7 Onehouse
  Rodeham
6 Shelland
9 Stowmarket
10 Thorney
  Torpe
  Torstuna
  Ultuna
  Weledana
1 Wetherden

Wangford (Wa)
5 Barsham
1 Beccles
2 Bungay
  Catesfella
  Croscroft
11 Ellough
17 South Elmham All Saints,
  St. Cross, St. James,
  St. Margaret, St. Michael,
  St. Nicholas, and St. Peter
8 Flixton
  Hatheburgfelda, Hetheburgafel
13 Homersfield
  Icheburna
9 Ilketshall St. Andrew,
  St. John, St. Lawrence,
  and St. Margaret
15 Linburne
3 Mettingham
16 Redisham
7 Ringsfield
18 Shadingfield
4 Shipmeadow
14 Sotterley
  Thicchebrom
10 Weston
  Wichedis
12 Willingham
6 Worlingham

Wilford (Wi)
29 Alderton
30 Bawdsey
5 Bing
6 Boulge
18 Boyton
7 Bredfield
12 Bromeswell
17 Capel St. Andrew
26 'Culeslea'
3 Debach
25 'Halgestou'
1 Harpole
24 Hollesley
14 Hoo
15 'Hundesthoft' -'tuf'
21 'Laneburc', -'burh'
19 Littlecross
4 Loudham
10 Melton
28 Peyton
27 Ramsholt
23 Shottisham
8 Sogenhoe
16 Stokerland
20 Sutton
13 'Turstanestuna', 'Thor-',
  'Thur-', 'Tor-'
22 'Udeham'
9 Ufford
2 Wickham Market
11 Wilford

SYSTEMS OF REFERENCE TO THE TWO VOLUMES OF DOMESDAY BOOK

The manuscript of the larger volume (here referred to as DB) is divided into numbered chapters, and the chapters into sections, usually marked by large initials and red ink. Farley did not number the sections and later historians, using his edition, have referred to the text of DB by folio numbers, which cannot be closer than an entire page or column. Moreover, several different ways of referring to the same column have been devised. In 1816 Ellis used three separate systems in his indices: (i) on pages i-cvii, 435-518, 537-570; (ii) on pages 1-144; (iii) on pages 145-433 and 519-535. Other systems have since come into use, notably that used by Vinogradoff, here followed. The present edition numbers the sections, the normal practicable form of close reference; but since all discussion of DB for two hundred years has been obliged to refer to folio or column, a comparative table will help to locate references given. The five columns below give Vinogradoff's notation, Ellis's three systems, and that used by Welldon Finn and others. Maitland, Stenton, Darby, and others have usually followed Ellis (i).

Vinogradoff	Ellis (i)	Ellis (ii)	Ellis (iii)	Finn
152a	152	152a	152	152ai
152b	152	152a	152.2	152a2
152c	152b	152b	152b	152bi
152d	152b	152b	152b2	152b2

The manuscript of Little Domesday Book (here referred to as LDB), in which the text of the Suffolk survey is preserved, has one column per page but is again divided into numbered chapters and the chapters into sections, usually distinguished by paragraph-marks. Modern users of LDB have referred to its text by folio number, e.g. 152(a) 152b. Farley's edition presents both *recto* and *verso* of a folio on one printed page. In Suffolk, the relation between the column notation and the chapters and sections is:

281a	Landholders	308a,b	6,44 — 6,52	338a,b	7,65 — 7,72
b	1,1 — 1,5	309a,b	6,52 — 6,62	339a,b	7,72 — 7,79
282a,b	1,5 — 1,20	310a,b	6,62 — 6,79	340a,b	7,79 — 7,92
283a,b	1,20 — 1,47	311a,b	6,79 — 6,84	341a,b	7,92 — 7,105
284a,b	1,47 — 1,62	312a,b	6,84 — 6,92	342a,b	7,105 — 7,119
285a,b	1,63 — 1,82	313a,b	6,92 — 6,100	343a,b	7,119 — 7,133
286a,b	1,82 — 1,98	314a,b	6,101 — 6,112	344a,b	7,133 — 7,143
287a,b	1,98 — 1,106	315a,b	6,112 — 6,127	345a,b	7,143 — 7,151
288a,b	1,107 — 1,115	316a,b	6,128 — 6,143	346a,b	8,1 — 8,9
289a,b	1,115 — 1,121	317a,b	6,143 — 6,162	347a,b	8,9 — 8,23
290a,b	1,121 — 1,122g	318a,b	6,162 — 6,177	348a,b	8,23 — 8,35
291a,b	2,1 — 2,13	319a,b	6,177 — 6,191	349a,b	8,35 — 8,46
292a	2,14 — 2,20	320a,b	6,191 — 6,202	350a,b	8,46 — 8,55
292b	Landholders	321a,b	6,202 — 6,214	351a,b	8,55 — 8,59
292b	3,1 3,9	322a,b	6,215 — 6,221	352a,b	8,59 — 8,78
293a,b	3,9 — 3,39	323a,b	6,221 — 6,232	353a,b	8,78 — 9,3
294a,b	3,39 — 3,61	324a,b	6,232 — 6,251	354a,b	9,3 — 12,1
295a,b	3,61 — 3,79	325a,b	6,251 — 6,267	355a,b	12,1 — 13,3
296a,b	3,79 — 3,94	326a,b	6,267 — 6,283	356a,b	13,3 — 14,3
297a,b	3,94 — 3,101	327a,b	6,283 — 6,301	357a,b	14,3 — 14,12
298a,b	3,101 — 4,6	328a,b	6,301 — 6,308	358a,b	14,12 — 14,20
299a,b	4,6 — 4,15	329a,b	6,308 — 6,317	359a,b	14,21 — 14,28
300a,b	4,16 — 4,22	330a,b	6,317 — 7,3	360a,b	14,28 — 14,42
301a,b	4,22 — 4,35	331a,b	7,3 — 7,10	361a,b	14,42 — 14,50
302a,b	4,35 — 4,42	332a,b	7,10 — 7,15	362a,b	14,50 — 14,59
303a,b	5,1 — 5,8	333a,b	7,16 — 7,26	363a,b	14,59 — 14,68
304a,b	6,1 — 6,8	334a,b	7,26 — 7,37	364a,b	14,69 — 14,75
305a,b	6,8 — 6,19	335a,b	7,37 — 7,49	365a,b	14,75 — 14,81
306a,b	6,20 — 6,32	336a,b	7,49 — 7,58	366a,b	14,81 — 14,90
307a,b	6,33 — 6,44	337a,b	7,58 — 7,65		

367a,b	14,90	–	14,101	394a,b	25,57	–	25,66	423a,b	38,12	–	39,3
368a,b	14,102	–	14,110	395a,b	25,66	–	25,78	424a,b	39,3	–	39,10
369a,b	14,111	–	14,120	396a,b	25,78	–	25,92	425a,b	39,10	–	40,4
370a,b	14,120	–	14,138	397a,b	25,93	–	25,112	426a,b	40,4	–	41,9
371a,b	14,138	–	14,166	398a,b	26,1	–	26,10	427a,b	41,10	–	42,1
372a	14,167			399a,b	26,10	–	26,12d	428a,b	42,2	–	43,5
	Landholders			400a,b	26,12d	–	26,20	429a,b	43,5	–	44,4
372b	15,1	–	15,4	401a,b	27,1	–	27,7	430a,b	45,1	–	46,4
373a,b	15,5	–	16,10	402a,b	27,7	–	28,1b	431a,b	46,4	–	47,3
374a,b	16,10	–	16,17	403a,b	28,1b	–	29,1	432a,b	48,1	–	51,2
375a,b	16,17	–	16,25	404a,b	29,1	–	29,11	433a,b	52,1	–	52,9
376a,b	16,25	–	16,31	405a,b	29,12	–	31,3	434a,b	52,10	–	53,6
377a,b	16,32	–	16,40	406a,b	31,3	–	31,20	435a,b	53,6	–	55,1
378a,b	16,40	–	17,1	407a,b	31,20	–	31,34	436a,b	56,1	–	59,2
379a,b	18,1	–	19,10	408a,b	31,35	–	31,44	437a,b	59,2	–	62,6
380a,b	19,11	–	19,18	409a,b	31,44	–	31,53	438a,b	62,6	–	66,1
381a,b	19,18	–	21,5	410a,b	31,53	–	31,60	439a,b	66,1	–	66,9
382a,b	21,5	–	21,16	411a,b	32,1	–	32,11	440a,b	66,10	–	67,3
383a,b	21,16	–	21,29	412a,b	32,11	–	32,23	441a,b	67,3	–	67,11
384a,b	21,29	–	21,42	413a,b	32,23	–	33,2	442a,b	67,11	–	67,19
385a,b	21,42	–	21,52	414a,b	33,2	–	33,8	443a,b	67,19	–	67,30
386a,b	21,53	–	21,69	415a,b	33,8	–	33,13	444a,b	67,30	–	68,5
387a,b	21,69	–	21,86	416a,b	34,1	–	34,6	445a,b	69,1	–	73,1
388a,b	21,87	–	22,3	417a,b	34,6	–	34,16	446a,b	74,1	–	74,15
389a,b	23,1	–	25,2	418a,b	34,16	–	35,5	447a,b	74,16	–	76,3
390a,b	25,2	–	25,17	419a,b	35,5	–	36,4	448a,b	76,3	–	76,16
391a,b	25,17	–	25,35	420a,b	36,5	–	37,1	449a,b	76,16	–	76,23
392a,b	25,35	–	25,52	421a,b	37,1	–	38,4	450a	77,1–4		
393a,b	25,52	–	25,57	422a,b	38,5	–	38,12		Colophon		